Christ Returns from
the Jungle

SUNY series in Transpersonal and Humanistic Psychology
—————
Richard D. Mann, editor

Christ Returns from the Jungle

Ayahuasca Religion as Mystical Healing

Marc G. Blainey

SUNY PRESS

Front cover image: Fardada holding a cup of Daime (photo by a Belgian daimista). Back Cover image: Portrait of Mestre Irineu, By: Jorge Patrocinio (published with permission)

Published by State University of New York Press, Albany

For information, contact State University of New York Press, Albany, NY
www.sunypress.edu

Library of Congress Cataloging-in-Publication Data

Name: Blainey, Marc Gordon, author.
Title: Christ returns from the jungle : ayahuasca religion as mystical healing /
    by Marc G. Blainey.
Description: Albany : State University of New York Press, [2021] | Series:
    SUNY series in transpersonal and humanistic psychology | Includes
    bibliographical references and index.
Identifiers: LCCN 2020058286 (print) | LCCN 2020058287 (ebook) | ISBN
    9781438483139 (hardcover : alk. paper) | ISBN 9781438483146 (pbk. : alk.
    paper) | ISBN 9781438483153 (ebook)
Subjects: LCSH: Religion and culture—Europe. | Santo Daime (Cult)—Europe. |
    Cultural pluralism—Europe. | Cultural pluralism—Religious aspects. |
    Europe—Religion—21st century.
Classification: LCC BL65.C8 B542 2021 (print) | LCC BL65.C8 (ebook) | DDC
    299/.93—dc23
LC record available at https://lccn.loc.gov/2020058286
LC ebook record available at https://lccn.loc.gov/2020058287

10 9 8 7 6 5 4 3 2 1

This book is dedicated to you, the reader

Figure 0.1. *Christ in the Wine Press*, By: Hieronymus Wierix (1619); Image copyright © The Metropolitan Museum of Art, Image source: Art Resource, NY.

from the chalice of this realm of spirits
foams forth for Him his own infinitude.

—G. W. F. Hegel, *The Phenomenology of Spirit*

Eu tomo Daime	*I drink Daime*
Para ver os meus defeitos	*To see my flaws*
Eu tomo Daime	*I drink Daime*
Para eu me corrigir	*To correct myself*
Não tomo Daime	*I don't drink Daime*
Para me engrandecer	*To exalt myself*
Porque o grande	*Because the Great*
É Jesus, está aquí	*Is Jesus and He's here*
...	
Eu tomo Daime	*I drink Daime*
E considero este vinho	*And consider this wine*
O mesmo vinho	*The same wine*
Que Jesus deu para tomar	*Jesus gave to drink*
Aos Seus apostoles	*To His apostles*
Disse: Em minha memória	*He said 'in my memory'*
Que é para sempre	*So that forever*
Esta Luz nunca faltar	*This Light never goes out*

—excerpt from hymn #14, "Em Minha Memória"
("In My Memory"), in *Livrinho do Apocalipse*
(*Little Book of Revelation*), by Padrinho Valdete

Contents

PART I

FRAMING AND TACKLING THE QUESTION: WHY SANTO DAIME IN EUROPE?

PART II

FROM AMAZONIA WITH LOVE

PART VI
FARDADOS' EXISTENTIAL VALUES

PART VII
APPLYING ANTHROPOLOGY TO
PUBLIC DEBATES ABOUT AYAHUASCA

APPENDICES

xii / Contents

Illustrations

Figures

Tables

Preface

Is there a meaning of life and if so, what is it? Or, for those who are confident there is no ultimate meaning, how can one be so sure? How *should* we go about interpreting and dealing with the human condition? Are resolutions to the perplexities of existence best pursued according to traditional religious dogmas? Or do the irreligious ideals of secular materialism provide a more reliable avenue for achieving and maintaining one's well-being? When saints and prophets of the world's many religions claimed to receive messages through dreams or visions, were these true revelations of divine will or were these delusional fantasies? Ought we to live our life as if this temporary existence is the only game in town or do our actions on Earth somehow determine our placement in an eternal afterlife? Although no person is equipped to definitively answer such foundational dilemmas of ideology, a diverse array of believing and unbelieving groups nevertheless act as if they epitomize proper standards of thought and behavior (a bias anthropologists refer to as ethnocentrism). As seen in humanity's violent history and in partisan conflicts of the present day, ethnocentric ideologues of all stripes are inclined to denounce as wrong any perspective that disagrees with their own.

Ongoing strife in Western societies between religious and nonreligious subcultures attests to each side's presuming that their respective viewpoint constitutes *the* metaphysical truth. But for a portion of onlookers, bitter tensions between opposing camps of this-worldly and celestial priorities suggest that neither the secular nor mainstream religious establishments offer a complete systematization of how to live optimally. Thus, many citizens of North Atlantic nations now feel agitated by what the philosopher Charles Taylor (2007, 15/598/676) calls "cross-pressure," in that "the debate in our society has to be understood as suspended between the extreme positions . . . represented by orthodox religion on one hand [e.g., Christianity, Judaism, Islam, Hinduism, and other large faith denominations] and hard-line materialistic atheism on the other." Despite mass media portrayals of dramatic clashes between secularist institutions and religious customs (e.g., abortion/euthanasia/death penalty debates, face-veil [*niqāb*] bans, church-state separations, and war), Taylor (2007, 5/302/423) identifies how some people's aversion to both cross-pressured extremes motivates affinity for alternative paths or "third ways" toward existential "fullness," a splintering he labels the "nova effect": "the steadily widening gamut of new positions—some believing, some unbelieving, some hard to classify—which have become available options for us" (see also Kearney 2011, 3). Yet because the discordant voices of the cross-pressured extremes demand so much attention in the public sphere, the unusual offspring being generated by this nova effect often go unnoticed. By contrast, anthropological approaches can shed light on overlooked social realities, including some of the interesting and controversial new ways that modern Westerners are seeking to transmute their cross-pressured angst. This book examines a small but provocative example of how resistance to contemporary cross-pressures can spur the flowering of peculiar new ritual activities.

Through fourteen months of fieldwork between 2009 and 2011, I gathered ethnographic data concerning the European expansion of *Santo Daime* (pronounced San-too Die-mee; Portuguese for "Holy Give-me"). Santo Daime is a new Brazil-based religion in which devotees drink a mind-altering beverage called *ayahuasca*. This bitter, brown fluid has a powerful capacity for altering human consciousness because it contains *N,N-Dimethyltryptamine* or DMT, a psychoactive chemical dubbed "the spirit molecule" (see Strassman 2001; St John 2015). Ayahuasca is ingested as a holy sacrament in Santo Daime rituals, much like the wine distributed in a Christian mass. However, most governments consider this to be a criminal act, designating DMT as a dangerous and illicit "hallucinogen." The arrival of this new spirituality thus represents an ethical dilemma for the "Free World": How can the liberalist value of religious freedom be sustained if the fundamental component of Santo Daime religious practice is not permitted? Anthropology, the discipline that strives to account for cultural variation, is tailor-made to intercede in debates about stigmatized populations because it can clarify otherwise obscure social phenomena. As an anthropological study, this book's focus on Santo Daime opens up a broader inquiry into how cross-pressured ideals underlying European social norms tend to exclude alternative ideas about the nature of mind and reality. Just as prejudices of class, race, gender, and sexual orientation are unmasked through ethnographic research, anthropological analysis can expose prejudices that afflict ostracized faith communities. The Santo Daime congregations in Europe demonstrate the transnational movement of a foreign spiritual organization. Conversions to exotic religions portend deeper shifts in how some Europeans are adapting to an increasingly interconnected planet. The clarification of this process is important because there remains much uncertainty among social scientists regarding why some Westerners are making unorthodox religious choices in what was thought to be an age of secularization (see Dawson 2003, 125). Hence, in presenting the results of fieldwork with Santo Daime groups in Europe, this volume offers empirical and empathic answers to the following question: *Why are some Europeans, who were raised within a social milieu dominated by secularism and mainstream Christianity, now choosing to adopt Santo Daime spiritual practices?*

A fully committed member of Santo Daime is known as a *fardado* (plural: fardados, for males only or both genders collectively) or a *fardada* (female, plural: fardadas). The blanket term *daimistas* is used when discussing both fardados and Daime devotees (a.k.a. *firmados*) who are not yet fardados. European fardados are prone to express key aspects of Santo Daime culture using the Brazilian language of Portuguese (a glossary is located in Appendix I). They wear white *fardas* ("uniforms") when attending ceremonial Daime *trabalhos* ("works"), where they imbibe ayahuasca while meditating, singing, and dancing for between two and twelve hours. Meaning "vine of the (dead) spirits" in the Peruvian Quechuan languages, ayahuasca is a concoction[1] of plants that originated among Amazonian indigenous peoples in Pre-Columbian times (Shanon 2002, 13–14). Fardados also refer to ayahuasca as "Santo Daime" or "Daime," illustrating how this drink is the pivot of the religion as a whole (Polari de Alverga 1999). As witnessed in the epigraph of this book, fardados also link the Daime brew to the holy blood/wine that Jesus served at the Last Supper. I met an Italian fardado who put it like this: "*I think that as a sacrament the Santo Daime* [beverage] *symbolizes the blood of Christ, so I think there is a presence of the Christic energy inside the Santo Daime.*" This same informant also characterized Santo Daime as a resurgence of the "original Christianity," in that it involves clandestine rituals with a mind-altering liquid (in this case ayahuasca instead of alcohol). Such statements distill my informants' understanding of Santo Daime ritual works as fusing the shamanic act of quaffing ayahuasca with the sacramental basis of the Christian mass. Yet as will become apparent throughout this text, fardados view Jesus as one example of a cross-cultural category of "Great

Spiritual Teachers," which they perceive as a special feature of all authentic religious traditions.

As an anthropologist, I carried out research that became the raw material for this book because of my continued frustration with divisiveness among factions of believers and nonbelievers. Through this work, I discovered that debates about ayahuasca spirituality go to the heart of cross-pressured frictions between secularism and religion in Western societies today. In particular, while most governments prohibit "hallucinogenic drugs," the ethnographic realities demand a reconsideration of pre-theoretic fears about substances like ayahuasca. For fardados, some of the botanical technologies developed by "New World" indigenous peoples are in many ways superior to the pharmaceutical drugs of Western biomedicine. Whether one accepts or rejects fardados' theology, the evidence imparted herein suggests we must at least contemplate their claim that ayahuasca rituals can act as a therapeutic "key to solutions." Regardless of belief, my informants' only prerequisite for healing in Santo Daime is earnestness to learn from the "meeting with yourself" occasioned in their ceremonies. By combining ethnographic methods with phenomenology, this book also engages existential currents in anthropology's emergent dialogues with secularism and theology (e.g., Asad 2003; Cannell 2010; Lemons 2018; Mathews and Tomlinson 2018; Robbins 2006, 2014).

Structure of the Text

While each section of this book addresses a specific topic, the sequential flow between chapters is intended as a progressive unfolding of answers to the central problem of the monograph: *Why is it that some Europeans are choosing to join the global daimista movement?* After presenting a basic overview of Santo Daime, Part I delineates a justification for mixed methods of participant-observation, interviews, and cognitive surveys with daimistas. During visits with informants, my strategy struck a balance between emphasizing fardados' personal testimonies about why they are drawn to Santo Daime and techniques for gathering statistical data. The reasons for employing certain sampling procedures are explained in terms of the exceptional demands of this research, which concerns a small, nonlocalized collection of Europeans who practice rituals that are illegal. When an ethnographer wants to cultivate empathy with members of a religion that is based around extraordinary experiences, one must immerse oneself in the research subjects' worldview. Following a discussion of my tactics of ethnography, the theoretical orientations of existential anthropology are applied to fardados' view of Santo Daime as a therapeutic form of mysticism. So as to frame subsequent chapters, some direct quotations from informants are included as representing fardados' perceptions of Santo Daime. I recorded 102 semistructured interviews with daimistas in Europe. Of these informants, eighty-seven are fardados, four are former fardados,[2] and eleven are "firmado" nonmembers who regularly attend Daime works. This sample includes daimistas born or living in fifteen different European countries (two fardado informants were Israeli expatriates living in Europe). In integrating theoretical implications with the results of ethnographic fieldwork, each section touches upon a separate aspect of the wider concerns of this study.

Part II presents an anthropology of Santo Daime's origins in South America. This section commences with a brief explanation of the chemistry and ethnobotany of ayahuasca. Next appears an ethnohistorical account of the first Europeans to come into contact with the brew through their encounters with indigenous peoples in the Amazon rainforest. The discussion then charts ayahuasca use in different cultural settings, including the employment of the beverage in its original shamanic healing and divination contexts among aboriginal groups, in the neo-shamanism of multiethnic mestizos, and in the syncretic "ayahuasca religions." This is followed by a chapter that locates the present volume relative to major publications in the field of Santo Daime studies. The section then closes by detailing my trip to Céu do Mapiá, the Brazilian headquarters of Santo Daime, where I interviewed tourists visiting from around the world. Thus, groundwork is laid for the ethnography of Santo Daime's rise in Europe, an emblematic case study for the global expansion of ayahuasca spirituality that has accelerated in recent decades.

Part III situates European daimistas relative to key scholarly debates about the place of religion within Western societies. On the surface, the expansion of this Brazilian religion runs against the grain of twentieth-century predictions about secularization trends in Europe. But the Santo Daime is just one of many new spiritual movements that are emerging alongside the decline of mainstream religions in the Western world. So while this is an ethnography focused on ayahuasca use and the Santo Daime doctrine in Europe, it is by necessity also a study of the much larger subculture of "re-enchantment" in the West (Partridge 2004). After considering the wider context of contemporary spirituality, the stage is set with a survey of the historical and cultural profiles of Santo Daime's international expansion across Europe.

Part IV concentrates on an ethnographic exposition of Santo Daime ceremonies. Through a systematic illustration of the dynamics involved in Daime works and the spiritual beliefs associated with these practices, the narrative enters the private ritual world of European fardados. For my informants, Santo Daime's eclectic ideological elements coalesce into a single harmonious unit, a mixture that constitutes the essence of their doctrine. During Daime works, daimistas regard the symbolic amalgamation of many religions into one as connected to transpersonal experiences that ayahuasca drinkers have relative to each other and the entire Cosmos. While the general public is largely unaware of the expansion of Santo Daime, this ethnographic account shines a light on behaviors that might at first glance seem dodgy to many readers. In concise terms, fardados believe that Santo Daime works help them to discover metaphysical solutions that beget practical solutions.

In moving toward a cogent answer to the question of why some Europeans are drawn to Santo Daime, Parts V and VI examine the results of two freelisting exercises implemented with fardado informants. Pursuing a standard cognitive anthropology focus on *schemata* (singular: *schema*)— what Roy D'Andrade (1995, 132) defines as "culturally shared mental constructs"—fardados were asked to "freelist" (i.e., spontaneously enumerate) the plants they regard as sacred as well as all the people they deem to be "Great Spiritual Teachers."

Part V expounds on responses to the first freelist test with European fardados. In accordance with classifying ayahuasca as an "entheogen," the data show informants' mutual reverence for certain psychoactive plants as "sacred." The chapters then proceed to elaborate on ethnographic findings about European fardados' conceptualization of Daime rituals. This is where existential modes of analysis help to tease out the spiritual aspirations of European daimistas. Following an emic blueprint that explicates informants' common view of Daime works as a mystical "key" or "mirror" technology, I then explain this etically as a "suiscope" mechanism for healing through self-observation. Ritualized self-confrontation is an introspective device promoted by many schools of mysticism. Daimista informants believe that sacred plant ceremonies can teach soteriological lessons equivalent to those bestowed by saints and sages from different cultures and time periods. To investigate this, I conducted auto-ethnographic experiments through "ethnophenomenological" methods, a venture that left me with a host of personal benefits but still without the desire to become a Daime member.

Part VI begins by presenting the results of a second freelist produced by European fardados. After hearing many informants mention the names of various people from whom they learned important life-lessons, fardados were asked to compile a list of all the "Great Spiritual Teachers" that they know. One gets a clue about the shared values of European fardados through the spiritual figures they mentioned, which include both ancient and modern personalities from a variety of backgrounds. The way informants describe the transcendence they seek through Daime is identical to a cross-cultural mind-state classified as *Cosmic Consciousness* (Bucke 1995[1901]). This integrating of diverse religious practices in a search for inner peace suggests that Santo Daime is symptomatic of a much deeper social transformation underway across the West. When their eclectic values are considered relative to cross-pressured extremes of secularity and conventional religiosity, European daimistas epitomize a third demographic that has (largely) escaped the notice of social science. Elaborating on sociologists' designation of Euro-American spiritual seekers as "Cultural Creatives" (Ray and Anderson 2000), "New Agers" (Heelas 2008), or "New Metaphysicals" (Bender 2010), I highlight how the expansion of Santo Daime typifies the Taylorian "nova effect" ongoing in Western cultures today. European fardados share with this new demographic an appetite for seeking innovative solutions to existential and ecological crises. These concerted methods of transcribed interviews and *cultural domain analysis* generate both qualitative and quantitative data; thereby, the empirical results present fardados' *integralist* or *perennialist* worldview as an alternative perspective from which to consider the tolerability of ayahuasca religion in Western societies.

Part VII concludes the book by assessing broader implications of this research in light of fresh scholarly appeals for compromise between secularist and religious voices in the European public sphere. Realizing a need for more balanced accounts of the continued intermingling of secularity and religiosity, for lack of a better word many social theorists now refer to European society as *post-secular*. For philosopher Jürgen Habermas (2009, 59–77), the label *post-secular* recognizes that both religious and secularist worldviews must learn to negotiate cooperatively with mutual toleration. One of the essential functions of anthropology is to render different cultural logics as mutually explicable. Consistent with the post-secular ethos, this book contributes to reconciling intercultural misunderstandings about ayahuasca mysticism that have heretofore remained intractable.

As the researchers Beyerstein and Kalchik (2003, 30) observe: "Where drug use becomes problematical is usually when another culture's socially approved drug is parachuted into a society that has not had the time and experience to adapt its informal controls to handle it . . . problems are most likely to arise when the newly exposed users lack models for safe usage that they can emulate." Unfortunately, resistance to such "models for safe usage" relegates the use of most mind-altering "drugs" to the underground, an unregulated setting where substances such as ayahuasca can be dangerous. Indeed, the ritual drinking of ayahuasca by committed practitioners of Santo Daime can appear unsavory when viewed from either a traditionally religious or an atheist-physicalist standpoint. By presuming that substances other than alcohol, tobacco, coffee, and pharmaceuticals are always unsafe, mainstream Western perspectives have tended to demonize "hallucinogens" that many other societies have long revered as therapeutic sacraments. Recently, however, medical scientists have begun to take another look at hallucinogens/psychedelics and are finding that the hazards of these materials have more to do with the context in which they are used than with the substances themselves (see Blainey 2015). This accruing evidence supports the claims of Santo Daime members, a community of European citizens willing to risk stiff judicial penalties in choosing to ingest ayahuasca. In line with the findings of a growing scholarly consensus, my ethnographic data intimates that ayahuasca has many psychotherapeutic applications. Through the ethnographic lens one understands that fardados sip ayahuasca not to have a casual "trip" with hallucinogenic imagery, but rather as an introspective steppingstone toward lasting emotional stability and existential repose. Daimistas say that ayahuasca rituals provide mystical solutions that help them to feel happier, healthier, and more fulfilled in their lives. With this in mind, after some important acknowledgments the next chapters will introduce the theoretical and methodological scope of the present study.

Acknowledgments

Before we begin, I want to first express my deep appreciation to the global Santo Daime family. All the pseudonymous informants mentioned in this book represent real people who patiently responded to my countless questions during fieldwork. I hope that by divulging firsthand observations about your beliefs and practices as a genuine spiritual community, this text will in some way help you in your struggle to attain religious liberty around the world.

I owe a great debt of gratitude to the many academic mentors I have been fortunate to work with over the years. In particular, for advice and constructive critiques on my research, I want to express heartfelt thanks to William Balée, Adeline Masquelier, Allison Truitt (Tulane), Pamela Klassen, Brian Rush (Toronto), Paul Healy, Roger Lohmann (Trent), Andrew Nelson (UWO), Kate Harper, Christopher Ross, Carol Duncan, and Daniel Maoz (Wilfrid Laurier).

I must express my gratitude to Tiago Jurua Damo Ranzi and his father Alceu Ranzi (as well as their colleagues Amelia, Antonia, and Diego) for acting as my local guides in Acre, Brazil. Furthermore, I thank the citizens of Céu do Mapiá (especially Padrinho Alex Polari) for their warm welcome and assistance during my fieldwork in the Brazilian rainforest. I also thank Jessica Rochester, Andrew Dawson, and Matthew Meyer for their invaluable preparatory advice about traveling in the Amazon.

I am grateful for the camaraderie I share with colleagues in the budding society of Ayahuasca Researchers. Specifically, I want to acknowledge fellow Canadian Ken Tupper for his friendship and professional advice, as well as Brian Anderson, Bia Labate, and the late John J. McGraw for their thoughtful comments regarding my interpretations of Santo Daime.

Much credit is due to James Peltz, Eileen Nizer, Kate Seburyamo, Sharla Clute, Michelle Alamillo, and Alan Hewat, who shepherded my manuscript through the many stages of the publication process at SUNY Press. Thanks to David Prout for expertly compiling the Index and I am also thankful for Jason Hashimoto's assistance with images.

For financial support, I am grateful for research funds provided by the Social Sciences & Humanities Research Council of Canada (SSHRC), the Paul and Elizabeth Selley endowment at Tulane's School of Liberal Arts, and the Murphy Institute Center for Ethics and Public Affairs. I am also appreciative that this research was conducted with the approval of the Tulane University Human Research Protection Program—Institutional Review Board (IRB reference #08-00025U).

I am privileged to have enjoyed the unwavering encouragement of a devoted family. Thank you so much Mom and Dad (Sue and John)! Everything I have ever achieved or will ever accomplish is entirely attributable to the unconditional love you poured on me throughout my life. Thanks to my dear sister Cara (Care-Care) for being the most dependable sibling one could hope for—we have always taught each other through a reciprocal dynamic whereby we are different and yet also very alike, and I look forward to continuing to share our mutual challenges and successes as we keep learning about life together. I am grateful to my parents-in-law Byron and Barb, my siblings-in-law (Ryan, Mikey, Kieva), and my niblings (Graeme, Hatley, James, Leo), all cherished additions to my family system who have been so gracious to welcome me as their son, brother, and uncle. To all my friends and family: I am glad you are in my life.

And last but the opposite of least, I must acknowledge that the most important source of reinforcement is my wife Darcie Leigh Blainey, without whom I could not have finished this project with my sanity intact. Darcie, you are the sacred mirror by which I discover more every day about how to mature as a human being. I look forward to growing with you in compassion and tenderness as we share the joys and adventures of raising our two intelligent, kindhearted children: Perth and Celine, I love you now and forevermore.

—Marc G. Blainey (Ontario, Canada)

Twitter @EthnoMetafisics

PART I

FRAMING AND TACKLING THE QUESTION

WHY SANTO DAIME IN EUROPE?

Figure 1.1. *The First Approach of the Serpent*, engraving by Gustave Doré (1866), published with permission from the Bibliothèque nationale de France (BnF).

The believer possesses the ever-sure antidote to despair: possibility; since for God everything is possible at every moment. This is the health of faith which resolves contradictions. The contradiction here is that in human terms the undoing [i.e., mortality] is certain and that still there is possibility. Health is in general to be able to resolve contradictions.

—Søren Kierkegaard, *The Sickness unto Death*

Encontrei uma chave	*I found a key*
Para ser feliz	*To be happy*
É fazer	*It's to do*
O que Jesus me diz	*What Jesus says to me*
. . .	
Se errar Deus perdoa	*If one makes mistakes God forgives*
E eu peço perdão	*And I ask for forgiveness*
Limpai a minha mente	*Cleanse my mind*
E o meu coração	*And my heart*

—from Santo Daime hymn #8, "Eu Encontrei uma Chave" (I Found a Key), in *Flores de São João* (*Flowers of St. John*), by Cristina Tati

1

Introduction

On Mother's Day 2005, I found myself hurtling down an Amsterdam highway in a compact car driven by a petite Dutch grandmother. In her mid-sixties at the time, Jacoba[1] is a veteran member of *Santo Daime,* a new religion from Brazil organized around the psychoactive beverage ayahuasca. Through prior email contacts I had made with a local congregation, Jacoba was appointed as chaperone for my first *trabalho* ("work" in Portuguese), the apt identification of Santo Daime ceremonies as performative and introspective labor. As I was then just a backpacker curious about why ayahuasca had found its way to Europe,[2] Jacoba kindly shepherded me to and from the rural outskirts of the Netherlands' capital city. Upon entering a little rented chapel where the ritual was held, she introduced me to her fellow *daimistas,* a term encompassing both uninitiated parishioners and full-fledged Santo Daime members (*fardados/fardadas*), those dressed in white, green, and blue *fardas* ("uniforms").

Noticing that I was confused by the whirlwind of activities and conversations going on inside the church, my fardada chaperone guided me to the registration table where I paid 30€ and signed my name in the official participants' log. She then handed me a small hymnbook before turning me over to the elderly fardado in charge of assigning individuals to their "place" on the "men's side" of the *salão* ("hall"). Although I have since acquired a deeper appreciation of Santo Daime works in Europe, a spiritual behavior that is the main subject of this book, my memories of this introductory ayahuasca ritual are mostly a blur due to an utter lack of bearings in 2005. After swigging my first glass of the ayahuasca, which fardados lovingly dub "Daime," I spent the next six hours trying but mostly failing to sing along with a seemingly endless string of repetitive hymns. To the accompaniment of guitars, flute, and a bongo drum, I clumsily attempted to dance back and forth in the manner of the daimistas, a task that became trickier the more the effects of the Daime kicked in. At phases where the music paused in between hymns, the sudden silence was accompanied by an uneasy sensation of being trapped in an intergalactic dream sequence resembling the final scenes[3] of Stanley Kubrick's (1968) film *2001: A Space Odyssey*. Whenever the music proceeded, I felt lucky not to be joining the ranks of fellow participants making loud retching noises as they vomited into plastic buckets at the back of the room. Amid all this, the foremost recollection of my first Daime work is that every time I closed my eyes, the ambient sounds of vocalized hymns produced in my mind's eye a vivid image of semi-naked tribal celebrations in Africa or South America—akin to *National Geographic* documentaries I watched as a child—but when I opened my eyes I was shocked to remember that these chants were being emitted by Europeans dressed in pristine formalwear. This was no ordinary church service!

Flash forward to a sunny afternoon in the summer of 2010. I had arrived back in Amsterdam and now sat across from Jacoba on the flower-covered balcony of her apartment. While my maiden Daime voyage had been a sightseer's whim five years earlier, her facilitation of that enigmatic experience inspired me to return to gather ethnographic data about Santo Daime groups in Europe. Now, as I record an interview with Jacoba, she speaks in accented but fluent English about what her life was like before she began attending Santo Daime works twelve years ago. She tells me that she had a distressing childhood, beginning with her birth in The Hague in 1941. She states that because her family was then taking shelter during World War II and there were "bombs falling around us . . . [we] had to go [into] hiding in the factory of my grandfather in Leiden." She then tells me that she was physically and psychologically abused by family members and teachers while she was a youth, attributing the pain inflicted on her to the projection of collective wounds suffered by Europeans at that time: "In Holland we are still in shock from the war; it's really very bad what people can do to each other." Claiming that these ordeals weighed heavily on her well into adulthood, Jacoba now radiates a sense of steely calm through her blue-grey eyes as she touts the psychotherapeutic effects of Santo Daime. She characterizes the ayahuasca "sacrament" as a spiritual being. She earnestly believes that the brew gives access to a divine interlocutor that can steer people who drink it to become better versions of themselves by helping them resolve internalized stings of past trauma: "I say all the time, the Daime (the spirit in the bottle [of ayahuasca]), that's my best friend: it cares about me, it corrects me, it makes me realize how I relate to other people (because I'm not always so nice to other people) . . . and I think that's the same person as God. . . . God has many faces."

Needless to say, fardados' view of the Daime beverage as containing a direct link to God is very different from the generally negative attitude about "hallucinogenic drugs" in Europe. For instance, Jacoba has two daughters, one of whom has two daughters of her own. She now has a close relationship with her granddaughters, but it took some time for their mother to let them visit with their grandmother again after she found out that Jacoba was involved with Santo Daime. Jacoba says she is hurt that some members of her family are staunchly opposed to ayahuasca. She tries to patiently accept that the stigmatized status of her religious orientation has caused such rifts in her family, but she confesses that "it is difficult!"

Whereas social bigotries can perpetuate laws that exacerbate the very problems they are designed to resolve, ethnography informs more effective public health and crime policies by shining a light on unseen realities lived by marginalized groups (Fleisher 1995, 5/243–47).[4] Based on stories of youths experiencing "bad trips" a half-century ago during the "psychedelic sixties," in Western societies so-called hallucinogens are assumed to be inherently dangerous. Popular fears about the hippie counterculture's promotion of psychedelics provoked a worldwide criminalization of this class of chemicals, enacted by the United Nations' Convention on Psychotropic Substances in 1971 (Beyerstein and Kalchik 2003; Spillane and McAllister 2003). Since then, 184 member states have signed this UN treaty, which obliges each signatory to also legislate their own national sanctions.[5] Globally, the *International Narcotics Control Board* (INCB) now adjudicates international prohibitions of these psychoactive materials (see Tupper and Labate 2012). Because DMT, the mind-altering molecule found in ayahuasca, is also officially classified as a banned "hallucinogen," Santo Daime rituals remain a punishable offense in most countries[6] (Horák, Novák, and Vozáryová 2016). Consequently, in many liberalist nations where the freedom of religion is enshrined, those whose religious convictions revolve around ayahuasca now risk incarceration. Even while ayahuasca's constituents are condemned in most places, Santo Daime has managed to earn full legitimacy in Brazil, as well as in small sections of Europe[7] (Netherlands, Spain), the United States (Oregon), and most recently in Canada.[8] In these exceptional localities, courts of law upheld fardados' right to practice their religion as superseding statutes that outlaw ayahuasca. On the other hand, the United Kingdom, Ireland, France, Portugal, and Germany have opposed this religious use of ayahuasca, arresting and in some cases imprisoning fardados for importation and distribution of an illicit substance (Dawson 2013, 31–35; Labate and Feeney 2012; see also Silva Sá 2010). By contrast, fardados flatly reject the terms *hallucinogen*—which implies that the substance engenders delusions— and *psychedelic*—reminiscent of hedonistic use during the 1960s. Instead, they prefer the terms *sacred plant* and *entheogen*. Meaning "to generate god/s within" in Greek, entheogen denotes "vision-producing" substances employed "in shamanic or religious rites" (Ruck et al. 1979, 146). This vocabulary of entheogens as revealing an inner divinity is crucial for apprehending fardados' nonconformist approach to life. Now, years later, sifting through the transcriptions of interviews I recorded with fardados across Europe, I find that the essence of these testimonies is neatly summarized in the words of Jacoba.

I had asked Jacoba why she chooses to participate in these Christianized ayahuasca works, a question I put to every fardado I met during more that a year of fieldwork in Europe. Jacoba paused, and thought for a moment before saying, "Of course, we come to the Daime because of our despair." When I invited her to elaborate on what she means when she pinpoints "despair" as a motivation for attending Daime works, she resumed:

> *It's despair . . . the feeling of estrangement . . . from others . . . and isolation . . . there is no unity at all. . . .*
>
> *Everybody is always looking for the answer of why we are here. What is this all about? You know, at my age sometimes I'm bored; is this all there is? I've seen everything of theatre, of art; it's all repeating itself. And then I found something so new . . . it is so intriguing, so fascinating, so fitting and logical. I thought it was a fantasy, but as a child I was connected with spirits. . . . So there was already a clairvoyance in me before I went to school, and then I was abused [at] school, very repressed . . . and all these layers you have to [take] them off, one by one, and that [took me] at least ten years [of Daime] works. . . .*
>
> *In a [Daime] work, in the beginning I got a lot of corrections. It's called "peia" [in Portuguese]; it's actually an "obstacle" you have to overcome . . . it's very good lessons . . . it's like suffering, but it's also good for you to be humbled. . . .*
>
> *What the Daime gives me is that I observe myself observing, and that means I can change. . . . You observe the observer*

observing, and that's why you can change yourself with the click of your fingers, because you see directly the implementation you have on others, but also on yourself, and you see the whole picture, like [from] a helicopter. . . . After Daime works it stays in you all the time, that's really the big progress you see [over] the years.

Peia is a complex concept. When taken in Jacoba's sense of "obstacle," *peia* is like the Daime form of karma. As will become more apparent in the ensuing chapters, daimistas view their ayahuasca ceremonies as a microcosm of life itself. They presume that whatever negative thoughts or actions a person puts out into the world will eventually come back as a corrective reaction from the universe (Schmidt 2007, 167). As a word for what outsiders might conceive to be a "bad trip" during Daime rituals, *peia* is seen by worshippers of ayahuasca religions "as a sign that something inside the person must be out of tune with the cosmic order," which is often "manifested as a physical symptom; thus, the act of vomiting is seen as an expulsion of pernicious matter, as an act of purification" (Henman 2009[1985]). Besides the physiological reaction of vomiting, *peia* can also convey the connotation of "aggression (as in 'beating up')," which accounts for devotees viewing difficult or horrifying ayahuasca experiences as a psychophysical "cleansing" (Soibelman 1995, 104). In a theological treatise that summarizes some of the basic tenets of Daime belief and practice, a widely respected daimista elder gives this gloss for *peia* (Polari de Alverga 1998, 212):

Peia—A purgative and mimetic process that sometimes occurs with the use of the sacramental Daime beverage. This is considered a cleaning of the physical level and a necessary discipline to unlock resistance and crystallization in the interior level.[10]

This seemingly upside-down interpretation of severe and harrowing episodes as therapeutic provides a convenient starting point for framing fardado perspectives on ayahuasca rituals. As such, the ways that daimistas describe the suffering in Daime works and in everyday life as ultimately restorative "processes" are mirrored by the psychiatric concept of "creative illness." According to Henri Ellenberger (1968, 443), to value the "good usage of illnesses" can appear like a "moral masochism" from the standpoint of physicalist biomedicine: "With the advent of Positivism, the hedonistic utilitarian notion came to prevail that [mental] illness is simply and exclusively a disorder of psychological origin, to be cured or to be prevented by scientific methods." But what might ordinarily be taken as a self-destructive drive to undergo torments that one should really try to avoid is the crux of disagreements between materialist approaches to psychotherapy and the initiatory trials of shamanic dismemberment or mystical death/rebirth experiences (Ellenberger 1968, 445–47). Such disparity means that strictly physicalist approaches to understanding Santo Daime cannot but misunderstand the perspectives of fardados. On the contrary, Jacoba's perception of sicknesses temporarily imposed by ayahuasca as signifying a healing of despair calls to mind notions from existentialist psychology. As an ethnography that brings existentialism to bear in explaining daimistas' entheogenic piety, the present study contributes to anthropological liaisons with philosophy and theology on the question of what it means to be human.

In advancing these new interdisciplinary ventures, the present text turns to various philosophers and theologians to draw instructive links between conventional Western thought and the unfamiliar social context of Santo Daime. To start, we turn to the nineteenth-century Danish philosopher/theologian Søren Kierkegaard, a founding father of existentialism who has long received scant attention from cultural anthropologists (the writings of Ernest Becker 1997[1973] are one major exception). Recently, Kierkegaard has been gaining notice in the now-blossoming subfields of existential anthropology, the anthropology of Christianity, and the anthropology of Santo Daime (Jespersen 2016; Lambek 2015; Rapport 2002; Tomlinson 2014; Willerslev and Suhr 2018). As displayed in interview narratives from European fardados, my informants are preoccupied with self-confrontation and faith as antidotes to existential anxiety and despair. Thus, I deploy perspectives from the existential anthropology of Christianity as an efficient framework for apprehending Santo Daime beliefs and practices.

Another key observation derived from ethnographic fieldwork and interviews is that European fardados disregard the dualist split between secular science and traditional religion as obsolete. For my informants, "belief" or "nonbelief" are beside the point of human flourishing. They say that they have jettisoned belief in favor of "experience" mainly because of the phenomena they must navigate within ayahuasca states of consciousness. They say Santo Daime provides them a dependable path for directly encountering a primordial source of healing and serenity that they could not find through the established secular and religious options in Europe. They value the otherworldly happenings of the Daime rituals as opportunities to effectively confront and resolve defects of their individual selves. But apart from the power of existential anthropology for elucidating alternative systems of thought, how does the ethnographer go about appreciating fardados' quest for self-enhancement through Santo Daime? Using visual and gustatory metaphors, one of my Belgian informants communicated the ineffability of experiences brought on by the Daime sacrament:

> *I can't tell with words . . . you can [only] have an experience to get close. . . . It's like [trying] to describe colors to a blind person . . . you know or you don't know. How do you explain the taste of chocolate to somebody who has never eaten chocolate?*

Despite the dubious identity of his key informant Don Juan, Carlos Castaneda (2016[1968])[11] was right that the most important anthropological insights about New World plant medicines can only be tapped by having expert informants guide us through the experience directly.

The dialectic compilation of both first- and secondhand data about what a specific cultural experience feels like comprises a method of inquiry known as *ethnophenomenology* (see chapter 2). Relationships between *existential* "analysis of what constitutes existence" and investigations into "the question of the meaning of Being" (*ontology*) are a cornerstone of *phenomenology*, an analytic technique defined by Martin Heidegger (1962[1927], 32–33, 58–63) as a "way of access to what is to be the theme of ontology." Thus, the ethnophenomenologist elects to temporarily set aside (or "parenthesize") their own personal biases when they submit themselves to the rites of a religious culture they are trying to comprehend (an ethnographic extension of the "phenomenological epoché" of Husserl [1960(1929), 20/131–36/150–51]).

I was initially drawn to study the anthropology of ayahuasca after reading *The Antipodes of the Mind*, a book written by cognitive psychologist Benny Shanon (2002). Through his text, Shanon proceeds to "chart" the "phenomenology of the ayahuasca experience," including meticulous chapters on contents/themes of visions, encounters with supernatural light, alterations of consciousness, and time. His report is based on his personal experience with the mind-altering brew at more than 130 ayahuasca rituals in South America (Shanon 2002, 41–45). But apart from his engrossing depiction of what is an almost unspeakable affair, I was taken aback by the following remark about outcomes of his fieldwork with ayahuasca drinkers:

> Personally, if I were to pick one single effect of Ayahuasca that had the most important impact on my life (there were many and the choice of one is not at all easy), I would say that before

> my encounter with the brew I was an atheist . . . and when I
> returned back home after my long journey in South America, I
> no longer was one. . . . I did not, despite strong encouragement,
> become a member of any of the groups I associated myself with
> nor do I have any intention of doing so in the future. But my
> [worldview] was radically changed. (Shanon 2002, 8–9/260)

Years later, having carried out my own participant-observation with Daime groups in Brazil, North America, and Europe, I now empathize with Shanon's statement of scholarly quasi-entanglement. It is inevitable that researchers of ayahuasca spirituality must eventually confront their own thoughts and feelings if they choose to repeatedly indulge in the brew themselves. Unlike Shanon, I was not a "devout" atheist going into my fieldwork; like most social scientists I was more of a disenchanted agnostic predisposed to cynical deconstruction of the theological beliefs underlying any organized religion. In the social sciences, this kind of incredulous agnosticism is usually synonymous with "methodological atheism" (Bialecki 2014; Dawson 2013, 196; see also Le Poidevin 2010, 46–53). But through painstaking observational experiments at Daime ceremonies, I likewise underwent shifts in my metaphysical outlook. Now, in no way have I abandoned my resolute commitment to the Enlightenment ideals of scholarly rigor grounded in verifiable evidence. What I have come to deny is the hasty arrogance in secularist "world structures" of "closed immanence" (i.e., absolute this-worldliness), whereby issues and questions beyond what can be empirically measured are devalued as "epiphenomenal" or not worthy of serious attention (Taylor 2007, 433–34/539–93).

Everyone experiences ayahuasca in a distinct way contingent on personality and mind-set. I myself faced a panoply of weird, frightful, sorrowful, agonizing, but also ecstatic, pleasurable, and even therapeutic sessions with ayahuasca. As someone who has always felt the presence of atheist/theist cross-pressures within and outside academia, my fieldwork with Santo Daime did result in what I now feel as a private reconciliation of these secular-religious polarities within my own thinking, a stance akin to Richard Kearney's (2011, 7) *anatheism*. Perhaps I would now identify as more of an awestruck agnostic, someone who feels content with "the openness and skepticism of science wedded to the zeal and exaltation of religion . . . the veneration of mystery wedded to the solemnity of [empirical] responsibility" (Schneider 2007, 33). I am still nonconfessional in my agnosticism[12] vis-à-vis both cross-pressured extremes because I have no idea whether the ultimate nature of the universe is divine or not; however, I am now more attuned to the inscrutabilities of existing as a human being and to a sense of wonderment about Nature that was absent prior to my fieldwork (see Tupper 2011, 224–36). Directly because of my Daime experiences, I now recognize a deep wisdom in the mythoses of the world's major religions that beforehand I would have viewed with haughty suspicion. For instance, the pluralistic way my informants conceptualize Jesus Christ and other Christian figures challenged and transformed residual bitterness I had held toward my Irish Catholic upbringing, which I had stridently rebuffed as a teenager. And even though I maintain contempt for the political and moral corruption that can fester within all human institutions, I have a newfound respect for the lessons of compassion, altruism, and forgiveness that constitute the ethical root of all great religious traditions. I do not feel comfortable counting myself as a "Christian," nor as a member of any religious group for that matter. But I am now proud to say that being an anthropologist does not preclude my admiration for the faith and charity exhibited by many religious believers.

"Cultural relativism," the bedrock of modern anthropology, underscores that all human beings think about and act in the world according to (or sometimes in defiance of) the system of ideological and behavioral norms within which they were reared. Contesting ethnocentrism, cultural relativism "strategically suspends moral judgement in order to understand and appreciate the diverse logics of social and cultural practices that, at first sight, often evoke righteous responses and prevent analytical self-reflection" (see Bourgois and Schonberg 2009, 7). Philosophers also acknowledge that each person has "pre-theoretic" beliefs/intuitions, which dictate one's degree of openness to ideas *prior to* one's making a decision to accept or reject them (see Güzeldere 1997, 2; Heidegger 1962[1927], 360; Velmans 2007, 348–49). As humans, we all habitually ignore inextricable connections between pre-theoretic values informed by our enculturation and the stances we take with regard to metaphysical conundrums, such as the underlying structures of conscious life. For example, is it better to assume that the observed world of external objects is the primary touchstone for acquiring knowledge? Or should our inner sense of subjective mindfulness be treated as the epistemological starting point? Does ayahuasca cause hallucinations that misrepresent the one true objective world or are these visionary dispatches from a spiritual otherworld that normally goes unseen? The kneejerk ways in which each reader reacts emotionally and intellectually to such dilemmas show how we are predisposed to liking or disliking certain ideas at the outset.

The discipline of anthropology as we know it today was born of scholarly aspirations for a general "science of humanity" dating back to the

Renaissance (Zammito 2002, 221–22/435–36, n. 9). Over the centuries, the "empirical [social] sciences of 'physical' and 'cultural' anthropology'" became divorced from "philosophical anthropology" as "a study of [humans] in the widest sense" (Macquarrie and Robinson in Heidegger 1962[1927], 38/n. 2) and "theological anthropology" as any "doctrine of human nature" held by religious believers (Jones et al. 2005, 1972). Yet as attested by William Adams (1998, 1), the philosophical "roots" still apply to anthropology as the only social science that "dares to suggest that in studying the Other, we may learn more about ourselves than we do by studying ourselves." While anthropologists studying religion need not adopt the positions of their research subjects, Joel Robbins (2006, 287) highlights the budding but "awkward relationship" between anthropologists and theologians, which requires anthropologists to show an "openness to the possibilities" presented by nonsecular Others: "The encounter with theology might lead anthropologists . . . to imagine that theologians might either produce theories that get some things right about the world they currently get wrong or model a kind of action in the world that is in some or other way more effective or ethically adequate than their own." It is not so much that theology undercuts secular approaches to anthropology, but rather that a genuine anthropology of religion is enriched by interchanges with theologians who write about the wider philosophical sense of anthropology. I agree with Robbins that rather than continuing to omit theology as inconsistent with the goals of sociocultural anthropology, new transactions with theologians can disclose important features of religious beliefs and practices that ethnographers might otherwise overlook. In the case of the present study, Jacoba's assertion that she "overcomes" her "despair" when ayahuasca helps her to "observe the observer observing" is most expediently illuminated by existentialist theologies about the relation between self and what is considered other-than-self.

For an initial example, I turn to Jacoba's optimistic view of *peia* as providing remedial insights into her despair and other detrimental defects in her personality. This positive spin on suffering is typical of fardados, and matches Kierkegaard's (1989[1849], 43–45) theistic "formula" for how a human self can surmount the "sickness unto death" he calls "despair":

> Despair is a sickness of the spirit, of the self. . . .
>
> The human being is spirit. But what is spirit? Spirit is the self. But what is the self? The self is a relation which relates to itself, or that in the relation which is its relating to itself. The self is not the relation but the relation's relating to itself. A

human being is a synthesis of the infinite and the finite, of the temporal and the eternal, of freedom and necessity. In short a synthesis. . . .

If a person in despair is, as he thinks, aware of his despair and doesn't refer to it mindlessly as something that happens to him . . . and wants now on his own, all on his own, and with all his might to remove the despair, then he is still in despair and through all his seeming effort only works himself all the more deeply into a deeper despair. The imbalance in despair is not a simple imbalance but an imbalance in a relation that relates to itself and which is established by something else. . . .

This then is the formula which describes the state of the self when despair is completely eradicated: in relating to itself and in wanting to be itself, the self is grounded transparently in the power that established it. . . .

Despair is the imbalance in a relation of synthesis, in a relation that relates to itself.

Such a poetic itemization of the relational dialectics inherent in being a human self simulates the way fardados conceptualize existential problems they try to address through Daime works. They likewise claim that ayahuasca rituals help them resolve personal conflicts through teaching them the benefits of self-surrender into "faith" in a higher "power" (Kierkegaard 1989[1849], 165). As will be made plain in later chapters, daimistas share Kierkegaard's inverse definitions of illness and health regarding the human self. To further contextualize how this corresponds to daimistas' worldview, one can refer to how Alastair Hannay (1989, 4–5) deciphers Kierkegaard's notion of despair:

Kierkegaard detects in contemporary life-styles, in the kinds of goals people set for themselves, in their ideals of fulfilment, a fundamental fear of conscious selfhood. He calls it "despair." . . .

Despair is not a disorder of the kind that should be rooted out or prevented. Indeed, from the point of view of spiritual development, there is something healthy about it. For one thing, even if it is clearly negative, despair is at least a sign of some first inkling of the requirements of such a development. . . .

The only way of escaping despair, therefore, seems to be to go through with it. The cure is for the self to "found itself transparently in the power which established it," but since transparency here requires full self-awareness . . . and full awareness of the self is the goal of spiritual development, the cure is simply not available until one reaches the point where continued denial of one's dependence upon God is an act of open defiance. Only then does the alternative—open acknowledgement of that dependence—become possible.

For Kierkegaard, despair is a symptom of any self that is malformed in its relation to itself because it is unacquainted with or actively evading deeper truths about itself (a parallel idea was later picked up in Jung's "assimilation of the shadow" [Dourley 2014, 127]; see also Maté 2018, xvii–xviii). Similarly, fardados are preoccupied with unearthing and resolving internal disharmonies, especially the ways disharmonies manifest in a self's actions upon the outside world. In concert with their introspective practice, fardados portray their inner journeys with ayahuasca as ultimately serving to help heal despair on the collective scale of human society.

Jacoba also justified her ayahuasca practice as an opportunity to "feel the unity" or commune with fellow human beings through transpersonal experiences afforded by the Daime sacrament. When I asked why she continues to attend Daime works, she responded:

> *Because there is so much to learn, every time you have something new. . . . One of the purposes in a [Daime] work is to feel the unity: you sing together, you concentrate together, you sit together in the round . . . so this is really a community form. Singing together around the light of the candles and the Cross, it's giving a feeling of community. . . .*
>
> *Yes, everybody has his own peias (obstacles), so you work alone on your things, but your neighbour is there; on both sides you have neighbours and maybe you [are working on] the same subject . . . you can feel the sorrow and the grief from others. You have your own as well, but you can share . . . directly.*

In conversations with Jacoba, she conceded that the Netherlands is a very nice country to live in because it is relatively wealthy and safe. But she also pointed to inequality, pollution, and for-profit exploitation of the Earth's resources as corollaries of despair in Europe. From fardados' perspective, this despair develops when human selves are not connected to each other through intimate social bonds, or, as Jacoba declared, "isolation and estrangement of people makes them crazy." Her language of "estrangement" echoes theologian Paul Tillich's (2014[1952], 51–52) rendering of existential despair as an "inescapable" and "desperate . . . anxiety of emptiness and meaninglessness." Like other European fardados, Jacoba contends that ostensibly positive aspects of modern civilization camouflage ways that secularized individualism, materialism, and consumerism express a spiritual impoverishment in industrialized nations today (see also Dourley 2014, 2/13). This Santo Daime value is like philosopher Martin Buber's (1996[1937], 92–95) distinction between the utilitarian I-It approach to interpersonal relations and the I-You approach of "loving" or "true" communities:

> The improvement of the ability to experience and use generally involves a decrease in [humanity's] power to relate. . . . Standing under the basic word of separation which keeps apart I and It, he has divided his life with his fellow [human beings]. . . .
>
> That institutions yield no public life is felt by more and more human beings, to their sorrow: this is the source of the distress and search of our age. . . .
>
> When the autonomized state yokes together totally uncongenial citizens without creating or promoting any fellowship, it is supposed to be replaced by a loving community. And this loving community is supposed to come into being when people come together, prompted by free, exuberant feeling, and want to live together. But that is not how things are. True community does not come into being because people have feelings for each other (though that is required, too), but rather on two accounts: all of them have to stand in a living, reciprocal relationship to a single living center, and they have to stand in a living, reciprocal relationship to one another.[13]

Like Buber's I-You relationship, Jacoba claims that reunion with fellow human you's and a cosmic You (God) in Daime rituals has led to the progressive healing of her despair. Through transcendent "unity" they experience with each other in the Daime rituals, fardados believe they can reconcile unhealthy separations between their individual selves and the rest of the universe.

Without needing to adopt fardados' worldview, the ethnographic evidence presented herein raises questions of interest to social scientists, philosophers, legal scholars, medical practitioners, and theologians: What does the emergence of ayahuasca religion portend about the undercurrents of belief and nonbelief in Europe? Should fardados' notion of ayahuasca as a spiritual sacrament be protected as a religious freedom or should Santo Daime be prosecuted according to the War on Drugs? Is it possible that Western societies have misapprehended the hazards and benefits of so-called hallucinogens, materials that many non-Western societies value as psycho-therapeutic medicines? These questions reflect broader public concerns about drug legislation and limits on freedoms of religious expression. Disagreements about where these limits should be drawn intersect with ideological fault lines about the regulation of human fulfillment, or "fullness"; this is why what Taylor (2007, 600) calls a "swirling debate" between the "cross-pressured fields . . . [of] belief and unbelief, as well as between different versions of each, can therefore be seen as a debate about what real fullness consists in." Therefore, in order to uncover the reasons behind Santo Daime's rise in Europe, this book will augment standard anthropological techniques through consultation with Western theologians. In keeping with an established tradition of philosophical anthropology,[14] I refer to existentialist and mystical theorists to help extract the cryptic nuances of fardados' worldview. As opposed to secularist rationalizations for religious behavior, I rely mainly on theological philosophers because their enchanted ontologies are more compatible with that of fardado informants. But before delving further into these theoretical and methodological issues, we must first introduce the Santo Daime as a community of individuals who perform ayahuasca rites in Europe. Following an overview of the social settings within which I carried out ethnographic research, this section closes by formulating the scope and thrust of the present volume.

Ethnographic Contexts

Regarding all new religious forms in Europe, it is extremely difficult to ascertain exact statistics. This is because there exists a wide variety of new religions on the continent—estimated to number more than two thousand distinct groups—all of which define full-time, part-time, exclusive, or nonexclusive membership in different ways (Barker 1999, 16–18). A conservative tally calculates that Europe has 353,000 practitioners of religions founded since the start of the nineteenth century; these "new religionists" had an annual growth rate of 0.39 percent during the decade of 2000 to 2010 (Melton and Baumann 2010, lvii/lxv). Another estimate holds that participants in "alternative" religions make up between 0.3 and 0.5 percent of the European population (Lewis 2004, 16). This latter estimate suggests that out of the 731 million people in Europe at the dawn of this new century, somewhere between 2.1 and 3.6 million citizens are involved with non-mainstream religions.[15]

Considering the concept of "religion," anthropologist Talal Asad has questioned the legitimacy of applying this concept cross-culturally. In *Genealogies of Religion*, Asad (1993) traces the Eurocentric construction of "religion" into a universal category used by Western scholars to explain non-Western peoples' institutions of the sacred (Asad 1993). He rejects as "externalist" those attempts by anthropologists to define what religion is according to functionalist (e.g., Malinowski 1939) or interpretive (Geertz 1973) schemes. Instead, he recommends that anthropologists train their efforts on understanding the "internal" aspects of religion, such as worshippers' subjective construal of ritual embodiment and traditional disciplines for cultivating an ideal human self (Asad 2006, 212/234–35/240). In speaking about his own analysis of medieval Christian monasteries (see Asad 1993), Asad underscores ritual practices as an act of "willing obedience." He characterizes "monastic disciplines not as something that comes from outside but as an internal shaping of the self by the self" (Asad interviewed in Scott 2006, 272). This is a compelling critique of studies alleging that the essences of particular religions can be detected via the outward traits of symbols, language, and practice. European fardados evince similar doubts about external categorizations of religion; they prefer to accentuate the subjective, noumenal dimensions of ritualized ayahuasca experiences as a direct encounter with God inside oneself. Notwithstanding Asad's sound critique of the religion concept, for practical purposes fardados do still liken Santo Daime to all other communal forms of worship normally described as "religion" (a complex issue we will return to later on). This shows how anthropologists must also be mindful of the perils associated with the "deconstructive impulse," and heed Matti Bunzl's (2005, 534) worry that "in our discipline, we spend far too much time deconstructing the key terms of social debate and far too little time analyzing how they function in the real world." Since the present text deals with European-born Daime adherents, the Western-centric meaning of "religion" is more appropriate than it would be in say, an ethnography on Australian aborigines. In discussing cross-cultural spiritual devotion, *religion* is herein understood to be any "organized belief in phenomena that cannot be demonstrated scientifically or empirically" (Balée 2012, 55).

The term *entheogen* serves the anthropological focus of this book, which conveys fardados' insider (emic) view that ayahuasca is a medicinal sacrament. However, the theological connotations of this term are antithetical to the pursuits of medical researchers who are more concerned with psychiatric and biological effects of substances like ayahuasca. Such scholars may not be interested in religious beliefs per se, but many are attentive to the therapeutic values of spiritual experiences. Thus, the term *psychointegrator* has been proposed for strictly scientific approaches to the synchronizing effects of these substances on body and mind (Winkelman 2000, 229). While this "psychointegrative" utility of ayahuasca is germane, the terms *entheogen* and *sacred plant* will be employed throughout this text because the divine qualities fardados attribute to the Daime beverage are essential to their religious practice.

Santo Daime was founded in 1930 by an Afro-Brazilian rubber tapper and border guard named Raimundo Irineu Serra, now known as *Mestre* (Master) Irineu. After emigrating from his birthplace in the Brazilian northeast to the Western Amazon region, Mestre Irineu began to experiment with ayahuasca by borrowing from local rituals he came across in the rainforest. In visions he experienced through ayahuasca, Santo Daime mythology holds that otherworldly guides informed Mestre Irineu he would be responsible for establishing a new spirituality. He continued to "receive" *hinos* (hymns) and instructions for instituting this new religion throughout his life. His Santo Daime *doutrina* ("doctrine") began to expand around Brazil and then to every inhabited continent following the Mestre's death in 1971 (see Barnard 2014; Meyer 2014). According to published approximations, there are now as few as four thousand (Labate, Rose, and dos Santos 2008, 27) or as many as twenty thousand (Dawson 2013, 5) Santo Daime members around the world. Although sociologist Andrew Dawson (2013, 5/203[n. 21]) provides a "rough guesstimate" of "between 4,000 and 6,000" daimistas outside of Brazil, he is right to point out that "the importance of Santo Daime resides not in its size but in its significance for understanding the respective character and dynamic interface of society and religion."

Through fieldwork, I determined that the first Santo Daime works in Europe were held in Spain, Belgium, and Portugal in 1989. At this time there were fewer than a dozen European fardados. When Groisman (2000, 16[n. 10]) conducted a survey in 1996, he reported twenty-nine individual Daime groups in eleven different European countries, with a total population of 324 fardados. Although Santo Daime grew by hundreds of fardados in its first six years in Europe, since 1996 its growth has leveled out to a more gradual pace. At international Santo Daime gatherings I attended in Amsterdam in 2009 and 2010, I spoke with participants representing eighteen European nationalities. In consultation with informants from around Europe, I learned that official works are organized across twelve European countries (Austria, Belgium, England, Finland, Germany, Greece, Netherlands, Ireland, Italy, Portugal, Spain, and Wales). Independent participants also travel to Amsterdam from the Czech Republic, France, Poland, Romania, Switzerland, and Ukraine (see Figure 1.2). In total, at the time of my fieldwork there were thirty-six Santo Daime groups in Europe, comprising some 700 fardados. Individual congregations refer to themselves and the wider Santo Daime community as an *igreja* ("church," usually consecrated with the prefix *Céu do* ["Heaven of" or "Sky of"], as in Céu do Mapiá).

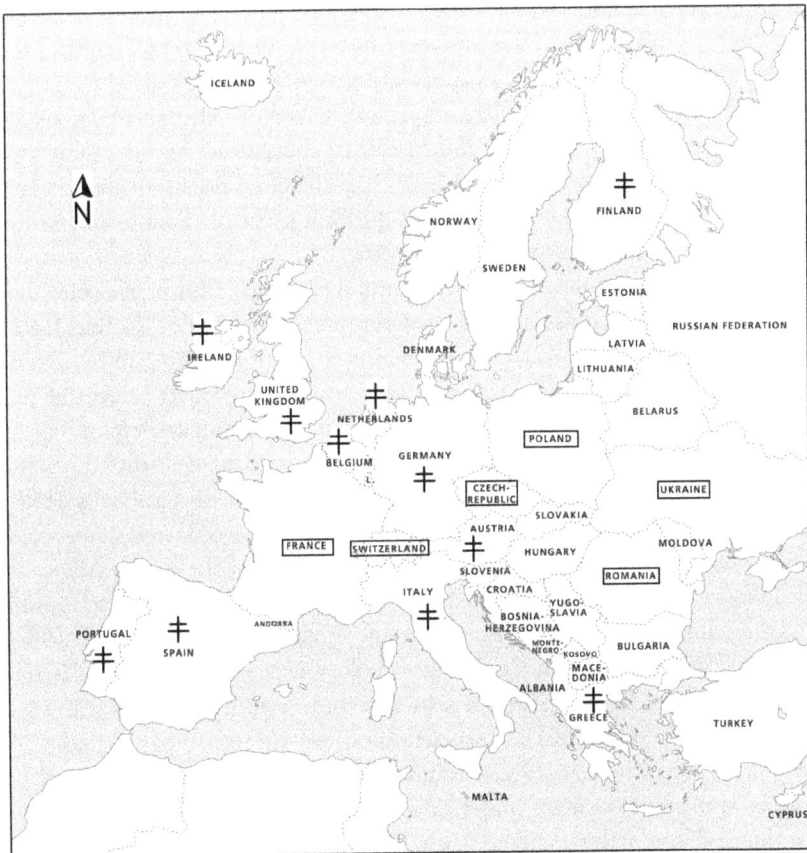

Figure 1.2. The European continent; countries in which Santo Daime congregations exist indicated by a double-armed cross (following the precedent set in Labate and Araújo [2004, 614; with Sandra Goulart]); black boxes indicate countries whose citizens attend Daime works in Amsterdam.

Santo Daime ideology is conventionally understood as made up of a mix of Catholicism, New World shamanism, Afro-Brazilian spiritualities, and European esoteric[16] theologies. The term *syncretism,* meaning "the combination of diverse traditions in the area of religion" (Shaw and Stewart 1994, 11), can apply to the Santo Daime because of its blending of components from several spiritual backgrounds. Such blending occurs to some degree in all circumstances of acculturation (i.e., when different cultures come into contact with one another). But as Droogers and Greenfield (2001, 31) note, "syncretism in itself does not indicate whether the two (or more) religions involved in the mixing process are influencing each other equally, or whether the process is asymmetric, with one dominating the other." My informants disapproved whenever I asked about contrasts between different syncretic aspects of Santo Daime. Fardados describe Santo Daime as an "eclectic, yet highly organized and spiritually aligned ritual form" (Goldman 1999, xxvi). They do acknowledge that there are different religious elements composing the Daime doctrine. However, they prefer to concentrate on how these elements' fuse into a new cohesive whole. It is therefore necessary for scholars to focus on the harmonious mixing of different spiritual traditions in Santo Daime as well as on its diverse syncretism.

Some scholars have classified Santo Daime as a form of "collective shamanism" (e.g., Groisman 2009; La Rocque Couto 1989; MacRae 1992; see Labate 2004a, 240–42), because each participant is seeking to both cure themselves and help the healing process of other individuals present at the ritual. This tendency tells us something about how some academics like to highlight the shamanistic (i.e., indigenous Amazonian) elements in Santo Daime (see Dawson 132–33; Labate and Pacheco 2011, 81–82; Narby 1998, 16–18). The shamanism notion is derived from the word *šaman,* meaning "one who is excited, moved, raised" in the language of the Tungus (Evenki) peoples of Siberia, and it entered Western parlance during the eighteenth century through writings of European and Russian explorers (Eliade 1964, 495–96; Walsh 2007, 13; Znamenski 2007, viii/3–5). Santo Daime is not directly associated with Siberian shamans, but daimistas do in some ways fit Joan Townsend's (2001) wider definition for the role of the shaman: "A shaman is one who has direct communication with spirits, is in control of spirits and consciousness, undertakes some (magical) flights to the spirit world, and has a this-material-world focus rather than a goal of personal enlightenment." But in my interviews with daimistas, they tended to temper the shamanistic aspects of Santo Daime with references to Christianity, Buddhism, Hinduism, Sufism (Islam), Kabbalah (Judaism), and Taoism.

However scholars brand it, clearly the Santo Daime doctrine melds a diverse range of religious traditions and ideas into a coherent new ensemble. It is perhaps best to generally conceive of Santo Daime as a kind of *eclecticism* (Groisman 1991; see Labate 2006, 206), since it combines the shamanic technique of ingesting an entheogen for healing purposes and the spiritist/esoteric penchant for mediumship with the mystical ambition of ecstatically uniting selfhood with God. As the field of Santo Daime studies continues to develop, it is crucial that scholars pay attention to subcultural differences between daimista communities from distinct parts of the world. For instance, while the mediumistic aspects of the Daime may take precedence in North and South America (see Dawson 2013), European daimistas express a point of view more in line with those authors who classify Santo Daime as a form of "mysticism" (Dias Junior 1991; Shanon 2002; Soares 2010; see Labate and Pacheco 2011, 76). Daimistas may emphasize different aspects of the multilayered Daime doctrine, but they agree that ritual consumption of the sacramental beverage induces "mystical experiences" (Polari de Alverga 1998, 36). We can thus also conceive of Daime as *shamanic mysticism* or *mystical shamanism*. Another terminological option is offered by Mexican anthropologist Mauricio Genet Guzmán Chávez (2008, 159), who labels Santo Daime as "Shamanic Christianity" because many daimistas believe their doctrine "represents the manifestation of Christ in the Amazon." However, as will become evident herein, even if the mystical shamanism of Santo Daime is largely based in Christianity, it also extends beyond this framing to encompass much more.

Since fardados are the most thoroughly committed and experienced class of daimistas, the present study centers more on fardados than non-member firmados[17] (i.e., daimistas who have yet to undergo a *fardamento* initiation rite). Interestingly, my informants refused to deem their decision to become fardados a conversion. As one attends more Santo Daime works and lives among the fardados, one comes to understand that the fardamento is more of an ordination. In a certain sense, in Santo Daime there is not one priest that oversees the congregation but rather everyone is their own priest. Here one witnesses how Santo Daime confounds Eurocentric notions of religion. Whereas hierarchical authorities oversee a flock of parishioners in ecclesiastical organizations such as the Roman Catholic Church, in Santo Daime churches each fardado partakes in a self-guided religious act. One of my informants compared her decision to become a fardada to a marriage ceremony. In undergoing the initiation ritual of fardamento, the newly minted fardado enters into a private relationship with the divine presence that is believed to exist inside all human persons, what Daime hymns refer to as the *Mestre Ensinador* ("Master Teacher"). Fardados say that by committing oneself to this inner study, the entheogenic drink reveals a mystical truth that all beings are extensions of one cosmic Being (i.e., God).

When I asked informants why they had become fardados, they gave a variety of explanations, but the central theme is summed up by a fardado from Belgium who said: "Santo Daime is the key to a lot of solutions." In a few words, this statement captures a range of idiosyncratic reasons behind my informants' initial attraction and long-term commitment to Santo Daime. Through a multiplicity of rationales that will be examined herein, European fardados are on a quest for "solutions." In dozens of recorded interviews, informants recounted to me how ayahuasca rituals directly improved their lives by guiding them to overcome their most difficult personal problems. They contend that Daime has repaired them emotionally, psychologically, and physically by helping them to heal various maladies, including depression, social anxiety, and alcohol/drug dependence (i.e., practical solutions). They say these practical solutions are a consequence of the Daime's instructing them in how to resolve mind/body/spirit dissonances of which they were previously unaware (i.e., metaphysical solutions).

In interviews, fardados said they are attracted to ayahuasca because it stimulates a mystical state of awareness. Hereby, the subjective boundary between the observing self and the observed world appears to dissolve. I have had this stunning sensation myself in the Daime rituals, and it is astounding to say the least. Fardados interpret this not as hallucination, but as a proof that all human selves are at one with a celestial Godhead. Santo Daime has also been classified as an "eco-religion" because adherents avow that the spirit of Father/Mother Nature is incarnated in ayahuasca (Schmidt 2007). Through the mixture of Amazonian plants in the brew, many fardados believe this androgynous deity teaches humans how to live more harmoniously with each other and with the natural world. Moreover, my informants drink ayahuasca because they believe it contains "Christ Consciousness" and that it cures by giving people direct access to other-worldly beings such as Jesus, the Virgin Mary, and a host of non-Christian spirit "guides." But these beliefs are unacceptable for most Euro-American medical and legal authorities, which currently banish ayahuasca and related substances as illegal "drugs" (Blainey 2015). At present, "Western policy-makers are reluctant to draw a line" between recreational uses of addictive drugs (e.g., heroin, cocaine) and the ritual uses of psychoactive sacraments that are relatively nonaddictive and nontoxic (Frecska 2011, 151–53).

The present text presents a detailed ethnographic portrayal of the Santo Daime religion as it is being executed beyond its geographical and social origins. Fieldwork I conducted in Brazil (one month in 2008) and Europe (fourteen months from 2009–11) was aimed at explicating fardados' belief in the safety and benefits of ayahuasca rituals. Though the majority of my informants are European-born, my purpose for spending time with them is decidedly because they have chosen to follow a spiritual tradition from Brazil. The reader will notice that a preponderance of data presented here comes from Belgian fardados. Fundamentally, I chose Belgium as my headquarters for researching the inception and subsequent growth of Santo Daime in Europe for three reasons: (1) Belgium's status as a microcosmic representation of Western European society; (2) Belgium's historical and geopolitical importance, centered on Brussels, for the past and future development of the European Union (see Blainey 2016); and (3) the fact that Belgium features one of the oldest Santo Daime outposts on the continent. Beginning in May 2010, my wife and I rented an apartment in Brussels for the year. We often peered out our window to glimpse, smell, and hear the typical happenings of this capital city of Europe: automobiles, trucks, Vespa scooters, streetcars, but also children, couples, and families conversing with each other in French, English, Dutch, Portuguese, Arabic, Turkish, Polish, German, and Mandarin. It was from this central location that I would make frequent trips to attend Daime works and interview daimistas all around Europe.

The Santo Daime Family in Europe

In the past, anthropologists were accustomed to working within a circumscribed village or district. With the rise of the internet and unprecedented transnational flows of ideas and people, scholars can no longer take for granted that the "local" exists as a static place (Gupta and Ferguson 1997, 15–16). There is an ebb and flow of Santo Daime social organization whereby fardados meet at ritual works at least four times a month,[18] between which they go back to their mostly separate lives. Daimistas' homes are geographically scattered across the continent. Thus, my field sites offered a unique methodological challenge for an ethnographer studying Santo Daime culture in Europe: namely, daimistas value the thirty or so hours they spend together at ritual works each month as sufficient for their religious community. For the most part, my informants live their own individual lives much like any other Europeans. They spend the bulk of their time outside of the church environment, going to their day jobs, raising children, and socializing with non-Daime friends/family. Of these more mainstream relationships, fardados only divulge their entheogenic practice to people they trust will accept this non-mainstream pastime. Although some daimistas do mingle with each other outside rituals (see below), there is no obligation to interact with fellow worshippers between Daime works.

The setting of ritual works is the rhythmic nucleus of daimista communities in Europe, meaning that the social nexus of their mutual interactions is transitory. Otherwise, Santo Daime is one of many other demographic subgroups that European daimistas belong to simultaneously. Considering interviews[19] collected during intensive fieldwork with Santo Daime churches in Europe (May 2010–May 2011), daimistas come from all socioeconomic classes and a range of religious backgrounds. Although most had either a Christian or atheist upbringing, some daimistas also participate in Buddhist, Hindu, or Islamic organizations. I conducted interviews with eighty-seven fardados from sixteen different European countries (this includes French, Romanian, Swiss, and Czech fardados I met at works in Amsterdam and two Israeli expatriates living in the Netherlands). Considering seventy-two informants whose personal data I collected (thirty-six males, thirty-six females), this sample has European fardados ranging from twenty-nine to seventy years old, with an average age of forty-six. They work in a variety of careers, mostly engaged in the service industries and the helping professions. In my overall count (with a few informants working more than one occupation), the Santo Daime groups in Europe feature at least thirteen teachers (of dance, music, theatre, language, schoolchildren, and the disabled), five nurses, five office workers, four gardeners/landscapers, four graphic designers, four practitioners of alternative therapies, four social workers, four small business owners, three artists, three psychologists, two medical doctors, two cooks, two journalists, two yoga instructors, two astrologers, and two Humanities PhD candidates. Other occupations include an architect, a kinesiologist, an industrial designer, an ambulance driver, a hospice care supervisor, a housekeeper, a secretary, a computer programmer, an arborist, a hotel manager, a massage therapist, a security guard, a photographer, a receptionist, a telephone operator, an economist, a baker, a jeweler, and a draftsman. Seven informants had retired from their jobs and three were currently unemployed (this unemployment rate for European fardados [4.2%] falls well below the EU societal average [>10%][20]). So other than being set apart by their dedication to Santo

Daime, the bulk of my informants typify a cross-section of the European middle class (see similar findings in Dawson 2013, 37/99/154–57). It is by converging to attend Daime rituals at regular intervals each month that participants distinguish themselves as a spiritual community. Thus, daimista congregations in Europe can be classified as "periodic" social groups.[21]

The personalities of the people who attend Daime works are diverse, to say the least. Several extraverted fardados admitted that as youths they were carefree bohemians who enjoyed a vigorous nightlife, while others are introverts who have long been teetotaling homebodies. But all fardados express that at some point in their life they became spiritually restless and noticed a hunger for deeper existential meaning. Prior to "finding" or "meeting" the Daime, many daimistas had previous training in a non-Daime form of spiritual practice. Of the fifty informants included in my core fieldwork in Belgium, there were those who had practiced or still practice forms of prayer in the tradition of Catholicism (three daimistas) or Islamic Sufism (two daimistas). They also include daimistas with experience in Hindu yoga (two), Buddhist meditation (seven), Taoism (one), and three had a background in native American or neo-pagan shamanism. However, for the remaining thirty-two informants Santo Daime was their first serious commitment to a spiritual practice. All European daimistas are associated with the wider trend of "spiritual seekers," Westerners who experiment with sacred disciplines from different cultural contexts. In general, these individuals are seeking methods that can help them endure life's difficulties with greater acceptance and grace. The common theme of today's spiritual seekers is described as a project to "resacralize the self" (Wuthnow 1998, 158–60). Daimistas personify this broader drift in the Western world: searching for alternatives to cross-pressures of traditional religion and disenchanted atheism, my informants want to be religious in a way that fuses a formal spirituality with the individual liberty prized by secular modernity.

Daimistas consider each other to be members of a "spiritual family" and it is common for fardados to refer to each other as "brothers and sisters" (*irmãos e irmãs*). This spiritual family is not confined to how much time members spend with each other in the physical realm. Such nontraditional social groups are an established subject of anthropological study. For example, fans who support European football (soccer) games constitute such a periodic community (King 2003, 13). Following Durkheim (1915, 349–50), even though the Santo Daime and soccer communities in Europe are composed of individuals who do not all live in the same neighborhood, their periodic assembly for collective ritual a few times a month is enough to sustain a sense of shared identity. The periodic rituals of Santo Daime offer an opportunity to understand how some Europeans are adopting new styles of social relationship by tapping into a globalized spiritual culture.

A mingling of Brazilian and European Santo Daime occurs through reciprocal tourism. European fardados often travel to Brazil in a kind of religious pilgrimage. When non-Brazilian daimistas bring their new religion home with them and begin to practice there, this resettlement creates a transnational network of Santo Daime's expansion. The European churches also regularly host "entourages" (*comitivas*) of Brazilian fardados for extended visits in Europe. During these sojourns, the visiting fardados stay with host fardados. European fardados are eager to improve their Portuguese and learn from veteran Brazilians, just as the Brazilian visitors are keen to improve their English as they impart expertise about the Daime. Brazilian daimistas are prone to view this cultural exchange in postcolonial terms, as a "reversed form of invasion" (Schmidt 2007, 229). However, a few European fardados complained to me that the exchange is occasionally too unidirectional. Although some informants may perceive Brazilian fardados as less open to learning from non-Brazilians, the latter will consistently discount such misgivings as gratuitous carping based in their own egotistical pride. As discussed in the following chapters, while there is considerable influence from Brazil, the Santo Daime communities in Europe are developing mainly according to local processes of socioreligious transformation.

At both the global and local level, the Santo Daime family is overseen by highly esteemed fardados referred to by the titles *Padrinho* ("Godfather") and *Madrinha* ("Godmother"), terms of endearment that mark them as authorities in the doctrine (herein shortened to Pd. and Md.). These titles are reserved for the most experienced fardados, and are bestowed only on those whose knowledge of the Daime doctrine is widely respected in their congregations. Officially, no Santo Daime member has unassailable say-so over any other. However, a hierarchy of social organization does exist when it comes to the practical matters of managing church affairs. Each Daime church is run by an individual male or female *comandante*[22] ("commander"). The commander will designate seasoned fardados to carry out various tasks (e.g., interviewing newcomers, upkeep of financial records, or overseeing the ritual space). By fulfilling such special functions, these members develop a kind of informal power within their congregations. On a national and international level, administrative duties are presided over by committee, whereby a group of fardado representatives is charged with making policy decisions for affiliated Daime churches. For instance, during my fieldwork it was a Dutch Madrinha and her most trusted confidante who served as president and secretary of a committee representing Daime churches in twelve European nations. Based in Amsterdam, members of this international board rotate for provisional terms.

Out of the fifty Belgian informants that contributed to my core research, nineteen (38%) are married, thirty-one (62%) are unmarried,[23] twenty-one (42%) have children, and twenty-nine (58%) do not have children; of the nineteen married daimistas, there are eight couples that attend Daime works together. It is not uncommon for daimistas to begin dating each other after meeting at the rituals. I witnessed three pairs of daimistas begin a courtship during my fieldwork. I also observed two instances of fardados' partners who were not involved in Daime become curious and eventually begin attending ritual works (but this is not universal, as discussed below). All daimista couples I met were heterosexual. Although homophobia appears to be present in some of the Daime centers of Brazil (Cavnar 2011, 61/64), I met individual fardados whose same-sex orientation was totally accepted in the European Daime communities. While there is much controversy about officially anti-LGBTQ2+ policies in the UDV organization and prejudice within some Brazilian Daime churches, the fardada scholar Clancy Cavnar confirms that she has "never heard of any gay or lesbian people in the Santo Daime having notable homophobic experiences in Europe or North America" (quoted in Hartmen 2019).[24]

In Brazil it is common (and legal) for children to fully partake in Santo Daime in the company of their parents. When scholars studied Brazilian adolescents who participate in structured ayahuasca ceremonies, they judged these youths to be "healthy, thoughtful, considerate and bonded to their families and religious peers" (Dobkin de Rios et al. 2005, 135). When these ayahuasca-drinking adolescents were compared to a control group, researchers found few significant differences between the two samples; overall, results reveal that the adolescents who attended ayahuasca rites consumed half as much alcohol (Doering-Silveira et al. 2005), and showed lower levels of anxiety, self-image, and attention problems relative to the control group (Silveira et al. 2005, 131). Thus, in Brazil, permission for children and pregnant women to drink Daime is officially recognized as an "exercise of parental rights" (Labate 2011a, 28–29).

Unlike in Brazil, children are generally not allowed to join Santo Daime ceremonies in Europe. Daime church leaders told me that this restriction is in place because the drinking of ayahuasca by children would only magnify the qualms of government authorities. As policy documents of the Belgian Santo Daime explicitly state: "The minimum age for participation in the ritual is 18 years of age."[25] Although children are largely absent from ceremonies and some daimistas' spouses are not interested in drinking ayahuasca, these loved ones sometimes attend nonritual events of the Daime community such as dinner parties. I met two married fardados' spouses who do not participate in Daime works, and it seemed that the non-daimista individuals in each couple respect their partner's spiritual choices. During my time in Brazil, I observed that family members who do not drink Daime are warmly welcomed into nonritual functions of the congregation. All fardados avow that drinking Daime is a deeply personal choice and that no one should be coerced into ingesting ayahuasca. Like choosing to be a priest or rabbi, my informants say that becoming a fardado is a spiritual "calling" that does not apply to everyone.

Much like any kinship structure, daimistas occasionally meet at social gatherings outside of the ritual atmosphere for meals, birthdays, administrative meetings, and scheduled hymn-singing practices. Many friendships develop between members of the church. European daimistas sometimes go on vacations together (e.g., to Brazil or other European Daime centers) and exchange reading materials. It is evident that fardados seek each other out for business opportunities. I observed informants perform babysitting, housekeeping, and yard work for fellow daimistas, tasks which were compensated monetarily. During visits I sometimes helped fardados watch over each others' children while the parents were at work. I also got to help a fardado who is an arborist trim vegetation for an elder fardada. But generally these nonritual meetings occur among subsets of daimistas that already live in close proximity to each other. As exemplified in my Belgian sample, I accompanied four Antwerp-area fardados to their regular lunch date, for which they meet at their favorite restaurant the day after Daime works. I joined the fardados of Liège for scheduled walks in the forest. There are also multiple fardados who live near each other in the regions of East Flanders, West Flanders, Luxembourg province, and Brussels. These daimista enclaves do interact socially with each other on a regular basis outside the works. However, other than smaller pockets comprising five or fewer individuals, many daimistas do not live near other daimistas, and thus only see their peers when they meet at rituals. This distinguishes most European Daime churches from those in the Netherlands and Spain, which are exceptions where daimistas live relatively nearer to each other and maintain more continuous contact. In addition, European fardados do keep up with one another and with fardados around the world by means of online social networks. Upon being invited to join these internet groups, I noticed daim-istas sharing links to spiritual websites and YouTube videos with each other. These online links are commonly related to Daime topics such as specific hymns or audiovisual footage of rituals in the Amazon rainforest. Fardados would likely not agree with their community being designated a "periodic" social group because from their emic perspective the Daime family is always connected spiritually. But for practical purposes of participant observation, the outsider's (etic) viewpoint of ethnography can only gauge social affairs in the physical world. In the Santo Daime, such tangible meetings occur mainly at ceremonial works.

Allures of the Ayahuasca Experience

After decades of neglect as a taboo subject, renewed medical and academic interest in the early twenty-first century is ushering in a "Psychedelic Renaissance" (Sessa and Johnson 2015). This is demonstrated by a surge in books about ayahuasca and other psychedelic substances published since the beginning of the century[26]. By 2008, the study of ayahuasca spirituality com-prised almost three hundred books and articles as well as more than eighty MA and PhD theses (Labate, de Rose, and dos Santos 2008, 42–48). The internet has stimulated popular interest in ayahuasca, with enthusiast web-sites exchanging stories about otherworldly visions and introspective journeys experienced under the effects of the brew (Tupper 2009). However, what it really feels like to undergo the ayahuasca experience is very difficult, if not impossible, to explain in words. Although public and professional awareness is rapidly growing, for most people ayahuasca remains a strange enigma. This book presents a balance of references, juxtaposing scholarly perspectives with daimistas' subjective accounts of what the Daime sacrament means for them.

Most of the time, after a person drinks ayahuasca they will begin to experience a reality that is very different from normal waking consciousness. When entheogenic substances are consumed in sanctified and clinical con-texts, this can bring on altered states of awareness that seem a lot like the qualities of mystical experiences (Griffiths et al. 2006; Pahnke 1963; Pahnke and Richards 1966; Winkelman 2001). Ranging from the gruesome to the sublime, this is an ineffable state that was described as the "antipodes of the mind" by Aldous Huxley (1990[1956], 92–93). Psychologist Benny Shanon (2002, 57), one of the world's leading experts on the cognitive effects of ayahuasca, characterizes the general impact of the brew thusly:

When the "force" strikes, usually around forty minutes after consumption of the brew, many are prone to vomit. It is a vomit like no other—drinkers often feel that they are pouring out the depths of both their body and their soul. . . . Usually, the harshest symptoms . . . occur during the first 90 minutes following the onset of the effect. During this time, visions can be very strong and the entire experience may be tough and even frightening. At times, the person . . . feels he or she is losing his or her senses and even going mad. Quite commonly, people feel that they are about to die. . . . With experience, however, the fear can be better managed and . . . drinkers usually begin to come to terms with the Ayahuasca experience and even enjoy it. Indeed, people may find that this experience presents them with moments of exhilaration and great wonderment.

While these difficulties are common during the first few sessions with aya-huasca, Shanon is correct in stating that there is a learning curve. Though it may seem perplexing that people would want to subject themselves to such agony, it is important to point out that the vomiting is most often associated with newcomers (see Beyer 2009, 213–14). The psychological shock and sudden onset of an unfamiliar state of awareness in one's initial ayahuasca experiences can bring on dread and nausea. But as Shanon notes in the above passage, these discomforts normally give way to cheerful feelings the more rituals one attends. Since he has personally consumed ayahuasca in more than 130 rituals, it is worth quoting in full Shanon's (2002, 41/339–40) phenomenological sketch of the brew's ego-dissolving effects:

With Ayahuasca, the divide between the self and non-self is blurred and the balance between the internal and the external changes. . . . First and foremost, under the intoxication, drinkers feel that they are more connected to nature and the cosmos at large. . . . Further, drinkers feel closer to other human beings and living organisms. The sentiments of love, empathy, and compassion common with Ayahuasca are corollaries of this effect. The closeness felt to the Divine and the Ground of all Being is another manifestation of the fundamental systemic change at hand . . . the barrier between the self and the world may dissipate to such a degree that individuality is indeed lost and the mental and the real become one.

Although such objective accounts are instructive, one ought to take seriously Shanon's (2002, 39) suggestion that the subjective feeling of the ayahuasca experience "brings us to the boundaries not only of science but also of the entire Western world-view and its philosophies." In my anthropological research, I found that European daimistas are dissatisfied with the abstract precepts of both traditional religions and secularism; instead, they are looking for direct experiences of otherworldly re-enchantment. For them, the ayahuasca experience appears as a promising avenue for curative self-exploration.

Through the course of this book, readers will gain access to a normally secluded religious community. My informants' opting for Santo Daime practice is the most conspicuous trait setting them apart from the European mainstream. The present text's focus on the apparatus of Daime ceremonies, in conjunction with daimistas' firsthand testimonies, is meant to capture the research subjects' life priorities. What does this unusual choice to become a fardado suggest about the shifting religious landscapes of twenty-first-century Europe? As the reader will see below, those Europeans attracted to Santo Daime are concerned with existential matters of holistic bio-psycho-social-spiritual well-being. By extension, this study will illuminate rationales as to why some Westerners are flouting their society's conventional belief systems, preferring a foreign spirituality to both the mainstream secularist and religious options.

2

How the Outsider Can
Understand Daimista Insiders

Despite the welcoming attitude Santo Daime members display to all new-comers, it can be cumbersome at first for an academic researcher to earn the trust of fardado informants. It is a delicate task to be an anthropologist collecting ethnographic data about European fardados because they are a vulnerable population, considered criminals by most governments. None-theless, the fardados were exceptionally patient with my many neophyte faux pas, which thankfully lessened as I learned the ropes of Santo Daime social norms. Fardados also approved of my nonconfessional status regarding their theological doctrines when they noticed that I aimed for a genuinely empirical approach to participant observation at their rituals.

Virtually every fardado I met expressed his or her willingness to pick me up at the nearest train station and host me in his or her home overnight in order to allow for the collection of anthropological data. Far-dados' residences are distributed widely across Europe. Through long-term fieldwork I visited many urban and nonurban contexts dotted across the continent. Santo Daime informants were interviewed in locations stretch-ing in all cardinal directions and in various landscapes and cityscapes. The majority of interviews were conducted during one-day meetings, either in restaurants, parks, or daimistas' residences. For example, these interviews occurred at cottages in the farming countrysides of Ireland and Portugal, apartment buildings in downtown Madrid and Vienna, modern suburban households in Germany and Switzerland, and during a stroll through the Kalmthoutse Heide nature reserve on the Belgium-Netherlands border. I sometimes met fardados' families, and cooked and ate meals with them. The recording of individual interviews allows the ethnographer to piece together similarities and differences in the backgrounds and ideologies of informants. The eighty-seven interviews ranged in length from eleven minutes to more than three hours, with a mean duration of just over one hour per fardado. In addition, I dwelt overnight in guestrooms or on couches at the homes of sixteen different fardados, stays that lasted between one and seven days (the average visit was for two nights). These visits offered me a chance to learn about fardados' daily lives in mundane settings, which complemented my interactions with them at Daime ceremonies.

Although I am not a member of Santo Daime, I delved into their rites just as an anthropologist studying Buddhism would train in techniques of meditation. My initial goal was to attend as many works as I possibly could. However, I soon realized that one has to pace oneself so as not to overexert body and mind. I have now participated in more than ninety ayahuasca rituals through fieldwork in Brazil, Europe, and North America. Of these, fifty-five were Santo Daime works in Europe. Attending these rituals is the most fruitful procedure for meeting new informants and developing rapport. While the frequency of works fluctuated over the fourteen months I was there, this is an average of just under four works per month. To put this in perspective, committed fardados attend between forty-three and ninety rituals arranged over twelve months of the official Santo Daime calendar (see Appendix II; see also Dawson 2013, 49–53). European Daime works are held in rental spaces, centuries-old Christian churches, fardados' residences, and also in the open-air of forested areas. These ceremonies can really be performed anywhere that can be assured to remain private, calm, and quiet.

In participant observation during Daime works, I initially aimed to heed David Gellner's (2001, 339) stipulation for "a minimal secularism, a kind of 'non-alignedness of religion'" among anthropologists; after all, "a fundamentalist who wandered, by error or design, into a course on the anthropology of religion would soon have to choose between being a good anthropologist and being a good fundamentalist." However, anthropologists who abide by this secular prerequisite have been inclined to see religion as founded upon supernatural beliefs that are incompatible with science (e.g., Harris 1979, 6; Wallace 1966, vi). The problem here is that in excessively trying to avoid "going native," a commitment to positivistic scientism subjects the ethnographer to yet another fundamentalist bias. Since I found this incredulous perspective needlessly encumbering during fieldwork with daimistas, I sought to sustain an aloof distance from the skepticism verging on atheism that too often pervades scholarly considerations of spirituality, particularly with Christian religions. In championing this more balanced approach, Fenella Cannell (2006, 3) writes:

> Anthropology sometimes seems exaggeratedly resistant to the possibility of taking seriously the religious experiences of others. Religious phenomena in anthropology may be described in detail, but must be explained on the basis that they have no foundation in reality, but are epiphenomena of 'real' underlying sociological, political, economic, or other material causes. It is not necessary to be a believer in any faith, or to abandon an interest in sociological enquiry, to wonder why the discipline has needed to protest quite so much about such widely distributed aspects of human experience.

Many social scientists are not at all interested in "taking seriously" the religious ideas of cultural "others." Anthropologists of this ilk are intent on displaying the deft capacities of secularist scientism to construe all spiritual beliefs as wishful fantasies (e.g., Guthrie 1993), or as Tanya Luhrmann (2018, 79) puts it: "Most anthropologists have insisted that God, or the gods, cannot be understood anthropologically except through an explicit decision to disavow the idea that such beliefs might be true." As noted by Katharine Wiegele (2005, 15) in her study of charismatic Catholicism in the Philippines, such reductive interpretations illustrate scholars' "tendency to ignore or dismiss or 'explain away' spiritual experience." This disparity in anthropological expositions of religion can only be rectified when objective (etic) construals of the evidence do not discount insiders' (emic) perspectives outright. Moreover, the results of my fieldwork with European fardados reinforce the notion that when scholars remain receptive to the emic value of religiosity for practicing devotees, science may have much to learn from mystical states of consciousness. Rather than get mired in the futile debates between theism and atheism, the present book accepts claims of both believers and nonbelievers as plausible epistemologies in and of themselves. This approach is more aligned with Luhrmann's (2012, xxiv) proper framing of "the anthropological attitude" as seeking "to understand how people interpret their world before passing judgement on whether their interpretation is right or wrong." I did not ever feel compelled to adopt the metaphysical beliefs of fardado informants. But in order to optimize ethnographic insights, I did strive to take seriously their explanations and advice about how one can most effectively approach and manage extraordinary sensations brought on by ayahuasca.

Ethnophenomenology and Existential Anthropology

When it is not constrained by atheist preconceptions, anthropology is well positioned to arbitrate in Santo Daime's clash with mainstream Western culture because of what Bruce Kapferer (2001, 344) calls the discipline's "willing suspension of disbelief."[1] As an important disclaimer, the reader of this book is going to encounter what might appear to be some very odd creeds, behaviors, and experiential accounts. In order to advance a deeper understanding of Daime spirituality, I ask readers of this book to try to maintain a similar suspension of disbelief as they learn about the anthropology of daimista worldviews.

By inspecting a religion that dispenses ayahuasca in a controlled setting, my research employs phenomenology as a "narrative strategy" for fostering "empathy" with people that the European public sphere deems irrational (Desjarlais 1992, 35; see also Csordas 1997; Desjarlais and Throop 2011).[2] In simple terms, "phenomenology is the study of structures of consciousness as experienced from the first-person point of view" (Smith 2013). Thus, in focusing on how informants subjectively interpret their lived states of awareness, my approach follows a line of thought stretching from the *anthropology of experience* established by Victor Turner (1982) to the *existential anthropology* of Michael D. Jackson (2005) and Albert Piette (Jackson and Piette 2015a). Contributing also to the subfield of phenomenological anthropology (Jackson 1996; Knibbe and Versteeg 2008; Ram and Houston 2015a), my work with European fardados pursues the approach of *ethnophenomenology*. A method originally formulated by German sociologists (see Knoblauch and Schnettler 2001), Eberle (2010, 135; 2014, 27) defines ethnophenomenology as developing empirical elucidations of "non-observable . . . subjective experiences" by recording and scrutinizing "the communicatively conveyed descriptions of extraordinary experiences . . . by everyday people." For the ethnographer trying to fathom a culture organized around extraordinary experiences, Kukla (1988, 151) writes that an essential aim of ethnophenomenology is to immerse "oneself in that culture's worldview in order to observe in oneself the effect of such an immersion." But while Kukla included the phenomenological observations of the immersed researcher, this option has been excluded by scholars who restrict ethnophenomenology to "extraordinary experiences that the phenomenological researcher never had," such as dreams, visions, and near-death experiences (Eberle 2014, 198, see also Orcutt 2019). In this view, ethnophenomenology is "quite a different approach" from *lifeworld analytic ethnography,* in which researchers "do not only rely on participant observation for their data collection, but also on . . . *observing participation* . . . a systematic phenomenological analysis of their own personal experiences as co-participants" (Eberle 2010, 135–36; see also Jackson 2013). Because of the nature of Santo Daime rituals, the present study will bridge these two methodological subcategories: the researcher does ethnophenomenology of an entheogenic "lifeworld" by comparing descriptions of fardado insiders with the extraordinariness of the researcher's ayahuasca experiences. It is through such ethnographic immersions that anthropologists can learn how to arbitrate in entrenched intercultural misunderstandings between Santo Daime ritualists and the outside world.

In keeping with Heidegger's (1962[1927], 348/496[n.xv]) origination of a philosophical bent for "existential anthropology," phenomenological methods are the empirical counterpart of ontological theorizing. As a work of Kierkegaardian anthropology, the present study recognizes that Heidegger's (1962[1927], 348/496[n.xv]) phenomenological, existential, and ontological (PEO) scope effectively secularized the theological *angst* of Kierkegaard. Jackson and Piette (2015b, 1/11) import this same relationship as the cornerstone of today's existential anthropology: "What characterizes the existential-phenomenological perspective is not only a refusal to reduce human experience to a priori categories such as the social, the cultural, the biological, or the historical, but a determination to open our minds to domains of human experience that fall outside of or defy the rubrics with which intellectuals typically seek to contain or cover . . . lived experience." Contrary to the scholarly habit of reducing complex human beliefs and behaviors to fit predetermined classifications, I am in agreement with Ram and Houston (2015b, 20) that "a better anthropology involves apprehending others' existential concerns and ordinary/extraordinary experiences through fieldwork and shared practical activity, evoking in writing what one has learned." Hence, to gain a more empathetic comprehension of their religious lifeworld, I documented the manners in which fardados advised me on how to pilot my ayahuasca experiences, as well as how they spoke about their own Daime encounters. I implemented their advice during the rituals in an effort to witness experiential parameters they describe as introspective "looking," the "holy light," an "open heart," and "ego-death." It is only through this ethnophenomenological immersion that the researcher can truly sympathize with daimistas, in that "during the highly charged process of self-awareness that is generated by the power of the Daime, they might at times feel somewhat disoriented and thin-skinned as their previous social facades and internalized cultural certainties are, over and over again, uncovered and exposed as illusions" (Barnard 2014, 683). Enacting the standard phenomenological *epoché* or "parenthesizing" technique of "abstention from position-takings" (Husserl 1960[1929], 20/95), the ethnophenomenologist endeavors to refrain from affirming or rejecting the legitimacy of experiencing extraordinary phenomena while these are underway. Ethnographers can use this "phenomenological reduction" or "bracketing" as a methodological "attitude" that carefully distinguishes the observable structure of an experience from personal prejudices of the observer having that experience (Csordas 2004, 172–73; Husserl 1960[1929], 32). With ayahuasca, this would mean that one does not spoil the opportunity to fully investigate what daimistas call a *miração* ("vision") by hurriedly dismissing it as mere hallucination.

Straddling the line between steadfast belief and adamant disbelief (what could be called "abelief"), the ethnophenomenologist's ideal niche in studying Santo Daime amounts to having one foot in and one foot out of the fardado social groups with which they deal. By participating in ritual works, I emulate Titti Schmidt's (2007, 22) research at the Brazilian Santo Daime hub of Céu do Mapiá; she discovered that "an important key to the heart of the members was [her] willingness to drink the Daime and to participate actively during the rituals. . . . According to them [she] would never understand anything about them or their work if [she] did not drink the brew." I share Schmidt's disinclination to become a member of Santo Daime.[3] But despite our lack of personal commitment, both Schmidt and I found that we secured the trust of informants by proving to them that we were earnestly willing to learn from ayahuasca. Schmidt (2007, 27) declares that Brazilian fardados were more open to providing ethnographic information to her once she began to participate in Daime works. Likewise, in my own experience with European fardados, it was clear that in order to be accepted by a Daime community, the ethnographer first has to demonstrate a capacity to face and cope with intense psychological and physical demands imposed by the ayahuasca.

Fitting in as an Ethnographer

Apart from a few informants who I could communicate with only in French, Portuguese, or (broken) Spanish, I conducted this research primarily in English. Even though this is most informants' second or third language after their native tongue, virtually all of them were adept at understanding my questions and expressing coherent responses in English. The abundance of competent anglophones in my sample reflects the relatively well-traveled, well-educated, and/or cosmopolitan tendencies of Europeans who become daimistas. Then again, the majority of hymns in all European churches are performed entirely in the main language of Brazil.[4] While not all daimistas speak Portuguese fluently (the hymnbooks contain local language translations for most hymns), the Portuguese language is marked with prestige among European daimistas. With the exception of members from Iberia and South America, daimistas' degree of Portuguese fluency correlates roughly with the frequency and length of their pilgrimages to Brazil.

After navigating the early stages of building mutual familiarity with informants, I began to assimilate. But I did not find out until the end of my fieldwork how daimistas perceived my presence among them. For instance, one of my final interviews was carried out with Saskia, a thirty-six-year-old Flemish language teacher who has been participating in Daime since 2007. She lives by herself in a row house apartment but keeps an active social life. She says that like many of her non-Daime friends of the same age, she had previously been a nonbeliever, agreeing that "if it is not proved by science, it does not exist." But since she first arrived at Daime out of curiosity, Saskia has found a deep faith in God. When I asked her what she thought about having an anthropologist hanging around all year, she replied:

> *At first, for me it was a little bit strange, because we are all studying the Daime. We are all a type of anthropologist, but in the astral world. We are all studying the world inside, what's happening there. And the first time that you said that you are making a study [of us] . . . [my] first reflex was: you have enough work with yourself* [laughs]. *But now, the more that you went to the [ritual works] . . . you take your place and you do it in a nice way.*

Her reflex was certainly correct. One quickly finds that in addition to conducting ethnographic work, an ethnophenomenological approach to Santo Daime requires a deep study of one's personal self. What daimistas call the "astral" is the otherworldly realm contacted through Daime rituals. They say that in the astral, one can interact with spiritual entities like angels or other "guides" such as Jesus, the Virgin Mother, saints, and other deceased figures. Saskia's view of all Daime participants as students of the human condition is a central element to be addressed in later chapters. Hugo, a Dutch-born fardado now living with his wife and two children in Belgium, answered the same question about the ethnographer's presence thusly:

> *I think it's helpful to see that [you] get into the same process, because [you're] doing works. That makes it easier, because I don't have to explain it on the literal side. . . . It's like talking to the irmão, to the brother.*

What he means is that many of the important aspects of Santo Daime are not relatable in words and that only by direct experience can one enter into the close-knit daimista brotherhood/sisterhood. Hugo is a thirty-seven-year-old industrial designer who has been attending Daime works since 2004. He did admit that because his wife and children are not involved in the Daime, it is difficult to share his experiences fully with them. Nevertheless, he maintains a happy and secure family life because his spouse is accepting of his Daime practice.

Officially, the ethnographer is considered a "visitor" at all of the Santo Daime churches they attend because they are not formerly enrolled as a member. Members pay a monthly due of fifty Euros while nonmembers pay between thirty and sixty Euros for each individual work[5] (I paid the nonmember fee for each work I attended). In the process of becoming acquainted with members of the Daime groups in Europe, they offered comments about my progress and politely critiqued my novice shortcomings just as they do with any newcomer. But unlike other nonmembers who attend these works, such as firmados preparing for fardamento initiation and independent "psychonauts"[6] attracted to ayahuasca but averse to joining any organized religion (Harvey 2012, 105–109), the ethnographer studying Santo Daime is a unique kind of visitor. My status as a visiting anthropologist was ambiguous because I was deeply invested in learning as much as I could about fardados' beliefs and practices (like the firmados), but at the same time I remained utterly uncommitted to Daime theology (like the psychonauts). As Courtney Bender (2010, 182) attests in her book on eclectic American spiritual seekers she terms "New Metaphysicals," social scientists tend to "ignore," "neglect," or "deflect" how such groups expose "entanglements" that "unsettle . . . the binaries of religious and secular institutional differentiation" (e.g., Dawson's [2013, 157–199] objective discussion of daimistas and "entangled modernity"). Bender (2010, 15–18) is right that although researchers may try to remain outsiders when they study and publish about Western spiritual seekers, they inevitably get "caught up" in informants' nonsecular interpretive agendas. Regarding ethnophenomenological research with Santo Daime, one cannot overlook these entanglements when the academic intentions of the scholar are reliant upon fardados' emic categorizations of ayahuasca states of consciousness. Put bluntly, my ethnography of European fardados would have been deficient had I not drunk ayahuasca with them nor sincerely implemented their guidance in the rituals. To reconcile this ambivalence, I turn to Graham Harvey's (2004, 171) endorsement for a supple "guesthood" in ethnographies of religion, which presumes it "vital to be open to the possibility of being changed, finding that those with whom we dialogue know more than we do about important matters, and welcoming the opportunity to revise lifeways and thought patterns." Since I am an outsider seeking to understand what it means and what it feels like to be an insider, I settled on assuming this stance of guesthood relative to daimista informants. My hope is that as the work of a guest ethnographer, the present text can build intercultural bridges between fardados and a mainstream society that is as yet unfamiliar with Santo Daime.

Answering the Research Problem

My methods are oriented around supplementary research questions concerning the multidimensional social implications of Santo Daime's arrival into non-Brazilian contexts:

- What personal traits are shared among Europeans who have converted to the Santo Daime?

- How do European fardados view the inclusion of ayahuasca in Daime rituals relative to their decision to commit to this religion?

- What features of the Santo Daime's eclectic belief system are most important to European fardados, and why?

Answers to these secondary research questions about personal attributes, the effects of ayahuasca, and religious syncretism jointly address my principal research objective of ascertaining why Santo Daime is drawing European devotees. In order to elicit relevant ethnographic information, in recorded interviews informants were asked questions such as:

- What initially attracted you to Santo Daime?

- Why do you continue to attend Daime works?

- How is it that Daime impacts your life positively/negatively?

- How has the Daime influenced how you think and feel about the meaning of human life and death?

- Can you describe what it feels like during a Daime work?

- In your opinion, what is the best way to approach and deal with ayahuasca experiences?

I then also inquired about particular details of Santo Daime worldview and about other topics that spontaneously came up in the course of each interview. Fardados' responses spell out justifications underlying the movement of the Santo Daime from Brazil to Europe.

As regards my research sample (eighty-seven daimistas in Europe), the nature of this ethnographic population requires several sampling considerations. Since my research involves a "special population" whose members are not localized as a residential community, random sampling methods are inappropriate[7] (Taylor and Griffiths 2005). Bernard (2000, 76) states that, typically, "life history research and qualitative research on special populations (drug addicts, trial lawyers, shamans) rely on judgment sampling" whereby researchers select "a few cases for intensive study." Philippe Bourgois (1999) has advanced a resolute defense of "the power of small samples" in anthropological studies of people who use illicit substances. He argues that purely "quantitative researchers do not understand the intensity of the relationship one must develop with each individual in one's sample to obtain information that addresses the cultural contexts and processual dynamics of social networks in its holistic context" (Bourgois 1999, 2158). Hence, the small population size of European daimistas and the fact that this study focuses on the ritual ingestion of a banned psychoactive substance necessitates a "judgment" (or "purposive") sample of fardados that agreed to an interview.[8]

The most straightforward way to attain an understanding of how drinking ayahuasca motivates Europeans' dedication to Santo Daime is to ask the fardados themselves. Asad (1996, 266) confirms that religious conversions in the West are normally expressed as narratives through which people apprehend and describe "a radical change in the significance of their lives"; often, "these narratives employ the notion of divine intervention; at

other times the notion of a secular teleology." Thus, I tape-recorded informants' spoken narratives about what initially attracted them to the Daime,
and about how their worldview has changed since they became fardados.
In these interviews, fardados were asked to recount how altered states of
consciousness induced by ayahuasca had impacted their lives.[9] Following
the style of Bourgois's (2003) book on New York crack dealers, the present
book includes numerous direct quotations that allow European daimistas
to enunciate their devotion to Santo Daime in their own words. But since
we are dealing here instead with ritualized ayahuasca therapy, the analysis of
fardados' spirituality will align with Thomas Csordas's (1997, 3) requirement
that ethnographers explain the "mechanism" or "experiential specificity of
effect in religious healing"; this means that the phenomenological "locus
of efficacy is not symptoms, psychiatric disorders, symbolic meaning, or
social relationships, but the self in which all these are encompassed." The
present text considers a group of people who espouse existential views of self
that are atypical relative to most other Europeans. This cross-cultural clash
demands anthropological scrutiny, the results of which will contribute new
avenues for conversation between the divergent ideological norms assumed
by fardados and the wider Western populace.

After a year of learning how fardados view the nature of existence,
certain patterns emerged in their explanations for why they attend Daime
works: they are seeking and are convinced that they are obtaining "solutions" to personal and interpersonal problems through ayahuasca rituals. As
an initial example I turn to the perspective of Nadia, a forty-two-year-old
massage therapist who lives with her husband and three children in the
Belgian province of Antwerpen. After attending Daime works informally
for three years, she became a fardada in 2005. Her husband is not a committed daimista, but he attends works with her a few times a year because
he finds them beneficial. Although Nadia had abandoned the Catholicism
of her upbringing, she found in her thirties that she had "a big desire for
something else." She remembers losing some of her longtime friends after
she realized she would rather attend Daime works than continue partying
at nightclubs. In evocative language that reveals how she approaches the
Daime experience, she described the results of her spiritual practice like this:

> It corrects my behavior in a very strict way. It makes me concen-
> trated in life, how I act towards other people, to my children, to my
> husband. I can't say it's always easy because you're born with some
> [mental] patterns that are very stuck sometimes. To be free of them

it takes a long time, but I feel very covered by the Santo Daime, because [these patterns] lead me in a certain way, they show me how to act from the heart . . .

For me, I'm grateful that I've met the Santo Daime, it's a wonder to me. . . . I've become closer to Nature, I'm more in touch with the universe. . . . I'm conscious about the Earth, about who I am. . . . It liberates you, but it's not always easy. . . . You lose friendships, but it's not bad because these are friendships that are not worth it. . . . Loneliness is a part you have to go through before you get liberation. It's like you go to the desert and it's heavy to walk. It's like a test in trust, you know, and sometimes you lose trust; you think "Oh, Santo Daime, is this really something good?" and you get doubts. I think everybody goes through that [fasting] in Santo Daime, or maybe not everybody but I did. . . .

Before I drink the Daime I ask for healing, and to harmonize again the situation, and then the Daime lets me see the solution. . . . Once you get to this concentration, once you really understand it, then some things come open again, and you come on all the levels, and there you see the solutions. But you have to concentrate yourself or nothing can happen. And that's also in your daily life: If your mind is distracted, and you go left and right, you're restless, down, depressed, so nothing can come in. And that's what the Daime also lets you see. The Santo Daime is for everyone, but I understand not everybody can understand it, or wants to understand. It's a certain language that you have to learn, and it takes a while. . . . To be humble. . . . more união [union] . . . you live more with your heart.

The theme of Santo Daime's ameliorative function arose in all of my interviews with European fardados. While any purported advantages of ayahuasca remain controversial relative to prevailing biomedical paradigms, fardados are proficient at verbalizing their own folk theories about how the Daime can heal. Nadia's language of "solutions" as related to learning how to live and act "from the heart" is common fardado parlance for valuing the transcendence of subconscious ego conflicts. Informants equate the sense of being a separate "ego" with the "mental" process of discriminating and segregating the world through intellectual concepts. While fardados celebrate the practical uses of human beings' mental faculties, they believe that this must be balanced with the heart's natural sense of "intuition." They posit that this spiritual function of the heart simultaneously links all individual beings to a single divine consciousness. As one veteran fardado said about the purpose of Daime works: "We work to open our hearts . . . and then you are ready to go to the Higher Consciousness." By this logic, in "opening" one's own heart through the dissolving of ego boundaries, one learns how to connect on an intuitive level with that which the mind usually segregates as other-than-self. Fardados explain that this energetic "synchronicity" adjoining everything in the universe is "very subtle," and thus it goes unnoticed when the heart is closed or when one lives too much in the mental-ego.

To tease out these emic conceptions, this book refers to fardados' language of Daime "solutions" as a multidimensional trope. Hereby, they claim that Daime affords solutions to daily problems by encouraging meta-physical solutions within a subject's consciousness. This core element of daimista worldview was demonstrated by a fardado I will call Gunther, a middle-aged psychologist from the Czech Republic. When I met him in a café he was adamant that I protect his anonymity, lest the Czech authorities try to impede his ability to travel to Daime works elsewhere in Europe. Gunther had already undergone intense training in Hindu yoga before he started attending Daime rituals in 1996. When I asked for his opinion about how Daime works can help people, he proceeded to explain what he sees as the precise "mechanism" of parallels between ideational "solutions" and psychophysical healing:

> *I think that one of the important mechanisms is the ego goes through the process of having its firm ground taken away from it, which creates tension, anxiety sometimes, and different responses to this. . . . One of the functions of the ego is to build defenses. And one of the first things is [Daime] breaks down the defenses . . . and then sometimes this is very painful because the ego is not prepared for it. . . . So I think in the long term, as people go through this repeatedly, it really teaches them not to build the defenses in the first place. So I think this is the personality growth that is based not on consuming Santo Daime, but on participating in the [Santo Daime] works.*
>
> *Another thing of course is people who do not have a strong enough ego can have problems. I met several cases that were definitely not helped by [Santo Daime]. . . . The ego itself is a difficult word,*

because it's also used in a negative way. For example, most of the New Age authors use it as a negative thing: you have to diminish your ego. . . .

What I mean by "ego" is a set of reactions, expectations, and beliefs that are developed to interface between the soul (or the self) and the world. . . . Of course it's a positive thing; we have to have [our ego] well structured so that we are able to work in the world; if we don't have it, we fall apart. . . . If we have [our ego] well structured, then we should (if we want to grow) work with it so that it's really serving us . . . loosening the hold of ego over the functioning of the whole system. . . .

INTERVIEWER: *This sounds a lot like what other fardados say about the relation between ego and humility; does Santo Daime teach about humility?*

GUNTHER: *Humility is [an] attitude which helps to let the ego mechanism dissolve, because with this attitude you are not feeding it, so it can dissipate, and you can face the situation anew. . . . Humility would definitely be part of the healthy ego, and it can also be part of an unhealthy ego, because you can apply humility to a situation when it's not appropriate . . . because humility can be a passive relationship to something or someone which might not be okay. . . .*

I think that's one of the problems with certain approaches to spirituality: they confuse the dissolution of the ego with evolution, with growth. How I understand it is ultimately, it is about the dissolution of the ego (like the dissolution of salt in water), but meanwhile we have to first make it loose and make it more efficient, and take away the most important garbage which is a part of the ego. And some approaches, for example drinking lots of ayahuasca [outside of a formal religious context], what they basically do is they really dissolve the ego on the spot. Which is good because it gives you the perspective . . . but then you have to come back to the ego [in daily life]. It doesn't make a saint out of you. If it would, then you would not need to come back to the ego. But you are not [a saint], so you then have to start [everyday] functioning again and the problem is if you just go by this [profane] approach, just shoot [the ego] blank, then start again [after the ayahuasca], I'm not sure that in the long term it's functional towards growth. For example,

*I know some people, they do psychedelics for this reason, because
they like to [dissolve] the ego, but that by itself is not the solution.*

This diagnosis and prescribed remedy for individual and social problems is
typical of European daimistas, in that they insist there are existential-phenomenological dynamics extending well beyond what is known about
ayahuasca's diminishing action on the neurological "default mode network"
(DMN) (see dos Santos et al 2016, 1240; Palhano-Fontes et al. 2019, 661).
While fardados do not associate inner "tension" with hereditary sin, they do
concur with Kierkegaard (1980[1844], 43–45/61/92–93) that "anxiety"[10] is
an ever-present discomfort about the "yawning abyss"; this father of existentialism also said anxiety is a "dizziness of freedom" for a being that is a
"synthesis of the psychical and the physical," as humans' mental imagining
of infinite "possibilities" is constantly overshadowed by the mortal finitude
of an animal body (see also Marino 1998). Kierkegaard's concept of existential *angst* as a primeval "dread" or "anxiety" is also described by Heidegger
(1962[1927], 227[n1]/356) as coming "face to face" with the "nothing"
of one's impending death. Further refining this topic of relations between
despair and existential anxiety as a reaction to the "threat of nonbeing,"
Tillich (2014[1952], 38/53) identifies how

> all human life can be interpreted as a continuous attempt to
> avoid despair. And this attempt is mostly successful. Extreme
> situations are not reached frequently and perhaps they are never
> reached by some people. The purpose of an analysis of such a
> situation is not to record ordinary human experiences but to
> show extreme possibilities in the light of which the ordinary
> situations must be understood. We are not always aware of our
> having to die, but in the light of the experience of our having
> to die our whole life is experienced differently. In the same way
> the anxiety which is despair is not always present. But the rare
> occasions in which it is present determine the interpretation of
> existence as a whole.

Daimistas share the existentialists' awareness of anxiety as a subliminal disquietude underlying all human affairs. From this angle, every human has
existential anxiety because we all find ourselves "thrown" into this life, a
baffling situation in which we are free to think whatever we wish even while
deep down we are uncertain about the meaning of it all and we are aware

we will one day perish from this place (see Becker 1973[1997], 155–156; Heidegger 1962[1927]). According to my informants, Daime works provide practical solutions because these rituals tend to intensify existential anxieties to the point where "ego" boundaries "dissolve" like a salt submerged in water. In this transpersonal state, anxiety is replaced by a feeling that observer and observed have fused into a single entity (i.e., a metaphysical "solution" of self and Cosmos/God).

Like other Western spiritual seekers (e.g., Bender 2010), when daimistas talk about "ego" they are calling attention to the divisive selfishness of individual subjectivities in conflict. In contrast to the popularized translation of Freud's "I" (*Ich*) as "ego,"[11] my informants believe that people's everyday egoic concerns are actually a preoccupation with a mirage that impedes social and spiritual evolution. As will be clear throughout the remainder of this book, fardados disparage egotism in an existential sense closer to the thinking of Buber (1996[1937], 112–15):

> Egos appear by setting themselves apart from other egos. . . . The purpose of setting oneself apart is to experience and use, and the purposes of that is "living"—which means dying one human life long. . . . The ego does not participate in any actuality nor does he gain any. He sets himself apart from everything else and tries to possess as much as possible by means of experience and use . . . The more a human being, the more humanity is dominated by the ego, the more does the I fall prey to inactuality.

But as Gunther emphasized above, in agreement with Huston Smith (2000, 33–43), ayahuasca is not by itself a remedy for the unhealthy ego and it can even be dangerous when consumed outside of well-tried ritual contexts. Gunther acknowledges the fact that ayahuasca is inappropriate for people who do not have a stable personality. It is true that ayahuasca poses more dangers for people with "abnormal metabolism or a compromised health status," such as those with blood pressure diseases, or schizophrenia or other psychotic tendencies; but otherwise, the risks of ayahuasca rituals are "minimal"[12] for average adults (Gable 2007, 24/29/31). Fardados emphasize the importance of ceremonial traditions and hymn lyrics as necessary guidelines for safely integrating the wider moral canons of the Daime "doctrine" into one's daily life. The ethical teachings of the Daime doctrine supposedly help people cultivate a healthy ego that is less officious after being "dissolved" in the ayahuasca experience. Subsequent chapters will cover this "solutions" trope as it pertains to the phenomenological elements of Daime experiences. This analysis of fardados' explanation of Santo Daime as an intertwinement of psychophysical therapy and existential salvation adds to the growing corpus of studies concerned with the anthropology of well-being (see Fischer 2014; Mathews and Izquierdo 2009).

When one tries to take seriously fardados' unorthodox view of existence, they are pointing out what they see as a fundamental flaw in Western civilization's habitual approach to human life. Fardados identify Europeans' overreliance on an egotistical sense of self as the source of most practical and existential problems. They claim that even if it is a necessary component of daily life, our ordinary experience of egoic divergence between the individuated observer and the observed world is fundamentally superficial. In accordance with scholarly reports about the entheogenic experience (Doyle 2012; Pahnke 1969), fardados explained Santo Daime as a "mystical" death or "letting go" of the ego. This view was expressed by Izaäk, a forty-eight-year-old graphic designer from Belgium who is also trained in the Asian alternative therapy of *shiatsu*. At the time of my fieldwork, Izaäk lived with his wife and their two kids in an urban East Flanders row house. Both he and his wife have been fardados since 2005. Izaäk described his ideal approach to the Daime in terms that echo Alan Watts's[13] writings on faith:

> *The mystical part is, in a way, always an experience of dying. So, [it's] what we're going to have in our last moment. Every Daime work is training for dying, so when the moment comes you'll be prepared. . . . It's total ego-loss. So your ego will always try to have control, even in the [ritual] work situations. At that moment, you just have to break through the membrane . . . it's a death of the ego at that moment, and then you go to a Higher Consciousness. And in a way the ego is still there, but it's not active anymore, it's on standby. But to pass that moment is the most difficult. Some people flip out, because you really have to let go. It's like going into the abyss and just trusting it. You don't have to grab a rock, you'll fall even faster [laughs]. So don't catch anything. If we're swimming, it's the same thing: you don't catch the water, you just get into the water.*

This ego-loss is not permanent, as the feeling lasts only a few hours, gradually dissipating after each work. Fardados say that Daime mystical practice just gives one a window of opportunity to see that one's being does exist beyond the ego. Analogous remarks were made by Alida, a middle-aged

Dutch fardada who works as a psychic therapist and a palliative care worker. Drawing on sixteen years of experience with Santo Daime, she also portrayed her ayahuasca experiences as a momentary death of the ego:

> *You die a lot of times in the Daime. . . . Your ego dies a lot of times. I've experienced many times that the Daime gives so much energy that you think, "I can't handle this." I collapse, I die! And then you don't . . . you only think that you die.*

Not unlike Kierkegaard's calling existential despair a "sickness" of the self (see Hannay 1998), fardados allege that overidentification with one's ego (through the dualistic belief that one is separate from external reality and distinct from other egos) has become a common mental illness in Western civilization. They believe that unhealthy dependence on ego causes people to fight with or dismiss one another, and can result in disharmonies of the self, which then manifest as physiological symptoms and social conflicts. Just as Kierkegaard valued self-reflexive anxiety as a " 'school' that provides [humans] with the ultimate education, the final maturity" (Becker 1997[1973], 87), fardados say that ayahuasca ego-death experiences teach them about faith as a "solution" to despair (see also Richards 2016, 60/104–12).

To supplement qualitative insights reaped through ethnophenomenological interviews and participant observation, I also employed standard techniques of cognitive anthropology to gather quantitative data about fardados' shared systems of meaning. This involved cultural domain analyses via two freelisting experiments. First, I asked dozens of fardados to list all the "sacred plants" that they know. The tabulating of their collective responses shows that they consider psychoactive or "entheogenic" vegetation and mushrooms as the most sacred exemplars of this category (see Part V). As seen in their responses to the second freelist and a triad exercise regarding "Great Spiritual Teachers," European fardados perceive an unbroken link between ancient and modern pursuits of spiritual enlightenment (see Part VI). Albeit couched in distinct cultures separated by vast spatiotemporal distances, my informants locate a universal and yet ever-evolving pinnacle of human fulfillment as achievable through different schools of ritualized contemplation. By concentrating on emic perspectives, the present study discloses that introspection is the main interest of most European fardados, a penchant that distinguishes this regional subculture from the mediumship that seems to predominate among Daime groups in North and South America (Barnard, forthcoming; Dawson 2013). All fardados are familiar with the writings of famous saints from a variety of historical periods and cultural contexts. They seek out mystical wisdom in all its forms as a source of practical advice about how to grow in existential maturity. Moving beyond Richards's (2016) theoretical suggestion that psychedelics can occasion mystical experiences when used in clinical settings, my book analyzes ethnographic data collected with actual mystics who practice a full-fledged entheogenic religion.

The present volume presents the findings of this mixed methods research, showing how fardados think about Santo Daime (both the beverage and the religion) in ways that can be rendered comprehensible to outsiders. A preliminary summation locates my informants as largely in agreement with an ideal of nonduality (an underlying union of opposites) that has been championed by mystics from different cultures and time periods (Wilber 1998, 12–15). Daimistas are aware of how their cosmology resembles what Western mystical authors speak of as the "Perennial Philosophy" (Huxley 2009[1945]), "egolessness" (Kornfield 2000, 74), or "holotropic" awareness (Grof 1998). At the same time, fardados speak of their spiritual beliefs as following the teachings of indigenous shamans and the "great spiritual teachers" of Hinduism, Buddhism, Taoism, Judaism, Islam, and Christianity. This predisposition to interpret different religious systems as built upon the same underlying truths is a topic that will be developed in later chapters. Prior to addressing the European context more directly, the next section will acquaint readers with the South American origins of Santo Daime and its ayahuasca sacrament.

PART II

FROM AMAZONIA WITH LOVE

Figure 3.1. *Execution of the Inca of Peru by Pizarro*, By: Alonzo Chappel (1533). Credit: Wellcome Collection (Creative Commons).

When two disciples begged Our Lord for a place on his right hand and on his left, he offered them instead the chalice that he had to drink as a thing more precious and more secure on this earth than is the possession of pleasurable things.

This chalice is death to the natural self, a death attained through detaching oneself from the world and bringing that self to nothing, in order that the soul may travel by this narrow path with respect to all its connections with the senses and to the spirit. On this way there is room only for self-denial and the Cross. Therefore Our Lord said through Matthew: My yoke is easy and my burden is light. And this burden is the cross.

—St. John of the Cross, *Ascent of Mount Carmel*

Before there can be a science of [humanity] there has to be the long-awaited demythification and reenchantment of Western [people] in a quite different confluence of self and otherness. Our way lies upstream, against the current, upriver near the foothills of the Andes where [indigenous South American] healers are busy healing colonists of the phantoms assailing them.

—Michael Taussig, *Shamanism, Colonialism, & the Wild Man*

3

Tracing Origins

The brown liquid called ayahuasca is the focal point of Santo Daime spiritual practices (Figure 3.2). Two basic ingredients are required to make ayahuasca. The primary entheogenic qualities of the brew come from DMT,[1] provided by leaves of the *Psychotria viridis* shrub or sometimes the vine *Diplopterys cabrerana*. But the potential effects of this chemical are neutralized when it is ingested orally by itself because our body's Monoamine oxidase (MAO) enzyme breaks DMT down in the stomach. Hence, the pulverized wood of the *Banisteriopsis caapi* vine is included in the brew because it contains β-carboline harmala alkaloids (i.e., harmine, harmaline, and/or tetrahydro-harmine). These β-carboline chemicals act as MAO inhibitors (MAOI). The inclusion of MAOI allows orally administered DMT to pass from the stomach into the bloodstream so that the drinker experiences the full force of the entheogen, usually lasting from four to twelve hours depending on the dose (Callaway 2006, 100–102; McKenna, Callaway, and Grob 1998, 67; Shulgin 2003, 109–10). This creation of an entheogenic beverage by combining plants whose chemical ingredients are inert—or inconspicuous[2]—when ingested alone represents an innovative technological achievement on the part of indigenous Amazonians.

The title of this book refers to Santo Daime's Amazonian origins in order to highlight that the European gaze upon far-flung "jungles" still recalls colonialist etymologies, denoting a tropical "area of land overgrown with dense forest and tangled vegetation" and "a situation or place of bewildering complexity or brutal competitiveness"[3] (cited in Roger 2012, 5). So while indigenous locals do not perceive the Amazon as so foreboding, such connotations of jungles are a fixture in the European psyche. In reply to

Michael Taussig's (1987) *Shamanism, Colonialism, & the Wild Man*, a classic ethnography about the hideous ways that Western imperialism reshaped life in Amazonia, the present volume assesses the recent importation of an Amazonian ayahuasca religion into the West. Like Taussig turned to Karl Marx and Walter Benjamin to reflect on European terror and shamanic healing in the Amazon, I consult existential philosophers and mystical theologians to illuminate a legacy of Europeans' effort to Christianize native South Americans that has resulted in the arrival of shamanic Christianity into Europe. In particular, I aim to demonstrate why European fardados are seeking to alleviate various forms of despair by drinking the vegetal tonic that Taussig's indigenous informants call *yagé*.

Figure 3.2. A cup of freshly made Daime tea—still warm, collected after the author participated in a *feitio* ritual at Céu do Mapiá in the Brazilian Amazon (Photo by author).

Traditional and Novel
Ayahuasca Practices in South America

The misty origins of ayahuasca date to sometime before the arrival of Europeans in South America. Routinely, the best conjecture that modern scholars can put forward for how pre-Columbian South Americans developed the basic recipe for ayahuasca is through "trial and error." But ethnobotanist Wade Davis (1995, cited in Narby and Huxley 2001, 289) stresses that this phrase ignores the socially ingrained skills and knowledge of indigenous peoples; they somehow managed to pair the distinct botanical requisites that are "orally inactive" by themselves, but when combined, "the result is a powerful synergistic effect, a biochemical version of the whole being greater than the sum of the parts." Davis proposes that instead of imagining the first discoverer of ayahuasca as having unwittingly stumbled upon the precise plant mixture, one must consider indigenous botanical knowledge as akin to experimental research by scientists in our own culture. Shanon (2002, 16) further extends this reconsideration of the origins of ayahuasca's botanical formula:

> When one thinks about it, the discovery of Ayahuasca is indeed amazing. The number of plants in the rain forest is enormous; the number of their possible pairings is astronomical. The common-sense method of trial and error would not seem to apply.

Alas, the prehistoric genesis of ayahuasca remains a mystery to Western science, since the initial commencement of any trial and error project with plants that are otherwise inactive when ingested alone is inexplicable in terms of secular rationality. Narby (1998, 11) underscores the indigenous explanation for how ayahuasca was invented: "It is as if they knew about the molecular properties of plants *and* the art of combining them, and when one asks them how they know these things, they say their knowledge comes directly from hallucinogenic plants." Many European fardados also reported to me their belief that they had received messages from intelligent spirits contained within the Daime sacrament.

The indigenous use of ayahuasca—which is called different names such as *yagé, caapi,* and *nixi pae,* depending on the cultural context—was first documented by José Chantre y Herrera, a seventeenth-century Jesuit priest who (citing an unknown, undated source) referred to it as a "diabolical brew (brebaje diabólico)" (Brabec de Mori 2011, 46n20; Ott 2011, 105).

The first outsiders known to have personally experimented with ayahuasca were the Ecuadorian geographer Manuel Villavicencio (1858) and the British botanist Richard Spruce. Both authors describe the ayahuasca intoxication as involving intense imagery, defining the overall experience as a predictable progression from dreamlike bliss to frightening anguish. Spruce drank "half a dose" of the tea in 1852, when he visited a native community on the Uaupés River (Amazonas, Brazil). However, he had to rely on the stories reported to him by "intelligent traders" because his own experimentation was interrupted before he could feel the brew's full effects:

> White men who have partaken of caapi in the proper way con-
> cur in the account of their sensations under its influence. They
> feel alternations of cold and heat, fear and boldness. The sight
> is disturbed, and visions pass rapidly before the eyes, wherein
> everything gorgeous and magnificent they have heard or read
> of seems combined; and presently the scene changes to things
> uncouth and horrible. . . . A Brazilian friend said that when
> he once took a full dose of caapi he saw all the marvels he had
> read of in the *Arabian Nights* pass rapidly before his eyes as in
> a panorama; but the final sensations and sights were horrible,
> as they always are. (Spruce 1908, 420–21)

Just as Spruce's account characterized indigenous ayahuasca rituals as nothing but a spectacle of masochistic confusion, psychoactive plants such as ayahuasca continue to be feared as poisonous narcotics by the majority of modern Western laypersons. However, when we pay attention to the minority voices of scientists and entheogenic devotees (see Luna and White 2000), these more empirically informed perspectives make it easier to understand why some people who are searching for answers to life's big questions are attracted to mind-altering plants.

Ethnobotany of Ayahuasca

It was Spruce (1908) who bestowed a scientific label on the vine that he learned was the main constituent of the ayahuasca. He identified it as a member of the genus *Banisteria* (later renamed *Banisteriopsis*) and added the *caapi* species name because it was the term that his native hosts used to designate both the vine and the potion made from it. In fact, as with the more popular term *ayahuasca* ("vine of the soul" or "vine of the dead" in Quechua), indigenous tongues often use the same name to refer to either the finished liquid or the *Banisteriopsis caapi* vine by itself (Beyer 2009, 207–208). This woody liana plant is widespread in the area east of the Andes mountain range, where lowland tropical forests are interlaced with tributaries feeding the Amazon River. The vine is well known in ayahuasca subcultures for its knotted helix shape, taking the form of a twisted rope as it climbs alongside and between the trunks and branches of larger trees. When either the cultivated or wild varieties of *B. caapi* are harvested[4] and cut into smaller chunks, it exposes the lobed cross-section of the vine's inner flesh. Here, one witnesses this vine's distinctive patterns of light- and dark-brown "bands . . . spiraling around the axis"[5] (Gates 1982, 10/112–14).

It was originally thought by early researchers that the primary psychoactive effects of ayahuasca were due to the chemicals in *B. caapi* (Reichel-Dolmatoff 1990[1972], 86; Schultes and Raffauf 2004[1992], 21–22). But tests in the mid- to late twentieth century hinted that it is actually the addition of leaves from DMT-containing plants that gives the tea its psychedelic qualities (McKenna 2005; Riba et al. 2003). It is now widely believed that the β-carbolines in *B. caapi* function mainly as inhibitors of the MAO stomach enzyme, which are required to potentiate orally administered DMT (a chemical with undisputed psychoactive properties). The chunks of vine are macerated into a pulp that is mixed with the DMT-containing leaves and boiled in water to serve as the basic elements of the beverage fardados call Daime.

Indigenous Entheogen Use in the Present Day

Today, the preparation of the ayahuasca drink varies cross-culturally, with different indigenous traditions known to have distinct modes for making the brew. Depending on the cultural context, the blending of ayahuasca's necessary DMT and β-carboline components is achieved by assorted combinations of locally available flora. Moreover, "a virtual pharmacopoeia of admixtures are occasionally added, the most commonly employed . . . are known to contain alkaloids, such as nicotine, scopolamine, and atropine," each of which contributes to how the finished product will affect the drinker's sensory experience (McKenna 2006, 41; see also Kaasik et al. 2020).

In general, it is known that ayahuasca is employed by indigenous peoples for a variety of practical purposes, including to prophesize the future, obtain otherwise inaccessible information, acquire spiritual protection, for pleasure/entertainment, or to diagnose and cure illnesses (Dobkin de Rios 1984, 175–76; see also Adelaars, Rätsch, and Müller-Ebeling 2006). Among shamanic traditions of the Amazon rainforests and the Andes, ayahuasca was probably preceded by alternative methods for introducing entheogenic agents into the human body. A widespread South American practice observed in both ancient and modern indigenous populations is the inhalation or "snuffing" of ground seeds from the genera *Anadenanthera* and *Virola* (which contain DMT and other psychoactive chemicals), occasionally combined with the chewing of *Banisteriopsis caapi* root. It is apparent that this "snuffing" practice dates back as much as four thousand years. Archaeologists have unearthed preserved *Anadenanthera* seeds and seedpods alongside the basic "snuffing" toolkit comprised of inhaler tubes, as well as trays for grinding and holding the snuff; all of which is often stylized with visionary motifs (Torres and Repke 2006; see also Schultes and Raffauf 2004[1992]; Von Reis 1972). It is also apparent that the ritual use of San Pedro cactus (*Echinopsis pachanoi*, containing the entheogenic chemical mescaline) has endured among peoples of the Andes and western coastal regions for at least three thousand years (Furst 1976; 109; see also Burger 1992, 64, cited in Torres 1995, 301).

Public and academic knowledge of ayahuasca increased with the renowned publications of poet-novelists (Burroughs and Ginsberg 1963), ethnobotanists (Schultes 1963), and anthropologists (Dobkin de Rios 1972; Harner 1973; Reichel-Dolmatoff 1990[1972]), often including personal accounts of the authors' own experimentation with imbibing. With these intellectuals' demonstration of alternative, non-Western viewpoints on psychedelic substances, Western scholars began making inroads into understanding indigenous perspectives on ayahuasca. Still, the ayahuasca experience confounds Euro-American notions of rationality, creating an awkward disparity between ethnographers who decline drinking the brew versus those who do experiment with it. The gravity of experiencing the brew directly is evidenced by Michael Harner (1973, 16–17), who wrote about being deeply moved when he participated in an ayahuasca ceremony with the Jívaro people of the Ecuadorian Amazon: "Transported into a trance where the supernatural seemed natural, I realized that anthropologists, including myself, had profoundly underestimated the importance of the drug in affecting native ideology."

The use of ayahuasca is widespread among many indigenous groups located in the western extremes of the Upper Amazon. This is the lowland jungle region encompassing eastern Peru, Ecuador, northwestern Brazil, northern Bolivia, and the southern forests of Colombia and Venezuela. At the time of completing his dissertation, Luna (1986, 167–70) counted more than seventy indigenous groups associated with the use of the *Banisteriopsis caapi* vine in "psychotropic preparations." Even though the exact geographical origin of ayahuasca is speculative, the best guess of scholars pinpoints the lower Napo River region of northern Peru as its likely birthplace (Zuluaga 2004, 132). Scholars generally agree that as with the dispersal of other cultural traits, knowledge and use of ayahuasca gradually spread to groups across the western Amazon basin and beyond (see Figure 3.3). However,

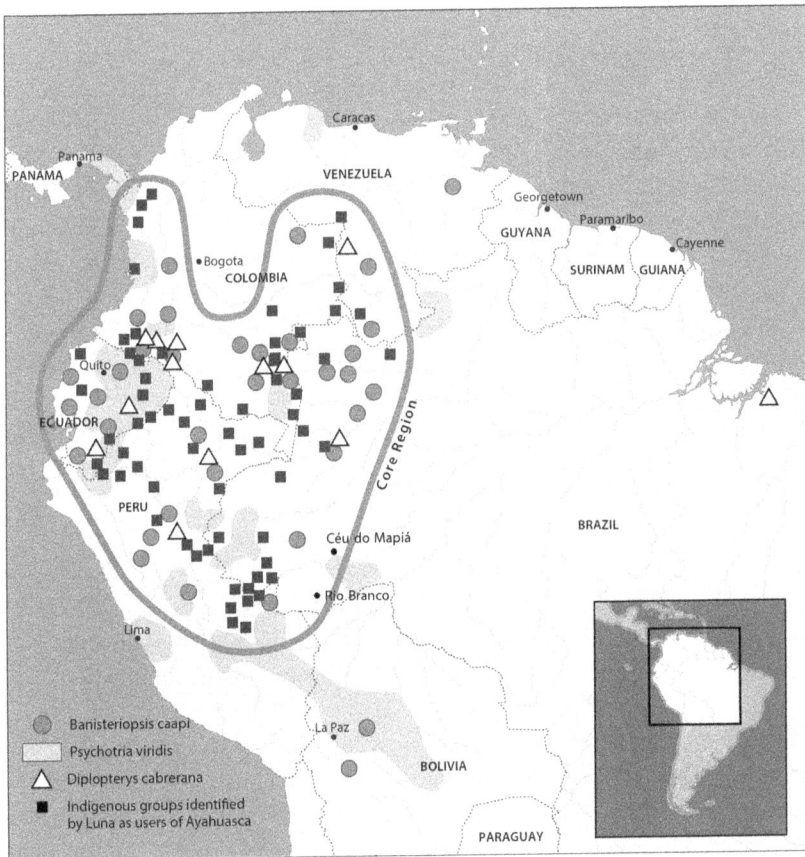

Figure 3.3. Map of ayahuasca vegetation and use in South America (assembled by the author with reference to Gates [1982, 117/212]; Luna [1986, 167–170]; Global Biodiversity Information Facility: https://www.gbif.org/species/2921300). For comparison, see Highpine (2008).

there is considerably less agreement regarding *when* the knowledge about how to make ayahuasca first emerged. It has become customary for both scholars and ayahuasca practitioners to reference the "millennia" that indigenous Amazonians have used ayahuasca (McKenna 2005; Polari de Alverga 1999, 137), with a proposed time-depth of "at least 5000 years" (Narby 1998, 154). But this premise has come under scrutiny. In a landmark paper, Peter Gow (1994, 91) first challenged this conventional wisdom by noting that ayahuasca shamanism "is absent from precisely those few indigenous peoples who were buffered from the processes of colonial transformation caused by the spread of the rubber industry in the region." In this way, Gow's hypothesis reverses the usual assumption that the extensive indigenous use of ayahuasca predated European intrusions; instead, he posits that urban mestizos ("mixed-blood" native/European peoples) adopted ayahuasca technology from remote indigenous groups they encountered while collecting rubber in the rainforest. In this scenario, use of ayahuasca was geographically restricted until colonial outsiders embraced this practice and transmitted it to other indigenous collaborators throughout the western Amazon. Pointing out the fact that archaeological discussions of ayahuasca are tenuously based on four-thousand-year-old receptacle objects that could have held any liquid (Naranjo 1986), Brabec de Mori has advanced a robust analysis of the ethnohistoric evidence for ayahuasca use in the eastern Peruvian lowlands. He concludes that in this region "the use of ayahuasca is probably less than 300 years old" (Brabec de Mori 2011, 24). Scholars must therefore heed Torres and Repke's (2006, 12) caution that entheogens consumed in liquid form

> present particular difficulties that complicate their identification in an archaeological context. Ingestion or preparation of such plants requires no paraphernalia that might be identified with certainty, and conjecture of such practices based solely on the presence of elaborate drinking vessels is insubstantial and unwise.

This interpretive prudence regarding inconclusive archaeological evidence must be upheld in future discussions. The uncertain antiquity of ayahuasca's use in South America demands a scholarly reassessment, especially given the recent discovery in Bolivia of an intact leather "ritual bundle" with a radiocarbon dating of approximately one thousand years ago; alongside snuffing paraphernalia, researchers found inside this bundle a "pouch" containing traces of "at least five psychoactive compounds" including DMT, the main mind-altering molecule in ayahuasca (Miller 2019). While the important question of ayahuasca's spatiotemporal origins will continue to inspire debate among researchers who study the Amazonian past, the present text concentrates on modern-day uses of ayahuasca by people from outside South America.

Ayahuasca Tourism

Partly as a result of interest spurred by scholars' publicizing the traditional uses of this powerful drink, from the late-twentieth century until today an increasing number of people from around the globe are now seeking out ayahuasca experiences. Because the alleged healing and transcendental properties of this plant beverage are disseminated by word of mouth, books, documentaries, and the internet, many individuals now travel to the rainforests of South America in search of psychophysical cures and spiritual enlightenment. It is not a surprise that many of these ayahuasca tourists begin their quest by attending ceremonies with what they assume are authentic ayahuasca shamans from native Amazonian communities. This is a logical pursuit, since ayahuasca originated among aboriginal peoples prior to the intrusion of European colonialism. But anthropologist Marlene Dobkin de Rios has called for governmental regulations of ayahuasca tourism, arguing that naive drug tourists are easy prey for opportunistic charlatans "out to get rich quick"; masquerading as ayahuasca healers, "these so-called 'neo-shamans' are mostly men without any special training, with little—if any—knowledge of disease process or biochemistry, and who are prone to use local witchcraft plants (read poisons) to ensure that their clients have a good trip" (Dobkin de Rios and Rumrill 2008, 72). The commercial incentives of ayahuasca tourism are enticing for otherwise poor residents of the Amazon, with foreign visitors shelling out between $300 and $500 for rituals that normally cost locals between $20 and $30[6] (Dobkin de Rios 2009, 167). While such reports raise grave warnings about tourists' safety and threats to Amazonian cultural heritage, other experts see this as a misreading of the situation.

According to some scholars, the (albeit problematic) cultural interactions between foreign outsiders and ayahuasca healers in the Amazon are an ongoing give-and-take, the social implications of which have yet to be determined. In response to Dobkin de Rios's disapproval of "drug tourists," Michael Winkelman (2005) published an article in which he reviews the personal testimonies of Europeans and North Americans he interviewed at an ayahuasca "retreat" in the Amazon. Winkelman counters the portrayal of ayahuasca tourists as impulsive hedonists, reporting that the pilgrims he met at the retreat were resolutely seeking improvements in their existential well-being. He concludes that his consultants' "principal motivations can be characterized as: seeking spiritual relations and personal spiritual development; emotional healing; and the development of personal self-awareness, including contact with a sacred nature, God, spirits and plant and natural energies produced by the ayahuasca"[7] (Winkelman 2005, 209; see comparable findings in Wolff and Passie 2018; Wolff et al. 2019). Similar motivations were reported by Veronika Kavenská and Hana Simonová (2015), Czech psychologists who note that ayahuasca tourists in South America also report worries, such as "lack of trust in the shaman or organizer, inaccurate information provided by the shaman or organizer, and exposure to dangerous situations." In analyzing the interaction of ayahuasca tourists and local peoples in the Peruvian ayahuasca market, Beatriz Labate (2011b) shows how both groups are actively engaged in symbiotic systems of negotiation and innovation. Evgenia Fotiou (2010) also repositions the debate away from viewing ayahuasca tourists as inadvertent accomplices in the continued destruction of defenseless local traditions. Instead, she highlights a perspective of "interculturality" whereby contacts between the cultures of Western tourists and Amazonian healers (curanderos) are viewed as a cooperative dialogue. Fotiou does acknowledge the obvious concerns about the ayahuasca tourism market fostering a profit motive among imposter "shamans." But rather than denouncing adjustments of presumably "authentic" indigenous and mestizo traditions to accommodate Westerners' desire for the "exotic other," she contends that

> people, including shamans, adapt constantly to new circumstances and as anthropologists have stressed, culture constantly takes new forms and should never be viewed as static. . . . Since cultures constantly reinvent themselves, every cultural act, including shamanism, should be considered authentic. (Fotiou 2010, 134–35)

For the purposes of the present volume, it is apparent that many Western ayahuasca "tourists" attend these rituals in the Amazon for reasons similar to European fardados' dedication to Santo Daime. Namely, Euro-Americans are drinking ayahuasca because they believe it can provide shamanic/mystical *solutions* to physical and psychological problems in their everyday lives.

Mestizo Ayahuasca Innovations

Despite the potential health and social risks posed by untrained swindlers and foolish travelers in the Amazon, the allure of ayahuasca remains. In fact, an entire industry of ayahuasca tourism now exists in the western Amazon region, centered in the urban hub of Iquitos, Peru. Skilled indigenous shamans in the rainforest are complemented by urban mestizos trained as genuine *ayahuasqueros,* a term "which denotes a healer who specializes in ayahuasca ceremonies" (Fotiou 2010, 64). Ayahuasca practices of mestizos (also known as *caboclos* in Brazil) aimed at medicinal and psychospiritual healing are more broadly known as *vegetalismo* (see Labate 2011b). In vegetalismo contexts, indigenous-inspired elements (such as the invoking of spirit beings and the singing of chants called *icaros*) are mixed with Christian traits (e.g., prayers and symbols from Catholicism). This combination of native and Christian components in vegetalismo reflects the general history of Amazonian mestizos, whose multiethnic identity is the result of contacts between indigenous groups and nonindigenous workers employed in colonialist industries (see Metzner 2006, 34; Tupper 2011, 207–208).

The seminal text dealing with vegetalismo practices is the PhD dissertation of Luis Eduardo Luna (1986). Luna focuses on how Peruvian *vegetalistas*[8] conceive of and utilize their *icaro* chants and the magic phlegm (*yachay*) hidden in their chests as "tools" in their shamanic trade. This author pays particular attention to vegetalistas' belief that their psychoactive plant medicines are *doctores* (doctors) or *vegetales que enseñan* (plants that teach): "It is their belief that these plants possess spirits from which they learn medicine, and from which they receive the magic phlegm and the magic chants or melodies" (Luna 1986, 16/63). More recently, Stephan Beyer (2009) has written a comprehensive examination of mestizo ayahuasca shamanism. He specifies exactly how psychoactive "plant teachers" are considered by vegetalistas as nonhuman beings that can convey information to humans who approach them properly:

> We must remember that the plant spirits are powerful and unpredictable; the relationship between shaman and plant is complex, paradoxical, multilayered. . . . The shaman "masters" the plant by taking the plant inside the body, letting the plant teach its mysteries, giving the self over to the power of the plant. There is a complex reciprocal interpersonal relationship between shaman

and other-than-human person—fear, awe, passion, surrender, friendship, and love. The shaman is the *aprendiz*, apprentice, of the plant; in return the plant *teaches* . . . by *showing*—the verb *enseñar* means both. (Beyer 2009, 61)

Followers of Santo Daime also view ayahuasca rituals as a state of consciousness that can only be "mastered" through a humble reverence for the spirits contained within the plants. Likewise, this shamanic idea that ayahuasca and other psychoactive plants are spiritual "teachers" that "teach" or "show" their human students otherwise hidden truths about disease, health, and the nature of the universe is also a central value of Santo Daime practice.

These non-Western forms of ayahuasca therapy are no longer restricted to distant rainforest locales. As ayahuasqueros perform ceremonies for tourists and train Western apprentices to lead rituals, new forms of "cross-cultural vegetalismo" are now linked into ongoing processes of globalization. Indigenous, mestizo, and even Euro-American ayahuasqueros now travel around the world, offering a product that their clients perceive as an "authentic" antidote to the dispirited complexion of consumerist modernity (Tupper 2009). In addition to the indigenous and vegetalismo contexts, new variations of ayahuasca practice are swiftly being "reinvented" in Brazilian urban centers. What have been termed "neo-ayahuasqueros" are independent individuals and groups engaged in modifying the more religious ayahuasca traditions toward more secular therapeutic ends (Labate 2004b). After receiving training in South America, some autonomous neo-ayahuasqueros have brought their brand of ayahuasca therapy to their European homeland. While the study of the South American neo-ayahuasquero scene is well underway, the emergence of similar practices elsewhere is a promising area for future research. Intercultural exchanges between Euro-Americans and Amazonians continue to expand. It is evident that just as Western medicine has provided new knowledge to non-Western peoples, the potential benefits of ritual ayahuasca use are gradually seeping into scientific awareness (see Anderson 2012; Beyer 2012; Fotiou 2012).

An intriguing prospect for Western medicine is the progress being made by self-styled ayahuasca healers who incorporate Euro-American therapeutic approaches in an effort to cure addictions to drugs such as cocaine and heroin. The most noteworthy example of this trend is the internationally renowned Takiwasi center in Tarapoto, Peru. Takiwasi is directed by Jacques Mabit, a French-born veteran of Doctors without Borders. Since 1992, Takiwasi has treated more than seven hundred patients in a program that involves a nine-month stay, during which they receive an average of twenty-five treatments with ayahuasca (Labate, Anderson, and Jungaberle 2011). Czech researchers who studied inpatients trying to overcome addictions to alcohol, marijuana, tobacco, and cocaine concluded that "the treatment at the Takiwasi Centre was effective in 27%[9] out of the 340 people treated during the years 1999–2008" (Horák, Verter, and Somerlíková 2014). To be sure, Mabit's effort to fuse indigenous and Western medical knowledge has not yet gained acceptance as a form of substance-abuse treatment outside of South America. Dr. Mabit and his colleagues explain that ayahuasca rituals can help individuals heal from debilitating psychological ailments like drug addiction because the brew instigates a deeply introspective mind-set whereby the subject must confront their repressed memories and emotions: "Those sessions allow the patient to release false psychic models, negative ideas, bad self-images, pejorative feelings (rage, hate, sadness, etc.), to correct personal perspectives, and to open up new horizons" (Mabit, Giove, and Vega 1996, 261). This logic agrees with the statements of numerous European fardados, who say that their experiences with Santo Daime were the primary aid that supported them in overcoming various addictions (see Part VII).

Emergence and Expansion of the "Ayahuasca Religions"

Santo Daime is the oldest of three Amazonian-based faith groups that imbibe ayahuasca as a sacrament in ceremonies combining Christian, Afro-Brazilian, and European influences; collectively these are classified as "ayahuasca religions" (Goulart 2004; Labate 2006, 2012a; Labate and Araújo 2004; Labate, MacRae, and Goulart 2010). Unlike the more sundry recipes found in indigenous and mestizo traditions, these ayahuasca religions share the same basic formula for their sacramental drink: *P. viridis* leaves and *B. caapi* vine boiled together in water.

It was in 1930 that an Afro-Brazilian man named Raimundo Irineu Serra, referred to by devotees as *Mestre* ("Master") Irineu, officially initiated the religious doctrine of Santo Daime (Figure 3.3). The details of Irineu Serra's life and teachings are mainly oral transmissions, but there is a standardized sequence of events in Santo Daime folklore. He was born in 1890 in São Vicente Ferrer, a small town near the Atlantic coastal Bay of São Marcos in the northeastern Brazilian state of Maranhão. After growing up as the grandson of slaves, the young Irineu Serra travelled to the Amazonian frontier region of Acre in 1912 to work as a rubber tapper. He would eventually settle on the outskirts of Rio Branco, capital city of Acre state, dedicating the remainder of his life to establishing ritual structures of the Santo Daime "doctrine" (see Moreira and MacRae 2011, 69; Meyer 2014). But before going into more detail, it is important to note the concurrent history that Santo Daime shares with the other ayahuasca religions.

Another ayahuasca religion called *Barquinha* (Portuguese for "Little Boat") was founded in 1945 by Daniel Pereira de Mattos (a.k.a. *Frei* [Friar] Daniel). Frei Daniel was also born in the northeastern Brazilian state of Maranhão and migrated to Rio Branco in his adulthood, where he eventually attended some of Mestre Irineu's Daime sessions. It was Mestre Irineu who gave some ayahuasca to Daniel and "encouraged him to pursue" his own

Figure 3.4. Portrait of Mestre Irineu (1890–1971); painted by Joanna Wernink; often displayed in the ritual space during Daime works in Amsterdam (published with permission).

"mission" of healing with *Daime,* as ayahuasca is also known by this name within the Barquinha doctrine (Frenopoulo 2006, 369). Unlike the other ayahuasca religions, the Barquinha organization has not expanded beyond the state of Acre, where it incorporates approximately five hundred members. Having had such close ties with Santo Daime since its birth, the Barquinha rituals resemble the interactive singing of Santo Daime works, albeit with a more nautical symbolic system and more emphasis on mediumistic healing (Araújo 2006). Like Santo Daime hinos, the content of songs performed in Barquinha rituals (called *salmos,* "psalms") are believed to have been received from beings in the astral otherworld and represent the core values of the doctrine. Also like Daime hinos, the salmos are deemed as revelatory truths to be interpreted intuitively by each individual who reads them while under the influence of Daime (Mercante 2006, 172).

A third ayahuasca religion, the UDV (*União do Vegetal,*[10] Portuguese for "Union of the Vegetal"), was founded in 1961 by José Gabriel da Costa (a.k.a. Mestre Gabriel) and is now based in Porto Velho, capital of the western Brazilian state of Rondônia. Mestre Gabriel was born in the northeast of Brazil in the state of Bahia but as a young man he traveled to the western Amazon to work as a rubber tapper. UDV "sessions" are more hierarchical and explicitly pedagogical than rituals of the other ayahuasca religions; during UDV sessions, lower-echelon disciples ask questions to designated *mestres* ("masters") whose answers impart spiritual knowledge. Much of this esoteric wisdom is restricted to members of specified ranks and UDV ritual songs (*chamadas,* "calls") are never written down. This organizational and ritual structure contrasts with the more egalitarian Barquinha and Santo Daime religions. But the UDV's interpretation of ayahuasca experiences as generating revelatory *mirações* (mind's-eye visions), divine light, and energetic "force" (which they call *burracheira*) parallels similar concepts in Santo Daime (Brissac 2006; Goulart 2006). Like Santo Daime, the UDV has recently begun to expand outside of Brazil and now has small communities in Europe, Canada, and the United States (Greenhouse 2006; Soares and de Moura 2011). The UDV is known for being proactive in advocating for the legalization of its holy sacrament, which it calls "Hoasca" or "the Vegetal." An international legal precedent was set in 2006 when the Supreme Court ruled in favor of UDV members' religious right to ritually consume ayahuasca in the United States: Chief Justice John Roberts wrote the majority opinion upholding the Religious Freedom Restoration Act, which had previously exempted the Native American Church's sacramental use of peyote in 1993, as also superseding the Controlled Substances Act with respect to the UDV (Bronfman 2011).

Since the first published analysis, a short encyclopedic entry about Santo Daime (Bastos 1979), scholarly interest in the ayahuasca religions has bourgeoned. However, in an exhaustive volume rightly described as a "Comprehensive Bibliography" of the ayahuasca religions, it is apparent that two significant gaps in the literature remain: the authors state that (1) "the transnational expansion of the UDV and Santo Daime, despite its importance, has been one of the least explored areas in studies of the ayahuasca religions," and that (2) their research "points to an enormous hole in English-language publications on Santo Daime . . . in the area of anthropology" (Labate, de Rose, and dos Santos 2008, 34/43–44). Focusing on Santo Daime, the present book will help impart these missing pieces in the ethnographic puzzle relating to the international expansion of ayahuasca spirituality. For the purposes of the present study's focus on Santo Daime, it is notable that migrants from the Brazilian northeast founded all three ayahuasca religions once they had settled in isolated urban capitals of the Amazon (Rio Branco and Porto Velho). Consequently, the roots of the ayahuasca religions must be traced back to processes of mass migration and an economic world system associated with the rubber boom-bust years in Brazil from 1850 to 1920.

Rubber Migrations: Global and Local

In 1839 Charles Goodyear, whose name was later immortalized in tires, accidentally discovered the process of rubber vulcanization. Through joining raw latex with sulfur, vulcanized rubber became a resilient material that revolutionized the railroad, manufacturing, clothing, mining, sports, and condom industries (Jackson 2008, 23–25; Taussig 1987, 94), which then sparked a world demand for raw latex. The harvesting of rubber tree sap for industrial consumption converged mainly on the Amazonian species *Hevea brasiliensis*, which was "far superior" compared to the "weak fine rubber" yielded by other species (Barbosa de Almeida 2002, 178; Stokes 2000, xiv). However, it took decades for infrastructure to develop to the point where rubber could be extracted in amounts suitable for supplying a global market. In fact, an efficient technique for extracting optimal amounts of rubber from a single tree did not become known to Europeans until 1855 (Dean 1987, 10).

Mestre Irineu was born into an impoverished setting where "the peasant exists on the periphery of society with little access to resources, no participation and no voice in the development of the region where he lives. . . . Drought, hunger and misery are words synonymous with Brazil's North-East" (Oakley 1980, 12). Between 1877 and 1888, a series of devastating droughts hit northeast Brazil (the states of Maranhão, Piauí, Ceará, Rio Grande do Norte, Paraíba, Pernambuco, Alagoas, Sergipe, and Bahia). In an effort to exploit the Amazon's supply of latex, rubber magnates enlisted most of their laborers from the drought-ridden northeast, a region whose inhabitants were "known throughout Brazil as the *flagelados,* the scourged ones" (Collier 1968, 45). Also, the Afro-Brazilian contingent of rubber migrants in the late nineteenth century followed from the coinciding of deplorable economic and agricultural conditions in the northeast with Brazil's official ending of slavery in 1888 (Matory 2005, 201). It is only logical that newly freed slaves leapt at the opportunity for self-employment in the lucrative rubber tapping industry. Unfortunately, they were at the same time entering an atrociously cruel situation, one where the ruling rubber barons inflicted violent abuses upon workers in the postcolonial extraction industries (see Taussig 1987).

Despite the high hopes of many aspiring rubber tappers, known as *seringueiros,* the system was organized disproportionately against the lowly extractors, favoring instead the intermediary creditors called *patrões* ("bosses"). A patrão would lend the new immigrants cash advances (with high interest), stipulating that the tappers sell back all their rubber exclusively to him. Regardless of this economic inequality, droves of young men flocked to Acre, a district acquired by Brazil in 1901 after prevailing in a territorial dispute with Bolivia (Dean 1987, 39–42). It is known that Irineu Serra traveled to the freshly opened rubber zone in his early twenties. He was accompanied by two Afro-Brazilian acquaintances, the brothers Antonio and André Costa, who were also from his hometown of São Vicente Ferrer (MacRae 1992, 48). In 1912, these men were moving into Acre at what seemed like a most ideal phase of the rubber boom, as the price of rubber had reached its all-time high in 1910 (Weinstein 1983, 141/214/232).

Unfortunately for the Brazilian rubber barons and eager new migrants like Irineu Serra, in 1876 an Englishman named Henry Wickham had smuggled out seventy thousand rubber seeds in "one of the most successful and far-reaching acts of biological piracy in world history" (Jackson 2008, 9–10). Although the Santo Daime founder had been part of a population increase in Acre "from 74,484 to 92,379 between 1910 and 1920," the bootlegged seeds had already founded a rubber industry in the British colonies of Asia; Asia then surpassed Brazil in rubber output for the first time in 1913 and produced more than ten times as much rubber as Brazil by 1919 (Weinstein 1983, 218/242). Nonetheless, the importance of the lingering Amazonian rubber industry for the initial formation and persistence of Santo Daime cannot be overstated.

Over the decade prior to the rubber industry's post–World War I collapse, Irineu Serra and his rubber-tapper peers had been experimenting with ayahuasca during their travels in the jungle. Granted that details concerning the early founding of Santo Daime are scarce, according to Brazilian anthropologist Edward MacRae (1992, 48–49): Irineu Serra's northeastern peers "the Costa brothers opened up a religious center in the [19]20's, called 'Círculo de Regeneração e Fé' (CRF) (Center for Regeneration and Faith) in the town of Brasiléia, Acre." These innovative ayahuasca rituals surfaced amid other syncretic religious movements formed by migrants importing their Afro-Brazilian belief systems from Maranhão (Monteiro da Silva 2004, 417). Both in the past and continuing into today, it was and is quite commonplace for residents of remote rubber-tapping camps (*seringais*) to employ ayahuasca by combining indigenous and nonindigenous ritual techniques (Labate, MacRae, and Goulart 2010, 3/6–7; Pantoja and Silva da Conceição 2006). After belonging to the CRF during the 1920s, Irineu Serra ultimately left to establish his own organization. When the Brazilian rubber industry finally folded, the corporate class that had ruled over the western Amazon went bankrupt. Many rubber tappers emerged as peasant managers of a regional economy detached from the rest of the world until World War II, when the allies needed rubber again after being cut off from the Asian supply (Barbosa de Almeida 2002, 181). This twenty-year hiatus in Acre's contact with the outside world coincided with the Daime founder's transition from common *seringueiro* to the renowned spiritual healer known as Mestre Irineu.

History of Santo Daime

At some unknown juncture during his wanderings as a rubber tapper in the rainforest[11]—likely somewhere in Peru—Irineu Serra was first introduced to ayahuasca by a group of multiethnic *caboclos* (see chapter 4 in Goulart 1996; Mendes do Nascimento 2005; Moreira and MacRae 2011, 88). Here, Irineu Serra's cultural predispositions are intriguing. In the Western Amazonian region of Brazil, *caboclo* refers to people with "Indian-white mixed blood" (Landes 1940, 391). However, in the Candomblé religion of Irineu's northeast birthplace "caboclos" refer to "Brazilian Indian spirits" identified as native counterparts of African-inspired spiritual beings called *orixás* (Matory 2005, 29). Jonathan Goldman (1999, xxii; see also Haber 2011), an American leader of a Santo Daime church that won its legal right to import and consume ayahuasca in Oregon, recounts the foundational story of the Santo Daime doctrine:

> [Mestre Irineu] saw a woman in the Moon who identified herself
> as the Queen of the Forest. She told him to go into the jungle
> by himself for a week to fast, pray, and drink the sacred tea.
> When he did this he was informed, to his total surprise, that he
> had a spiritual mission: He was to establish a new spiritual path
> to be called the Santo (Holy) Daime. He came to understand
> that the woman with whom he was communicating was in fact
> an embodiment of the Divine Feminine. . . . He also came to
> understand that she was instructing him to create a religion that
> would center around the direct experience of the divine forces
> contained both in the forest and in the astral plane. Access to
> these subtle realms would be facilitated by drinking of the sac-
> ramental tea that, in its new context, was to be called Daime.

On Monday, May 26, 1930, Irineu Serra held his first *trabalho* ("work") at Vila Ivonete on the margins of Rio Branco (Dawson 2013, 8–10/18; Moreira and MacRae 2011, 131). This ritual was open to the public and attracted many former rubber tappers, particularly fellow Afro-Brazilian and caboclo peasants who made up the greater part of Irineu's early following (MacRae 1992, 50). According to Dawson (2007, 71–72), as former rubber tappers continued to settle in the urbanizing outskirts of Rio Branco,

> a combination of growing popularity and escalating persecution
> led Irineu Serra to seek a move from Vila Ivonete. This was made
> possible by the donation of a tract of land by the then Governor
> of Acre, Guiomar dos Santos, who had already been instrumental
> in safeguarding Irineu Serra and his religious community from
> the attentions of the local police force. Originally known as
> "Custódio Freire," the land donated by Guiomar dos Santos
> is today named "Alto Santo" and serves as the headquarters of
> the "Universal Christian Light Illumination Centre" (*Centro de
> Iluminação Cristã Luz Universal—CICLU*) founded by Irineu
> Serra after his community's arrival in 1940.

The political clout that Irineu Serra was able to muster is astonishing, given that he was consistently persecuted by police due to his subaltern racial and economic status (de Assis 2020). Nonetheless, Mestre Irineu's fame in the region grew so briskly after 1930 that membership in a local branch of the church was commonplace. This trend continues in Acre today, as even though most locals proclaim a Catholic identity, the Santo Daime doctrine is established as a conventional feature of Acrean society (MacRae 2004, 29; Meyer 2014).

Many fardados believe that Mestre Irineu was "a reincarnation of Jesus" (Dawson 2007, 76). After the Mestre's death in 1971, a sizeable portion of his followers pledged themselves to Sebastião Mota de Melo, referred to as *Padrinho* ("Godfather") Sebastião (Figure 3.5). Born on an Amazonian rubber plantation in 1920, Pd. Sebastião was a *caboclo* man who trained as a spiritist medium in the tradition of Allan Kardec while making canoes and tapping rubber to support his family. Sebastião first drank Daime at Alto Santo in 1965 after someone suggested that Mestre Irineu could help him treat an acute liver illness he was then suffering from. Recalling his first Daime work, Sebastião reported having received a "spiritual surgery" wherein two astral "doctors" removed from his abdomen three insectile parasites that were causing his sickness (see Barnard 2014, 674–675; Dawson 2013, 20/130; MacRae 1992, 56; Polari de Alverga 1998, 24/60; 1999, 69–70/74–75). An instant convert, Sebastião and his family became daim-

Figure 3.5. Portrait of Padrinho Sebastião (1920–1990); painted by Joanna Wernink; often displayed in the ritual space during Daime works in Amsterdam (published with permission).

istas and he eventually developed his own form of Santo Daime, which he branded with the acronym CEFLURIS[12] (in English: "Eclectic Center of Flowing Universal Light Raimundo Irineu Serra").

Legends state that both Mestre Irineu and Pd. Sebastião prophesized the globalization of Santo Daime (Polari de Alverga 1999, 6/18). During the 1970s, the Alto Santo CICLU community continued while Pd. Sebastião maintained a separate CEFLURIS community outside Rio Branco called Colônia 5000, effectively creating a split between these two Daime denominations. In 1980, Sebastião moved his center of operations north onto a rubber plantation known as Rio do Ouro, in the state of Amazonas. However, the Rio do Ouro daimistas were later evicted by the owner of the property. The eviction compelled Sebastião and his followers to make an arduous journey farther north, where in 1983 they founded a permanent base at Céu do Mapiá on a tributary of the Purus river (MacRae 1992, 58–59). Years of consolidating a foothold at Mapiá overlapped with the beginnings of a national expansion for CEFLURIS, which in 1982 formed Céu do Mar in Rio de Janeiro, the first Santo Daime church outside the Amazon (Labate 2012a, 96). The current head of the CEFLURIS branch of Santo Daime, Padrinho Alfredo—son of Pd. Sebastião and his widow Madrinha Rita (Figure 3.6)—was born in 1950 on the Adélia rubber plantation,

Figure 3.6. Portrait of Madrinha Rita (1925–); painted by Joanna Wernink; often displayed in the ritual space during Daime works in Amsterdam (published with permission).

near the Juruá River in Amazonas state. It is in this same region that Pd. Alfredo has founded a new community called Céu do Juruá, which now complements Mapiá as an important CEFLURIS settlement in the rainforest (Schmidt 2007, 66).

4

The Current State of Santo Daime Studies

Brazil and Beyond

In their foundational publications on Santo Daime, Brazilian academics have focused on tracing the history of how different religious ingredients—indigenous shamanism, Afro-Brazilian traits, folk Catholicism, Kardecism—were combined into a multifaceted new whole. Yet Labate and Pacheco (2011, 72) critique early ayahuasca scholars' "tendency to conflate the historical formation of Santo Daime itself with the various authors' personal representations of this religion as constructed through time and in relation to Brazilian society." For instance, Goulart (1996) contends that Santo Daime can best be understood as an outgrowth of the post-rubber boom confluence of indigenous and Afro-Brazilian customs with a strong infusion of folk Catholicism and Kardecism. On the other hand, Cemin (1998) refutes the notion that post-rubber boom social fluctuations played a dominant role in the shaping of Santo Daime. Instead, she asserts that the doctrine exhibits influences from pre-rubber boom modes of indigenous shamanism and folk Catholicism. While anthropologists have been intent on dissecting syncretic components, which could be seen as a cultural bias of scientific approaches to the world, fardados themselves prefer to envision Santo Daime as a medley of spiritual traditions convening around universal truths (Dawson 2013, 36). The spiritual backgrounds of European fardados are diverse to say the least: Christian, Buddhist, Jewish, Islamic, even atheist. But they are less concerned with the distinct origins of particular religions and are instead engrossed in the mind-altering effects of Daime works in the present day. Just by confronting and navigating the experience of Daime rituals, fardados believe that each individual receives appropriate lessons for overcoming their attachments to egotism.

The only book-length study dealing exclusively with the Santo Daime in Europe is Alberto Groisman's PhD dissertation, based on fieldwork with three churches in the Netherlands (Groisman 2000). This text provided the first long-form documentation of Santo Daime's expansion outside of Brazil. In his quest to understand the "transposition" of Santo Daime from Brazil to a European context (i.e., the process of how it was incorporated into a Dutch setting), the author focuses heavily on the "trajectories of groups and individuals, basically the way they interpreted and applied their perception of what Santo Daime is" relative to their personal histories (Groisman 2000, 19). He argues that the Santo Daime in the Netherlands fits what he terms "postmodern religiosity," paralleling other New Age groups in its stress on individualism and "experiential knowledge" (see Groisman 2000, 242–243). While this outsider's (etic) perspective is informative, Groisman's dissertation all but ignores his informants' insider (emic) explanations for *why they* say they are attracted to Santo Daime. This study also grapples with an incongruity: that the ethnographer had many more years of experience and familiarity with Santo Daime practice compared to his Dutch informants.[1] Later sections will report the results of my testing Groisman's hypotheses, which entailed asking fardados directly about whether they agree with his conclusions.

In terms of recent work in the field of Santo Daime studies, the last two decades have seen an exponential increase in publications, especially in the English language. In particular, the collaborative work of Labate and colleagues has made significant inroads in marshaling research on the ayahuasca religions. The edited volumes *O Uso Ritual da Ayahuasca* (*The Ritual Use of Ayahuasca*) (Labate and Araújo 2004), *Ayahuasca, Ritual and Religion in Brazil* (Labate and MacRae 2010),[2] *The Internationalization of Ayahuasca* (Labate and Jungaberle 2011), *Ayahuasca Shamanism in the Amazon and Beyond* (Labate and Cavnar 2014a), and *Plant Medicines, Healing and Psychedelic Science: Cultural Perspectives* (Labate and Cavnar 2018a) embody an indispensable corpus of reference material. In terms of Europe, the first section of the *Internationalization* book contains a chapter by the Dutch historian Wouter Hanegraaff (2011), who theorizes about challenges posed by the introduction of ayahuasca spirituality into Netherlander society. Hanegraaff (2011, 94/97–98) discusses what he calls the "million-dollar . . . problem" confronting scholars of ayahuasca religions, and he advocates for ethnophenomenology as a research imperative in this subfield:

Ayahuasca drinkers are bound to claim that scholars cannot possibly understand their religion unless they have personally experienced what happens to an individual under the influence of the sacrament. Most modern scholars are bound to reject this argument as a classic example of the "Ottonian bugbear" according to which only insiders can understand what their religion is all about. If they are right, the implication is that drinking ayahuasca is irrelevant to studying ayahuasca religion: it suffices to look at the doctrine and observe the rituals as an outsider. I argue that such critics would indeed be right in the case of the kinds of religion which tend to be most familiar to us, and which [Rudolf] Otto had in mind as well. But in the case of religion grounded in the deliberate induction of altered states, the situation is different because the experiential dimension is not peripheral but central, and hence a different methodological stance is required: otherwise, the implication would be that scholars may study everything about such religion, but are allowed to ignore precisely what is most central to the religion in question. Such an approach could not but lead to a distorted view of the object of research. . . . There can be no doubt that having personally ingested the sacrament at least once, within the ritual context of the religion in question, scholars will thereby have learned essential things about it that they would not be able to learn in any other way.

The second section of the *Internationalization* book concerns the potential medical applications of ayahuasca and includes a chapter by the prominent fardado intellectual Alex Polari de Alverga (2011). While the final section of this book is very helpful in offering firsthand historical and legal details about the rise of Santo Daime in France, Italy, Germany, and the Netherlands (Bourgogne 2011; Menozzi 2011; Rohde and Sander 2011; van den Plas 2011), only the chapter on Spain includes information collected by a professional social scientist (López-Pavillard and de las Casas 2011). More recently, scholarly experts have increasingly begun to weigh in on the global "diaspora" of Santo Daime (see Labate and Cavnar 2018b; Labate, Cavnar, and Gearin 2017; Watt 2017). Indeed, a new edited volume on what is termed the "World Ayahuasca Diaspora" boasts chapters exploring the use of ayahuasca in Britain and Ireland (Hobbs 2018; Watt 2018).

Another major scholarly publication dealing with the expansion of this new spirituality outside of Brazil is Andrew Dawson's (2013) book *Santo*

Daime: A New World Religion. Building on earlier tomes by MacRae (1992) and Schmidt (2007), at the time of publication Dawson's became the foremost Santo Daime textbook written in English. This treatise is to be commended as a meticulous introduction to Santo Daime's historical development in the Amazon and the movement's subsequent globalization. Dawson (2013, 5) makes a justifiable appeal to the sociological tactic of investigating "novel religious phenomena as practical-symbolic barometers of overarching social transformation." He is likewise correct that "daimista belief and practice is by no means exempt from the commoditizing forces and dynamics constitutive of entangled, Western late-modernity"; and yet, despite concentrating his concluding interpretations on socioeconomic factors, he admits that daimistas' "views, values and behaviour . . . are fundamentally irreducible to being straightforward expressions of commodity consumption" (Dawson 2013, 175). Although he acknowledges that daimistas' "emic terminology rarely matches that of conventional academic discourse," Dawson (2013, 127) nevertheless collapses these emic concepts into "established etic categories." Thus, Dawson's more etic (outsider) approach demands scholarly interlocutors to clearly articulate emic perspectives on why some people from around the world are attracted to Santo Daime. Counterbalancing Dawson's objectivist focus, the present text seeks to augment etic analyses with bottom-up attentiveness to the ways in which fardados frame their Daime practice.

Dawson (2013, 189) characterizes the global expansion of Santo Daime as "Amazonian religiosity . . . radicalized at the hands of an urban-professional constituency drawn from the new middle class spawned by entangled late-modernity." This is a multiplex theoretical classification that speaks to Taylor's (2007, 5/302/423) ideas about a "nova effect" of new spiritual options being generated by secular-religious "cross-pressures." But such etic categorizations of specific religious communities tend to misrepresent devotees "as mere followers, a mindless mass . . . [instead of as] people with choices" (Wiegele 2005, 15). In pigeonholing Santo Daime as merely a reflection of the "non-mainstream, alternative religious scene" (Dawson 2013, 2), there is a tendency to overlook the special allure of the ayahuasca sacrament for fardado informants. This disconnect is most evident in a paucity of observations about the ayahuasca experience, which Dawson (2013, 54–56/196/206[n23]) restricts to a few brief comments from the "detached" perspective of "methodological atheism." Thus, while the two works deal with some of the same subject matter, the present text complements Dawson's monograph by advancing new ethnophenomenological understandings of fardados' standpoint from the inside out.

The present volume also expounds upon the "introspective idiom" of mystical self-transformation that is largely overshadowed by Dawson's (2013, 134–37) focus on the vogue of spirit mediumship in Santo Daime. Certainly, debates about the appropriateness of mediumship are arising as a major concern for daimistas and scholars of Santo Daime alike. Daime leaders are obviously intent on training Europeans in the arts of embodying spirits, as this seems to be a priority when Brazilian fardados visit established daimista congregations in the Netherlands (see Schmidt 2007, 211–13). But at the time of my fieldwork incorporation of spirits was still negligible across the European daimista communities,[3] a situation that differs from mediumship proclivities found with many Daime groups in North and South America. In fact, not for lack of trying I attended only two works dedicated to mediumship during my time in Europe. Both of these rituals were at large international gatherings in Amsterdam, and while incorporation of spirits was present, it was noticeably subdued relative to full-blown "Illumination Works" of mediumship I have witnessed with Daime in North America (see Barnard, forthcoming).[4] Although there were a few veteran fardados in Europe who occasionally "incorporated" spirits during Daime works there, the topic hardly ever came up during more than a year of fieldwork and interviews.

One exception to this general rule of restrained mediumship in European Daime circles is the case of Ireland, where one Brazilian Padrinho has exercised considerable influence. While the reader is referred to Barnard (forthcoming), Dawson (2013), Luke (2014), Sarrouh (2020), and Schmidt (2007) for thorough treatments of spirit incorporation in ayahuasca ceremonies, the following quote from an Irish fardado gives a sense of the pro-mediumship Daime subculture:

> We know we're very safe when we're in our place. . . . So the other night it was on Good Friday . . . I could feel the energy building and building (and at this stage I'm not afraid of the sickness anymore, I know what's happening). I could feel the energy and I'm one of these people, whatever way I'm made, a very big energy comes through me (I even frighten them in Brazil when the beings incorporate into me and come through me, [they're] very strong). And so I could feel the entity coming in, I could feel the entity was there. And then you allow those beings to manifest (it's an act of compassion) . . . and then I was able to clean (it was all just noise, there was no [material vomit]). . . . It's infamous the amount of noise that comes through me. . . . So in the space of two minutes,

it was a huge clearing of energy! . . . Whether to allow the beings to incorporate or not, it's partly choice and it's partly not. It has to happen. That's the point of the works for the beings [we incorporate], because it's the suicide that happened an hour ago, or it's the person who died on the operating table, or it's the car accident, or it's the grandfather who was drinking [alcohol] all his life and then he just died.

This is a typical account of how it feels when a daimista "allows" a suffering or confused "entity" from the astral otherworld to temporarily enter their body in order to be "cleaned" or "cleared" in the divine light afforded by the Daime. But as noted by Dawson (2013, 134–44), the popularity of mediumship in Daime is "unevenly expressed across the movement," as many daimistas and entire congregations are either incredulous about, disinterested in, or outright averse to the practice of incorporating spirits. This is apparent in my recent fieldwork with daimistas in Canada and the United States, where the custom of incorporating spirits is more palpable. Here, I encountered much mediumship but also some strong opposition, such as this opinion from an American fardada now in her sixties:

The ideology of Daime incorporation, as I learned it when I joined the Daime, is the following: you can indiscriminately allow any "suffering spirit" to come in, because you are protected by the Daime and because they can and will be healed if they come into the body of a person who is under the Medicine. At first, I thought: Wow, this church does very high level work indeed, healings in the astral! I came into the Daime believing that the leaders must know what they are doing. I have now come to believe that none of the leaders of CEFLURIS/CEFLURGEM churches really know what they are doing, and they are endangering people spiritually as well as psychologically. Why is it supposed to be the job of us living people to heal screwed-up dead people, anyway? We have enough on our plate as it is, living life here on the physical [level] with our own healing challenges. There are plenty of other beings in the astral dedicated to assisting the dead.

Daimistas are taught to believe that Sebastião practiced incorporation mediumship during Mestre [Irineu]'s lifetime and that Mestre approved of that and even encouraged it. This is because it is a matter of record that Sebastião was already a practicing medium before he met Mestre. But what is obscured is the fact that he practiced Kardecist mediumship—that is to say channeling, not incorporation. Kardecism explicitly opposes incorporation (although Kardecist concepts have been absorbed into Umban-daime⁵) and pure Kardecism is still very widespread in Brazil. The loose use of the term mediumship in the Daime obscures the difference, and the fact that [with] most of the world outside the Daime, when it uses the word mediumship, this does not mean possession or incorporation. Indeed, people's legitimate spirit helpers have no need or reason to take over their bodies. An entity that comes to occupy a person's body has some other agenda than to help that person. Indeed, promiscuously opening to any entity that comes along is an invitation to spiritual parasitism. Mestre was perfectly familiar with Afro-Brazilian possession cults from his childhood in his home state of Maranhão, and he intentionally chose to leave it out of the practice he taught.

Recalling Pd. Sebastião's training as a Kardecist medium, this fardada's concern about the dangers of mediumship echoes the warnings of the French spiritist codifier Allan Kardec (1874, 311–12), who cautioned that spirit "possession," or more specifically "obsession . . . is one of the greatest dangers of mediumship; it is also one of the most frequent; so we cannot take too much pains to combat it." In this way, a determined subset of fardados opposes any intermixing of spirit possession and ayahuasca, claiming that the "incorporation" of astral "entities" is an illegitimate and even harmful innovation frowned upon by Mestre Irineu. Although European daimistas accept interaction with astral spirits as a feature of Daime's "palimpsestic repertoire," in no way were my informants "preoccupied" with incorporation to the extent implied by Dawson (2013, 117). During an interview with a prominent British fardada I refer to as Julia, I mentioned the relative lack of mediumship in Daime works on the European continent. Affirming that there is not much spirit incorporation among UK daimistas either, Julia theorized that the emergent mediumship craze in Daime is due mainly to a handful of charismatic leaders, particularly the Brazilian Padrinho referred to above. While this Padrinho made occasional visits to European Daime centers in the past, he has focused his energies on developing his style of the doctrine in North America. Julia justified the scarcity of mediumship in Europe as indicative of her fellow fardados being unfamiliar with such practices: "In Brazil, I think that they grow up with this understanding of the spiritual realms. . . . It's normal to them, whereas over here, those channels seem to be shut down and people don't know how to use them; it's not that [spirits] are not there, it's that we just don't quite know that they're there." She proposed that even when mediumship works like *Mesa Branca* ("White Table") and *São Miguel* (St. Michael) are performed, most European daimistas might feel something strange occurring to them but have no idea what to do about it. She thinks that in order for mediumship to take root more firmly in Europe, local fardados would need steady training from expert Brazilians, guidance that is not yet readily available to most European daimistas. Perhaps things will change as the years unfold, and it will be interesting to see if incorporation-style mediumship begins to grow in Europe as it seems to be growing in the Americas. Either way, we must be careful not to overemphasize the centrality of mediumship within the Daime as a whole. In future studies of theological diversity within the global Daime movement, I would suggest that daimistas' assenting or dissenting perspectives on mediumship present scholars with a natural branching of Mestre Irineu's tradition in real time, similar to divergent interpretations of the founder's intentions leading to schisms between Mahayana and Theravada Buddhism or Sunni and Shia Islam.

It is patent that the way scholars conceptualize their own interpretive relationship with Santo Daime determines the extent to which their analyses capture ideological realities of daimista informants. Although I agree with Dawson (2013, 184–85) that overly apologist writings about Santo Daime are suspect, I do not share his reluctance about taking fardados' point of view seriously. Scholars' keeping theological perspectives at arm's length has been one of the "pitfalls of the study of religious change" because it is deaf "to the possibility that spiritual transformation and experience can sometimes be a significant motivation" (Wiegele 2005, 15). Although recent increases in the popularity of spirit possession are outwardly remarkable, this can distract from what some of Dawson's (2013, 134) informants value "most" about their Daime practice: "the most important thing is the encounter with your true self . . . the journey inward is all that's needed . . . to take the radical change in myself inward and meditate and contemplate." The present text opens a deeper study into the culture of European fardados, specifically their characteristic tendency to prize that which Dawson (2013, 137) terms the "introspective" idiom of humanity's interface with spiritual realms.

On the opposite side of the spectrum is *Liquid Light*, by the religious studies expert G. William Barnard (forthcoming). Compared to Dawson's (2013) secularist breakdown of Santo Daime, Barnard's book complements my book in the reverse manner. What I mean is that as a self-styled "schol-ar-practitioner" (Barnard, forthcoming), Barnard is himself a veteran fardado within one of the mediumistic Daime lines that has taken North America by storm. Though Barnard's book pairs well with the present volume through its intriguing explorations of Daime mysticism and ayahuasca phenomenology, there are two key differences with respect to what I deal with herein. First, while Barnard actually stakes out declarations about what Daime experi-ences mean for the true natures of reality and consciousness, my agnostic approach to an existential anthropology of European fardados makes no such ontological claims. Secondly, Barnard's "insider" status as a member of Santo Daime is balanced by his appeal mainly to philosophers of psychology (William James and Henri Bergson). This contrasts harmoniously with the ways my outsider ethnophenomenology of daimista social and ritual life is fleshed out through reference to philosophical theologians. Counterpoising the present book's community-wide scope, which surveys collective schemas of rank-and-file daimistas, Barnard's "first-person" reflections constitute the scholarly autobiography of a single fardado (fittingly, he is a well-respected and established professor of religious studies). Otherwise, I have less critical comments for Barnard's book because, unlike Dawson's neglecting of expe-riential dimensions, the former author personifies a well-documented case study of one American fardado's fascination with entheogenic otherworlds, the very topic I develop on a collective scale though this ethnography of daimistas in Europe. I encourage readers to consult both Barnard's and Daw-son's books to obtain a well-rounded appreciation for the interdisciplinary and international scope of Santo Daime studies.

While there is a great deal of merit in strictly etic and entirely emic analyses of Santo Daime, the present study is the first to pursue a balanced ethnophenomenology of fardados' mysticism. In what follows, I tackle this issue with an uncommitted receptivity to Daime that bridges interpretive gaps between the remote atheism maintained by many social scientists (e.g., Dawson 2013) and erudite memoirs penned by fully committed fardados (e.g., Barnard, forthcoming; Polari de Alverga 1999). As an outsider gathering insider data about the global fardado movement, fieldwork that became raw material for the present book, I began my participant-observation journey by traveling to South America.

5

Passage to "Heaven" of Mapiá

In the summer of 2008, I traveled to Rio Branco in the Brazilian Amazon, the veritable nerve center of ayahuasca religion where one has access to different offshoots of Santo Daime, UDV, and Barquinha. In Rio Branco I attended two Barquinha rituals, one work with the Alto Santo line of Santo Daime, and toured a UDV facility (called a *núcleo* ["nucleus"], although I did not get a chance to attend a UDV session there). I also visited Mestre Irineu's tomb, which is located at the last stop of a bus called the "Irineu Serra." From Rio Branco, it takes five hours by taxi along a very rough road to reach the town of Boca do Acre in Amazonas state. From Boca do Acre I caught a *canoa* (motorized canoe) that was already on its way to deliver supplies to *Céu do Mapiá* [Portuguese: "Heaven of Mapiá"].[1] It takes three hours to ride up the Purus River until the canoa turns onto the *igarapé* Mapiá, a smaller "stream" that empties into the Purus. For the next four hours the canoe stopped along the way to visit modest dwellings of caboclo families, each of whom warmly welcomed the boat's crewmen and the young *gringo* (foreigner). The residents of these homes served us meals of local fish, capybara (a large jungle rodent), and sides of rice and *macaxeira* (cassava), with raw sugar cane for desert. After we spent a cold sleepless night in a hammock at a pit stop called *Casa Grande* (Big House), the boat embarked early the next morning to travel five more hours along the igarapé until finally reaching Céu do Mapiá.

As the present-day "Mother Community" of CEFLURIS, Céu do Mapiá is a prime pilgrimage destination for Brazilian and foreign tourists, a migration that is increasingly sparking curiosity among Western social scientists. American geographers have attempted to track the "global networks" of human and botanical life that flow in and out of Céu do Mapiá (Lowell and Adams 2016). The interviews and observations garnered in this ethno-geo-graphical perspective show promising paths for future study. But attending a sample of four Daime works over the "brief" period of three weeks lacks the depth needed for ethnophenomenology to be effective with ayahuasca religions; this might account for the researcher's underwhelmed reaction to the Daime experience (Lowell 2013, 23). In an article discussing two months of fieldwork conducted at Mapiá, the British sociologist Andrew Dawson (2010)—whose work was discussed in the last chapter—examines delicate insider-outsider statuses that must be navigated by researchers who drink ayahuasca in the Daime works. I faced similar awkwardness with informants during my initial months of fieldwork in Europe, but found that with ample time my guesthood status within the community became more stable. My fifteen months of ethnophenomenology was modeled after the example of Swedish researcher Titti Schmidt (2007), whose monograph on her fifteen months of fieldwork at Mapiá encompasses a thorough ethnographic survey of the Daime doctrine as an "eco-religious movement." In her book, Schmidt provides a comprehensive account of how residents of Mapiá conceive daimista ritual practices as a universal touchstone for interpreting the human condition. Recognizing the anthropological importance of religious pilgrimage sites for the global communities they serve (Eade and Sallnow 2013), it was necessary for me to visit Céu do Mapiá, the base of Santo Daime's international expansion.

At the Pousada São Miguel, one of the original structures of Céu do Mapiá that now serves as a hostel, the room I rented was a far cry from my later home in Brussels (see chapter 6). From my Mapiá bedroom I looked out the window onto a lush, green garden speckled with a rainbow of flowers and butterflies. Sounds of insects buzzing and birds chirping were only occasionally disrupted by a gas generator or motorboat. The São Miguel Inn was an ideal location for meeting new international visitors who arrive at Mapiá without having prior arrangements to stay with locals. I conducted short interviews with visitors from all over the world, including people from Brazil, Columbia, Argentina, the United States, Mexico, Ireland, Poland, Spain, South Korea, and Japan. These interviews would help to lay the foundation for my subsequent research with fardados in Europe and North America.

The community of Mapiá consists of one thousand permanent residents; 70 percent are local caboclos and 30 percent come from elsewhere in Brazil or from abroad (Schmidt 2007, 74). But because of increases in tourism and permanent residents, the main church building I attended in 2008 will soon be replaced by a new ceremonial structure with capacity for more than two thousand people (Guimarães 2019). The people I met in Mapiá spoke about many different types of personal revelations, but the common denominator revolved around the capacity of Santo Daime to alleviate struggles of daily life. A young fardada from Texas explained that prior to her first Santo Daime work she had been having negative feelings toward members of her family. But she said that after drinking Daime, "every resentment I ever had for my family was lifted, instantly." A daimista from Spain who studies psychology responded upon being asked what her Daime experiences have done for her personally: "It's given me strength to believe in myself and what I can do . . . it's given me support in my faith." In trying to explain how and why Santo Daime delivers these positive outcomes, Javier (a fardado from Columbia) said in a Portuñol mix of Spanish and Portuguese that the ayahuasca sacrament helps to reveal the supreme love of God:

> With Santo Daime one can encounter a Higher Power. The Santo Daime is a drink of power, a sacred plant which is made to purify devices because the Santo Daime is able to show something better out of matter, such as to realize God is inside and outside of everything. When we fear, the Santo Daime is looking for love. Thought is steady in the light. We can realize that there are things besides matter: spirit.[2]

It is a common premise among fardados that many forms of human suffering can be resolved by making personal contact with a universal source of love and light through the "sacred plant." This idea was echoed by Malcolm, a fardado from California who described to me how Daime changed his life:

> I was going through a lot of personal/emotional problems. It was a really difficult time and [the Daime] just cleaned everything out. It felt like the weight was just lifted and I felt clear, I felt open, I felt at ease. It took a little time, a few works, but knowing that that is what occurred, I just really focused on wanting to understand and study the tradition.

He went on to explain that he had come to Mapiá to deepen his knowledge of the Daime so that he could return home to help fortify his daimista community there. At the time of these interviews, I was still very inexperienced with Daime works. But as Malcolm indicates, as one continues to attend works such feelings of inner clarity and relief become more common.

The works I attended at Mapiá were very demanding, a common hurdle for neophytes partaking in their first full *hinário* ("hymnal") works during the *Festa Junina* ("June Festival"). Regular Daime works usually last about six hours, but Santa Missa funeral services can be as short as two hours and full hinário works can be as long as twelve hours with an hour break in the middle. These works often involve an experiential journey into the source of one's deepest sense of observing "I." This can be described as "ego-death," or the dissolving of barriers between the conscious observer and the observed world (see Doyle 2012). Such an ego-death is often accompanied by perceptions of encounters with what my informants describe as supernatural energies and otherworldly spirit beings. I never saw any spirit beings during my time in the Amazon, but during one of the last works there I "saw" the church's variegated central pillar animatedly growing longer, larger leaves while the entire church pulsated with waves of ethereal energy. The next day, I went to inspect the church pillar—its leaves were no larger than before. Whereas this "vision" in the ritual was clearly a hallucination from an objective/materialist standpoint, the memory of it still feels to me subjectively as a direct engagement with what spiritual believers interpret as "hierophany" (see Eliade 1964, xxii–iii).

One special work I participated in was the *feitio*, a Portuguese title for the "making" of the Daime beverage (see Barnard forthcoming; Cemin 2010, 47–52; Dawson 2013, 50–53). Through this highly ritualized process, feitio participants treat the ingredients of the Daime with special care at each stage of preparation. The botanical constituents are gathered in a consecrated building known as a *Casa do Feitio* (House of Making). Then the leaves of *P. viridis* (called *Rainha*[3] ["Queen"]) are carefully cleaned by females (*catação*) while the woody bark of the *B. caapi* vines (*Jagube*) is painstakingly scraped (*raspação*) and then pulverized with wooden mallets (*bateção*) by males (Figures 5.1, 5.2, and 5.3). Since the participants also ingest fresh warm Daime brew during this work, the entire feitio is viewed as an initiation rite. Reverence for the cosmic relationship between human-student and plant-teacher is underscored by the immense exertion invested over several hours of processing the leaves and vine (Polari de Alverga 1999, 146–47). One gets an experience of just how grueling it is to crush the vines with a mallet for hours on end (I learned the hard way that novices' hands tend

Figure 5.1. Females carefully clean bugs and other impurities off the *Rainha* leaves (photo by Dutch fardada, published with permission).

Figure 5.2. The men crush the *Jagube* vines with wooden mallets—*bateção* (photo by Dutch fardada, published with permission).

Figure 5.3. The hammering action of *bateção* creates a vine pulp (photo by Dutch fardada, published with permission).

to get torn up with blisters). When the female Rainha leaves and the male Jagube vine are combined and cooked with water (Figure 5.4), fardados believe that by uniting these two plants the feitio ritual imbues the Daime beverage with a divine spirit (Cemin 2006, 267–72).[4] Specifically, through singing of hymns and meditative focus the feitio workers turn ayahuasca into Santo Daime, a sacrament that for them is literally imbued with Christic energy. Adapting indigenous myths about "the creation of [ayahuasca] from the body of a primordial divine being," Daime adds the Catholic concept of *transubstantiation,* where "one who drinks sacramental wine takes Christ's essential nature and very blood within his or her own body" (Jones et al. 2005, 848). For fardados, this physical-chemical solution of plants symbolizes spiritual solutions that are the keys to salvation; as discussed in Parts V and VI, by working with Daime, fardados believe they mystically solve inner conflicts, and spur practical processes of healing and personal improvement.

I first began to hear about the idea of Santo Daime being a gateway to practical and metaphysical "solutions" in one of my final interviews at

Figure 5.4. The mixture of the vine and leaf plant materials is boiled in water using wood-burning ovens (photo by the author).

Mapiá. When I asked an Irish fardado who built a house for himself at Mapiá why he thinks people struggle with problems in their life, Riley pondered the question for a moment and proceeded to give a meticulous answer:

> *I think people tend to stop feeling and start thinking and then try to work things out . . . especially people from the West because we're conditioned to try and work things out and try to understand them in an intellectual way. We like to try and figure out how things*

work . . . when the true path to everything is feeling. The true language of life in its purest sense is to be able to connect with each other without words, and if you can use your feelings as a means of communication, you'll understand so much more. Because the amazing thing about the universe is that as humans, we use words in a way that they lie; words aren't the truth, feelings are the truth. And people tend to tell people what they think they want to hear, when if you're tuned into your feelings and you spend time in anybody's company, in any situation, you'll feel what's going on much quicker than you'll hear what's going on. . . . The more you tap into this, the more your heart becomes open, and the more open your heart is, the more the ability is to receive love, and generate love. . . .

Once you start loving yourself, your family, your friends, strangers, you radiate that love, but you get it back, and getting it back you're receiving this unconditional flow of energy from the universe, which gives you all that you need. Everything that you ever could wish for in this life and the next life is contained in that one message of love and light. And the path that we are all on is very interesting, because most of us try to figure it out in our heads, we're always going, "What should I be doing?" instead of switching it off and thinking, "My path is illuminated by the light." But it's a strange situation: the light illuminates your path, but you can't see the light, you can only feel it. Then when you feel it, the light reveals itself from within and you realize that everything that you need is within you, and once you get into that cycle, your (what I would call) True Life or New Life . . . opens up and you end up walking in this great space . . . where stuff happens around you in an effortless way, and the thinking goes, and the struggle goes!

And the idea that all the tasks or things that were issues (like the idea of work and all these labels) melt away into nothing, and life takes care of what you originally thought were problems. Nothing is a problem because now, as you perceive a problem to arise, the solution is arriving at the same time, so what happens first is the solution, you never see the problems . . . and this is the New Era of how we all need to function and that's the goal: for all the people on the planet to reconnect to each other and to stop thinking and stop putting conditions in the way of everything. My only message is: to feel is the only path.

Fardados view the tendency to rely more on mental "thinking" as a double-edged facet of Western culture. They do realize that mental thought is indispensable for any intellectual achievement. But they also see Western culture's resolute dependence on thinking as causing people unnecessary suffering and confusion when they are confronted with emotional problems in life. Ignacio, a fardado from Spain, corrected me when I asked him about his "thoughts" and "opinions" about what Daime means for his life. He cited his introduction to yoga as first awakening him to a mental calmness that he now continues to cultivate with his Daime practice:

> *Thoughts and opinion don't have any interest [for me] . . . what I consider important is experience. . . . For many years I was thinking about everything and trying to understand life in this level of the mind. And with Yoga . . . I realized that all the energy and attention I was giving to this asking about life, I was taking from simply living; so, when I understood this, I tried to correct it because my choice is living. I still think, but I think [about] what is necessary . . . because [thinking is] a tool. It's not God, it's not me, it's a tool.*

Santo Daime devotees try to avoid overthinking human life. Instead, like Sufi mystics, daimistas focus on developing and placing trust in what they believe to be natural senses of intuition found in the intelligence of the "spiritual heart" (Frager 1999, 2/21–46). Daimistas' endeavor to rouse the spiritual heart through introspective prayer is akin to Eastern Orthodox mystics, for whom "the heart has a double significance in the spiritual life: it is both the centre of the human being and the point of meeting between the human being and God . . . both the place of self-knowledge, where we see ourselves as we truly are, and the place of self-transcendence. . . . The heart is the primary organ of our being, the point of convergence between mind and matter, the centre alike of our physical constitution and our psychic and spiritual structure" (Ware 1974, 18–20). Tapping into this "experiential" or "feeling" aspect of the self (located in the center of the chest), rather than identifying exclusively with mental thoughts in the head, is seen by fardados as an advancement in one's personal evolution. They believe this goal of developing an "open heart" is facilitated by participating in Daime works. Since the ayahuasca experience feels like a dissolving of the cerebral ego-self, fardados also interpret this event as revealing a core self located in the heart *chakra* (the Sanskrit term for "wheels" or corporal energy centers, a concept borrowed from the Asian tradition of tantrism [Jones et al. 2005, 8992–93]). But as daimistas warned throughout my fieldwork, sacred plants can only display pathways to solutions for people who ingest them. The plants do not solve problems magically. In an interview with Sibila, a Mexican indigenous healer who traveled to Mapiá from her home land, she instructed:

> *When you drink ayahuasca or peyote, the plant, in many ways, does not heal you; what it does is it shows you your patterns, your behaviors, and I think this is where a lot of people don't get it. So it wakes you up, and now how am I going to take these patterns that I see and try to change them? . . . So a lot of people don't change because they keep drinking and drinking and drinking [Daime], but they can't see their patterns and then [they don't] really try to change them in their life with their families, with their friends, their interactions. We say: "The Ceremony actually starts when the plant ceremony ends."*

So even though many people are drawn to attend ayahuasca rituals for therapeutic reasons, the drinker's willful intention and determination to implement the lessons learned in Daime works is necessary for success. I would later learn that these concepts are also appreciated by European fardados, who assert that Daime rituals are really like a reproduction of daily life. They cherish Daime works as an opportunity to face one's problems in a condensed form. It is during these rituals that solutions to one's problems are revealed. But these lessons must be incorporated in normal life between rituals to have any lasting benefits. As my time in Mapiá came to a close, my plans began to shift toward the long-term fieldwork I would carry out in Europe.

In Mapiá, one of my final interviews was with a revered elder of the CEFLURIS movement, Padrinho Alex Polari. I asked him what I should expect from the Belgian Santo Daime? He said that even though the churches in Spain and the Netherlands are more well-known, Belgium was one of the first countries where Santo Daime took root in Europe. He said that this is a difficult time for the European churches because there is very little comprehension of the sacramental use of ayahuasca in Europe's public sphere. Instead, there is legal discrimination of Santo Daime as the use of a "hallucinogenic drug." He sees this as a "mystification" of the truth. He also said that in the *casa da Bélgica* (house of Belgium) "today there is a fragmentation of the groups" where some people have split away from the CEFLURIS line and have begun to hold non-CEFLURIS Daime works. When asked about his views regarding scholarly research into Santo Daime, he expressed his approval for the many studies that are currently underway across the world. He said that now is a "very important opportunity" because this is a time "of much union and also a lot of dialogue between the traditional knowledge of forest peoples (the importance of spirituality in these sacred plants), and also with science, with the state."[5] I hope the present text can help advance ongoing intercultural dialogues, fostering growth of mutual understandings between mainstream Western society and newly arrived entheogenic religions like Santo Daime.

Although I had wanted the fast boat that can travel from Mapiá to Boca do Acre within six hours, only the slow canoa was available for my departure. Unlike the twelve-hour trip to Mapiá, because it was now going with the current of the *igarapé*/stream (but against the current of the Purus river) the boat was able to make it to Boca do Acre in a little over ten hours. After having participated in a total of ten ayahuasca ceremonies during one month in the Amazon, I returned home to Canada physically exhausted but anthropologically energized. I looked forward to beginning core fieldwork with the Daime congregations in Europe, a new frontier for daimistas and researchers alike.

Presenting data assembled during long-term fieldwork, the next sections comprise a systematic ethnography of Santo Daime, chronicling observations and direct testimonies that arose out of my contacts with European fardados. A dialectic symbiosis ensues, as etic analyses are punctuated throughout by quotations from daimistas enunciating their subjective experiences, intentions, and beliefs. When one gains intimate access to communities of European fardados (as the reader will do throughout this book), it becomes clear that their Daime practice is geared primarily toward enhancing well-being through introspective rituals. Like many spiritual contemplatives throughout history, fardados believe in the mystical principle that meditative prayer followed by active compassion to others in the outside world can resolve most if not all of life's problems. In dialogue with the emic viewpoints of fardado informants, the next section presents a social history of Santo Daime's expansion across the European continent.

PART III

BACK TO THE OLD WORLD

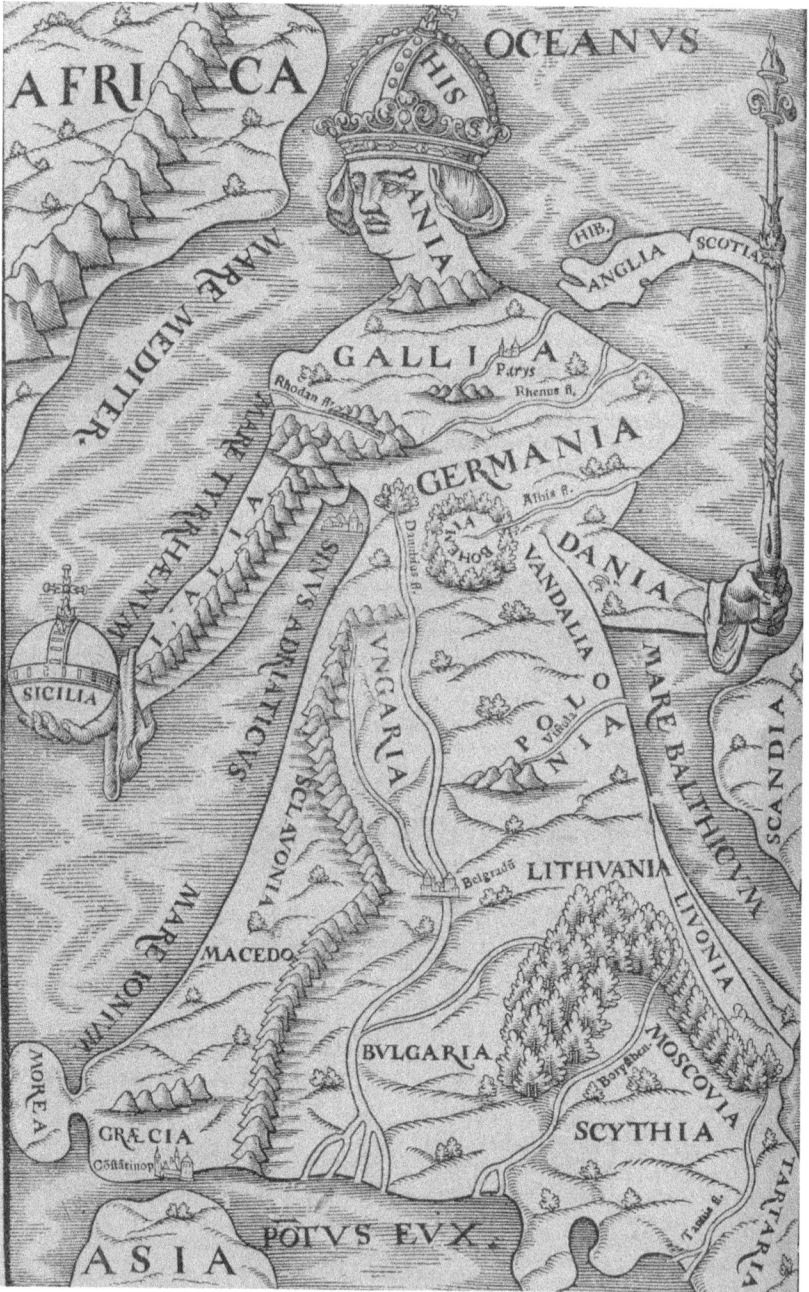

Figure 6.1. *Europe as a Queen*, By: Sebastian Münster (1588); Source: Digital Collections, The Newberry Library (Public Domain).

I watched his skinny calves, and the naked, bloody feet that continually stumbled and tripped. He was running now, gazing constantly at Assisi: he had suddenly been invaded by a sense of urgency, of great longing. But when we reached the walls his knees gave way and he stopped.

"Brother Leo," he asked in a gasping, supplicating tone, catching hold of my arm, "do you remember how on that night on the Mount of Olives Christ lifted his arms to heaven and cried, 'Father, let this cup be taken from me'? The sweat was pouring from his forehead, Brother Leo. He was trembling."

"Calm down, calm down, Francis". . . .

I spoke to him softly, sweetly, because I was afraid of his fiery eyes. But he was far, far away on the Mount of Olives, and did not hear.

"He was trembling," he murmured again, "He was trembling . . . but he seized the cup and drank it down in one gulp, right to the bottom!"

—Nikos Kazantzakis, *St. Francis: God's Pauper*

É o Reino da Verdade	*It's the Kingdom of Truth*
É a Estrada do amor	*It's the Path of love*
E todos prestar atenção	*And everybody must pay attention*
Aos ensinos do Professor	*To the teachings of the Professor*
Os ensinos do Professor	*The teachings of the Professor*
É quem nos traz belas lições	*Bring us beautiful lessons*
Para todos se unir	*For everybody to come together*
E respeitar os seus irmãos	*And respect one's brothers and sisters*
Respeitar os seus irmãos	*To respect one's brothers and sisters*
Com alegria e com amor	*With happiness and with love*
Para todos conhecer	*For everybody to know* (one another)
E saber dar o seu valor	*And to know how to give your value*

—excerpt from hymn #118, "Todos Querem Ser Irmão" ("All want to be Brothers"), in *O Cruzeiro* (*The Cross*), by Mestre Irineu

6

Santo Daime and the
Re-Enchantment of Europe

I first arrived in Belgium in the summer of 2009 for two months of exploratory fieldwork. Having already carried out preliminary research in the rainforests of Brazil a year earlier, I was struck by the stark contrasts between these two field sites. Even though I was studying the same religious tradition in both locales, the steamy Amazon jungle had given way to the concrete jungles of urbanized Europe. Instead of spiders, snakes, and bats, I was now confronted with pigeons, transit strikes, and the constant threat of expert pickpockets.

I emerged from the downtown Bruxelles-Nord/Brussel-Noord train station into a congested and yet strangely tranquil city characterized by a mishmash of centuries-old architecture with ultramodern high-rises. Taken together, the assortment of buildings conveys a stylistic blend of influences from surrounding European nations. At the same time, Brussels's cityscape is flecked with exceptional specimens of Art Deco and Art Nouveau forms popularized by designer-architect Victor Horta (1861–1947). Numerous large walls are splashed with bold-colored murals depicting famous Belgian comic book figures such as Tintin, Gaston Lagaffe, and Lucky Luke. These officially sanctioned murals (an initiative of the Brussels Comic Book Museum) are accompanied by illicit graffiti-type paintings of monochromatic arachnids, dinosaur skeletons, and other animals by street artists like Bonom and Roa. The unassuming little nation of Belgium is not the setting one might imagine for ritualized consumption of a mind-bending Amazonian beverage. Yet this is precisely why it was a perfect context to observe how the Santo Daime's deployment of this enigmatic plant concoction is spreading throughout the world. My intention was to spend more than a year in Europe trying to understand fardados' dedication to Santo Daime, particularly the question of why some individuals are choosing to repeatedly undergo the ayahuasca experience. As I walked the Brussels streets in search of my hostel, I was surrounded by the smog and hubbub in this bustling capital city of Belgium, which simultaneously serves as the headquarters of a shaky European Union.[1]

Before getting in touch with local daimista contacts, I wanted to orient myself to my new surroundings. The first few days were spent exploring the downtown core of Brussels, wandering in and out of the gorgeous Grand Place (Grote Markt in Flemish [see Davies 1996, 626–27]), the central square of the city teeming with tourists who meander around its shops and buskers. I made a point to savor the delicious flavors of world-famous Belgian chocolate, *frites*,[2] and waffles, as well as the best beer[3] on the planet. For the ethnographer, such abundant visual and appetizing delights afforded recreational relief in between the occasionally gut-wrenching ordeals that accompany regular ayahuasca use. In addition, European daimistas are generally kind and hospitable people. Relations with research informants, many of which developed into good friendships, provided a source of emotional support. This was essential for a young anthropologist studying a ritual format that challenges each participant to directly confront their deepest personal weaknesses. The omnipresence of the Belgian sensual and social value of *gezelligheid* (Flemish for sociability, coziness, or snugness) served to offset the arduous and sometimes excruciating challenges that one undergoes in Daime works. Through in-depth ethnographic analyses of Daime groups in Europe, this section of the book reveals the processes according to which small groups of people in the West have embraced a spiritual tradition from the postcolonial periphery.

Even as anthropology navigates its "existential" (Jackson and Piette 2015b) or "ontological" turn (Bessire and Bond 2014; Heywood 2012; Holbraad and Pedersen 2014), with few exceptions (e.g., Heelas 2008; Magliocco 2012; Srinivas 2012) the discipline remains largely aloof to what has been called a "re-enchantment of the West," with many Euro-Americans now discovering and adopting new ways of being religious (Partridge 2004, 44). As demonstrated more robustly by sociologists of religion (e.g., Arweck 2006; Bender 2010; Dawson 2013), it is individuals seeking opportunities for re-enchantment who are drawn to new spiritual formats as an alternative to the Christian and secular heritages of Western culture. According to Eurobarometer polls, the dawn of the twenty-first century finds that as many as "four in five EU citizens have religious or spiritual beliefs" (European Commission 2005, 9). While 20 percent of European Union residents are nontheists, there are 51 percent committed to a traditional belief in God. The rest of the EU population includes 26 percent of respondents who vaguely "believe there is some sort of spirit or life force" and 3 percent who "don't know" (European Commission 2010, 203–205). This 26 percent segment espousing unconventional forms of spiritual belief is key to understanding that shifts away from mainstream churches do not entail that "the fate of our times is characterized by rationalization and intellectualization and, above all, by the 'disenchantment of the world'" (Weber 1948[1922], 155). Exploring emergence of novel religious minorities through the lens of Santo Daime, the present book demonstrates how state opposition to an unorthodox form of re-enchantment discloses the normative power of cross-pressured extremes in mainstream Europe.

Because Europe is not a homogeneous culture, regional diversity on the continent must be taken into consideration. Surveys show that the Czech Republic, Bulgaria, and Sweden are the most secularized nations in Europe, because they score the lowest on church attendance and "importance of God" measures. In contrast, Poland and Ireland boast the highest European rates of church attendance and reliance on God (Halman and Pettersson 2003, 63). According to data from the World Religion Database (WRD) reported by Johnson (2010, lvi/lxv–lxvii), during the first decade of this century the number of atheists (AT) and agnostics (AG) expanded modestly in most of Europe. By 2010, these nonreligious groups represented 10.8 percent (2.1% AT, 8.7% AG) of Southern Europeans, 14.5 percent (2.4% AT, 12.1% AG) of Northern Europeans, and 21.6 percent (2.8% AT, 18.8% AG) of Western Europeans. Yet during this same decade, the total proportion of nonbelievers actually contracted when the entire continent is considered, with annual rates of decline at −1.88 percent for agnostics and −2.2 percent for atheists. This skewing of the continent-wide data is due to pronounced declines of atheists and agnostics in Eastern Europe, where in 2010 they were 8.5 percent of the population (7.0% AG, 1.5% AT). As it develops beyond the postcommunist legacy of suppressing religiousness, Eastern Europe has experienced a "slight religious revival" since the end of the Cold War (Müller and Neundorf 2012, 559). In terms of Western Europe, the WRD figures project that traditional Catholic and Protestant Christians will shrink from almost 131 million (67% of the population) in 2010 to just over 111 million (59% of the population) through 2050. Conversely, all other religious groups have seen increases in the twenty-first century. From 2000–2010, the data show annual growth of atheists (+1.3%) and agnostics (+1.9%) occurring alongside growth in many non-Christian religions in Western Europe, including: Muslims (+0.59%), Jews (+0.45%), Buddhists (+1.07%), Hindus (+1.51%) and "New Religionists" (+0.45%) (Johnson 2010, lxv–vii). All told, the persistence of residual believers in Europe casts doubt on secularist predictions about religiosity's impending extinction.

After more than a century of defining itself as a discipline specializing in cultures of non-Western peoples, the theory and methods of anthropology are now increasingly being applied to European society, the cradle of Western thought. For most of its history, anthropology did not apprehend Europe as an opportunity to think ethnologically about industrialized Western societies. According to Susan Parman (1998, 193), until recently the discipline's "most promising candidate for critical self-reflection, Europe, remained largely orientalised—Europeanist anthropologists paying lip service to the notion of 'complex society'" while their writing concentrated on the lives of bucolic peasant communities. Yet considering how interrelated economic and identity crises in Europe are now reverberating across global markets invested in the EU project, there is a pressing need to make better sense of Western culture's original homeland.

As outlined above, the present book draws attention to a new spirituality that is finding supporters in urban centers across Europe. Inquiring into why hundreds of Europeans have chosen to convert to Santo Daime instead of following a local religious tradition, my research confronts the more general issue of religion's place in the Western world. After being neglected for more than a century in anthropology's quest to understand non-Western locales, a recent turn to studies of secular modernity has placed Europe at the center stage of twenty-first-century social science.

Religious Modernity in Europe

Peter Beyer (1994, 111) acknowledges that the "diverse manifestations of religion in our world reflect the global context in which they operate." As a multitude of cultural forms are increasingly subject to forces of globalization, the economic and social relationships between West and non-West are paralleled by a reciprocal transfer of religious traditions. Anthropology has traditionally studied the non-Western "Other" (see McGrane 1989). This has led to some of the discipline's greatest contributions, as anthropology's unique theoretical standpoint discredits prejudice and xenophobia by advocating cultural relativity. However, Hefner (1998, 86) observes that "anthropologists who rightly challenge the application of secular-modernization narratives to the non-Western world are sometimes less critical of these theories' portrayal of religion in the modern West." As pointed out by Paul Rabinow (1996, 36), the postmodern critique triggered appeals to "anthropologize the West," venturing to show "how exotic its constitution of reality has been" and emphasizing "those domains most taken for granted as universal." Notwithstanding these advances, Csordas (2007, 259; 2009, 1) laments that "in one of the most vital contemporary arenas of scholarly debate in the human sciences, that which deals with world systems, transnationalism, and globalization, the role of religion remains understudied and under-theorized." My research discerns reasons for the transnational adoption of Santo Daime by Europeans, which occurs despite the long-held presumption that Europe is undergoing a teleological process of secularization.

As for the classic secularization theory's claim that any surviving religious beliefs are increasingly confined to secluded domains, it is true that the public (i.e., governmental) influence of religion is on the wane in Europe. But undue preoccupation with this trend obscures other intriguing social transformations that loom as direct repudiations of the secular norm. While sociologists, historians, philosophers, and religious scholars continue to debate chronological census data showing a decline in church attendance (Bruce 1992; McLeod and Ustorf 2003; Ziebertz and Riegel 2008), ethnographic facts are being ignored. Some anthropologists have demonstrated how Europeans are adapting Christianity (Badone 1990; Coleman 2000, 72–86), Judaism (Buckser 1999), and Buddhism (Obadia 1999) to global forces of modernity. Curiously, the secularization debate has been largely oblivious to the fact that in Western countries "the most dramatic and unanticipated" fluctuations in the spiritual landscape are due to the rise of New Religious Movements (Rambo 2003, 211).

Elisabeth Arweck (2006, 351) defines New Religious Movements (NRM) as "religious groups and movements which arose in the West since the Second World War, where they emerged as a new phenomenon, even if their roots reached further back in history." The growth of these groups in Europe is detected as an inverse correlation. In places where attendance at traditional religious institutions is declining, the popularity of NRM is on the rise (Stark 1993, 389). Of the multiple types of NRM, Santo Daime beliefs are routinely tied to the so-called New Age (but there are important distinctions, as discussed further in Part VI). New Age spirituality is notoriously difficult to define because of the ambiguity of its boundaries (Sutcliffe 2003, 9–30). However, it became clear through my fieldwork that fardados share with New Agers the belief that "the earth is a conscious, living organism" (Hanegraaff 1998, 157) and the "monistic assumption that the Self itself is sacred" (Heelas 1996, 3). But rather than lumping it into the nebulous category of New Age, it is more accurate to link Santo Daime to the more definitive class of Euro-American "nature spiritualities." Followers of nature spiritualities are frustrated by materialism's disenchantment of humanity's relation to the biosphere. They try to "overcome this cultural alienation and relate with nature as a living and inspirited cosmos" (Greenwood 2005, vii). Even though these nature-oriented rituals may appear new, practitioners are often keen to trace the origins of their spiritual practice to premodern traditions.

Ethnographers have published works on the subsistence of folk healing practices (Lambek 2007; Lüdtke 2009) as well as twentieth-century varieties of "paganism" related to nature spiritualities in Europe. Prominent examples of the latter include studies of *Wicca* (modern witchcraft), which some European communities willingly espouse (Luhrmann 1989) while others fear it as sorcery that must be cast out by magical "unwitchers" (Favret-Saada 1980). There have also been studies of European neo-shamanism (Blain 2002), an assortment of new forms of spirituality alleging their authentic rehabilitation of rites inherited from ancient Europeans. Still, despite extensive sociological, historical, and psychological literature on conversions to NRM in the West, Lorne Dawson (2003, 125) indicates that "a crucial and easily overlooked element of mystery remains about why people choose to be religious, especially in so radical a manner." It is possible to get a hint as to why this mystery endures when one considers how most ethnography is infused with secular presuppositions. For example, Luhrmann's study of British witchcraft (1989, 13) ponders why "apparently irrational beliefs are held by apparently rational people." My research endeavors to unravel this "mystery" as it pertains to a small group of Europeans whose embrace of a foreign ayahuasca religion presents an affront to post-Enlightenment standards of "rationality." In so doing, the ethnographer must maintain impartiality regarding whether Europeans' commitment to Santo Daime is any less "rational" than the worldviews of their mainstream Christian and secularist peers.

For the purposes of the present text, it is especially important to note details spelled out in Turney-High's (1953) chapter on rural Walloons' "magico-religious" worldview. Here, the author places special emphasis on his informants' commitment to residual healing traditions of Celtic origin. The Celtic priests called Druids are depicted as a kind of ancient European shaman. This author says that during his fieldwork, it was apparent that apart from heavy influences of Catholicism, Walloons still hold mythical beliefs in gnomes, sacred trees, and magical folk remedies, and that *makrale* is a Walloon "word for shamanism [containing] a root connected with death and the shades of the dead" (Turney-High 1953, 227–28). Coincidently, aspects of Turney-High's study are reflected in my own fieldwork, with many European daimistas voicing similar neo-pagan sympathies. Expressing deep sadness when this topic arose in an interview, one German fardado dated the overthrow of native European animism to the "Massacre" or "Bloodbath" of Verden in AD 782. He bemoaned that the Frankish king Charlemagne (*Karl der Große*) had arranged for 4,500 Saxons to be put to death because of their refusal to convert to Christianity (see Flierman 2016, 183/189).

Much like North American seekers (Bender 2010, 157–162), European fardados evince "metaphysical nostalgia" for a spiritual "homeland," a longing that propels them to experiment with non-Western spiritualities even while they remain somewhat wary of cultural appropriation. During one of my interviews with Gilles, a French-born fardado who is now a naturalized Belgian, he told me why he follows Santo Daime and also regularly participates in *temazcal* ("sweat lodge") ceremonies, both spiritual paths normally associated with the Americas:

People ask me: "Why do you go so far? Why don't you work on a spiritual path that's in your roots?" But that's my roots and that's our roots! I think it's very important to understand that the Christian roots here in Belgium go back fifteen hundred years more or less.[4] So before, we've got . . . Celtic tradition. . . . If you go deep, everywhere in the world there was more or less the same type of belief, the same type of structure, and the same type of tradition: to honor Nature, to honor the mystery, to see Man as part of Nature, and not Nature as part of Man. And so, if you just look at the archaeological research of Belgium, when they find a very old place most of the time they will find a circular house where they did the sweat lodge! You know, I'm not playing indian when I'm doing sweat lodge, I'm just going back to my European roots. Here in Europe the Vatican killed tradition, just cut the line. Most of the time when I go to South America, they speak about how bad the White men were for the indian. But please! They were bad before with us! . . .

> *For example, I'm quite annoyed when I go to South America, the people think that the Christian Vatican made the worst [colonization] in the Americas. But that's not right! They killed thousands of our elders here. They completely destroyed the culture. In America they didn't succeed, they succeeded in part. . . . [But] there's no roots anymore here. . . . We are not playing indians; we are coming back to our memory, to honour it.*

Living with his non-daimista wife and children in Brussels, Gilles is a fifty-year-old human resources consultant who began his Daime practice in 2001. He also teaches *Biodanza* (*bio* [Greek: "life"] + *danza* [Spanish: "dance"], or "dance of life"), a globalized musical movement therapy developed in the 1960s and 1970s by Chilean psychologist-anthropologist Rolando Toro Araneda.[5] In traveling to the Andes Mountains several times, Gilles underwent an extensive education with indigenous shamans, so that he now also considers himself a "medicine man." In this sense, he believes that his training in the ritual techniques of the New World is essential to revitalize the shamanic knowledge of his ancient Celtic ancestors. This sentiment expresses a tendency of European fardados to downplay the differences between peoples in favor of stressing a mystical or shamanic inheritance shared across cultures.

A disdain for institutionalized Christianity places some fardados in the "spiritual but not religious" (SBNR) category of Western re-enchantment (see Bender 2010, 3/11; Fuller 2001; Wuthnow 1998). And yet many other fardados agreed that Daime could be considered a religion. One example is Henriette, a thirty-five-year-old school teacher who discovered the Daime while travelling in Brazil during her twenties. She met and married a Brazilian fardado, who now lives with her and their two children in suburban Brussels. She alternates between attending works with different daimista churches in Belgium, and concurs with other European fardados that Daime meets her needs more effectively than the spirituality of her upbringing:

> *Yes, because "religion" is you restore the bond with God. That's what happened for me [with Santo Daime]. Because before, the Catholic religion didn't function as a religion for me because I couldn't really feel God. Well, I could think about it, like a man with a beard that's watching you or something, but not really.*

Here she is drawing on religion's Latin etymology of *religare* as "to re-tie" or "to re-bind" (Csordas 2004, 163). While the anti-institutional attitude is shared by many fardados, they value ceremonial ayahuasca experiences because they believe this provides direct access to "sacred knowledge" (see Richards 2016). Or, according to another Belgian fardado:

> *I'm okay with the word* religion *because it refers to religare: "re-connects" and "re-unification".* . . . *I have a hard time connecting with the word* faith *or* belief, *because it implies something which is blind, which is something that you have to accept without it being explained. In part it's true, but it's not because I just believe it blindly, it's because I've experienced it through the ayahuasca . . . so it's more [about] experience than blind faith.*

Though the word's true origin is controversial, my informants approved of the etymology of "religion" as meaning " 'to reconnect'—from the Latin *re* (again) and *ligare* (to connect)" (B. Taylor 2007, 11). They believe that the entheogenic action of Daime allows them to experientially "reconnect" with God inside their own consciousness. When I first met Felix early on in my fieldwork, we were both newcomers to the Daime. At age thirty-six, he works as a graphic designer in East Flanders. Felix's curiosity about my research project led to us becoming fast friends, and I observed as he transitioned from uncommitted firmado to a deeply devoted fardado now playing guitar in the Daime works. At the time, Felix lived near the building where Flemish Daime works are held; upon his invitation, I stayed the night on the couch in Felix's apartment following almost every ritual I attended in Flanders. Since it is difficult to sleep the night after a Daime ritual—a common side effect of ayahuasca is temporary insomnia—Felix and I would converse for a few hours after each work. The topic of the aforementioned quotation would frequently arise in these late-night chats. In a process that is common in the conversion narratives of my informants, Felix initially strained to square his estrangement from traditional Christianity (which he rejects as authoritarian) with his growing esteem for the Daime doctrine. Eventually, he decided to become a fardado because he did not perceive Daime as domineering.

Since their religious practices are still considered deviant, most Daime groups in Europe are compelled to hold rituals in secret. But European daimistas allowed me access to their rituals and expressed willingness to participate in ethnographic research because they do not want to live in the shadows. Both during and immediately following my fieldwork, several Daime communities in Europe were raided by police, resulting in the arrests of fardados in Great Britain (August 2010) and Portugal (October 2011). Although all those arrested were released on bail, they were charged with importation and possession of a controlled substance (a jailable offense), their Daime sacrament was confiscated, and legal proceedings are ongoing. At the supranational level, the protection of religious freedom is decreed in Article 9 of the European Convention on Human Rights (ECHR),[6] a law that applies to all EU member states. But it is unclear whether these protections would extend to daimistas because this decision hinges upon whether or not the EU Court of Human Rights in Strasbourg would classify Santo Daime as a bona fide "religion." Shining an ethnographic light on the realities of Santo Daime in Europe will provide anthropological details for governments now wrestling with this clash between drug policies and religious freedom.

Transnational Developments of Santo Daime

Abridging the chronology of Part II, historical entanglements that led to the formation and global expansion of Santo Daime run as follows: From the sixteenth to the nineteenth centuries, Europeans brought African slaves and Christianity to South America, a continent inhabited by native populations, some of whose ritual practices utilized ayahuasca; after slavery was formally outlawed in Brazil in 1888, many young Afro-Brazilians sought to work as rubber tappers in the Amazon, an economic opportunity prompted by the contemporary rise in Euro-American demand for rubber; beginning in the 1920s, Mestre Irineu and other rubber tappers combined the Afro-Brazilian and Catholic elements of their upbringing with Amazonian indigenous practices of ayahuasca consumption; in the late twentieth century, the Santo Daime becomes regionally and then nationally popular in Brazil, eventually attracting devotees from around the world. While ayahuasca rituals have also been exported to North America, Central America, Asia, Africa, and Australia (see Labate, Rose, and dos Santos 2008, 27; Labate and Feeney 2012; Gearin 2015, 2017), the present study of Santo Daime highlights how Europeans' colonization and Christianization of the Americas has come full circle with the arrival of this eclectic form of shamanic Christianity in Europe. As attested in Part II, even though Santo Daime in Brazil is well researched, the reasons for the doctrine's transnational expansion remain understudied, incentivizing this timely analysis of the European case.

The non-Brazilian awareness of Santo Daime began with a trickle of foreign travelers reaching the community of Padrinho Sebastião in the 1970s. This is revealed in the Colônia 5000 guestbook signatures of visitors from Argentina, Bolivia, Peru, Colombia, Venezuela, England, France, Germany, Italy, Portugal, Switzerland, Israel, Japan, and Canada (Fróes 1986, 48, cited in Groisman 2000, 84). In fact, the most experienced living European fardado that I had the chance to meet during fieldwork is the current *Madrinha* ("Godmother") of Daime in Italy, who reported that she and some Italian friends had visited Colônia 5000 in 1978–79. At early stages of Santo Daime's expansion (which principally involves the CEFLURIS branch and its offshoots), it is typical for new groups to begin as a small congregation called a *ponto* ("point"). After a few years of development and growth, pontos can eventually be given official designation as an *igreja* ("church"). The first Daime ponto outside of Brazil was a small American congregation in Boston, Massachusetts, inaugurated in 1987 (Groisman 2000, 16). It has been previously reported that the earliest Daime rituals in Europe began informally in Spain in 1985, and that a fardado representing Céu do Mapiá visited Spain to oversee the first official Daime work in Europe on March 19, 1989, "a date which in that particular year coincides with the beginning of Easter week" (López-Pavillard and de las Casas 2011, 365). But during fieldwork I discovered that this same Mapiá representative also traveled to Belgium to supervise works there immediately following the March 1989 works in Spain. Unlike some of the larger European countries (e.g., Labate and Jungaberle 2011, Groisman 2000; Weinhold 2007), the Daime community in Belgium has not yet been addressed in any scholarly research.

I had initiated contact with the Belgian Santo Daime through email. After receiving a response and talking on the phone with a fardado charged with duties of managing an internet website for the Flemish Daime group, I acquired contact information for Lars, a fardado who had previously served as commander of the original Belgian church. Lars had retired from his commander role in 2001, but he continues to regularly attend works as a respected elder. Upon my arrival for fieldwork, Lars offered to host me at his house for several days to assist me in finding my bearings. It was fitting that my first recorded interview was carried out with Lars, who is the most veteran fardado still residing in Belgium—the first Belgian daimista moved to Céu do Mapiá in the late 1990s. At fifty-five years of age, Lars is an unmarried landscaper living in rural Flanders. Invoking "the established Brazilian narrative of cultural confluence" (Dawson 2013, 89), Lars explained why he thinks Santo Daime appeals to some Europeans:

People are searching for something, something that puts them on a higher level. People want to be conscious in their life, I think. They're searching for that. Not to be put asleep all the time, by consumption and by watching television and going to sports. They want to be active. They want to find something that fits to themselves that is out of the common culture, the common lack of consciousness in this society. So, when you find something that appeals to your deepest self, you want to know more about it. And I think there the Santo Daime has a big role to fill. But the Santo Daime's not for everybody. It doesn't have the ambition. . . . It's a doctrine, it's a school where you can learn to deal with your own life, with the mysteries of life. It gives answers to those very profound questions: What is the meaning of life? I don't know! [laughs] But it gives you a direction. That's also why it works, for example, for drug addicts, or ex-drug addicts; they see a new direction in their life, and so they can overcome their addiction.

And, we have the addiction to materialism; we want a new car. All our culture is about having things. And with the Santo Daime you see you don't need that anymore. You need to have some comfort in life. Everybody wants to have comfort, and that's a good thing. But it's not the main goal anymore. You can look through it. You don't have this enormous hole anymore in your soul, that stays empty, that the shopping center can't fill.

We are the land of the Godless. All over Europe, all over America. There are still the ancient, the old religions, like in Belgium [we have] Catholicism, Christianity in Europe. But they don't appeal anymore to the people. They are burned out, there is only form. But every man has that need for spirituality. And people fill that with materialism. . . . They're searching for it, but they don't find it. Or there's also the success of the Eastern religions like Zen Buddhism or Tibetan Buddhism or even Islam. And also Christian fundamentalism . . . but sometimes it's too strange to fit in this society. To become a Tibetan monk is not obvious in our culture, or to become Islamic in Belgium, it's difficult also. Because there never has been a translation of these religions, of these philosophies into Western society. [Santo Daime] is even weirder! When people come to take Santo Daime, it is something from the South American indians, but because it has Christian roots, it's also a Christian doctrine. . . . We use the names of the Christian saints like São José or Jesus. For us it's easy to understand. We can imagine something when we hear the name São José (St. Joseph): okay, that's the father of Jesus. And Maria, Mary, we know who she is. All this Christian mythology, we understand.

Me myself, I consider Mestre Irineu as a prophet, someone who brings a holy message from the Divine. Also, he brought this doctrine. He was the in-between between the [South American] indians and the Western civilization. He translated the Ayahuasca into Daime. He was Brazilian but he was a black man. He was like a synthesis between indian, African, and European. Between red, black, and white. . . . Some people in the Daime they say it's like you had Jesus, and he gave his lessons. And then, Mestre Irineu renewed those lessons. He planted this holy doctrine again in the world a second time. The second arm of the cross. You must find that out yourself, everybody's different.

As he recapitulates the idea that every human's "search" for well-being is rooted in a desire to experience a "higher" consciousness—what Charles Taylor (2007) calls "fullness"—Lars also conveys here the common assumption that mainstream religious values are declining in Europe (Catholicism, in the case of Belgium). So alongside remnants of the once-pervasive community of practicing Christians, there is now a substantial segment of the population that is nonreligious (i.e., secular materialists). Lars also expresses the belief of fardados around the world that the double-armed ✝ Cross of Caravaca (Figure 6.2), one of the main symbols of Santo Daime, represents the return of Christ. Daimistas interpret this not as Jesus coming back to earth as an individual, but rather that the liquid Daime brew is itself a "key" to *parousia*, through which access to the spirit of "Christ Consciousness" can be obtained inside each person who partakes of this ayahuasca religion (Polari de Alverga 1999, 2/16/25/155/173–74; see also Barnard, forthcoming; M. Fox 1988). MacRae (2006, 398[n5]) explains that this "important Daimista symbol is a Byzantine cross supposed to have been introduced to Spain by the Knights Templar, and which has since had strong occultist connotations. . . . [During the colonial period], its name was used in a compilation of prayers that were used by healers and magicians in Spain, Portugal, and Latin America." While the Daime cross also resembles the Roman Catholic cross of Lorraine or the Patriarchal cross of Orthodox Christianity (with the upper beam representing an INRI titulus), on Caravaca crucifixes Christ is often nailed to the upper beam, suggesting Second Coming connotations more closely

Figure 6.2. Double-armed cross at Céu do Mapiá, Brazil (photo by the author).

aligned with daimista symbology (see Hildburgh 1940, 242–43). I have also seen numerous examples of Caravaca crosses fashioned from the Jagube (*B. caapi*) vine that is used to make ayahuasca, implying that by drinking the Daime beverage one takes the wood of Jesus's cross into one's body.

While Santo Daime is largely Christian in form, Lars articulates fardados' common conviction that Mestre Irineu's "doctrine"[7] is a "synthesis" of universal truths that apply to all humans regardless of cultural upbringing. It is through disciplined drinking of the Daime sacrament—itself a synthesis of distinct chemical ingredients into a homogeneous solution—that daimistas believe they can transcend superficial divisions between different religious traditions, making contact with the common source of all spiritualities. Lars proved to be a crucial gatekeeper, the first in a long line of fardados who introduced me to the history and diverse social landscapes of Santo Daime in Europe.

7

National Profiles

In the formative years of Céu do Mapiá (1982–83) there were a handful of foreigners participating in works and helping the primarily Brazilian population to institute their new community. Two of these European inhabitants of Mapiá, a Spanish man and a Belgian woman, eventually imported bottles of the Daime sacrament to their home countries in 1985 (López-Pavillard and de las Casas 2011, 365) and 1989 respectively. In this chapter, I track the sequences through which this new religious movement expanded into several European countries during the late twentieth and early twenty-first centuries. For some of these contexts, reference will be made to existing scholarly literature (e.g., France, Germany, Ireland, Italy, Netherlands, Spain, UK). But in others (e.g., Austria, Belgium, Finland, Greece, Portugal), this represents a pioneering analysis of local Daime activities. These national profiles stitch together recollections of interviewees representing all European nations where fardados were residing at the time of my fieldwork. The chronological narratives—whose relative length corresponds roughly to each Daime community's age and size—are accompanied by brief ethnographic observations concerning the wider implications of the churches' presence in each country. Taken together as an impressionistic portrait of daimista communities across the continent, these national overviews establish the first composite ethnohistory of Santo Daime in Europe. In framing each country as a specific subculture within the European daimista community, the national profiles convey this text's broader interpretation of the rise of new mystical practices in the West. Accordingly, spread of the Daime in Europe in the late twentieth and early twenty-first centuries is an occurrence of religious "glocalization," whereby social trends imported from abroad are adjusted to fit cultural norms at the local level (Robertson 1992, 173–74). Despite being one of the first places where Daime took root in Europe, I consider the Belgian daimistas last because the concentration of my ethnographic focus there resulted in a deeper database.

Spain

I had the opportunity to interview the brother of the first Spanish daimista at his apartment in 2011. Now one of the chief fardados in Spain with more than twenty years of Daime experience, José was twenty-one years old when in 1987 he and some friends were invited by his older brother Florentino to partake in a ceremony with a "mysterious liquid." Florentino spoke to them about Padrinho Sebastião, the Amazon rainforest, and the Daime. At that time, José was uninterested in any sort of religious doctrine and disliked the idea of taking "drugs," but he was enthralled by stories of adventure deep in the jungle. In our interview, José wanted to emphasize that he had initially arrived to the Daime free of all expectations.

When the group of five or six friends arrived at their cabin in the mountains, Florentino played Pink Floyd music and some Mestre Irineu hymns on a stereo while they took the Daime. José recalls that the ritual went all night, and that he traveled internally like an "astronaut." He recounted to me how at one point they made a campfire, and as he looked at the flames there appeared a "bisonte" (bison) like those in the Paleolithic cave at Altamira, Spain. The visionary animal kept changing form before his eyes. All night, José says, he "traveled around the small things of the mind and the big things of the universe." He told me that as a young man he was not especially religious. Although like all Spanish children he had studied religion in school, he had never had a spiritual experience like this before. Also, because he was ignorant of the tendency for ayahuasca to not mix well with alcohol, the next day he went out partying and got so sick that he vomited in the street. This same group of friends took Daime two or three more times that year (1987). The next year (1988) Florentino returned to Brazil but left a bottle of Daime behind for his brother. José and his companions imbibed a few more times but the experiences were not as "deep" as the first time. In hindsight, he observes that none of these instances constituted official Daime works, but instead, "it was hippie, free; we took Daime, put on classical or New Age music, [then] meditated, walked in the forest, without leaders, only a [small] group of friends." They also drank smaller doses of Daime in these experimental sessions because they only had the one bottle to share.

José traveled to Mapiá and stayed for two months in late 1988. Through Florentino he met Pd. Sebastião, and then he and his brother traveled to Machu Picchu in Peru for what amounted to a total of three months in South America. He stops the interview momentarily to retrieve and show me a photograph he took of Pd. Sebastião and Md. Rita while he was in Mapiá. He says that Pd. Sebastião talked and explained a lot. José did not understand the Daime patriarch's caboclo dialect of Portuguese, but Florentino acted as translator. Pd. Sebastião apparently prophesized that José would one day be the leader of the Santo Dame in Spain. But José says that he was not then very fond of taking Daime within the rigid structure of the Padrinho's doctrine, and that he much preferred to drink it by himself quietly. However, he did enjoy the work of making the Daime (feitio) in Mapiá, which at that time was "a small village, very basic . . . very rustic." The more works he attended there, the more the doctrine began to appeal to him, such that he now claims that this trip to Mapiá "changed my life." Upon his departure, Pd. Sebastião gave him a bottle of Daime. When they returned to Spain, José and Florentino began preparations for the first official works in Spain (1989). In their historical review, López-Pavillard and de las Casas (2011, 366) report a total of 250 fardados now practicing Daime in Spain. At the time of my fieldwork there were six churches (three in Catalonia, one near Basque country, one in Toledo province, and one in the Balearic Islands), as well as numerous smaller pontos or "points" scattered throughout Spain (see also Apud and Romaní 2017). In disclosing the vague regional whereabouts of congregations in countries where Daime is not yet fully legal, I refrain from giving exact locations so as not to compromise the anonymity of my informants.

Even though it is not the main reason that he continues to work with the Daime, José expressed his approval of historical upshots that are signified by the continued globalization of this doctrine of Christianized shamanism—or is it shamanized Christianity?

> When Padrinho Alfredo came to Spain in nineteen-ninety-two, it was five hundred years after Columbus discovered America; and the Red Way . . . also made its first work in Europe that year. For me, spiritually it's our way of returning this [event]: the Spanish go there with a cross [and] the indians came here with spiritual plants. For me, the [story] of the conquerors is a political question;

> *[it's] the same history as the beginning of time, because one people conquer or exterminate another people. . . . For me it's important that at this time when Padrinho Alfredo came here in nineteen ninety-two he spoke about this. . . . In Spain at this time, [the whole] country was celebrating the five hundred years of Columbus [arriving] in America.*

José said that in 1992 Pd. Alfredo's *comitiva* (entourage) attended a Red Path[1] peyote work where the indigenous leader of that ritual spoke about the same topics, and how he had been designated at a meeting of the grandfathers in Mexico "to present to [Westerners] our grandfathers' secret to save the world." José concluded the interview by expounding on the revolutionary meaning of the Red Path elder's statement: "This is the message, the mission that the grandfathers received [from the astral] in several parts of the world; this is the last time for some things, [and] now the world is *balançando* ("shaking/rocking"); for me, it's not the end of the world . . . but at the time, I had so many visions about this." It is open for debate whether such an account of sharing indigenous entheogens is a European daimista's convenient gloss for what might otherwise be construed as cultural appropriation. Nonetheless, this fardado's interest in the end times is consistent with Dawson's (2013, 80–94) astute observations about "Daimista millenarianism," fardados' widely held conviction that their Daime sacrament heralds the dawn of a "New Era" (*Nova Era*). At the very least, the global spread of entheogenic spirituality portends an expanded Western awareness of mind-altering substances that have been employed as medicines by aboriginal peoples for centuries.

As will become apparent in the following reviews of different Daime communities in Europe, the intercultural encounter between an Amazonian ayahuasca religion and Western legal authorities customarily begins with criminal prosecution of the former by the latter. For more than a decade José and his daimista compatriots have been embroiled in a lengthy effort to garner legitimacy as a registered religious organization in Spain. According to a summary of this legal history published by López-Pavillard and de las Casas (2011), in 2000 three daimistas were arrested and imprisoned after they were found with ayahuasca in Madrid. At that time, the charges of possessing an illegal drug were justified by police because ayahuasca "contains an active psychotropic substance known as DMT . . . which [can] cause great health damage producing hallucinogenic effects which create a moral dependence on the 'guru' or 'shaman' who leads the ingestion, and, at the same time, a physical dependence on the substance" (López-Pavillard and de las Casas 2011, 367). This event launched ongoing juridical wrangling in Spain between the antithetical concerns of prohibitions against the DMT chemical in ayahuasca and daimistas' claim to religious freedom. As is the case elsewhere in Europe (see below), Spanish daimistas remain in legal limbo because they present their government with a Catch-22: authorities want to maintain constitutional protections for religious freedom while at the same time continuing to outlaw the sacrament at the heart of Santo Daime practice.[2] This is where anthropologists can help resolve the fray of cross-cultural misunderstandings, in that ethnography provides a powerful tool of arbitration to distinguish between facts and paranoia. Therefore, even though this book is not meant as an apologist account of the Daime in Europe, the etic and emic analyses offered herein cannot help but dispel some of the ethnocentric prejudices and opposition that daimistas confront around the world.

After the interview, José arranged for my wife and me to visit a Daime community where fardados reside year-round in the rural periphery outside of Madrid. When we arrived by bus near the site of Cielo de San Juan (or Céu do São João [CdSJ], the languages being so close that they feel comfortable using Spanish for their church name) we were greeted by two kindly ladies who brought us by car to the church compound. It was quite striking to see a Spanish Daime settlement fashioned after the model of Mapiá. There were houses or trailers of all shapes and sizes encircling a central church attached to a communal kitchen and mess hall (my wife and I paid a small fee to stay in a guest bedroom in the main building). As far as I could tell, this is the only permanent community in Europe where daimistas live, eat, and sleep only meters from a church structure that they own rather than rent. The permanent salão of CdSJ is a large rectangular space that was flooded with natural light during the daytime work I attended. The floors are painted with lines to demarcate where rows of participants are to sit/stand during the works. The most conspicuous item in the room is the Wiphala flag, a politically charged symbol that signifies daimistas' support for indigenous movements in Spanish-speaking South America. Certainly, this space saves a lot of time and energy for the local daimistas, who do not have to set up and take down the ritual paraphernalia, as is the norm elsewhere in Europe. It is also much safer for people to walk rather than drive to their homes after a work. In fact, many daimistas I met in Europe spoke yearningly about the sense of civic identity within Brazilian Daime centers. European fardados hold the Brazilian model of collectivist living as an ideal that they would one day like to fulfill in their home countries, once it is legally permissible to do so.

My wife has no interest in entheogens herself, so she read a book and went on a walk in the surrounding countryside while I participated in a daytime Mother's Day work (exactly six years to the day after my maiden Daime experience in the Netherlands). After the work I mingled with the Spanish fardados, communicating in a hybrid Portuñol inflected with English words. I eventually reencountered one of the fardadas who had brought me from the bus station and she agreed to record an interview. I learned that Madrona is a sixty-year-old divorcée who is trained as a past-life regression therapist. She told me that she had begun her Daime career fifteen years earlier at the same time that she began the process of divorcing her husband because of irreconcilable differences. At that time, she was one in a small Daime group living in different places around Madrid. Following her divorce, people began to come to her large house to take the Daime there. Then she bought a small house figurine and put it on the main Daime table during their works. She referred to this act as a "creative visualization"[3] aimed at their collective need for a place to live and do rituals together. She claims that the miniature house she put on the Daime table was the same exact architectural design as the farmhouse that now serves as the main building of the CdSJ community. Following this interview, my wife and I were lucky to be offered a ride back into Madrid with a Spanish fardada who had to run errands in the city.

Portugal

Immediately following our sojourn in central Spain, we made our way by train to visit fardados near the Portuguese cities of Lisbon and Porto. Through informants, I had learned that after the first European Daime works were held in Spain and Belgium in Spring 1989, the doctrine was then inaugurated in Portugal in September of that year. They referred me to the Brazilian man who had first brought Daime to Portugal when he emigrated there in 1986. In his native Brazil, Adão had been raised in a family tailor-made for Santo Daime discipleship, in that his mother had an intense interest in Umbanda and his father was a practitioner of Kardecist spiritism. Yet he himself had never felt the inclination to practice any religion until he went back home to Brazil and visited with an old friend who was involved in Daime. Adão then participated in some works in Rio and

São Paulo and was moved by the music (he now interprets the vomiting and instance of fainting he endured as painful lessons or "peia"). When he returned to Lisbon, he organized Daime works there with some of his close friends in late 1989.

As this small group amassed in the early 1990s they met Tiago, a man from the north of Portugal who had independently discovered Daime while traveling in Brazil. Tiago had also brought the Daime home with him and began to rehearse the doctrine with his social contacts in the local music and capoeira scenes. Through the 1990s the two small groups from the Porto and Lisbon areas independently held works and occasionally came together for important dates on the Daime calendar. Eventually, these two groups collaborated in organizing a visit from Pd. Alfredo and his comitiva of musicians. However, Adão laments that this larger gathering attracted a group of about twenty people acquainted with ayahuasca shamanism. He says that as these two groups continued to drink ayahuasca together, the new situation "diluted" the smaller cadre of Portuguese fardados who had before then been holding works in his house. In a manner not uncommon among daimista communities around the world, personality clashes developed into broader frictions and fissures. Adão began to sour on organized religion and he left the doctrine because of his "disappointment" with how Brazilian leaders handled disagreements among Portuguese daimistas—and yet he is careful to state that he holds no ill will toward the Daime, which he still considers "beautiful."

There are now approximately thirty fardados comprising five Daime groups in Portugal (two in the Norte region, two near the central coast, and one newer ponto in the southern region of Algarve). I arranged to meet the commander of one of the Lisbon groups for an interview, a sixty-year-old retired tradesman whom I will refer to as Justino. He founded a Daime community called Jardim de São Francisco (Garden of St. Francis) in 2005. As we sat on a bench facing the Atlantic Ocean, Justino affirmed that it would be okay for me to publicize that there are Daime activities ongoing in his country: "It's not legalized, [but] it's not forbidden . . . the more discreet [the better]"; he assured me that it would not be a problem to publish about the Portuguese Daime in a book because he believes that people do not pay too much attention, as they are more interested in economic concerns. But less than five months after I had conducted the interview with Justino, he was arrested for possessing thirty liters of ayahuasca, which authorities confiscated as an illicit "hallucinogenic substance." It is worth mentioning that the European Monitoring Centre for Drugs and Drug Addiction (EMCDDA) is located in Lisbon, capital of the country with the most progressive drug policy in the Eurozone. Portugal's new policy decriminalized all drugs and replaced imprisonment with substance abuse treatment programs[4] (EMCDDA 2011, 21–23). In view of mounting empirical evidence confirming the safety and potential benefits of entheogens ingested in controlled contexts (see Part VII), European governments' management of Daime churches is a test case for the legitimacy of the EMCDDA's mission statement: "The EMCDDA exists to provide the EU and its Member States with a factual overview of European drug problems and a solid evidence base to support the drugs debate."[5] Unfortunately, the facts about entheogenic practices continue to be eclipsed by residual paranoia and propaganda, which undergird the enforcement of prohibitions that label all nonmedical drug use as "abuse."

I attended one Daime work held in a natural area on the periphery of Porto with the church commanded by Tiago, the initiator of Daime in northern Portugal. They set up the central table (*mesa*), other ritual accoutrements, and padded mats upon which to sit in a small clearing amid the trees. The ruined remains of old buildings were scattered around what was once farmland that has since been reclaimed by forest. In usual Portuguese fashion, the cross in the middle of this mesa was accompanied by a statuette of the Lady of Fátima (see Jones et al. 2005, 7148), a national symbol derived from a coronated Marian apparition that corresponds to the "Queen of the Forest" in Daime lore. The Daime brew was dispensed near where a cross, candles, and pictures of Mestre Irineu were placed on a natural rock outcropping that Tiago referred to as the "grotto." During the warmer months, such open-air works "in Nature" are prized by European daimistas as an opportunity to commune with the animistic forces of wind, water, earth, sun, clouds, animals, and vegetation. At the close of the work, a couple visiting from Brasilia introduced their form of Daime mixed with UDV, so they sang a UDV chamada and a Hindu Mantra about Ganesha. Following this, Tiago led the group in a prayer dedicated to water, for which they opened the cap off a plastic bottle of H_2O and placed it on the mesa.

In an interview with some of the fardados from the Porto church, they spoke about how they go about welcoming new members relative to ayahuasca's liminal status in a country that has decriminalized all psychoactive drugs. Tiago's wife Margarida, a thirty-four-year-old part-time office worker and fulltime mother, put it this way:

> *Daime is not a secret line, but it has to be discreet. . . . In the countries where we really don't have a legal position, we have to be more secret. . . .*

> *It was the position of Mestre Irineu: you can't invite people to go to the churches. It has to be an inner call, so when someone comes to us and starts to talk about something that she knows about this spiritual line, or have a conversation that we feel that she maybe can find herself in this spiritual line, then we talk about it with the person. Otherwise, we don't say anything.*

As a small aside, many of my fardado informants from elsewhere in Europe betrayed a lighthearted envy of Portuguese daimistas, who do not have to grapple with learning a new language to sing the Daime hinos.

Germany

A firsthand report on the rise of Santo Daime in Germany has been published by Rohde and Sander (2011). In their account, they confirm both that the first Germans visited Mapiá and the first Brazilian Daime representatives visited Germany in 1990.[6] There were fifty fardados in Germany at the time of my fieldwork (see Rohde and Sander 2011, 340, 349), a community made up of nine distinct churches and points distributed throughout the country (located near or in the states of Baden-Württemberg, Bavaria, Brandenburg, Hesse, North Rhine-Westphalia, Saxony, and Schleswig-Holstein). One of the smaller communities is independent, but the other eight German Daime groups are collectively joined in an organization called *CEFLU São Miguel* after St. Michael the archangel, patron saint of Germany (see Wilson 1994, 52). I attended a weekend set of works in the west of Germany where I interviewed some of the local fardados who were staying in cabins on a rented campground. Of the fardados I met, most had traveled from the south of Germany, but others had traveled from farther away, such as a contingent that arrived from Switzerland. One of the key interviews I conducted was with Hermann, the current leader of the German churches. Hermann has been involved with the Daime for fourteen years. When I asked him about the status of his religion in Germany, he identified two contrasting relationships that his congregation continues to navigate: (1) they are considered criminals by the German government, but at the same (2) they are engaging in a cordial if sometimes fraught research collaboration with scientists at the University of Heidelberg.

In September 1999, a Daime retreat in Germany was raided by federal police armed with automatic firearms. Over the next year, the police arrested several leading members of the German Santo Daime and confiscated many liters of their ayahuasca sacrament. This episode is also documented by Rohde and Sander (2011, 344–47), who note that "the consequences of the raids for the German church were that a lot of members and friends of the Santo Daime religion abandoned their connection to the church, fearing to lose their jobs or other penalties . . . that could arise from practicing this religion." The direct impact of this traumatic event for the local Daime community is apparent in the fact that in 1999 there were approximately one hundred fardados in Germany, twice the size of the present-day population. Because of the aggressive reaction of the government authorities, Hermann was among a group of German daimistas living in exile in the Netherlands when I interviewed him on New Year's Day 2011.

In the hopes of gaining scientific legitimacy for their legal struggle, the German daimistas agreed to participate in a long-term study of their members and ceremonies with scholars at the University of Heidelberg. As part of Heidelberg's "Ritual Dynamics" research initiative, this collaboration has already occasioned numerous publications dealing with ayahuasca (e.g., Labate and Jungaberle 2011; Loizaga-Velder and Verres 2014; Schmid 2011). However, there have arisen quarrels about the way some of the Heidelberg scholars have presented their findings. In particular, the German daimistas are concerned that there has been a lack of consultation with them prior to the public dissemination of research results. Hermann and other representatives of the German fardados were "very hurt" when they read Jan Weinhold's (2007) article on the "Failure and Mistakes" he observed in their Daime rituals.[7] Hermann sought to personalize why he and his colleagues took offense to this article by asking how I would feel if someone presented a scientific analysis entitled "the Mistakes of Marc Blainey." He admitted that mistakes happen in all rituals—in fact, Hermann admitted he once accidently set off the fire alarm in the middle of a Daime work when he attempted to ignite incense with embers from an outdoor campfire. But he said that for daimistas such mistakes are of only a secondary importance as lessons about what to do differently in the future. Hermann stressed that Weinhold's preoccupation with errors overshadows what daimistas view as the more significant therapeutic and spiritual successes granted through their Daime practice. This is certainly a common ethical predicament confronted by any social scientist that studies and writes about people who have the ability to read ensuing publications. In one infamous example, Nancy Scheper-Hughes's (2001, 126) ethnography of a rural community pursued a "counterhegemonic" depiction of mental well-being in Ireland. In reflecting on the strong rebuke she received from informants, who took exception to what they saw as her unfairly negative portrayal of them, she gives the following response: "Anthropology is by nature intrusive and it entails a certain amount of symbolic and interpretive violence to the 'native' peoples' own intuitive, though still partial, understanding of their part of the world" (Scheper-Hughes 2000, 127). She is correct that the anthropological exposition of any culture is necessarily a warts-and-all enterprise. In offering an honest portrait of daimista culture as I saw it, I expect that informants might dislike some of what I write about them. But since the prevailing hegemony regards daimistas as dangerous drug addicts, ethnography also counters this stigma by demonstrating that they are anything but.

After the interview with Hermann, I participated in a Daime work with German fardados. Uncharacteristically, the large room in which the work was held had been decorated with flags of all the countries German fardados recognize as places from which at least one serious daimista hails[8] (this does *not* mean that Daime works occur in all these countries). Hermann added that the official flag of Iran was conspicuously absent because Persian daimistas do not accept the legitimacy of the postrevolutionary regime.[9] In total, forty-one flags were included in this gesture of global solidarity. Sorted by continent, the following flags were displayed:

SOUTH AMERICA: Peru, Columbia, Ecuador, Chile, Uruguay, Argentina, Brazil

EUROPE:[10] **Austria**, **Belgium**, **Czech Republic**, Denmark, **Finland**, **France**, **Germany**, **Greece**, Hungary, **Ireland**, **Italy**, **Netherlands**, **Poland**, **Portugal**, **Romania**, Russia, Slovakia, Slovenia, **Spain**, Sweden, **Switzerland**, **UK** (one flag representing daimistas in **England**, **Northern Ireland**, and **Wales**), and the twelve-star standard of the European Union

NORTH AMERICA: United States, Canada, Mexico

AFRICA & MIDDLE EAST: Morocco, Lebanon, Israel, and Palestine[11]

ASIA & OCEANIA: Japan, India, Australia, Armenia[12]

Verifying that Daime works occur in many (not all) of the above places, Dawson (2013, 34–35) mentions two more nations where daimistas are present, whose flags were not hung by German fardados: South Africa and New Zealand[13] (see also Labate and Loures de Assis 2017, 66).

The German Daime groups remain steadfast in their belief that prohibitions against sincere sacramental devotion to ayahuasca are based largely upon an intercultural misunderstanding. As voiced by Rohde and Sander (2011, 349):

> The [Santo Daime] church wishes to enter into an open and sincere dialogue with state authorities and is open for scientific investigation and cooperation with governmental institutions, with the aim of cooperatively finding a way to perform their Human Right to practice this peaceful religion in Germany on a legal basis. . . . As in many other Western countries, the law enforcement institutions in Germany were not prepared to face the reality of this process [of Santo Daime's globalization] in an appropriate and proportionate way, and therefore confused the religious practice of a small group of spiritually committed citizens with drug trafficking.

These authors go on to conclude that the Santo Daime case represents an illegitimate repression of religious freedom, under Article 9 of the European Convention on Human Rights: "Ayahuasca religions like Santo Daime establish a modern cultural model to experience the *mysterium tremendum* of existence, which should be considered a birthright for every human being that seeks spiritual or simply human education" (Rohde and Sander 2011, 349). Much the same sentiments were expressed to me by other exiled fardados currently enduring state persecution while continuing to hold clandestine ayahuasca works throughout Europe.

The Netherlands

The Dutch Santo Daime churches may not have been the first, but they are now arguably the most sociopolitically dominant fardado community in Europe. This is mainly due to the early and sustained achievement of full legalization for the doctrine in this tiny northwest corner of the continent. Subsequently, three Daime groups in the Netherlands feature as many as 150 fardados who regularly welcome fellow daimista visitors from across Europe and abroad. The prominence of the Dutch Daime churches has resulted in their having thus far garnered more academic attention than any other daimista population outside of Brazil. In refining the chronological and sociocultural surveys published previously[14] (see Groisman 2000; 2009; van den Plas 2011; Hanegraaff 2011), the present text situates the Netherlandish Santo Daime as a nucleus of religious freedom within a broader transnational network of clandestine ayahuasca religiosity.

While Groisman (2000, 177–95; 2009, 193–95) refers to a third group in the province of North Holland founded by a Brazilian immigrant from Mapiá, I did not encounter anyone from this group during my fieldwork. Hence, I will focus here on the two Dutch Daime churches led by fardados born and raised in the Netherlands: Céu da Santa Maria (CdSM) in Amsterdam and Céu dos Ventos (CdV, Heaven of the Winds) in The Hague. In interviewing some of the founding fardados of each group, I found that they corroborated Groisman's (2000; 2009) history of the Dutch Santo Daime. I then met with two couples in The Hague and performed four separate interviews with them: Anneke, a fifty-four-year-old woman who works as a cook for disabled people, her fifty-year-old gardener husband Leon (serving respectively as a guardian and the commander in CdSM), as well as a fifty-year-old nurse I will call Ienje, and her husband Maurits, a fifty-three-year-old professional artist (leaders of the CdV). They told me that during the 1980s they were part of a Dutch *sannyasin* commune as followers of the Indian mystical guru Osho (a.k.a. Bhagwan Shree Rajneesh). In the years preceding the guru's death in 1990, members of the Dutch commune had begun experimenting with psychoactive substances like psilocybin mushrooms, MDMA, and LSD. They were reading a lot of the psychedelic literature (e.g., Timothy Leary, Terrence McKenna, Stan Grof) and one day the group came across an article about Santo Daime in an American magazine called *Shaman's Drum* (Richman 1990/1991). Through their contacts in the psychedelia world they met a German daimista who helped them to organize a 1993 visit to Amsterdam by a comitiva of fardados from Mapiá (including an accordionist, guitarist, singer, and a commander who spoke English). This was followed a few months later by a trip to Céu do Mapiá, where all six of the Dutch neophytes who traveled to the Amazon became fardados on New Year's Eve (see Groisman 2000, 138; 2009, 193). It was not long before as many as twenty of the old Osho group's members decided to become fardados too, a core constituting what would become the CdV.

The CdSM developed along a parallel but separate path to that of CdV. In contrast to the collective conversion of old Osho devotees in The Hague, the Amsterdam Daime church formed around an elderly Dutch woman now known by the honorific title "Madrinha" in European Daime circles. Born in 1945 and abandoned to a monastic orphanage at the age of three, Md.

Geraldine Fijneman[15] came to ayahuasca as a form of faith-based therapy after being diagnosed with brain cancer in early 1992 (see also Groisman 2000, 158; Groisman 2009, 193). In the middle of that year she drank Daime for the first time. In her own words, here is the way Md. Geraldine told her story of how she believes Daime helped her to defeat cancer, transcribed from an interview I conducted at her apartment in 2011:

> MD. G: *The doctors in the hospital said I had a tumour of seven-point-five centimeters on the brain stem. And they said operation was very dangerous, so they offered me chemotherapy and radiation, and I refused because I don't believe in it. And I know to be able to heal you need to believe in something, otherwise you cannot receive it. So I said "I won't do it," and they said: "But do you know how dangerous it is? We give you three months to half a year [to live] if you don't come to us." But I said, "I won't do it." And then three weeks later I met Santo Daime. I met a man in Italy and he invited me to do special healing works with shamans. I went to Italy and there I met Padrinho Alfredo, and I knew already by the first glass [that] this is going to help me, I felt it. So three months [later] I was in the Amazon, at first in the center of Mestre Irineu in Rio Branco, and Mapiá after that. There [they] gave me a lot of Daime to bring to Holland and to drink every day (at three a.m.), because I didn't have time to lose. I was drinking a little bit every night; he said: "And the last bottle you have you can share with your friends." So after a year I shared that last bottle, and [those] people liked it so much that they also went to travel to Mapiá.*

> INTERVIEWER: Why didn't you believe in the chemotherapy?

> MD. G: *Because my whole life I didn't believe in chemical drugs . . . I lived in a different way. And something inside me knows that you need to believe in it to be able to be healed, to receive it. I always say to people who ask me: "If you believe in chemo, you will be healed, but most people are doing chemo because they are afraid to die."*

> INTERVIEWER: What do you think was the underlying cause of the disease?

MD. G: *I think it's timing. Because it started already when I was born [during World War II]. I was taken by forceps; an airplane came over with a bomb . . . that's why the tissue on the right side of my head started to dig in a bit . . .*

INTERVIEWER: How did the Daime cure you, then?

MD. G: *When I was drinking the first glass of Santo Daime, I knew this was going to help me because it is bigger than I am. And there I have trust. Chemotherapy is not bigger than I am, that's made by man; [Daime] is made by plants, it is a creation of God.*

No doubt such extreme naturopathic loyalties would be very alarming to mainstream physicians. Yet Md. Geraldine's crediting her faith in Daime with the abatement of her terminal cancer was the only such instance I encountered in Europe. By contrast, most European fardados praised the accomplishments of conventional Western biomedicine—albeit with a disclaimer that they feel materialist approaches tend to ignore nonphysical sources of and solutions to disease.[16] This was evident in my interview with Alwin, a Friesian fardado from the northern Netherlands who uttered his belief that the Daime and Western medicine can be complementary:

My physical and non-physical world, these two are one. So I can have a solution for a problem in two directions: I can . . . change my body to change inside, but I can change inside to have a solution for my body. They work together. So you can use the regular medical way and you can use things like Santo Daime . . . but you need to change both. When I change inside, I found the solution for outside. If you have a cancer, you can drink Santo Daime to change your inside world. In the meantime, use what [Western medicine] found for the physical world. Maybe these two ways give you the possibility to live longer.

Owing to both her tale of healing and her reputation as a saintly personality, many of my informants referred to Geraldine as the "Madrinha of Europe." Although I can neither confirm nor disprove the veracity of the Madrinha's cancer cure story, it nevertheless serves European fardados as a parable for the healing powers of the Daime.

Every fardado I met expressed their belief that most physical and psychological sicknesses are communications from one's true spiritual (or Higher) self. In accepting that some terminal illnesses are incurable because of divine will, Daime logic holds that most psychophysical maladies serve a "signal" function of bringing attention to sicknesses of the spirit; daimistas prefer to view all physical and mental sickness as symptoms caused by a single egotistical refusal "to surrender to the voice of God" (Schmidt 2007, 177). Their theories about how Daime stimulates worldly cures by resolving disharmonies of the internal psyche concur with existentialists such as Kierkegaard (1989[1849], 50–51), for whom a "sickness of the soul" is rooted in "the torment of contradiction in despair." There is no better source than the Madrinha of Europe to communicate local daimistas' ideas about sickness and health of the egoic self:

> *The Daime is giving you advice. . . . First thing you have to clean . . . otherwise you cannot receive the knowledge because you're blinded by your own ego. So there you start: the Santo Daime helps you to clean, it's a whole process. . . . I know that I'm not free of my ego yet. I think the majority on Earth is not free of the ego. . . . The goal is that the ego is not interrupting anymore, because you need a healthy form of ego to create. The sick ego is to put your self in front in a way that keeps you [from] your goal. In the hymns we say, Mestre na frente [Master in the front], not the ego. . . . Mestre is what we follow, . . . the Mestre is Jesus. . . .*
>
> *The ego has many forms, many expressions. . . . It is very easy to say, "What an ego that person has!" Many times ego is behind [it] when you look very sad, you need a lot of attention because you're complaining, that's also ego. . . . [The Daime] cleans all these layers of conditioning, that has to do with the ego, . . . from your parents, from the influence from outside, . . . a lot of times you are doing what they expect from you, you don't even think, "Do I really want that?"*
>
> *When you are born you grow up, you have to form your ego (otherwise you cannot create), and after that the ego becomes so ill because of all kinds of [external] influences, that you have to drop the ego again. . . . I think a sick ego is very dangerous (you can hurt yourself and others a lot with it), but [with] the healthy ego you can create beautiful things. . . . [A healthy ego] realizes the traps, that it is not yourself who is doing that fantastic thing, but*

it is God who works through you . . . we are inspired. . . . You
have to open yourself up for that and to allow it, and then you
need to work on your ego . . . because the ego is always proud that
he's doing it. . . . Most illnesses are coming out of this: the wrong
understanding.

Instead of claiming that daimistas want to wholesale "eradicate" or "anni-hilate" the ego (Dawson 2013, 91), it is more accurate to attend to their subtle but crucial emic bifurcation of "sick" ego versus "healthy" ego—this is similar to the distinction in Sufism between the "tyrannical" self (*nafs*) and the "pure" self (Frager 1999, 3–4). Later chapters will explore in detail why daimistas consider an ego's health or sickness as tied proportionally to one's degree of self-awareness. For the time being, it is important to note that for daimistas a sick ego is that which operates unconsciously. By con-trast, a healthy ego is progressively attained through "cleaning" out thoughts and feelings that have been warped by one's overreliance on fixations of the egoic "lower self" (see Dawson 2013, 18). Like Md. Geraldine, they seek to diminish the "sick" aspects of their ego in favor of cultivating a "healthy ego," whereby the Higher self is liberated from or "free of the ego," or lower self. As will be demonstrated throughout the remainder of this book, daimistas seek to overcome mental and bodily diseases by viewing their suffering as a constructive process that guides them toward choosing faith over egotistical despair. Not unlike Kierkegaard's existentialist "formula" for faith overcoming despair,[17] daimistas consider a healthy ego as one that has learned to submit itself to God's will, especially when faced with any kind of suffering. Before the reader judges daimistas' stories about ayahuasca healing—such as the allegedly miraculous remission of Md. Geraldine's brain tumor—one must remember that this is no different from traditional narratives of religious therapy found the world over. Whereas biomedicine relegates faith-healing success to placebo or stress reduction effects, fardados are certain that reli-gious devotion can help one survive life-threatening illnesses; and even when God and science agree that it is the end of the road, daimistas know that surrender to a Higher Power helps one cope better with a terminal diagnosis.

After sharing her last bottle of Daime with some of her compatriots in 1993, Md. Geraldine worked with the fledgling community of Dutch fardados to initiate what became the CdSM. During the following two years, the groups in Amsterdam and The Hague started holding most of their works separately, but these two do come together to celebrate important Daime holidays. According to Ienje, prior to any legal trials the CdV and

CdSM had been founded as independent Daime churches which she calls "twins . . . from the same seed." Following the 1999 arrest of two prominent Dutch fardados, these churches successfully defended their case for religious freedom—they have been officially authorized to practice Santo Daime in the Netherlands since 2001 (van den Plas 2011). And yet European daimistas were recently reminded about the fragility of their hard-won religious freedom when a new legal ruling put the legalized status of ayahuasca "on pause" in the Netherlands (Hartman 2018).

Because so many fardados from around Europe and the rest of the world regularly descend on the Dutch capital, my fieldwork brought me to Amsterdam more than anywhere else outside Belgium. The "big works" (coinciding with major dates on the Daime calendar)[18] are intricately coordinated events wherein well over one hundred participants are registered, supervised, and guided throughout their time in the salão. The two main ritual spaces that are normally rented for Daime works are a large church within Amsterdam proper and a smaller church outside the city limits. Each contains a large room with adjoining chambers that are used to prepare food and for separate male and female areas to change into and out of ritual clothing. Teams of local and foreign fardados are responsible for a variety of tasks that are necessary for managing such large assemblies. These include leaders from Brazil, the Netherlands, and elsewhere in Europe acting as commanders of the central table, administrators who work the registration table, guardians of the ritual space (*fiscais*), kitchen staff, and a crew that sets up and takes down the salão before and after each work. Through participant-observation during works I attended in Amsterdam, I experienced how fardados approach these tasks (e.g., washing dishes, moving chairs, cleaning floors) as components of the overall Daime ritual. The mystical ideal that fardados learn within the works is to carry a state of prayerful mindfulness into all of one's everyday activities. The ritual niceties of Santo Daime works will be discussed in greater detail in later sections.

Italy

Although I have yet to attend a Daime work in Italy, I was able to gather interview data with Italian fardados. One of these conversations was with Chiara, among the first Italian daimistas who drank Daime in 1978–1979 with Pd. Sebastião at Colônia 5000. Because of her deep history with the doctrine, some daimistas from elsewhere in Europe refer to Chiara as a

Madrinha, but this is not a universally accepted designation, as it is with Md. Geraldine. Chiara said that unlike the early pilgrims from Spain and Belgium (who began to hold works in their home countries in 1989), she did not organize Daime works in Italy until 1992. By the mid-1990s there were four points in Italy: one in Lazio led by a Brazilian immigrant, one in Tuscany linked to a large Brazilian church through the Netherlands daimistas, another in Lombardy, and Chiara's church in Umbria. Only Chiara's group lasted through this initial phase, and it is mainly from this base church that the Italian Daime community grew into its current form.

At the time of my fieldwork there were approximately seventy Italian fardados (Menozzi 2011, 387) operating at least six distinct Daime congregations located in the environs of the following regions in Italy: two in Liguria, and one each in Umbria, Emilia-Romagna, Piemonte, and Marche. The two most established churches are those in Umbria and Emilia-Romagna, where the entire Daime calendar is celebrated. Then again, I was notified that the Umbria church had temporarily suspended its works beginning in the summer of 2010 because of ongoing police investigations. As detailed in a book chapter by Menozzi (2011, 379–381), the Italian daimistas have endeavored to practice their religion with "total transparency" by filing application documents to qualify as a legal religious entity in 2003. Alongside these efforts, since 2004 the Italian Daime community has faced criminal prosecution on multiple fronts, with twenty-seven liters of their sacrament seized and dozens of their members arrested. The Italian daimistas' judicial odyssey achieved some provisional restitution when their Daime beverage was returned to them through the Italian Ministry of Health in early 2011. Paraphrased by Menozzi (2011, 387), a recent judge's ruling "declared the acquittal of the case because . . . there is no evidence . . . to demonstrate that ayahuasca/Santo Daime can be included on the list of controlled psychotropic substances, in the terms clarified by the Supreme Court of Cassazione in Rome." The status of Santo Daime in Italy is still ambiguous, however, as investigations by Italian legal and medical authorities are ongoing. As with the case in France (see below), exoneration of daimistas on a technicality does not preclude the government's passage of new legislation specifically outlawing ayahuasca.

In contrast to the many European fardados who make a clear separation between the Amazonian-based Santo Daime and institutions such as the Vatican in Rome, Chiara was determined to impress upon me that the Daime is tantamount to the teachings of mainstream Christianity. When I asked her to compare the Catholicism she grew up with to the ayahuasca spirituality she now professes, she said:

I'm a Catholic and I'm Santo Daime also. . . . For me, it's the same. . . . For me, the essential message of the Pope and [that] of Mestre Irineu [are] . . . the same lessons. . . . So for me, there is no problem of separation. Differences exist, but I consider them a richness, not a problem . . .

The message is the same . . . but a different medium. . . . Each [religion] has its particularity. For example, in Nature, different trees . . . all coexist. Each is a form of divine creation. So all is good . . . it depends on what you like. What's important is to practice . . . for everyone it's the same: we are very much in the head more than the heart; it's mysterious . . . [but] I know that I encounter God and Christ with Santo Daime . . .

I have many Catholic friends [that] like Santo Daime; they drink Daime and believe it is a good thing . . . [but] the average Italian doesn't have much interest.

Despite the obviousness of non-Christian elements in their spirituality, fardados do frequently equate lessons they learn from Daime with the teachings of Jesus Christ (see Part VI). This topic also arose in an interview I conducted with Prospero, a thirty-five-year-old business consultant who has been practicing Daime since 1998 and is now the commander of a Daime point in Emilia-Romagna. Unlike Chiara, Prospero avowed a more nuanced demarcation between his daimista view of Christianity and the declining popularity of institutional Catholicism:

Here in Italy, we have Saint Francis (and Saint Francis decided to remain inside the Catholic Church). He was the prophet of the reconciliation [between] spirit and Nature. This is very important in our history, because in the Middle Ages, the body and Nature were considered at an inferior level with respect to the soul and the spirit. But this brought a split, a division between [material] creation and the soul/spirit. And Saint Francis was the prophet that first of all talked about the reconciliation [between] the Creation and Nature. So his famous poem "Cantico di frate sole" ["Canticle of the Sun"], . . . it's a hymn that says "Brother Sun, Sister Moon, Sister Water, Brother Fire, and [so on], and this is considered the maximum expression of this spirituality linked with Nature. We can say that the spirit of the Franciscans was really, truly shamanic, and very integrated with Santo Daime doctrine. We can say that the hymn "Sol, Lua, Estrella" ["Sun, Moon, Star"] of Mestre Irineu has many words that can be the same that Saint Francis said.

By reinterpreting the spiritual system of a great Italian Catholic saint as "shamanic" animism (see Harvey 2006), Prospero epitomizes daimistas' embrace of ayahuasca Christianity as helping to rectify what they see as the disease of spirit-matter dualisms. Numerous fardado informants reiterated this diagnosis of the ontological "split" or "division" between mind and body as a pathological trait of modern Western culture (see also Metzner 1993; Schmidt 2007, 142). Such an outright censure of Post-Enlightenment selfhood by twenty-first-century Europeans invites the ethnography of daimista theologies pursued in this text. In another sense, daimistas' framing of mainstream Western culture as unconsciously suffering from an existential malady informs their interpretations of why they face opposition across Europe, as they did recently in England.

United Kingdom

Along with dozens of Daime pilgrims from around Europe, I had already paid my registration fees for a continent-wide "meeting" of daimistas (called an *encontro*), to be held in the south of England in Autumn 2010. However, while I did meet English fardados in Amsterdam, I never ended up having an opportunity to participate in a UK Daime work. This is mainly because a few weeks before the encontro was set to take place, UK authorities arrested and charged British daimistas with importation of an illicit substance. I did get to interview Julia, a fifty-year-old fardada from England who has been drinking Daime since 2003. She explained to me how she felt "persecuted" when she and six other fardados were arrested before being released on bail. However, right before their legal trial was set to begin in 2012 the British authorities dropped the charges when they eventually realized that the daimistas would probably win the case (see Walsh 2017). From British informants' perspective, this preemptive action suggests that the government recognized fardados' claim for constitutional[19] rights but feared that a definitive acquittal would set a precedent for other entheogenic groups seeking religious freedom. But the damage had already been severe for Julia, who in the meantime was dismissed from her job as a social worker due to being charged with a serious crime. But as is typical of daimistas, she framed personal and collective suffering as divinely ordained, a test of faith that many of my interviewees referred to as a necessary "process": "Although we were believers and my faith grew stronger through the whole process, we felt it might mean that going to prison would be part of that process of us gaining our right to exist." She informed me that before these arrests there were three small groups in the UK (one each in the central and southern regions of England and another small point in Wales). During my fieldwork, there were between forty and fifty fardados living in the UK, one of them in Northern Ireland, two in Wales, and the rest living in England. But in the past when comitivas from Brazil visited the UK, Julia reported that as many as two hundred people would come to those works.

Julia related how the origins of her Daime community date back to the early 1990s, when the doctrine was introduced to the UK by a Brazilian couple. These Brazilians had originally taken Daime to Japan. While they were in Japan they came into contact with an Englishman who accompanied them on a trip to Brazil before inviting them to the UK for the first time. In these early years the Brazilian couple would visit the UK once or twice a year to help train the British daimistas. Contrary to the primacy of CEFLURIS in mainland Europe, none of the groups in the UK are affiliated with CEFLURIS. Because of this, the UK groups did not have close relations with the rest of the European churches until the 2010 police raids. The UK daimistas' solidarity with their European peers grew when the latter sent an outpouring of advice and prayers to the British fardados who were arrested. Julia described how the UK fardados then led their European counterparts in resisting an attempt by Brazilian CEFLURIS leaders to strengthen their oversight of the Daime's international branches. In Julia's words, the Brazilian Padrinhos and Madrinhas "wanted more control [with the Daime groups in Europe], and they wanted to know the names/addresses of everybody in our churches, they wanted to know how much [Daime] we drink, where we get it from, how much money we take, . . . which on one level is fine but we didn't want to be reined in and strapped down." At the same time as the British public's outcry for Brexit was gaining steam, European Daime leaders renegotiated with Brazilian leaders a continuation of their right to handle most of their own affairs, and the UK Daime groups were officially recognized as "friends of CEFLURIS" who would retain their independence.

I interviewed another British fardado in late 2010. At sixty-four years of age, Rocky is a retired music producer who had recently left his native England to settle in Amsterdam, one of the few places where Daime was then tolerated as a religious right. Beyond being fed up with the illegality of his religion—his primary motivation for leaving Britain—he did not mince words about a broader disaffection he feels toward his homeland:

> *England is fucked! Ever since Thatcher we kind of joined with America. We didn't join Europe; England joined America, you know, corporate laws where anything goes, relaxing rules, which caused this economic crisis. I don't include England in Europe. For me England feels like a third-world country to the extent that the difference between the rich and the poor is so great that it causes unhappiness . . . , There's obscene riches (e.g., bankers), [while] other people have two jobs just to pay the rent. It's absolutely mad . . . I did get pissed off with England and I couldn't stand it anymore.*

These words are even more striking with the hindsight of the 2016 Brexit vote, in which a slight majority of the United Kingdom opted to separate from the European Union. Although Rocky's passionate opinions are uncharacteristic relative to the generalized apathy about politics found among most European fardados, a heightened agitation about governmental affairs is more common with those living in countries that have prosecuted daimistas. I interviewed Rocky in Amsterdam in 2010, but since that time the UK government has stepped up its prohibition of mind-altering agents by seeking to criminalize all psychoactive substances (other than alcohol and tobacco), a "blanket ban" that ignores the recommendations of senior psychiatric researchers in the UK (Gayle 2015). Along with their brothers and sisters around Europe, UK fardados are caught within a broader political clash between conservative antidrug mentalities and the progressive push for decriminalizing drugs advocated by more liberal parties (Perraudin 2015).

Ireland

In Spring 2011 I traveled to a remote village in the Irish province of Ulster to attend a ritual with the local Daime community. With the assistance of a young Irishman I had met at the Daime works in Amsterdam, I arranged to meet up with the church's commander on the edge of town, where my bus from Dublin had dropped me off. Right on time, a car drove up and I was greeted by Seamus, a fifty-year-old man who runs a small business with Keira, his forty-two-year-old fardada wife. The couple hosts a full annual calendar of Daime works on their eco-farm, where they live in a circular structure made of wood and straw with their teenage children. Seamus showed me around his property on the Republic of Ireland side of Ulster near the Northern Ireland border, which included a compost toilet located in a greenhouse and a converted barn where the Daime rituals are held, affectionately referred to as "the Ark."

Before any daimistas had arrived for the work to be held that night, I sat down for an interview with Seamus. He remarked that he and Keira were long-time devotees of the Hare Krishna before they became fardados, and they both still consider themselves devotees of that movement.[20] Upon the invitation of a fellow Hare Krishna devotee (now deceased), Seamus had his first Daime experience in County Tyrone (Northern Ireland)[21] in 2001. Seamus then helped to develop this Irish Daime group with the support of a fardado from Wales and they benefited from periodic visits by fardados from England. He is now the leading Irish fardado and has represented his fellow daimistas in ongoing legal wrangling since he was arrested, jailed, and released on bail in 2006. He dated the arrival of Santo Daime into Ireland to the early 1990s, but he noted that the doctrine was not firmly established in the country until his church was founded in 2001. I was informed that approximately twenty-five practicing fardados and dozens of non-fardado visitors attend the three Daime congregations in operation at the time of my visit (Seamus's church in Ulster, with two smaller pontos located in the provinces of Munster and Leinster respectively). When I asked Seamus how he conceptualizes the appeal of ayahuasca in Europe, he argued that the Daime was derived from animistic ideologies not unlike those found in pre-Christian Ireland:

> Even though you have these different periods in history of oppression, you had it very much in Ireland with the invasion and the oppression of the original indigenous culture, which kind of continues on. . . . And Ireland was one of the first countries to actually suffer from . . . the dominating culture that's very much pervasive on the planet at the moment. . . .
>
> But that actually was a very high culture here that was really put down . . . so there was an oppression of the shamanic culture [in Ireland]; and I can see what the Portuguese did to the indigenous [peoples] in Brazil was the same patriarchal oppression of native traditions. So the Daime for me is the very tolerant, peaceful, indigenous, native appreciation of Mamãe Natureza (Mother Nature); it

*comes back up through the Christian belief, which became corrupted,
but then the Daime kind of de-corrupts it, and it purifies that to
what it originally was.*

In equating the colonization of both Ireland and the Americas, Seamus
reinterprets a nationalist narrative of pre-Christian Celtic populations (see
Davies 1996, 221–22/275–76; Wilson 1994, 72) as analogous to the
aboriginal cultures of the New World. As he sees it, because the Daime is
a form of "shamanism for Christians," his ayahuasca practice helps to put
right the painful legacy of Christian assaults on nature-oriented paganisms
in both Europe and the Americas.

Immediately following my interview with Seamus we were joined by
six other attendees for the Daime ritual, which included his wife Keira, two
other fardados, and three non-fardado visitors. Besides the standard Daime
accoutrements (see Part IV), a salão located on the upper floor of the Ark
building was decorated with two paintings depicting the Virgin Mary and a
big white flag upon which were printed three symbols of this Daime church:
a green clover, a yellow Celtic harp, and a nimbused Celtic cross. The work
itself was ordinary by Daime standards, except for my hosts' conspicuous
routine of saying the Our Father and Hail Mary in Irish Gaelic after they
were done in English and Portuguese. When I later asked him about this
custom, Seamus said that they had not always done this, but that when they
first tried saying the prayers in Irish a photo of Mestre Irineu "jumped" off
of the wall, which they took as a sign that the Daime spirits approved of
this glocalization gesture.

Just as with Daime works held all over the world, the Irish celebrants
gathered after the ritual to commiserate about their experiences. Yet even
this phase of the work had an Irish flavor, as one of the visitors played the
guitar while he serenaded the group with a beautiful folk ballad. I learned
that he was a homeless man for whom this had been his first Daime work.
In speaking to him, he claimed that he did not feel any effect of the ayahuasca, but he was grateful to Seamus and Keira for letting him squat in
the Ark to rest a few days before he rambled on in search of work. Due
mainly to the presence of a Canadian ethnographer, the group's conversation turned to advice about how best to comprehend Ireland and the Irish
Santo Daime. After hundreds of years of interethnic and interreligious strife
on the island, Seamus also credited the Daime works with healing historic
wounds that colonialist and civil wars had inflicted on his country. As evidence of this he pointed to the fact that the local Daime works welcome

fardados and non-fardado visitors from both Ireland and Northern Ireland. In an exploratory article on Irish fardados, Gillian Watt (2014, 53) also cites her informants' conviction that the Daime consoles the spirits of their ancestors as it also heals modern-day people who are carrying emotional baggage inherited from past generations. Underlining the distress that is still endured by modern Irish people, I listened to a fardado from Northern Ireland bemoan the sectarian violence that is prevalent in his hometown. He lamented that even though Catholic members of his family are harassed by Ulster loyalist gangs, he feels that he cannot tell the police because he fears that these "bad boys" would retaliate by burning his house down. He also reminisced about how poor his family was when he was a child, in that he and his five siblings all slept together in one small room. As the night drew to a close, such stories of hardship intensified my appreciation that I was offered a straw bed in the Ark to rest on before leaving the next morning.

Austria

In Austria, I participated in a work in the east of the country, after which I interviewed a group of four male fardados (at that time there were no Austrian fardadas). One fardado came only for the interview because he was at his job during the ritual, so I was the fourth of four people present at this work. Thus, Manfred and Axel (two men who co-manage this small congregation) asked me to sit in a seat at the central table with them, a position that at larger works is reserved for the most experienced fardados. With the lowest turnout of all the Daime rituals I attended in Europe, it was a *cura* or "healing" work held in the stark white living room of Manfred's small urban flat. In a land known for composers such as Mozart, Haydn, and Schubert, the musical ritual of Santo Daime in this case included only the singing of hymns accompanied by maracás, since there were then no Austrian fardados who could play an instrument. Through an open window, the frequent sound of streetcars rattling along the cobblestone streets was another reminder of how far this ayahuasca rite has traveled from its Amazonian birthplace.

In contrast to the perceived equivalence of Daime and Catholicism among the Italian fardados, Austrian interviewees theorized that the waning dominance of conservative Catholicism in their country is now leaving a legacy of "resentment" about Christianity. None of the Austrian fardados professed sympathy with Catholicism and instead, Manfred and Axel interpret the Daime through a Buddhist lens. Because of what he believes to be the overly aggressive and even abusive tactics of twentieth-century Catholic education, Axel maintained that many Austrians have an ill will toward Christianity that persists "even if they become Buddhists; they keep this resentment, . . . they never make peace with their own childhood experience." In agreeing with Axel, Manfred's brother Alfons deemed his Daime practice as a means to resolving this resentment:

> *For me it's a process to heal my Catholic origins, because when I was twenty I was very angry. . . . But these enemies, they have to be healed by forgiveness. . . . My childhood (concerning the Catholic church) was not good. . . . Normally people think if you forgive, then you say yes to what they did to me. It is not so; you can forgive the Catholic Church while [still] saying it is not right.*

This same attitude was common among European fardados who had been raised Catholic, some of whom admitted their deep misgivings about Christian elements in the Daime doctrine. Several informants told me that the Daime helped them to confront and rectify their false perceptions of Christianity, in that they now distinguish between rather than conflate the messages imparted by Jesus Christ versus the institutionalized Church.

According to the Austrian fardados, Daime works have been held in their country since the mid-1990s, when they were first introduced by visitors from Brazil. However, it was not until Manfred visited Mapiá in 1998 that the doctrine found a stable foothold in Austria. The following year, Axel joined Manfred as together they journeyed as Daime tourists around Europe and South America. After honing their practice mainly in Amsterdam and Brazil, they became fardados in 2006 and were appointed by Md. Geraldine to be co-organizers of the Daime in Austria. Although they have yet to confront any problems with legal authorities in Austria, the local fardados told me that they expect to eventually face police action similar to that experienced by colleagues in Germany. One of the Austrian fardados alluded to the fact that Vienna is where (in his words) the "anti-drug cartel meets." Indeed, it was the Austrian government who invited representatives from all UN nations to its capital city, where they instituted a global ban on chemicals such as LSD and DMT by signing the "Convention on Psychotropic Substances" in 1971.[22] Vienna is now also the headquarters of the United Nations Office on Drugs and Crime (UNODC), which adjudicates the worldwide war on drugs by periodically updating the 1971 Convention.

Yet the hegemonic status of international prohibitions treating entheogens like ayahuasca as a criminal problem (termed the "Vienna Consensus") is now being challenged by the attempts of a new "Vienna Declaration" to reframe the debate as a public health issue (Tupper 2011, 153).

Greece

Although I was unable to make it to Hellas to participate in works there, I did manage to perform an interview with the Canadian-born founder of the Greek Daime community. Jason first got involved in the Daime in 2001 at the age of twenty-two while he was working and studying in southeast Brazil. Having been raised by immigrant parents, he had learned to speak Greek but had never actually lived in Greece. He and his wife became fardados in Brazil. During one of the works there, he says, the Daime spoke a personal message to him, declaring: " 'We will go to Greece!" He says without really planning it, within six months he and his family were living in Greece. While there, he began to pine for the Daime and he realized that he would have to take it upon himself to organize works in his new home. So he went to Mapiá in late 2003-early 2004 and received Pd. Alfredo's blessing to conduct works in Greece. He said that this is how it works when a fardado wants to open a new church: "To demonstrate your humility, you're supposed to ask for permission to conduct the works . . . as a sign of respect [to the] parent church." Until recently, there were six fardados in Greece. But since Jason and his wife left to live in South America, there remain four fardados in Greece who welcome many non-fardado visitors into Daime works held in the northern part of the country. Although Daime churches tend to be quite welcoming to new members, Jason insists that becoming a fardado is not for everyone. He states that one's being called to be a fardado is "for the Daime to decide," and that people who are not totally committed to the doctrine are better off remaining as visitors.

When I asked him how his Daime practice influences his understanding of Greece's current socioeconomic problems, he gave a detailed answer that typifies the general critique that European fardados level against modern Western culture:

> *I see that as the logical conclusion of a world in which people have lost their sense of community, they have lost their sense of spirituality, and they've lost their general sense of unity with anything except for*

material goods or instant gratification or satisfying what I would call the "lower needs" of humans. The crisis of Greece is a crisis of capitalism (what in Daime we call "the world of illusion"). And I think that my perspective as a fardado, maybe I have something of a privileged view of things. I hope that doesn't come across as sounding kind of arrogant, but it just seemed like the natural conclusion to me. When you look at the way culture has developed in the West (and in many senses Western culture began in Greece), maybe it's ending there as well [laughs]. Because you see the system as it's been set up does not function: everyone is just looking after their own interests, their own backside as it were.

And Santo Daime is really all about community. In Europe, I know they are still struggling with these kinds of things. But you see this much more clearly in Brazil: the people who drink Daime, people who are fardados, they're very much into a sense of family, community, unity, and supporting one another on every level; not just the material level, but emotionally, and spiritually, energetically, cosmically. And when you see a society that has lost all of those things, that's really lacking all of that, I think the logical conclusion is that this thing will eventually collapse. Maybe that's just my somewhat jaded view as someone who pursues a spiritual path, as someone who believes that this is one of the most important things that we should be focusing on in our lives, and not a new Mercedes or a shiny new villa.

So I think that the crisis of Greece is a crisis of Western culture; it's a crisis of a world of capitalism and credit, which serves only to make people suspicious of each other and to make people feel isolated. Because also when people feel isolated, they're more easy to control, they're more easily terrorized in a way; I'm not talking explosive devises, I'm talking about the terror that is the six o'clock news, that's just trying to make people feel uncomfortable, make people feel that they are not secure, that they need to look to organizations like their governments, or police, or military to provide security for them. Whereas someone like myself, I believe that security comes with peace and tranquility, and love and forgiveness towards your fellow man; this is what brings you security, this is what ultimately brings you peace and happiness. . . .

Greece in particular, oh my God, they have so much history that it's a weight almost. . . . Greece being the founding place of a

*lot of the ideas that in the West we hold true as ours, which [distin-
guish] us from other societies; things like democracy and philosophy,
and a lot of the fundamental things of science and mathematics and
the Pythagorean theorem, they have their origins in ancient Greek
culture. And that's great! I'm not trying to discount those. It's just
that thirty-five hundred years later, what's going on in Greece now
within the idea of a European community? What role does Greece
play in that society, in the rest of the world? But all of that history,
instead of being something that can illuminate people, these things
tend to be a bit heavy. And maybe part of that is because they look
back at how the society was in Greece and the ideas that came out
of that culture, and then they see where they are now, and they
go "My God, how far have we fallen?" And maybe that tends to
make people a little bit upset or complaining about things, looking
to blame others sometimes.*

This is a lucid example of daimistas' inclination to reinterpret events of
the secular world as symptoms of a karmic momentum underlying both
individual and collective life (see Dawson 2013, 100–101). When Jason
cites Daime hymns' repeated reference to "the world of illusion" (*o mundo
da ilusão*), he broaches what Dawson (2013, 61/93/106/177/186–92) terms
daimistas' "paradoxical" relationship with physical reality, in that "Santo
Daime's world-rejecting aestheticism couples a heartfelt symbolic denial
of the world with the concerted enjoyment of its contents." In this way,
daimistas' enchanted view of nature and history is not unlike that of more
established religions such as Hinduism and Christianity. For daimistas, it is
not in itself a sin to relish this-worldly relationships and experiences; and
yet they do prioritize the *longue durée* of human existence as governed by
divine laws that ultimately reward selfless acts of humility and generosity
while selfishness rooted in arrogance and greed is inevitably punished.

Finland

Since 2004 the tiny Santo Daime ponto of Finland has been operated by
a married couple who hold ritual works near their home in the north of
the country. I conducted a joint interview with them at the apartment of a
Dutch fardada they stay with during regular visits to Amsterdam. Marjatta is
a forty-seven-year-old homeopathic healer and Teemu is a fifty-seven-year-old

retired art teacher. They stated that along with one other Finnish fardado and a fardado expatriate from Belgium, their group only performs Daime *cura* ("healing") works that occasionally welcome in drug addicts seeking treatment (see Bouso and Riba 2014; Labate and Cavnar 2014b; Fernández and Fábregas 2014). When I interviewed them in 2010, they were unfazed by the threat of future legal problems that may result from this unauthorized form of addiction therapy in Finland:

> MARJATTA: *I'm really ready to go to court, I'm even ready to go to prison for Santo Daime. It is such a good thing, it is the best medicine that I have ever met.*

> TEEMU: *I'm [also] ready to go to court. . . . It's obvious that the [government] officials have to accept this sooner or later.*

Even though the Finnish government softened its drug laws in 2001, so that now most drug offenders are reprimanded with a fine, the official policy still considers possession of any illegal drug to be a jailable offence (EMCDDA 2011, 24). They both said they are committed to Santo Daime because they believe it makes it possible for them to have a personal and therapeutic relationship with Christian divinity. Referring to the Lutheranism of his upbringing, Teemu insists that he had tried to find spiritual fulfillment there, "but I never found Jesus, I never found God; it was only written things."

These two Finnish fardados travel to Amsterdam several times a year because they want to train intensely in the Daime doctrine so they can better manage the works they hold with their home community. When I asked about how this foreign ayahuasca religion fits with their Nordic heritage, they were sentimental in comparing the Daime hymns to the Finnish epic mythology called *Kalevala* (see Davies 1996, 818). With transparent glee Teemu proclaimed that he "found the perfect music" in Santo Daime, describing daimista hymns as "pretty much the same" as the Kalevala songs he grew up with:

> *[Kalevala] is always sung . . . it's the same kind of melodies, they're always received, they are never composed; they sing in a circle also, it's a shamanistic tradition, it's like Santo Daime exactly. . . . It enhances community life, . . . you learn everything by singing. . . . So when you ask this question "Do we turn into another culture?," no, we recognize our own culture through Santo Daime . . . it's like coming home.*

To this, Marjatta added that "it's the same system of singing: you have two lines and you repeat." Of course, there is a vast spatiotemporal difference between the Finnish peasant tradition of two men joining hands in singing *Kalevala* together and the Daime's twentieth-century emergence in the Amazon. But as pointed out by Dawson (2013, 102–103), the "relativizing holism" of daimistas' worldview is disposed to interpret all genuine spiritual systems as "expressions of one and the same all-encompassing, universal reality." Hence, Teemu and Marjatta proceeded to list commonalities they notice between the intoned folklore of the *Kalevala* and the hymns sung in Santo Daime: a performance goes on for many hours and the lyrics are about topics such as otherworldly journeys, supernatural beings, astronomy, vegetation, healing, sexuality, and general advice on how to live well.

Moving beyond the countries in which Daime works are regularly (if discreetly) staged, I now turn to data collected with fardados who live in countries where these rituals are not openly performed. I made contact with the daimista communities of the following nations when they had traveled to either Belgium or the Netherlands to participate in Daime works there, mostly at large international daimista gatherings in Amsterdam.[23]

Czech Republic

When I traveled to Bohemia to deliver a lecture on Santo Daime at a university there, I also interviewed two Czech fardados living in that vicinity. Both of these informants are psychotherapists who claim that ayahuasca rituals are therapeutic and also that their Daime practice makes them more effective in sympathizing with their clients' troubles (see parallel findings in Horák, Hasíková, and Verter 2018; Horák and Verter 2019). In a busy café I met with Gunther, who helped pioneer the Czech Daime community when he first pilgrimaged to Mapiá in 1996. Eventually, after forging a relationship with CdSM in Amsterdam, he and his wife became fardados and now they escort a handful of Czech daimistas to attend works in other European countries. Wary of the Daime's forbidden status in their homeland, a few Czech fardados have immigrated to the Netherlands in search of a more permanent refuge. Having been reared within a family that "was always very suspicious about religions," Gunther initially found spiritual fulfilment through the meditative traditions of Asia. Like the Hare Krishna fardados in Ireland, he now considers himself affiliated with both Hinduism and Santo Daime:

Because my daily practice is yoga and the Daime works are not every day, and Amsterdam is far away. . . . [Eastern spiritualities and Santo Daime] are very different of course, but there is one basic thing that is common: that without concentration you have no spirituality. And yoga is more pointing towards this; Santo Daime has it as a part (not as a main part), and I feel very strongly how it helps me in the Daime works if I do yoga and meditation [outside the works]. It's a double-edge [sword] to travel for Daime, because it is a help but it is also more difficult to keep the practice because of the overnight traveling.

Gunther's upbringing is not abnormal in the Czech Republic, which has the lowest level of traditional belief in God (16%) of any European country. However, besides the 37 percent of committed Czech atheists, this leaves half of the country's citizens (44%) who reject traditional theism even while they espouse beliefs in "some sort of spirit or life force" (European Commission 2010, 204; compare European Commission 2005, 9–10).

I also met with Agnes, an unmarried fardada who like Gunther maintains her commitment to Hindu philosophies as a supplement to her Daime practice. Sitting at the kitchen table in her suburban flat, she said that her religious life was first sparked by an encounter with Kundalini yoga. Her spiritual search brought her to Mapiá in 2003, where she says she was surprised to find herself forming a relationship with Jesus Christ; detached from the Catholicism that she had abhorred as a child, she says that the Daime inspires her to view Jesus through the lens of her Hindu training as a divine "avatar" (see Polari de Alverga 1999, 170). She describes the state of Czech religiosity this way: "A lot of people in our Republic, they believe in something higher, but they are not really practicing." Agnes's observation concurs with that of Czech sociologist Zdeněk Nešpor (2010, 70), who concludes that "despite the fact that Czechs are stronger opponents of church religion than other Europeans they can hardly be understood as 'atheists' but rather unchurched and 'uncertain' in religious issues." This tenuous spiritual commitment was on display when a colleague brought my wife and me to Christmas mass at the Cathedral of St. Bartholomew in Plzeň. Contrary to my guide's assurances that few people attend church in his hometown these days, the cathedral was packed to standing-room-only as children and adults lit candles sourced from the "peace light of Bethlehem." These Czech parishioners may not be stalwart attendees during the year, but they do continue to link their celebration of Christmas with attending mass that day. Czech fardados share their compatriots' uneasy relationship with Roman Catholicism, but they behold their Daime practice as a personal rediscovery of Christian principles outside of the Vatican's establishment.

Switzerland

During a trip to the Swiss Confederation, I visited two local fardados whom I had originally met in Amsterdam. My most sustained contact was with Oswald, a fifty-three-year-old graphic designer in a German-speaking canton. He said that he and his wife were first introduced to Santo Daime in 1998 through a local LSD-assisted therapy group they were frequenting at the time. He is now a senior Swiss fardado and he leads fellow daimistas on regular pilgrimages to Amsterdam to partake in the big works held there. During a forest stroll near his house, Oswald distinguished the therapeutic rationale that initially attracts many Europeans to the Daime from his own reasons for seeking experiences with ayahuasca and other so-called psychedelics:

> *There are different reasons of course. For sure, people who have health problems, some who don't trust* [mainstream] *medicine, and some who hear from [mainstream] medicine that there is no help. So if you know that you might die in the next three or six months, you'll try everything, . . . and the other* [reason] *is for sure that people suffer* [because] *we don't have a spiritual system. We are out of religions. People are spiritually homeless; people are looking for something, and there is a lot of bullshit around; so they look for serious things, and for sure* [Daime] *is serious. It comes from the Amazon, from native people; we look at them and say, "If you are able to survive in the Amazon then there is not* [much] *wrong with what you are doing."*
>
> *And I know a lot of people who are really suffering because they don't have a spiritual system. For thirty years I was really an atheist. So for me, I was not really looking for spirituality, it came into my life, but (because my parents had already left the Catholic Church), I'm not baptized; so it was not the most important thing for me to find a religion I trust. [For me in Daime works], it's more the opposite; it's, "Ugh, always singing to Jesus and Maria, what am I doing here? This is not really my world." But a lot of people are really looking for a religious system they trust.*

And I would say the [reason] *I came* [to Daime] *(and I'm not the only one) is a little bit more the drug experience. . . . I've never tried heroin, I've never tired cocaine, I'm not interested in this because I know what big problems you can have with that; but with LSD, if you read serious stuff, you see this is not really a dangerous thing. If the setting is okay, very intelligent people say, "This is an interesting thing; try this!" But with heroin and cocaine, people don't say that. . . . I don't want to hurt myself, I don't want to die. I don't want to [commit] suicide, so I'm careful with what I'm doing. But I'm interested in opening my consciousness. I'm interested in substances if I know it's not bad for me.*

Beyond the typical claims of ayahuasca's therapeutic functions, Oswald believes that the Daime also appeals to some people as an opportunity to ingest a psychoactive material which they carefully differentiate from addictive narcotics like cocaine and heroin. Swiss fardados said that even though ayahuasca is not yet legal in their country, they are optimistic about the future because their government has proved to be quite progressive with respect to illicit drugs. For example, Swiss authorities have been supportive of empirical studies with the mind-altering chemical LSD, which was discovered by the Swiss chemist Albert Hofmann in 1938. Recently, Swiss psychiatrists gave LSD to patients suffering from terminally ill diseases and found that this substance acted to reduce anxiety without negative side effects when it was administered within a controlled psychotherapeutic setting (see Dolder et al. 2016; Gasser et al. 2014).

Oswald confirmed that there have been Swiss daimistas since at least the late 1990s and that now there are between ten and twenty Swiss fardados. He said that Swiss daimistas must be discreet because even though the psychotherapeutic potentials of LSD are taken seriously, most Swiss citizens would be suspicious of a mind-altering sacrament employed in a religious context. Actually, both Swiss fardados I interviewed claimed that when they first learned about Daime, they initially spurned it as a "sect." They stated their feeling that the Swiss public associates any small unknown religious group as akin to the Order of the Solar Temple, famous because forty-eight of its members committed mass suicide in Switzerland in 1994 (Riding 1994). Like many informants around Europe, the Swiss fardados argued that their religion should not be lumped in with dangerous cults. They say their main reason for this distinction is because unlike the brainwashing found in cults like the Solar Temple, daimistas are discouraged from pressuring people to join Daime rituals and that people are free to leave the Daime whenever they please.

France

Of all the countries where it is present in Europe, the harshest opposition to Santo Daime has occurred in France, whose public sphere is dominated by a political doctrine called *laïcité*. A characteristically French form of secularism, laïcité (English: *secularity*) is not easily translated. Growing out of a desire to exterminate the Catholic-aristocratic alliance that was overthrown during the 1870s, it was in 1905 that the government of the Third French Republic enacted a law officially enshrining the separation of church and state. Although the "degree" to which secularism is now enforced in France is more "rigorous" than elsewhere in Europe, the 1905 French law also protected freedom of religion; that is, except for religious forms that pose a threat to "public order" (Jansen 2006, 475–76/759[n2]). In essence, French "Laïcité strictly calls for a state that is free from an official or exclusive religion; yet this freedom is commonly understood in France as an absence of religious expression in the public sphere" (Chelini-Pont 2005, 612). As Selby (2012) displays in her ethnography of Islamic women in Paris, the dominance of laïcité in French society privileges secularists' right to denounce spiritual practices over and against the aspirations of religious minorities.

In 1999, six fardados were arrested and jailed in France because they were accused of the following offences: "acquisition, use, sale and international traffic of illicit substances pertaining to a sect" (Bourgogne 2011, 354/362[n6]). International police coordination is suggested by the fact that the raids in France happened in the same year as legal action against Daime in Germany and the Netherlands and the UDV ayahuasca church in the United States (Bronfman 2011). In January 2005, French daimistas were acquitted on the technicality that only the chemical DMT was prohibited and not the plant-based ayahuasca brew itself. However, the French government moved swiftly and by April 2005 the botanical constituents of ayahuasca were officially labelled as illicit *stupéfiants* (English: "stupefacient"), a term whose verbal root "to stupefy" presupposes that the Daime causes a nonsensical intoxication or "stupor" (see Bourgogne 2011, 357/402).

In Amsterdam, I met Christophe, one of the originators of the Daime community in France. Now in his sixties, his first Daime experiences in 1996 coincided with a period of midlife crisis as he was then in the midst of a difficult divorce and the successful business he had created was in turmoil. At the time, he says, his daughters were suspicious of the Santo Daime and considered it a dubious "sect" that uses a dangerous "drug." I encountered numerous European fardados who faced a similar lack of understanding and support from kin who knew about their Daime practice, a situation that sometimes contributed to their estrangement from their families. It is for this fear of rebuke that many of my informants did not disclose their Daime practice to extended family, coworkers, and friends.

Christophe told me that there were two Daime groups in France by 1997, one in the north and one in the south. He said that there were as many as forty people participating in the northern French Daime group by 1998. He was among the fardados arrested in 1999, and he spent a total of three weeks in prison before being released for the remainder of the trial. When I asked him what life is now like for his contingent of fardados residing in the only country that has passed legislation to specifically outlaw Santo Daime, he sighed:

> *Everyone is afraid . . . and for us . . . it is extremely heavy on our shoulders. We hide. . . . My neighbors, they do not know who I am; I am obliged to hide. It's sad . . . because . . . Santo Daime gives us access to openness, and we are . . . obliged to be closed. So it's hard for us to live. But we must have patience, calm, and we have eternity for [justice]. We will continue to [practice elsewhere] with humility and discretion.*[24]

During my fieldwork, I met five French fardados who were attending Daime works as religious refugees in Belgium and the Netherlands. This regional overview of the Santo Daime across Europe now concludes with a thorough assessment of congregations in Belgium.

Belgium

In addition to its being one of the first places Daime took root in Europe, I focused the bulk of my fieldwork here because Belgium embodies a historical, geographical, and cultural microcosm of the continent as a whole. In brief, the ethnic-linguistic tensions within Belgium between a Germanic-speaking north (Flanders) and a Romance-speaking south (Wallonia) mirror a regional divisiveness felt at the supranational level of the European Union (see Blainey 2016a). The Belgian Daime community has not escaped this tendency toward mutual fragmentation. At the time of my fieldwork there were approximately sixty fardados composing four distinct Daime groups in Belgium: one in Flanders, one in Wallonia, and two in the capital region of Brussels.

In terms of religion, the nation of Belgium is a byproduct of a Christian schism wrought by the Reformation, its national borders having been formed out of the Catholic southern Netherlands when this region separated from the Protestant northern Netherlands in 1830 (Blom and Lamberts 1999, 480). The divide between Catholic and Liberal Belgians is a testament to the cultural context within which Belgium materialized out of nineteenth-century ideological mayhem. It is a quirk of history that nation-states of Europe, formed along religious borders, now represent bastions of secularism. In Belgium it is difficult to determine whether religion has any significance at all. Renée Fox (1988) struggled with this question in a paper titled "Is Religion Important in Belgium?" She explains that even though there have been steady drops in church attendance and loss of interest in Catholicism, this does not mean that Belgians have opted for secularism instead of spirituality. Amid the prominence of Catholicism and secularism, one finds an awkward cohabitation of enchanted and disenchanted leanings in the modern Belgian approach to life (R. Fox 1988, 305/641). David Voas (2009, 161) identifies "fuzzy fidelity" as the presence of an aloof group of people maintaining "some loyalty to tradition, though in a rather uncommitted way." Such fuzzy fidelity is commonplace in Belgium, where the ethical values of many nonpracticing citizens remain "loosely and distantly connected with their Catholicism" (R. Fox 1994, 169; see also Piette 1992). Speaking of this widespread discomfort, Taylor's (2007, 599) cross-pressure diagnosis notes that Westerners "are torn between an anti-Christian thrust and a repulsion towards some (to us) extreme form of reduction"; in response to this dilemma, it is only natural that some people would "invent new positions." The arrival of Santo Daime, an unambiguous turn to entheogenic reenchantment, brings historical tensions underlying European social life to the fore.

The founder of Daime in Belgium, a female art teacher from Brussels and one of Lars's closest friends, discovered the doctrine while on a trip to Brazil in 1981. During this journey, she eventually made her way to Colônia 5000 in the western Amazon, which served as the command center of the CEFLURIS Santo Daime prior to its relocation to Mapiá. Over the next few weeks, as she participated in her first ritual works where ayahuasca is consumed, she befriended Pd. Sebastião. Because he had trouble pronouncing her francophone name, he nicknamed her *Pedrinha* ("little stone").[25] When it was time to leave, the Padrinho supplied this young woman with a batch of ayahuasca to take home with her to Brussels, thus giving nascence to Santo Daime in northern Europe. She would practice Daime privately for the next eight years, making frequent return trips to Brazil where she became directly involved in the early formation of Céu do Mapiá. In due course, in February 1989 she led an unofficial ayahuasca ritual near Brussels with three friends (including Lars), a month before the Mapiá visitor arrived from Spain to administer the first official Daime work in Belgium.

Roots of the four Belgian Daime groups lie in the now defunct *Céu da Lua Nova* ("Heaven/Sky of New Moon"), the country's first official organization, formed in 1992 by attendees of the first work there in 1989. These first four Belgian fardados were then haphazardly joined by visitors, with alternating works held in Brussels and West Flanders attended by as few as two and as many as twenty people. Despite the irregularity of participation this early church[26] persisted with the core members, ensuring that the full calendar of works was executed, often in open-air settings "in Nature." A gradual accumulation of new fardados developed through the late 1990s until the first of multiple rifts occurred in Autumn 2003. During a work, one of the original four fardados received instructions from the astral world that it was time for her to open a new group in Belgium. She gained the approval of Brazilian leaders from Mapiá and opened a new church near Brussels called *Céu da Luz* ("Heaven/Sky of Light"). This split marked the initial surfacing of a latent friction that still exists between the churches in Belgium. Interpersonal tensions between church leaders follow the trend of recurrent Santo Daime fissions since the death of Mestre Irineu, while also manifesting conflicts that are uniquely Belgian. Although fardados cite social discord stemming from the ethnic/linguistic divide and personal dislike of particular authority figures, travel distance is the principal concern that informants provided in explaining why ruptures have occurred between the churches in Belgium. So, for many Belgian daimistas it was just a practical decision to attend Céu da Lua Nova if they lived closer to where it held works in Bruges and to frequent Céu da Luz if they lived closer to Brussels. On the other hand, it is revealing that the respective memberships of these two churches were almost exclusively Flemish- and French-speaking. These two separate groups operated independently for a few years until the commander of Céu da Luz and her husband left the Daime in Spring 2007 because the time commitment of leading a church was infringing too much on their family obligations. As the members of Céu da Luz now had no commander, they decided to join with Céu da Lua Nova. In acknowledging this reconciliation of Belgian daimistas into one group, the joint church was rechristened in late 2007 as *Céu da União* ("Heaven of Union"). Today, Céu da União (CdU) is the oldest and most sizeable church in Belgium, consisting of approximately thirty fardados and many non-fardado members that attend regularly. During my fieldwork, CdU works were conducted in a rented nineteenth-century chapel in East Flanders, usually attended by between fifteen and forty people.

One year after the consolidation of Céu da União, tensions between certain individuals resulted in another split, with a woman from Brussels (the cousin of the former Céu da Luz commander) deciding that she would start her own church in Wallonia. She traveled to Brazil and after much contemplation opted to open what was then one of the first churches in mainland Europe not affiliated with the CEFLURIS "line" of Daime. She named the new church *Céu do Arco-Íris* ("Heaven/Sky of Rainbow"), which gathered for its first official work in the summer of 2008. Holding works at rented spaces in the province of Namur, Céu do Arco-Íris (CdAI) was composed of twenty fardados at the time of my fieldwork. Much as CdU is affiliated with the CEFLURIS hub of Céu do Mapiá, CdAI is linked to a church in Rio de Janeiro state called *Céu do Dedo do Deus* ("Heaven/Sky of the Finger of God"), the leader of which serves as "spiritual advisor" to CdAI. Arising out of the CdAI commander's musical expertise (she is an expert luthier),[27] the performance of Daime hymns in this church is markedly slower and softer than the more rapid and vigorous sounds characteristic of CEFLURIS ceremonies. Besides the fact that this church is made up mostly of francophones while CdU has a majority of Flemish speakers (though there are members of both Belgian linguistic groups in each church), some fardados cited their preference for the music at CdAI as a reason they attend this newer church. Since CdU and CdAI comprise the most experienced Belgian-born fardados, the bulk of my fieldwork revolved around rituals and spending time with members of these two churches.

In addition, two other Daime organizations are based in Brussels, called *Rendezvous avec Soi* (French for "Meeting with Yourself" [RaS]) and *Casa da Cura Mestre Irineu* (Portuguese for "Mestre Irineu House of Healing" [CCMI]). While their devotees are mostly Belgian-born, both of these Daime groups are managed by young Brazilian married couples affiliated with the Brazil-based church *Céu Sagrado* ("Sacred Heaven/Sky"), located in the state of São Paulo. The founders of RaS and CCMI were already good friends in Brazil, but they proceeded to become more independent of each other once they arrived in Belgium. The male founder of RaS came to Belgium in 2006 and made contact with members of CdU. He and his wife chose Belgium because they had read on the internet that Belgium is the "Heart of Europe." Having come from a non-CEFLURIS background, he became interested in establishing his own Daime group modeled on the Céu Sagrado template but oriented toward European sensitivities. RaS basically constitutes a nonreligious alternative more palatable to those Europeans who are loath to ally themselves with the rigid dogma of their Christian upbringing. The name of RaS accurately portrays the practical function of Santo Daime as it is construed in Europe, literally as a "meeting" with one's deepest "self." Participants at RaS rites do not wear uniforms (hence there was no differentiation of fardados and non-fardados). While ceremonies of RaS include the singing of hymns from Mestre Irineu, individual attendees were encouraged during an "improvisation" section of rituals to perform for the group with musical instruments, regardless of their skill. Also unlike CdU and CdAI, there is only faint reference made to Catholic saints or Jesus in RaS rituals, and significantly less emphasis was placed on religious imagery within the ceremonial space. For example, while it is customary for photographs of famous personalities from Santo Daime and other mystical traditions to be placed around the room and on the central altar for traditional works, these were replaced by various rock crystals at RaS. The only "religious" symbol to be found was the apparently indispensable double-armed Caravaca cross at the center of the altar. It is apparent that RaS acts as a relatively informal introduction to the ayahuasca experience; after this more casual ceremony, initiates seem prone to become more interested in the strictly controlled rituals of mainline Santo Daime. The Brazilian couple who founded and manages RaS told me they perceived Europeans as being generally distrustful of new spiritualities; thus, they have consciously scaled back the "religious" facets within their ayahuasca ceremonies. These immigrants' impression is most likely derived from a suspicion in Europe of "brainwashing" in new religious movements, a sentiment exhibited in the rigorous surveillance and persecution of so-called sects in Belgium and France (Fautré 1999; Richardson and Introvigne 2001).

Whereas I attended numerous rituals with the CdU, CdAI, and RaS groups described above, it was quite difficult to gain access to the second Brazilian-run group, CCMI. Among daimistas in Belgium, CCMI is considered to be "more closed," as opposed to the other "more open" groups. These metaphors of "closed" and "open" refer to the amount of restrictions a group maintains concerning receptivity to new participants. It was quite simple for me to gain admission to most churches by just asking for contacts and accompanying a member to a work, but it was not until the twelfth of my fourteen months in the field that I secured approval by email to attend some CCMI works (not for lack of trying). More than in the other three Belgian groups, the leaders of CCMI are shown greater deference by members of their congregation, and they are referred to by the honorific titles of Padrinho and Madrinha despite being a generation younger than the CdU and CdAI commanders. The man who would become Padrinho of CCMI began in 2007 to provide private ayahuasca sessions for Belgian clients. Eventually, he gathered these separate individuals for group works, which led to the formal organization of CCMI in 2009, now consisting of twelve fardados and several regular visitors. It became apparent in speaking to CCMI fardados that the group's "House of Healing" moniker is a decisive framing of this group around spiritual therapy. Indeed, a sizeable proportion of disciples at both Céu Sagrado in Brazil and CCMI in Belgium are attracted to these centers because of a substance abuse problem (e.g., cocaine, alcohol). While tobacco[28] and moderate alcohol consumption are tolerated in the Belgian-led CdU and CdAI, all psychoactive substances other than ayahuasca (considered a "medicine") are ardently discouraged in CCMI, which advocates strict abstinence as key to a healthy lifestyle. In the words of the CCMI commander, unlike the curative qualities of Daime, all other psychoactive substances can make people addicted to "bad energy."[29]

The success of RaS and CCMI in Belgium has not gone unnoticed at these groups' patron church in the south of Brazil. In particular, since the leaders of RaS and CCMI managed to obtain steady employment upon immigrating, they were also able to bring their children from Brazil to attain educational opportunities in Belgium. The perceived prospects of a higher quality of life for his family spurred a third member of Céu Sagrado to attempt to found his own group in Belgium. I was present when this third man came from Brazil and was hosted as a special guest in a work with CdAI. Here he performed a selection of his own received hymns as an advertisement for subsequent works that he would lead in Antwerpen province. In an interview with this man, he was adamant that works in Europe lacked a standard of steadfastness that Brazilians call *firmeza*—the Portuguese word for "firmness," which fardados consider as an essential trait for enduring personal obstacles both inside and outside of Daime works (see Barnard 2014, 681–84). For instance, he disapproved of the small mattresses provided for people to lie down on in European works. However, his two works in Antwerpen (designed to encourage this heightened firmness) proved too severe for many of the neophyte attendees, and ultimately he failed to establish a committed following. CdAI also hosted a young female guest from *Céu do Gamarra* (in Minas Gerais, Brazil), who then arranged her own work in Belgium's Limburg province. This was the state of the four Belgian Daime churches when I left the field in May 2011. But things changed after the October 2011 arrest of the RaS church leader.

CdU had previously sent a formal letter through their attorney to the Belgian government, explaining exactly how they were using ayahuasca in their Daime rituals. They had interpreted the government's nonresponse to the letter as implicit approval of their spiritual practices. Then the RaS arrest provoked Belgian authorities to open a formal investigation of Santo Daime, as had previously occurred in other European countries. It is worth noting that unlike Catholics in other parts of Europe, since the founding of their country Belgian Catholics have assented to laws protecting religious freedom (Strikwerda 1997, 27–28). In essence, Belgium encapsulates the pan-European tension between these two major streams of religious and secular thought, touting the progressive freedoms of the Enlightenment while remaining loyal to inherited Christian norms. Although modern Belgium mimics the French hostility toward nontraditional forms of religion (according to state-sponsored secularism, or *laïcité*), Belgians also adopted a more Dutch-style system of "pillarization," wherein the freedoms of particular ideological communities are mutually protected. Dobbelaere (2008, 78) distinguishes Belgian laïcité from the French variety in that the rights of unbelieving secularists (*laïques*) in Belgium have been "institutionalized . . . alongside six recognized religions (Catholic, Protestant, Jewish, Anglican, Orthodox and Islamic)." This government-legal compromise regarding minority groups displays how Belgian liberalism exists as a fusion of qualities found among its neighbors to the north and south. For now, Belgium appears to be following the French rather than the Netherlands with regard to Santo Daime. Most recently, in 2014 daimistas' appeal for religious freedom was denied by the district court of Bruges. Imposing monetary fines on Flemish daimistas, the judge reaffirmed ayahuasca's illegality in Belgium because it contains "a hallucinogenic drug" that presents "a danger to public health"; this verdict was reached despite the court openly admitting "the fact that the risk of dependency on ayahuasca is considered minimal in the latest scientific findings, that the users of the tea claim to experience beneficial and even therapeutic consequences by using the tea, that risks are limited because of the controlled setting . . . that the effects on health are temporary and that until now no serious side-effects which lead to hospitalizations are known" (Belgium 2014, 5–6). It remains to be seen whether future court cases in Belgium will go the way the Netherlands did previously, in officially permitting ayahuasca rituals, or the way of France, where Santo Daime has always been strictly prohibited. As legal processes ensue, CdU and CCMI members now attend works outside Belgium, CdAI temporarily ceased works out of fear that police would intrude, and RaS (a.k.a. *O Centro Eclético Espiritual Encontro com seu Eu*) is now based in Brazil and the Netherlands.

Whereas virtually all new religions are referred to pejoratively as *sectes* ("sects" or "cults") in France, the Belgian anti-sect commission makes a crucial distinction between benign and harmful sects. As reported by Belgian legal scholar Paul Lemmens (1999, 87–89), the commission's report defines a tolerable "sect" as "an organized group of persons who have the same doctrine within a religion," while a "harmful sectarian organization" is "a group with a philosophical or religious vocation, or pretending to have such a vocation, which in its organization or practices engages in harmful illegal activities, harms individuals or society, or affects human dignity" (see also Ferrari 2006, 12–13; Torfs 2005). Of the criteria listed in the commission's report as traits that designate a sect as "harmful," none apply to the Santo Daime doctrine as it is regularly practiced around the world.[30] During fieldwork, I did not personally witness any form of physical, psychological, sexual, or financial abuse in the Daime congregations I visited. My informants never urged me to convert to their religion, nor did I ever observe any form of aggressive recruiting, as there is a fundamental taboo against pressuring people to participate in Daime works. I met four former fardados who had freely quit the church, all of whom expressed their gratitude and positive feelings for the Daime. Fardados repeatedly affirm that individuals should attend only when "called" to the Daime out of their own free will.

While the CEFLURIS roots of Daime in Belgium echo the trend of these churches' expansion across Europe, at the time of my fieldwork only one of the four Belgian groups was affiliated with CEFLURIS, while the other three were non-CEFLURIS. Of these four, it is interesting to consider distinctions between the two churches run by Belgian-born commanders, and the two groups led by Brazilian immigrants. The respective characters of the four groups range from CdU's more orthodox adherence to the doctrine as practiced by their Brazilian sponsors to RaS's nonreligious adaptations. In this way, the two Belgian-run churches tend to embody a more conventional approach to Santo Daime practice (with CdAI having made some slight adjustments), whereas the Brazilian-run groups espouse a more adaptational method for modifying rituals to fit European tastes. For instance, Lars told me about how CdU struggled to find a linguistic compromise for giving instructions in the works, which are announced in between the singing of Portuguese hymns. After first trying to translate announcements into both French and Flemish (too cumbersome), then trying English (not everyone speaks it), the leaders of CdU finally settled on Portuguese. Even though few CdU members speak Portuguese, this decision was viewed as an impetus for encouraging them to learn the original language of Santo Daime. The three non-CEFLURIS groups in Belgium represent the first international satellite centers for their sponsoring churches in southern Brazil, which are themselves breakaways from CEFLURIS. The creative license exemplified by diverging from CEFLURIS (which had itself separated from Mestre Irineu's original Alto Santo line) is emulated in Belgian groups that implement "softer" musical performance (CdAI), or more secular and less dogmatic rituals (RaS). CCMI has gone so far as to introduce new elements that are not officially part of Santo Daime doctrine, alternating conventional works with what are termed "ayahuasca sessions," inspired by their Padrinho's affinity for the indigenous Yawanawa culture of South America. Linguistically, although the other Belgian groups always sing in Portuguese, announcements during CdAI works are in French with Flemish translations for important details, while RaS and CCMI operate entirely in French.

It is likewise intriguing to note differences in self-identification between the more conventional and the more adaptational Daime groups in Belgium, as the standard "Céu" prefix is conspicuously absent from RaS and CCMI. This intentional move away from the conventional church names beginning with "Céu" marks these adaptational systems as resembling the more experimental character of "neo-ayahuasquero" groups in urban Brazil (see Labate 2004b). On the one hand, the freeform innovations and loose spiritual connotations of RaS are the reason its members refer to it as a "spiritual group" rather than a "church." While the label *church* is appropriate to describe the institutional nature of CCMI, it is distinguished from CdU and CdAI by its unequivocal emphasis on aboriginal shamanism and addiction therapy. While the members of CCMI retain close contact with Céu Sagrado, the deviations of RaS from the standardized Daime doctrine suggest that it is not an official *igreja* sanctioned by the authorities in Brazil. Regardless of whether they achieve official church status, it is clear that CCMI and RaS have identified a previously untapped market for Santo Daime alternatives in Europe, as their works in Belgium also attract people from France and the Netherlands. The French visitors are to be expected, since Santo Daime is prohibited in France. Remarkably, the Dutch members of RaS and CCMI were willing to make the drive south because they prefer these less religiously oriented ayahuasca works to those in the Netherlands, where CEFLURIS is the only Daime option. Before their arrest, the RaS leaders had begun scheduling regular works with about ten participants in Amsterdam to meet the demand in that city. But as the arrest put their immigration status into question, the leaders of RaS returned to Brazil and reinstated RaS based in São Paulo state. Belgian members of CdAI, RaS, and CCMI continue to organize group pilgrimages to their patron churches in southern Brazil, just like the decades-long tradition of CEFLURIS-affiliated fardados travelling to Mapiá.

Taken together (Table 7.1), the above national profiles mean there were approximately seven hundred fardados in the European Santo Daime at the time of my research (2009–2011).

Table 7.1. Summary of Santo Daime's International Profile in Europe

Nation	Year of Official Arrival	Approx. # of Fardados	# of Daime Groups
Austria	2006	4	1
Belgium	1989	60	4
Czech Rep.	N/A	3+	N/A
Finland	2004	3	1
France	1997 *(shut down in 2005)*	5	N/A
Germany	1990	50	9
Greece	2004	4	1
Ireland	2001	25	3
Italy	1992	70	6
Netherlands	1993	150	2+
Portugal	1989	30 to 40	5
Spain	1989	250	6+
Switzerland	N/A	10 to 20	N/A
UK	early 1990s	40 to 50	3
TOTAL	—	**~700**	**40+**

I was unable to determine the total number of non-fardado visitors and firmados because official records are not kept for these itinerant daimistas. Yet we can venture an extrapolation based on data showing that out of three hundred people loosely "connected to the centers of the Santo Daime in Italy," 130 are firmado "members" of the doctrine and 70 are full-fledged fardados (Menozzi 2011, 387). Out of the roughly 550 daimistas in Spain, 250 are fardados and 300 are non-fardados (López-Pavillard and de las Casas 2011, 366). Since these stats more or less match the proportionality of daimistas I observed at rituals around Europe, we can verify that there are at least an equal amount of firmados and fardados (in fact the former probably outnumber the latter). We can thus make a conservative guesstimate that there are more than 1,400 people formally patronizing Daime works in Europe in the early twenty-first century (the actual number is probably much larger). Without further ado, the discussion now turns toward European fardados' perspectives on how and why the metaphysical solutions attained in Daime works can lead to practical solutions in the everyday lives of participants.

PART IV

SANTO DAIME "WORKS"

Figure 8.1. *Christ and angel with chalice on Mount of Olives (Gethsemane)*, By: Pieter de Bailliu, after Peter Paul Rubens (1660); Published with permission from The British Museum.

Our Lord never asks us for sacrifices that are beyond our strength. It is true that sometimes this divine Savior makes us taste all the bitterness of the chalice which He presents to our soul. When He asks the sacrifice of all that is most dear in this world it is impossible, apart from a very special grace, not to cry out as He did Himself in the Garden of His agony [Gethsemane]: "Father, let this chalice pass from me . . . nevertheless, not my will but Yours be done." It is most consoling to remember that Jesus . . . experienced our weakness, that He trembled at the sight of His Own bitter chalice, the very one which He had once so ardently desired to drink.

—St. Thérèse of Lisieux, Letter to Father Maurice Bellière

An imaginary divinity has been given to man so that he may strip himself of it like Christ did of his real divinity. . . . A woman looking at herself in a mirror and adorning herself does not feel the shame of reducing the self, that infinite being which surveys all things, to a small space. In the same way every time that we raise the *ego* (the social *ego,* the psychological *ego* etc.) as high as we raise it, we degrade ourselves to an infinite degree by confining ourselves to being no more than that. When the *ego* is abased (unless energy tends to raise it by desire), we know that we are not that.

—Simone Weil, *Gravity and Grace*

8

Framework for Curing the Ego

The European daimista community gathers regularly at the Amsterdam church of *Céu da Santa Maria* (CdSM), the largest and most well-known Daime church on the continent.[1] Fardados from all over the world travel to CdSM, especially for "festival" works (a.k.a., "big" or "long" works, because they are expanded in duration, with a greater than average turnout). At rituals around Europe—mainly at the international gatherings in Amsterdam—I met Daime participants from Argentina, Bolivia, Brazil, Chile, Colombia, Ecuador, Surinam, Canada, the United States, Guatemala, Sint Maarten, Turkey, Israel, Tunisia, Malta, Morocco, Cape Verde Islands, and Iran.

I frequently accompanied Belgian informants to festival celebrations in Amsterdam, held on the same dates every year according to a fixed calendar of official ceremonies (see Appendix II). While fardados consider all works important, they place special emphasis on the birthdays and death dates of prominent figures in Daime lore. These big works often involve dancing (*bailado*) while singing an entire *hinário* (hymnbook/hymnal), which can take as many as twelve hours to complete. During dancing works, participants rotate between three types of dance depending on the beat of the hymn, all paired with a particular rhythm of the maracá percussion: the *march* (taking three steps right, then three steps left), the *waltz* (swaying back and forth without moving feet), and the *mazurka* (a Polish-inspired stepping in place, swiveling the body continuously from facing left to facing right). While Belgian works usually include between ten and forty people, at the big works in Amsterdam it can feel like a spectacle because the relatively large crowds, sometimes exceeding two hundred attendees, swell the capacity of the church.

According to Hugo, a fardado who performs the role of ritual guardian at CdU (see below), the particular setting of Daime rituals is what he called

173

a *kader* (Dutch for "framework"), which steers the ayahuasca experience toward specific goals. He contrasts this framework of ceremonial works with the independent (or *psychonautic*) use of entheogens that he experimented with before he found Santo Daime:

> *To see the kader* [framework], *to be in relation with the experience but guided as a structure, so this was the whole thing which was missing . . . in all the times before (when I used entheogens independently). Because that was just the experience by myself, going through and seeing what happened and what came by and what was there, but then most times you are left behind, not in a confused way but . . . it was always by itself, always in the moment. It was not so much related to . . . the bigger understanding. . . .*
>
> *To get deeper into the plants, I think* [the framework is] *needed. You need guidance, not a physical, but a sort of mental guidance towards awareness. . . .*
>
> [For example, the ritual Daime] *music you can describe as a really close relation to energy, vibration. Energy is difficult to grasp, but with music it comes much closer, not for the understanding, but for the tensions in what the vibration did. So in this sense, it's full on, it's there. So, you can speak about tones and about the singing: bringing the music, the tones into your body in the vibration . . . that's it!* [The lyrics of the hymns], *they help with the process in that time in that moment for you. So everybody will read them on a different level, on a different reflection. And they help you to overcome fears, for example, to come into the trust, to come into the understanding.*

So it is evident that Daime works are considered a programmatic framework in which music guides what is simultaneously an individual and a collective experience. With the aid of this ritual format, fardados see themselves as coming into contact with astral energies through an entheogenic sacrament. Although there are numerous variations in the form and order of these rituals depending on the particular location and purpose of the work, what follows is a distillation of the quintessential facets of conventional Daime works as they are carried out in Europe. After detailing the intricate ritual mechanisms that contribute to Santo Daime as an introspective technique, the discussion proceeds to explain fardados' folk theories about how this ritual practice engenders various *solutions*.

Inside the Ritual Space

When arriving at a Daime work in Europe, one encounters a lively and deliberate buzz of activity. Daimistas converse while setting up chairs, tables, stands for musical instruments, and other basic ritual equipment, a process that must be reversed after the work if it takes place in a rented *salão* ("hall," the physical room in which Daime works take place). Once preparations are complete, the salão consists of a hexagonal arrangement of chairs or chalk lines on the floor[2], all facing either a rectangular or a six-pointed-star-shaped central table (Figure 8.2). This is likely an "African-derived" configuration of the ritual space (see Stewart 2005, 112–113).

Occupying the geographical midpoint of the salão, in the middle of the table is placed a double-armed Caravaca cross sculpture, often with a rosary draped over it and sometimes ornamented with favored symbols such as the crescent moon and six-pointed star; around the cross are placed fresh cut flowers in a vase, photographs of Daime personages and Christian icons, incense/smudge sticks immersed in a pot of sand, four lit white candles (with a fifth placed under the table), and the personal hymnbooks[3] and *maracás* of fardados who will sit around the table for the work (Figures 8.3 and 8.4). These latter

Figure 8.2. An overhead view of a dancing work at Céu da Santa Maria in Amsterdam (photo by a Belgian fardado, published with permission).

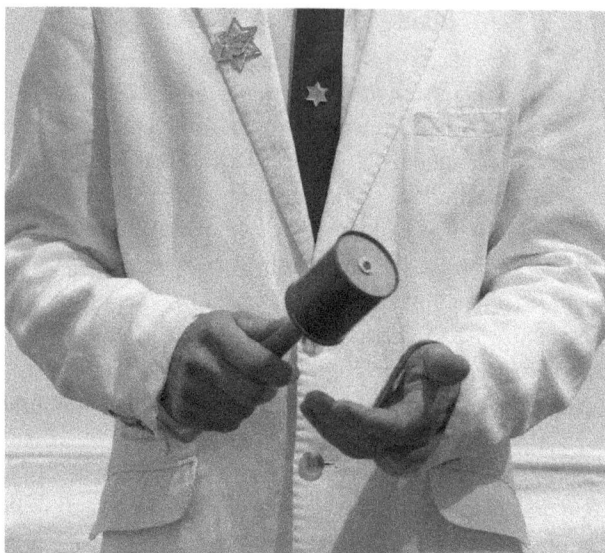

Figure 8.3. The hand-held *maracá* is the main percussive instrument in Santo Daime music (photo by a Belgian fardado, published with permission).

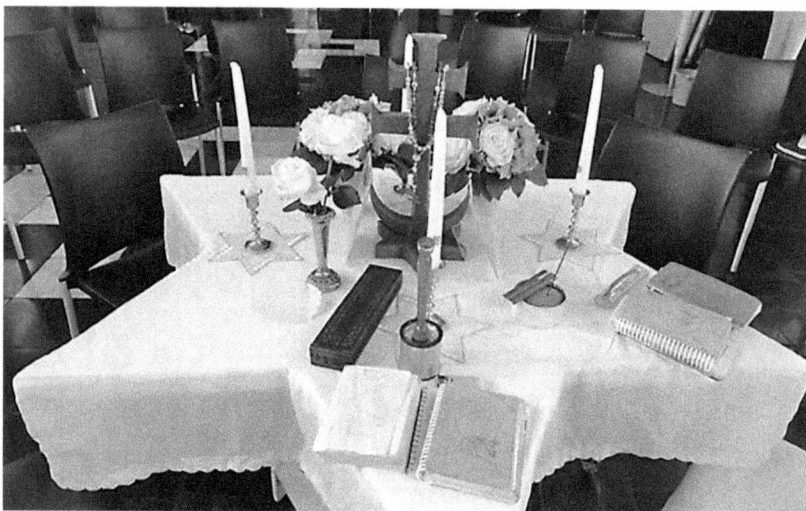

Figure 8.4. The ritual space of Daime works involves rows of chairs organized in a hexagonal shape. All face the central star-shaped table. On the table are placed a cross sculpture (in the middle), candles, flowers, incense, a maracá, and hymnbooks; for dancing works, chairs are removed and participants stand in the same hexagonal layout (photo by the author).

items are two iconic personal objects in the daimista toolkit: hymnbooks have a distinctive spiral binding and maracás are rattle instruments made of tin cans containing metal ball bearings, decorated with sparkly designs.

In Brazil, the atmosphere of the salão is reminiscent of "Afro-Brazilian *terreiros* . . . [as] many daimista churches string paper or material strips along the roof space by way of reproducing the forest canopy" (Dawson 2007, 80). For special festival works, European Daime churches simulate this visual display by hanging across the ceiling a smaller number of multicolored cardboard flags in blue, yellow, green, pink, and white. Festival works also include the occasional loud bang of fireworks, to simulate Mestre Irineu's firing a shotgun at the sky as a source of comfort during his first ayahuasca rituals, alone in the jungle (Mendes do Nascimento 2005). Other objects placed with exacting care and intention around the salão include a larger "Daime table" at one end, displaying similar objects as the central table alongside a stately piece of *B. caapi* vine, large bottles of Daime liquid, glass serving jugs, and stacks of Duralex[4] "Picardie" tumblers in which the sacrament will be served. Distributed throughout the room are larger photographs/paintings of revered personalities from Santo Daime or other spiritual traditions (such as Mestre Irineu, Pd. Sebastião, Md. Rita, Jesus Christ, Virgin Mary, Ramana Maharshi [see Appendices IV and V]). To energetically purify the room, incense paraphernalia for *defumação* ("smudging") include eagle feathers (for wafting), candles, charcoals, a knife (for chopping), and a Bic lighter. Sticks of *Palo Santo* (Spanish for "Holy Wood," from the tree species *Bursera graveolens*, are mixed into a "cocktail" of Lavender (*Lavandula* spp), Myrrh (*Commiphora* spp), White Sage (*Salvia apiana*), and assorted "Amazon herbs" from Mapiá, all placed within the shell of an abalone mollusk (*Haliotis* spp), used because it embodies the four elements: it is a sea animal (water), it has natural holes to channel oxygen onto the incense (air), it is made of calcium (earth), and the incense is ignited (fire). The fardado in charge of the CdU defumação reasoned that this species of shell "is what native Americans use for smudging." Resting stations outside the central hexagon include extra chairs, jugs and glasses of drinking water,[5] thin mattresses and blankets for those who need to lie down during the work, plastic buckets for vomiting ("purging"), various sound amplifiers and instruments (guitars, mandolins, violins, accordions, flutes, djembe drums, and/or electric piano), as well as *Florida Water* cologne.[6] Fardados also often carry personal objects in their hands or pockets, such as white/beige sweaters, chair pillows, hymnbooks, water bottles, and maracás. In some of the old chapels where Daime works are held in Europe, the rock floor is inscribed with the names of the deceased who are buried underneath.

Before being admitted to a Daime ritual, all newcomers must undergo an "intake" interview whereby a church authority scrutinizes whether the candidate's intentions are genuine and tries to rule out psychotic/schizophrenic symptoms. Shortly upon arrival, the visitor joins with committed fardados to wait in line for formal registration at a table located near the entrance of the salão. Each person signs their name on the attendance list, pays their entrance fee, and purchases a new hymnbook if they do not already own the text that will be sung at this particular work. Neophytes are then gathered together with a designated fardado who prepares them for what to expect in the work and attempts to answer any last-minute questions the new people might have. It is easy to distinguish the fardados because they are all wearing either their "blue" (navy blue/white) or "white" (white/green) *fardas*—the two types of "uniforms""—including a "star" brooch and women's white farda adding a "rose" brooch. Unmarried fardados wear the star brooch on their left (heart) side while married fardados wear the star on their right side. An iconic symbol of the fardado identity, this silver-dollar-sized six-pointed star usually contains the image of an outstretched eagle taking flight above a crescent moon, the symbol that is also shown in white upon a green field on the official Santo Daime flag (see Wilson 1994, 80). The star brooch is made of metal (or less often wood) and is always pinned to the chest of both male and female fardados during ritual works (Figure 8.5). For the

Figure 8.5. The "star" brooch—as an official insignia, fardados "receive their star" in the fardamento initiation rite (photo by a Belgian fardado, published with permission).

most part, fardados' grooming aesthetics vary from person to person such that they are indistinguishable from the European population. However, there are always a few fardados sporting characteristically daimista hairstyles that celebrate the ageing process; for women this is long, undyed hair left free to trail behind their back, and for men this is a long fleecy beard like that worn by Pd. Sebastião.

The *farda* uniforms worn by fardados, a custom designed by Mestre Irineu (Figure 8.6), are what most strikes the outsider. The white farda is worn for special occasions (e.g., weddings, annual "festival" works, local church anniversaries), and consists of a navy blue necktie with all-white dress shirt, pants, and blazer for men, while women wear a white, long-sleeved collared blouse and white ankle-length pleated skirt, accented with a green sash, a collection of multicolored ribbons suspended from one shoulder, and a shimmering tiara on their head (see Dawson 2007, 74). This white uniform resembles the mostly white garb, colored ribbon sashes, and tiaras worn in Baile de São Gonçalo; Labate and Pacheco[7] (2004, 331–34) show how the Baile de São Gonçalo, a Portuguese tradition that spread widely throughout Brazil in the mid-nineteenth century, influenced the eclectic religiosity of Maranhão and would have been a regular spectacle in São

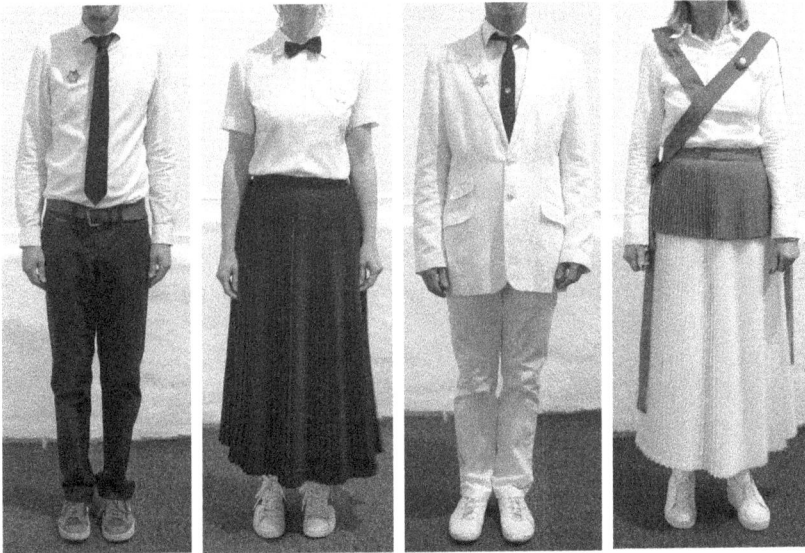

Figure 8.6. Fundamentals of the Blue and White fardas as worn by female and male fardados (photos by a Belgian fardado, published with permission).

Vicente Ferrer during Mestre Irineu's childhood. It was in 1936 that Mestre Irineu introduced "the *farda* and the *baile* or *bailado* (a synchronised and repetitive dancing)," based on what he could remember about the Baile de São Gonçalo he had seen in his youth (Groisman 2000, 80). However, modifications to both the uniforms and dances of Santo Daime were made following Mestre Irineu's return trip home to Maranhão in 1957, when he noticed inaccuracies in his initial memories of the São Gonçalo (Labate and Pacheco 2004, 334). The standard blue farda (worn at regular works) consists of a white long-sleeved shirt, navy blue necktie, and navy blue pants for men and a short-sleeved, collared white blouse, navy blue bowtie, and navy blue ankle-length pleated skirt for women—this blue farda is deliberately meant to look like a school uniform (Groisman 2000, 79), as all fardados are considered "students" of the Daime. Shoes seem to be the one article of clothing that can vary, as fardados' footwear may include sneakers, sandals, loafers, or even bare feet.

As the time for commencing the work approaches, chattering voices quiet down and then cease as each individual is ushered to their assigned "place." Following official doctrine (outlined in a CEFLURIS [1997] manual called "Norms of Ritual"), attendees are organized with fardados closer to the central table and visitors closer to the outside of the hexagon, women on one side and men on the other, with three separate age sections on each side in male/female collections of (1) elder married/unmarried (2) younger married, and (3) younger unmarried. All these sections are arranged according to participants' height, each concentric "line" ascending in order from shortest to tallest. As aromatic incense smoke wafts through the air, participants open their hymnbooks[8] and introductory defumação hymns signal that the work is about to begin.

Daime works are officially opened with prayers, which always include the Catholic editions of *Pai Nosso* ("Our Father") and *Ave Maria* ("Hail Mary"), as well as invocations from esoteric spiritual traditions[9] that inspired early founders of the doctrine. When the commander deems it necessary he/she will announce that it is time to drink Daime. Then the first of two or three "doses" of Daime is served, with the initial one being the largest and subsequent doses containing smaller amounts of liquid.[10] Participants form a queue to receive the drink at the serving table (fardados go first), with one line on the male side and one on the female side. The "dispatchers," fardados who pour and deliver each dose of Daime, have been trained how to serve the sacrament via mentorships with more experienced elders; in Europe the dispatchers are male and female depending on the gender they are serving, while in Brazil it is a males-only role (see Cemin 2010, 52).

Each person is served their dose of Daime and the single-use glasses are stacked until they are picked up by fardados who take them to a nearby kitchen for washing in preparation for the next dose.[11] Depending on the purpose of the work and readiness of attendees, the Daime served can range from weaker to stronger varieties.[12] Jeremy Narby's (1998, 6) description of ayahuasca as "extremely bitter" is quite accurate, although I would add that it frequently has sour undertones. Beyer (2009, 212) is more explicit: "The ayahuasca drink . . . has an oily, bitter taste and viscous consistency that clings to your mouth, with just enough hint of sweetness to make you gag." Many ayahuasca drinkers often carry mints or raw ginger, which they slip into their mouth to offset the harsh aftertaste and concomitant nausea. The range of taste from repellent to slightly pleasant is a quality that seasoned fardados discuss much like wine connoisseurs; the highest quality product is a thick brew designated *mel* ("honey") because its flavor verges on pleasing to the palate. Other fardados told me that they refuse to cut the Daime's flavor with mints, preferring instead to receive with total gratitude what they believe is a bitter medicine gifted to them straight from God.

After drinking their dose of the Daime sacrament, each attendee is expected to "work" on their individual self while also making a concerted effort to generate a shared spiritual "energy"—also called the "force" (*força*) or the "current" (*corrente*)—a transpersonal vigor that flows within and between all the participants. This topic arose in conversations with Etienne, a thirty-nine-year-old fardado from CdAI who works as a registered nurse in southern Wallonia. I visited him and his family at their cabin in the wooded Ardennes region. Although his wife does not attend Daime works, they did nevertheless get married in a Daime wedding ceremony at CdAI. He agreed to participate in an interview in exchange for me helping him move dozens of freshly cut logs from the top of a hill on his property down to a firewood stack at the side of his house. When asked to describe what happens at a Daime work, Etienne explained it like this:

> *Santo Daime works have a special energy. . . . People are sitting in a certain way and all the energy is concentrated over the table. . . . As a person individually you get higher in energy, but all that energy doesn't stay in you, it just goes there, it's a flow. . . . The center of the flow is over the table, and all the energy goes there and goes up to the Astral and from there goes back to all the persons. . . . So by getting focused as an individual person, but adding all those individual persons together, then it's not anymore individual, it's collective.*

This description of the work is similar to that of Frederik, a forty-seven-year-old bachelor who works as a psychotherapist and astrologer. Frederik has been attending Daime works since 2005 and he became a fardado in 2006. He always sits at the table in CdU because he leads the singing for the men's side during the works. When I visited him at his large home in the remote Flemish countryside, he used daimista terminology of the "current" (Portuguese: *corrente*) to describe the mysterious "energy" that appears in Daime works:

> *When I feel there is a current, it usually starts at the table, at the center, and so we feel that something is changing in the energy. We feel it physically, we feel it emotionally, we feel it in the presence around us. And then the current goes out, so that you have the first rows, and then the second and the third and the fourth and so on. . . . I find it very difficult to put a word on it. I think it's a combination . . . it's energy, it's light, it's matter, it's non-matter, it's strength, it's something powerful, sometimes you can smell it, sometimes you don't, sometimes there are colors, sometimes there are no colors; so it also depends because it's different every time.*

This uncanny phenomenon regularly appears in Daime works. Another helpful perspective on this ectoplasmic "force" or "current" energy comes from Irma, a fifty-seven-year-old social worker who has been a fardada in her native Germany since 1996. In my interview with her, she described how synchronization of participants' singing and dancing potentiates a cooperative building up of this energetic current:

> IRMA: *The harmony of the current is very important, because it's an energy current, and the flowing is beautiful when everything is in harmony . . . and then the energy can rise . . . it's light, it's healing energy. . . .*
>
> INTERVIEWER: What does the current heal?
>
> IRMA: *Everything: the body, the spirit, the mental . . . all our bodies.*[13]
>
> INTERVIEWER: How does the dancing impact the "flow" of the current?

IRMA: *When we dance the march, the waltz, and the mazurka,* [the body moves like] *a number eight, the form of infinity* [∞]. *The singing is a beautiful healing too. It's a vibration inside of the body. So the rituals of Santo Daime are a mystery, a big healing.*

Within nondancing rituals, in order to optimize the current's curative "flow" between and within participants' bodies, everyone is advised to sit up straight in their chair without crossing their feet, legs, or arms—gently clasped hands seem to be acceptable, but the ideal is a hand resting on each lower thigh. Fardados believe the overlapping or intertwining of physical extremities can cause energetic blocks, which discourages healing flows of the current during their works.

Some fardados claim that in Daime they experience out-of-body journeys through alternate dimensions, a phenomenon called "astral projection"[14] or "soul-flight" (see Dawson 2013, 127/134–37/208[n2]; Meyer 2014, 188/293). When I asked Lars to explain daimistas' shared intention of opening a bridge to spiritual otherworlds, he responded in typical daimista fashion by dismissing the ego "veil" or "curtain" as an illusory construction that erects dualistic boundaries separating this world and the "astral":

I think the human brain makes the separation between the material world and the astral world. But in fact, there is no border. The ratio [reasoning mind] can't experience the astral world because it's part of the material world. But our consciousness lives in both worlds; both worlds that are in fact one world. Here around us are plenty of spirits and astral beings and God is here and angels, but we don't see them. We [act] like they don't exist, and they also [act] like we don't exist [laughs]. It's like a veil, the veil of Isis,[15] is taken away. The curtain opens, you can see what is behind. We see in fact there is no curtain. We make the curtain.

The occult notion of an otherworldly "astral plane" is associated with the Theosophical Society, a nineteenth-century Euro-American spiritual movement (see Bender 2010, 165–72; Leadbeater 2005[1896]). Theosophist practices of investigating and interacting with astral dimensions were also present among similar "esotericist organizations" that influenced Mestre Irineu as he developed his eclectic Daime doctrine (Meyer 2014, 167–70). Cemin (2006, 281) highlights the prominence of this astral realm in fardados' awareness as "the creative source of everything that exists, being represented on earth by the [Santo Daime] leaders and the Sun, Moon, Earth, Wind, and Sea, being the Light of the Heavens, whom one must love," all of which is reinforced in the hymn lyrics. At the same time, the astral is the abode of what fardados call the *Santa Luz* ("Holy Light"), roughly equivalent to that which major world religions term the Holy of Holies, Nirvana, or Heaven (see Shanon 2002, 273–83).

European fardados explained their experience of the Holy Light (*Santa Luz*) in Daime works as a direct encounter with an otherworldly source of unitive radiance. Below are some examples of fardados' outlook on the Holy Light, starting with Saskia who said:

> *It would be beautiful to live in the Holy Light every minute! Some-times in the Daime I feel in the Holy Light, and it feels like you are surrounded by light, and everything inside is light, and I can feel my cells and their great spaces, and in the great spaces there is a big light. So in the whole body, everything is enlightened. . . . I think the Holy Light is when you awake the light inside of you, and that you can let it burn: the Christ in you, it's the Christ that wakes up.*

A similar enthusiasm was expressed by Lambert, a fifty-eight-year-old art teacher who currently serves as commander of the CdU church in Belgium. Lambert has been involved in Santo Daime since 1995. When I asked him about the Holy Light he described it as a "mystical experience" that sometimes appears during Daime rituals:

> *They say it is an astral Light. . . . The Santa Luz is real! In the Daime it is a reality, it is there! And when you are lucky, in a good moment you can come completely in the Light. This is one of the mystical experiences you can have. You feel the strongest in the Light. You feel love in the Light. And then you feel everything, you become it, you feel it, and you know it, and it is Everything when you come in the Light. And during the works, we have moments that we all come in the Light . . . it becomes clear, really. It becomes very clear.*

I also raised this issue with Lotta, a Dutch fardada who works as a nurse and in her spare time helps organize international Daime gatherings in Amsterdam. A well-respected elder in European fardado circles, Lotta was fifty-three years old and had been drinking Daime for sixteen years when we met for an interview in her bachelorette apartment. She rendered the Holy Light as a curative element of the Daime practice:

> *The Holy Light burns away all the worries, can burn away all the sicknesses, because that cannot exist there in the Light. . . . Santo Daime gives a lot of Light. . . . The cleaner you get . . . the more* [Light] *you can carry . . .* [and as Buddha urged in his final instructions, you can] *be a Light unto yourself.*

Here, Lotta speaks of the Holy Light as a purgative agent that purifies any parts of the self that are antithetical to divinity. This take on "sicknesses" and "worries" being "burned away" in the Light recalls Kierkegaard's (1980[1844], 155) optimistic view of suffering anxiety and "dreadful torments" as "through faith absolutely educative, because it consumes all finite ends and discovers their deceptiveness." Indeed, fardados regard the Daime sacrament as "liquid light"[16] because it can induce direct experiences of this Holy Light, which allegedly provides one with therapeutic results. Later (in Part V), I will discuss how fardados explain the mechanisms of Santo Daime healing in more detail.

The ritual use of ayahuasca is also an incentive for European daimistas in search of what Durkheim (1915) termed "collective effervescence," a transpersonal sensation of bonding with fellow humans through communal ceremony (see also C. Taylor 2007, 482). But my informants stressed that the actual *feeling* of direct encounters with spiritual entities, energies, and lessons portrayed in the Daime hymns is impossible to capture in direct words. These sentiments were articulated by Werner, a fifty-eight-year-old retired telephone operator who has been attending Daime works since 2002. Werner trained intensively with a Hindu yoga teacher before he found the Daime, but he claims that he learned the same mystical truths in both of these spiritual disciplines. Referencing Daime concepts in Portuguese, he used a gustatory analogy to explain the extraordinary sensation of cosmic "oneness" that is accessible through Daime works:

> *The goal of the works in the Santo Daime is união* [union]. *You feel that you are one with everybody. . . . The first part of the works are always a little bit individual: you have to clean yourself. You have to look at your doenças* [diseases], *and after a time*

> *when that is cleaned . . . you feel that everybody is more in that*
> *oneness. . . . Santo Daime is a cleaning work and it helps us to*
> *get connected with that oneness.*
>
> *If you want to know it you have to taste it and you have to*
> *drink it and then you know what it is. . . . It's like drinking wine.*
> *It's like, we can talk all day about wine: wine is made like this*
> *from those grapes. And then you have talked about it, and then you*
> *think "Now I know everything about wine." But when you drink*
> *it, then you know it! And it's the same with that oneness. When you*
> *have that experience of oneness, everything disappears; your thoughts*
> *disappear, your emotions disappear, and there is just deep, deep,*
> *deep happiness, deep oneness. Once you experience it, then you know*
> [what it's] *about. That's the point where your spiritual path begins.*

Werner enjoys this feeling of interpersonal oneness in the Daime works, an extraordinary experience aided by an entheogen that dissolves his sense of separation from other human beings and the rest of Nature. My informants say that through Daime they "clean" the egotistical "diseases" that mark everyday divisions between their inner self and the outer world; thereby, they say they see more clearly that they are not separated but fundamentally connected to all beings on both sides of the astral veil.

To coordinate such delicate meetings between the human domain and astral realms, there are specific roles that some fardados hold during rituals. Thus, every work needs a *comandante* ("commander"), who guides the operation of the works from a lead position at the table. Also sitting at or near the table with the commander (depending on the number of people in attendance) are the *músicos* ("musicians") who play guitars and other instruments to accompany the singing. The usually female *puxadoras* or less often male *puxadores* ("pullers") are responsible for knowing all the hymns by heart and they use their loud voices to instigate and "pull" the singing of the entire congregation. Another crucial function is supplied by fardados serving in the role of *fiscal* (plural *fiscais*, Portuguese for "supervisors" or "guardians"), who are responsible for maintaining order in the salão and for aiding persons having difficulty handling the ayahuasca experience. Acknowledging the significance of all the roles listed above, the this-wordly value of fiscais must be emphasized as a vital cog in the engine of Daime works because their "supervision" (*fiscalização*) upholds the integrity of the ritual space. Fiscal guardians are an essential safety valve, particularly for newcomers struggling to come to grips with intense psychophysical modifications that can occur after the ingestion of ayahuasca. Another internal document, entitled "Guidelines for Guardians" (CEFLURIS n.d.), advises new fiscais about their complicated duty to assist those in need without letting their own ego hangups disrupt the healing processes of individuals in the work:

> As with everything within the Daime, the main teacher is the power itself. The ultimate source of guardianship is provided by the All that Is; all that is Nature, all that is Love, and all Divine Beings. The Daime will teach each guardian how to best fulfill their role, based on their relationship with the power and their own sensibilities. . . . The main guidelines when caring for people are, to make your first priority your own alignment with God, to maintain harmony, and, to keep your interactions subtle and minimal, yet firm. The most important work going on is between each person and the Daime. Even kind actions can interfere with that process. Keep talking, touching, and eye contact to a minimum. If it is absolutely necessary to speak to someone, do so after a hymn is completed, and then say as little as possible. . . . If a person is throwing up, you can hold the bucket for them and keep their hair out of the way, if they need the help. They may be handling things very well on their own. Often the most helpful thing that you can do is remember that each person is Christ, and treat them with that level of respect, tenderness, and love. . . . Always allow harmony to prevail. If someone doesn't want to do what you think is best, go along with their needs, unless someone will be harmed. . . . ABOVE ALL, TRUST IN GOD. The Daime Knows What The Daime Is Doing.

The Norms of Ritual further describes how "the good fiscal must be serene, gentle and at the same time persuasive and firm when it is about solving problems and situations that bring harm to the harmonious flow of the work" (CEFLURIS 1997). In cultivating this ideal demeanor, skillful fiscais command respect from all participants in the work, and will work with fellow fiscais to address any problems that arise. While guardians endeavor to resolve issues in the salão without restraining participants, "occasionally this may also be necessary, usually with inexperienced individuals, who, under the effect of the brew, behave in a troublesome or aggressive manner" (MacRae 1992, 105).

Since collective ritual is the most important aspect of daimista religious life, I attended as many different types of work as possible. All official Daime churches hold "Concentration" works on the fifteenth and thirtieth of every month. As the name implies, these bimonthly Concentration works entail periods of silent meditation at planned junctures within the ritual. During these phases of personal introspection, each individual "within the force of the current, of the spiritual energy of the elevated minds and of the protection of our spiritual guides, [tries] to attain a state of contemplation, of complete rest, serene and without thoughts, in which [one attempts] to merge the observer, the observed and the act of observing into one" (CEFLURIS 1997). It is this feeling of mystical union of self and what might usually be considered not-self, which my informants spoke of as a metaphysical solution that leads to therapeutic solutions in life outside the works (see Part V). Besides standard Concentration works every two weeks, there are a variety of rituals organized throughout the year that include *Cura* ("Healing") works (with "Star" and "Cross" varieties), baptisms, weddings, and *Santa Missa* ("Holy Mass") death memorials; any of these might incorporate a *Fardamento* initiation rite, wherein new members officially become fardados by "receiving their star." Md. Geraldine, the matriarch of the European daimista community, summarized some of the different kinds of Daime work this way:

> *You can take me as an example: every work is different for me. Because every time you work on another kind of thing, so sometimes you have an easy work (only light), sometimes you have a very hard work because Daime always gives you what you need. Sometimes you need to go through a hard process in order to let go. . . .*
>
> *[In] a Concentration . . . you can go deep inside, you can go in meditation, contemplation . . . you become one.*
>
> *And then you have the Curas, a special work for cleansing the blockages. . . .*
>
> *Santa Missa is a work especially for the [discarnate] souls, it's a charity work. You're not sitting there for yourself, you're sitting there to generate energy and light for the souls who are coming there for that, to help them, . . . because so many souls are dying; they had a difficult life on Earth, and they die, and they go to another realm [where they] also have difficulties, so they need help because they [were] not in the Light when they died. So we help them: we pray for them, we sing for them. . . .*

A Cross work is what you do when nothing else helps, when somebody is taken over by the negative energy, then you can do a Cross work. You can compare it with an exorcism, like the Catholic Church has. . . . Everybody has a cross in his hand . . . praying. . . .

A Star work is the same as a Cura, only with a small group, and in a Star work you go deeper and deeper because you drink more Daime, and that's why you're doing it in small groups, not in big churches. . . . You help in that [work] because it is better that there [is] oneness between the people, because . . . [sometimes] they are too busy with "I don't agree with this, I don't agree with that." All are different! It is not that one is better than the other. We have to learn to see that things are different in the world; but not with judgment on it, that's not the meaning; just look at it like a child [would].

I partook in several Santa Missa works, a kind of astral funeral. Santa Missa participants write the names of deceased (or sometimes still living) loved ones on a piece of paper, which is placed with charitable intention underneath the cross on the central altar—these pieces of paper are burned to ash after the work is completed, symbolizing the named soul's subsequent liberation. Daimistas conceptualize the séance-like Santa Missa as opening a heavenly portal for souls who are struggling to find/maintain a connection to the divine Light. As the Madrinha indicates, Curas are focused on "cleansing the blockages." By this she means that Curas allow for a purging of egotistical fixations, which tends to result in more vomiting and "heavy" body discomforts at these works. In addition, popular Brazilian rituals of Umbanda have more recently been incorporated into the CEFLURIS line, with "Umbandaime" works such as *Mesa Branca* ("White Table") and *São Miguel* (St. Michael) spirit-conjuring rites (see Barnard, forthcoming; Dawson 2013, 49–53/142–48; Schmidt 2007, 145–63). Although I attended one Mesa Branca and one São Miguel ritual during fieldwork, these mediumship rites are as yet scarce in Europe compared to their prevalence at Daime churches in North and South America.

While I did do several regular Curas, I did not have an opportunity to attend the "Cross" or "Star" categories of Cura, which are respectively reserved for resolving individual spirit possessions and collective disputes that arise within a Daime community. Star works are private affairs for resolving touchy interpersonal quarrels within a specific daimista congregation, so leering anthropologists are not really invited. Regarding the Cross works, prominent fardados in Europe and North America told me they are aware that on very rare occasions Daime will exacerbate problems for a specific subset of people; indeed, medical professionals confirm that ayahuasca can "precipitate psychotic episodes in persons with a predisposition to such states" (Anderson et al. 2012, 174; see also Bilhimer et al. 2018; dos Santos 2013a, 71). As far as I know, my European informants take this as reason enough to refuse entry to individuals who have psychotic or schizophrenic tendencies. While I have never heard of a Cross Work being performed outside Brazil, leading fardados insist that the spiritual "doctors" at Mapiá can expel dark forces from a "patient" by performing this Daime form of exorcism. Lotta described the Cross Work this way: "it's a short work (it takes only one hour), and it's special; nine people around the table and the patient (the one who gets healed), and you ask the Master to get rid of this spirit, so that the spirit can also get loose and go to the Light." Dawson (2013, 128) reports that attendees intone the "Prayer to Dispel the Curses of Evil Spirits and Infernal Demons" to patients that have been diagnosed by experienced daimista healers as demonically possessed. The German commander Hermann said that if there are any hidden neuroses or psychoses within a person, the demonic parasites causing these symptoms will come out with the Daime. He figures that people who routinely suppress internal turmoil will sometimes act out, scream, cry, laugh, or have a temper tantrum in a ritual because this suffering is exposed when they drink Daime. He stresses that he believes this to be a transitory or liminal crisis that predictably leads to existential and psychospiritual "catharsis through the holy plant." Anneke, the veteran Dutch fiscal, assured me that her experience in guardianship shows that these bouts of psychosis are "usually a temporary passage; people sometimes go wild, and after a while they calm down." Needless to say, this conceptualization of psychosis and schizophrenia as caused by demonic forces is diametrically opposed to the biomedical model according to which Western societies operate (see Labate and Jungaberle 2011; Polari de Alverga 2011, 208–11). From a biomedical perspective, schizophrenics or psychotics (estimated to be 1.3 percent of the general population) are not considered psychologically stable enough to handle an entheogen; however, psychologist Robert Gable (2007, 30) avows that for nonpsychotic adults, ingesting the psychoactive chemical found in ayahuasca (DMT) "is not a triggering event for sustained psychosis."

While each type of work possesses a distinct purpose of repairing individual, social, and/or astral disharmonies, all Daime rituals are directed toward a mystical intent verbalized in the "Consecration of the Space" prayer recited at the beginning. This lengthy prayer acts to sanctify the salão by emphasizing that the only presence in the room is a Divine Being composed of Harmony, Love, Truth, and Justice—a fourfold motto of Daime morality. The prayer identifies this entity as God, stating that "God is the essential Life of all beings, the health of body and mind." The prayer ends by proclaiming:

> In the most perfect communion between my lower self and Higher Self,[17] which is God in me, I consecrate this place to the perfect expression of all the Divine qualities that are in me and all beings. The vibrations of my thoughts are the forces of God in me, which are stored here and radiate to all beings.

Again, this transcendent state of union (or metaphysical solution) between humans and the conscious spirit of all Nature is the ultimate goal of Daime devotees. It is no surprise that ritual use of an entheogenic substance believed to "reveal the divine within" is tied to a theology of *panentheism,* which "understands God and the world to be inter-related with the world being in God and God being in the world . . . [seeking] to avoid both isolating God from the world as traditional theism often does and identifying God with the world as pantheism does" (Culp 2009; see also Barnard, forthcoming). The fusion of these multifarious aspects of God in Daime works is deemed to occur inside the subjective being of each participant who is willing to open their heart and mind to the ritual experience. The mystical realization of panentheistic union between the human self and the divine is underscored in hymns sung at Daime works, such as:

Eu estou com Deus	*I'm with God*
Deus está em mim	*God is within me*
Eu estando com Deus	*I being with God*
Deus é o meu caminho	*God is my path*

—Padrinho Sebastião # 143[18]

Following each service of ayahuasca, the participants then take their places in the salão to commence hours of singing and meditating geared toward manifesting this spiritual intention.

When the phantasmagoric journey of each work reaches completion, closing prayers are recited and it is announced that the work is "closed." A round of applause follows and attendees' faces often express happy relief that they have braved another work. The clapping then converts into singing of *Parabéns* ("Happy Birthday" in Portuguese)[19] and all members whose birthday is near are brought up to the front to be serenaded.[20] Then everyone hugs the people in their immediate vicinity, congratulating each other on a "good work" (*bom trabalho* [in Portuguese], *goed werk* [Dutch], or *bon travail* [French], etc.). Now begins a social time, with the striking up of various conversations and the serving of prearranged refreshments (fruit, cake, hot tea, juice, nuts, and confectioneries). Participants change out of their white uniforms into street clothes before crowding around a food table to snack on the available cuisine. Since the effects of ayahuasca are still present for a few hours after an intense Daime work, food and drink taste quite different than they normally do.

Discussions immediately after a work are generally relaxed and jovial, with everyone basking in the exquisite afterglow of the entheogenic ceremony. But this is not a time for idle chitchat. Instead, the norm is to focus on commiserating about subjects related to Santo Daime. Sometimes newcomers who had a particularly difficult work will be seen resting or talking through their experience with a commander or fiscal. For neophytes like me, this post-work social time is an opportunity to ask questions to experienced fardados about how to best handle difficult or strange situations encountered during the work. While I initially approached fardados with intellectual questions related to the underlying theory of my anthropological research, I quickly learned that such topics were seen as "too mental." In downplaying intellectual thinking as an ego activity, daimistas prefer to talk in terms of "feeling" and "getting in touch" with the "vibrations" of spiritual entities and one's "Higher Self." Gradually via exposure, ethnographers can become more adept at engaging with daimistas in their mystically inclined speech style.

Music and the Ethical Lyrics of Daime Hymns

Aptly titled *Opening the Portals of Heaven*, a pivotal publication by Labate and Pacheco (2010) has instituted the comparative study of music in the Santo Daime and UDV ayahuasca traditions. The authors emphasize Santo Daime as a "musical religion" because ritual ingestion of the sacrament is inextricably tied to the performance of and personal engagement with chanted *hinos* ("hymns"). Through the expansion of CEFLURIS and its offshoots, "the number of hymns today is in the thousands, forming a corpus that keeps growing" (Labate and Pacheco 2010, 31/92). These hymns are considered by daimistas in biblical terms as a "third testament" (Labate and Pacheco 2010, 30/89; Schmidt 2007, 88), witnessed in the way members refer to particular hymns like passages of holy scripture.[21] Furthermore, it is accurate to state that adepts of ayahuasca religions behold their ritual music as "a kind of sign of experience which metonymically condenses the religious experience as a whole" (Labate and Pacheco 2010, 94). Thus, one cannot overstress the centrality of singing hymns accompanied by instrumental music within Daime works[22] (see also Labate, Loures de Assis, and Cavnar 2017).

Santo Daime hymns are a type of mantra composed of short lyrical verses with vertical lines indicating stanzas to be repeated. I admit that the first few times I heard the Daime hymns I found them quite tedious, and initially the text appeared to be vague and even silly. Yet my informants frequently cited the music as one of their favorite aspects of Daime practice. The more I participated in the Daime works, the more I gained an appreciation for the resplendence of musical harmonization that occurred whenever the phenomenon fardados call the Holy Light arrived. I was also thankful for the mooring of reassurance these hymns offered during turbulent phases of the rituals. As one informant told me (quoting a Brazilian Padrinho), paying close attention to the hymns during particularly difficult works can be like "holding onto the tail of a camel in a sandstorm." In delving past surface connotations, hino lyrics take on the form of polysemic texts,[23] much like modernist literature or religious holy books, because they can have different subjective meanings for different people at different times. This polysemic flexibility is augmented within the confines of the Daime ritual. So when reading the lyrics one must remember that daimistas "consider themselves as following a 'musical doctrine' and that the hymns only reveal their full strength when sung to the sound of 'maracás' and under the effect of the sacred brew" (MacRae 1992, 126). Nevertheless, even from a sober perspective it is possible to outline some elementary facets of the Daime doctrine as delineated in the hymns.

Explaining how hymns comprise the basic gospel of Santo Daime because they are "received from the astral, or the spiritual kingdom,"[24] the church's principle historian, Lúcio Mortimer, opens Mestre Irineu's *O Cruzeiro* ("The Cross") hymnal with a well-known story about how the Mestre initially refused to sing when he was recruited by the Queen of the Forest:

> It was the Spiritual Virgin Mother who taught him and ordered him to sing to His brothers. The hymns of the Cruzeiro are this

revelation: words that are new, beautiful and simple, explaining an old teaching. It's the fruit of Daime and its powerful teachings. From this hymnal comes down a multitude of hymns praising God and His Creation. To speak about the real meaning of the Hymns is a very difficult task. However, despite my ineptitude, I am certain that by loving these songs in my heart, I am fulfilling myself completely in the Spiritual Life.

As noted by MacRae (1992, 126), daimistas believe that the Santo Daime doctrine is summarized in the final twelve hymns of Mestre Irineu's hymnal, a subsection called the *Cruzeirinho* ("Little Cross") that is performed at the end of most works. Here are some examples of these summary phrases from the Cruzeirinho: "The teachings of the Professor bring us beautiful lessons. . . . To respect one's brothers and sisters . . . and learn to appreciate one another" (MI#118); "This path of love inside my heart, I ask Jesus Christ to give us salvation" (MI#120); "Whoever seeks this house and arrives here, encounters the Virgin Mary, she gives you your health" (MI#122); "I take this drink which has an incredible Power, it shows all of us here in this Truth" (MI#124); "I tell everybody the hymns are teachings us. . . . The Holy Mary is Supreme. . . . She sent me here to be a teacher" (MI#125); "The House of my Father is in the heart of the world, where all Love exists there is a profound secret. . . . It's in all humanity, if we all know each other here in this Truth" (MI#126). While Mortimer is correct that decoding the "real meaning" of Daime hymns is difficult, if not impossible, because the interpretation is inherently subjective, these excerpts from the Cruzeirinho do insist on this: when one drinks Daime, one gains entry to a storehouse of teachings provided by a spiritual "professor" contained both in the beverage and inside every human being; this "Master Teacher" (*Mestre Ensinador*), which represents Jesus and the divine Feminine + Masculine essences present in all Nature, instructs the drinker in how to access universal "Truth" and wisdom about the human condition; the core thrust of these lessons revolves around values of unconditional compassion and love for oneself and every other being, principles that mirror the teachings of Christ and other spiritual sages (see Part VI).

Calling attention to the fact that music is a major component of ritual alterations of consciousness found cross-culturally, Shanon (2011, 290) observes that "ayahuasca amplifies an effect intrinsic to music, and in turn, music provides extra fuel for ayahuasca's psychoactive effects." The Norms of Ritual manual describes how Daime music carries the spiritual current which envelopes all participants in a harmonic energy, eliciting a dissolution of the boundaries that normally separate individuals from each other and from the rest of the Cosmos:

> The dancing and the music generate an energy that is channeled by the vibrations of the maracá. All this propitiates an inner work of spiritual uplift and expansion of consciousness, which supports the *mirações*, the insights and diverse teachings that occur during the work with every member of the current. The hymns guide our ritual expedition. They awaken, encourage, advise and instruct us so that we may be able to make our inner dive, always within the protection of the current. The *firmeza* ["firmness"] of the current rests within the *firmeza* and consciousness of every brother and sister and his/her obedience to the rules of the work. (CEFLURIS 1997)

Miração (plural: mirações) is Daime terminology for "visionary states produced by the beverage" that can be considered a kind of "shamanic flight" or "mystical perception," as explained by Mapiá elder Alex Polari de Alverga (1996):

> This is the summit of the ritual's work. During this lengthy journey, the self unfolds; it remembers and resolves certain karmic problems; it channels energy to heal itself and others; it obtains revealing and emancipating insights for its conflicts; and experiences all types of ineffable states of mystical perception, of comprehension of the universe, love for humanity, premonitions or future events and synchronicity. As a result of all these stages, we are given the possibility of experiencing total ecstasy and a feeling of blessedness. It is important to note that everything described is processed in an inner connection with the music, the singing, the dance, and the rhythm of the maracás.

Visions and other perceptual modifications that are a hallmark of the ayahuasca experience[25] are thus guided in Daime rituals by the music and textual meanings aroused by the hymns. This same notion of music providing a structural framework for entheogenic experiences has also been noted with indigenous ayahuasca rituals (Andritzky 1989, 80–81). Accordingly, entheogenic visions are highly esteemed for their capacity to precipitate "self-knowledge, the assimilation of the message of the hymns, social integration, spiritual healing, and salvation of the soul" (Abramovitz 2002, 21).[26] Rather than interpreting them as "hallucinations," daimistas are attentive to insights received through mirações and are keen to integrate these existential teachings into their daily lives. However, even though mirações are what attracts many newcomers to Santo Daime, veteran fardados cautioned that rather than edifying lessons, improperly framed psychedelic visions can become empty infatuations of one's ego. Such caveats reiterate St. John of the Cross (2010[1618], 66), who advised fellow mystics that "in order to come to this essential union of love in God, the soul must take care not to lean on visions that take place in the mind, or on forms or figures or particular objects of the understanding." Similarly, fardados consider Daime visions as like the bardo "projections"[27] enumerated in the Buddhist text *Bardo Thödol*, known in the West as the *Tibetan Book of the Dead* (Evans-Wentz 1980[1927]); this text suggests that images of otherworldly beings should be treated as archetypal guideposts to unifying oneness, rather than as things in themselves. For instance, whether one encounters a scary monster or an angel, my informants say it is important to recognize that visions merely convey lessons about how one can evolve spiritually by shedding egoic complexes. Veteran fardados are aware that spiritual seekers tend to get distracted when they focus too much on encountering otherworldly beings. Etienne, a fardado from CdAI, referred to these as "side effects" of the ego, which can "trick" one into focusing too much on the privilege of relating with spirits. He warned that this is "a big trap, because you get stuck" in the pride of possessing elite knowledge rather than remembering that the learning process is an unending practice of humility. Werner echoed other Daime elders in downplaying the content of visions, stating that the goal is really to learn how to "live in union with your family, with your friends, that you see how you can keep the harmony, stay in that loving way. . . . That's the most important thing, and that's what the Daime is helping us to realize: to stay in our hearts." Unlike the dualistic focus of the egoic mind-brain, the spiritual "heart" symbolizes fardados' ideal of cultivating sensitivity to an underlying unity of all beings. The themes of ethical instructions broached in the many hymns are wide-ranging. Below are some wordclouds[28] extracting the most prominent words found in some exemplary hymnals (Figures 8.7 to 8.11):

More specifically, one finds a cross-section of the Daime's fundamental virtues in this excerpt from Padrinho Alfredo's hymn #27:

Figure 8.7. Wordcloud for all hymns in Mestre Irineu's hymnal *O Cruzeiro* ("The Cross"). The most frequently cited words include *mãe* ("mother"), *virgem* ("virgin"), *deus* ("God"), *vós* ("you"), *sempre* ("always"), *todos* ("all"), *amor* ("love"), and *filho* ("child").

Figure 8.8. A wordcloud from Pd. Sebastião's hymnal *O Justiceiro* ("The Justice Maker"). The most frequently cited words include *mestre* ("master"), *irmãos* ("brothers"), *pai* ("father"), and *aqui* ("here").

Figure 8.9. A wordcloud from *Flores de São João* ("Flowers of St. John"), a well-known hymnal by Brazilian fardada Cristina Tati. The most frequently cited words include *marcha* ("march"), *vamos* ("let's go"), *vou* ("I will"), and *coração* ("heart").

Figure 8.10. A wordcloud from *A Pilgrimage to the Angelic Realm* (a hymnal received in English by Frederik, a Belgian fardado in Céu da União). The most frequently cited words include *light, angel, sacred/holy,* and *soul.*

Figure 8.11. A wordcloud from *Doçura da Luz* ("Sweetness of the Light"), a hymnal received by Cécile, the commander of the Belgian church Céu do Arco-Íris. The most frequently cited words include *luz* ("light"), *amor* ("love"), *deus* ("God"), Jesus, and *verdade* ("truth").

Vou receber minha Mãe	I'm going to receive my Mother
Dentro do meu coração	Within my heart
Para eu poder caminhar	So I can walk
Neste mundo de ilusão	In this world of illusion

Vou colocar minha Mãe	*I'm going to place my Mother*
Bem juntinho do meu Pai	*Right next to my Father*
Vida, paz e harmonia	*Life, peace and harmony*
Com isto nos satisfaz	*With this we are satisfied*
Amor, verdade e justiça	*Love, truth, justice*
Fé, firmeza e consciência	*Faith, firmness, and consciousness*
Serenidade, respeito	*Serenity, respect*
São partes da providência	*Are parts of providence*
Calma e tranquilidade	*Calmness and tranquility*
Obediência e coragem	*Obedience and courage*
Humilhação e prudência	*Humility and prudence*
São partes desta imagem	*Are parts of this image*
Este é o amor divino	*This is the Divine Love*
Do trono celestial	*Of the Celestial Throne*
Que resplandece nas matas	*That shines in the forest*
Iluminando todos iguais	*Illuminating all equally*

Daimistas consider a hymn as a map or blueprint that teaches them how to nurture such traits so as to transmit "divine love" in one's daily life. It is not by merely conceiving the merit of these ethical-emotional values that Daime hymns guide fardados' personal integrity. Rather, Daime experiences foster an explicit confrontation with the—often repressed—features of one's personality that do not live up to these moral standards.

In a straightforward hymn called *Confia* ("Trust"), the lyrics of MI#119 advise devotees about how to handle and capitalize on their Daime experiences:

Confia, confia, confia no poder	*Trust, trust the power*
Confia no saber	*Trust the knowledge*
Confia na força	*Trust the force*
Aonde pode ser	*Where it can be*
Esta força é muito simples	*This force is very simple*
Todo mundo vê	*Everyone can see it*
Mas passa por ela	*But they pass by*
E não procura compreender	*And don't try to understand*

Estamos todos reunidos	*We are all together*
Com a nossa chave na mão	*With our key in hand*
A limpar mentalidade	*Cleaning our mentality*
Para entrar neste salão	*To enter this temple*

All the hymns employ symbolic language, such as the "key," which opens inner doors to uncover latent knowledge. The *Daime* (literally "give-me") is a catchall term referring to the doctrine organized around this sacramental beverage and the capacity of these rituals to act as a skeleton key for unlocking internal "blocks" that cause problems in people's lives; sometimes the Daime doctrine is referred to as a "golden key" that is a "key to all my discernment" when it is "consecrated in your heart" (PA#106/120/142). The next section will have more to say about fardados' descriptions of Daime rituals as a key technology or tool for psychospiritual transformation and healing. For now, let us look more closely at what the hymns have to say about Santo Daime symbology.

Eclectic Symbolisms of Santo Daime Ideology

There are numerous ideological elements contained in the hymns, all of which work in unison to guide introspective journeys of the Daime experience. To begin with, there is an assortment of spiritual beings (both anthropomorphic and abstract) whose energetic powers are summoned regularly. These include the *Mãe* ("Mother," an essence of the divine feminine referred to with various names such as "Celestial Mother," "Queen of the Forest," and "Divine Virgin Mary") and *Pai* ("Father," dubbed the "Eternal Father" or "Sovereign Lord/King/Creator"), often cited together as paired aspects of one androgynous God. From Afro-Brazilian influences, the hymns identify a pantheon of deities (*orixás*; e.g., *Yemanja*, *Ogum*) and indigenous *caboclo* spirits[1] (e.g., *Tucum* and *Currupipipiraguá*)[2] that "come from the Astral" (MI#64). The hymns entwine allusions to Afro-Brazilian spirits with Judeo-Christian biblical figures such as Jesus Christ (of whom Mestre Irineu is considered an avatar), St. John the Baptist (avatar: Pd. Sebastião), King Solomon (avatar: Pd. Alfredo), and King David (avatar: Pd. Alex) (see Dawson 2013, 123).

By merging Christian concepts with eclectic non-Christian theologies, it is believed that Mestre Irineu renewed a genuine connection between human beings and the Divine Absolute, a situation he termed *Juramidam*. Juramidam refers to "the major spiritual entity" permeating the doctrine (Goulart 1996 [Chapter 4,[3] n7]) and at the same time refers collectively to all the members of the Santo Daime "family" (Schmidt 2007, 88; see also Barnard, forthcoming). More specifically, according to MacRae (1992, 55) daimistas' work in the astral plane is conceived of as a war or a battle against weakness, impurity, doubt or illness. The daimistas are the soldiers or "midam," who alongside Jura (God) make up the Juramidam Empire, a source of strength for the obedient, the humble and the clean of heart. Thus, Juramidam means God or God and his soldiers, a notion of the divine which is both individualistic and collective.

The all-encompassing spirit of Juramidam, revealed inside and between daimista participants, simultaneously contains all beings and values of Santo Daime as one within itself.

Although it was difficult for most informants to communicate the enigmatic qualities of this entity, Juramidam was defined quite lucidly by José, a veteran fardado from Spain who juxtaposed it with the egotistical discord that seems to reign in earthly affairs:

> *The hinarios [received by an individual daimista] explain the experience of the spiritual life of this person; Mestre Irineu is always speaking about . . . every day people put Christ [on] the cross when they don't practice union, don't practice love, don't practice harmony, and Mestre Irineu's hinario speaks intimately about these things. . . .*
>
> *For me, the Juramidam Empire represents all the [opposite] things: a place, a spiritual empire. . . . Juramidam is a thing in the astral that people want to go to . . . it's the kingdom of harmony, love, truth, [and] justice . . . a kingdom of the Light. For me, in the spiritual Light all is truth, all is union, all is harmony, all is love, all is perfect, like Nature. Nature is for me the representative of Juramidam in our world, because it's perfect.*

For fardados the essence of Nature's "perfect" moral balance is embodied in the Daime sacrament, which they claim has the capacity to forge a new covenant between human beings and Heaven. Daime elder Pd. Alex Polari de Alverga (1999, 252) identifies Juramidam as "the Divine Being who lives in the spiritual drink," noting that "the hymns speak of Juramidam as being the new manifestation of Christ in the forest." This Daime theology resembles two major concepts in Catholic Christology. The first is *Hypostatic Union*,[4] described by Edward Schillebeeckx (1963, 30–31[n64]/57) as Jesus's demonstration of "a divine way of being [human] and a human way of being God": "In Christ the redemptive love of God has become an historical reality . . . and through the Hypostatic Union—Jesus' humanity assumed in a divine person which thus becomes the ultimate goal of all humanity—Christ is not merely morally representative of all [humankind]." Secondly, it is clear from daimistas' explanations of their ayahuasca rituals that they are attempting to reenact the *kenosis* (Greek: "self-emptying")[5] of Jesus Christ—such a total relinquishment of one's self-centered desires in deference to Divine Will is an ideal which is also implicit in the existentialist theology of Kierkegaard (Law 2013, 1/53; see also Chávez[6] 2008, 157; Hegel 1977[1807], 439/492). In Santo Daime, Juramidam highlights a prospect that all human beings can find this mystical Christ quality within themselves, a goal that is facilitated through ritually drinking the Daime sacrament. Juramidam summarizes how fardados conceive of existential turmoil within and between individual human beings as taking on cosmic proportions. Such ideas evoke the alchemical Christologies of Carl Jung and Jakob Böhme, for whom Christ[7] signifies that all of "humanity dwells in both time and eternity as the finite site of the resolution of divinity's eternal struggle for integration" (Dourley 2014, 112/121). So while the Daime sacrament contains the Juramidam being, it is also said to embody the divine illumination of Christ. Together with the Holy Light, connotations with Christ consciousness mark Juramidam as the ultimate metaphysical solution in Santo Daime, signifying daimistas' goal of experiencing firsthand the spiritual merger of God and humanity as one unified Being/being. By postulating a divine-human linkage wrought by a community of Christlike warriors, Juramidam typifies why "entheogen" is an apt label for capturing ayahuasca's emic function within Santo Daime.

The array of Daime visual symbols includes overtly Christian icons (crosses, images of Saints, Jesus, and Mary) alongside a mixture of non-Christian motifs (six-pointed stars, crescent moons, hummingbirds,[8] trees, flowers, avian wings, and the plants used to make ayahuasca). References to these icons swirl together in the hymns, inferring an interwoven harmony of human spirituality and the natural environment. It is because of this clear parallelism between welfares of the human and natural realms that Schmidt (2007) designated Santo Daime an "eco-religious movement." Above all, however, the double-armed Caravaca cross (*cruzeiro*) acts as a kind of symbolic *axis mundi* in Daime life. During works, force/energy from the astral is said to emanate from the center of the table, with the double-armed cross acting as the focal point. While there is hardly any reference to Christ's resurrection, the hymns stress Jesus's suffering on the cross as emblematic of the need to maintain faith in Divine Love even when faced with immense pain, doubt, and fear. As Lars explains:

> *In the Daime they don't accentuate [Christ's resurrection]. In the*
> *Daime you don't have this feast of Easter. Easter doesn't exist in Santo*
> *Daime because they say, "Christ is alive." Why feast his re-birth?*
> *Because he's alive! They feast the Semana Santa [Holy Week], with*
> *his suffering and his death. The suffering of Christ, you can also*
> *translate it into everybody's life: the suffering through life and death.*

On this topic, fardados tend to interpret Christ's resurrection as an allegory. In the words of Madrona, the Spanish divorcée, she touched on the symbolism of Christ's death and resurrection as a divine teaching, an important subject we will return to later in Parts V and VI:

> *When we are singing the hinos . . . Jesus is you. Jesus means "I*
> *am." Because Jesus was a Master, he came to teach us that we are*
> *God . . . I am!*
>
> *I am the resurrection and the life! Jesus means that you find*
> *yourself, not him! Jesus Christ is you! I am also "I am," you are*
> *"I am" . . .*
>
> *He had to die to have the opportunity to resuscitate . . . and*
> *in Santo Daime works you die; and then after you die in the Santo*
> *Daime, you also resuscitate as Christ.*

Likewise for Jeannette, a Belgian fardada who was employed in a laboratory at a Flemish university before switching to pursue a career in financial consulting. At age sixty, she is now retired and divides her time between taking care of her grandchildren and receiving clients for her astrology practice. She had been attending works at CdU since 2005, when she first learned about Daime through her contact with Frederik, who is also an astrologer. After recently taking her star to become a fardada, during an interview in her urban townhouse she stated:

> *For me the resurrection is what the Daime tells us every time.*
> *Every time when we can contact the Higher Self, that's what Jesus*
> *[taught] with the Resurrection: you leave your body, and you'll be*
> *back . . . every time when we take Daime, and we travel, it's a*
> *possibility to [experience] that we are bigger than our body, that we*
> *are bigger than what we can experience with the eyes, the nose, the*
> *senses. And that's the resurrection. So it's the way that I put it into*
> *life: you have to be whole, and there is more every time.*

Thus, one's enduring of travails during the singing of the Cruzeiro and other hymnals is akin to each individual participant standing "at the foot of the cross" (e.g., MI#7; PS#40, 49, 50, and 88; PA#106). As the hymns suggest, this climactic experience can be so acute that it is interpreted as identifying personally with the agony of Christ's sacrifice; "to firm in" the divine light and love contained within the symbol of the crucifixion is considered a means of strengthening one's own faith (MI#7, GG#27, PS#26, PA#96). Notably, the curricula of most Daime hymns appear not at all interested in the famous stories of Jesus's miracles (e.g., curing the blind, raising Lazarus, the fish and loaves, walking on water). Instead, like Jung and Hegel (see Dourley 2014, 151–163), the Daime doctrine is much more focused on the tangible teachings of Christ and his personifying resolute trust in the face of unspeakable torture. The parallels with Christ's accepting the bitter "cup" of immanent execution in the Garden of Gethsemane are unmistakable (Matthew 26:39; Mark 14:36; Luke 22:42).

It is also no coincidence that the Star of David (an icon of Judaism related to the Seal of Solomon) and the crescent moon (the main insignia of Islam) are converged with a Christian cross in Daime iconography. Consonant with the "Theosophical Glossary" of Helena Blavatsky (1891; see Hanegraaff 1998, 443–455), in Daime these symbols represent a belief in the inheritance of esoteric wisdom presumably shared in common by ancient Egyptians, Persians, Chinese, Greeks, Druids, and Hindus. A few of my informants evinced an awareness that these occult symbols indicate the ways Daime founders were influenced by writings and rites of European esotericism groups such as Theosophists, Masons, Anthroposophists, and Rosicrucians[9] (Dawson 2013, 16–18/94; Moura da Silva 2006). European fardados interpret this conflation of esoteric icons as denoting Daime to be a common meeting ground for *all* authentic spiritual mystery schools. In this respect, daimistas are not unlike followers of the Bahá'í faith, a Persian–Middle Eastern religious movement that views all genuine spiritual systems as projections of a single divine source, presuming that there is really "only one religion, which develops according to human evolution" (Jones et al. 2005, 739). I met Jewish fardados educated in the Kabbalah, fardados trained as Islamic Sufis, and other fardados who were experts in Buddhist or Hindu meditation and yoga; all affirmed that Santo Daime was helping them to reach the same primeval truths of Holy Light, pervasive love, and cosmic unity that they had learned about in other mystical formats with which they are affiliated. Instead of isolating these different religious backgrounds, fardados consider Daime to be a "melting pot" where the common truths of otherwise discrete spiritual traditions are homogenized. This accords with Dias Junior's (1992, 47) depiction of cooking the holy drink as signifying how the eclectic Daime "doctrine can be seen as a cauldron where different influences blend together" (cited in Labate and Pacheco 2011, 76). Such notions of brewing multiple elements into a liquid mixture fit with the "solutions"[10] trope proffered herein: the material "solution" of plants and chemicals in ayahuasca also emblematically symbolizes a metaphysical "solution" between the observing self and a universal God-Nature, the drinking of which in turn catalyzes practical "solutions" for daimistas' well-being. Hence, the mystical union of all existence is promulgated by the hymns' repeated references to harmonic synergies shared between symbolic concepts. In synchronized contemplation, these symbols act as signposts pointing to the oneness of all things.

In hymn #1 (entitled *Harmonia Cósmica* ["Cosmic Harmony"]) in a hymnal of the same name by Padrinho Zé Ricardo, one finds these atypical lines recited after conventional references to Christian and Afro-Brazilian entities:

Viva a Mãe e Aurobindo	*Hail the Mother and Aurobindo*
E Massahanu Taniguchi	*And Masaharu Taniguchi*
Viva Buda, Viva Krishna	*Hail Buddha, Hail Krishna*
Viva Gandhi e o Dalai Lama	*Hail Gandhi and the Dalai Lama*[11]

This same hymn closes with stanzas celebrating a concept of "unidiversity": a recognition that the amalgamation of "love, light, [and] eternity" found in different religious traditions is a sign that humans in different times and cultures have achieved the same state of being "one with God and the Universe." The Belgian adaptational group CCMI placed Buddhist and Hindu statuettes on either side of the cross upon the table for their works. To invigorate the collective energy of the salão, most Daime works include a series of *Viva!* ("Hurrah!") calls at occasional junctures between hymns, with senior fardados (usually male) initiating "Viva!" exclamations for various Daime symbols and personages, and the congregation responds with a concerted "Viva!" As an adaptation, the CCMI commander includes unconventional calls such as "Viva Buddha" and "Viva Krishna" in addition to more conventional calls of "Viva Mestre Irineu" and "Viva a Rainha da Floresta" (Hail the Queen of the Forest). He explained that these are all part of the astral energy that the Daime contains. While there is no public reference to such Buddhist or Hindu entities in CEFLURIS works, many of these prominent spiritual figures from outside Santo Daime are also privately revered by more conventional groups of fardados (see Part VI).

Apart from all the symbols reviewed above, it is curious that the snake—a major indigenous symbol of ayahuasca—is largely absent from Daime iconography. This is a conspicuous omission, given that many daimistas are aware of Jeremy Narby's (1998, 187) book *The Cosmic Serpent*; in this book, the Amazonianist ethnographer links a predominance of snake imagery in indigenous shamanism to the ayahuasca vine's double-helix shape and cross-cultural appearances of two interlaced serpents, such as in the ancient Greek "staff of Hermes," a.k.a. the "caduceus" logo of modern Western bio-medicine. Likewise, in his exhaustive survey of ayahuasca in South America, Shanon (2002, 118) emphasizes that in both his own ayahuasca visions and those of his informants, "serpents are the most common animal and, in fact, the most common single content item reported." Notably, according to Monteiro da Silva's (2004) assessment of the doctrine's Afro-Brazilian roots, "the words *Daime* and *Juramidam* (the most important spiritual entity in Santo Daime) supposedly possess a secret meaning associated with the cult of Dá, the sacred serpent of the Fon" people from West Africa (Labate and Pacheco 2011, 74). Hints of such esoteric serpent knowledge within the Daime are suggested in a work of visual art called "Cross-Eyed Snake," created by the daimista scholar Clancy Cavnar (see cover image: Labate and Pacheco 2010). There does appear to be another noteworthy correspondence, whereby a common indigenous Amazonian notion that "the mother of aya-huasca is a snake" (Narby 1998, 34–35)—a "guide" or "teacher" also called the "Ayahuasca *mama*"—is somewhat akin to a feminine/maternal essence within the Daime sacrament, revered by fardados as "the *Rainha da Floresta* (Queen of the Forest) and the Holy Virgin (the two are often regarded as being the same persona)" (Shanon 2002, 115–116).

The relative paucity of snakes in Daime symbolism is also puzzling because of the significance of serpents in Judeo-Christian traditions. Out-standing examples include associations of the serpent with deceptiveness in the Garden of Eden (Genesis 3) and—recalling the ancient medicinal "rod of Asclepius"—Moses's placing of a bronze snake sculpture onto a staff or pole to miraculously cure Hebrews' envenomed snakebites while they wandered in the wilderness (Figure 9.1; Charlesworth 2010, 256; Num. 21:4–9; see Shanon 2008, 59–60). It is interesting to note the resemblance of the snake affixed to Moses's staff in the wilderness to the rosary draped over the cross on the central altar of Daime works—for example, perhaps the Marian Fatima figurine on the altar at an outdoor Daime work in Portugal (Figure 9.2) suggests the divine

Figure 9.1. *Le serpent d'airain* ["The brazen serpent"], engraving by: Gustave Doré (1878), published with permission from the Bibliothèque nationale de France (BnF).

feminine reconciling the snake of original sin via the snake/serpent of Mama Ayahuasca. One intriguing instance of a daimista explicitly discussing serpents as a sign of the eternal feminine is the "Oh Mother God" dream reported by Barnard (forthcoming), in which this fardado religious scholar recounts his

Figure 9.2. Marian Fatima figurine on the altar at an outdoor Daime work in Portugal (photo by the author).

vision of a "huge brass cauldron . . . filled with serpents" that represented for him "the Life Energy of the Daime." This can be compared to a story from Mestre Irineu's disciple Luíz Mendes do Nascimento (2005), who recounts in an interview biography of the Mestre that while contemporaneous rubber

210 / Christ Returns from the Jungle

tappers believed the "caboclos . . . who took this drink had a satanic pact," Mestre was still curious enough to join them for a ritual. During the Mestre's first ayahuasca ceremonies, instead of visions of serpentine Mama Ayahuasca, Mestre Irineu was bombarded with visions of Christian crosses—only later did he have his fateful encounter with Clara, aka the Queen of Forest. While much remains to be explored by future researchers, for now I feel confident in asserting that these stories gesture toward the need for a reassessment of habitual demonizations of snakes and the feminine within Christian theology.

The only one of my European interviewees to go into detailed speech about snakes was Antoon, an elder Dutch man who had already completed sixteen years of intense training in indigenous ayahuasca shamanism (he emphatically identifies as *not* a daimista). When I asked Antoon what he thinks ayahuasca can teach us about the nature of consciousness, he said:

> *I have a different* [perspective] *than the Santo Daime, so it may be interesting to understand this shamanic approach towards the plants. According to the indigenous people of the Northwestern Amazon (Columbia, Peru, Brazil, this is the area where* [Ayahuasca] *probably originates), for these people, life came from the stars. The first ancestors came on the back of a mythical Anaconda from the Pleiades* [star cluster], *and they landed on Earth. So Ayahuasca and Anaconda are one, it's the same. You know the Big Snake? The way the vine grows is like an anaconda. So drinking ayahuasca is connecting with the source of life, it's connecting with your ancestors.*

Although the topic of serpents was not an issue that surfaced during my fieldwork and interviews with daimistas, future research might examine interesting questions such as: How do daimistas reconcile the different spiritual meanings of snakes in indigenous shamanism and in the Bible? Do daimistas see any connections between the Garden of Eden serpent and European settlers' incursions into the Amazonian "garden" with disruptive intent/actions? Is perhaps the snake a metaphor for the tempting voice of the self-centered human ego more generally? If yes, does God intend for this egoic serpent to be destroyed, or should it be healed by mystical/sha-manic/alchemical integration? In other words, are the devious snake of Eden and the historically devious European colonists forever evil or can they be redeemed by a confrontation with the Amazonian serpent of ayahuasca? In relation to the snake's role in the original sin at Eden's "Tree of Knowledge" and Moses's curative snake sculpture on a pole, does Jesus's self-emptying (*kenosis*)[12] in the "garden" of Gethsemane and His sacrifice on a wooden cross perhaps represent what daimistas term Juramidam, a narrative archetype of salvation that can recur in the life of each human being? Is this at all related to Santo Daime's double-armed Caravaca cross, symbolizing that the ayahuasca sacrament is itself a way for Christ's Second Coming to be personified through the ritual suffering of daimista devotees? With the latter two questions I am thinking of William Blake's illustration of a scene from Milton's *Paradise Lost*, depicting the head of a dead snake affixed to the crucifix by the same nail that penetrates Christ's feet (see Figure 13.1). Further, if the *B. caapi* vine can be perceived as cosmic serpents intertwined like a caduceus, then the *bateção* action of pulverizing the vine with mallets in the feitio rite would seem to call to mind the hammering action of nailing Jesus to His cross. Is the ritual consumption of Daime perhaps like imbibing the wood of the cross, thereby collapsing the executioner's snake-ego and the humbling power of the ayahuasca snake into one mystical experience of death-rebirth? Similarly, is the fardadas' cleansing (*catação*) of the *P. viridis* leaves meant to evoke the end of the passion narrative (Luke 23:55–56, Luke 24:1–3), when Jesus's female followers were responsible for preparing spices to anoint the body of Christ for burial? I honestly do not yet know the answers to such questions. From what fardados told me, I get the impression that with the help of an indigenous medicine they seek to reenact these Alpha and Omega points of the Bible at every Daime work, a syncretic encounter of one culture's ayahuasca snake rectifying the original sin of the other culture. Considering the medicinal symbolism of the caduceus or rod of Asclepius alongside the "ophidian Christology" in depictions of St. John the Evangelist holding a snake-filled chalice,[13] we are faced with a blatant alchemical implication of serpents as healers, namely: the transmutation of poison into antidote via surrendering one's self-centered egotism to a divine Higher Power (Charlesworth 2010, ix/5/14/411–414/485/590n#214). Future theologians might advance fruitful studies of ayahuasca in light of what Princeton religious historian Elaine Pagels (1989, 31) says about an ancient Gnostic interpretation of the Genesis creation story,[14] which depicts "Eve as the spiritual principle in humanity who raises Adam from his merely material condition"—this text explicitly mentions that "the Female Spiritual Principle came in the Snake, the Instructor" and that "the arrogant Ruler cursed the Woman . . . [and] . . . the Snake" (see also Pagels 2011). I hope future scholars of Daime can illuminate us on this topic, perhaps by directly asking knowledgeable fardados to interpret the ideology of serpents within their religious doctrine. Then again, since serpents are sometimes interchangeable with dragons in Jewish and Christian iconography (Charlesworth 2010, 212/226; Henderson and Oakes 1990; Rev. 12:9), we will revisit the meaning of "dragon-snakes" near the end of this chapter.

Outside the Ritual Space: Supplementary Trends

Mention must also be made of some peripheral practices that are customary among many European fardados, but are by no means an official part of Santo Daime doctrine. These include the ingestion of both mundane and obscure natural substances loosely associated with the expansion of ayahuasca culture in Brazil, the acquiring of lustrous crystals, and spiritual books that some fardados deem as equivalent to Daime teachings.

For instance, most European fardados more or less lean toward an organic diet (known colloquially as *bio* in Europe). But this is not universal, as the meals I shared with fardados ranged from a totally vegan potluck feast to fast-food hamburgers. Although many daimistas opt for vegetarianism, others like to eat meat, such as those who served me delicious horse salami in Flanders and urged me to try local wild boar in the Walloon Ardennes. While fardados generally prefer to be responsible consumers—a value that accords with their belief that all actions are reciprocal—veteran Daime members staunchly disapprove of moral chastising. On one occasion after a work in Amsterdam, a novice daimista reproved me for bringing nonorganic raisins as a contribution. An elder fardado who overheard these judgmental remarks later approached me and expressed his disagreement with the novice's comments; this fardado said that there are no rules in Santo Daime about what one cannot eat/consume, but that he himself does seek out natural as opposed to processed foods, as well as foods that have been produced ethically. While many fardados around the world abstain from alcohol, viewing it as a destructive habit, a substantial number of European fardados enjoy alcoholic drinks, but always in moderation. A prominent Brazilian disciple of Mestre Irineu named Luís Mendez do Nascimento (2005) proclaims that Daime cured him of his own "vice" or "spiritual disease . . . [of] alcoholism," reporting that Mestre Irineu enjoyed alcohol responsibly in the early era of Santo Daime's history—however, apparently after a new decree from the Holy Queen of the Forest, Mestre began to formally scold daimistas who regularly drank alcohol to excess. In Belgium, a culture that cherishes its beer, the commander of the CdU church said that he still appreciates a bit of alcohol now and then, smiling as he affirmed to me that "it's in the blood."

During the intermissions of ritual works, some fardados use *rapé* (pronounced *hap-EH*, Portuguese for "snuff"), a powder made from tobacco and the burnt bark of trees such as "pau-pereira" (*Platycyamus regnellii*).[15] Rapé, the use of which was borrowed from South American indigenous groups, is administered on oneself or from one person to another via a jointed tube with one end inserted in the nostril and the other end in the mouth for blowing air through. The main purpose of this snuff is to provide a temporary calming effect that at the same time sharpens the mind's focus as one enters the Daime work. Some fardados also ingest rapé in their homes when they use it as a complement to silent meditation or as a sleep aid.

After the works of RaS and CCMI, the commanders of the ritual invite participants to take *kambô*, a secretion collected from the glands of the giant leaf frog (*Phyllomedusa bicolor*). These Brazilian-run Daime churches also offer separate kambô sessions open to all Belgian daimistas, but not all daimistas take kambô—in fact most members of CdU and CdAI seem to shy away from it. In sequence, each patient sits in a chair and allows the commander of either RaS or CCMI to burn seven tiny wounds into a biceps, leg, or sometimes other parts of the body with a small wooden ember. Then the fresh scars are removed with paper towel so as to directly introduce globules of the kambô paste. The onset of effects is almost immediate. Onlookers watch and assist as the kambô initiates vomit profusely into buckets and then rush to the nearby restroom to commence unstoppable diarrhea. Enthusiasts allege that kambô cleanses the body energetically and has fortifying properties (see Labate 2012b).[16] Because the ethnographic method of ethnophenomenology requires the researcher to go beyond passive surveillance toward direct engagement with informants' lived experiences, I underwent the kambô ordeal twice with RaS. Not only did the same outward bodily reactions occur, but both times I was temporarily seized by what seemed an almost unbearable physical discomfort. During the peak of the kambô, one feels as if on the verge of total collapse. After a few moments of this agony, the effects subside, leaving only a euphoric state of deep comfort tinged by a great sense of relief. This alternative medical practice needs further empirical studies to confirm or deny the anecdotal evidence of its safety and benefits. On isolated occasions daimistas offered me *sananga* eyedrops and a swig of tobacco juice, less common but increasingly popular options imported from Amazonian shamanic traditions (see Labate and Coutinho 2014, 192; Wilbert 1987). I tried each of these once, found both unpleasant, and decided to await the results of future biomedical studies before ever sampling sananga or tobacco juice again.

In their private lives at home, many European fardados are wont to use Bach Flower Remedies, consisting of little brown bottles that contain distilled liquid sourced from different flower species. The liquid is dropped and mixed into a glass of water, which is then quaffed down. These concentrates of particular flower species are believed to deliver a range of health and emotional benefits (Bach and Wheeler 1997). Unlike the scientific rationales of Western medicine, daimistas' confidence in the efficacy of these flower essence treatments are based in a conviction that rudimentary components of Nature can heal when correct knowledge is applied. Many fardados told me they are concerned about the implications of new EU regulations decreed in 2011 under the "Traditional Herbal Medicinal Products Directive"; while this law was meant to address the fact that "the use of herbal medicines in Europe is on the rise," it has upset communities who advocate and use folk remedies not recognized by the state (Dente 2011, 636). Daimistas are not just concerned about the prohibition of psychoactive entheogens, but they believe that nonpsychoactive folk remedies like those mentioned above are being banned because these threaten the profits of the pharmaceutical industry.

Placed throughout many fardados' homes are rock crystals of various colors, shapes, and sizes. These were also placed on the central table in some Daime works, particularly the more adaptational varieties of RaS and CCMI. At one work with CdAI, the commander presented a fardado with a large purple crystal as a birthday gift in a public presentation following the ritual. Upon being asked about the large collection of crystals placed throughout his Antwerpen apartment, a fardado who works as a Western-style physician said: "They contain the most sacred light that you can find on this earth." These crystals are a prototypical object of New Age devotion, and are sold in specialty shops throughout North America and Europe (Laqueur 1997, 36–37). Just as Christian, Afro-Brazilian, and indigenous elements were included in Mestre Irineu's original inventory, some New Age ideas are now being incorporated into the Daime doctrine along with Asian and Middle Eastern traditions.

Parallel to these trends in consumption habits, fardados' homes are regularly adorned with images and symbols from a variety of different religious backgrounds, usually accompanied by a large collection of books dealing with a host of spiritual topics. It would be beyond the scope of this analysis to account for all of the mystical avenues explored by individual fardados.[17] But although it is not directly associated with the Daime doctrine, one book that is especially cherished by many European fardados is a large volume called *A Course in Miracles* (Schucman 2007[1976]). The text of *A Course in Miracles* was transcribed by Helen Schucman, a professor of medical psychology at Columbia University, with the aid of her colleague William Thetford, who helped her to edit and ultimately publish the final volume. From 1965 to 1973, Schucman heard an "inner voice" dictate the Christian message of *A Course in Miracles* to her, and she wrote down these words even though she considered herself an atheist (Hanegraaff 1998, 30). The "combined volume" of *A Course in Miracles* consists of a main theoretical section that is meant to be read in tandem with a "workbook" section comprised of specific lessons to guide short stints of daily meditation. The book as a whole embodies a strong statement of panentheism, agreeing with Daime doctrine in its proclaiming that God is in everything and everything is in God. In offering existential advice, the Course also contends that the world perceived as outside is merely a "projection": "The world you see is what you gave it, nothing more than that. . . . Therefore seek not to change the world, but choose to change your mind about the world" (Schucman 2007[1976], 445). Its emphasis on a divinity located in the interior world of the conscious subject parallels the basic teachings of most mystical philosophies. The Course's text pinpoints the main hindrance to realizing inner and outer peace as the widely held egotistical belief in a division of internal self and external not-self. Fardados say that in Daime works they learn that everything in the outside world is intimately connected to their own self and vice versa. This realization inspires them to abide by the Christian "golden rule" ("Do unto others as you would have them do unto you") not as a moral axiom, but as following from the essential unity of self and other.

European daimista vernacular is clearly influenced by *A Course in Miracles*, which pathologizes "anxiety" and "despair" as ego "fantasies," since "preoccupations with problems set up to be incapable of *solution* are favourite *ego* devices for impeding learning progress" (Schucman 2007[1976], 67/170/177/341). Many daimistas consider *A Course in Miracles* a comprehensive blueprint detailing how the ego is the "great deceiver" (Schucman 2007[1976], 416), refuting the modern notion of disenchantment by equating the Nietzschean scheme with ego neuroses: "The ego is at war with God. . . . The death of God, if it were possible, would be your death" (Schucman 2007[1976], 486). Fardados' views about how Santo Daime effects the ego are expressed by Etienne's response when I asked why he participates in ayahuasca works:

To cure. Basically that's the main point: to cure myself from my ego, and to help people to cure themselves from their ego. By taking ayahuasca, to get so sensitive to myself, to get so sensitive to other persons, just to try to live together in harmony, just that. . . . [Western psychiatry] *made an entire system to cure the ego . . .* [but] *the problem is the ego makes himself a system to cure himself, so of course it doesn't work, because ego is tricky . . . So he made a structure to have this feeling to be okay, but it didn't work, because the ego himself is the problem. . . .*

For me, [Santo Daime is] *a complete way. . . . All spiritual ways have the same goal: to get out of the ego. . . .* [The ego is] *what makes living so difficult for everybody, so just to cure that. To make living just simple . . . happiness, that's about it. . . .* [Ayahuasca] *doesn't solve the problem, it shows you where the problem is. . . . So after, it's your decision to just look, and to change or not look and not change. But it will not do the work for you, it's just (for me) a very fast way if you decide to move fast. . . . It just depends on the intention. . . . You give a direction and then the ayahuasca just guides you to this intention. . . . The idea is not to get rid of the ego, the idea is to ask the ego to serve, and to show him that he has more interest by serving than by trying to keep the power.*

Contra Dawson (2013, 18/91), fardados are clear that the goal of curing the ego does not mean that one has to "annihilate" the ego.[18] Rather, as Frederik indicates, the goal is to realize how belief in one's individual separateness (i.e., ego) is merely a practical concern in daily life, while at deeper levels of reality all beings are united as a single divinity of "Higher Consciousness":

For me, my ego is a part of me that is not me [laughs]. *It's all kinds of things that help me to survive and to have a life here on earth. So it's very useful, there are very useful things in it, and I've learned a lot through it. And I also need my ego to put things into form, because without my ego I would be nothing of course. But it's my ego that has to serve my consciousness and not the other way around. . . . Getting the ego into a place where it is loyal to the Higher Consciousness, then it is really tamed. Because you can tame something, but it stays quite wild or vicious, and it just waits until it can get you in some way, that is not tamed. By tamed I mean it's loyal, it's faithful, and it knows that you will care for it, that it can make mistakes and it will be forgiven.*

Once the perils of identifying with one's egoic conditions are exposed through working with Santo Daime (or any other mystical practice), fardados believe that the ego can play a new role in the service of one's "true self" or "Higher Consciousness."

The reasons for the popularity of *A Course in Miracles* among European daimistas are exhibited in a discussion with two fardados who attend CdSM in Amsterdam; when asked what was the most important lesson she had learned from Daime, Charlotte, a fifty-two-year-old Belgian social worker who has been an active daimista since 2006, told me how both *A Course in Miracles* and Santo Daime help people to "dissolve/resolve" their ego:

> *ego loslaten* ["to release ego"]. . . . *If you're singing the hymns, all blocks within yourself are being opgelost* ["dissolved/resolved"] . . . *they cease to exist. . . . It's the thing that shows and lights all the blocks[19] you have, and all the things that keep you separated. . . . It shows the Christ awareness . . . and it helps you to let go of the ego. . . . In the end, Daime is just a liquid, and it's you that has to do it. . . . You can drink liters and liters of Daime, but if you're not working yourself, there's no point. It will probably not help you if your own intentions are lacking or missing or not there.*

Charlotte's Dutch boyfriend told me that *A Course in Miracles* can serve as a "key" to the ego:

> *For me it's such a key. . . . It really helps me connect what I experience in the Daime* [to] *my daily awareness. . . . So much is explained there about how the ego works, and how it confuses people instead of showing them something that's more true. And ego is just illusions creating more illusions and fears.*

All fardados I spoke with identify ego illusions as the main source of suffering and illness. This "ego" is the same sense of individual human actors as secluded from external forces that has been exalted in secular modernity, what Taylor (2007, 262/300) calls the "buffered" identity. In contrast to the buffered self, fardados are more likely to agree with *A Course in Miracles* that

218 / Christ Returns from the Jungle

suffering stems from "sleeping" human beings' identifying with their dualistic ego; my informants say people would be wise to "awaken" to the divine will that flows within and between all beings (see Schucman 2007[1976], 118–19/182). In short, fardados believe that inside each person is a divine quality shared in unison at the core of all existence. According to European fardados, *A Course in Miracles* is simply a more detailed verbalization of lessons they receive from introspective journeys embarked upon in Daime works. Fundamentally, in the modified states of consciousness available in Santo Daime, fardados seek to experience a meditative awareness of the observer observing itself, a beatific and curative revelation of the primordial source of being. They believe that it is from this unique vantage point, where observer and observed are witnessed as a single entity, that any and all ego conflicts can be resolved.

Confronting and Reforming Egoic Anxiety

My informants report a broad variety of examples for how their Daime experiences have "corrected" their habits and beliefs, both in terms of detrimental qualities of their individual character as well as what they see as destructive aspects of their cultural upbringing in Europe. In other words, Daime works are considered a means to "working" toward becoming an evermore-enlightened human being. Fardados from outside Brazil also receive hymns, either in Portuguese or in their native language. Frederik, the Flemish fardado from CdU, received an entire hymnal in English that touches on the concept of "ego," which does not typically show up in hymns from Brazil. For example, from Frederik's hymn #7 called "Pluto's Angel":

> *I'm the destroyer of old patterns*
> *I don't like the ego's tricks*
> *I'm not fond of mind creations*
> *That will make your true soul sick*

As is witnessed throughout the present study, the concept of ego, a mental construct of separation, is central to how fardados interpret the Daime experience. Universally, my informants claim that commitment to conceptual dualisms—i.e., self-other, body-mind, matter-consciousness, science-religion, Nature-God—causes psychological and physical conflict inside and between human selves. They concede that abstract dissections of reality can certainly be helpful in scientific endeavors. But they say that by ignoring social inter-dependence in favor of rugged individualism, Westerners have lost sight of the proverbial forest for the trees.

This common daimista outlook is exemplified by Karel, the fifty-year-old manager of a hotel in a downtown urban center in Belgium. Even though Karel has been participating in Daime since 1995, his wife does not attend these rituals at all. He portrayed the "ego" as a maladaptive selfishness that obstructs social and psychological harmony, a problem that he believes Daime can help solve:

> *The ego is the one you have to fight, of course. He is the one who says "This is my piece of ground". . . . If there would be no ego, definitely no wars. . . . All your conditionings are your ego because you want to hold onto them. No, it's just blocking you from your essence, from divine happiness and ultimate wisdom. . . . For me . . . [it is] the entheogen, the sacrament basically, which helps you to go into the layers of your subconscious so it becomes conscious. You have to unravel all your conditions that actually make you sick or make you worried or make you afraid or make you angry.*

Fardados view of "ego" as a conceited element of the human self that thinks it should be in charge of the universe is widespread in popular mysticism discourses (e.g., Bender 2010). This term has become so ubiquitous in the late modern spiritual zeitgeist that it shows up in a self-help book written by a Catholic priest (Rohr 2011, xxiv):

> The human ego prefers anything, just about anything, to falling or changing or dying. The ego is that part of you that loves the status quo, even when it is not working.

This present-day metaphysical trend resembles Kierkegaard's earlier analysis of existential "defiance" as the "despairing misuse of the eternal in the self to want in despair to be oneself"; daimistas cherish their ego-death experiences as chances to "leap *to* faith" (Ferreira 1998, 207), just as Kierkegaard (1989[1849], 98–99) operationalized despair as "the corridor to faith": "through the eternal the self has the courage to lose itself in order to win itself." By contrast, daimistas value humility (Portuguese: *humildade*) as a measuring stick of spiritual maturity. The prominence of humility as a central virtue of the Daime doctrine was very appealing to Jason, the young founder of the Greek daimista community. In paraphrasing a modest depiction of the Daime that he heard from a prominent Brazilian Padrinho, Jason said, "Here is a church without a church, preacher, temple. . . . It's a church that is within you: you are the pope, priest, sinner, sufferer, saviour and the saved and everything; no lies, no hiding." Jason claimed to know psychotherapists who say that two sessions with Daime are better than years of clinical treatment, where people hide from their counsellor, talking and talking but all the while keeping their defense mechanisms up to avoid directly facing their subconscious ego neuroses:[20]

> *The Daime is medicine for that split mind* [of egotism]. . . . *You can't hide from yourself when you're in the* [Daime] *work; things take place and that's your work. I can't explain it to you, no one can explain it to you. We all just help each other along. And that to me is extremely reassuring.*
>
> *When I meet Padrinhos and Madrinhas in Brazil who are working with this thing for years, they will turn around and say to you: "I have a lot to learn still; I'm working on this every day just like you are; so why don't you come help me, and I'll help you, we'll help each other," and there won't be any sense of identity that "this is my church, or this is my doctrine." It's just the work, it just happens, it just is. And that's very comforting.*

When I asked him why he attends Daime works, Jason remarked that it was my simplest question in the interview and yet the most difficult for him to answer:

> *I think it's probably in step with the common thread that you have heard from other fardados throughout Europe, and probably what you would hear throughout the world: The works give me, personally, a sense of peace with myself and with the world around me. They bring me a wonderfully fulfilling sense of community, of belonging to something that is greater or larger than yourself. The works provide a great opportunity to learn about humility, which is something that in my opinion is possibly the most lacking attribute in Western civilization; we've all been taught to believe that we know it all about everything all the time. And the works are a constant reminder that there are all sorts of things that we don't know yet, and that provides a forum to continue learning.*

> *I can quote lots of hymns that say exactly the same: how import-*
> *ant it is to be humble, and as much as you walk along this path,*
> *the brighter the star shines, the more light you will have. . . . You're*
> *continuing on a path that you're managing to improve yourself on*
> *some level. . . . I think that there are many corollaries between*
> *the lessons of Santo Daime and Buddhism: the path somehow is*
> *the goal . . . don't try to achieve some great fantastic shining thing*
> *at the end. The path should be the enjoyment, you should enjoy*
> *very much just working on yourself and working together with*
> *your brothers and sisters; and this is perhaps the greatest reason of*
> *all why I enjoy works and why I go to works: because I want to*
> *have that sense of unity with my fellow man, I want to feel like*
> *there are others around me who support me and help to provide*
> *that sense of community, which again I think is something that is*
> *terribly lacking* [in Western societies].

My informants tend to classify the Daime as akin to other mystical con-
frontations with one's inner domains. Long-term benefits of the introspective
struggle to overcome egotistical discord within oneself and between self and
others have been recognized since ancient times in Buddhist, Hindu, Islamic,
Jewish, Christian, and shamanic traditions (Grof 1998, 150–52; Kornfield
2000, 38–41). Santo Daime has spread throughout the world mainly because
its eclectic receptiveness to all forms of mystical practice makes it adaptive
to devotees from different social climates.

One of my key informants early in fieldwork was Waudru, a retired
music teacher who in 2011 was already a thirteen-year veteran of the Daime.
At age seventy, Waudru is famous in the European fardado community for her
skilled playing of the violin during ritual works. She now lives in the Brabant
countryside, where she is constructing a spiritual retreat center. But during
my fieldwork she lived with three generations of her family in a three-story
house in downtown Brussels. At this time she was helping her son and
daughter-in-law raise their three young children. For a week, I stayed with
her family in a guestroom at the house, helping cook, clean, shop, and take
care of her grandchildren. Waudru has long struggled with depression, and
at my last visit with her she was suffering from an acute bout of melancholy.
Like most daimistas, she sought the Daime as a therapeutic aid to help her
through what she views optimistically as a "process" of spiritual maturation.
Waudru preferred to view her current state of sadness as a temporary mystical
passage or "dark night of the soul," a topic we will return to in Part V.

Walking around her neighborhood with her, Waudru repeatedly pointed out the Catholic persona of St. Michael (*St. Michel* in French). Images of this patron saint of Brussels are installed throughout the city. Not only is the representation of the archangel battling a dragon or devil a prominent symbol of Belgium's capital, it is also a common element in Daime iconography (see Figure 9.3). It is thus illuminating to compare the daimista interpretation of St. Michael to the mainstream Christian view of snakes/dragons as evil. According to James Charlesworth's (2010, 210) fascinating book *The Good And Evil Serpent: How a Universal Symbol Became Christianized*: "A considerable amount of early Christian art depicts the serpent or dragon as the enemy defeated by Christ; sometimes the snake appears at the foot of the cross." In an effort to describe what Santo Daime practice can teach humans about subduing their ego, Waudru expressed her allegorical interpretation of St. Michael:

Figure 9.3. Statue of the archangel St. Michael, near Place Ste. Catherine, Brussels (photo by the author).

St. Michel and the Dragon, the two are us. It's the same person. . . . To accept all of you, the dark, to accept yourself even if you are jealous, even if you are lazy, if you have an ego, if you are judging, we are [all] *like that. Jesus says, "Love the other as you love yourself," and the first thing is to see how imperfect we are, to accept it, to love it, and to change if you don't like it.*

And the dragon is all that: all the monsters who are in us, all the comparisons. To think you are more or you are less, it makes the same confusion and the same disharmony. . . . St. Michel says to the dragon "I see you. I know that you are me," . . . because on the statue you see even the dragon has wings. So, "You are me and I am you, but there are things that I don't let come inside of me, it has to go back to the earth and the earth will heal it" . . . that is the Higher Self and the lower self. That's it exactly: The lower self is the dragon . . . you don't let that be the center of you. That is the way.

Through firsthand knowledge of mystical states of consciousness in Daime rituals, fardados learn to contact their divine "Higher Self," the aspect of consciousness they associate with St. Michael in the astral otherworld. Gradually, they say, they learn to supplant their egotistical "lower self" by choosing to allow the Higher Self to govern their daily decisions and actions. Here, they draw on the "alchemical" symbolism of St. Michael and his "earthly 'avatar' St. George" (*São Jorge*), where "to 'kill' the dragon is not to eliminate it but to tame it, to leash it, to order it, to use its power towards spiritual ends" (Wilson 1994, 52/56–63).

Daimistas' absorption with inner scuffles between a divine Higher Self and an egoic lower self fits with existentialist analyses of what it means to be a human being. For instance, Kierkegaard's (1980[1844], 155) Christian ontology apprehends human selves as composing a "synthesis" of animalistic and angelic forces, the clash of which culminates in anxiety:

If a human being were a beast or an angel, he could not be in anxiety. Because he is a synthesis he can be in anxiety; and the more profoundly he is in anxiety, the greater is the man—yet not in the sense usually understood, in which anxiety is about something external, about something outside a person, but in the sense that he himself produces the anxiety. Only in this sense can the words be understood when it is said of Christ that he was anxious unto death.

As previewed above, such conundrums align neatly with Heidegger's (1962 [1927], 290–99) "anxiety in the face of death," Tillich's (2014[1952], 128–42) "courage of despair," and Buber's (1996[1937], 144–47) anxious "stirring of the creature between the realms of plantlike security and spiritual risk." For daimistas and existentialist thinkers alike, only by unswervingly confronting this inbuilt anxiety about life and death can one positively reform oneself toward more enlightened states of being. For Kierkegaard (1990[1851], 76–77), as for daimistas, one "must die to the world and to oneself" before one can overcome such angst:

> A life-giving Spirit . . . is not a *direct* heightening of the natural life in a person in *immediate* continuation from and connection with it . . . no, it is a new life, literally a new life—because, mark this well, death goes in between, dying to, and a life on the other side of death—yes, that is a new life. . . .
>
> Therefore, death first; you must first die to every merely earthly hope, to every merely human confidence; you must die to your selfishness, or to the world, because it is only through your selfishness that the world has power over you; if you are dead to your selfishness, you are also dead to the world. But naturally there is nothing a human being hangs on to so firmly—indeed, with his whole self!—as to his selfishness!

Later on, I will analyze more fully the reverence for earning eternal life through faithful surrendering to death that European fardados share with mystical and existentialist theologians (see Parts V and VI). But prior to this, to demonstrate the heuristic conditions of ethnophenomenology I feel it is pertinent to first share a series of auto-ethnographic accounts from my fieldnotes. The final chapter of this section explores a sample of the kinds of nonordinary perceptions one can encounter within Santo Daime rituals.

10

Being-in-the-Astral

An Auto-Ethnography of Ethnophenomenology

Of course, as all fardados are aware—and I can attest to this after undergoing many dozens of Daime ceremonies—every work is different. Perhaps the best explanation would be to say that there are infinite varieties of ayahuasca experience. Even though one can never know exactly what to expect, there is a continuum whereby Daime works fall within a range between the following: intensely "beautiful" (full of Light, love, and pleasant feelings of harmony), severely "heavy" (feelings of nausea and confronting one's biggest fears, which daimistas consider as forms of *cura* ["healing"]), or disappointingly lackluster[1] (boring, an absence of feeling the brew's effects). Often combinations of these are experienced through the course of a single work. The heavy works can be quite challenging, and participants tend to vomit more during these rituals. Nevertheless, in all works fardados share a core intention of inner purification in search of mystical solutions to the ego. They then seek to enact the lessons of these solutions within their daily lives (see Sudhölter [2012, 53–54/58] for similar findings with Dutch daimistas).

While experimentation with dangerously addictive substances like heroin pushes personal and professional limits too far (e.g., Agar 2006, 172–74), I decided that ethnophenomenology with Santo Daime was feasible because a growing scientific consensus suggests that ritualized ayahuasca use is relatively safe and nonaddictive (see dos Santos 2013a; Fábregas et al. 2010; Gable 2007; Halpern et al. 2008). As documented thoroughly by Shanon (2002), ayahuasca is like other entheogens in that these substances have a variety of potential qualities largely dependent upon mind-set and environmental setting. Even though I have concentrated on the mystical aspects of the Daime experience, because these were the most important to my informants, in no way does this exhaust the myriad of strange and abnormal effects that ayahuasca has upon those who drink it. For instance, my research did not encounter the same keenness for spirit possession and mediumship that has been well documented with Daime groups in North and South America (Barnard forthcoming; Dawson 2013, 126–33). In establishing the ethnophenomenological breadth of *being-in-the-astral*[2] as presented to me by fardados in Europe, I include the following auto-ethnographic accounts to show how an agnostic ethnographer can still be swept away by the mind-body tumult of the ayahuasca experience.

The burden for any scholar who studies people engaging in entheogenic rituals is to authenticate his/her own perspective vis-à-vis that of the informants. Historically and today, social stigmas against the drugs under consideration here force a dilemma on academics who want to base interpretations upon the collection of all pertinent data. The extent to which the taboo status of entheogens impairs scientific rigor is indicated by Brian Anderson (2012, 55) in his exploration of ayahuasca's potential as a treatment for depression: "Although self-experimentation is often done in psychedelic research—to satisfy both the ethical goal of being able to empathize with one's research subjects and the technical goal of being able to validly interpret the resulting data—it is rarely mentioned in scientific publications for fear of the accusation of having lost one's objectivity." As opposed to the suspicion with which self-experimenting investigators are met in the medical sciences, most social scientists studying ayahuasca have operated on the conviction that they must be *participant*-observers if they are to produce accurate portrayals of entheogenic practices. The reasoning behind such unorthodox procedures is similar to the classic epistemological parable known as the "knowledge argument," which goes something like this: A scientific genius named Mary is trapped for her entire life in a totally black-and-white room. Through colorless television lectures and the printed word she has absorbed all of the knowledge about color that can be conveyed through these sources. Yet when she finally leaves the room to enter the outside world, she learns something new about the nature of color when her visual cortex is introduced to it for the first time. This thought experiment underlines the fact that besides the objective knowledge one can acquire from secondary reports, there is also a subjective kind of knowledge called "qualia, the properties that characterize what it's like" to actually undergo something (Alter 2007, 396). Therefore, a scholar who reads all of the literature on ayahuasca and interviews many informants without actually dipping into the brew themselves is a lot like Mary studying color before she leaves the black-and-white room: they are well-informed about objective data but they are totally ignorant about what it really feels like to experience their subject of study. This is why I resolved to supplement my more conventional ethnographic fieldwork and interviews with a pursuit of anthropological knowledge that can only be gathered through the methods of ethnophenomenology.

Ethnophenomenological approaches have produced a vast assortment of auto-ethnographic accounts, a corpus that is too big to review here in its entirety. Even a cursory glance at some of the major publications in this field reveals the hodgepodge of ayahuasca's effects, exhibiting the brew's enigmatic hallmark as producing all kinds of enjoyable, benign, and ghastly sensations. On the one hand, there are the tame observations of Schultes, who recognized the brew's ethno-botanical significance even though he claimed he "never got sick" with ayahuasca and only saw "colours, no visions" (Davis 1996, 155). On the other hand, there are Taussig's (1987) gut-wrenching recollections of vomiting amid visionary "montages" during "*yagé* nights" he spent with shamans in the rainforests of Columbia (see Beyer 2009, 213–214). There is also a spectrum of auto-ethnographic writings about Daime works, from Dawson's (2013, 54–56/196/206[n23]) more "detached" remarks about swelling hands, sensorimotor changes, and heightened emotions, to the full-blown magical realism found amid in-depth narratives by Barnard (forthcoming), Luke (2020), and Shanon (2002, 184; e.g., listening to a mosquito sing Mozart while it sat on the tip of his nose). In short, it would seem that anything can happen, or seem to happen, under the influence of ayahuasca! Due to mind-body outcomes running the gamut from gentle to stormy and from sweet to bitter, another prerequisite of scholarly self-experimentation with ayahuasca concerns the need for the researcher to undertake the experience repeatedly. Thus, it was only after his first time with ayahuasca that Wade Davis (1996, 194) could discern how his neophyte "confusion of random visual and auditory hallucinations without form or substance was only a crude approximation of something indescribably rich and mysterious." So we witness many different reactions, no doubt evoking the crucial import of mind-set in determining an individual's immediate and subsequent interpretations of ayahuasca experiences. In this chapter, I stand on the shoulders of these ethnophenomenological precursors by disclosing what it was like to be a temporary guest inside the Santo Daime subculture of Europe.

As an ethnographer trying to understand why fardados choose to drink ayahuasca, it was apparent that the most accurate means for tackling my main research question was to take part in the rituals as informants do. Through participating in more than a year of Daime works across Europe, I grappled firsthand with the vigorous and multifarious alterations of body-mind perception that are engendered by ayahuasca. Plunging myself directly into the Daime, my own sensations and thoughts under the brew's influence became raw material for soliciting informants' advice about how they navigate their Daime voyages. Yet executing this seemingly straight-forward method of ethnophenomenology is not easy. By participating in the full annual calendar of Santo Daime during my fieldwork, I subjected myself to a broad array of ayahuasca happenings, from the reassuring to the terrifying, from the blissful to the nauseating, from the mundane to the uncanny. For critics who might charge that drinking ayahuasca somehow discredits my objectivity as an anthropologist, I would challenge them to justify how one would otherwise assess social settings within which the brew is ingested. As daimistas regularly attest, one cannot appreciate the subjective effects of ayahuasca if one does not personally undergo the intellectual and emotional demands imposed by the brew (see Schmidt 2007, 22/27). I venture that such direct immersion into Daime works is a prerequisite for formulating etic questions in such a way that they make emic sense to fardado interviewees, such that researchers can prompt informants to speak about esoteric concepts in a clear way. It is equally impossible to otherwise do interpretive justice to the diversity of joys and difficulties that can transpire within a single Daime work. Daimistas acknowledge that Daime ceremonies can range in intensity from mild to strong, opposite extremes that they describe respectively as "light works" and "heavy works." In order to provide a representative taste of the panoply of experiences generated by Daime rituals, what follows are some ethnophenomenological synopses based on selections from my fieldnotes.

For me, the ayahuasca frame of consciousness is like nothing I have ever experienced in my normal waking state. Here are some general trends I noticed over the years since my first Daime experience in 2005. I have a difficult time drinking the ayahuasca brew because of the intense flavor, and so for particularly bitter batches I have to pinch my nose to swallow the allotted portion in multiple gulps—like some daimistas, I took to keeping Tic Tacs[3] in my pocket to help with the aftertaste. A common trait is an uneasy excitement that gathers across the group after each participant has consumed the brew and there is a realization that the ritual has passed beyond the point of no return. But the more one rehearses this performance, the more this nervousness about not knowing what one is in for is tinged with a certain assurance that come what may, the rituals usually end with emancipatory gladness. Approximately one hour after ingesting the ayahuasca, the activation of odd psychophysical effects can arrive as anything from a trickle to a flood. Sometimes it is a flushing of the body while in other moments it can be a mental sensation of rushing thoughts or exaggerated emotions. One can become acutely aware of one's bloodstream, stomach contents, or what feels like immaterial fluids coursing through a maze of arteries, veins, and entrails. There can be spells of synaesthesia, the blending or swapping of senses, such as when one can feel sounds or hear sights. One may also sometimes hear, smell, or taste things more intensely (e.g., thuds, flowers, or incense), and one can even come across sounds, scents, and flavors that do not seem to have a physical source. But apart from the more eccentric incidents reviewed below, the most obvious alterations that take place in a Daime work are associated with one's visual faculties.

A general quality I detect when under the influence of ayahuasca is that everything I observe appears to be imbued with some sort of intersubjective sentience. Even when the work is held in a setting one has never visited, the Daime can foster a sense of eerie familiarity with one's own self and the external surroundings. Many daimista informants aptly portrayed this tender feeling as "like coming home." When the "force" of the ayahuasca takes hold, my entire perceptual field changes from one dominated by alterity (Buber's I-It) to an inscrutable sense of dialogue (Buber's I-Thou). Any stimulus can take on a special significance that is subjectively meaningful. Sometimes this can be an uplifting encounter, as features that had been mundane beforehand suddenly take on a fascinating tenor, such as when cloud formations, woodgrains, or chipped paint manifest as strikingly gorgeous images and forms. Portraits, photographs, or other static pictures can stand still even while at the same time they gyrate and breathe with alluring splendor. Vegetation appears to hum a buzzing sound as the same plants glow with a hue that somehow looks green and purple simultaneously. Birds, insects, or any other organism that enters the ritual space seem to know why they are there; one's observation of these animals is met automatically by the anthropomorphic suspicion that they are transmitting extrasensory communications. In this impressionable state one could swear that the coinciding of sudden fluctuations in sunlight or the wind with certain hymn lyrics or meditative insights are expressions of pathetic fallacy; in other words, it is almost as if the environment is purposefully interacting with the human observer by shifting in concert with existential dynamics of the Daime work. Other times, one's body and the ambiance of the salão strike a tone of hostility. In such urgent situations, one's inner sense of self feels alienated by inhospitable surroundings and perhaps ensnared in woeful suffering. In both their pleasant and unpleasant forms, these unusual displays become especially pronounced when one meets another human being who may or may not also be on ayahuasca.

Depending upon one's outlook at the time, other individuals can appear menacing, angelic, or anything in between. In my own Daime career, any effort to remind myself that my faculties were not functioning normally did not hamper my amazement at how differently people look during Daime festivities. Although they are not the type of thoughts that one would have in normal circumstances, very compelling interpretive projections can surface in the ayahuasca-infused mind before one has had time to rationally discredit them. Once, I fretted during an entire work because I unwittingly took the mannerisms of a daimista dancing in front of me to be those of a malicious demon hell-bent on my destruction. On a few occasions I could not shake the suspicion that I was in the midst of ghosts temporarily visiting the world of the living. But by far the most common sight is that of daimistas' faces and white uniforms shining radiantly, as if they had accomplished some sort of sublime transfiguration.[4] These ways that one's imagination can get carried away are why direct eye contact and informal communication between people is minimized during the Daime rituals; participants are urged to focus on their own personal journey until social mingling resumes at the intermission or aftermath of the work.

Such classically "hallucinogenic" yields of the ayahuasca-tinged psyche are paralleled by physiological strains inflicted by the brew, usually resulting in the irrepressible discharge of vomit, sweat, tears, or, much more rarely, diarrhea. In the context of their rituals, daimistas refer to such corporal releases as the "purging" of pent-up thoughts, memories, and emotions. Individual daimistas differ widely in personal reports about the frequency and kind of their purging. It is not unusual to hear someone weeping mournfully during the meditative part of a Daime work. I have shed tears a few times when I was touched by loveliness or sadness during the rituals, and I did once soil my white pants soon after the end of a Daime work. One informant who tends to purge in the former way told me that "crying is like a balm for the soul." With regard to vomiting, one Belgian fardado said he believes you can look into the bucket of puke like an oracle to see what "dark" sides of yourself have just been expelled. In the main, my informants certify that the vomiting lessens over time as long as one does not relapse back into the very vices that the purging is meant to expunge. They are prone to cite Pd. Sebastião's warning to his followers: "Do not be as dogs"⁵ (see Polari de Alverga 1999, 127/180). In elaborating on the importance of this lesson, a young Brazilian fardado visiting Dutch Daime churches opined about such common mistakes during an interview in his Amsterdam hostel:

> *Hopefully he won't do like the dogs do: puke out everything that they just ate that was not good for them and go eat it up again. . . . They go* [to the work], *they learn, "Thank you God!" . . .* [and] *two weeks later they forget everything they learned, go use the drugs again, go to the bar, do everything wrong again, and then they ask, "Why don't things go right for me? Why am I puking every time in the work?" No, the Daime keeps cleaning you out, and you go and you get that crap that the Daime helped you push out, you get that crap off the floor, you scrape it up, and you put it back in your mouth and you swallow it back again. You're doing everything you used to do before you went to the Daime.* [If] *you don't change your life, the Daime doesn't change you.* [If] *you change your life with the Daime, the Daime changes you a lot!*

And yet the need to vomit can reappear for anyone at any time. I am told this is because either the person has been contaminated by bad energies during their life outside the ritual or sometimes nausea can pass from a neophyte to a veteran daimista who must then vomit by proxy. I can recall vomiting within or immediately after an ayahuasca ritual on at least seven separate occasions thus far, always a humbling affair that feels both disgusting and liberating at the same time. I have experienced what the fardado describes above, where I could feel that what I was vomiting up was a lesson from earlier Daime works that I had failed to put into practice in my daily life. I do recall these upchucking events as involving fractal visions of kaleidoscopic "spirals and vortices" (see Mikosz 2009). Outside of a handful of works that I left with aftereffects of nausea persisting until the next day, more often than not I feel positively refreshed after a Daime ritual. The deliverance one relishes at the conclusion of a Daime work is often tied to the subsiding of extremes faced during the ritual, the taxing volatility of entheogenic excursions that Huxley (1990[1956]) famously compared to "heaven and hell." Although brief—so as not to digress too far—I will now relate a few auto-ethnographic anecdotes to lay bare how my agnostic mind-set handled its immersion into the sacramental rites of Santo Daime. I begin by describing some of the more laborious episodes before moving on to examples of ways Daime can also elicit bizarre and pleasurable effects.

One particularly agonizing Daime experience occurred when I was late in leaving my apartment for a work in Amsterdam and so I hurried to pack my bags and catch the train. As I arrived at the Central Station in Brussels, a thought flew into my mind that there was the possibility I had left the coffee maker in my kitchen turned on but empty. Recalling that I had double-checked my apartment before I left, I now remembered that when I looked at the coffee maker's plug, I had decided to leave it plugged in. In keeping with the anxious disposition I inherited from my father and paternal grandmother, on the train ride to the Netherlands I began to cultivate a worry about the coffee maker. By the time I arrived at the Amsterdam church and the Daime work began, this worry had developed into a near certainty that I had burned down the apartment building and had perhaps killed my neighbors in the process! Throughout the ritual's first half I endured mental images of firefighters failing to rescue the people victimized by my negligence. I also envisioned the prospect that I would be charged with manslaughter and nervously imagined being confined to a jail cell. The vision of the burning building expanded into a multisensory embodiment of conflagration, such that it felt as if I was engulfed in emotional flames. Through correspondence between my fear and my subjective sensations, I gained a stark appreciation for why daimistas label such ordeals as a "heavy *cura* [healing]." Indeed, it was by consciously working through this specific worry that I began to feel as if my tendency to fret about things beyond my control was being forcibly dissipated. Yet in the face of such distress, my inclination to lament this predicament only increased my misery. Finally, during the mid-work break I phoned my neighbors, who confirmed everything was okay with our building. Even though the work ended with relief (as most Daime rituals do), the dreadful terror I had passed through was a tutorial about how entheogens can be conditioned by one's preexisting mind-set. When I later asked fardados what they do when they come upon a heavy ayahuasca work, they uniformly suggested that "surrendering" or "relaxing" into all unavoidable suffering helps them cultivate patient forbearance or *firmeza* both inside and outside the rituals.

I later had a chance to implement this advice in a protracted dancing work in Germany where the entire hinario of Pd. Alfredo was performed over twelve hours. After the first fifty hymns or so I began to fatigue with the constant singing and marching back and forth, and it evolved into one of the toughest ayahuasca works of my ethnographic career. It was as if gravity's pull on my body was amplifying and I realized why informants use the word *heavy* to describe the great mental and corporal torment that can be brought on by the Daime. At one point, the horrid weight of my limbs was joined by an acute nausea in my abdomen. I went to vomit into a nearby bucket but nothing came out except a couple of fierce dry heaves. Even though participants who are struggling have the option of sitting or lying down at the outskirts of the ritual space, I was determined to show my daimista hosts that I was strong enough to persevere. So I promptly returned to my assigned dancing place, where the anguish resumed. In line with texts I was then reading about the Buddhist Four Noble Truths, a vivid impression of suffering (*dukkha*) emerged whereby my sense of self became wrapped in what appeared to be shiny green and red leather. The more I resisted this vision the more tightly the taut leather entombed me, pushing me to the point where I just gave up and accepted that escape was futile. At the time, it seemed like I would be trapped in this hellishness forever. Fortunately, having survived dozens of other long drawn-out Daime rituals, I tried to trust that this too would eventually pass. When the work did at last come to a close I collapsed onto the floor in utter exhaustion. In speaking with the German Daime leader the following day, Hermann declared that while it is good to have firmness in bearing discomforts that arise in Daime, if we need to vomit or take a rest it is usually best to heed that craving. He said this is how Daime highlights the balance required in everyday life, in that even as we strive for the ideal of staying in our place for the entire work, we should never be ashamed of our limitations. He contends that this experience teaches one to intuitively discern when it is appropriate to stand firm or humbly surrender.

As I had wrestled with different degrees of psychophysical heaviness numerous times in the Daime works, I inquired about how to better handle such phenomena with Cécile, commander of the CdAI church. She recommended that one can "just call the Light" in any difficult situation inside or outside of a Daime work. Like the word *dai-me* means "give me" in Portuguese, she characterized this as a visualization technique of surrender and supplication to the "Holy Light." I had an opportunity to test this suggestion in the later stages of a Daime work in Belgium, when I was suddenly struck by all-encompassing pain. Without warning, a severe hurt invaded my consciousness and all the cells in my body. At the time, this

interruption seemed to represent to me a condition of chaotic dismember-
ment. This pain increased steadily until it aggrieved me to the point that
I almost emitted a loud scream. Staying silent so as not to disturb others,
I just squirmed in my chair for a while as I tried vainly to find some
modicum of solace. As it got to be too much to bear, I remembered what
Cécile told me about "calling the Light"; so, downright forlorn, that is what
I did and about thirty seconds after I began to concentrate on the goal of
inviting a hypothetical luminescence, the heavy energy departed as quickly
as it had arrived. I sighed and was left feeling tired but thankful that the
oppressive pain had lifted. Thank goodness this is the only time that I have
ever experienced physical pain in an ayahuasca work. I never heard any
informant talk about having such pains (nausea, fatigue, and dread are the
more common symptoms of "heavy" works). This goes to show that even
though ayahuasca can function in unexpected ways, daimistas learn to apply
certain meditative strategies to deal with the many challenges that arise in
Daime rituals and in daily life.

From the stories above, the reader may detect why Daime rituals are
called "works." Unlike the recreational or hedonistic use of "psychedelics"
with which mainstream Western society is more familiar, fardados approach
the ceremonial consumption of ayahuasca as an opportunity to "work" on
boosting their faith in the face of adversity. Virtually all the Daime rituals
I have attended involved some element of hardship (e.g., boredom, angst,
doubt, queasiness, resentment, sadness) that by the end of the work predictably gives way to feelings of immense rejuvenation. To illustrate how
Daime works are not only about coping with afflictions, I now turn to
recount a sample of other perceptual upshots that can attend the intake of
entheogens like ayahuasca.

The weirdest phenomenon I have ever witnessed took place when
I visited with the more unregulated RaS group as it hosted an outdoor
Daime work on a wooded property south of Brussels. I have no idea why,
but most of the time when I partake in Daime rituals held "in Nature"
I have a "light work" in which I feel almost no effects of the ayahuasca.
At first, this particular work was no different, as even after we had taken
a second dose of Daime I felt no changes in perception. However, at one
point an odd noise drew the group's attention to a patch of forest about
twenty meters from where we were sitting. The singing of hymns halted and
when I looked over I beheld two blond tufts of hair peeking out above the
underbrush. They looked like the heads of small children bobbing up and
down amidst the sounds of juvenile giggling. As I stared bewilderedly, trying

but failing to ascertain what I was beholding, some of the other people in the ritual began to laugh out loud as they pointed in the direction of the little visitors. The blond heads snickered again, in turn setting off another round of laughter amongst the daimistas. This back-and-forth laughter lasted for about a minute until the blond tufts scurried out of sight. At this point the energetic force of the Daime sacrament came to the fore and I struggled to maintain my composure. I saw that another man who was having trouble was allowed to wander by himself into the adjoining forest (unlike the other groups in Belgium, RaS did not employ fiscal guardians to prevent such an act). Returning at the close of the work, this man then vomited profusely in the middle of the ritual space. When I met this man after the post-work feast he was covered in a bluish-white dust, which I supposed was tree pollen. In the customary fashion we hugged to congratulate each other on a "good work," at which point I noticed a cloud of his accumulated dust puff out into the air around us. Upon coming out of the hug I was surprised to find that a soft blue haze now dominated my entire field of vision! Disoriented by this sudden optical adjustment, I was stunned to find myself transported into what in that moment looked to me to be a life-sized Smurf village. Akin to the *Schtroumpfs* comic strip about little blue gnomes created by the Brussels artist Peyo, I observed what seemed like a downtown of mushroom buildings, some of which had blue corporate logos mounted over their doors. Astonished, I then watched what my mind interpreted as Smurfette driving by us in a blue Mini Cooper automobile! As a resolute agnostic, I was dumbfounded by what I was seeing. Looking back, now I can detect how my vulnerable state of consciousness may well have been projecting residual memories of my childhood—I was an avid viewer of the Smurfs television show and I had even dressed as a Smurf for my first Halloween.

When I asked a fardada interviewee what she thought about my Daime-induced "meeting" with chortling sprites and blue gnomes, she referred to the mythic trope of "going through a door" by which humans now and again access otherworldly planes of existence (see "crack between the worlds" in Castaneda 2016[1968], 149–152). She intimated her belief that entheogens such as Daime open a portal to "side worlds," positioned horizontally to complement the vertical worlds of Heaven and Hell. She talked about the stereotypical image of gnomes with a laughing face as evidence that some humans have contacted a species of creatures with this same identifiable feature. With regard to the scene above of a group of Daime participants seeing giggling blond heads, I can fathom two possible explanations to counter daimistas' interpretation of this as the revelation of a spiritual domain: either I was part of a collective hallucination or perhaps what we saw were some local youngsters who had stumbled upon the ritual. But in terms of my ethnophenomenological focus, I am less concerned with labeling what I saw as either real or hallucinatory than I am with the very fact that ayahuasca causes people to have dreamlike meetings with what appear to be supernatural beings. Regardless of whatever theories might be advanced by disenchanted skeptics, many daimistas are certain that tales about dwarfs, fairies, elves, extraterrestrials, angels, and the like are rooted in true encounters with humanoid entities (see Davis et al. 2020). This belief is similar to Middle Eastern folklore about *djinn* or jinn beings, which are "ontologically intermediate, somewhat like the Greek *daimonia* and the Judeo-Christian angels and devils" (Jones et al. 2005, 2279–80). During my subsequent research with daimista mediums in North America, these informants drew my attention to the meaning of the six-pointed star in Daime symbology, identifying it as the "Star of Solomon" (see Cemin 2010, 45). Mixing occult legends with stories from Islamic scripture, Daimista mediums suggested to me that Solomon's Star evokes the talismanic powers of the biblical King Solomon. Indeed, the Qur'an reports that Solomon enslaved many jinn into forced labor "bound together in chains" (Qur'an, Surah 34: 12–14, 38: 34–38), some say with the help of a bestarred signet ring. Conversely, Daime mediums work with an opposite intention of liberating rather than enslaving "suffering spirits" that often arrive with arms bound behind their backs into the Daime ritual space, seeing this as a cosmic emancipation of spirits trapped in an otherworldly karmic prison. Personally, I remain unconvinced that all myths reflect authentic yet concealed alternate universes—and yet I cannot disprove this theory either. Still, I can now sympathize with why spiritual seekers are drawn to the Daime as a path to bolstering their enchanted take on the nature of reality. Despite my reticence to share fardados' conviction that the Daime actually unveils otherworlds populated by spirits, an ethnophenomenological outlook enables the ethnographer to explore beyond the confines of presupposition. Such receptive immersion forges empathy with informants' ritual practices, an approach that then calls attention to anthropological questions that might otherwise be neglected.

Though open-eyed sensual modifications also transpired when I attended the more traditional Daime works, they tended to be less dramatic (e.g., visual irregularities or hypersensitive tactility/smell/sound). My informants also encouraged me to take part in periods of closed-eyed, silent introspection—or "concentration"—which happen between the singing and dancing phases wherein it is difficult to focus on anything but keeping up with the music. Once, in one of these meditative interludes during a large Amsterdam work, I had a deeply comforting *miração* of a big egg-shaped aura surrounding my body. In my mind's eye this ethereal cocoon looked like an oil painting swirling around me in black and white, then multicolored waves. After a few minutes my attention drifted toward my stomach area, where I discovered what I envisaged as a large cast-iron pot sitting on top of a fire. At times, it felt like an invisible hand would come by to stir the pot and tend to the fire underneath. It was apparent to me that I should ideally keep the heat and cooking at a moderate level; not too low, so that the pot continues to cook, and not too high, so as to avoid overflow of the contents. The inside of the pot was never shown to me, but I felt as if this "vision" was a metaphor for my emotional equilibrium. I had an inkling that whenever the liquid in this cauldron reached a rolling boil, this symbolized my impatient temper getting the better of me. On the other hand, if the blaze were to cool off too much this would indicate a depletion of my passionate drive to put forth effort and achieve goals. Whether one calls it a hallucination or a *miração*, this cooking pot and fire in my belly really seemed as if I was peering into aspects of my being that are normally beyond my cognitive reach. Again, disagreements about the ontological labels used to designate such visions as real or unreal are less interesting than the lasting result of satisfaction that I had grasped new self-knowledge about how to maintain my existential stability.

On many other occasions within these works I gained a tangible awareness of what informants mean when they talk about a *união* ("union") of one's own mind-body with other people and the rest of the universe. Usually, the onset of this ecstatic sensation was enhanced when I contributed to the collective singing of the hymns. Even though I had read about Durkheim's concept of collective effervescence (1915), this theory of transpersonal transcendence became a concrete actuality whenever the atmosphere of união arrived in the Daime sessions. Although I could still see my skin as a barrier between my inside and outside, I was overwhelmed by an intuitive notion that this routine dualism between self and not-self had been subverted by a more fundamental oneness. The spectacle of my own individual identity having melted away into an almost total fusion with my social and physical environment was routinely accompanied by a deeply pleasurable mood. There was the undeniable presence of a pulsating orb of pure light that enveloped both my body and my inner consciousness. When

I asked fardados about this, informants consistently connected what they refer to as the "Holy Light" with a spiritual "illumination" or "enlightenment" that occurs when one accesses divine realms. For example, my key informant Felix metaphorically rendered the ego of the thinking mind as like a fog. He said that when one enters a state of ritual meditation, the fog separating an individual being from the cosmic whole tends to lift, allowing the light of heaven to shine through. As Part V discusses in greater detail, the Daime doctrine emulates other mystical systems in deeming exchanges with the "Holy Light" as an epitome of spiritual success.

Then there is the inflammatory topic of spirit possession, channelling, or "incorporation" that is prized in some branches of Santo Daime (see Dawson 2013, 128–31). Even while most European daimista lines tend to muffle mediumistic practices, there have been many times that it has felt as if a nonphysical being was knocking on the doors of my selfhood during a ritual. At the time, I actively resisted the idea of allowing incorporation to occur because I have no interest in inviting or even playact inviting foreign entities to occupy my body. Yet even without trying I once "met" each of my deceased Grandfathers through ayahuasca. Although I never knew my maternal grandfather Gordon Hamill (a Presbyterian minister who died when my mom was ten), once during a Daime ritual I had the eerie yet comforting sense that his ghostly presence was hovering just over my right shoulder. My paternal Papa Bill Blainey Sr. died while I was doing fieldwork in Europe, so I could not attend his funeral back in Canada. In the course of an ensuing Daime work in Belgium, it felt like my Papa arrived in such a way that he first was beside me and as I recognized him he proceeded to move *into* me, until it suddenly felt like he was looking out through my eyes. I had long experienced a friction or clash of personalities with my Papa, a moneyed lawyer who approved of my academic success but never seemed to value my chosen field of study. Yet as "he" observed the Daime work via my visual faculties, "he" and "I" seemed to relax into a mutual empathy, forgiveness, and acceptance regarding each other. The sensation of his persona mingling with my own Dasein lasted until I ate a Destrooper butter crisp biscuit at the end of the work (delicious!). Then the cookie started to make me nauseous and when I spit out the bolus it appeared as if my Papa left with it and had by this means left my body! Some of my informants would interpret these as real-life encounters with my dead grandfathers, while others would perhaps say it is a symbolic confrontation with my own memories and neuroses—perhaps guilt about missing Papa's funeral? When I told the story about incorporating my departed grandfather to Seamus, a pro-mediumship fardado in Ireland, he responded by characterizing Daime mediumship as a charity for disincarnated spirits:

> *Yeah, your grandfather is a real person, and he still exists. He's real, and it's the same with every single one of us. We're real! Yeah, we have this body now, but when we lose our bodies we don't have our body, so everyone thinks we've disappeared but we haven't. We're still there! And the earthbound spirits are the ones who have never done anything during their lives, they don't know where they are, and they're lost then. The spiritual works then gives them an opportunity to move to the Light, to move to the next incarnation, or to the subtle realms, you know? As Jesus says, "My [Father's] house has many mansions." So the divine reality is very very vast, [whereas] we're very limited here. Earth's a kind of a training school, that's the way I see it anyway. The Daime is the training school in the training school [laughs].*

As an awestruck agnostic, I am enthralled that this *imaginal* experience happened to me, but I remain uncertain about whether it really was the spirit of my dead grandfather or just a remedial yet hallucinatory psychodrama (see Kripal 2014, 251–53). Either way, as an existential anthropologist I appreciate the profoundly personal benefits of this anomalous event, whereby I "felt" I had made peace with the conflict between my Papa and myself—notably, this alleviation of my grief did not depend upon my belief that the trance actually involved my real grandfather. It is remarkable that the agnostic perspective of ethnophenomenological receptiveness allowed me to gain some therapeutic benefit from being open to experiences during the ritual, rather than erecting skeptical barriers that actively repress and deny the qualities of such modified awareness.

Thus concludes my auto-ethnographic sketch of ethnophenomenology with Santo Daime in Europe. Certainly, the daimista perspectives reviewed in previous chapters challenge us to reflect more dispassionately about both enchanted and disenchanted approaches to metaphysical topics, such as the natures of consciousness and reality. Moving forward to the final sections of this book, the analysis now turns to the emic and etic takeaways of Santo Daime for religious believers, scholars of religion, and policymakers. The anthropological essence of worldviews that fardados share in common was encapsulated in my interview with Werner, the Belgian fardado who found his way into Daime through meditative yoga practice:

In the work of the Santo Daime, spirit is one. There are many teachers, like Jesus [and] Buddha, but above them it's one Light. And they are just the transmitters of that Light. . . . When you see all the teachers before you, and that they are all together in that same Light, it's difficult to talk about it because it's a feeling that . . . we are all that Light. You too!

We have a [mind-set] that separates everything: that is low, that is high, that is better, that is [worse]. . . . But everything is God; that's how a realized master looks at things.

To fully appreciate daimistas' search for effective antidotes to existential suffering, it is necessary to move beyond the "rational" thinking of philosophy (e.g., Buber 1996[1937], 176–77) to the transcendent realms of introspective contemplation explored by mystical theologians. In shifting to dig deeper into what fardados look to get out of ayahuasca experiences, the next chapters elaborate on their understanding of Daime rituals as a mystical technology. With their shared intention of experiencing and nurturing a feeling of harmonious nonduality, it is evident that fardados value mystical reformations of selfhood. Ethnophenomenological observations and cognitive domain analyses reveal ways informants envision Daime rituals as a "key" that unlocks "solutions" to existential pains felt inside all human selves.

PART V

THE MYSTICAL TECHNOLOGY
OF SANTO DAIME RITUALS

Figure 11.1. *Celestial Rose: Dante and Beatrice gaze upon the highest Heaven* (The Empyrean), engraving by Gustave Doré (1869), Canto XXXI, *Paradise, Divine Comedy* by Dante Alighieri (1265–1321). Published with permission from the Bibliothèque nationale de France (BnF).

Behold, the Kingdom of God is within you.

—Jesus Christ (Luke 17:21)

For it is quite certain that, when we empty ourselves of all that is creature and rid ourselves of it for the love of God, that same Lord will fill our souls with Himself. . . . The words of Jesus Christ our King and Lord cannot fail; but because we ourselves fail by not preparing ourselves and departing from all that can shut out this light, we do not see ourselves in this mirror into which we are gazing and in which our image is engraved.

—St. Teresa of Avila, *Interior Castle*

11

A Key to Solutions

The entheogenic beliefs and practices of Santo Daime detailed in previous chapters are presumed to be dangerous in mainstream Western cultures. However, the theoretical vantage of an ethnology of metaphysics (i.e., *ethnometaphysics*) can help demystify such cross-cultural clashes by underscoring how and why human groups encourage individuals to assume assenting, dissenting, or neutral attitudinal stances regarding particular claims about the nature of reality. The ethnometaphysical scheme of anthropologist Charles Laughlin (1997) categorizes as *polyphasic* those cultures that treat different states of consciousness as sources of distinct cognitive abilities and benefits. It is clear from testimonies presented herein that fardados hold a polyphasic view regarding the Daime's mind-altering effects. Distrust of entheogens is linked with the *monophasic* cultural category, which captures the modern Western propensity for restricting knowledge claims to information gleaned in the normal waking state of consciousness (Laughlin 1997, 479). Like conflicts between religions and secularisms, polyphasic postures strike the monophasic worldview as illogical, and the monophasic position appears blinkered to a polyphasic worldview (Blainey 2010, 2016b; T. Roberts 2006, 105; Walsh and Grob 2005, 1).

Anthropologists researching entheogen-users are charged with earnestly considering informants' polyphasic avowal that these substances are safe and advantageous when used in ritual contexts. The ethnographer thus establishes him/herself at the intersection of an inter- and intracultural disagreement: mainstream edicts in the West outlaw substances that non-Western cultures have long used as medicinal sacraments. This is a crucial matter for fardados, whose religious use of ayahuasca is imperiled because of widespread "cultural conditioning" that has "pre-categorized" entheogens as "irrational" and "irresponsible" (see Hanegraaff 2014, 395).

The term *entheogen* invokes contexts where people use substances like ayahuasca not for just a casual "trip," but rather with the intent of getting in touch with their innermost memories, emotions, and beliefs. Many cultures throughout history and across the world have treated entheogens as holy sacraments (see Schultes et al. 2001). Examples of these practices range from the entheogenic Eleusinian cult of ancient Greece[1] to the modern-day use of mescaline-containing cacti by indigenous people in the Americas (Calabrese 2013; McGraw 2004, 204–51; Smith 2000). As discussed earlier, Daime members believe that ayahuasca contains the spirits of Christ and Mother/ Father Nature, primordial intelligences that impart existential teachings to humans who drink the brew.

In order to get a more precise sense of European fardados' shared spiritual values, I administered two "freelisting" exercises (see Quinlan 2005). Serving as the springboard for this section, the first freelist questionnaire elicited the names of plants that fardados consider sacred. In the second freelist (presented in Part VI), I asked fardados to list all the people that they regard as Great Spiritual Teachers. Once enough freelists had been collected,[2] the data was processed using Anthropac (Borgatti 1991), software that sorts how a social group prioritizes items within a "cultural domain." Stephen Borgatti (1994, 265), the creator of Anthropac, defines a cultural domain as "a set of items which are, according to informants, of a kind." Once a cultural domain is identified, freelists provide information about the relative significance of specific domain items according to the "Smith's *s*"[3] measure of cognitive salience. Such inferences presume that more significant entities in the minds of informants are mentioned earlier and with more frequency than less significant entities (de Munck and Sobo 1998, 79).

Fardados' Domain of "Sacred Plants"

In the first freelist test, I elicited responses for fardados' cultural domain of "sacred plants."[4] Upon being asked to list all the plants they consider sacred, informants from around Europe mentioned a total of sixty-five specific items. The first dozen or so most salient items are all psychoactive substances employed by some cultures in entheogenic rites:

Table 11.1. European Fardados' Sacred Plants Domain ranked by Smith's *s*

Rank	"Sacred Plants"	Frequency	% of Freelists that include item (n = 42)	Smith's *s*
1	Ayahuasca	42	100%	0.830
2	Peyote	33	79%	0.530
3	*Cannabis*	34	81%	0.488
4	Mushrooms	31	74%	0.461
5	San Pedro	28	67%	0.400
6	Iboga	20	48%	0.204
7	Tobacco	11	26%	0.128
8	Datura	8	19%	0.087
9	Jurema	6	14%	0.079
10	*Amanita muscaria*	7	17%	0.078
11	*Salvia divinorum*	5	12%	0.058
12	Sage	4	10%	0.046
13	Coca	5	12%	0.034

Only mind-altering plants occurred with a Smith's *s* value > 0.05; in total, 29 (45%) of the sixty-five "sacred plant" items have psychoactive properties. The remaining collection of thirty-six non-psychoactive items included five plants with purported medicinal properties (e.g., *Digitalis*), eight trees (e.g., oak, juniper), four plants with ritual significance (e.g., incenses such as myrrh or palo santo), and fifteen foods or spices (e.g., passionfruit, basil, thyme). Ten of the "sacred" items are not plants at all (e.g., MDMA, LSD, mushrooms, alcohol, kambo). Though the majority of fardados' "sacred plants" have nothing to do with Santo Daime, they were aware that many of these materials have been employed elsewhere for spiritual or therapeutic purposes. The complete list of fardados' sacred plants can be found in Appendix III.

The most prominent items in fardados' cultural domain of sacred plants include examples of psychoactive flora and fungi that have been valued as holy sacraments at one time or another. First, all forty-two respondents mentioned ayahuasca,[5] the sacramental beverage employed in a variety of traditional indigenous and new syncretic settings (see Part II). Second, resuming a pre-contact indigenous practice of northern Mexico, the Native American Church's use of the peyote cactus (*Lophophora williamsii,* containing *mescaline*) is now recognized by the United States and Canadian governments as a protected religious freedom (Calabrese 2013; Schultes et al. 2001, 144–55). Third, various crossbred species of *Cannabis* (containing the psychoactive molecule *Tetrahydrocannabinol* [THC]) were used for entheogenic purposes in ancient Hindu traditions, and are a central feature of modern-day religious practices such as Sadhus in India and the Rastafarians of the Caribbean (Schultes et al. 2001, 92–101). Fourth, ancient Mesoamericans and twentieth-century Mazatec shamans in Mexico engaged in the ritual use of mushrooms imbued with the entheogenic alkaloid *psilocybin* (Schultes et al. 2001, 156–163). Fifth, the pre-Columbian consumption of mescaline-rich San Pedro cactus (*Echinopsis/Trichocereus pachanoi*) is mirrored among present-day aboriginal groups in the South American Andes region (Schultes et al. 2001, 166–169). Sixth, followers of the Bwiti religion of West Central Africa ingest the *Tabernanthe iboga* root (containing *ibogaine*) in their initiation rites (Schultes et al. 2001, 112–15). Seventh, various types of Tobacco (*Nicotiana* spp.) can be considered among "the most important shaman plants in South America" (Schultes et al. 2001, 134). Eighth, common shrubs of the *Datura* genus, with their "thorn apple" fruit and fascinating flower structures, are a vessel of precarious deliriant molecules associated with the highest spiritual ideas of cultures around the world (Schultes et al. 2001, 106–11). Ninth, various species in the *Mimosa* genus are called "Jurema" in eastern Brazil and are known to be useful ayahuasca analogs because their "root husk" is rich in DMT (Schultes et al. 2001, 49/138–39). Tenth, it has long been suggested that the red-capped mushroom *Amanita muscaria*—speckled with distinctive white "warts"—might have played a role in inspiring the originations of shamanism and Hinduism; although unproven, this is an attractive theory for fardados given that ingesting dried *Amanita* flesh delivers the entheogenic alkaloid *muscimol* (Schultes et al. 2001, 34/82–85). Regarding items 11 and 12, because fardados mentioned both entheogens and cooking spices as "sacred plants" it was unclear whether some freelist mentions of "sage" were meant to indicate *Salvia divinorum*, a psychoactive plant from Mesoamerica that contains *Salvinorin A* (see Schultes et al. 2001, 56/164–65) or common kitchen sage (*Salvia officinalis*). Finally, as a mild stimulant that is unlike its derivative form of powder cocaine, the leaves of *Erythroxylum coca* are sacred to indigenous peoples of the Andes (see also Rätsch 2005).

Just as a shared interest in altered states of consciousness inspires them to seek out ayahuasca, I met European fardados who had experimented with some of the other "sacred plants" listed in Table 11.1 above. Although I was unable to verify exact numbers, during fieldwork numerous fardados divulged that they had personally experienced *Cannabis* (i.e., marijuana) and psilocybin mushrooms in the past. The former is not surprising, considering that Cannabis is "the world's most widely used illicit drug" (Hall and Degenhardt 2007, 393). A recent survey by the European Monitoring Centre for Drugs and Drug Addiction (EMCDDA 2011) found that seventy-eight million people (23.2% of the EU populace aged 15–64) had smoked Cannabis at least once during their lifetime.[6] Psilocybin or "magic" mushrooms are also a popular psychoactive option throughout Europe. Across EU countries at the beginning of this century, between 1 percent and 8 percent of youths aged fifteen to twenty-four admitted to having experimented with mind-altering mushrooms (van Amsterdam et al. 2011, 424, 427). With some of the more exotic plants not easily available in Europe, I met two fardados (one Frenchman, one Dutchman) who had tried San Pedro cactus, the same Frenchman was the only informant who reported experience with peyote, and three fardados (one French woman, one Dutchman, and one Finnish man) claimed to have sampled Iboga. Though the recreational use of "hallucinogens" is common knowledge in Western societies, many fardados around Europe mentioned that they first learned about entheogenic ceremonies through their own private research. Only a handful of informants professed that they had had no prior experience with illicit psychoactive substances prior to encountering ayahuasca.

Attuned to broader subcultures of "psychedelic" spirituality that have spread throughout Western societies since the 1960s (Ray and Anderson 2000, 115), fardados are remarkably well-read concerning the topic of sacred plants. Most often, it was by searching for mystical and shamanic websites on the internet that they first stumbled upon entheogenic literature. On their bookshelves I noticed daimistas own many volumes that deal with entheogens, including some of the monographs that are referenced herein (e.g., Narby 1998; Shanon 2002; Strassman 2001). The famous writings of Carlos Castaneda (2016[1968]), which discuss the shamanic use of peyote, mushrooms, and *Datura*,[7] were also cited by some fardados as having stimulated their interest in entheogens. Whenever they meet, daimistas are inclined to exchange their respective knowledge about entheogenic materials. They regard the Daime beverage as akin to the other entheogens mentioned above, in that it is a sacred plant employed in controlled ceremonies. In likening entheogenic "teacher plants" to human educators, European fardados concur with the approaches of aboriginal Amazonians and neo-pagan Westerners (MacRae 1992; York 2005, 96). This idea is emblematic of *animistic* worldviews associated with shamanism, which posit that all of Nature is alive. In animism, natural entities such as animals, plants, and geographical locations are associated with attendant "spirit" beings (Harvey 2006). Such animistic approaches to psychoactive plants and mushrooms conflict with the mainstream Euro-American view of "hallucinogens" as harmful drugs.

Therapeutic Functions of a Sacred Technology

Therapeutic potentials of the brew are a major theme in the multidisciplinary field of ayahuasca studies (see Labate and Cavnar 2014b). In Europe, Janine Schmid (2011) and colleagues have reported on semistructured interviews conducted with fifteen participants in ayahuasca rituals, seven of whom are members of Santo Daime. Examining participants' "subjective healing theories" about *how* ayahuasca can cure, Schmid et al. (2010, 201) report that of the fifteen informants, seven "declared that they had successfully 'healed themselves' with the help of ayahuasca" but that there were five "disorders ayahuasca seemed to have had no influence on (migraine, fibromyalgia, prostate cancer, pain/knee, pyelitis)." Many of my informants also claim to have achieved profound healing through Daime rituals. However, fardados told me they are attracted to the Daime beverage *not only* as a medicine for existing health problems, but also as a source of practical remedies to common sociological and existential dilemmas in human life. Thus, in delineating my informants' emic beliefs about the curative powers of Daime, this chapter also accounts for what Schmid (2011, 252) designates as "unspecific changes" triggered by ayahuasca rituals.

Numerous European fardados claimed that psychosocial and health problems in their lives had been healed or alleviated through participating in Santo Daime, including:

- addictions (cigarettes, alcohol, and cocaine)
- depression
- social anxiety
- loneliness
- mourning/grief (divorce and death)
- post-traumatic stress (sexual/physical/psychological abuse, war)
- attention deficit disorder (A.D.D.)
- arthritis
- chronic fatigue syndrome

These can be added to disorders that Brazilian daimistas believe are treatable with ayahuasca, a long list that includes "skin problems, respiratory diseases, contagious infections, hepatitis, diabetes, leprosy, malaria, worms, dysentery, digestive problems, anaemia, fevers, influenza, mental disorders, and other problems connected to the nervous system" (Schmidt 2007, 65; see also Barnard 2014, 679–680). My European informants also reported that Daime has spurred improvements in their general quality of life, including positive increases in:

- happiness
- confidence
- inner peace
- humility
- harmony with non-daimista family members, friends, and work colleagues

When European fardados were asked if ayahuasca rituals had impacted their lives negatively in any way, most could not think of anything. Some said the only negatives were temporary insomnia and feeling tired the day after a difficult Daime work. Others expressed regret that they could not speak openly about their ayahuasca routine to some of their friends and family. Although they carry on with mainstream social lives, daimistas said they felt somewhat isolated before having access to like-minded people in Santo Daime. In fear of being arrested, they are careful to remain discreet about their entheogenic practice. Yet they also view the prospect of legal action as a necessary element in the Daime's struggle for religious freedom.

Fardados allege that they have achieved astoundingly positive results through working with Santo Daime. Not only do they assert that the Daime experience can help to heal personal and social conflicts, but they also contend that it can help repair current discords between humans and the natural environment. Cemin (2006, 279) recounts how daimistas view the outcomes of their ayahuasca rituals thusly:

> Daime reconciles man with himself, with his social milieu, his history, position and culture, and with the milieu of origin of the product which is essential to Daimistas: the forest, because "Daime is from the forest, the doctrine is from the woods," and, for example, Daime harmonizes man with the whole cosmos

represented by the woods, the stars, and the visible and invisible,
physical and spiritual beings that inhabit them.

It is understandable that the above claims stimulate curiosities of people
around the world who are seeking psychosocial healing and/or those who
are concerned about ecological crises such as deforestation and declining
biodiversity. Through interviews, I urged informants to explain *how* their
commitment to Santo Daime helps them realize such an idyllic state of
being. As explicated by Saskia, a fardada from Belgium:

> *I think Daime can heal. But not Daime, belief can heal. Daime
> helps . . . only if you're open for it. If you are still closed, you get
> ill. . . . It's not the ayahuasca that heals you, but it helps you to
> have more insight in your life so that you can change it. But if you
> can look at it but not change your life, then the illness will stay.*

In the following quotations from European Daime members, the reader will
get acquainted with daimistas' emic justifications for how enchanted uses
of ayahuasca can act as a "key" technology that fosters personal "transformations" (see also Cougar 2005; Schmidt 2007, 141–44; Dawson 2013,
91–111). Subsequently, for the purposes of anthropological clarification,
I then endeavor to translate these emic concepts into corresponding etic
formulations of introspective mysticism.

One Flemish banker who was preparing to soon become a fardado told
me his main intention for participating in Santo Daime is to "integrate [my]
demons" and to transform "sorrow into serenity." In the words of another
veteran fardado I will call Alwin, a Friesian playwright and theatre director
who lives with his fardada girlfriend in the Brussels suburbs:

> *One of the most difficult things I transformed was revenge to love.
> For me that was very hard. . . . The Daime helps you to do it. It's
> a big help to transform. Once I said "I want to be happy." Then
> I thought someone would give me that. And now I know it's just
> work! Now I found something that gives me the possibility to change
> myself! . . . It's amazing!*

Of course, all religions provide what their devotees consider as practical and
spiritual guidance or support for dealing with difficulties faced in daily life.

Fardados are no different from followers of other religions in the belief that their doctrine affords liberation from bodily and psychological suffering. My highlighting of fardado informants' repeated use of words such as *solution* is not meant simply to communicate the obvious point that their religious practice aids them in adapting to hardships and appreciating wonders of the human condition. Rather, I refer to their language of "solutions" as a multidimensional trope, whereby variations in the related meanings of this word serve to convey to outsiders the emic (insiders') perspective on Daime's capacity for all-purpose healing. Thus, in fardados' interview transcripts there is a recurrent reference to finding practical "solutions" through working with the Daime; at the same time, this text propounds an ethnometaphysical discourse, pinpointing fardados' captivation with the notion of two or more elements becoming one. Fardado interviewees often used words that connote the conjoining of two entities, such as: *connected, communion, link, contact, touch, engage, lock, bind/bound, combine/combination, unite/union, synthesis, dissolve, mix, integrate/integration/integrating,* and *balance.* In direct relation to European fardados' language of "solutions" is their characterization of Daime rituals as a complex technique that acts as a "key" to accessing these solutions. As discussed earlier, fardados believe that by nurturing currents of Holy Light in Daime works, they can incarnate that energy, which helps to allay the amount of suffering in themselves and the world at large. While this idea is outlandish to secularist nonbelievers, fardados believe that Daime rituals constitute a precise method for gathering and directing divine energies, which heal the participants by dissolving ego barriers.

In both ancient and modern times, certain cultures have recognized that the safety of entheogens is optimized when people with expert knowledge use them in appropriately ritualized settings. Scholarly researchers have also realized that the nature of entheogenic experiences depends largely upon the mental "set" of the individual ingesting the entheogen (i.e., expectations, preparedness, emotional stability), as well as on the physical and social "setting" within which it is consumed (e.g., the difference between a laboratory experiment and a rock concert) (see Zinberg 1984). Likewise, far removed from nonchalant or recreational attitudes toward entheogens that caused so much trouble in the 1960s, Daime members appreciate that the cooperative intentions (set) and context (setting) of ayahuasca drinking are imperative. For instance, when asked to state the difference between using and abusing entheogenic substances, the commander of the Belgian Daime church CdAI said:

> *For me, using [ayahuasca] in a good way is: put yourself in connection*
> *with God, with your sacred part, putting yourself in prayer, and*
> *be attentive to what happens along the process. . . . It's important*
> *for me to do that in group, not alone. Santo Daime is not to do*
> *alone. The group: at least two, three, four people . . .*
>
> *It's also a tool: there's the plants, the prayer, the songs, the*
> *music, and the group. Because there is the "egregore"[8] . . . the sum*
> *of the spiritual energies of the people is a whole thing in itself. It*
> *has its own strength and connection. Christ said: "If two or three*
> *people are put together in my name, I will come."*

Cécile is fifty-six years old and works as an elderly-care nurse. Born in Brussels and now living in Liège province, she has been involved in Daime since 2003, when she was introduced to the doctrine by her cousin (a woman who was present at the first Daime work in Belgium in 1989). Cécile's reference to Daime rituals as a multiplex "tool" in the quotation above introduces a crucial analogy for understanding how fardados' conceive of their ayahuasca practice.

It has been suggested that entheogens can be considered as "cognitive tools" in and of themselves (Tupper 2002). For fardados, it is actually the entire structure of Daime works that forms a composite tool of which ayahuasca is one of many components; recalling the details of Part IV, these include specialized ritual constituents (such as music), the group atmosphere, and the intention of participants, all essential elements of set and setting that work in concert with the Daime sacrament. This is similar to how shamanic "technology" has been depicted "as a group of techniques by which its practitioners enter the 'spirit world,' purportedly obtaining information that is used to help and to heal members of their social group" (Krippner 2000, 93). Psychological anthropologists have previously framed shamanic/mystical techniques as "technology of transcendence" (Walsh 1989) and "cultural technology of consciousness modification" (Calabrese 2008, 339–340). In a congruent manner, Labate (2011b) introduces the hybrid notion of *tecnologias do sagrado* ("technologies of the sacred") in her dissertation on global networks of Peruvian ayahuasquero shamanism.

Fardados also invoke architectural metaphors to describe the instrumental functions of Daime rituals. Extending their "family" of "brothers and sisters" trope of domesticity, "the category 'house'[9] designates the 'moral community' " in daimista discourse (Cemin 2006, 280; see also Meyer 2014, 12). References in Daime hymns to the "holy house" (*casa santa*), "palace," or "temple" also denote the astral "*casa*" revealed by the ayahuasca sacrament, the literal home of one's own subjective consciousness (see Schmidt 2007, 137). One Belgian daimista I will call Gabe used the cultural metaphor of cleaning his house to speak about how Daime acts like a "key" to sustaining health of the individual self:

> *The fact of going* [to Daime works] *gives me the confidence of having one key. Okay, I can get mixed, I can get lost in society. I can get contaminated by the stress, by the purposes of other interests that try to affect me. But already I have one key. . . . It's not because I clean my house once that it's clean forever. I'm clean if I have the discipline to clean my house every weekend, for instance. I'm clean, also, if I have the discipline not to dirty my house. . . .* [Santo Daime] *is the key to myself, it's the key to this Higher Self.*

My informants repeatedly used this "key" metaphor to describe how Daime rituals help them in their life. Another example is Leon, the commander of the Amsterdam CdSM church who overcame his addiction to cigarettes after he had been involved with Daime for many years:

> *I used to smoke tobacco, and I was drinking Daime. During a Concentration* [work] *some voice came to me and said, "What are you doing? When the work is finished you go outside right away to smoke a cigarette, don't even say thank you to your brothers and sisters, now you are cleaning yourself and you go outside and put this bad thing inside you again; so it's no use to drink Daime."*
> *This was very strong, and then I asked for help, and at this moment some things jumped out. . . . This is cleaning, and getting understanding that if you don't take care of your temple (your body), other things come inside your temple. Because you leave the doors open, other things come and they get inside and after a while you are not in control, you don't have the key to your temple. So when you come to the Daime, you have to get the key to your temple and you have to expose these . . . spirits from the lowest* [realms], *who bring the addictions, the sex, the drugs.*

Barnard (2014, 681) has it right that fardados tend to conceptualize Santo Daime in technological terms, believing that "over time, with tremendous self-effort and discipline, little by little they learn how to become increasingly translucent conduits of Divine Power, Light, and Love." The related goal of reaching one's "Higher Self," or an ideal state of consciousness beyond the ego and its many neuroses, will be further developed throughout the remainder of this text.

When fardados asserted that Daime works help them in their daily lives, I asked them to elaborate on how this process occurs. Astrid, a Flemish fardada, emphasized the importance of orienting her "intentions" according to the concept of *firmeza* ("firmness") as a major factor determining the lessons about ego she receives during the Daime works:

> For me *firmeza* is knowing your goal. It's not being distracted by bad thoughts, or by ego. It's knowing who you are and what you're part of. And it's having this connection with the universe: not being disturbed by bad things, by negative things. . . . I just go [to Daime works] with certain intentions. For instance, when I have a fight with a person . . . sometimes I'm not even really aware that I'm struggling, but I know there's something wrong. And then I ask in the work "Please Daime, help me to find out what the problem is." And very often I get the solution. But very often I also feel that the Daime wants me to find it out for myself; that I need to do it myself. Or sometimes it's not the time to solve the issue already. But it always gets solved anyway. Daime or no Daime, it always gets solved anyway.
>
> But Daime gives me the strength to look at it and to handle it like I should. Sometimes you need to think about it but sometimes you just need to let it go. . . . For me, ego is the thing that cuts off your connection with the universe and with other people . . . and it comes in different forms, it's a challenge. The good thing is ego makes you grow. So we shouldn't say it's bad or not bad. It exists, and you need to overcome it in life. I think once you've done that, you can die peacefully [laughs].

Astrid is a thirty-nine-year-old receptionist from Antwerpen province who has been attending Daime works since 2006. Like other fardados who live in the northern part of Antwerpen, she prefers to make the trip to Amsterdam to attend the CdSM church. Although she has dated fellow daimistas, she was single at the time of our interview. In the quotation above, one witnesses the fundamental meaning of the word *Daime* (Portuguese: *Dai-me* ["Give me"]) as a request for understanding and aid concerning common human problems.[10] Astrid pronounces a typical explanation of how daim-istas approach their Daime experiences as an orchestrated opportunity to ask questions to the spirit world about hindrances in their lives. Here the Daime works are a kind of divination practice of receiving knowledge from the astral otherworld, if only the drinker will have the courage to "look at" his/her own subjective being.

Depending on the nature of the problem, the otherworldly "teacher" that is conjured through the Daime is seen as a universal source of guidance that assists the daimista in overcoming their difficulties. When fardados speak about the mechanism of Santo Daime solutions, they use words such as *trigger, transform,* and *tool,* describing it as a kind of catalyst that can unlock any personal obstacle. In the words of Karl from Flanders:

> *Daime is the key to that state of conscious spirituality.* . . . *If there's a solution in a room and you're standing in front of that room but the door is locked* [laughs] . . . *you can't get to it* . . . *a lot of stuff is in front of us to go to an essence. Daime is the key to go through there and go to the solution.* . . . *Daime, in a sense, it's already an* oplossing [Dutch: solution] *itself* . . . *what Daime does is confronts you to a condition which is not correct yet, makes you sick* . . .
>
> *What you do in Daime is actually alchemy. What is alchemy? From lead, you make gold. Okay, as a metaphor: from a very bad condition, jealousy, you make true love. Daime does that* . . . *Daime shows you, gives you a path, the key to find all these things that were incorrect or work against you, small parts of your ego, and turns them into gold. It's an alchemical process: make a goal of it, and just look, look, look. Then you take a solution, make another solution, to have an alchemical process in your own body. What is alchemy? Well, it's finding the Holy Grail at the end. Make the potion* . . . *because if you do Daime works (and you've done works), it brings you first into your everyday reality and you see yourself.* . . . *So, it all boils down to your condition, what people mirror at you. Everybody mirrors each other, we play a role towards each other.*

Here, Karel conveys the essence of fardados' view that imbibing the liq-uid-spiritual "potion" in Daime rituals acts as both a physical and psycho-logical "key" or catalyst to practical and metaphysical "solutions." The ways my informants think of the ayahuasca sacrament are reminiscent of Hegel's

(1977[1807], 493) foaming "chalice" of "infinitude," the esoteric "elixir" of the "Philosophers' Stone" (Corbett 1983, 326), or Jungian-inflected reframings of the alchemical *Magnum Opus* ("Great Work")[11] (see Dourley 2014, 1–36/43/54; Hanegraaff 2014). Rather than searching for the "Holy Grail" or converting lead into gold in the outside world, these metaphors show how fardados seek "boiled-down" solutions through mystical experience. This idea of Daime as a key that unlocks inner solutions is reinforced in the hymns, such as the lyrics of PA#91, which locate the source of "salvation" as the inner Jesus: "It is in me, it is in everyone . . . you are all light that illuminates all darkness . . . you are the key of the Astral." Both Astrid and Karel place special importance on the "intention" to "look" at what is presented to one's consciousness upon entering the Daime experience. According to fardados, having right intent—such as trustful openness toward what the Daime has to teach, as opposed to wanting the ego to control the experience—is a basic component of the ideal mind-set.

Fardados' notion of ayahuasca rituals as a "key" to accessing practical and metaphysical *solutions* also evokes Michel Foucault's (1988, 18) theorizing on "technologies of the self": "specific techniques that human beings use to understand themselves . . . so as to transform themselves in order to attain a certain state of happiness, purity, wisdom, perfection, or immortality." Some authors have likened entheogens to technological utensils designed to help an observer peer into otherwise inaccessible realms; it was decades ago that writer Alan Watts (1965, 25–26) and psychiatrist Stanislav Grof (1976, 32–33) used the language of microscopes and telescopes to depict how entheogens can magnify normally hidden aspects of the subconscious self. More recently, psychologist William A. Richards (2005, 378) endorsed this analogy: "As the telescope is to astronomy, or the microscope is to biology, so are entheogens to psychiatry and especially, to the psychology of religious experience." While these comparisons fit nicely with fardados' conceptualization of Daime rituals, no one has yet named this new type of "scope" instrument! I propose the term *suiscope* (Latin *suī-* ["oneself"][12] + Latin *-scopus* ["an instrument for observing, viewing, or detecting"][13]) as a neologism that best characterizes fardados' technological portrayal of Daime works. Thus, the ayahuasca is not so much a tool by itself as it is one essential cog in the multipart equipment of the Daime ceremony as a whole. Understood in this etic manner, the ritual apparatus of Santo Daime acts as an introspective device that helps one to look at oneself (i.e., a sui-scope). Just as technologies such as microscopes and telescopes make it possible for humans to gaze upon distant realms of the very small and very far away, so does the suiscope of Daime rituals permit the observing self to observe itself. Like other systematic endeavors of observation, the Daime suiscope allows individuals to learn/gain new knowledge[14], in this case self-knowledge (i.e., autognosis). According to my informants, the suiscope of Santo Daime helps them achieve medical and existential solutions by revealing new information about aspects of their psyche with which they were previously unfamiliar. If fardados' claims are seriously considered, it is possible that just as microscopes and telescopes have triggered revolutionary breakthroughs in microbiology and astrophysics, entheogenic rituals could divulge potential advances for psychiatry (Richards 2005). Such was Hannah Arendt's (1998[1958], 257–58) comparison of Christianity to the momentousness of Galileo's invention of the telescope: "Like the birth in a manger, which spelled not the end of antiquity but the beginning of something so unexpectedly and unpredictably new that neither hope nor fear could have anticipated it, these first tentative glances into the universe through an instrument, at once adjusted to human senses and destined to uncover what definitely and forever must lie beyond them, set the stage for an entirely new world and determined the course of other events, which with much greater stir were to usher in the modern age." So what is it that happens when one looks earnestly into the suiscope furnished in Daime works? And how does this experience of looking through the suiscope provide solutions? In short, for fardados Daime works are meant to act as a crucible of the human self, wherein one's conscious awareness is fixed into a state of observing itself.

The collective task of each attendee making contact with this deepest dimension of selfhood is the main goal of Daime rituals in Europe. According to informants, when one looks inside oneself during a ceremonial work, one "confronts" the inner observer, the deepest source of subjective consciousness located underneath the noise of our thoughts and emotions. Werner, a Belgian fardado with a background in Hindu meditation,[15] called this inner observer the "witness," the "light," and the "True Self":

> *Sometimes the confrontation with aspects of yourself that are painful, you don't want to see them because everybody is afraid. The Santo Daime is a big confrontation. . . . When you don't know that you can find peace, happiness inside [yourself] . . . then you try to find that happiness and the things that you need. Everybody needs to feel home, to feel good, to feel comfortable inside; I don't mean materially, but to feel at rest and at peace in yourself. When you*

don't have that experience, then you have to find it outside. So most people . . . they try to find that happiness outside but sometimes they do crazy things for it: sometimes they think, "When I have a lot of money, then I will be happy," or, "When I have a lot of sex all the time then I [will] feel good," or, "When I can eat very good things every day" . . . or drinking [alcohol]. . . .

But most people, the first thing that you experience when you look inside is what is covering that happiness and that well-being: your judgments and all your conditions. And you have to go through that before you reach the Light in yourself or the beauty in yourself. . . . You have to look to clean, and that looking is cleaning yourself. And when the Daime came for me, it was a big cleaning. To clean all those layers that I was not, but that I had in my cells: the judgments, the hate, all these negative things I also had in me. Because you are the world. Everything that exists in the world exists in you. So you have to dive deep into yourself. And when you dive in yourself, you are confronted with all those doenças [diseases]. You have to look at those doenças to clean them. Looking is the Light. Seeing it is the Light. When you see it, it disappears: when you see your fear, your fear disappears; when you see your hate, your hate disappears. . . . All those experiences of hate, experiences of jealousy, experiences of happiness, are temporary. But behind all those experiences is the Silence. . . . The Silence is the witness. It's the mirror in yourself that is your True Self. . . . The goal is to connect with your True Self, that's the goal of life . . .

When there is fear, look at it. When there is jealousy, look at it. That looking at it is the Light in yourself. The Light makes that shadow (that fear or that hate)[16] *disappear. That's the doorway, that's a very simple thing. . . . We are not this body, we are not our mind, but when you think you are your mind and your emotions . . . the emotions make you sick. Because that is not the truth. You are just being. That's what you are. It's the emotions that make the body sick. . . . I have experienced fear in the Daime sometimes because I still have that fear in me. And the fear sometimes comes very heavy, and . . . [by] just looking, it's gone. . . . The disconnection is when you think that you are your emotions . . . when you think that you are your thoughts . . . when you think that you are a big man, or when you think that you are nothing. Because it's a lie . . . you are just being.*

What Werner calls "the mirror in yourself" is located at the headwaters of subjective consciousness inside each human being. So just as some microscopes and telescopes employ catadioptric mirrors to expose the very small and very distant, the Daime suiscope also works with a mirror principle to reveal the observer to itself. Describing perhaps the most literal form of self-"reflection," this mirror metaphor surfaced again when Lambert, the commander of CdU, was asked about his intentions in drinking Daime:

> *It is always to work on myself. To try to see what I do not see. To see the mirror, to look in the mirror. . . . I can fulfill my very big hunger [for] spirituality in the Santo Daime. I do not need other things anymore. I have enough with this. . . . To live without this spirituality, I would miss it very much. . . . Spirituality is to go in yourself, and to connect with your Higher Self. . . . It is difficult to make a connection with your Higher Self when you are not used [to it]. In the Santo Daime, you have a sacrament who is helping you to connect with your Higher Self. . . . The lessons you get from your Higher Self (God in yourself) bring you to the harmony . . . and you feel better. You feel what you should not do and you feel what you should do. Your Higher Self knows what's good for you. . . . It is God in yourself. God is everywhere, but He's also in yourself. So with the Daime, you connect with yourself, God in yourself.*

By looking at that which looks, treating one's innermost self as an entheogenic oracle, fardados say that the observer sees that it is essentially one and the same with whatever it observes.

Similarly Sieglinde, a thirty-eight-year-old German artist who has been partaking in Daime for four years, said that she was drawn to ayahuasca because she was seeking help for her chronic struggles with the "chaos" of the human condition. In a manner that conveys a normal sequence for the ayahuasca experience (see Taussig 1987, 321–26/429/438–46; Shanon 2002, 41/57/339–40), she portrayed the mystical death/rebirth nature of the Daime ritual as a "confrontation" with an inner "mirror":

> *At the beginning you get in touch with all your negativity. . . . Slowly it starts to become somewhat uncomfortable. . . . In every sense of my being I feel a change and heaviness, and it's this slow confrontation with my shadows, with my dark side, with the things I don't want to see and I don't want to be responsible for and which*

I project into the outside. . . . I often also feel the sickness in my body. For a long time I felt my own chaos in the form of . . . my own guilt and shame . . . but I know that by going [to Daime] I will break through it. . . .

It's like this bent mirror which makes everything very big, so I was able to see my chaos. . . . [The first time] was Hell. . . . And then I thought "I have to die, it's the only way [out]." And then there was this [thought]: "What will your parents think if you die? You cannot do this to your parents!" So I was not able to let go. And then I asked for help so much that I couldn't even breathe . . . and I came to this birth trauma again every time in a different form. . . . And then I really asked for help to the guy who led the ceremony, and I said, "I've lost my mind," and he said, "Your mind will find you". . . . Then at one point it happened: I found my heart and love and a new life. It was a new birth!

All this talk of light and mirrors recalls how scholars have tried to put into words the utmost effects of ayahuasca (Shanon 2002, 273–83/381–82) and entheogens in general (Smith 2000, 10–13/74–75). According to fardados, when one observes suiscope reflections in the inner mirror, one generally sees the impurities of one's ego reflected back as visions, insights, and lessons specifically geared to each individual's "conditions." In general, informants report experiences with ayahuasca similar to those summarized by Sudhölter's (2012, 9) Dutch informants: "They go up to heaven or descend into hell; others travel through a wide range of 'other realities' . . . visions of, or communication with supernatural beings: from religious figures like Jesus and Mary to aliens and 'beings of darkness' "—the latter known also as *espíritos sofredores* ("suffering spirits"). Yet in pinnacle moments of the Daime experience (i.e., after one has done the purgative work of "cleaning" the inner mirror), the reflection is so clear that the ego barriers separating self and not-self dissolve, leaving only what is felt to be a vibrant, unadulterated Light. This revelation is not limited to entheogens, as the "mirror" analogy for suiscope introspection is also found in mystical doctrines of Christianity (e.g., John of the Cross 2010[1618], 63–66), Islam (Huxley 2009[1945], 276), and Zen Buddhism (Watts 1999[1957], 20/91–93/97/142), as well as in Jewish, Hindu, Taoist, and ancient Maya traditions (Pendergrast 2003, 31–32). Recalling the biblical language of Paul,[17] a paraphrased view of the fourth-century Christian monk Evagrius and a quotation from the twelfth-century Scottish theologian Richard of Saint Victor both describe what happens in states of deep meditative prayer:

> The purified mind sees itself, its truest self, its true state. The self it sees is luminous. The luminosity that permits it to see itself is the *divine light*. . . . It also sees and knows by seeing— indirectly, as in a *mirror*—the uncreated, immaterial light that God is. (Harmless 2008, 153)

> Let whoso thirsts to see his God *cleanse his mirror, purge his spirit*; and when thus he has cleansed his mirror, and long and *diligently gazed in it*, a certain brightness of *divine light* begins to shine through upon him, and a certain immense ray of unwonted vision to appear before his eyes. . . . From the beholding of this light, which it sees within itself with amazement, the mind is mightily set on fire, and lifted up to behold that *Light* which is above itself. (quoted in Underhill 1914, 115)

This same suiscope principle is a common metaphor in the mystical teachings of Sufi Islam. As non-Christian examples, we see matching principles of purification via introspection upon an inner "mirror" in paraphrased translations of the poet Rumi and the theologian Al-Ghazzali:

> Every time you really look at your false self, you die. After thousands of repeated deaths, you begin to realize what in you lives forever, lives beyond all schemes and fantasies. What you have been searching for all your life will start to appear. Rub and go on rubbing a filthy *mirror* and however filthy it is to start with, eventually the pure glass will begin to be revealed, and shine. (Harvey 1996, 136; see Arberry 2009[1947], 17/26/38/125)

> Your heart is a polished *mirror*. You must wipe it clean of the veil of dust that has gathered upon it, because it is destined to reflect the light of divine secrets. (Frager 1999, 21)

The mystical statements above are identical to how fardados describe the Holy Light they encounter in Daime works. Through mystical techniques such as reading sacred scripture (see Kierkegaard 1990[1851], 25–26/35–36/43–44),

meditative prayer, or entheogenic rituals, practitioners of mysticism believe
that one can polish the inner mirror of selfhood until egotistical distortions
vanish entirely. As with Rumi above, an unclean mirror is covered in the
"filth" of egoic passions, repressed memories, and emotional hangups. By
working to clean (or literally purge) these illusions through Daime, daimistas
say they earn a new perspective from which they can bask in the Light of
oneness with all that is.[18] Linking with the Daime theology discussion in
Part IV, fardados believe that when many individuals are attuned to this
Holy Light at the same time, they combine as *Juramidam* to open portals
to the astral otherworld.

Santo Daime hymns and prayers attest to the curative properties of
this inner divine Light, as in PA#67:

Eu entrei em entendimento	*I entered an understanding*
Entre meu eu e material	*Between my self and matter*
Sou luz expulso doença	*I am light, I expel sickness*
E destrincho a causa dela	*And I unravel the cause of it*

The "Prayer of Charity" text recited in Daime works[19] concludes with the
following appeal to God: "Give us the simplicity that will make our souls
the *mirror* where Your image must be reflected." Fardados concur with the
mystics that when not obscured or inflated by an egocentric outlook, the
root of subjective consciousness = infinite Light = Absolute Oneness = God.
Daimistas say this sensation emanates from the "heart" (chest) region where,
unlike dualistic "thoughts" of the egoic mind/brain, one has the "feeling"
that everything in existence is an outgrowth of a unified field of "Higher
Self" or "Higher Consciousness." Whereas fardados say devotion to the ego
creates an uncomfortable feeling of isolation, leading to manifold types of
emotional anxiety/despair and psychophysical sickness, the realization of
total oneness with a panentheistic divinity erases this suffering, replacing it
with inner peace and outer well-being. According to the methods of ethnophenomenology, I applied my informants' suggested techniques of trying to
look at my own sense of observation. In doing so, I was initially met with
very uncomfortable sensations that from the mystical point of view would
be described as rubbing egoic filth off of my inner mirror. However, after
facing this bitter suffering, I then regularly broke through to experience a
deeply comforting sense of omnipresent light and peace. Even though I
am not a daimista and I did not adopt their belief system for myself, the
suiscope device still had practical benefits for me; the arrival of this inner

luminescence coincided with my most personally meaningful and rewarding Daime works. For instance, it often seemed that conceptual obstacles in my fieldwork and daily life were resolved in these intense meditative events that fardados would construe as a merging with the Holy Light.

After experiencing this type of mystical illumination for themselves, fardados are prone to interpret all of external reality in the same way, believing that the observed outside and the internal observer are two aspects of a single conscious being. Once again the looking glass principle applies, so that all of external reality is taken to be a reflection of the internal mirror. A Course in Miracles portrays this insight thusly: "Perception is a mirror, not a fact. And what I look on is my state of mind, reflected outward" (Schucman 2007[1976], workbook page 451, Lesson #304). In other words, fardados see an underlying "solution" of what is usually sensed as a divide/ boundary/veil between the inner ego-self and outer not-self. Instead, everything in existence is conceived as an extension of one's own self. But this is no narcissistic solipsism. Rather, in daimista logic it follows that when one sees that which is "other" (i.e., all other people and all of Nature) as part of one's self, one is more likely to care about the well-being of the other; simultaneously, one is less likely to want to attack or hurt others if one's own well-being is acknowledged as tied to the well-being of the other.

Appreciating the "mystical" qualities of Daime rituals, Soares (2010, 68) captures the implications of the suiscope in-sight:

> There is no paradox . . . the revelations being precisely the awareness of this coincidence, the matrix of acknowledgement of the holy unity, which reconciles, with the supreme connection it brings about, matter and spirit, self and other, individual and collectivity, the human and the natural, the natural and the cosmic whole, the cosmic whole and the deity, and—through this association—the human and the divine.

To be sure, fardados are quick to point out that this is not unique to Santo Daime. They often state that different mystical practices from around the world and throughout history have provided these same basic teachings. Prior to their membership in Santo Daime, the overwhelming majority of my informants had been raised according to the beliefs and traditions of either a Christian or a secularist/atheist background. These two main ideological options in Europe flow out of premodern and modern currents of Western culture from the twentieth century. As my informants had experimented with different forms of traditional religious and modern secular routes throughout their lives, they ultimately found that Santo Daime satisfied their spiritual and existential needs. This brings us back to the central question of the present book: Why are some Europeans electing to follow an ayahuasca religion from Brazil instead of accepting the secular and religious traditions of their homeland?

12

Fardados' Conception of
Santo Daime as a Mystical Path

Much of human activity is organized around the solving of problems. In all times and places, humans seek to alleviate various forms of suffering (hunger, poverty, violence, illness, unhappiness) and overcome obstacles (disabilities, injustice, marginalization, catastrophe). For many cultures throughout time, spiritual or religious systems evolved to explain and manage common difficulties that are part and parcel of the human condition. Contrarily, the modern Western view of secular disenchantment tends to reject the notion that problems and solutions have anything to do with the supernatural because it holds that nothing exists beyond the physical world. According to Charles Laughlin (1999, 465), modern European-derived culture can be characterized as "materialist," in that it is "primarily concerned with tracking external events while in the waking state" (see also Johnson 1985). Such a portrayal is similar to Benjamin Whorf's (1941) model of the Standard Average European (SAE) worldview, wherein the aggrandizement of externality relegates internal consciousness to an epiphenomenal domain of the "imaginary." Today it is assumed by many people in Western cultures that problems appear for various reasons but that ultimately they have to be managed with appropriate *external* responses: physical problems come from bad hygiene, or bad nutrition, or bad luck, and must be treated with behavioral changes or surgery or pills; psychological problems come from bad experiences or bad brain chemistry, and must be treated by psychotherapy or pharmaceuticals; relationship problems derive from disloyalty, bad compatibility, and bad habits, and can be settled by finding new relationships;

geopolitical problems originate with bad people or conflicts between different groups of actors. Most Westerners learn how to navigate the practical challenges of existence through trial and error, along with the support and guidance of peers. The general message is: if you want to be happy, the best way to secure this emotional state is to engage in the external system of work and rewards, thereby acquiring physical and social comforts that can engender your contentment.

In contrast to this materialist approach, spiritual traditions categorized as forms of mysticism explain human suffering very differently. For mystical practitioners from different cultural traditions throughout the ages, the main sources of and solutions to most human problems are found within. Many world religions have mystical branches affiliated with them, ranging from faiths where mysticism composes the main body of teachings to mere off-shoots that persist in a quasi-official status relative to church orthodoxy. In distinguishing between mysticism and regular religious institutions, theorist Evelyn Underhill (2002[1911], 72) underlines that the mystic seeks "not to *know about*, but to Be": "Mysticism, in its pure form, is the science of ultimates, the science of union with the Absolute, and nothing else, and the mystic is the person who attains to this union, not the person who talks about it." Carmody and Carmody (1996, 4) render a mystical experience as "a direct encounter with ultimate reality, the very foundation of everything that is." However, as these authors recognize, language does not do justice to the intensity of a mystical experience. The reason for this is that in normal waking awareness, the individual observer perceives a distinction between the self and the other-than-self. Thomas Csordas (2004, 163–64) draws attention to the "ineffable" relationship between self and not-self as "the phenomenological kernel of religion"; he proposes that in removing the sense of a self-other divide (or *alterity*) "the mystics have discovered that the wholly other can be modulated into the wholly one and that it is equally awesome either way" (see also Steinbock 2009). Since time immemorial, groups of mystically inclined people have found it necessary to devise highly regimented disciplines to organize and construe these "awesome" bonds between self and otherness. I found that fardados share the mystics' theory of life. They believe that ayahuasca rituals help them to generate mystical experiences through which they can intuit solutions to their problems. Before wading farther into European fardados' peculiar ideas, it is important to first understand controversial ambiguities that bedevil the interdisciplinary study of mysticism.

The etymology of the term *mysticism* (*mystikos*) comes from the Greek verb μυω (*muo*), meaning "to conceal" or "to close," adopted by figureheads of the early Christian church to designate "secret" or "hidden" components of their rituals (Gellman 2014; Parsons 2011a, 3). But because the modern use of this vocabulary originated within Christianity, some scholarly critics disapprove of applications of the adjective *mystical* to non-Christian societies. In general, the major fault line in this debate pits the *perennialist* (or *traditionalist*) recognition of mystics from different cultures as working with the same universally accessible states of rapture against *constructivist* (or *contextualist*) positions, which prefer to discriminate between ritual contemplativeness associated with specific sociocultural settings (Kripal 2014, 71–73; Stoeber 2015). In parsing this debate, William Parsons (2011a) has published a helpful survey of the complex inconsistency in intellectuals' treatments of the term *mysticism*. For instance, it has been rightly suggested that if mysticism indicates some sort of direct relationship with a monotheistic Godhead, it is inappropriate to classify Buddhists as "mystical" because they do not admit the existence of a supreme deity (Gimello 1979, cited in Parsons 2011a, 4). Despite some critics' contentions that "mysticism" is an invention of Euro-American academia, I am in agreement with Michael Stoeber (2015) when he argues: "Even if the modern concept of mysticism were wholly a social construction created for scholarly analytic purposes, it is a field that certainly gives apt voice to a phenomenon that has been present to human spiritual experience since very ancient times—that is, a private and individual condition of consciousness with significant affective and communal components, be it intertwined historically with the contemplation of scripture, the practice of liturgy, ascetic activities, contemplative meditation, or other religious activity." The disagreement between perennialists and constructivists parallels an old debate in anthropology between "lumpers" and "splitters" (see Ford and Steward 1954, 55). To be sure, I do appreciate the "splitter" concern of constructivist colleagues, as it is by all means necessary to delineate sociocultural particularities if one wants to examine contrasts of ethnology. At the same time, because European daimistas are engrossed with mystical traits shared in common between different groups of people, in what follows I must prioritize this emic outlook of my informants as more in keeping with the "lumper" proclivities of thinkers who ascribe to perennialist schools of thought (e.g., Schuon 2013).

To reconcile divergent perspectives on mysticism, Jerome Gellman (2014) singles out "two, related, senses of 'mystical experience.'" When professional scholars of philosophy, psychology, and religious studies write about this topic, they typically mean Gellman's narrow definition of mysticism as "unitive experience": "a phenomenological de-emphasis, blurring, or eradication of multiplicity," exemplified by existential states described as "the oneness of all of nature, 'union' with God, as in Christian mysticism, the Hindu experience that Atman is Brahman (that the self/soul is identical with the eternal, absolute being), the Buddhist unconstructed experience, and 'monistic' experiences, devoid of all multiplicity." Conversely, the "wider" sense of mystical experience would include any polytheistic, spirit possession, mediumistic, and nontheistic states of altered consciousness. Gellman (2014) defines this expanded sense of a mystical experience as "a (purportedly) super sense-perceptual or sub sense-perceptual experience granting acquaintance of realities or states of affairs that are of a kind not accessible by way of sense perception, somatosensory modalities, or standard introspection." But Parsons (2011a, 3–5) cautions researchers to be aware of two misapprehensions with respect to what mysticism is: (1) the colloquial merging under the "mysticism" umbrella of ritualized formats that scholars would prefer to isolate with specific labels such as "shamanism," "Gnosticism," "spirituality," and "esotericism"; and (2) "the failure to discriminate between episodic experience and mysticism as a *process* that, though surely punctuated by moments of visionary, unitive, and transformative encounters, is ultimately inseparable from its embodied relation to a total religious matrix: liturgy, scripture, worship, virtues, theology, rituals, practice, and the arts." Parsons (2011b, 211) also remarks on how contemporary parlance tends to confuse the "wider" sense of mysticism with a loose commitment to a "spiritual but not religious" SBNR identity (see Bender 2010; Fuller 2001). He affirms that for many laypeople today, "modern mysticism and modern spirituality have become interchangeable terms (mystical experiences are seen as part of, indeed the culmination of, the spiritual path)" (Parsons 2013, 48). As long as one stays mindful of these background debates, Parsons (2011a, 3–4) approves of the wide perennialist definition as a basis for comparing different systems of ritual contemplation; accordingly, one can "point to St. Teresa of Avila, the Zen master Dogen, the Sufi al-Hallaj, or the Hindu sage Sri Aurobindo as 'mystics'; the Enneads, the Upanishads, or the Zohar as classic 'mystical texts'; and Ramakrishna's vision of Kali, St. Paul's ascent to Paradise, and Buddha's attainment of Nirvana as examples of 'mystical experiences.'" The results of my research with European fardados suggest that the practitioners, hymns, and rituals of Santo Daime can likewise be considered alongside other kinds of mystical personalities, texts, and experiences. Moreover, considering the ethnophenomenological approach pursued herein, we can bear in mind Evgeny Torchinov's (2003, 45) proposition that comparative studies of mysticism "may supply philosophy with new impetus to overcome the difficulties of its traditional approaches, thus opening new horizons and unknown dimensions of our understanding of reality." I now want to reflect on ways that European fardados combine traditionally narrow definitions of theological "mysticism" with the more modern, wide connotations of spiritual experiences and practices classified as "mystical."

The narrow sense of Daime mysticism was present in an interview with Agnes, a fardada psychotherapist from Czech Republic. After intense training in Hindu Kundalini, Agnes says she rediscovered her esteem for Christianity through her Daime experiences. When I asked her how the Daime compares to other religions, she responded:

AGNES: *It depends what you mean by religion . . . for me now,* [Santo Daime] *is really a Christian way. When I read a lot of books from Christian mystics (Saint Teresa, Saint John of the Cross), it helped me very much on my way because I have really had very similar experiences* [in Daime]. *For me it's the school of real Christianity. So it is religion in one way, but not the same as official religion. It's very difficult to answer this question.*

INTERVIEWER: How is Daime related to mysticism?

AGNES: *The steps of the Dark Night. . . .* [In Daime works] *I had horrible experiences of various feelings that were one hundred times stronger than I could imagine in my psychotherapeutic* [training] *(because you know, when you are a psychotherapist you must also experience the* [psychoanalysis] *on yourself). But these experiences* [of my psychotherapeutic training] *were only kindergarten play compared with* [Daime] *. . . I learned a lot about grief and hope and love. . . . I had two difficult years where it was very, very difficult in my Santo Daime group. And I really felt such great loneliness because I was trying to [be the puxadora for our Daime group] and I was alone, I had nobody to learn from and it was really difficult. So in terms of relationships with people in the group, it was really the most difficult [time] I have passed through.*

INTERVIEWER: Are all mystical traditions teaching the same lessons?

AGNES: *Yes. These lines are opened from "upstairs," not done by people "downstairs." So they have a lot of similarities; it's only to some groups of people it fits more this way or that, but in the end, it's the same. . . . I think that several lines can be more appropriate to the historical time. Because if you do Kundalini mahayoga, you must sit several hours a day; how can you connect this now with life in this historical period? I think Santo Daime is really appropriate* [today] *because you can learn so much in one lesson, and then . . . you have a lot of opportunities to practice in your normal life.*

Agnes's view of Daime mysticism invokes "steps of the Dark Night"—this is the "road to union with the divine" through "a most lofty path of dark contemplation and dryness" celebrated as "cleansings" or "purifications of the soul" by the sixteenth-century Spanish mystic St. John of the Cross (2010[1618], 8/11). Hence, this fardada's conviction that all mystical traditions teach the same lessons through different disciplinary modes reiterates Underhill's (2002[1911], 168–69) classic theory of the "Mystic Way," stipulated as five "phases in a single process of growth; involving the movement of consciousness from lower to higher levels of reality": (1) Awakening or Conversion, (2) Self-knowledge or Purgation, (3) Illumination, (4) Surrender, or the Dark Night, and (5) Union. This five-step scheme probably oversimplifies what is really more of a meandering journey. My informants constantly reminded me that whatever union (Step 5) one achieves only brings one back to new awakenings (Step 1). They would agree with the modern mystic Jack Kornfield (2000, 116/123–38) that counter to popular stories about famous holy men and women attaining permanent inner peace, there is "no enlightened retirement":

> Systematic depictions of spiritual stages can make it seem as if the path is simple, linear, and progressive, as if spiritual life were a step-by-step development of oneself over time. In one way, the maps are correct, and we do gradually purify, open, release, and stabilize over the years of spiritual practice. But whatever happens does not happen in a straight line. Whether in the monasteries of Burma and Tibet or in the accounts of Christian, Jewish, and Sufi mystics, we almost never see anyone whose past is simply

linear. . . . There are always changing cycles—ups and downs, openings and closings, awakenings to love and freedom, often followed by new and subtle entanglements. In the course of this great spiral, we return to where we started again and again, but each time with a fuller, more open heart.

I did meet daimistas, usually relative newcomers, who clearly believed that the Daime and other mystical disciplines could lead to a state of unwavering serenity and freedom from suffering. But elder fardados were more likely to view the Mystic Way as like the dialectic of Kornfield's "spiral," as constantly facing new lessons through perpetual cycles of pleasurable and painful growth. For example, a Dutch man told me he still considers himself a beginner at each Daime work he enters even though he has been a fardado for more than a decade. Nevertheless, for purposes of demonstration, Underhill's five phases read like a general outline of the kinds of mystical experiences that my informants recounted as benchmarks in their Daime vocation.

Awakening or Conversion

Some European daimistas had already received mystical initiation through other means prior to their first ayahuasca experience. But for many others their introduction to Santo Daime provoked what Underhill (2002[1911], 176) calls "that decisive event, the awakening of the transcendental consciousness." A striking example of this mystical "awakening" was relayed to me by Eleonora, an unmarried thirty-seven-year-old Flemish fardada who works as an "energetic healer" with clients looking for alternatives to Western medicine. She told me that before she first found the Daime in 2005, she had been struggling with depression and debilitating arthritis in her hands. In a story about a *miração* she had in one of her first Daime works, she spoke of being lifted up into the clouds where she saw Jesus Christ and she sat down next to him:

> I said: "I don't even believe in you Jesus!" (Because I wasn't brought up with religion. . . . I never believed in my life). . . . He showed me how safe the world is . . .
>
> At that point I could release so many fears that I had. . . . I felt the pain coming out of my body with the vibrations of the [fardados'] singing. . . . I didn't have any swellings anymore . . . my

> *depression was gone. . . . After a few days, the [arthritic] pain*
> *came back, but I knew I had just seen that it is possible to heal*
> *myself. . . . The depression didn't come back.*

In realizing "it is possible to heal myself," Eleonora verbalizes a standard daim-ista diagnosis that symptoms of psychophysical ailments are indicators of one's subconscious existential disorders (see Polari de Alverga 2011). She went on to claim she had also met God in the Daime works: "I saw Him too . . . a big beam of light." Eleonora declared that in these mystical awakenings, the Daime helped her "remember" that in one of her former lives she had known God, but something had caused her to banish God from her life. She had felt guilty when she first learned this, but this "God" figure told her that there is no such thing as guilt, and that she should "just be happy."

Like fellow daimistas, Eleonora blamed unhappiness and sickness on "habits," which develop when a person constructs egoic self-identities not in harmony with his/her true needs:

> *We create ego from when we are a little child. . . . Everybody*
> *wants to be liked, to be approved . . . so everybody builds up his*
> *ego to be liked, to be accepted by everybody. . . . When you grow*
> *up, most people notice that it doesn't work anymore. . . . When*
> *[the ego] is not helping you, the Daime shows you. Then, you can*
> *have a look at it, and also you can find out why do I have this*
> *habit? Why did I create this habit and does it serve me still? And*
> *if not, what can I do to change it? . . . For me, the time when I*
> *became a fardada . . . for me that was laying down a part of my*
> *ego, to put on the uniform.*

For daimistas with an irreligious past, this waking up to a repressed longing for spiritual connection inaugurates another mystical process, whereby false identities are discarded in favor of one's true aspirations.

Self-Knowledge or Purgation

For Underhill (2002[1911], 198), the stage of Purgation through Self-knowl-edge is "a getting rid of all those elements of normal experience which are not in harmony with reality: of illusion, evil, imperfection of every kind." For daimistas this is a never-ending facet of the mystical life. All of my informants idealize a courageous striving toward self-improvement through greater self-knowledge, a process they believe is accelerated by their Daime practice. This is poignantly illustrated in the case of Leon, a former heroin addict who now serves as commander for the CdSM congregation in Amsterdam. When I visited him at the home he shares with three other fardados, he answered my question about what it is like to experience the Daime:

> A very strong experience. It's very difficult to explain it in words what happens inside you. It is hell and heaven at the same time: moments that you really can feel very bad, but in the same moment you can feel what has happened is very good, it's the cleaning; when I arrived in Santo Daime I had many things to clean, many years of using drugs, drinking alcohol (a lot of sex, drugs, and rock and roll), not eating good food; so when you come to Santo Daime you clean many things that are inside you; you can call them the demônios [demons] who are inside you, you have to expose them. . . .
>
> [Daime] takes out the bad things that are inside you . . . and it gives you an understanding of why you are using drugs, why you have addiction. . . . I was already clean [of heroin] before Daime (I went to a therapeutic community and spent more than a year there). . . . [But] when I did all this therapy and spent all this time working on myself (getting rid of the addiction), I didn't feel I was healthy; this really completed in the Daime. [In the Daime] I got more understanding of why things happen in life, why you get addicted . . . the Daime put light on it. Santo Daime is light; it's like things that are in the dark come in the light, and then you can get rid of it. . . . The light is Nature, the stars, the sun, the moon. . . . When somebody asks me, "What is Santo Daime, can you explain?" I say, "No, if you want to know, come drink. That is the only way to understand . . . to have the experience". . . . That is the good thing about Santo Daime—it is very correct, very precise: what you put in is what you get back. It's like in life also: if you do good, you get good back; if you do bad you get bad. Doing bad in life I know very well, I have a lot of experience. . . . Because before I didn't know what I was doing here in this world (why I'm here, what is this?). I always felt that things were not right. . . . I never had a reason to be here. And after the Santo Daime, now I feel I have something to live for . . . and with the Daime you can help [others] also.

It is noteworthy that even though he had quit using heroin, Leon claims he did not feel he "completed" his cure of the underlying reasons for his addiction until he met the Daime. Leon is like other fardados in his sourcing of self-destructive behavior to subconscious "demons" that must be "exposed" in order to be "cleaned." Although they are less concerned with supernatural possessions and mediumship compared to daimistas in the Americas, fardados I met in Europe are just as focused on ritual procedures for discovering and expelling egoic fixations, impulses, and obsessions. In code-switching between spiritual and psychological rationales for the purging of inner "demons," informants assured me that the Daime performs a healing function by shedding light on hidden aspects of one's consciousness.

Illumination

After having their first awakening and the purgative revelations that follow, Europeans who decide to become fully initiated fardados do so because they believe the Daime to be a reliable technique for accessing mystical knowledge and shamanic healing. For Underhill (2002[1911], 233), the stage of Illumination signifies "the great swing back into the sunshine which is the reward of that painful descent into the 'cell of self-knowledge'. . . . The mystic now has a veritable foothold in that transcendental world into which they penetrate now and again." Whether their first steps into the mystical life had occurred inside or outside of Daime, informants' commitment to this doctrine is solidified when their self-experimentations with ayahuasca begin to bear lasting psycho-spiritual fruit. This shift to a deeper respect for the illuminative "power" of Santo Daime is exemplified by Margarida from Portugal. She had already been involved in spiritual self-reflection for many years before she first drank ayahuasca. But it was only in her first couple of Daime rituals that she found what she calls "proof" of realms beyond the material:

> *At a certain time I felt a group joy . . . that was the most important thing I felt the first time. . . . But the second time I had a much stronger experience. . . . It was more remarkable . . . I started to feel that that power, it has a truth. We started to feel harmony, and started to think that there really exists something that is not the material world that we're used to seeing. I had already experienced that, because I was a mystical person. I read a lot at that time.*

I like Tarot. . . . But when I started to feel the power of Daime,
then I really started to know what is the spiritual world. It was
really a proof that there is something more than this dimension.

While this subjective "proof" is not the empirical kind that scientists collect,
the modifications of perception that one can "feel" in the Daime rituals act
as corroborating evidence for people seeking to directly experience spiritual
otherworlds. Margarida's allusion to Tarot cards as "mystical" shows how
fardados' sense of mysticism includes occult divinatory practices borrowed
from Western Esotericism. Although not ubiquitous, Tarot cards were a
popular pastime for many daimistas across Europe. This wider reading of
mysticism is of the New Metaphysicals type (see Bender 2010, 51/55), part of
a late-modern social phenomenon we will concentrate on more fully in Part
VI. For now, it is necessary to mention my informants' emphatic disclaimer
that every illuminative wonder and insight they receive through their Daime
practice is counterbalanced by very grueling intervals of doubt and fear.

Surrender, or the Dark Night

To designate what results after many "oscillations between 'states of pleasure'
and 'states of pain,'" Underhill (2002[1911], 381) adopts St. John of the
Cross's "Dark Night" metaphor to mark the penultimate step along the
Mystic Way:

> The most intense period of the great swing-back into darkness
> which usually divides the "first mystic life," or Illuminative Way,
> from the "second mystic life," or Unitive Way, is generally a period
> of utter blankness and stagnation, so far as mystical activity is
> concerned. . . . The self is tossed back from its hard-won point
> of vantage. Impotence, blankness, solitude, are the epithets by
> which those immersed in this dark fire of purification describe
> their pains.

Waudru, a well-known elder fardada and Daime violinist from Belgium, had
just returned after a temporary hiatus from Daime when I interviewed her
on a small plot she owns in the rural outskirts of Brussels. Raised by atheist
parents who taught her that "to believe in God is to be naïve," Waudru says
she was the only person in her family with a desire for spirituality. After

marrying and having two sons, she was devastated when her husband left her for another woman. Beset by grief over the tragic end of her marriage, a friend invited Waudru and her son to a Zen monastery in the United States. Waudru spent a year in the monastery training in Za-Zen contemplation. Although she deems Zen as similar to the Daime, she prefers how the latter alternates silent meditative sessions with exuberant dancing and singing:

> *The source is the same, but I feel much more strong in my body with the Daime. With Za-zen you have to stay immobile and silent. . . . I did it, but I am not sure that I could do it again. . . . In the Daime . . . I feel the pleasure of being in life, of breathing, and I am also connected with the angels of music. I am completely in the service of the musicians, so I am very happy that I can play an instrument.*

But even though she says she has found much consolation and emotional healing in thirteen years of Daime practice, when I knew her in 2009–2011 she was suffering bouts of intense despair over revived feelings of loneliness and abandonment. She assured me that she was not suicidal, but she said she was so sad that she sometimes hoped she would die. In the depths of this desolation, Waudru also did not want to be in the company of her beloved music:

> WAUDRU: *When I went in my dark night of my soul, I didn't touch my violin. . . . I didn't want to play anymore. . . . No joy of living . . . I didn't want to live anymore.*

> INTERVIEWER: What do you mean by "dark night of the soul"?

> WAUDRU: *This deep suffering was in me, since childhood and before. . . . I was in the war, my father was Jewish, it was dangerous, he didn't want a child. . . . What I passed through, what made the difference between a depression . . . and what I had, I think that mine is a mystical illness, shall I say . . . an illness of the soul. Why did I have an illness of the soul? Because my soul was asking for that, and I received the answer. . . . It's not a depression . . . it's soul pain. And so antidepressants don't help.*

A common daimista inclination, Waudru reframes her existential tribulations as a test of faith within an ultimately beneficial process of mystical growth.

In her view, the "dark night" period she had recently confronted was the climax of a long battle to overcome depressive mood swings rooted in wounds of having been neglected by her father and forsaken by her husband. When I left Belgium, Waudru was still struggling with melancholy. However, she was firmly convinced that she would find salvation through her continued participation in the Daime works. This belief is akin to the mystical theory that one's withstanding of Dark Nights of the Soul are a blessing that helps one to grow in faith toward ultimate states of Union with the divine Absolute. In order to achieve this feat, the mystic must incessantly choose to surrender in faith to whatever God wills. Designating faith in God as the only succor that can sustain someone through such darkness, Kierkegaard (1990[1851], 82) calls the acme of this stage the "night of hopelessness":

> Faith is against understanding; faith is on the other side of death. And when you died or died to yourself, to the world, then you also died to all immediacy in yourself, also to your understanding. It is when all confidence in yourself or in human support, and also in God in an immediate way, is extinct, when every probability is extinct, when it is dark as on a dark night—it is indeed death we are describing—then comes the life-giving Spirit and brings faith. This faith is stronger than the whole world; it has the power of eternity; it is the Spirit's gift from God, it is your victory over the world in which you more than conquer.

Much as Kierkegaard (1990[1851], 20) seeks to instrumentalize "the horror of spiritual trial," fardados attend Daime works "to arouse restlessness oriented toward inward deepening." This is an old mystical formula: as long as one trustingly capitulates throughout devastating dark nights, the symbolic deaths of false aspects of one's ego give way to a process of salvational coalescence with the eternal soul or Higher Self (see Dourley 2014; Rohr 2011, 43–51).

Union

Only after one has surrendered fully to the Dark Night phase does it become possible to reach what Underhill (2002[1911], 413) calls "Union": "the final triumph of the spirit, the flower of mysticism, humanity's top note: the consummation towards which the contemplative life, with its long slow growth and costly training, has moved from the first." If there is someone to whom most European fardados would turn first to convey the mystical apex of Daime practice, it would be Md. Geraldine; in my interview with her, she described the state of being that is achieved through mastery of Daime works as "oneness" (see Partridge 2018, 17–19):

> *It is energy: you receive [it], then you pass [it on]; and that's why when it starts, the energy is coming in by the table, and then it goes further, and at the top of the pyramid, that's God. . . . You have to work on yourself [so] that you can reconnect the heart and the mind energy, that it becomes one thing: that you sync with your heart, connected with your mind . . . you're vertically connected with the Higher. . . . Then we have the oneness in the group because we are all connected. . . .*
>
> *When the work is perfect, then everybody has to understand this. We have people who are drinking Daime fifteen years and don't understand it, and we have people who drink Daime one or two times and understand more of this; it has to do with the energy development of the soul (it's also different for everybody); and Daime is open for everybody, so you have all* [kinds of people who come] *there.*

Her devotion to all-encompassing "oneness" also came across when I asked about God's gender:

> *I think that because we have the perception as human beings, we can only explain things like we recognize. But there is something much bigger than what we know. And I think* [God] *has nothing to do with Man or Woman, that's why I always say: "My Father and my Mother are One" (that's my personal opinion). . . . I don't see God as a person; God manifests Himself as a person, otherwise you cannot see him, you cannot recognize Him; but God is Light, God is Love, God is a stone, God is a leaf on a tree . . . but you can also talk about Maria is the Mother . . . the Earth is female, and Heaven is male . . . together it's one. . . .*
>
> *For me personally (because I don't believe in this or that), I believe in oneness. That's the purpose of the* [Santo Daime] *work: you sit there in the formation, and you are connected with God. . . . We are horizontally connected, but we are also vertically connected with God; so we are with each other in oneness through God. . . . I think*

Europe needs [oneness]*! Because what I see is in general, Europe is ruled by mind. . . . The ego separates. . . .* [But if the ego is cleaned] *. . . then the ego realizes that he is one with everybody.*

Having traversed the cycle of mystical experience multiple times throughout her Daime career, Md. Geraldine enunciates a view that directly corresponds to Underhill's "Union" phase of the mystical path, when all opposites are realized as one and the same.[1] The ways daimistas describe the peak experiences of Daime mysticism can be both *kataphatic* (describable) and *apophatic* (beyond words) (Gellman 2014). For instance, Frederik is an apophatic fardado:

> *When it comes to mystical experiences, the mind cannot comprehend what's happening . . . that is understanding with my Higher Consciousness. So it's an understanding that could not be understood by my mental brain. No, not at all. And that's why it's so difficult when you have mystical experiences to say something about it, because to express it you need the mind, but my mind doesn't have words for it.*

On the contrary is Leon, a fardado formerly addicted to heroin who now serves as commander of the Amsterdam Daime church. When I asked him to describe what human existence is from the Daime point of view, he proceeded to convey the kataphatic content of Daime mysticism:

> *We are one, but we are connected with* [both] *the Higher beings and with the Lower beings, with the* seires divinos [divine beings] *and with the* zombeteiros [mocking spirits] *who are in darkness (the cemeteries and these kinds of places), addicted people. But in the Daime you work with both, you work with whatever comes. . . .*
>
> *I don't believe in Hell . . . no, we create hell on earth I think. Hell is when you make a mess of your life and when you are in a really bad situation, when you are really addicted; many people live in very bad conditions. I don't believe that we go to a Hell or Heaven; no, Heaven and Hell are here already, we create them. It's not something like the Catholic Church or other religions say (if you don't behave good here you go to Hell). . . .* [no, it's actually] *Heaven and Earth:* [as above, so below], *and there is even underground!*

> *Have you ever traveled under the ground with Santo Daime? You've never felt so bad that you really cannot keep your head* [up]*? . . . These are very deep experiences. . . . I think that is more in the beginning. Also, more in the beginning you normally have the strongest* mirações [visions]*. . . . You go all over the place . . .* [but after a while] *you know how to handle the force. It's like if you go on a horse,* [at first] *you fall off many times, until you learn to keep the* [reins] *and you travel far with the horse. In the beginning you fall and you get hurt, you step up again and you fall down again. The Santo Daime is a very strong force, and in the beginning you are nothing. You even feel like you are really dying, and you have to let go; don't give resistance to this and then it* [will] *pass by. But if you contract, if you hold things in your body, and you go to deep experiences* [it will] *not feel very comfortable. After, you feel very good! But during, you'll pass some difficulties. But that is life; life is not only nice beauty, it also has another side.*

It is only because of my thorough ethnophenomenological experience in Daime works that Leon's narrative sounded like something other than the byproduct of an overactive imagination. To link daimistas' emic ideas to mainstream philosophy and theology, what Leon is describing here is very similar to the despair and anxiety Kierkegaard sees as symptomatic of paradoxical syntheses between finiteness and infinity within each human self. Likewise, Md. Geraldine proclaimed that her goal in Santo Daime and in life is to connect Heaven and Earth, the divine and the animal within yourself, "and then you become one."

By reading Daime practice through the lens of archetypal paths of mysticism, we can come to appreciate fardados' approach to physical and mental illnesses as stages of spiritual growth. Rather than trying to avoid or resist psychophysical miseries, daimistas are prone to welcome mystical ego-deaths as part of a recurrent process whereby "the dissolution of the mind beyond all differentiation is the basis of the deepest freedom and the root of a restorative resignation" (Dourley 2014, 94). This is why the British fardado Rocky said in his interview: "I think that most of the 'mad' people are the sane ones and I think that most so-called 'sane' people are the mad ones." Here, the active veneration of "creative illness" among indigenous shamans and religious mystics (Ellenberger 1968) finds agreement with the existentialist's "sickness" of self as an entranceway to salvation. As such, Daime devotees follow religious doctrines that invert materialist definitions of healthiness, in that suffering from despair is considered a virtue while denying that one is in despair is a sign of sickness (Kierkegaard 1989[1849]). Here, the existential theorists concur with mystical practitioners that "courage" in the face of despair/anxiety is a universal ideal for being human: "The striving for union with ultimate reality, and the corresponding courage to take the nonbeing which is implied in finitude upon oneself are a way of life which is accepted by and has shaped large sections of mankind" (Tillich 2014[1952], 147). Focusing on informants' reverence for "Great Spiritual Teachers" from a variety of eras, places, and cultural contexts, the next chapters will delve further into existential values that mark European daimistas as both similar to and distinct from other religions. In this way, etic evidence is marshalled to interpret daimistas' emic schemata of mystical Perennialism, demonstrating primary reasons why they are choosing to enlist in this foreign religion.

PART VI

FARDADOS' EXISTENTIAL VALUES

Figure 13.1. *Michael Foretelling the Crucifixion to Adam* (Illustration to Milton's "Paradise Lost"), William Blake (1808), Photograph © 2019 Museum of Fine Arts, Boston.

When the striving one droops under the prototype, crushed, almost despairing, the Redeemer raises him up again. . . . [Lord Jesus Christ] you left your footprints, you, the holy prototype for the human race and for every individual, so that by your Atonement the saved might at every moment find the confidence and boldness to want to strive to follow you.

—Søren Kierkegaard, *Judge for Yourself!*

We deal here with . . . a small but ever-growing group of heroic figures, living at transcendent levels of reality which we immersed in the poor life of illusion, cannot attain: breathing an atmosphere whose true quality we cannot even conceive.

—Evelyn Underhill, *Mysticism: A Study in the Nature and Development of Spiritual Consciousness*

13

Timeless Wisdom

So far, the most direct attempt to answer the question of *why* some people across Europe are adopting Santo Daime is found in the work of Alberto Groisman. In a recent book chapter, Groisman (2009, 186) speculates that since some Dutch fardados expressed regret about the history of European colonialism, he believes people become members of Santo Daime to bestow "reparations" to the native peoples of the Americas. While his efforts are commendable, Groisman's conclusions do suffer from certain misreadings of the ethnographic situation. Of course, Groisman was indeed picking up on a general sentiment among European fardados, such as when Margarida, a fardada from Portugal, talked to me about her countrymen having been the first European settlers to arrive in Brazil: "It's a . . . historic exchange; we go to Brazil yesterday, and now Brazil comes to us through Santo Daime; so when we went there, we took with us Catholicism, and then we obliged the indians to accept that religion, and now [Daime is] a way to say, 'I'm sorry . . . your religion is so beautiful, we are learning so much with you'. . . . It's a very beautiful . . . syncretism . . . now [that] we are taking [interest in their] religion." The Dutch fardados I met did sympathize with sufferings inflicted upon indigenous peoples of the Americas, but they distanced themselves from the notion that they must "clean the heavy karma" of colonialism (Groisman 2009, 195), instead saying things like, "I forgive myself for my ancestors." When I showed Groisman's (2009, 186) theory[1] to European fardados, they all rejected it as the principal reason for their participation in Santo Daime. For example, one elder of the Dutch Santo Daime remarked that Groisman's reparations theory is too "narrow-minded" an explanation. I also asked the commander of CdU in Belgium if he agrees with Groisman's theory that European daimistas are motivated by the history of imperialism, and he responded:

> Not at all. I haven't thought about this, no. I do not at all have a feeling with this. Here [Groisman 2009, 186], this is something in the past with the people who were living then, and in this sense I do not have anything to do with it. . . . Yes, of course [colonization] happened, indeed . . . [but] I do not feel guilty.

Numerous other informants avowed that this hypothesis of a "reparations" motive does not represent European daimistas as a collective. Among my informants from the Low Countries, several recognized that Groisman relied on the author of a self-published booklet, who is more concerned with "cleaning of karmic bonds" than are most European fardados (Bogers 1999, 4).

There has also been a tendency to interpret the global expansion of Santo Daime in the West as tied to recent developments of late modernity (see Dawson 2013; Groisman 2000). Certainly these explanations capture some of the causal links between the globalization of ayahuasca and new forms of enchantment that have appeared in the West during the late twentieth and early twenty-first centuries (see Heelas 2008, Bender 2010, Fuller 2000, 51–89). Citing Paul Heelas (1996), Groisman (2000, 110) does correctly identify some of the traits that European fardados share with "New Age" devotees: "New Age introduced in its project of self a new type of individualism, which replaced what can be called 'modern' 'libertarian' individualism, in which the material 'necessities' of the 'ego,' consumerism, prosperity and pleasure—were the main concerns, with a 'postmodern' individualism, in which the 'sacred' 'necessities' of the spirit—transcendence, creativity and aesthetics . . . could be satisfied." Yet the terms *postmodern* and *New Age* are not in themselves accurate tags for Daime in Europe. The postmodern is defined as "incredulity toward metanarratives" (Lyotard 1984, xxiv), but fardados are inclined to trust in the cosmological and theological doctrines of various mystical traditions. As Wouter Hanegraaff (Hanegraaff 1998, 9) has noted, the "New Age" is a "poorly defined label which has different meanings and connotations for different people." For this reason, "New Age" is more of a "buzzword" with a "wide and often vague use" for describing "the amorphous nature of the phenomena it refers to" (Hanegraaff 2002, 249). Although its popular use began to crystalize during the 1960s, the moniker "New Age" is now being abandoned as denoting "a superficial and 'flaky' spirituality" (Znamenski 2007, xi). Because the subsequent "commercialization" of this nebulous "counterculture" renders it inauthentic to many, Hanegraaff (1998, 17[n49]) predicted that "the term 'New Age' will probably not survive the twentieth century as a generally-used label."[2] Moreover, identifying New Age groups apart from the wider population is practically impossible because New Age ideas have become fashionable beyond their point of origin. In fact, many mainstream Christians assent to characteristically New Age beliefs such as channeling, astrology, and reincarnation (Gallup and Lindsay 1999; Lewis 2004, 16; see also Csordas 1997, 26/54). Boundaries of the New Age concept are so fluid that it becomes impossible to tell who does and does not belong to this group.

Besides these terminological issues, the main problem with the New Age[3] category is that it misrepresents the seriousness of fardados' Daime practice. Of course, some New Age enthusiasts are attracted to Santo Daime by the promise of ecstatic visions and personal exploration. But the intense exertion and dedication that is required for long-term learning in Daime eventually deter those looking for a spiritual quick fix. In contrast, Soares's (2010, 66) linking of Santo Daime to an upsurge of a "new religious consciousness" is more applicable because he notes that fardados' commitment is "closer to Spartan discipline than to a vague, pervasive 'hedonistic narcissism.'" My informants do accept that some New Age ideas have been absorbed as one among many other elements within Daime's multifarious cosmology. But fardado informants largely dismissed the "New Age" as *zweverig* (Dutch: "woolly") or as "faith without *firmeza* [firmness]" because they see it as shallow pseudo-spirituality. As one fardado reacted when asked about Groisman's labeling of Daime as New Age: "I don't think so; I think New Age began in the sixties in the hippie time, [whereas] Santo Daime is really old." Although the 1960s "hippie" era can be traced to the nineteenth-century Romantic period[4] (see Ray and Anderson 2000, 142/148), fardado informants assume that Daime is directly allied with the invention of ayahuasca in Pre-Columbian South America. In addition, daimista activists in Germany associate Daime ontology with strains of religious philosophy going all the way back to ancient Greece:

> The concept of a subtle metaphysical astral plane of existence has its origins in the philosophic mysticism of neoplatonism where it was first postulated by Proclus. The concept was known in alchemical and hermetic traditions and popularized in the 19th and 20th century by the teachings of Theosophy and Neorosicrucianism. (Rohde and Sander 2011, 350[n10])

Even if the term *New Age* does not suffice, there must nevertheless be a home-grown aspect of European fardados' worldview that engendered a receptivity to Santo Daime. This brings us back to our original problem: If people's concept of self is culturally constructed, why are some Europeans reared in a secularist or traditional Christian context attracted to a foreign spiritual practice like the ritual use of ayahuasca? Breaking new theoretical ground, I will now seek to satisfy Hanegraaff's (2011, 99) petition that insofar as the rise of Daime in Europe is concerned, "the very foundations for an adequate scholarly study of 'entheogenic religions,' including aya-huasca religions, still need to be created." Through etic and emic analyses of the way European fardados make sense of their chosen spirituality, this penultimate section locates such foundations in enchanted metaphysical systems that have persisted throughout Western history.

Fardados show disfavor for the dominance of materialism that was ush-ered in with post-Enlightenment modernity. Although it may seem perplexing from a secularization perspective, the trend of Europeans joining Santo Daime is comprehensible as part of a long-term movement in Western societies. There have always been subcultures resisting the physicalist values of the Enlightenment due to a deep personal preference for idealism. Isaiah Berlin (1979, 1) coined the concept of a "counter-Enlightenment" (dating back to the ancient Greeks) as a fixed opposition to the Enlightenment "proclamation of the autonomy of reason and the methods of the natural sciences, based on observation as the sole reliable method of knowledge, and the consequent rejection of the authority of revelation, sacred writings . . . and every form of non-rational and transcendent source of knowledge" (see also Hanegraaff 1998, 411–12). Hence, the oppositional disparities in post-Enlightenment systems of thought—e.g., Leibniz versus Voltaire, Spinoza versus Descartes, Kant versus Hume—such that each era produces champions of either sub-jectivist or objectivist epistemology. We still see this dichotomy between soft and hard ontologies playing out in parochial religion versus science "debates" between prominent public intellectuals. Charles Taylor, a student of Isaiah Berlin at Oxford, is also intrigued by enduring doubts about secularization narratives, and is not surprised that spiritual alternatives continue to pop up in the West. In his book *Sources of the Self*, Taylor (1989, 32–43) traced historical developments in Western concepts of self, critiquing the "ethno-centrism" of the prevailing Euro-American view that "what we are 'really' is separated individuals."[5] In his more recent book, Taylor (2007) updates his discussion of how the notion of a "buffered identity"—roughly equivalent to fardados' notion of the *ego*—has acquired an unquestioned status in secular modernity. He contrasts the "transcendent" worldview of premodern enchantment with the "imminent frame" of disenchanted secularism: convinced that the source of mind is confined to individual animal selves rather than imbued throughout Nature, "the buffered self begins to find the idea of spirits, moral forces, causal powers with a purposive bent, close to incomprehensible" (Taylor 2007, 539). But while Taylor (2007, 552–553) recognizes that this "immanent" view is now the established norm, he also stresses the "sense of loss" that many modern subjects feel as a latent longing for transcendence, such that receptivity to enchantment persists. As the current century emerges, social scientists are recognizing that the decline of conventional religions does not portend a waning of all spiritual strivings. Contrary to Weber's prediction that modern scientific rationalism would breed "disenchantment," psychological anthropologist Pascal Boyer (2008, 1038–39) summarizes how the latest

> findings from cognitive psychology, neuroscience, cultural anthropology and archaeology promise to change our view of religion. . . . The evidence shows that the mind has no single belief network, but myriad distinct networks that contribute to making religious claims quite natural to many people. . . . By contrast, disbelief is generally the result of deliberate, effortful work against our natural cognitive dispositions—hardly the easiest ideology to propagate.

Rather than viewing the rise of Santo Daime and other "new" religious movements as a sudden resurgence of religious zeal following a period of universal secularization, it is more plausible that this is a continuation of an ever-present subgroup of Europeans with spiritual affinities. This penchant for spiritual belief and practice endures as a continually evolving counter-Enlightenment discourse within modern Western consciousness. On the one hand, it is evident from interactions with fardados that they share a keenness for newfangled spiritual pursuits. On the other hand, Santo Daime is being adopted by Europeans who are also intent on rediscovering sacred knowledge from Axial religiosities that began thousands of years ago.

In line with modern American "mystics" profiled by Bender (2010), fardados in Europe are simultaneously complicit in and cynical about dominant hegemonies of capitalism, materialism, and consumerism. However, exclusively synchronic depictions of Santo Daime as "New Age" fail to account for a deeper heritage at play, in that daimistas must be understood as just the latest in a long history of Europeans oriented toward contemplative lifestyles. Rather than confining the transnational daimista movement to modernism and postmodernism, we must also attend to geographers who observe that Santo Daime is being

> drawn into, and its practitioners embrace, an anti-modern discourse merging indigenous therapeutic and spiritual knowledge with demands for social justice and deep ecology. This is somewhat surprising, however, since shamanism and indigeneity are grafted onto, more than rooted in, the religion's history and traditions. (Lowell and Adams 2016, 15)

More accurately, European daimistas carry on a counter-Enlightenment legacy congruent with theistic strains of existential philosophy (e.g., Kierkegaard, Buber) and other mystical or occult traditions of Europe (e.g., Evelyn Underhill, Simone Weil, Rudolf Steiner). The esotericist elements of Santo Daime's foundational ethos reflect that "European-derived movements provided a theoretical framework for interpreting ayahuasca" (Meyer 2014, 193). Just as with Bender's (2010, 4–7) "New Metaphysicals" in the United States, European daimistas are "*entangled* in social life, in history, and in our academic and nonacademic imaginations." From this more inclusive scale, the anthropologist studying Daime is not only faced with a new spirituality organized around an indigenous entheogen from the New World. Having interviewed dozens of daimistas, I think the more riveting issue is that European expansions of ayahuasca religion manifest Western mythologies about an ideal human type—the "inner-worldly mystic"—a popularized psychology about holy dispositions of introspectiveness found across different cultures throughout time; it is this more recent "view of mysticism, focused on the individual and shorn of its rootage in a specific religious matrix, that has carried weight for the proponents of modern spirituality" (see Parsons 2010, 18–19). In this manner, Santo Daime embodies a novel reinsertion of inner-worldly mysticism into the framework of organized religion.

Other scholars have documented the authentic personal desires that are driving individual agents to join this new religious practice. As illustrated by the "suiscope" metaphor from chapter 11, there exists a broad consensus that the core of Santo Daime is "autopoiesis," a "transformation of the self" toward "self-betterment" (Schmidt 2007, 141–44; Dawson 2013, 106/118–19/178–82/226). Surveying this global movement, Barnard (2014, 678) proposes that one of the most important reasons why individuals become members of the Santo Daime tradition and continue to engage in this difficult and demanding path of inner purification is not primarily due to the depth of the religious understandings, or even because of the profound mystical and visionary experiences that frequently occur, but rather, perhaps primarily, and crucially, because of the physical, moral, emotional, mental, and spiritual transformations that they perceive within themselves and within others as a result of drinking the Daime.

The results of my fieldwork likewise show that spiritual and therapeutic self-transformation is the chief goal among European daimistas. Probing into fardados' intentions for a ritual curing of the ego, previous chapters outlined my informants' emic perspective of "solutions" to inform new etic perspectives on the medicinal potentials of ayahuasca. Understanding Santo Daime as a "suiscope" conveys how fardados explain the mechanism of their ceremonial introspection as catalyzing upgraded versions of selfhood. To excavate deeper into this pivotal theme of existential anthropology, the present section outlines fardados' belief that Daime works help them to be more like Jesus, Buddha, the Virgin Mary, and other great spiritual teachers of lore.

European Fardados' Domain of Great Spiritual Teachers

When 32 fardados from Belgium (16 males, 16 females) were asked to list all the Great Spiritual Teachers[6] (GSTs) that they know, I had expected to acquire a list that would show a heavy emphasis on Christian figures and leaders of Santo Daime. But as seen in Table 13.1, the names they mentioned spanned a wide array of spiritual traditions from different historical eras. The collective list of 146 Great Spiritual Teachers (GSTs) cited by Belgian fardados includes not only religious personalities, but also ancient philosophers, modern scholars, famous artists/musicians, informants' personal friends, and even supernatural entities such as angels (see Appendix IV). Broken down by geography, the list includes 54 (37%) people from Europe, 33 (23%) from Asia, 14 (10%) from South America, 13 (9%) from North America, 13 (9%) from the Middle East, and one (<1%) from Africa.[7] The list also included 11 names of nonhuman entities from various spiritual traditions (e.g., 4 angels, 2 bodhisattvas), seven items that cannot be fixed geographically (e.g., "Daime people"), and three entire cultures (e.g., Maya,

Table 13.1. Belgian Fardados' Domain of Great Spiritual Teachers Ranked by Smith's *s*

Rank	GST Name	Frequency	% of Freelists that include item (n = 42)	Smith's *s*
1	Jesus Christ	27	84%	0.639
2	Buddha	22	69%	0.535
3	*Mestre Irineu*	15	47%	0.313
4	Gandhi	10	31%	0.212
5	*Pd. Sebastião*	8	25%	0.171
6	Mohammed	6	19%	0.141
7	Krishna	5	16%	0.134
8	Virgin Mary	8	25%	0.105
9	Dalai Lama	7	22%	0.105
10	Eckhart Tolle	6	19%	0.090

India, Arabs). Setting aside two ambiguous items ("friend" and "my psychotherapist"), the remaining list of 123 items designating past or present human beings includes 102 (83%) males and 21 (17%) females. This list of 123 human names can also be divided historically, with 31 (25%) of the personalities having lived before the seventeenth-century Enlightenment and 92 (75%) having lived during or after the Enlightenment. Out of 83 names from Belgians' GST list that can be reliably grouped into specific religious categories, these can be broken down as follows:

7 (8.4%)	Buddhist
2 (2.4%)	Chinese (Taoism, Confucianism)
18 (21.7%)	Christian
15 (18.1%)	Daimista
21 (25.3%)	Hindu
4 (4.8%)	Islamic
1 (1.2%)	Jewish
9 (10.8%)	New Religious Movements / New Age
5 (6.0%)	Occult / Theosophy / Anthroposophy
1 (1.2%)	Zoroastrian

We see a similar array of ancient and modern names from multiple different religious traditions in continent-wide GST data collected with 42 fardados

Table 13.2. European Fardados' Domain of Great Spiritual Teachers Ranked by Smith's *s*

Rank	GST Name	Frequency	% of Freelists that include item (n = 42)	Smith's *s*
1	Jesus Christ	34	81%	0.650
2	*Mestre Irineu*	23	55%	0.298
3	Buddha	16	38%	0.259
4	Osho	15	36%	0.239
5	Dalai Lama	13	31%	0.179
6	*Pd. Sebastião*	13	31%	0.154
7	*Pd. Alfredo*	11	26%	0.103
8	Krishnamurti	7	17%	0.100
9	John the Baptist	6	14%	0.099
10-A	Virgin Mary	9	21%	0.095
10-B	Gandhi	6	14%	0.095

from around Europe (a sample that includes two Israeli immigrants who were then living in Germany and the Netherlands). Comprising a sample of 21 males and 21 females, I collected GST freelists from Daime members with the following national origins: Dutch (6 fardados), Spanish (6) German (4), Portuguese (4), French (3), Italian (3), Austrian (2), Czech (2), English (2), Finnish (2), Irish (2), Israeli (2), Swiss (2), Greek (1), and Romanian (1).

As seen in Table 13.2 (above), the top ten names on GST freelists from fardados around Europe (Smith's *s* > 0.09) expose both similarities and disparities compared to Belgian fardados. Even while seven of the top names are the same in both datasets, some highly salient GST names at the local Belgian level have lower salience from the continent-wide perspective of fardados across the rest of Europe, and vice versa. The total list of 196 GST names provided by European fardados also encompasses religious leaders, philosophers, scholars, artists/musicians, informants' personal friends, and supernatural entities (see Appendix V). Setting aside 52 ambiguous items (e.g., mother, children, Inca, Hopi), the remaining 144 names of historically documented human "teachers" include these ratios: 121 (84%) are male and 23 (16%) are female, 41 (28%) are pre-Enlightenment and 103 (72%) are post-Enlightenment figures, and they are geographically split between Asians (47 or around 33%), Europeans (37; 26%), North Americans (25; 17%), South Americans (17; 12%), Africans (4; 3%) and those from the Middle

East (14; 9%). I can discern specific religious affiliations for 112 names on Europeans' GST list, distributed as follows:

14 (12.5%)	Buddhist
5 (4.5%)	Chinese (Taoism, Confucianism)
17 (15.2%)	Christian
17 (15.2%)	Daimista
24 (21.4%)	Hindu
4 (3.6%)	Indigenous Peoples of the Americas
4 (3.6%)	Islamic
8 (7.1%)	Jewish
11 (9.8%)	New Religious Movements / New Age
7 (6.2%)	Occult / Theosophy / Anthroposophy
1 (0.8%)	Zoroastrian

These breakdowns of the collective freelists suggest that fardados tend to revere a geographically and historically diverse range of spiritual teachers, but with more emphasis placed on post-Enlightenment males from Asia, Europe, and the Americas. However, with the most salient teachers—i.e., those that were mentioned many times and occurred nearer the top of individuals' freelists—there is a balance between ancient and more modern names.

After the freelists were compiled, I visited the eight Belgian fardados who had provided the longest freelists to carry out follow-up interviews[8] (this subgroup consisted of four males and four females). Below, I review how these fardados' interpreted the occurrence of the top ten names on the GST freelists. Rankings in the Belgian dataset is prioritized because the closer contact I had with Belgian fardados permitted me to apply greater scrutiny to their GST freelists.

First in Both Belgian and European Freelists: **Jesus Christ** (7–5 BCE—30–33 CE)[9]

Regarding Jesus Christ, a fardado from CdAI said, "I'm not astonished that Jesus came in first position here in Belgium, because most of the people here (even if they don't believe in Christ), they grow [up] in this type of approach." All informants concurred that due to European heritage and the Christian background of Santo Daime, Jesus's appearance as the most prominent spiritual teacher is to be expected. A majority of European fardados were reared as Christians—the lion's share as Catholics—but many reject what they see as the institutional corruption of mainstream churches more interested in power and moral guilt than in teaching about love and forgiveness. On the other hand, many daimistas credit Daime with helping them rediscover their connection to Christ, a bond that dates back to their childhood education. As Frederik from Belgium told me:

> Because of our history. Because of our faith. We are a very, very Catholic country. And although many say we are not Catholic anymore, we still are. I think a lot of fardados took a teaching of Jesus out of the very narrow-minded kind of Catholic religion and put it into perspective. And I think that the Daime also opens the other dimensions of the energy of Jesus, and not the narrow-minded things that we all learned here in school.

The culture of Christianity in Europe gives a partial explanation for why Jesus is the most prominent GST on fardados' freelists. As discussed in previous chapters, daimistas' conception of Jesus is quite distinct from the average European's. As one fardada told me: "Ayahuasca, we say that it's Jesus, that it's Jesus in another form." Jesus Christ was the only name on the GST freelist of Justino from Portugal, who explained this by saying: "There are others but they all come from him."

Arguing that Mestre Irineu is a divinely sanctioned "vessel" for uniting Christianity with Afro-Brazilian spiritualities and the indigenous ayahuasca traditions, Frederik responded this way to my question about whether the teachings of Jesus are contained in the Daime doctrine:

> I believe they are in a very subtle and humble way. You can also read it in a lot of hymns, certainly in the hymns of the Mestre. What I like so much in the hymns of the Mestre is that there is no judgment at all, and that's why I appreciate it so much. So yes, in certain hymns and hinarios you can feel, taste these teachings of Jesus. Yes I do believe that. . . .
>
> When [Jesus] came to earth, of course he was a vessel as well. I believe that everyone who incarnates in a physical body is here to be a vessel. But when you see his path and put him out of that body, then we're talking about something very different. Because being able to channel the divine the way [Jesus did], then I only can try to imagine how many paths that specific soul must have been wandering [in past lives].

With some exceptions (Araújo 2001; Barnard forthcoming; Madera 2009; Oliveira 2009), disproportionately few scholarly treatments provide in-depth analysis of Jesus's magnitude in Santo Daime—the present book aims to help remedy this lacuna. As a ready example of Jesus's centrality, notions of the Holy Mass and the Last Supper are evoked in the epigraphic hymn #14 of Pd. Valdete (brother of Pd. Alfredo, son of Pd. Sebastião), which says, "I drink Daime and consider this wine; the same wine Jesus gave . . . to his apostles." With Brazilian congregations, it may well be true that "the popular Catholic identity at the core of Santo Daime belief and practice is somewhat removed from the Catholic Christianity of the modern West" (Dawson 2013, 14). Not so for fardados in Europe, many of whom draw on their Catholic/Christian upbringing to reinterpret their Daime practice along the lines of books such as *The Coming of the Cosmic Christ* (M. Fox 1988) or *The Psychedelic Gospels* (Brown and Brown 2016; 2019).

What is so striking about Christ's returning to Europe in the form of Santo Daime is that it provides an alternative rubric for Europeans raised according to more mainstream understandings of Jesus. Perhaps residual bitterness about Christianity meant that a few fardados (five Belgians, eight Europeans) did not include Jesus in their GST freelists. Yet even fardados who deny any personal dedication to Jesus still evince relief at the ways that Daime has rehabilitated their previously resentful views of Christianity. This attitude is exemplified by Oswald, a fardado from Switzerland who was anti-Christian when he began with Daime:

> What I see is that, especially people who really believe in God, who want to have a religious system, they see what happened with the Catholic Church, with sexual abuse of children; I mean it's hard to be a Catholic these days, with all the information you have; It's hard to be Islamic, it's hard to be a Jew; in all the big traditions it's hard to be there. A lot of people are very believing, they want to be in a religious system, but since the whole world is so transparent . . . these people who really want to be in a religious system are suffering. . . .
>
> Most of the loud atheists in our society would have a very hard time to sing [for] so many hours about Jesus and Maria, because they are just making jokes about everything religious. So it really depends on what kind of atheist you are. . . . Because I always said, "I don't know!" that's more agnostic, and an atheist is somebody who really says, "I know there is no God." I mean,

how do you know? You can really believe that there is nothing, but you don't know, nobody really knows. . . . Sometimes if there are discussions on TV about does God exist?, I really feel some (not all) of the atheists are as small-minded as very stupid religious people. . . . But to be honest, I guess everybody has to say (if he has an open mind), we don't know!

I still don't know. . . . There was a time I realized I have so much resistance in my system; if there are some lines in the [Daime] hymns with Jesus, and you have to repeat them, I didn't repeat them. . . . I realized, okay, [there's] still resistance; but now I hope I have [recognized] deeply in my system [that] there is nothing wrong with Jesus; the Jesus energy is love, is justice, is alegria *[joy], is all the good things. . . . So even if you are atheist, you have to say there is for sure nothing wrong about Jesus. If people love each other, if there is justice on Earth, that's the best. . . . You can really say there are so many [bad] things about the Catholic church, about all the religions, but I have never heard somebody saying Jesus was a bad guy. . . . So I believe in the great shamans, they do big healing things; okay, Jesus might have been a shaman! He was a good guy.*

For fardados the Daime sacrament is a shamanic vehicle or mystical tool through which they can develop an intimate relationship with the astral energy of Jesus and other spiritual teachers. In line with Kierkegaard (1990[1876], 160–61), most European fardados regard Jesus as the undisputed spiritual teacher "prototype," whose "life must have been designed from the very beginning": "Just as the essentially Christian always places opposites together, so the glory is not directly known as glory but, just the reverse, is known by inferiority, debasement—the cross that belongs together with everything that is essentially Christian is here also." In the Daime ritual space, the second coming of Christ is denoted by the double-beam cross, which reminds daimistas about the greater purpose of sufferings they endure through ayahuasca. Unlike Kierkegaard, daimistas broaden their idea of Christ to include saints and prophets that have appeared in all genuine spiritualities throughout time. While the following names are also prominent in the minds of most daimistas, none of them match Jesus's high cultural salience. In short, fardados think all great spiritual teachers are famous examples of God's divine Light arriving into the world in human form, an archetype epitomized by Jesus Christ.

Second in Belgian / Third in European Freelist: **Gautama Buddha** (c. 566–486 BCE)

Unlike Jesus's foreseeable appearance as an important figure in a Christian context, Buddha is not so predictable here because he is not traditionally part of the Santo Daime doctrine. However, fardados did affirm that "Buddhism is quite well known" in Europe. Lars explained why he admires Buddha:

> *Buddha is an important message. He gave a teaching of how you can fulfill your life without illusion, without suffering, and he gave all the steps: follow this and you have rebirth in Nirvana, you'll become one again with the One. And he doesn't speak about God, it's only about humans, about our psychology, our mind.*

So even though their hymns officially evoke Christian, Afro-Brazilian, and indigenous Amazonian entities, fardados see the teachings of the Buddha and the Daime doctrine as complementary ways to reach personal enlightenment. Pd. Alex Polari is well-known in the global daimista movement as a proponent of implementing Buddhist knowledge into the Daime.

Third in Belgian / Second in European Freelist: **Mestre Irineu** (1890–1971 CE)

Prior to reaching his grownup height of "almost two meters (6.56 feet)," the founder of Santo Daime Raimundo Irineu Serra was born on December 15, 1890 (Mendes do Nascimento 2005; Moreira and MacRae 2011, 39/70). Although an adult identification card gives his birth year as 1892, Bill Barnard (forthcoming) affirms research by Moreira and MacRae (2011, 70) that updates the record with a newfound baptismal certificate, listing Irineu Serra's year of birth as 1890. This would mean that Irineu Serra died on July 6, 1971, having lived fourscore years to the age of eighty. The man who would become the Mestre (Portuguese: "Master") was born to Sancho Martinho de Mattos and Joana D'Assunção Serra, but Irineu later adopted his piously religious mother's surname after his father abandoned the family when he was a boy (Mendes do Nascimento 2005; Moreira and MacRae 2011, 69–72). He spent his childhood and young adulthood in his hometown of São Vicente Ferrer (Maranhão state, Brazil), a village of about eighteen thousand present-day inhabitants located 280 km southwest of the state capital at São Luís (Cavnar 2011, 27; Labate and Pacheco 2004).

With its hub and main *casas* (houses) descended from slave-trade diasporas in São Luís, *Tambor de Mina*[10] was the main religion of Afro-Brazilians in turn-of-the-century Maranhão. Since Tambor de Mina is related to the broader Afro-Brazilian spirituality known as Candomblé, it is important to recognize how the cultural context of Irineu Serra's formative years influenced his creation of Santo Daime. The sway of Tambor de Mina was weaker among populations located outside the capital, where Afro-Brazilian communities tended to incorporate indigenous Amazonian elements into their spiritual practices.[11] J. Lorand Matory (2005, 120) reports that many established Candomblé temples "were quite comfortable with the simultaneous or hybrid adoration of Roman Catholic and African divinities."

During the 1890s, a descendant of slaves such as Irineu Serra would have been taught whatever vestiges of Afro-Brazilian religion had endured amid his community in the face of a dominant Catholic hegemony. Living in the hinterland outside São Luís, he was separated from the more regulated forms of Tambor de Mina because of the lack of any means for swift transport between his hometown and the capital in the early twentieth century. He was most likely exposed to a hyper-syncretic rural faith called *pajelança,* what Labate and Pacheco (2004, 315) define as "a religious manifestation formed from elements of popular Catholicism, indigenous cultures, Tambor de Mina, [and] folk medicine." It is therefore evident that intermixing propensities in Santo Daime date back to this diverse religious initiation the Mestre received during his youth in northeast Brazil.[12]

While social scientists have been very interested in piecing together Mestre Irineu's personal history (Dawson 2007; Labate and Pacheco 2004), European fardados are less concerned with his ethnic heritage. Instead, my informants emphasize the exemplary persona of the Mestre as a distillation of all the values espoused by the Daime doctrine. For instance, an elder Belgian fardada (Waudru) claimed that when she was traveling in Brazil with Luiz Mendes, a contemporary of Mestre Irineu, he told her that the Mestre was distinguished by his "nobility and simplicity." Frederik said that he is not surprised that Mestre Irineu appeared very high on fardados' GST freelists "because you're asking the question to people in the Daime . . . My line in the Santo Daime is the Mestre, he's my compass."

Even as every fardado would agree that Mestre exemplifies the purity of heart and spiritual genius of all Great Spiritual Teachers, it is important to note that Mestre did not live a spotless life. For instance, he habitually smoked tobacco and he was a serial monogamist who left at least one of his children fatherless when as a young man he abandoned their mother, perhaps because she disapproved of his drinking ayahuasca (Mendes do Nascimento 2005; see also Barnard forthcoming). And yet despite his all-too-human qualities, the Mestre is revered among modern daimistas because even amid intense social conflict he was known throughout his adopted homeland for radiating a Christlike commitment to "harmony, love, truth, and justice," which he infused into the Daime doctrine and his many hymns. Mestre Irineu is thus seen as a personification of ethical and mystical values that comprise the fabric of the new religion he founded. Like Frederik, fardados told me that they turn their awareness to his image as a psychospiritual "compass" both during works and in daily life. More details on the life of Mestre Irineu can be found in biographies by Barnard (forthcoming), de Assis (2020), Labate and Pacheco (2004), Mendes do Nascimento (2005), or Moreira and MacRae (2011).

[Note: I group together the next few teachers in order to capture the prominence of Hinduism in the minds of European fardados, as made evident by the fact that the majority of GSTs mentioned in their freelists are from India. Daime mysticism is also quietly spreading to India. I know this because I met a Brazilian fardada at Alto Santo in Acre, who lives part-time in India.]

Fourth in Belgian / Tied for Tenth in European Freelist: Mohandas Gandhi (1869–1948 CE)

The moral leader in India's quest for independence from British colonization, Gandhi is revered the world over. Fardados' dislike of barriers erected between religious identities is evoked in Gandhi's refusal to limit his own spiritual affiliation when he said, "I am a Christian and a Hindu and a Moslem and a Jew." Fardados also concur with Gandhi's critique of modern Christianity:

> If then I had to face only the Sermon on the Mount and my own interpretation of it, I should not hesitate to say, "Oh yes, I am a Christian." But negatively I can tell you that much of what passes as Christianity is a negation of the Sermon on the Mount. . . . Jesus possessed a great force, the love force, but Christianity became disfigured when it went to the West. It became the religion of kings. (quoted in Fischer 1954, 130–131)

Fardados likewise disparage the corruption and hypocrisy of powerful religious institutions. In contrast, Jeannette from Belgium explained why she admires Gandhi:

He showed the power of integrity. . . . His belief and his life were one: he believed that you have to go this way and he [went] this way; he took responsibility . . . and he communicated a lot. And he's near to us; the words of Jesus and Buddha, they are far away, but Gandhi is closer in time to us.

This attention to the time periods in which a GST lived is an important chronological feature of fardados' spiritual orientation, discussed in more detail below. But before we go farther into these temporal issues, let us first consider the other salient personas on fardados' GST freelists.

Thirty-second in Belgian / Fourth in European Freelist: Osho (1931–1990 CE)

As discussed earlier in the historical overview of Dutch Daime congregations, fardados in Europe have long maintained ties to the Rajneesh, or Osho, movement organized around the charismatic guru Bhagwan Shree Rajneesh, aka Osho. Osho is a controversial character, to say the least, a scofflaw scholar whose global following included some of the founding daimistas of the Netherlands (Groisman 2000, 25/127–28[n91]). In the following passage from Osho (1995, 147), one senses why his pan-religious message appealed to many modern seekers:

> The whole art for the new humanity will consist in the secret of listening to the heart consciously, alertly, attentively. And follow it through any means, and go wherever it takes you. . . . But don't follow rules imposed from the outside. No imposed rule can ever be right, because rules are invented by people who want to rule you. Yes, sometimes there have been great enlightened people in the world too—a Buddha, a Jesus, a Krishna, a Mohammed. They have not given rules to the world, they have given their love.

While Osho's ideas echo some of the same themes present in daimista mysticism, since Osho's 1990 death (the same year Pd. Sebastião passed away) European fardados have slowly drifted to more Daime-centric priorities. It is also interesting to note the disparity in Osho's ranking on the two freelist datasets, showing that fardados in Belgium are less associated with Osho allegiances that still linger among fardados elsewhere in Europe.

Thirteenth in Belgian / Eighth in European Freelist:
Jiddu Krishnamurti (1895–1986 CE)

An India-born figurehead of the Theosophical movement. Like Osho and other gurus who are overly exalted by some followers, Krishnamurti's glorified status among his spiritual devotees too often obscured very human foibles (see Kornfield 2000, 139–40). I did not often hear daimistas discuss Krishnamurti, but his published sermons do address the same antidotes for overcoming "agony and despair" as one finds in the Daime doctrine:

> To live completely, wholly, every day as if it were a new loveliness, there must be dying to everything of yesterday, otherwise you live mechanically, and a mechanical mind can never know what love is or what freedom is. . . . To find out actually what takes place when you die you must die. This isn't a joke. You must die—not physically but psychologically, inwardly, die to the things you have cherished and to the things you are bitter about. (Krishnamurti 1969, 76–78)

As outlined in the present text, Krishnamurti's words neatly overlap with daimista discourse on the shamanic and mystical themes of detrimental egotism. Though interviewees barely alluded to Krishnamurti outside the freelists, a couple of daimistas did note that they had read his books.

Seventh in Belgian / Seventy-fourth in European Freelist:
Krishna (? BCE)

According to Hindu mythology Krishna is a deity that incarnated on earth in multiple different forms throughout ancient history.[13] Fardados are aware of this, and as one informant put it: "Krishna is more a concept than a person." But they nevertheless expressed fondness for the enlightened qualities ascribed to Krishna, who "more than any other figure symbolizes divine love . . . divine beauty . . . and a quality of purposeless, playful, yet fascinating action" (Jones et al. 2005, 5248). Jeannette smiled as she said:

> *[Krishna] is a happy one. Krishna is the possibility to have more than one life because you have the different [forms] of Krishna. The living Krishna is one, but then you have Krishna in this form*

and Krishna in that form. I think it is what will happen with us . . . that we have more than one life in one body. And it's kind, it's very nice with Krishna, no? When you look at a picture of Krishna it's all love, it's all pleasure, it's all colors.

Much like Krishna represents death and rebirth of the soul in Hinduism, spiritual reincarnation over many lifetimes is generally accepted as a cosmological principle in Santo Daime.

I also witnessed Hindu influences in the ostensible popularity of Kundalini and various other forms of yoga among daimistas around Europe. In Ireland, there were pictures of Krishna in the salão, demonstrating the importance of Hare Krishna in the spiritual lives of many, but not all, Irish fardados. Ennis, a young fardado from Ireland, said he attended a local work wherein all participants could hear an invisible flute being played by an invisible flute player, and he suggested that this was Krishna participating in the work with them. Ennis also said Krishna and Christ are very similar, and he proposed the portmanteau "Jesus Krishna." Then again, Keegan, a fardado from Northern Ireland, said he was never interested when daimista colleagues tried to sell him on Hare Krishna, saying to them: "Krishna is fine for you, but I have Christ and that is all I need." Still, some daimistas' attraction to Krishna is unsurprising when we consider words attributed to this Hindu god in *The Bhagavad Gita* scripture (Chapter 13: verses 12/15–17):

I will tell you of the wisdom that leads to immortality: the beginningless Brahman, which can be called neither being nor nonbeing. . . . It is both near and far, both within and without every creature; it moves and is unmoving. In its subtlety it is beyond comprehension. It is invisible, yet appears divided in separate creatures. Know it to be the creator, the preserver, and the destroyer. Dwelling in every heart, it is beyond darkness. It is called the light of the lights, the object and goal of knowledge, and knowledge itself. (Easwaran 2004, 206)

To reiterate, for fardados the practical take-home messages of the Daime doctrine are virtually indistinguishable from mystical philosophies set out in the Bhagavad Gita or the teachings of Buddha, Sufi masters, and contemplative Christian writers.

Fifth in Belgian / Sixth in European Freelist: **Padrinho Sebastião**
(1920–1990 CE)

Sebastião Mota de Melo was born into meager circumstances on a *seringal* (latex production area) near Eurinepé on the Juruá River (Brazilian state of Amazonas). His family was derived from " 'traditional' mixed-race populations, known locally as *caboclos,* formed over the centuries through the mixing of indians with a small but steady stream of white and Afro-Brazilian immigrants to Amazonia" (Hall 2007, 153). It appears that he was raised in some sort of spiritualist tradition, since his mother was "a medium, but because her gift was not developed correctly, she became possessed by obsessive spirits, which tormented her with increasing frequency" (Polari de Alverga 1999, 66). Following in his mother's footsteps, the young Sebastião eventually encountered an Afro-Brazilian man from São Paulo named Mestre Oswaldo,[14] who practiced a form of spiritist mediumship in the Kardecist tradition (MacRae 1992, 56). Sebastião eventually became a spiritist medium himself. By invoking astral powers given to him when he summoned "two spiritual guides, Professor Antônio Jorge and Dr. Bezerra de Menezes," he achieved fame as a healer throughout the vicinity of Rio Branco (Polari de Alverga 1999, 67–68).

But it would not be until 1965 (at age forty-five) that he would cross paths with Mestre Irineu (Groisman 2000, 75/82). As legend has it, Sebastião became afflicted with his own illness, a severe liver ailment for which he sought treatment from the eminent Mestre Irineu, whose supervised ayahuasca sessions were said to have curative qualities (see chapter 3). Sebastião became a regular attendee at Mestre Irineu's Daime gatherings, and grew to be a prominent member of Alto Santo in his own right. After the Mestre's death in 1971, Sebastião formed the *Centro Eclético da Fluente Luz Universal Raimundo Irineu Serra* (CEFLURIS), which is now the most popular and widespread Daime organization in the world (Goldman 1999, xxvi–vii; MacRae 1992, 56). His CEFLURIS doctrine included mediumistic innovations that were previously absent in Mestre Irineu's practice, such as the Afro-Brazilian *Umbanda* tradition from southeast Brazil. After his death on January 20, 1990 (MacRae 1992), Pd. Sebastião was succeeded by his son Pd. Alfredo, who now serves as head of the worldwide CEFLURIS line of Daime (Groisman 2000, 85–86/93). In recounting the importance of Pd. Sebastião, Lars said:

> *He brought the same message as Mestre Irineu, but he brought it to the West. He brought this message all over the planet. . . . He said we have to live ecologically. We must be in harmony with Nature,*

*and that's something Padrinho Sebastião added. Mestre didn't talk
too much about it* [in his hymns]. . . . *I always followed the line
of Padrinho Sebastião because this contact with Nature was important for me; we Western people, we need Nature, don't forget that.*

As discussed earlier, Santo Daime can be categorized as a nature spirituality
or eco-religious movement (Schmidt 2007). The beginnings of a global
expansion for Santo Daime's environmentalist message are thus attributed
to the efforts of Pd. Sebastião.

Twenty-ninth in Belgian / Ninth in European Freelist:
John the Baptist (BCE–32 CE)

The biblical forerunner who christened Jesus Christ, João Baptista is frequently
called upon in the Daime hymns. As mentioned earlier, Pd. Sebastião is
considered to have been an avatar of John the Baptist (Dawson 2013, 123),
with his *O Justiceiro* ("The Justice Maker") hymnal representing an Amazonian "voice of one calling in the wilderness, 'Make straight the way for
the Lord' " (see Jn. 1:23 and Is. 40:3). Yet whereas the prophetic career of
John the Baptist preceded that of Jesus in the New Testament, in Daime the
sequence is reversed, with Pd. Sebastião coming after Mestre Irineu (avatar:
Jesus) to spread the Daime founder's new Christian gospel.

Thirty-eighth in Belgian / Seventh in European Freelist:
Pd. Alfredo (1950–present)

The leader of the CEFLURIS branch of Santo Daime is in some daimista
circles considered an "avatar" of King Solomon (Dawson 2013, 123). For
all practical purposes Alfredo serves as a sort of pope figure, overseeing the
global Daime movement from his headquarters at Céu do Mapiá and Céu
do Juruá, Brazil. He has received and is still receiving many hymns which
are compiled into hymnals such as *O Cruzerinho* (the Little Cross), *Nova
Era* (New Era), and *Nova Dimensão* (New Dimension).

Sixth in Belgian / Twenty-third in European Freelist:
Mohammed (570–632 CE)

As the founder of Islam, the name Mohammed was well known to Belgian
fardados, even if they were not entirely familiar with the details of his life
and teachings. Fardados' ecumenical leanings welcome the teachings of all

religions that are founded on love of God and love for fellow human beings. Fardados believe this was the central message of both Jesus and Mohammed, but that the original teachings of the founders of Christianity and Islam have been distorted by ego. For Saskia, who works as a language instructor for Muslim immigrants learning to speak Flemish Dutch, there is a distinction between the teachings of Mohammed and that of fundamentalist Islam:

> *If you grew up in Islam . . . he will be a great teacher. . . . For me that's a difficult thing because of the Islam of today. For them. . . . they said the only right teaching is the teaching of Mohammed, because he was the last prophet. . . . I'm sure that he was a great prophet, but not greater than others. So he's near the line of Jesus. . . . It's beautiful when people become the light, when people are enlightened, you cannot be greater than that.*
>
> *That's one of the beautiful things in the Daime, I think, because* [it's] *culture mixed together. . . . Daime is open, that's the beautiful thing for me from Daime, that it's not* godsdienst [god-service], *it's not a belief system. . . . The Daime is a religion but not with the strict rules, it's more open.*

So while fardados embrace Mohammed as a GST, they critique any narrow dogma that fails to notice universal truths promoted by all great spiritual traditions. They admire the peaceful and devout aspects of Islam, particularly the mystical school of Sufism. Daimistas would recognize their own sha-manic flight experiences in the story of Mohammed's "Night Journey . . . to heaven . . . accompanied by Gabriel and escorted by attendant angels" (Wilson 1994, 38/82). Indeed the daimistas' ranking of Mohammed as one of many great spiritual teachers agrees with the Qur'an: "Muhammed is no more than a Messenger; many were the Messengers that passed away before him"; akin to Santo Daime's linking of the Abrahamic faiths, the Muslim Holy Book instructs readers to "make no distinction between any of the Messengers" from Judaism, Christianity, and Islam, and see all these "People of the Book" as the "same Religion" (Surah 3-144, 4-152, 4-163, 4-171, 42-13 [Ali 2004, 41/60/62/321]; see Frager 1999, 14/39/57–60/175). Whereas Muslims typically believe Mohammed was the final Messenger that God sent (just as other Abrahamic canons tend to presume a terminus of prophethood), European fardados instead believe that Allah continues to send such Great Spiritual Teachers into the present day.

Eighth in Belgian / Tied for Tenth in European Freelist:
Virgin Mary (BCE–1st century CE)[15]

It is noteworthy that the only female name among the fardados' top ten GSTs is a historical figure of which very little is known. I asked fardados why Mary would be the only female on their freelists. The leading puxadora for the CdU suggested that this is because, historically, women could not communicate in the publicly overt ways that men could, an idea that was also mulled over by the monastic hermit Thomas Merton.[16] In the words of Lars, the former commander of CdU in Belgium:

> *The Virgin Mary, she has no teachings, she's only the mother of Jesus. But she became the symbol of the Eternal Feminine, and she gives this message. What makes her a saint, a divinity, is that she said to God, "Do with me what You want." She's humble, she gives a message of humility, of confidence in God. . . . She's the Great Mother, it's the* Rainha da Floresta [Queen of the Forest].[17]

All interviewees agreed that even though females' contributions are understated throughout patriarchal history, the Virgin Mary epitomizes qualities of both human and divine motherhood. For example, Clara is a thirty-four-year-old school teacher who began her Daime practice in 2002 at the age of twenty-six. Despite their youth, she and Saskia provided some of the longest GST freelists, indicating their extensive knowledge of this cultural domain. A soft-spoken single woman who attends CdU, Clara explained the importance of the Virgin Mary this way:

> *We don't know so many female teachers in history. Maybe they were there, I don't know. Like the stories about Mary Magdalene, that she was the woman next to Jesus, or probably before Jesus also there were more women that were more important. But I think that history changed that way of seeing. Maria, she's well known but she also was the mother of Jesus. So it was he who took the most important part. It's like she was in the background. . . .*
>
> *I think at the moment [the Virgin Mary is] one of my favorites. There's a lot of pain in the world at the moment, and it goes fast, and for me I can feel very unsure. Maybe that's also something collective. I think it's a very important energy that she*

> *embodies. For me she embodies the most loving mother. Like even if you're totally at the end and there's nobody any more, then she is still there with her arms open and with her softness, to take you and bring you to her heart.*

As a universal source of faith and unconditional motherly love, the Virgin Mary is an archetypal figure for fardados, representing a primeval femininity that can be called upon for support and comfort in times of disquietude.

It is daimistas' devotional commitment to the Virgin Mary and other canonized saints that marks Santo Daime as closer to Catholicism than other Christian denominations. As detailed in Part II, Christianity was introduced into Santo Daime via "folk Catholic" elements from the widespread yet sporadic influence of the Vatican across colonial South America. Thus, traditions such as Marian devotions (e.g., praying the rosary) and reverence for saints' hagiographies dominate Santo Daime in a way that resembles Catholicism[18] and Eastern Orthodox more than protestant Christianities. Accordingly, there is a major emphasis in Daime hymns on the "Virgin of Conception" (*Virgem da Conceiçao*) or the "Sovereign Mother" (*Mãe Soberana*) as embodied in Nature's bounty, the moon, forests, flowers, and bodies of water. From this angle, one can read any reference to Virgin Mary in Daime hymns as a loving glance to the eternal feminine divinity in Rosicrucian alchemy[19] and the Goddess personification of Mother Nature in "pagan" animisms such as Wicca: thereby, Daime fits neatly into the categories of Dark Green Religion (Taylor 2010) or Eco-Religion (Schmidt 2007). During a Mother's Day work in Toronto that began with all participants reciting the Holy Rosary[20] prayers together, I once heard two commanders lead a special prayer to the "the Virgin Mary, Mother Earth"; in a short sermon, the church leaders suggested that by showing gratitude to our own mothers we give thanks to the Gaia-like "Her" for being so patient with us humans: "She takes all of our pain on Herself, and also takes our garbage." And one final note to tie in to an earlier discussion about serpents in indigenous Mama Ayahuasca cosmology and daimistas' reverence for the Queen of the Forest: I leave it to future scholars of Daime to decode the meanings of traditional Catholic depictions portraying the Virgin Mary "perpetually crushing the snake beneath her heel" (Hall 2004, 57).

Ninth in Belgian / Fifth in European Freelist:
Dalai Lama (1935–present)

A tireless advocate for universal compassion as humanity's greatest ideal, the Dalai Lama (a Nobel Peace Prize Laureate) is credited with bridging cultural and spiritual gaps between East and West. Speaking about his place in a cyclical history, Lars tied the Dalai Lama's contemporary message to all GSTs:

> *He's of our times, and that's his importance. He translates again this ancient message of brotherhood.* . . . [The Dalai Lama] *also says,* "Oh, it's good that the Chinese kicked us out of Tibet, because now our religion is spread all over the world. . . . Thank you Chinese" [laughs]. *So he's a very great example of love and tolerance and spiritual life.*
>
> *But in fact, he doesn't bring a new message. He's Buddhist, he's a follower of Buddha. He incarnates it again. The history of philosophy is a history of incarnation, and every few hundred or thousand years there's a person who brings the same message adapted to that era. Like Buddha in his era, then later there's Jesus, later there's Mohammed, and in several parts of the world also.* . . .
>
> [Santo Daime is] *all over the world by now and it says "Preserve Nature, have love, believe in God, believe in the Higher Self, have spirituality, Awake!" In the Daime hinos, they speak about* "o povo" [the people]. *Most people are sleeping, are living the world of illusion. What Buddha* [and] *Jesus talk about: be awake! Be awake for the Higher message! Make your life spiritual!*

The Dalai Lama is a living representative of what fardados believe is a universal truth that has been preached by all GSTs throughout history. Recalling the daimista concept of *peia* ("obstacles"), the introspective orientation that Daime shares with Buddhism is crystallized by the Dalai Lama (2005, 189/227) thusly:

> When we engage in ritual practice, we sometimes encounter obstacles. These obstacles are not external but internal; they are delusions of our own mind. The real enemy, the destroyer of our happiness, is within ourselves. . . .
>
> If we change internally—disarm ourselves by dealing constructively with our negative thoughts and emotions—we can literally change the whole world . . . we can begin to bring about a spiritual revolution of kindness, compassion, patience, tolerance, forgiveness and humility.

Though Buddhists tend to avoid mind-altering substances, Douglas Osto (2016) has demonstrated that many Western Buddhists began their awakening with psychedelics. Just like Daime, fardados say GSTs provide the opportunity for individuals to wake up to inner peace and joy instead of sleeping in illusions of dualistic tension and egocentric despair. Fardados stress that even though GSTs appear in all cultures in all time periods, it is up to each person to recognize existential truths when these are imparted by spiritual sages or plant teachers.

Tenth in Belgian / Eighty-ninth in European Freelist: Eckhart Tolle (1948–present)

Eckhart Tolle is a German-born Canadian author. After having been touted by Oprah Winfrey, Tolle (1999) became world famous as the author of a book called *The Power of Now*. He is now one of the most well-known spokespersons for reenchantment subcultures in Western societies. Some fardados did not agree with the inclusion of Tolle as a GST alongside the other names discussed above—indeed, having been listed by only one European fardado, Tolle is not a very important GST for fardados outside Belgium. However, six Belgian fardados mentioned him on their freelists because they believe he is reiterating the same spiritual truths championed by other GSTs in a way that is recognizable to modern Western readers. Clara was especially enthusiastic about Tolle's placement among other GSTs on the collective freelist:

> *I am very happy to see him here because he's really a person of these days, and these days are so different than the days before. It's so hard to find stability or some teaching that can bring you stability. . . . [Tolle] can show people to find rest in your heart at those moments. He really does his very best without big prophesies; still he gives very important lessons. If you read his books or if you see his DVDs, it really touches you directly. You see that he lives it and he's a great teacher because he knows [how] to bring over this knowledge that he embodies.*

Tolle's philosophical priorities clearly match those of European fardados. The way that my informants talk about "ego" is identical to Tolle's (1999, 22/181) discussion of ego as "a false self, created by unconscious identification with the mind . . . the ego perceives itself as a separate fragment in a hostile universe, with no real inner connection to any other being, surrounded by other egos which it either sees as a potential threat or which it will attempt to use for its own ends." Seeking introspective "limit-situations" in their ayahuasca rituals, fardados try to put Tolle's (1999, 216–19) theories about mystical transformation into practice:

> Become an alchemist. Transmute base metal into gold, suffering into consciousness, disaster into enlightenment. . . . As far as the still unconscious majority of the population is concerned, only a critical limit-situation has the potential to crack the hard shell of the ego and force them into surrender and so into the awakened state. A limit-situation arises when through some disaster, drastic upheaval, deep loss, or suffering your whole world is shattered and doesn't make sense anymore. It is an encounter with death, be it physical or psychological. The egoic mind, the creator of this world, collapses. Out of the ashes of the old world, a new world can then come into being.

An elder fardada referred to all GSTs as the "flowers of humanity," a phrase she no doubt borrowed from Tolle's (2005) book *A New Earth*. In also grouping together the teachings of GSTs such as Jesus and Buddha, Tolle (2005, 6) suggests that the human species is now prepared to "flower" or "awaken" beyond ego consciousness on a grand scale. My informants concur with Tolle that all GSTs preach the same message of shifting from an egotistical self to a sense of personal connection with cosmic harmony. European daimistas use similar language to Tolle (1999, 154–55) to express a belief that looking "beyond the veil of form and separation" brings "the realization of oneness," and thus one can witness how "all love is the love of God." Fardados are inclined to look at human dramas from the more-than-meets-the-eye perspective of astral otherworlds; in turn, while the human forms of famous GSTs take on associations of distinct cultural formats, on a more fundamental level fardados consider them as angelic expressions refracting a singular Absolute Godhead (see Wilson 1994, 52–53). Thereby, daimista logic presumes that the realized souls of deceased GSTs (e.g., Jesus, the Virgin Mary, Mestre Irineu, Pd. Sebastião, etc.) can be conjured through intercessory prayers and occasionally encountered personally within Daime rituals. However, the historical context of each GST is still important to fardados for considering the applicability of their common message today. Whereas Eckhart Tolle is the top Europe-born GST on Belgian freelists, I also want to mention that at number Thirteen, St. Francis of Assisi was the most prominent European GST for fardados from Europe (see Kazantzakis

2000[1955]). The temporal connotations of all these GSTs became even more clear-cut when the cultural domain data from my Belgian sample was tabulated further.

Delving Deeper into the Belgian Sample

The mixture of historical and geographic backgrounds exemplified by the most prominent names on the GST freelist made more sense after dispensing "triad" tests to fardados from Belgium.[21] A pen-and-paper triad test involved taking the top ten freelist names[22] and combining them into multiple groups of three called "triplets" (Borgatti 1994, 271) or "triples" (Borgatti 1999). The function of a triad test is to prompt informants to make "similarity judgments" (D'Andrade 1995, 48), in that it gets "people to define what attributes they use to distinguish among items" in a cultural domain (Borgatti 1999, 142). In the triad test, informants are asked to circle the one item that they judge to be "the most different" (Borgatti 1999, 142). By doing so, informants imply that the other two items are comparatively alike[23] (Borgatti 1994, 271). Many fardados found the triad task difficult, expressing their aversion to making distinctions between wise spiritual masters that they believe are teaching the same mystical truths. Two fardados (one male, one female) even refused to complete the triad test because they claimed it was impossible to identify differences between GST items. This reticence to segregate GSTs is consistent with daimistas' proclivity for seeing "solutions" or unifying resemblance between what outsiders would consider as disparate elements.

Nevertheless, twenty-six Belgian fardados completed the triad test (thirteen male, thirteen female; twenty-two had also provided freelist data, four were new recruits). Anthropac utilizes these data to produce various kinds of diagrams that portray a visual illustration of how informants view the similarity-dissimilarity of items within a cultural domain. In digging further into the meaning of GSTs for Belgian fardados, Anthropac generated two diagrams that display the similarity judgments made by respondents in the triad tests. First, the software created a two-dimensional map (called *multidimensional scaling* [MDS])[24] that gives an idea of how fardados cluster items into groups (D'Andrade 1995, 64–69). Secondly, the database also yielded quantitative relations that can be depicted as a bar-graph of *hierarchical cluster* analysis (Figure 13.2).[25] The results of the triad test (n = 26) demonstrate how different spiritual teachers are arranged relative to each other in the minds of Belgian fardados (see Appendix VI). For follow-up interviews with eight informants who provided the longest freelists, levels of similarity formulated by the hierarchical cluster analysis were inserted into the MDS map, which resulted in the visual diagram of Figure 13.3 (see Bernard 2011, 363; Bernard and Ryan 2010, 117–119/180–183).

```
        M K B J V M P G D E
        D R D C M I S D L T

                          1
Level   6 7 2 1 8 3 5 4 9 0
------  - - - - - - - - - -
  1     . . . XXX . . . . .
  2     . . . XXX XXX . . .
  3     . . . XXX XXX XXX .
  4     . . XXXXX XXX XXX .
  5     . XXXXXXX XXX XXX .
  6     XXXXXXXXX XXX XXX .
  7     XXXXXXXXX XXXXXX .
  8     XXXXXXXXX XXXXXXXXX
  9     XXXXXXXXXXXXXXXXXX
```

Figure 13.2. Hierarchical cluster analysis of triads from Belgian fardados' GST domain.

GST Hierarchical Clusters

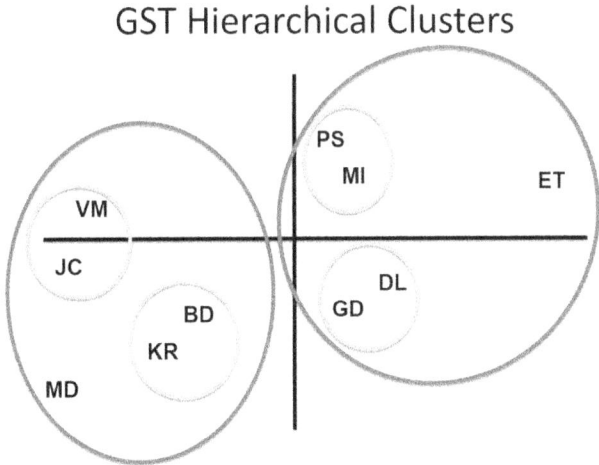

Figure 13.3. A graph based on the output of triads for Belgian fardados' GST domain; the image combines a multidimensional scaling map with results from the hierarchical cluster analysis.

Belgian interviewees were asked to give their interpretations of the top ten GSTs and the distribution of these names in the multidimensional scaling map (Figure 13.3). One fardada stated it simply: "They are all good examples of the positive vibrations we are looking for." Another fardada agreed that these GST "are examples," and elaborated by saying that "they are a little bit [of Higher] consciousness that came into the material, so they all bring things for the whole world . . . from the Source of Being." This concurs with fardados' view of the heavenly astral realm as a place of oneness that can be accessed through mystical practices such as Santo Daime. The GSTs are those who incarnate this divine essence and thus transport it into the human world. But when Saskia looked just at the list of ten names (*before* she had seen the hierarchical cluster diagram) she observed three distinct groups: (1) "great masters of the world that [are] well known to everybody" (Jesus [JC], Buddha [BD], Krishna [KR], Virgin Mary [VM], Mohammed [MD]); (2) "teachers associated with Santo Daime" (Mestre Irineu [MI], Padrinho Sebastião [PS]); and (3) "teachers of today" (Eckhart Tolle [ET], Dalai Lama [DL], Gandhi [GD]). After considering the significance of each GST individually, informants were asked to survey the different levels of similarity identified by the hierarchical cluster chart.[26]

In these follow-up interviews, fardados provided relatively consistent justifications for why certain items clustered together the way they did. For instance, for Level 1 there was a general consensus that Jesus and the Virgin Mary were the most similar GST names because of Belgians' Christian heritage. I interviewed Paulette, a forty-two-year-old fardada, in the rural Walloon homestead she shares with her Sufi/fardado husband Thibault. Paulette is a kinesiologist who has been attending CdAI works since 2008. She reasoned that:

> *We are in a Catholic region* [in Belgium] . . . *The Virgin Maria is the mother of Jesus, and she has a very big importance for Christians: she is the mother, and Jesus is a little bit the father. The masculine and feminine divinity in Christianity* [is] *a representation of even power, yin-yang.*

This ontological value of complementarity and balance is seen by fardados as a quality shared between mystical Christianity and Taoism. My informants were similarly frank about why Mestre Irineu and Pd. Sebastião were strongly linked (Level 2): "That's the Daime of course!"

With regard to the perceived similarity between Gandhi and the Dalai Lama (Level 3), while some fardados surmised that they are alike because they are both from Asia, the most common interpretation was that both these GSTs are known as champions of nonviolence. A biography relates how "Gandhi's nonviolence was first of all a creed of personal ethics which included truth, love, service, scrupulous methods and means, nonhurting by deed or word, tender tolerance of differences, and desirelessness or, at least, moderation in the pursuit of material things" (Fischer 1954, 132). This statement could also apply seamlessly to the values cherished by both the Dalai Lama and fardados.

For Level 4, Saskia explained why fardados would consider Buddha as closely related to Christian figures such as Jesus and the Virgin Mary:

> *He was also an enlightened person. The difference, I think, between Christ and Buddha (you can put them both near each other because they both are enlightened people), Jesus shows us how to be the light and Buddha shows us the way to the light, how you can go to the light, shows that path.*

For Level 5, when Krishna joins the group on the left, most fardados were stumped as to how he fit with Jesus, Mary, and Buddha, but Saskia suggested that it had something to do with time: "Krishna is ancient . . . older than Buddha and Jesus but still, ancient time." With Level 6, fardados also had less to say about why Mohammed was clustered with the group on the left, but Lars suggested that he is "one of the important teachers of mankind, and . . . his inspiration is Christianity and Judaism." As the levels of clustering were revealed to them piece by piece, fardados tended to focus more on the aspect of time.

Divisions based on the historical time when a GST lived really emerged for people when they were shown the Level 7 cluster, where Mestre Irineu and Pd. Sebastião join Gandhi and the Dalai Lama. Saskia rationalized the division this way:

> *For two reasons:* [On the Left], *these are more people from history, years and years ago, and where all the big religions came from like Islam, Christianity and Hinduism . . . and these are also the really enlightened persons. And these persons* [on the right] *they have levels of enlightenment, but I think they are not so high as* [on the left]. *These* [on the right] *are more recent people.*

Other fardados concurred that the reason for this perceived difference between the famous names of ancient people (on the left) and the names of well-known modern GSTs (on the right) is because only the most exceptional spiritual figures remain relevant over long periods of time. In this way, they did not expect all names on the right to still be well known thousands of years from now. For example, at Level 8 Eckhart Tolle is the farthest outlier. Looking at this, fardados acknowledged that they have read his books and that "he's very popular in Europe." But as is demonstrated by the response of Thibault, a fifty-six-year-old psychologist and CdAI musician from Liège, those GSTs on the left had a "big mission" to fulfill. He said those on the right have a "little mission" to pursue "in a particular time" period. Like other fardados, Thibault approved of Tolle's remote place on the cluster analysis because he is literally on a lower "level" relative to the "big big big geniuses": "There is no comparison . . . the same difference between me and Beethoven, that's Eckhart Tolle in front of Buddha or Krishna." Even if it is to different degrees, the unifying factor of this cultural domain is that all the GST have important psychospiritual lessons to teach humanity.

For fardados, the GSTs imply that all people are students of life trying to learn lessons in order to advance to greater self-awareness. By extension, they see the Daime doctrine as the curriculum of a "spiritual school" or a "school of being." In an interview with a Dutch fiscal, he told me he considers the Daime the "University of Universities." My informants testify that the Santo Daime "university" teaches them the same lessons that the GST teach. They contrast these mystical lessons with both the scientific materialism instilled by secular education and the moralism of dogmatic religious institutions. After hearing many informants refer to Santo Daime as a "school," I asked a Belgian fardada how she distinguishes between her career as an elementary school teacher and the teachings of the Great Spiritual Teachers. Clara responded:

> *The things in* [secular] *school are things that are important for the structure of the way we are living here* [in Belgium]. *So the government chooses what is important for students to know to help develop the country.* [Whereas] *I think Great Spiritual Teachers are universal knowledge . . . some collective wisdom that can help to have a positive development in the world, in yourself, and without boundaries. . . . If you study psychology or philosophy at university, there are subjects that can teach the matter, but that's not the same as the person who lives the matter. . . . I think a big difference can be that [Santo Daime is] the experience, you go into the experience. So it's not only theory, but . . . you sometimes get insights because*

you live it. Or as the Santo Daime says: maybe you can change your way of thinking. . . . So a spiritual school is more like living and searching and trying out things more than only studying the theory.

In sum, the GSTs mentioned by European fardados are for them "mediators between human and divine" affairs who represent elements of the ideal human being (see Macquarrie 1996). Within the astral school of Santo Daime, fardados conceptualize themselves as pupils learning directly from the examples set by saintly figures throughout the ages.

After the interviews were conducted and the freelist results tabulated, I fathomed that fardados cannot just be categorized as a subgroup of New Age hippies or late-modern consumers because they are simultaneously committed to age-old religious values. Instead, fardados' mixed admiration for founding figures of ancient religions *and* twentieth-century spiritual leaders demands an entirely different template to explain the worldviews they espouse. Their conflation of old and new is puzzling until one looks to popular ideas about cross-cultural mysticism that Huxley (2009[1945], vii/21) glossed as the Perennial Philosophy (*philosophia perennis*):

> The fully developed Perennial Philosophy has at all times and in all places given fundamentally the same answer. The divine Ground of all existence is a spiritual Absolute, ineffable in terms of discursive thought, but (in certain circumstances) susceptible of being directly experienced and realized by the human being. This Absolute is the God-without-form of Hindu and Christian mystical phraseology. The last end of man, the ultimate reason for human existence, is unitive knowledge of the divine Ground—the knowledge that can come only to those who are prepared to "die to self" and so make room, as it were, for God. Out of any given generation of men and women very few will achieve the final end of human existence; but the opportunity for coming to unitive knowledge will, in one way or another, continually be offered until all sentient beings realize Who in fact they are.

In agreement with this Perennial Philosophy, daimistas' critique of the institutions of Western Christendom parallels Aldous Huxley's (2009[1945], 242–43) diagnosis of how gospel teachings were "overlaid by wrong beliefs that led inevitably . . . to wrong actions"; this revolution of ontological priorities saw Jesus's focus on the otherworldly Kingdom replaced by "an immense increase in technical and governmental efficiency and an immense increase in scientific knowledge—each of them a result of the general shift of Western [people's] attention from the eternal to the temporal order, first within the sphere of Christianity and then, inevitably, outside it." Charles Taylor (2007, 348–49) also observes this "shift in cosmic imaginary" or "transition between the two great cosmic outlooks" that occurred in post-Enlightenment thought: "The Cartesian subject had lost the kind of depth which belonged to a 'nature' which was part of a cosmic order, where the discovery of what I really am requires that I come to grasp this nature by studying the orders of human social life and the cosmos." Just as Huxley (2009[1945], 77) decries "the apocalyptic religion of Inevitable Progress," whose "creed is that the Kingdom of Heaven is outside you," fardados attribute various contemporary maladies to the secularist momentum of modern Western civilization (for a historical critique of this ideology, see Green 2019).

It is not that fardados reject or denounce science, technology, or globalization—in fact they admire these achievements as ultimately good for humanity; rather, it is the lopsided dominance of secular materialism that they see as a hollowing-out of humanity's entheogenic aptitudes. Fardados assert that spiritual disenchantment causes imbalances in human life—at both the individual and collective level—leading to undue suffering, illness, and confusion. They emphasize a "confluence narrative" that reckons Santo Daime as a fated apex of perennialism, "an historical nodal point combining the accumulated spiritual wisdom of the world at large" (Dawson 2013, 89). Many European daimistas urged me to look into various forms of alternative literature, to compare famous figureheads of Western thought with the writings of unconventional philosophers that operate outside the campuses of mainstream universities. An example of this is my interview with Ines, a sixty-five-year-old retired woman from the Netherlands who enjoyed waxing philosophical whenever we spoke at ritual works. Denoting her archetypal role in the Daime as "the thinker" or "a teacher," she tried to explain what she knew to be ultimately beyond words:

> *I live my life always with science, which I experience as helpful in this world. . . . But for me the "pre/trans fallacy" of Ken Wilber* [27] *is a very interesting point for all who come from more individualist cultures. This is a huge paradox. On the one hand, when you open the book in drinking the Holy Drink* [of Santo Daime], *you get the deepest original information from the gnosis. . . . For me as a fardada this comes first.*

The gnosis is called the gnosis because we don't know [laughs]. . . . *It's entering the mystery. And it's because it's beyond material concepts, and language is a part of the material world. . . .*

Science is part of the material world. Wittgenstein[28] *already said: "What you cannot say you cannot talk about." That's the essence of the gnosis: you cannot talk about it. That's why the* [Daime] *hinos are poetic, they are symbolic. One of the mistakes of the* [more traditional] *churches is that they took the symbols as the* [earthly] *image of the unearthly world (that's why you have poetic language); because if you make it too concrete, it's* [then] *part of the material world and the spirit's gone. . . .*

Science is neutral. Science is an instrument to give names to what has no name . . . and sometimes we have totally the wrong concepts [e.g., Galenic physiology or geocentric astronomy]. . . . *The work of science is to try to find the most valuable concept. And now* [science] *has lost its roots. For me, all that is left in science is a word-game . . . so what we experience, we distort it into what we already "know." And what we do not know, we cannot see, we cannot recognize. So science is important, but it's a tool. . . .*

[With ayahuasca] *there is so much to do research on, it is such a rich research field; here you see in vivo the coming together of two very different cultures (when people from abroad and the cities drink the Holy Drink of the Queen of the Forest). Most of the research* [about Santo Daime seems to be] *"drugs" oriented: Does it do harm? Is it a sect? What happens in the brain? These are all research on the easy, detectable objects. This is science for science (and for legalization!).*

My big question for sociology, psychology and therapy is: How does it influence the lives of people and what mechanics play a role there?

The Santo Daime will teach you and bring you to where you have to be. But if a book is published listing almost all [the visionary] *images people can encounter while drinking ayahuasca,* [readers] *will not be educated* [about what Santo Daime really is]. . . . *Daimistas have another way to learn.*

Taking the advice of informants, I discovered that daimistas are plugged into a constellation of paradigms found in books on "integral" epistemology, which have popularized the notion of an imminent fusion between science and spirituality in the West (e.g., Ray 1998; Wilber 2000). Unlike the flighty New Age concept, the "integral" label captures a cohesive demographic undercurrent in North Atlantic societies, a perennialist branch from the counter-Enlightenment of which Santo Daime's expansion is a conspicuous symptom. This perennialist subculture offers a clear-cut demarcation of the wider community to which European fardados belong. The "solutions" theme arises again as fardados share a preference for "an integral culture that can bring together the traditional and the modern" by incorporating "a great heterogeneous mélange of movements, organizations, and trends" (Ray and Anderson 2000, 93/171). Rather than seeing a dichotomy between ancient religions and modern sciences, fardados appreciate that both physicality and spirituality are necessary considerations in human life. Or as Ken Wilber (1998, 102) writes: "Physics deals with matter, biology deals with the living body, psychology deals with the mind, theology deals with the soul, and mysticism deals with the direct experience of spirit—so an *integral approach* to reality would include physics, biology, psychology, theology, and mysticism."

In the next chapter, I uncover ways that fardados' perennialist doctrine offers glimpses into *integralist* subcultures emerging in the twenty-first-century Western world, which in turn will help to further disclose why Santo Daime has expanded across Europe. In closing this chapter, I must briefly address how Daime perennialism fits into academic debates within transpersonal psychology.

Although many of my daimista informants were aware of first-wave transpersonal writers such as Grof and Wilbur, none of my informants expressed awareness of more recent waves in scholarship, such as the groundbreaking work of Jorge Ferrer (2002; 2017) and Steve Taylor (2016). If one really wants to get into the weeds of how daimistas can be categorized by transpersonal theory, for purposes of intellectual classification Daime theology can best be described as a *"participatory perennialism"* or *"soft perennialism"* (see Ferrer 2017, 263). In manifold ways, the ethnophenomenological research comprising the present text directly responds to an apparent consensus among contemporary scholars "that transpersonal psychology would benefit from more phenomenological studies; as [Steve] Taylor suggested, phenomenological research could help to ground, enrich, and even revise traditional accounts of both spiritual transformative processes and the creative mystery" (Ferrer 2017, 264; see also Taylor 2016, 37–38 [Endnote #8]).

Daimistas would no doubt highlight their astral and suiscope experiences in Daime as empirically undermining Ferrer's (2002, 87) strong claim that the "spirituality espoused by the perennial philosophy is not the conclusion of cross-cultural research or interreligious dialogue, but an inference deduced from the premise that there is a transcendent unity of reality, a single Absolute that underlies the multiplicity of phenomena and towards which all spiritual traditions are directed" (see also Partridge 2018, 240–249). At the same time, daimistas would recognize the historical fluidity and branching of their own perennialist religion in Ferrer's (2002, 145) "participatory" demand for an organic "multiplicity of transconceptual disclosures of reality." Considering my ethnographic findings, the very nature of the Daime religion proves it is not necessary to jettison the entire perennialist paradigm. As opposed to claims of theological stasis or finality by more exclusivist transpersonal endeavours, Santo Daime is a participatory system of perennialism because it explicitly celebrates that human relationships with the ground of Being are an endless unfolding of infinite newness.

The vast majority of veteran daimistas would likely be receptive to Ferrer's (2002, 92) warning that in its more arrogant or "hard" forms "perennialism tends . . . to recede into dogmatism and intolerance towards different spiritual world views" when adherents fall prey to "universalist and objectivist assumptions" about their subjective mystical experiences—indeed, fardados regularly censure unwise novice daimistas when sometimes the latter become convinced that Daime is superior to other mystical formats. It is crucial here to underscore divergence between "splitter" tendencies of scholars, who reject any "naive perennialism" that acts "as if all religions really are saying the same thing" (Kripal 2014, 72) and daimistas' "lumper" ideology that views it as naive to dismiss spiritual universals (see Ford and Steward 1954, 55). Because the Daime faith is geared towards a cosmopolitan openness to various different ways of conceiving alliances between Godhead and humanity, daimistas' worldview personifies the "soft perennialism" compromise proposed by transpersonal psychologist Steve Taylor (2016, 35):

> From the soft perennial perspective, it is unnecessary to claim that all spiritual states and stages of development are essentially equivalent, only that they are different aspects and perspectives of the ranges of potential expansive psychological experience beyond the limitations of one's normal state. This gives the soft perennial perspective more leeway to account for the differences across spiritual traditions, often downplayed in hard perennialism. . . . [The] soft perennial perspective honors the spirituality of indigenous cultures, without denigrating them as pre-egoic or immaturely spiritual. The spirituality of post-axial

cultures is not higher or superior to pre-axial ones. . . . [The] soft perennial model differs from traditional [hard] perspectivist perennialism in a number of important ways. It differs in its open endedness—that is, its lack of a conception of a specific end point to spiritual development. It differs in its view of spiritual development as a deepening and expansion of one's relationship with the phenomenal world rather than a transcendence of it. It differs in its primary ontological feature of an allpervading spiritual force that is fundamental rather than a transcendent and ultimate other. Because soft perennialism views spiritual development as a process of awakening or opening to vast ranges of more expansive experience rather than in terms of encountering or experiencing a differently conceived spiritual absolute, this allows for a great deal more plurality than the traditional [hard] perspectivist approach.

Thus from the ethnophenomenological evidence presented herein, we see that daimistas embrace Santo Daime as a pragmatic ontology of healing that can be termed a soft perennialism. In any case, most daimistas do not want to get too preoccupied with all the academic hairsplitting of transpersonal theorists (see Hartelius 2017; Taylor 2017). Instead, the daimistas I met prefer to focus on optimizing practical therapeutic outcomes of mystical ceremonies rather than to overthink otherworldly experiences that for them are beyond the capacities of human cognition anyway. With all this in mind, in the next chapter it is to be assumed that such a "soft" or nonexclusivist perennialism is meant whenever the word *perennialism* is applied to Santo Daime.

14

The Aims of Santo Daime Perennialism

As detailed above, because of their eclectic combination of Christianity, Afro-Brazilian systems, indigenous shamanism, and European spiritisms, ayahuasca religions surely represent a unique manifestation of ritualized psychospiritual healing. In practical terms, future research could delve into ostensible similarities between Daime and other esotericist pedagogies such as Rudolf Steiner's Anthroposophy (McKanan 2017) or the Diamond Approach of A. H. Almaas (2017). If one wants to locate fardados among the buffet of organized faith options in today's world, it is most productive to classify Santo Daime as a perennialist religion because of its interfaith recognition that all mystical theologies are different pathways for achieving the same goals of eternal salvation and direct encounters with Godhead. Although relatively small in membership, the global sweep of newish perennialist reawakenings suggests a modest yet fascinating subculture that could be considered a Neo-Axial Age. After a brief ethnological comparison of Santo Daime with two more well-known perennialist traditions—Bahá'í and Swedenborgianism—the chapter will proceed to explain the core theology underlying daimista beliefs and practice.

In many ways, Daimistas' reverence for common threads they perceive in an eclectic array of holy people is comparable to the "New Era" doctrine of "progressive revelation" in the Bahá'í faith; worldwide, five million members of the Bahá'í religion consider Moses, Jesus, Krishna, Zoroaster, Buddha, Mohammed, and all other genuine "prophets" as "Messengers," "Manifestations of God," or "Light-bringers"—Note: just as with the origins of Bahá'í in nineteenth-century Persia, the Santo Daime began in an

Amazonian context far removed from the Western New Age movement (Esslemont 2006[1923], 4–6/16/117/135–37/141/312). We can likewise speak about a progressive revelation in the perennialism of Daime theology (see chapter 13). There are echoes of the Christian story also, in that Bahá'ís believe the birth of their religion was originally proclaimed by a John the Baptist–type figure known as the Báb. After predicting the coming of a new messiah "Whom God shall manifest," the Báb was assassinated in Iran in 1850 (Esslemont 2006[1923], 20–24). Bahá'ís believe that the Báb's prophesy came true in the person of Bahá'u'lláh, whose controversial formation of the perennialist Bahá'í religion within Islamocentric contexts of the Middle East led to his decades-long imprisonment in exile. The way Bahá'u'lláh embraced his suffering recalls the *firmeza* with which daimistas approach travails of all kinds—for instance, Bahá'u'lláh wrote: "By God, though weariness should weaken me, and hunger should destroy me, though my couch should be made of the hard rock and my associates of the beasts of the desert, I will not blench, but will be patient, as the resolute and determined are patient, in the strength of God, the King of Preexistence, the Creator of the nations; and under all circumstance I give thanks unto God" (Esslemont 2006[1923], 39). Apart from these links of perennialist open-mindedness shared by Bahá'í and Daime, the virtual lack of collective ritual in Bahá'í is a considerable distinction between the two faiths. Actually, I perceive the greatest ethnological fecundity in comparisons of Daime with Swedenborgianism.

It is instructive to observe how Swedenborgians' concept of a perennialist "New Church" resonates neatly with the spiritual priorities of Daime practitioners in Europe. The "Church of the New Jerusalem" that formed in England in 1787 around the ideas of Swedish scientist/mystic Emanuel Swedenborg (1688–1772) now comprises an estimated fifty thousand adherents across all inhabited continents (based mainly in Europe, North America, and South Africa);[1] indeed, it is remarkable to consider daimistas' adulation of Mestre Irineu alongside Swedenborg's belief "that the Africans were humanity's most enlightened race, being more in contact with their inner nature" (Chryssides and Wilkins 2014, 413; see also Williams-Hogan 2003). The most erudite fardados are aware of their doctrine's resemblance to Swedenborgianism; this is witnessed in Stephen Larsen's Foreword to Polari de Alverga's *Forest of Visions: Ayahuasca, Amazonian Spirituality and the Santo Daime Tradition* (1999), considered essential reading for new daimistas in the CEFLURIS line:

Swedenborg postulated a world of spirits adjacent to and in intimate contact with this one. We may be consciously or unconsciously in the presence of spirits all the time; and they may influence us for good or evil, depending on their natures. This belief also seems to permeate the Daime tradition. Careful ritual protections accompany the Daime works and ceremonies, so that contact with the "good" spirits is maximized and interference from the "bad" spirits is warded away. . . . In both traditions there is an idea of sin, not so much as invitation of divine wrath as an erroneous understanding. Enterprises that fail to inquire into divine intentions are doomed to failure—not through divine displeasure but through estrangement from the flowing source of all life, and failure to acknowledge the interconnectedness of all things. . . . Swedenborg called this same principle *influx,* and maintained that the Divine flows into all things as into a vessel, that humankind is merely the recipient of an overflowing of the Divine. The real goal of spiritual practice, therefore, is to prepare a place—to use truth and love to cleanse and chasten oneself to receive more adequately the Divine. . . .

Probably the single most important agreement of the two systems is the notion that all the good intentions and profound meditation . . . are useless unless brought into daily practice. . . . Swedenborg placed in importrance loving one's neighbor after loving the Lord. Practical and charitable expressions of one's affections allow love, an inexhaustible source of renewal of Divine origin, to flow through one's life into the community. And lastly Daime and the Swedenborgian path complement each other in providing a daily and intimate spirituality and praxis, a way of working on oneself, to the Christian tradition.

Daimistas would also sympathize with the Swedenborgian theory of *correspondences,*[2] a proposal that all natural phenomena can be deciphered as reflections of the celestial order. Other key Daime/Swedenborgian parallels include the two traditions' preoccupation with encountering astral realms populated by angelic/demonic beings, their worship of Jesus's teachings, their belief that the Bible is a true (yet largely metaphorical) revelation from God to humanity, and their perennialist conviction that one does not need to be a Christian to earn a place in Heaven. Or, as Swedenborg (1980[1764], 370–71) wrote:

Those born outside the [Christian] church are human beings equally with those born within it; they have the same heavenly origin, and like them they are living and immortal souls. They also have some religion by virtue of which they acknowledge God's existence and that they should live aright. . . . It may be protested that they have not been baptized, but baptism does not save any who are not washed spiritually, that is, *regenerated*, of which baptism is a sign and reminder. . . . Furthermore, those outside the church have a clearer idea about God as Man than Christians have, and those who have a concept of God as Man and live rightly are accepted by the Lord . . . Christianity obtains only in Europe; Mohammedanism [Islam] and Gentilism [paganism] are found in Asia, the Indies, Africa, and America, and the people in these parts of the globe are ten times more numerous than those in the Christian part. . . . What then is more mad than to believe that only these latter are saved and the former condemned, and that a man has heaven on the strength of his birth and not on the strength of his life?[3] (emphasis added)

A central tenet of Swedenborgian perennialism is the doctrine of *regeneration*,[4] denoting a sequence of "periods" or "stages" of spiritual illumination occuring throughout the life of every person's eternal psyche, with or without their awareness: "Step by step we advance from being nonhuman to being somewhat human though only a little, then more and more up to . . . when we become [God's] image" (Dole, Cooper, and Rose 2011, 275). But Swedenborg says the regeneration process can often get stymied by the temptation of human selfishness. He writes that people addicted to "self-love" are enslaved by what he calls the *proprium,* which "is nothing but evil" and sounds a lot like fardados' interpretations of egotism: humanity's "proprium is infernal and consequently love of it is diabolical . . . self-love is the devil, and lusts with their enjoyments are the evils of his kingdom, which is hell" (Swedenborg 1980[1764], 179–80/334). It is no surpsise that a forerunner of the present book repeatedly cites Swedenborg to outline the supernatural phenomenology of ayahuasca (Shanon 2002, 110/113/162/226/239/273). Of course, one clear disparity is that Swedenborgians do not have a psychoactive sacrament and their rituals operate like a perennialist Anglicanism, whereas daimistas use ayahuasca to travel in person to what would appear to be the same kinds of otherworldly realms chronicled by Swedenborg.

In appealing to the wider definition of mysticism, daimistas agree theoretically with Gellman (2014), who says that scholars focus too much on distinguishing between different mores for interpreting mystical experiences, while mystics themselves care only that these are reliable means to psycho-spiritual maturation: "Typically, mystics, theistic or not, see their mystical experience as part of a larger undertaking aimed at human transformation . . . and not as the terminus of their efforts." Similarly, as emphasized by the Belgian fardado referred to herein as Izaäk, the ultimate end of Santo Daime is not to have mystical insights but rather, "You have to work with it, do something with it" in everyday life. Unlike hermits or monks that live apart from the world, the religious values of daimistas (like Baháʾís and Swedenborgians) center on a desire to embody fruits of mystical visions in one's dealings with the outside world. This is where fardados also share existentialist theologians' misgivings about exclusively "immersive" (Buber 1996[1937], 131–44/159–60/177) forms of mystical prayer that verge on navel-gazing (Kierkegaard 1980[1844], 81–82/242[n2]). As developed in preceding chapters, such existentialist lenses can help us to further flesh out the aims of Daime mysticism.

Although scholars disagree on whether or not Kierkegaard was himself a mystic (Nelson 2006, 436), the Danish father of existentialism was well acquainted with many Christian (mainly "Rheno-Flemish") mystics and his thought "drew from mystical and spiritual literature on such crucial issues as the meaning of self-denial, spiritual guidance, the imitation of Christ, divine pedagogy, or human responsiveness to God" (Šajda 2015, 177). Cognizant of Thomas à Kempis's (2003[1418], 9) optimistic view of "adversity" ("It is good for us to have trials and troubles . . . these things help us to be humble and shield us from vainglory"), Kierkegaard (1990[1876], 203–204; see also Šajda 2015, 171–72/176) insists on an "imitation" of Christ as the prototypical devotee: "To suffer for the doctrine . . . to find joy and blessedness in . . . torture not only to force himself not to scream but to be so victorious over himself and the pain that when others looked at him it would appear as if it were a pleasure and that this was not an artful deception but that it actually was so terrible to him." This equipoise amid "fear and trembling," which Kierkegaard (2003[1843], 77/101) calls "humble courage," is practically identical to fardados' value of *firmeza* ("firmness") within ayahuasca sufferings and everyday life; such a "mystical theology" is the cornerstone in St. John of the Cross's (2003[1619], 46–47/89) prescription for reading the "dark night" as a "happy chance" for alchemical illumination:

that is, in the darkness of my understanding and the constraint of my will, in affliction and anguish with respect to memory, remaining in the dark in pure faith, which is dark night for the said natural faculties, the will alone being touched by grief and afflictions and yearnings for the love of God. . . .

This was a great happiness and a good chance for me. . . . And my will went forth from itself, becoming Divine; for, being united with Divine love, it no longer loves with its natural strength after a lowly manner, but with strength and purity from the Holy Spirit.

And finally, by means of this night and purgation of the old man, all the energies and affections of the soul are wholly renewed into a Divine temper and Divine delight.

Yet even while such exclusively Christian programs contrast somewhat with the eclectic mysticism of Santo Daime, I am stressing here how well-known existentialists and mystics can clarify the otherwise exotic soteriology of daimistas.

Data from European fardados show that in renewing medieval Eck-hartian ideas about "total self-divestiture of . . . the [personal] will" as "the breakthrough" gateway to salvation (Dourley 2014, 188), the "way of the cross" is now part of today's mystical discourses via popular authors such as Eckhart Tolle (1999, 218–226). Embracing existential angst and despair as tools for forging deeper faith in God's Will, again one can understand fardados' conception of GSTs through Kierkegaard (2003[1843], 90–95), specifically his designation of "Knights of faith" such as Abraham, Jesus, and the Virgin Mary. These biblical "knights" all personify perfect faith because during episodes of immense uncertainty and torment, their "great" trust in God was unyielding: "Thus to live joyfully and happily in this way every moment on the strength of the absurd, every moment to see the sword hanging over the loved one's head and yet find, not repose in the pain of resignation, but joy on the strength of the absurd—that is wonderful" (Kierkegaard (2003[1843], 79). Noting tacit links between Kierkegaard's Knight of Faith paradigm and cross-cultural mysticism, philosopher Agnė Budriūnaitė (2009) reaffirms the connection I am drawing here, that "the mystical experience neither contradicts nor negates existential experience, but embraces and transcends it as existential experience embraces and transcends the everyday experience." Thus, Kierkegaard's Knight of Faith concept and his focus on the imitation of Christ as prototype neatly parses daimistas' emic preoccupation with Great Spiritual Teachers as a cross-cultural category of the fully realized human ideal.

Whereas existentialist theologians tend to remain within mainstream Judeo-Christian traditions, daimistas are more aligned with Aldous Huxley's Perennial Philosophy in looking beyond these conventions to encompass any ways humans achieve spiritual awakenings; like fardados, Huxley (2009[1945], 48–49) classifies a host of "saints" or "avatars" from Christianity, Judaism, Hinduism, Buddhism, Islam, and Taoism as all "a divine incarnation . . . [who had] passed beyond selfness and had become the bodily and mental conduit through which a more than personal, supernatural life flowed down into the world." European fardados see their Daime practice as learning to imitate the comportment of Jesus Christ[5] and the Virgin Mary as well as non-Christian GSTs, whose lives demonstrated deep faith unmoved by external and internal difficulties. Daimista theology lionizes this archetype of heroic surrender to Divine Will, what Kierkegaard calls the Knight of Faith, but Daime extends this to include all great holy men and women who display total self-abandonment in the face of existential trials. Even while many fardados may agree with Kierkegaard that Christ is the "prototype," they also include the mystical teachings of Buddha, or the nonviolent actions of Gandhi, or prominent fardados' stewardship of the Santo Daime movement as the work of non-Western Knights of Faith (see Buber 1996[1937], 138–43). For European fardados, a humble courage of *firmeza* during dark nights of the soul is *the* fundamental lesson bestowed through the exemplary lives of all Great Spiritual Teachers (see chapter 13).

Although my informants are acutely aware of how the element of time is an important factor (because the divine is expressed in different ways in different eras), they are adamant that all GSTs ("Knights of Faith") teach the same mystical lessons. When fardados were shown the cluster map, they concurred in their explanation for its division into two main clusters at Level 9: one on the left with JC, BD, VM, MD, and KR, and one on the right with MI, PS, GD, DL, and ET. As an example, Frederik stated upon looking at the cluster map:

> *I think these* [on the right side of the GST cluster map] *are the contemporary representors of some of the teachings of these great souls* [on the left]. *They come from a different religion, but when you put them together it all comes down to the same thing. It's Buddhism, it's the Daime, it's Christianity, it's all the same message:*

> *love, understanding, humility, no ego, peace, all that. . . . The pure*
> *messages are all the same.*
>
> *But when power is involved in the message, then it goes wrong.*
> *Then you have a religion that says women are less important than*
> *men, for example. That already is enough for me to stand aside,*
> *because then we're leaving the truth. . . . And it also happens in*
> *the Daime, some people say "Daime is the only pure religion." Ugh,*
> *there we go again!*

So while fardados respect the teachings of all GSTs, they mostly isolate individual spiritual teachers from associations with institutional religiosities.[6] While systematic dissection may be important for an anthropologist administering cultural domain analyses, for fardados the distinctions between different religions or between religious figures are an odious distraction. In accord with the basic themes of Santo Daime worldview, my informants believe that the same existential truths are universally applicable, cross-culturally and throughout history. Their perennialist focus on valuable lessons they can learn from every different spiritual tradition, past or present, infers that fardados favor an *integralist* (aka *transmodern*)[7] outlook on the world.

Unlike the rejection of both traditional and modernist "metanarratives" by postmodernism (C. Taylor 2007, 716–19), which Latour (1993, 46) diagnosed as "a symptom [of modernism], not a fresh solution," transmodernity designates the embrace of hybrid metanarratives. In seeking integralist resolutions to diachronic conflicts, the transmodern implements compromises between old and new wisdoms with

> a spirit of hopefulness; a desire for wisdom; a concern with religious and transcendent and spiritual themes; a rediscovery of the importance of truth, beauty, goodness and harmony; a concern with simplicity and the quest for a mature and balanced understanding of experience. It will not be so much a spirit of new theories or ideologies, but of an *integration* of existing valid intellectual approaches, including those from the pre-modern tradition. (Vitz 1998, 113–14)

Considering the previous chapter, we can safely say that fardados' GST lists express an integralist (transmodern or soft) perennialism that combines ancient and modern worldviews into a coherent new whole. Fardados are convinced that it is possible to resolve ethnic conflict, heal economic disparities, cure psychological illnesses, and avoid ecological crises through integrations of what are usually seen as mutually exclusive domains of science and spiritualities.

Seeking to situate fardados' perennialist values, the results of this cognitive domain analysis call to mind a transmodern demographic in North America and Europe, sometimes called *Cultural Creatives*. In a book on this topic, sociologist Paul Ray and psychologist Sherry Ruth Anderson report on "thirteen years of survey research on more than 100,000 Americans, hundreds of focus groups, and about sixty in-depth interviews that reveal the emergence of an entire subculture of Americans" (Ray and Anderson 2000, 4/349–50). They contrast the *Cultural Creatives*—abbreviated below as CC—with two other Euro-American subcultures labeled *Traditionals* and *Moderns*. These three Western subcultures are characterized according to their divergent sociopolitical values. Concerns of what Ray and Anderson (2000, 30–32) call the *Traditional* subculture (estimated to make up "24.5 % of the U.S. population, or 48 million adults") "are not primarily about politics" but more fundamentally "about beliefs, ways of life, and personal identity"; these authors' catalogue Traditionals' shared values as including strict gender roles, more fundamentalist approaches to religiosity, conservative views of sexuality, suspicion of ethnic others, and rural ideologies such as an ardor for firearms. Existing as a polar opposite view on human life, the *Moderns* subculture has long been the dominant "taken-for-granted perspective" within secularized politics and popular culture in the West. Moderns represent 48 percent of the U.S. populace (93 million adults), a mainstream ideology made up of "people who accept the commercialized urban-industrial world as the obvious right way to live" (Ray and Anderson 2000, 25–30); the authors identify the Western-centric values and opinions of Moderns' as organized around moneymaking, physical appearance, consumerism, materialism, and scientism. By contrast, fardados are people seeking solutions to cross-pressures between traditional religion and secular modernity in twenty-first-century life. Fardados do not see such conflicts as necessary, preferring to emphasize options for integrating certain aspects of Traditional and Modern value systems. Indeed, this is like what Ray and Anderson (2000, 94) call the CC subgroup, which is averse to both extremes in the "culture war," opting instead to "head off in a third direction that's neither left nor right, neither modern nor traditional." Ray and Anderson (2000, xiv) pinpoint the shared values of CC as more collectivist, environmentalist, spiritually curious, optimist, anticonsumerist, and xenophilic/philoxenic toward sociocultural others. These theorists perceive a "comprehensive shift" of worldview, as the dawn of this century found the

CC subculture comprising 26 percent of U.S. citizens (50 million adults) and at least the same proportion of the population in Europe (Ray and Anderson 2000, 4–5). This would mean that out of five hundred million people in the European Union populace, roughly 123 million (24.5%) are Traditionals, 240 million (48%) are Moderns, and about 130 million (26%) hold values that fit the Cultural Creatives CC category (calculations reached with reference to CIA World Factbook 2008).

As Ray and Anderson (2000, 215–23) point out, CC subcultures grew out of the civil rights and women's movements in the 1960s-1970s, and these activists became key players in the subsequent environmental and LGBT movements. With significance to the present discussion, a central facet in historical developments of this integralist movement is the interest of many CC in the "consciousness movements." This collection of spiritual techniques imported into Western culture in the late twentieth century[8] reads like a list of Santo Daime traits as discussed herein. These eclectic sociopolitical trends parallel a "spiritual revolution of belief" in the West among devotees of "inner-life spirituality," a miscellany of introspective practices sometimes associated with experimental use of "hallucinogens" (Heelas 2008, 49/73–74). Even as he criticizes Heelas's reductionist assessment of integralist "spiritualities of life" as "New Age romanticism and consumptive capitalism," Dawson (2013, 170–82) himself depreciates the globalization of Santo Daime as mainly due to socioeconomic factors of daimistas' "mystified consumption," driven by etic forces of "commodity capitalism and its commoditization of the late-modern subject." By contrast, emic portrayals in the present study suggest that a more accurate picture of Daime in Europe attends to fardados' sincere reverence for perennialist mysticism. And like the broader CC subculture, European daimistas demonstrate a transmodern desire to bridge "an old way of life and a new one" in order to "carry forward what is valuable from the past and *integrate* it with what's needed for the future" (Ray and Anderson 2000, 87).

Hence, the integralist or transmodern category offers a more precise account of serious perennialist subcultures in the twenty-first-century Western world, as distinguished from trends vaguely catalogued as narcissistic "self religions" (Heelas 1991) or ambiguous spiritual jumbles glossed as "new metaphysicals" (Bender 2010). While they are like other reenchanted seekers who are "mourning" the loss of "a religious worldview or common-culture" by actively trying to reestablish "connection with the religious past," daimistas' focus on community well-being takes them well beyond the self-absorbed omphaloskepsis of "inner-worldly mysticism" (Parsons 2010, 23–24). As noted earlier, Santo Daime can also be less disparagingly classified as a nature spirituality (Greenwood 2005, vii) because like neo-paganism and *Wicca* groups across Europe, Daime rituals and spiritual beliefs are oriented toward reconciling with the Earth's biosphere. Ray and Anderson (2000, 14) underscore that "all Cultural Creatives have 'green' values." Just as fardados devalue selfish interests of the ego, religious environmentalism grows out of their belief that individuals' true interests are tied to ecological sustainability and the welfare of all humanity. Similarly, the Santo Daime could be called an "eco-religion" (Schmidt 2007) or a "dark green religion" (B. Taylor 2010). This "eco-centric" or "biocentric" system of values espoused by daimistas and other integralist CC resembles aboriginal cosmologies in the New World: "Rather than seeing the planet as a pyramid with humans on top, it sees the Earth as a web of life, and humans as just one strand in the web: what we do to the Earth, we do to ourselves; we belong to Nature, not nature to us; we have obligations to Mother Nature, not just for us" (Ray and Anderson 2000, 167). Fardados have faith that their ayahuasca sacrament embodies the spirit of a Gaia-like deity, which teaches humanity how to live in harmony with the natural environment. In essence, European daimistas are eco-religious, interfaith perennialists[9] as distinguished from secularist and theological Moderns who dominated the twentieth century.

Instead of throwing out either the ideals of the Enlightenment or the counter-Enlightenment, new integralist-transmodern subcultures view the reenchantment of Euro-American society as an inevitable reaction to overemphasis on materialism. In the words of Karel, a Belgian fardado:

> *It is a phase. . . . People will have more and more material* [wealth] *and say, "How can we not be very happy? Why are we unhappy with all our material?" And then they will have to look for something else, because more and more and more and more doesn't satisfy them anymore. And where's satisfaction? What is true happiness? True happiness is giving to somebody and seeing that you get it back almost immediately. . . . It's not like taking and grabbing it and defending it and fighting about it. No, it's actually giving it away and all of a sudden you get more. I might lose all my wealth, I don't need more because I'm not attached to it. And then all of a sudden you find, oh my goodness, this happiness* [laughs].

Here Karel is practically restating the theories of Charles Taylor. Taylor (2007, 310) also remarks on how many modern subjects are seeking meaning and "a recovery of transcendence" by reconnecting to "Nature," because, in their view, "we are cut off, divided from ourselves; we have to be brought back to the 'natural.'" He links the feelings of malaise in this era of secular disenchantment with many people taking "a position between the two extremes, shying away from materialism . . . and yet not wanting to return to . . . far-reaching beliefs about the power of God in our lives" (Taylor 2007, 431). Indeed, fardados see both extreme secularist atheism and extreme religious fundamentalism as merely two expressions of the same egocentric problems.

Santo Daime members are distinct from the general thrust of the counter-Enlightenment because fardados are not really "counter" or adversarial to the Enlightenment. In fact, they share Moderns' embrace of the technological advances and civil rights achieved through industrial modernity and liberalism. As declared by Emmanuel, a newly minted fardado from Belgium:

> *Science doesn't give a spiritual heaven. All existing people have something which is superior to them, like a religion. . . . They believe in something higher, spiritual. But science has broken down all these structures and said, "No, no. Just believe what we say is right"' and, "We can measure it, we take tests in laboratories." But that leaves people without. . . . They have nothing to hold onto in their life. Just objective facts like science gives, but that's not enough. . . . I think we need something which is higher than us, it makes us humble. Humbleness . . . it's important because I think all the negative things in the world, like wars and even rows between people or disagreements or fighting, all the negative aspects in society, they come from all these egos which are fighting. And if your ego is going down, then you feel united. Ego disunites people.*
>
> *To see that we are only tiny . . . Daime makes surely my ego less, because it gives you lessons. Because if you take Daime, it gives you like a slap in the face: "Oh you think you are The Man?". . . . Actually, [Santo Daime is] going back to the roots of Catholicism and Christianity, but we don't have all these popes and priests. We talk directly to the spirits of heaven. So it leaves one more free I think, because you have no intermediates. . . . Nobody imposes on me. . . . That's what I also really appreciate in Daime: they leave you free. There's no obligation whatsoever.*
>
> *Harmony. It's like something timeless. Something very ancient, like a tribe performing a ritual. It can be five centuries ago we are dancing there, or in the future. It has no time. For me it's one*

*of the most difficult things to describe how you feel when you do
a Daime work. It's hard to describe feelings, I think, because even
words can have a different meaning for me than for you. You can
read a book about a fire . . . but you won't know what fire is
unless you feel it, you see it, you touch it, and you burn yourself,
and you know what a fire is. . . . It's like very subtle energy. . . .*

*I think you can be a scientist and a daimista at the same
time. It would be good if more scientists were daimistas, because
as I told you if you take science as your new God and you don't
have this spiritual framework to place yourself into the universe,
you forget that you're only so tiny.*

At fifty-nine years of age, Emmanuel is a retired arborist who now lives by
himself in social housing. He related that he suffered from social anxiety
prior to getting involved with Santo Daime in 2009—he had taken his star
in the fardamento ceremony only two weeks before my interview with him
in late 2010. His spiritual journey began with a strict Catholic upbringing,
which he subsequently rebelled against during his twenties. After studying
philosophy in university he became an atheist who believed that "science
is God." Eventually, he began to thirst for spirituality, which led him into
a deep personal study of Zen Buddhism and yoga. But he realized that he
was missing a connection with fellow human beings, and he says that ayahuasca rituals have offered him "a highway into a spiritual life." He credits
the Daime for resolving his unease with group worship and with reviving
his Christian faith. He now views his atheist phase as naively conflating
Christ's message with institutional Catholicism. Fardados lament that most
Moderns' dismiss all spirituality, viewing this an unwise reliance on a
myopic materialism. Many Moderns are certain that technological progress
proves Western societies' superiority over so-called primitive or premodern
ideologies. But as with the integralist subculture in general, fardados see
achievements in manipulating the material world as distinct from mystical
truths that have remained universally valid since ancient times.

Like all participatory perennialists, fardados want a compromise that
celebrates the achievements of both ancient spirituality and modern science
(see Ray and Anderson 2000, 298–301). The way that Ray and Anderson
(2000, 316) assess the CC subculture applies directly to the emic inclinations of European fardados:

In the twenty-first century, a new era is taking hold. The biggest
challenges are to preserve and sustain life on the planet and find

a new way past the overwhelming spiritual and psychological emptiness of modern life. Though these issues have been building for a century, only now can the Western world bring itself to publicly consider them. The Cultural Creatives are responding to these overwhelming challenges by creating a new culture. With responses directed toward healing and *integration* rather than conflict and battle, they may be leading the way.

With CC, one can recognize a Western subculture whose values harmonize with those of European fardados.[10] Fardados agree with other integralists that narrow self-interest on a global scale fuels mutual destruction, whether through war or escalating ecological crises. According to this logic, future calamities can be avoided if humans choose instead to recognize that each individual's health is bound to the health of other people and the rest of Nature. Like other CC, fardados focus on the this-worldly and otherworldly simultaneously. As the Daime hymns constantly remind: *Eu vivo neste mundo*, "I live in this world" (MD#5, PS#98). The basic message of many Daime hymns is that one must deal with this earthly world as it presents itself, but one can also appeal to the astral realms for grace and guidance. Yet even as this CC category captures some of the sociopolitical affiliations of Western daimistas, it does not account for why a tiny fraction of inte-gralist-transmodern personalities are attracted to this ayahuasca spirituality in particular. Fardados' ultimate goal is to become like GSTs: progressively melding the ordinary world of one's senses with the spiritual otherworld of infinite light and oneness, such that mystical love becomes an ever greater part of everyday life. For fardados, ritual consumption of ayahuasca helps them to perpetually achieve personal growth and improvement. They believe that by communing with the entheogenic beverage, they learn to follow examples set by GSTs.

When they were shown the output for both the Sacred Plants and GST freelists, fardados stated that all spiritual masters and entheogenic rit-uals teach the same lesson. In fardados' view, this lesson is that the entire universe *is* God, a panentheistic notion of primordial unity at the base of all reality. When asked about her suggestion that the Great Spiritual Teachers and sacred plants teach the same lessons, a Belgian fardada I call Astrid explained:

> *Yes, of course, absolutely! It's just another way to get there. . . . You have these plants who open [you] up, so you can see what the*

Cosmos is about (or inside you, outside, it's everywhere of course). Like Jesus was here on Earth, [the Great Spiritual Teachers] *come from the other side; like the plants bring you up,* [the GSTs] *came down to help us . . . in fact it's just different representatives of the same thing . . . it comes from the same source. Like you say "God" or "Allah" or whoever, it's the same . . . it's just another name for something . . .* [The sacred plants] *are a tool to bring this connection back with the universe.*

This quotation demonstrates fundamental elements of the Daime worldview. In particular, fardados value a homogenized *solution* of spiritualities, seeing all religious traditions as growing out of the "same source." Astrid's folk theory evokes a reciprocity of contact between the human realm and the astral world. As the Belgian fardada Henriette said, it is "complementary":

I think it's kind of complementary. I think the plants help us to understand the teachings of those [great spiritual] *teachers. So for me,* [the Daime is] *just a way of opening your mind to those teachings. Because sometimes the hymns, when you read them at home, it's such simple language. Sometimes it seems like it doesn't say anything. . . .* [But] *then you get in the work and you do the whole sequence of hymns, and you can get really profound teachings that you couldn't have ever imagined.*

In this daimista view, Great Spiritual Teachers are divine beings who incarnate into human form in order to impart knowledge about the ultimate oneness of all things.[11] Daime theology is in this way in agreement with the Bahā'ī religious tradition, which teaches that "divine messengers and prophets appear in the course of time, but every prophet or divine manifestation brings the eternal religion, clothed in new garb" (Jones et al. 2005, 739). But unlike followers of Bahā'ī, daimistas believe that entheogenic plants make lessons of the GSTs more accessible. They propose that these sacred plants can transport a person who ingests them directly to that otherworldly place of oneness. Fardados say they are able to successfully commune with this spiritual essence by committing themselves to the rituals and eclectic doctrine of Santo Daime.

Issues of ideological heterodoxy arose in an interview with José, the Daime elder from Spain. Acknowledging a broad array of fardado personalities, he offered his two cents on similarities and divergences he perceives between the Daime and Catholicism:

I was always Christian . . . my sons had their first communion in the Catholic church, no problem; I go with them sometimes to [Catholic] *Church on Sunday mornings . . .* [but I'm] *not Fundamentalist; I don't believe too much in the Pope, but I feel Christian . . . and I have sympathy for the Catholics.*

I feel like a Christian, not Catholic because Catholicism has some differences with us [daimistas]. *. . . Catholics don't believe in reincarnation, and when you take Daime, you see deeper. . . . And the hierarchy is very structured with* [Catholics], *and I think the Daime is more eclectic. . . . Santo Daime doesn't have a code of moral ethics* [or] *religious mandates. . . . For* [example], *if you want to* [divorce] *a woman, or practice abortion, it depends on your conscience. . . .* [Homosexuality] *also: nobody can say you're bad. In the Santo Daime there are* [what I would call "fundamentalists"] *and there are "hippies"; the* [fundamentalists] *work every day, pray* [oração], *do the works on the exact day. . . .*

In our church there are a small group who are very funda-mentalist: the fiscais [ritual supervisors] *control the people . . . they prefer to join twenty persons* [at a work] *on Monday* [rather] *than change the work to Sunday or Saturday because Mestre Irineu said blah, blah, blah; or don't allow homosexuals, blah, blah, blah. . . . I think it's necessary, because everyone has his piece of cake; because if the church doesn't* [want to] *appear* [as] *a fundamentalist church, it's necessary for the hippies to appear; and for the hippie "all is possible" way* [not to overtake] *the church, it's necessary for some fundamentalists* [to remind about] *the rules. Equilibrium . . . for me some parts I feel more doctrinally, and in other parts I feel more hippie. . . . Also, the Santo Daime is a religion of the anti-religion rebels. Many people who arrive to the Santo Daime are very rebellious.*

This is one of the differences between Catholicism and the Daime; because the Catholics use the culpa [guilt] *. . . and Santo Daime, for me, is freedom, because you don't need anybody* [to] *inter-mediate between your heart (your spirit),* [and] *the Divine. . . . You can sit in the seat, very humble, very simple, and do the things the Master tells us to do.*

With ethical issues such as abortion and same-sex marriage, Madrinha Geraldine confirmed that in the European Daime community "we don't interfere in the private life of people . . . they have to decide themselves [because] everybody is responsible for himself." She also emphasized that at a young age she was adopted by an authoritarian Catholic community when her father drowned and her mother could not take care of her alone:

> Graças a deus [Thanks to God] . . . *from when I was three years old until I was seventeen I was brought up in a Franciscan monastery in the South of Holland. I came out* [and] *I never wanted to go to church anymore; I met the Santo Daime and it gave Jesus and Mother Mary back to me, because as a very sensitive child I already sensed* [with these Franciscans] *that "hey, this is not what Jesus and Maria meant"* . . . *they are not living what they talk about,* [it's] *just talk. . . .*
>
> *My purpose in life is to learn to live the Daime* hinos [hymns], *not only to sing them. . . . Even many Brazilians who understand Portuguese, they don't really live the* hinos; *sometimes you see people in Europe or in America who don't understand the [Portuguese] hymns, but understand and live the doctrine more, because they are sensitive for the energy and the teachings they receive.*

As she was then the undisputed figurehead of Daime in Europe, Md. Geraldine expresses the quasi-libertarian morality of daimistas. While they believe strongly in principles of right and wrong behavior (e.g., many daimistas have a preference for pro-life positions and monogamy), at the same time they are adamant that each human individual must be left to make their own choices in life. Such a nonjudgmental position grows out of daimistas' distrust of human-made laws and mores, preferring to focus more on universal love and forgiveness rather than on egoic refereeing of others' actions. Md. Geraldine also conveyed a strong aversion to religiocentrism when I asked about her list of Great Spiritual Teachers, which she said are emissaries of:

> GERALDINE: . . . *the same God; only God manifests himself in different ways, in the culture you understand . . . it's all the same.*

> INTERVIEWER: But different religions seem to fight each other?

> GERALDINE: *That's also the ego; they think always that their religion is THE religion. No, you choose the religion you fit the best in; I choose Santo Daime because . . . I think it's all one. . . . Whatever you look at, you are; what you eat, you are; the one who sees his*

object, he's the object also. . . . [Daime] *opens your consciousness . . . that's why* [mainstream authorities] *want to stop this kind of thing. . . .* [But] *they can never take the treasure in your heart away from you.*

Just like all veteran fardados in Europe, Md. Geraldine recaps what Huxley (2009[1945], 242) wrote about the core perennialism that cuts across a diverse range of mystical theologies:

> The aim and purpose of human life is the unitive knowledge of God. . . . In the past the nations of Christendom persecuted in the name of their faith, fought religious wars and undertook crusades against infidels and heretics; today they have ceased to be Christian in anything but name, and the only religion they profess is some brand of local idolatry, such as nationalism, state-worship, boss-worship, and revolutionism.

And yet like daimistas' "entheogenic" aspirations, Huxley's (2009[1945], 241) review of perennialist philosophies detects a larger cosmic plan at work across human history:

> The soul or character incarnated in the child is of such a nature, owing to past behavior, that it is forced to select those particular parents. And collaborating with the material and efficient causes is the final cause, the teleological pull from in front. This teleological pull is a pull from the divine Ground of things acting upon that part of the timeless now, which a finite mind must regard as the future. . . . The works of God have to be manifested . . . again and again, with the infinite patience of eternity, until at last the creature makes itself fit for the perfect and consummate manifestation of unitive knowledge, of the state of "not I, but *God in me.*"

As with all perennialisms, the belief in a "teleological" undercurrent of every soul's perpetual movement toward the divine "unitive" Light (albeit over many lifetimes) tends to engender an integralist universalism in daimista theology. Multicultural GSTs listed by my informants represent for them the pinnacle of a pan-human journey as achieved within different historical and social contexts. Or as described by Justino, an elder fardado from Portugal:

What I think is souls are not the same age: we are all equal, but I believe that some souls are more mature, some are less mature. The Santo Daime is a path that demands a lot. You have to really change in daily life. Because if you don't change, maybe you will get some discipline . . . so there are some people (although they have good intentions), but they are not prepared to change so quickly as [Daime] *requires. You have the ritual, you have the teachings, you have the drink, you get your insights, you have the message in the hymns, you get more in contact with your Higher Self; so you cannot say you don't change because you don't know, because you have all the warnings and teachings, and the path you have to follow. So if you don't follow, it's because you don't want* [to]. . . . *Because if you don't have the will power, Hell is full of good intentions. You need the will power to put the intention into practice. . . . Daily life is very difficult to follow many instructions you receive.*

The Higher Self is my spirit, my divine part. . . . I believe this is the one [from which] *you get intuition, the one* [from which] *you get teachings, insights; it is the one* [that] *sometimes puts words in your heart. Everything you do good is your spirit in you, everything you do bad is* [the ego in] *you. . . . If you are really connected, if you are conscious, if you are observing, you tend to do good things. . . . But if you are not conscious, you act from your attachments. That is the "little me." . . . The majority of people are not conscious, so they don't live in contact with the Higher Self. It's there, but . . . normally you get so involved in the routine of daily life, your problems, you are not conscious. . . . Because scientists . . . their job is* [to] *prove two and two are four . . . and scientists can go* [to Santo Daime unconsciously] *and cannot* [see anything] *because they are blocked.*

Santo Daime is for me the Higher Self. . . . The current, the singing, and the drink, it gives you the conditions for you to connect more with your Higher Self. So in reality, Santo Daime is the Higher Self because it's him who's going to teach you, not the plant itself. Because we live in a dense [energy], *they say the New Era will be a lighter energy; here* [now] *our consciousness is not very expanded. . . . God respects the free will of everybody. If you don't want, He respects. But if you open the window a little bit, the light will go in.* [laughs] *. . . What is God? Pure love? Love is light, is* sabedoria [wisdom], *so it's true.*

Again this is a fardado resonating with Huxley (2009[1945], 141), who proposes that while unconscious framings of the egoic self lead inevitably to internal and external conflicts, mystical realization can help one reframe reality in service of perennial illumination: "[Humans] must live in time in order to be able to advance into eternity . . . [he/she] must be conscious of [him/herself] as a separate ego in order to be able consciously to transcend separate selfhood; [he/she] must do battle with the lower self in order that [he/she] may become identified with that higher Self within [him/her], which is akin to the divine Not-Self." Or elsewhere: "It is by losing the egocentric life that we save the hitherto latent and undiscovered life which, in the spiritual part of our being, we share with the divine Ground" (Huxley 2009[1945], 106). In fact, it was Huxley's experiences with mescaline that cemented his position as a "proponent of . . . psycho-mystical, and highly eclectic perennialism" (Parsons 2008, 116–18). Like Huxley, fardados are drawn to entheogenic sacraments because they want to do more than just follow instructive teachings of past and present GST. Instead, fardados' chief ambition is aimed at actually tasting the existential acuities of perennialist figures such as Jesus Christ, Buddha, or the Virgin Mary.

Beyond Egocentricity:
Cosmic Consciousness as the Primary Objective in Daime

In previous chapters we learned that fardados conceive of drinking ayahuasca as not just like communion wine, but as also reenacting Christ's accepting the bitter cup of faithful submission in the Garden at Gethsemane, presaging a crucifixion of the individualized ego; as Jesus surrendered the flesh to unleash his eternal spirit, fardados believe that Daime works help them to forge alchemical renewals of the covenant between earth and heaven, humanity and God (i.e., *Juramidam*). European daimistas believe Daime mysticism affords solutions to the existential sickness of despair, which they believe is endemic in Western cultures. Rather than mainstream traditions of European religiosity, they are attracted to opportunities for directly encountering enlightened or illuminated states of mind. Emulating examples set by elder fardados recognized as masters of the Daime doctrine, to learn to weather heavy ayahuasca works with *firmeza* is a skill of faithful perseverance that daimistas then try to apply in the challenges of daily life. This schema matches other systems that prize suffering and death of the psychological ego as spiritually restorative. Here I am thinking of Carl Jung's take on the crucifixion as an archetypal "pleromatic process,"[12] or conceptualizations of Christ's passion as a symbol of God's love for humanity, such as in the thought of Simone Weil (2002[1947], 87): "The abandonment at the supreme moment of the crucifixion, what an abyss of love on both sides." Fardados likewise believe the more consistently one faces the oblivion that lies beyond egoic selfhood, the more one's faith will grow to resemble that of Great Spiritual Teachers. The ayahuasca rituals help with "observing [one's] own soul" toward contacting that which "traditional mystics have referred to . . . as 'the Void,' 'the One,' 'the infinite'" (Shanon 2002, 204). As far as fardado informants are concerned, such feats are the zenith/bedrock of psycho-spiritual well-being and so the quest to attain these inner heights/depths is their main reason for engaging in Daime works.

Preceding chapters have demonstrated that fardados value what they call "Higher Consciousness" or the "Higher Self." They believe that this Higher Consciousness is a divine aspect in all persons, wherein each human being is joined to the universal Godhead. The explicit suggestion that entheogenic substances can encourage truly mystical experiences has been advanced by various scholars through the years (e.g., Grof 1998, 260–61; MacLean, Johnson, and Griffiths 2011; Pahnke 1963). Psychologist Walter H. Clark (1969, 18–19) likened the "chemical ecstasy" of entheogens to a sensation of divine union written about by the fourteenth-century priest Jan van Ruysbroeck. There are also those who are skeptical that ingestion of a psychoactive substance could result in authentic mysticism. The most well-known detractor was R. C. Zaehner (1961), who denied Huxley's (1990[1956]) claim that mescaline could produce mystical awareness because no outside "drug" could possibly replicate true theistic contact (see Parsons 2008). The late Huston Smith (2000, 20/23–24) disagreed with this skepticism. As a religious scholar, he accentuated set and setting as important stimuli that regulate how one experiences and interprets entheogenic experiences. He acknowledged that whenever hallucinogens are taken with nonreligious intent, at best one gets a fleeting sense of holiness. On the contrary, in a context of "faith" and "discipline," such as that found with entheogenic organizations like the Native American Church and Santo Daime, real mystical content can appear (Smith 2000, 31). Smith (2000, 74–75) refocuses attention on correlations between the aspiration for entheogenic awakening and the adage of William Blake: "If the doors of perception were cleansed, everything would appear to man as it is, infinite."

Much scholarly writing on spiritual reenchantment in the West has highlighted William James's (1985[1902]) opus on *The Varieties of Religious*

Experience (see Barnard, forthcoming; Bender 2010; Hanegraaff 1998). However, the data collected from European fardados demand fresh considerations of a relatively unsung perennialist, who frequently corresponded with James and hypothesized a common mystical inheritance within all authentic religious traditions: the psychiatrist Richard Maurice Bucke (see Parsons 2013). Through a detailed survey of cross-cultural mysticism, Bucke[13] (1995[1901]) traced similarities in the experiences, teachings, and life course of some of the great spiritual and artistic sages of world history. He proposed *Cosmic Consciousness* as an official designation of traits that comprise an as-of-yet unacknowledged human faculty of enlightenment. Bucke's list of those who display the genius qualities of Cosmic Consciousness includes Emanuel Swedenborg and also many of the same names that fardados listed as GSTs, such as Gautama the Buddha, Jesus the Christ, Mohammed, William Blake, Moses, Lâo-tze, Socrates, and Spinoza (see Appendices IV and V). One sees in both Bucke's list and fardados' GST lists the same kinds of mystic attributes occurring in both Western and non-Western contexts.[14] Decades before Huxley (2009[1945]) wrote about the perennial philosophy, Bucke's (1995[1901], 357) theory of Cosmic Consciousness as the attainment of mystical realization included a formula that recalls the typical Daime awakening: "subjective light . . . moral elevation . . . intellectual illumination . . . the sense of immortality." In essence, my informants' explanations of the ayahuasca experience and the teachings of GSTs smack of this *Cosmic Consciousness*. Smith and Tart (1998, 98) were the first to compare the entheogenic experience with Cosmic Consciousness as "a specific type of mystical experience." Based on the lead author's comparison of his own LSD trips and his purported encounter with a spontaneous mystical episode, these researchers conclude that the LSD experience does not in itself bring about Cosmic Consciousness (Smith and Tart 1998). As was noted above, even if mystical states are set apart as ecstatic union with the divine, psychological reactions to entheogens vary according to the set and setting of ingestion. It is true that consumption of substances such as LSD and ayahuasca does not *cause* states of Cosmic Consciousness. Then again, the resemblance of Bucke's list of those who attained Cosmic Consciousness and fardados' list of GST hints at a common ideational paradigm. Even though none of my interviewees indicated to me they had read Bucke's book, their repeated claim that the Daime sacrament helps them to access a "Higher Consciousness" suggests that they are using a different name for the same mystical state. Responses from fardados show that in Daime rituals one can often have moments of enraptured timelessness, a state which resembles Aquinas's beatific vision, the *samadhi* or *moksha* of Hinduism, near-death experiences (NDEs), Gustave Doré's illustrations of Dante's *Paradiso*, or astronauts' overview effect. It is also amazing the degree to which Bucke's Cosmic Consciousness is recapitulated in Richards's (2016, 211–212) thirteen "insights from the [psychedelic] frontier where science and spirituality are meeting."

To test if fardados consider the lessons of Daime as comparable to how Bucke described outcomes of Cosmic Consciousness, informants were asked (after responding to the GST freelist) whether they agree that the Daime experience

> shows the cosmos to consist not of dead matter governed by unconscious, rigid, and unintending law; it shows it on the contrary as entirely immaterial, entirely spiritual and entirely alive; it shows that death is an absurdity, that everyone and everything has eternal life; it shows that the universe is God and that God is the universe, and that no evil ever did or ever will enter into it. (Bucke 1995[1901], 17)

Fardado interviewees who were shown Bucke's definition agreed that their participation in Daime works had revealed to them a condition equivalent to Bucke's concept of Cosmic Consciousness. As Eleonora responded upon reading the above quotation: "Yes, I agree . . . I can really find myself in it." Lars, one of my key informants whose more than twenty years in the Daime makes him the most experienced fardado in Belgium, reacted to Bucke's portrayal of Cosmic Consciousness thusly:

> *I completely agree. It's very beautiful . . . a lot of religions say the same. Hinduism comes close to this: Everything is spiritual. You see, there's no separation between material life and spiritual life, it's all the same. It's science and we who made this separation. . . . We are part of Nature, but a lot of people forget that. We live like we are not a part of it; we live in cities, you never see a tree, or you never feel the sunshine; we have air-conditioning. If you want, you can live like that, without being in contact with Nature.*
>
> *During my life, I was like that. I lost this contact. Before then, Nature was like a friend, a mother, it was interesting and a lot of joy. I felt good in it, I was always in the woods. And then I went to live in the cities and I got ill, and I forgot that, because*

you can forget. Then I took Daime. The first time. . . . I saw the
trees alive and I saw the sun, the moon, it was magic! And then
later I went in the woods for a walk and I said, "Whoa! Everything
is alive again!"

Writing over a century ago, the way Bucke sketched the features of Cosmic
Consciousness is reminiscent of fardados' testimonies about the Daime: "Like
a flash there is presented to his consciousness a clear conception . . . an
immense WHOLE, as dwarfs all conception, imagination or speculation,
springing from and belonging to *ordinary self consciousness,* such a conception
as makes the old attempts to mentally grasp the universe and its meaning
petty and even ridiculous" (Bucke 1995[1901], 73–74). By "self consciousness" Bucke means the common perception of oneself as an individuated
observer distinct from other such selves and the rest of reality. This is what
fardados refer to as "ego" consciousness. In asserting that through Santo
Daime "it's possible to realize" the same state of enlightenment demonstrated
by GST, one informant told me that "in the Daime, there are several holy
people . . . they are like living saints." In answering our original problem
of why some Europeans are committing to Santo Daime, fardados told
me that through their ayahuasca rituals they are not only seeking but also
finding and tapping into a Cosmic/Higher Consciousness beyond the ego.

Like Bucke (1995[1901], 22–82), fardados view Cosmic/Higher
consciousness as a potential evolutionary advance in the human species.
In contrast, both Bucke and fardados view hardline dualism, or the belief
that mind does not have causal effects upon physicality, as an outmoded
approach to life.[15] For instance, Marta is a thirty-seven-year-old single mother
who prefers to travel to CdSM in Amsterdam with other fardados from
Antwerpen. As a fardada who is also a certified physician, she admonished
egotistical thinking as a prevalent infirmity:

That's old thinking. That's a separation of dualistic thinking. The
dualistic is a cause of a lot of pain and suffering, and in Nature
you can get above it. . . . So, the outside, inside, it's the same. I
think that if we make connection with our Nature again, then
healing is being aware of the bigger context. . . . Because we live
in a world with a lot of what we call "civilization," we're getting
apart from our own Nature. . . . [Daime shows] that everybody's
really unique, but that at the same time we're connected, and that
we are part of a bigger thing. Like, you have cells in the body

making tissue, and those tissues make organs, and then organs make a human person; and also we are cells in another tissue, and we're forming also the world. . . . It's like microscopic: I am a collection of different things, small things, and at the same time I'm a small thing in a bigger context, and so to be connected again with the smaller parts and with the bigger parts at the same time. . . . [Daime is] parts of the forest that you drink, so you have the vibrations of the forest in your being, so it makes resonance with your own Nature.[16]

Daimistas thus agree with author Charles Eisenstein (2011, 1) that the major problems facing today's world are the result of fundamental errors in Western culture's "story of self," which glamorizes "the discrete and separate self: a bubble of psychology, a skin-encapsulated soul, a biological pheno-type driven by its genes to seek reproductive self-interest, a rational actor seeking economic self-interest, a physical observer of an objective universe, a mote of consciousness in a prison of flesh." In contrast to fardados' view that each human self is intimately connected to and continuous with all other selves and entities in the universe, the ego is the ordinary view that each self is an isolated unit.

Many daimistas report experiencing ecstasy and bliss during and after the ayahuasca rituals. Werner from Belgium spoke of this occurrence in his first Daime work:

I had the experience of oneness the first time. It was everybody: when I looked at the people in the room who were singing, it was like I was in heaven! The feeling that I had was so divine! The feeling of everything is so beautiful, everything, we are all one. . . . Everything is God!

But one must be careful not to mistake a passing experience for an enlightened finale. I was told as much by Joachim, a middle-aged Flemish fardado with a graduate degree in physics—he left academia to become a housecleaner because he said the latter is "more honest." In our conversations he talked a lot about humanity's universal search for inner peace, and he was adamant that physicalist egotism prevents many Western scientists from appreciating "that life is alive." When I asked him why he thinks most people cannot find this peace of mind if we are all looking for it, he responded by referring to the Great Spiritual Teachers:

Because people look at illuminated people and want to be illuminated, and they wait and are disappointed. But there is a misunderstanding about enlightenment: to really be in peace in this life, you need to be illuminated many, many, many times, and once, at a certain moment you see a flash of light, this first illumination, and then you know that it exists. But in the course of all the difficulties of your daily life, you forget and you cannot hold this flash of light. Then it comes again for a little bit longer, and you can hold it a little bit more. And this is a big effort and a long study to make the light in yourself last longer. Then if you are a very good student and very patient, then you can make it shine so that other people can perceive it. So it's really ridiculous to look at these illuminated masters as something outside of yourself. It's not like that. There are many people that are illuminated, but there are few people who shine the light through to the others. That's the difference. . . . People can hold it in a different degree, and then if you can really hold it, you can shine and you are like these masters that have been on earth.

Daimista theology, what I call entheology, does not require a rejection of responsibilities in the outside world, only that the starting point must first be set within, a sequence through which one learns how to act with more compassion in dealings with the outside world. Like Joachim's advice about cultivating one's light of illumination, great spiritual masters like St. Teresa of Avila (2007[1577], 57) promote the effectiveness of prayerful introspection as "founded upon a truth—namely, that God is within us." But fardados are just as comfortable accommodating a less theocentric slant on personal enlightenment, like the practical principles of Lao Tzu:

Within, within
This is where the world's treasure has always been. (Verse 62;
see Star 2008, 80)

Not only is "the Daime" virtually synonymous with "the Tao" of Taoism, but there is little daylight between how fardados speak of "the Daime" and "the Dharma"[17] of Buddhism. Similar arguments could be made about Daime's concurrence with mystical outlooks in Jewish Kabbalah (Jones et al. 2005, 7533–39) and Islamic Sufism (Frager 1999). Here daimistas are in lockstep with Matthew Fox's (1988, 230) avowal that "there is only one great underground river [of divinity], though there are numerous wells into it—Buddhist wells and Taoist wells, Native American wells and Christian wells, Islamic wells and Judaic wells." This is why one finds some Taoists, Buddhists, Jews, Hindus, Muslims, and indigenous people within the global daimista movement. Even while a handful of fardados harbor resentful attitudes toward Christianity, findings of the past two chapters reflect the dominant force of Jesus in daimista culture.

This present ethnography of Daime in Europe exhibits how the "existential attitude" of mysticism (Tillich 2014[1952], 114–75) is displayed by an entire community. This study also shows how the emic approach of existential anthropology can help inject new voices and perspectives into public debates about well-being, mental health, and ontology. As Bender (2010) affirms, the "new" spiritualities in the West are only the latest manifestations of older strands in Euro-American worldview. When metaphysical reenchantment in the West is traced back farther, we find ancestral lineages of European daimistas in the global spread of colonialist Christianity, esoteric Kardecism, and neo-Rosicrucianism, all of which melded together with Afro-Brazilian rites and indigenous shamanism upon reaching the Brazilian Amazon (see Dawson 2013; Meyer 2014). From the perspective of Santo Daime, these European pedigrees have returned from the "jungle" with a new message from the "Queen of the Forest," the spirit of Mother Nature who allegedly speaks to fardados through a sacramental beverage.

Given that Santo Daime is not yet considered a religious freedom in most of Europe, the establishment of scholarly evidence on this topic necessitates a reevaluation of how ayahuasca is legally regulated. According to anthropological relativism, one can see how the tension between monophasic and polyphasic ideologies is simply a misunderstanding between a dominant culture and an unfamiliar subculture. From the standpoint of human rights (see Tupper and Labate 2012), policies forbidding "hallucinogens" could be framed as a direct breach of polyphasic believers' *cognitive liberty*; this is the freedom that neuro-ethicist Wrye Sententia (2004, 223) defines as respect for "every person's fundamental right to think independently, to use the full spectrum of his or her own mind, and to have autonomy over his or her own brain chemistry." The Santo Daime religion endorses ethical principles of honesty, selflessness, and the cognitive liberty stance of leaving each person to make his/her own decisions about their states of consciousness. Present bans on entheogens are based on the dangers of their recreational use, as the law in most countries does not yet recognize scientific verdicts that regulated, ritualized uses can be beneficial. In the final section, our analysis closes with a discussion of how this intra- and intercultural debate could be settled through open-minded compromise.

PART VII

APPLYING ANTHROPOLOGY TO PUBLIC DEBATES ABOUT AYAHUASCA

Figure 15.1. *Europe supported by Africa and America*, By: William Blake (1796), ©
Victoria and Albert Museum, London.

The concepts that the self is made in its relations with others and is formed in relation to emanations of light lead to the mystical view of union and engulfment of the self, and likewise to the problem of edges that are both yearned for and, at times, quite frightening.

—Courtney Bender, *The New Metaphysicals*

Many follow Jesus up to the breaking of the bread, but few as far as drinking from the chalice of his Passion. Many admire his miracles, but few pursue the shame of the cross. Many love Jesus as long as no difficulties touch them. . . .

So, as a good and faithful servant of Christ, brace yourself to bear the Lord's cross with valor; out of love for you he was nailed to it. Be ready to bear many hardships and every kind of misfortune, for you will surely experience them wherever you are and wherever you may try to hide. It must be so. There is no way to avoid it; you can only endure it patiently. Drink lovingly of the chalice of the Lord if you wish to be his friend and to share his life.

—Thomas à Kempis, *Imitation of Christ*

15

The Cosmopolitics of Entheogenic Healing

Ayahuasca is not everyone's cup of tea, so to speak. More widely, distaste for any belief in sacred scriptures or supernatural entities is pervasive in much of the Western world today, particularly in intellectual circles. Indeed, disenchanted materialism, also called "physicalism," still represents the dominant ontological paradigm among Western scientists (Baruss 2003, 20; Frith and Rees 2007, 9) and philosophers (Alter 2007, 396; Seager 2000, 340). Ideologies of physicalism regularly coincide with placing confidence in the empirical sciences as a progression towards a conclusive theory of everything, faith in attainable objectivity, reductionist interpretations, atheism, and the notion that the whole of reality is closed under physics (Stoljar 2009, 12–13). And yet, today many other people remain steadfast in their ongoing search for supraphysical purpose, a fundamental human propensity that the psychiatrist Viktor Frankl (2006[1959]) delineated in his famous book *Man's Search for Meaning*. After recounting his theory that commitment to belief in life's meaningfulness is what helped him and others survive Nazi concentration camps, Frankl (2006[1959], 77) acknowledges that "it is impossible to define the meaning of life in a general way." Nevertheless, he highlights how each of us can discover existentially personal meanings that make even the most intense suffering more endurable:

> In some way, suffering ceases to be suffering at the moment it finds a meaning. . . . In accepting this challenge to suffer bravely, life has a meaning up to the last moment, and it retains this meaning literally to the end. (Frankl 2006[1959], 113–14)

Frankl's (2006[1959], 98) technique of existential *logotherapy* as a "meaning-centered psychotherapy" is in alignment with how daimistas view their devotion to ayahuasca mysticism (see also Hartogsohn 2018). As we learned from previous chapters, a subsection of Europeans frustrated with mainstream religions and secularisms are now embracing Daime as a venue for ritualized anguish that begets the detection of new meanings in their life—they push themselves to their existential limits without having to face real life-threatening dangers as Frankl did. Daime is thus a mystical logotherapy, in that daimistas seek to cure what Frankl (2006[1959], 138–48) terms modern Western culture's "mass neurotic syndrome" of " 'existential vacuum,' a feeling of emptiness and meaninglessness," which they consider the main cause of pervasive "depression, aggression, [and] addiction."

Unavoidably, fardados' claims—that ayahuasca engenders existential healing and that this Daime sacrament represents a return of Christ in vegetal form—antagonize what Kierkegaard (1990[1851], 96/150) labeled the "secular mentality":

> The secular mentality considers Christianity to be drunkenness, and Christianity considers the secular mentality to be drunkenness. . . . The [secular] world, as is natural, speaks . . . simply and solely about this world, does not know and does not wish to know that there is another world—another world would indeed be a perilous discovery for "this world."

One gets a sense of this "secular mentality," for which religious beliefs are unreasoned "drunkenness," from a letter the co-discoverer of DNA Francis Crick sent to Cambridge University's *Varsity* newspaper. Here the biophysicist explained his view that disbelieving "humanism" is superior to Christianity:

> I do not respect Christian beliefs. I think they are ridiculous. If we could get rid of them we could more easily get down to the serious problem of trying to find out what the world is all about. (Crick 1966)

Such hard-core atheist enmity against Christianity (and spirituality in general) would likely also extend to Santo Daime, which accepts Christian ideals as coequal with a host of other mystical doctrines (e.g., indigenous shamanism, Judaism, Buddhism, Hinduism, Taoism, Islam). Despite the intriguing ethnophenomenological data presented above, it is unfortunate that antireligious scientism is alive and well within a prominent subcommunity of psychedelic science. For instance, Robin Carhart-Harris,[1] the Ralph Metzner Distinguished Professor of Neurology and Psychiatry at University of California at San Francisco, is a foremost researcher in the growing field of psychedelic psychopharmacology. While daimistas would certainly celebrate the Carhart-Harris team's research findings about psychedelics' therapeutic potentials (e.g., Scott and Carhart-Harris forthcoming), one wonders at his lack of objectivity in public statements he has made about his humanistic beliefs. In a 2013 interview with philosopher Jules Evans, Carhart-Harris said:

> For a materialist scientist, I don't believe the theory that people gain access to a metaphysical or spiritual realm [with psychedelics], I think what they have access to is the vastness of the human mind, which includes their entire history—which isn't just human. It's very easy to become less than objective, to believe that things are really happening, that the walls are breathing . . . but they're not.[2]

Likewise, in a valuable publication laying the scientific foundations for "a Unified Model of the Brain Action of Psychedelics," Carhart-Harris and Friston (2019, 335–36) express an excessive amount of opinionated worry in their discussion of "What to Do About the 'woo'?":

> Psychedelics have an interesting history of association with pseudoscience and supernatural belief. One interpretation of this is that a strong psychedelic experience can cause such an ontological shock that the experiencer feels compelled to reach for some kind of explanation, however tenuous or fantastical, to close an epistemic gap that the experience has opened up for them. This is an important matter, particularly as increasing numbers of people are likely to be experimenting with psychedelics in the coming years—but it is also a rich topic that deserves a separate discussion piece of its own . . . as it is a problem that speaks to the special value of a naturalistic approach to psychedelics, as well as a responsible one that includes provision of education (e.g., about the importance of psychological preparation and integration) alongside careful engineering of the experience itself. . . . If done properly, tenuous magical explanations can then be challenged appropriately (although not during the experience

itself—as to do so would be inappropriate) in the skeptical, self-correcting fashion that is intrinsic to the scientific method. Reliable and robust models of natural phenomena, of the sort that science endeavors to discover and finesse, serve us best, as they are less likely to betray us, leaving us open to logical fallacies, dogmatism, absolutism, and an emotional and existential instability. . . . The phenomenon of spiritual bypassing is relevant in this work. . . . Spiritual bypassing may be understood as an escapist defense, dressed up as a spiritual awakening. Combining psychedelic therapy with a secular wisdom teaching, such as can be found in nonreligious Buddhism for example . . . as well as depth psychology . . . may have considerable value in this regard, helping to ground psychedelic science and medicine, while inoculating against evangelism.

As a psychedelic researcher, I want to emphasize that Carhart-Harris and his colleagues deserve praise for their impressive work in the "naturalistic" laboratory. But as an anthropologist, I cannot help but problematize the hypocrisy of scientists flippantly dismissing theologies in which they are untrained while at the same time decrying enchanted psychonauts' lack of scientific expertise. What such scientistic "evangelism" neglects to mention is that nobody can quantitatively measure metaphysical theories either way, and yet all too often materialist-atheists remain unaware that their unchecked animus against religious meaning-making is itself based on blind faith in ontological physicalism. Of course, empirical methods are a legitimate firewall when it comes to harebrained credos that contradict scientific evidence, which can lead to many hazards when foolish superstitions and overzealous spiritual dogmas are pursued unquestioningly. At the same time, scientistic prejudices against spiritual interpretations of psychedelics ignore that all human ideas need to be regulated; in truth, many potential dangers must also be curtailed in secular science (e.g., weaponization of new technologies or genetically modified human babies). Heading into the future, a better anthropological approach must guard against all misuse of psychedelics while maintaining an agnostic appreciation of responsible entheogenic experiments in both science and spirituality (see Blainey 2010; Steinhardt and Noorani 2020). Another area that is sure to spark controversy are the flourishing for-profit motives of new corporatations such as Compass Pathways (see Goldhill 2018; Noorani 2019). Future ethnophenomenologists should compare the scientistic and capitalist paradigms above with the new Center for Psychedelic and Consciousness Research[3] at The Johns Hopkins University School of Medicine, which includes members of its research team who explicitly lean into explaining psychedelics as vehicles for "Sacred Knowledge" (e.g., Richards 2016).

All told, while antireligious stances of the secularist mindset seem to omit the wisdom and knowhow of indigenous entheogenic traditions and newer Perennialisms such as Santo Daime, I am inclined to think there is room for a variety of tactics. Secularized or medicalized psychedelic therapy is well suited to atheist clients, for whom religious symbology may be uncomfortable and could negatively disturb their psychedelic session. But for the many spiritually minded people in Western countries, whose well-being is oriented around looking for enchanted meanings, the present book shows that mystical/shamanic approaches to entheogens can help to heal existential despair. Therefore, an anthropological approach would endorse mutual respect for both secular and spiritual modalities rather than mutual derision. My ethnographic reporting demonstrates that there is much practical value in the mystical framework of daimista rituals. Such benefits of the ceremonial suiscope in Santo Daime might be dulled by stripping away religious symbolism from ayahuasca. At worst, spiritually naive settings may be unsafe if therapists are not trained in the religious background of those to whom they administer ayahuasca. At best, it would be a missed opportunity for a client's spiritual/existential growth if therapists devalue ensuing visionary experiences as medically insignificant.

Contrast the secular mentality with outlooks of ayahuasca drinkers, who tend to spiritualize the world while viewing atheist "presuppositions" of "the materialist tradition established by the naturalists of the 18th and 19th centuries" as a "blind spot" of modern science (Narby 1998, 132–45). The Jungian theologian John Dourley (2014, 186) describes the discomfort this blind spot can cause, whereby "science and technology, valuable and inevitable though they be, reduce the knowable to the yield of the senses in relation to nature as something to be measured and manipulated, [while] the within, though not directly discounted, suffers the fate of the irrelevant." Mindful of cross-pressured tensions between secularist scientism and traditional Christianity in Western societies, Santo Daime is proof that a reenchanted subsection of Europeans is formulating new entheogenic meanings of life. In these final chapters, I discuss anthropological ramifications of continuing clashes between materialist and theistic conceptions of reality, an intracultural divide of cross-pressures that is stoked by the arrival of entheogenic religions into Western countries.

As preceding chapters have demonstrated, fardados depict being phys-ically and psychologically healed by Daime as an introspective process of "cleaning" or "purifying" the ego to uncover "infinite" light of the Higher Self. This is the same suiscope phenomenon discussed in chapter 11, where "the individual self dissolves and becomes an observer that is fused with what is observed and with the very act of observing" (Schmidt 2007, 159). Fardados share the belief that anyone can embark on the path to Cosmic Consciousness through a variety of mystical practices, such as meditation, yoga, praying, or the ritual ingestion of entheogens. At present, all except the last of these practices is accepted as a healthy pursuit in Western cultures. Counter to mainstream suspicions that ayahuasca is dangerous, fardados trust that within the proper set and setting the ritualized use of their Daime sacrament is just as safe and effective as other mystical practices. Here is an intercultural conflict about the nature of consciousness, which existen-tial anthropology is uniquely equipped to adjudicate. The present text has sought to show practical applications of existential anthropology, in that this approach can familiarize readers with what might otherwise appear to be abstruse human behaviors and beliefs. Thus, existential anthropology can be a great leveler of xenophobic reflexes that keep people from seeing themselves in each other, witnessing a common humanity beneath superficial differences—this can be a powerful force to counter the divisiveness and hatred we see in our world.

From an etic perspective, Santo Daime practice appears very strange; scholarly expositions in this vein can only go so far in challenging the hegemonic status quo. However, when the emic perspective is illumined via anthropological analyses, outsiders get a chance to glimpse the human condition they share with daimistas, in that we are all faced with similar kinds of existential problems. Even though I still cannot say that I believe in what my informants believe (i.e., animistic theism aimed at contacting and interacting with entheogenic spirit beings), my ethnophenomenological observations confirm that daimistas' understanding of ayahuasca is more informed than the mainstream presumption that this beverage is danger-ous. Secular societies do not have to agree with daimistas' spiritual beliefs in order to recognize the latter's constitutional rights to drink ayahuasca. In fact, as empirical data is accumulating, an interdisciplinary consensus is emerging which corroborates daimistas' conviction that their sacrament is safe and can have therapeutic properties.

As renewed attraction to entheogenic therapies is rapidly emerging in Western societies, there is a parallel "renaissance" in psychedelic scholarship underway (Sessa 2012). A quick search on Google Scholar will reveal a bounty of recent publications announcing that psychedelics/entheogens such as iboga, psilocybin mushrooms, ayahuasca, mescaline cacti, LSD, and empathogens/entactogens like MDMA have untapped medicinal applications (e.g., Carlini and Maia 2017; dos Santos et al. 2016; Haden, Emerson, and Tupper 2016; Tupper et al. 2015; Winkelman 2015). Another new study published in the *Journal of Psychopharmacology* suggests that psychedelic use may encourage people to be less violent (Thiessen et al. 2018). When considering ayahuasca specifically, the recent publication of an edited book on therapeutic uses of this brew signals the advent of new collaborations between Western biomedicine and traditional Amazonian knowledge on a host of health issues (Labate and Cavnar 2014b). A snapshot of research published in scholarly journals also finds promising functions for ayahuasca in the following areas of psychotherapy:

- **Addiction** (Apud 2020a; Argento et al. 2019; Barbosa et al. 2018; Hamill et al. 2019; Loizaga-Velder and Verres 2014; Thomas et al. 2013)

- **Depression** (e.g., Anderson 2012; Osório et al. 2015; Palha-no-Fontes et al. 2019)

- **Suicidality, panic, and hopelessness** (dos Santos et al. 2007; Zeifman et al. 2019)

- **Eating disorders** (Lafrance et al. 2017)

- **Grief** (González et al. In press)

- **Quality of life and wellbeing** (Barbosa et al. 2009; Ona et al. 2019; Tupper 2008)

The present ethnography of Santo Daime further suggests possible psychiatric applications for ayahuasca, especially in fields concerned with treating pathologies of meaning such as logotherapy and transpersonal psychology (see Clark 1998). Alas, such therapeutic potentials are currently stymied by a legacy of outright bans against entheogenic substances. It is a conspicuous breach of secularism's reliance on science for umpiring "truth" that the entrenched culture of prohibition denies empirical verdicts while upholding fearful stigmas in the Euro-American legal and medical sectors. However, directly contradicting justifications for proscribing "hallucinogenic" substances, the emergent science indicates that ayahuasca and many other psychedelics are nonaddictive, cannot cause lethal overdose, pose less psychosocial harm than either alcohol or tobacco, and have potential medical applications (Blainey 2015; Carlini and Maia 2017; Cormier 2015; Nutt et al. 2007; Pollan 2018; Tupper et al. 2015; Winkelman and Sessa 2019).

Just as with psychedelics in general, the central "quagmire" here is that ritual uses of ayahuasca for therapeutic purposes blur the line our culture maintains between religion and biomedicine (see Ellens and Roberts 2015). Certainly, any substance must be subjected to tests of safety and effects before it is approved for medical uses. The empirical evidence reviewed above suggests that ayahuasca is not a harmful or addictive substance within controlled settings. Thus, wholesale prohibition disregards scientific evidence that the effects of entheogens depend on whether or not they are used in a suitable setting by capable people with an appropriate mind-set. Scholarly reports like those listed above do not support Western societies' conventional grounds for arresting, jailing, and prosecuting local fardados. Such a conflict fits within the jurisdiction of what Belgian philosopher Isabelle Stengers (2005, 995) calls "cosmopolitics" (*cosmopolitiques*), a tactic for intercultural peacekeeping that recognizes the impossibility of "a 'really neutral,' anthropological, category" for normative ethics, because "anthropology is also us":

> The cosmopolitical proposal is incapable of giving a "good" definition of the procedures that allow us to achieve the "good" definition of a "good" common world. . . . The cosmos must therefore be distinguished here from any particular cosmos, or world, as a particular tradition may conceive of it. It does not refer to a project designed to encompass them all, for it is always a bad idea to designate something to encompass those that refuse to be encompassed by something else. In the term cosmopolitical, cosmos refers to the unknown constituted by these multiple, divergent worlds, and to the articulations of which they could eventually be capable. (Stengers 2005, 995; see also Latour 2004, 454; Stengers 2010; Stengers 2011)

Of course, this cosmopolitical diplomacy of cultural relativism does not extend to extremes of moral relativism, and thus excludes hateful ideologies such as neo Nazism and other violent supremacisms of that ilk. Before I attempt to further clarify the cosmopolitical fracas surrounding daimistas in Europe, I first want to lay out the very real liabilities intrinsic to Santo

Daime social life, as well as the compassionate yet pragmatic protocols by which daimistas seek to surmount these glitches.

A Word on Risk Management and Conflict Resolution

There is apparently a high attrition rate for neophyte daimistas. I managed to interview four former fardados, all of whom expressed gratitude for the lessons and personal growth they had acquired through years of Santo Daime involvement. However, the former commander of Céu da Luz in Belgium did evince sadness over her fardado colleagues' disgruntled reaction to her departure from the doctrine. I also met an ex-fardada from Central Europe who complained of feeling cruelly snubbed by silent treatment when she disagreed with the leaders of her church. Indeed, I did hear some current fardados express disappointment in those who had "quit the Daime." Though I do not have access to exact statistics, all of the former fardados I spoke with listed the following as reasons for their having left the church: ayahuasca rituals demand a lot of time/energy, aversion to church politics, and they all concluded that after they had received the spiritual insights they needed from Daime it was time to move on. Anecdotal evidence from some interviewees gives an impression that a large number of Europeans experiment with Daime a few times out of curiosity but find that it is not for them. One long-time Belgian fardado told me that he sees "many people come to one or two works and they enjoy it . . . and then they leave and never return." Hermann, leader of the Daime in Germany, told me that over a decade of his attendance at big works in Amsterdam he has observed thousands of visitors come only once or twice. He estimated that for every four new fardados, three end up quitting eventually because they tire of the constant self-transformation that is required in attending dozens of works per year.[4] Those who do stay must endure their own mystical hardships while also navigating the politics of a dynamic religious community.

Partitions of Daime groups in Europe mirror tendencies toward "intense secession processes" found with ayahuasca religions in Brazil, where cycles of segmentation, expansion, and diversification comprise a "circular movement of fabrication and constant multiplication of ritual practices and symbolic systems" (Labate, MacRae, and Goulart 2010, 4–5). Whereas CEFLURIS epitomizes the adaptational predilection of Daime in Brazil, the CEFLURIS churches in Europe are the most conventional congregations because they attempt to maintain doctrinal principles imported directly from Mapiá.

Contrast this with the adaptational non-CEFLURIS churches such as CdAI, RaS and CCMI in Belgium, which demonstrate how Daime's expansion is not a series of splits, but rather more like the organic branching of a tree. Instead of rejecting their CEFLURIS roots, CdAI and CCMI works include the singing of prized hymns received by Pd. Sebastião. A book by the leader of Céu Sagrado, the Brazilian patron of RaS and CCMI, pays respects to CEFLURIS and hails Pd. Sebastião as a "propagator of Santo Daime" (Neto 2006, 16/22). But official tributes notwithstanding, there remains tension between the leaders of different Daime groups in Europe. This is very similar to diversification in other so-called New Age groups. For instance, one finds disagreements in Wicca, occult esotericism, and paganism circles between old-fashioned conservatives and more liberal splinter groups concerned with "creative reinterpretation" of tradition (Hanegraaff 1998, 86–87/382–383). Because any future regulatory frameworks will need to establish legal distinctions between acceptable and unacceptable uses of ayahuasca, it is important to consider ways that Santo Daime is disposed to the same pitfalls that threaten optimal functioning of any human group.

As with the "discord and rivalry" found between different ayahuasca organizations in Brazil (MacRae 2010, 196–199), from time to time European daimistas can be heard criticizing one another. But beyond the clear ethical violations I feel obliged to divulge below, I will not go into too much private detail about interpersonal spats between individual daimistas—indeed, numerous Daime hymns warn against detrimental impacts of idle gossip and backbiting, as for example in Mestre Irineu #78, which calls for an end to the spreading of "bad news" (*má notícia*).[5] By and large, fardados' complaints had to do with "power struggles" between different views about how the doctrine is most accurately followed. This is not unlike competing factions that exist in mainstream religions and smaller esoteric guilds alike: all "have their traditionalist conservatives and their liberal-minded modernists" (Hanegraaff 1998, 408). On the other hand, the many individuals who have succeeded in integrating the Daime hymns' teachings of unconditional love, acceptance, and oneness hardly ever spoke ill of fellow daimistas, nor of any fellow human being, for that matter. While some bitterness and mutual distrust continues between the leaders of different Daime denominations, the general membership of each group displays little to no animosity. Instead, fardados assured me that these disputes were merely growing pains of the church's expansion, and they were confident that over time these wounds would heal as the European churches moved ever closer toward harmony.

Fardado informants frequently certified that there are imperfect people in all religious groups and that Santo Daime is vulnerable to the same problems that can emerge in every social organization. No religious group is immune from what Jack Kornfield (2000, 139–57) brands "dirty laundry," the potential dangers of misused power, money, sexuality, and mind-altering substances.[6] When left unchecked, the immoral intentions of a few can result in hurt feelings and victimization that are at odds with the objectives of healing and comfort that people hope to achieve in spiritual communities. Because fardado informants are adamant that the Daime community is constantly learning how to improve itself, I will list here infrequent yet nevertheless existent hazards I observed during fieldwork.

Financial disputes are usually avoided because each Daime church upholds a policy of sharing detailed balance sheets with its membership. But as mentioned by Dawson (2013, 73–74), money is a "sensitive topic" for daimistas because their ideal, to provide Daime for free, is undermined by the great expense of purchasing and transporting ayahuasca from abroad; so while it is strongly "suggested" that members pay a monthly tithe, officially the cash paid to attend rituals is considered a "donation" and fees are negotiable for cash-strapped members. However, a single circumstance I learned about with one of the independent Daime groups in Belgium shows how such arrangements can be breached. When police raided a Daime work in Brussels in October 2011, their arrest of the male leader of RaS had nothing to do with ayahuasca. Actually, it was due to a complaint of a former member alleging that the RaS leader had used finances allocated for the group's collective purchase of land in Brazil to stake his personal claim on said land—whether or not this is true I could not confirm either way. This serves as a cautionary tale for daimista churches about the need to ensure adequate oversight and contractual agreements when it comes to fiscal matters.

Though I did not witness it directly, on rare occasions I heard credible reports about sexual improprieties committed by daimistas. In one case, a furor surrounded one charismatic Padrinho (well-known in Daime as a gifted ritual commander), when he was caught having used his status to seduce female daimistas who were not his wife (see Monroe 2017). This infidelity also displayed carelessness on the part of Brazilian church leaders, some of whom "covered up and ignored" these "serious ethical transgressions" for years (Rochester 2012, 14). One fardada told me that even though infidelity is counter to Daime morality, the offenses were initially excused because of this Padrinho's reputation as a powerful medium that can "open channels"; with hindsight she grieved that too many daimistas failed to pay heed to "difficulties in his material/physical life [because] in his spiritual work he's extraordinary." Only after many daimistas' objections had mounted was this Padrinho eventually suspended from his role as a commander in Daime works. I am aware that he has since been readmitted to the church hierarchy after publicly repenting and reforming his ways. Although this Padrinho has been forgiven by many but not all of his peers, such "dirty laundry" can accrue in any organization that permits those in positions of authority to overstep moral boundaries without consequences. In the early twenty-first century, a much worse violation shook a Daime church in North America when it was discovered that a prominent member had made sexual advances on an underage minor. One fardada I talked to about this assault pitied the perpetrator as "an ill man"; she avowed that daimistas must guard against infiltration by "pedophiles" just as the Catholic church needs to expel "predator" priests. This daimista culprit was subsequently "ejected" from the church and the rest of the community continued on without him. Just as some ayahuasca shamans from South America have been accused of raping female patrons (Dobkin de Rios and Rumrill 2008, 98), it is evident that Daime is susceptible to the same sexual misconduct and abuses of power against which all social bodies must struggle.[7]

There is also the tricky question of catastrophes that can and do result from irresponsible uses of ayahuasca. One undeniable safety concern is Daime participants driving automobiles too soon after the ritual. It is typical for organizers of Daime works to ensure that attendees wait until the ayahuasca's effects have subsided before they get behind the wheel. Only once did I feel unsafe in a car driven by one of my informants. This was after an unofficial work organized independently in Belgium by a daimista tourist from Brazil. There was little to no supervision of participants during and after this work, something very out of the ordinary. Stupidly, I hitched a ride with a newly minted fardado who I realized was not in a condition to drive only after he began to scream at the top of his lungs whenever we went through a tunnel, and there were many tunnels. Though this was a singular event that does not in any way represent the rigorous "guardianship" upheld by established Daime churches, it goes to show that there needs to be vigilance about not allowing people to drive vehicles if they have yet to sober up. In a more extreme example of risks, two daimistas were assassinated in 2010 when a troubled young man with a history of drug abuse shot and killed a famous Brazilian cartoonist who led a Daime church in São Paulo and his son. The killer had been attending the local Daime church seeking a cure for his addictions. This occurrence led to a national debate in the Brazilian media about whether Santo Daime should still be permitted (Labate et al. 2010). Although this was a very unusual event in the history of Daime, it shocked the global daimista community. My informants cite this incident as demonstrating the need for careful screening of new initiates.

In Belgium, informants reported two perilous incidents that occurred during the twenty years that Daime works have taken place in this country. On one occasion, a paranoid newcomer ran out into the streets in the middle of a work. This man scurried to a nearby fire station and brought two on-duty firefighters to the Daime work. Upon arriving at the location of the ritual with this frightened man, the first responders left him in the care of the fardados there because all they saw was a group of people dressed in white quietly seated in meditation. Another time, fiscal supervisors had to physically restrain a man who moved to loom over the central table and tried to distract other participants with loud vocal outbursts. Afterward, the man wrote down his difficult experiences in his English diary, which he shared openly with me:

> Now I'm back home and I'm still flinching with embarrassment every time a memory comes up. I don't know what it all meant. I can see different possibilities, other than that it meant nothing at all and was just a heap of ugliness.
>
> One meaning is that I went through one of my worst fears. Another is that—in a very extreme way—I dropped all masks and said everything that was going on inside me uncensored. It was complete, raw honesty. Perhaps I wanted to know the effect that would have on people's appreciation of me. Perhaps I wanted to see how they would feel about me if they saw me sabotage a beautiful session with all the ugliness that was inside of me (a lot of things I said to be provocative, without meaning them).
>
> I'll see what the next days bring. For now, I'm not sure if I ever want to do this again, but on the other hand, I don't want to end like this either.

He did end up going back to do a few more works, and when I interviewed him as a part of the current study, he expressed sincere gratefulness for the lessons he had learned through Daime. Beyond this specific incident, fardados voiced their empathy for all those who have a painful ego-death in Daime, but they view it as ultimately a curative event. It bears repeating that this is a very uncommon occurrence and the results are temporary. All powerful technologies carry some risk, but except for those who have a latent or acute psychotic illness, the risks of participating in structured ayahuasca rituals are very low for average adults.

To be clear, there have been a small number of fatalities[8] associated with ayahuasca ceremonies, all of which are linked to various factors including poorly supervised imbibers, lack of screening, accidents, or toxic botanical additives that do not appear in the traditional Daime recipe of *B. caapi* and *P. viridis* (dos Santos 2013b; Gable 2007). Three prominent examples include a grisly infanticide during an ayahuasca ceremony run by a cult leader in Chile,[9] the suicide of a Canadian tourist[10] who stabbed himself during an ayahuasca retreat in Peru, and a self-defense homicide by a Canadian tourist, who killed a British tourist when the latter grabbed a knife to attack the Canadian at an ayahuasca retreat center in Amazonia.[11] I also heard reports from European fardados[12] about an incident in Japan where a mentally disturbed man apparently left a very badly organized Daime work there and set fire to a building, resulting in several deaths. I cannot find documented confirmation of this story, but it highlights a reckless lack of supervision for ritual participants that seasoned fardados frown upon. As frightening as these stories may be, it must be stressed that ayahuasca-related mortalities and injuries are very rare. To put this in perspective, one is compelled to note that Western societies do not criminalize automobiles, airplanes, or firearms even while gruesome details of fatal mishaps with these technologies continually appear in the news. As far as I can tell, after more than twenty years on the continent there had been no deaths due to ayahuasca rituals in Europe up to the time of my fieldwork. Still, lethal episodes that have occurred elsewhere stand as evidence running counter to anarchistic views held by a few people I have met in the entheogenic community, who tend to rebuff the idea that some formal regulations are necessary.

Contrariwise, the alarmism of mainstream media opposition to psychedelics is entirely at odds with the scientific findings. This is apparent in European newspaper articles that have portrayed the Santo Daime as a "drug-fuelled religion" (Boggan 2008). The popular assumption that substances such as ayahuasca are inherently noxious "drugs" persists even though there is no empirically verified evidence that Santo Daime is unduly dangerous (Labate and Feeney 2012, 160). The fact is that like all powerful tools (such as a car or a knife) or thrill-seeking hobbies (skydiving, whitewater rafting, horseback riding), ayahuasca can be benign when employed within sensible limits but it can be dangerous when used irresponsibly or when precautionary measures are lacking. Therefore, as with any other risky behaviors that are legal only because they are regulated, the religious use of ayahuasca must be subject to some ground rules to optimize benefits and minimize threats. While ayahuasca is generally nontoxic, the brew might be contraindicated for people who take prescription drugs called *serotonin reuptake inhibitors* (SSRIs) to treat depression (Callaway and Grob 1998). There is also a need for much more research to determine risks that ayahuasca may pose to youths, pregnant women, or those with "hepatic, neurological, and cardiovascular dysfunctions" (dos Santos 2013a; 2013b, 179/184–185). But beyond this, current psychopharmacological research suggests that for most adults, "the controlled/ritualistic use of [ayahuasca] has a good safety profile, and . . . [ayahuasca] can have therapeutic effects on the remission of some psychiatric disorders such as major depression and substance dependence" (dos Santos et al. 2016, 1244).

Most of the above exceptions to the otherwise safe and orderly functioning of Santo Daime would be alleviated or totally solved by decriminalizing daimista rituals, making them subject to oversights just as with other religious groups. This would lift some of the pressure daimistas might naturally feel when they fear that it would bring legal problems for the entire Daime movement if they expose individual wrongdoers. For their part, if daimistas turn a blind eye to foreseeable mishaps and criminal abuses or negligence within their ranks, this is what really threatens the viability of their practice. Indeed, daimistas' aspiration to be tolerated as a genuine religion within Western societies hinges upon their ability to demonstrate that such infractions will not be tolerated within the church. These warts of financial disputes, sexual violations, inadequate screening, and driving under the influence are safety issues that governments and churches will have to work out when and if they move to normalize Daime activities. On one hand, it is necessary to point out such irregularities, and I remark on these shortcomings because I know fardados pride themselves on their willingness to face hard truths. As one elder fardado told me, all darkness must eventually "come to the light." On the other hand, I do not share the scholarly penchant for concentrating on social conflict to the exclusion of daimistas' more distinctive preference for always striving toward reconciliation.

The history of Santo Daime's expansion across Europe, as related above, shows that daimistas sometimes disagree to the point of schism. Dawson (2013, 69–76) is technically correct that daimistas can also be observed in active "competition" for hierarchical supremacy. But it is misleading to argue that Daime rituals are "marked by cultic competition," such that "interpersonal rivalry" and "self-promotional status claims" are the most pertinent ethnographic details (Dawson 2013, 76). I fail to see why one would find this so noteworthy, for it is plain that all human groups display internal competition. Rather than witnessing the homeostatic balance of antipathy and altruism that exists in every culture, social scientists' preoccupation with an "ontology of violence/struggle" reflects how few "secular thinkers really escape a first principles commitment to a view of the world in which difference naturally leads to forceful conflict that can only be contained or ameliorated by some use of counter-force" (Robbins 2006, 289–290). It is true that personality differences lead some daimistas to jealousy, hurt feelings, and acrimony. But as is properly highlighted by Schmidt (2007, 200), disputes between daimistas, "even minor quarrels, are commonly looked upon as failures . . . to understand the reasons behind the conflict and your own part in it" (see also Schmidt 2006). In place of misapprehending discord in Daime communities as an end in itself, a thorough ethnography notices that fardados embrace conflict resolution as a pathway to spiritual evolution. We see this in the optimistic spin Julia puts on painful rifts exposed during British daimistas' legal troubles, an adversity that proved to her

> *how much of a community we really are, and how much we become like family. And it doesn't mean that we all love each other; sometimes we don't even like each other, but we're family. If you're a daimista, you're a daimista. Going through the legal process taught me this so much, because it brought out some different behaviors in people and I saw a lot about people in it (some of it was very hard indeed); but despite all of that, I realized that no matter what, we are the daimista family. . . . It's a very profound, unifying thing. . . . There's something very powerful that connects us, it's very bonding.*

There are petty antagonisms among my informants, but most daimistas see these as ultimately galvanizing counterforces of love and respect that can be cooperatively forged by drinking Daime together (see Barnard 2014, 683). Such a spiritual perspective recognizes that "in betrayal and the misuse of power we encounter the failures that come with the territory of being human, . . . out of our errors and frailty come some of our most profound lessons" (Kornfield 2000, 156–157). We see acknowledgment of this in the "decree" of Mestre Irineu, which reminds that "neither intrigue, nor hatred, nor even the slightest disagreement" is justifiable between fardado brothers and sisters; instead, the Mestre dictated an ideal that "everyone who drinks this Holy Beverage should seek not only to behold beauties and splendors, but also to correct your flaws, thus working towards perfecting your own personalities."[13] Whereas squabbling exists in all social contexts, it is exceptional that fardados tend to dovetail criticism of other people with affirmations about their own need to cultivate compassion and forgiveness. As the research in this book attests, daimistas see their efforts to resolve community frictions as contingent upon alchemical healing the Daime accomplishes through transmutations on the individual level.

Rather than get mired in overstressing the universally human trait of interpersonal conflicts, of greater anthropological significance is the fact that fardados are modern mystics who pursue introspective solutions to exterior problems (see Bender 2010). One gets this impression from Eleonora, a young Belgian fardada who said she was initially attracted to Santo Daime because she wanted "to find peace." When I interviewed her as we sat on a bench outside the chapel before a Daime work, she explained her conviction that

> most people come to the Santo Daime because they want to learn about themselves. It's not an easy way, so . . . that's something that binds us. . . . I believe that there's nothing outside us that's not inside us. So, people mostly judge everything that's outside them and say "That's bad and that's bad and that's bad," but they don't have a clue that all these things also live inside them and they can only do something about it and make it better by healing these parts in themselves. . . . Like war . . . look at the war in yourself. You can't help the war outside; you can stop the war in yourself, and if a lot of people do that, then the world can change. Therefore, I think it's so important to heal everything in yourself.

When one really listens to fardados, their mystical intent operates just like "the Jungian alternative to archetypal conflict settled by war in the external forum shifts the battlefield to the internal forum" (Dourley 2014, 168). Fardado ethics locate the burden of responsibility squarely on the individual observer, making it impossible to differentiate between oneself and a person or issue that one wants to judge negatively. Fardados are for the most part very hesitant to heap blame for worldly woes on any external individual or group. Instead, they prefer to emphasize how ayahuasca rituals teach them to focus on fixing their own personal imperfections. They describe humans' inner domain as either in "harmony" or "blocked." Harmony is seen as our natural state of nonduality, while ego "blocks" stem from a delusional belief in separation between self and not-self. They understand that "blocks" are a common part of human life, but they strive to "dissolve" these blocks so as to achieve greater states of inner and outer unity.

Throughout this book, I have explored as thoroughly as I can the main problem of my research: *Why are some Europeans choosing to dedicate themselves to Santo Daime spiritual practice?* I found that European daimistas are seeking metaphysical and practical solutions to internal and external conflicts through their participation in ayahuasca rituals. In terms of metaphysical "solutions"—like the chemical melding of two previously separate substances—a male member of CCMI told me that Daime is a way of "connecting to the Absolute," a melting of the self into the divine source of existence (he did not feel comfortable with the loaded word *God*). As for practical solutions, a female daimista in Brussels related a common narrative of how working with the Daime sacrament can gradually lead to one's personal growth and self-improvement. Although Yanette is not a committed fardado, she claims that Daime works have helped her to overcome her addiction to cigarettes and her lifelong struggle with chronic "melancholy," a disorder that worsened after the death of one of her parents. She had initially sought assistance through shamanic-style ayahuasca ceremonies, but she found that in these rituals she "didn't have enough support." She eventually learned about Santo Daime works. She said that Daime affords her an atmosphere of interpersonal reinforcement that helps guide her through the difficulties of the ayahuasca experience:

> *I think* [Santo Daime] *is a divine being, a kind of healer. It tracks down things that don't belong in your system . . . like illnesses, thoughts, and emotions. . . . It tries to have you change your mind or the way you feel in your heart about it. But it's not always easy at that moment when that is happening; you don't want to* [change] *because you're so used to it . . . it's too difficult, it's much too heavy to accept and to overcome and to transform . . . You have to work with it . . . then it can give real positive benefits. . . . It's nothing obscure, nothing ambiguous, nothing strange. Then you can see it's really something pure.*
>
> *But first it confronts you with the opposite effect. . . . In the beginning when I drank Daime I saw Hell, it was horrible: it's dark things, it's a dying, thinking you lost your mind, thinking people*

are against you.[14] *. . . Now the Daime is helping me get a little bit more confidence to trust people. . . . I now interpret it that it's okay to live your life in a good way; if you try to help people, if you try to work, if you try to love people, to be responsible for the environment and to clear yourself from bad habits like drinking alcohol, swearing, smoking (everything that's not good in fact),*[15] *and you really work on yourself and also your mind every day and you try to develop and to purify and to get better, I think you get a lot of rewards and that's what's happening now with me, finally.*

Despite such hellish tribulations, daimistas trust that the mystical experiences provided by Daime works foster practical enhancements in their daily lives by bringing devotees face to face with repressed emotions, uncomfortable memories, and other destructive thought patterns (see Dourley 2014, 93–97). Scholars have acknowledged this in passing with regard to Daime in Brazil, such as when MacRae (2006, 396) affirms Brazilian daimistas' belief that "every time someone takes the brew they have the opportunity of entering into direct contact with God and, if deserving, they might then be able to find *solutions* for problems they may be facing and even be healed of terminal illnesses, as many followers claim to have been." All the same, daimistas are aware that their otherworldly incentives must be balanced with attention to worldly concerns, otherwise they are prone to traps that befall all religious groups.

The main conflict of Santo Daime is not among fardados, but between all daimistas and the wider societies in which ayahuasca rituals are prohibited. That is why I want to shine a light on daimistas' view that the oppression they suffer due to criminalization of their unorthodox religious practice offers them yet another chance to have faith in the face of despair. European fardados continue their ayahuasca rituals despite state opposition because they believe that they are on the right side of history. The present text serves to encourage liberalist political authorities to heed scholarly knowledge by reconsidering the legal status of entheogenic religions, such as Santo Daime. Regarding daimistas' clash with the social settings in which they operate, the etic analysis of informants' emic perspectives in this book models how anthropology can contribute to public debates about entheogens in the Western world. This entails an appeal to the *post-secular*, a cosmopolitical compromise rooted in mutual humility of believers and nonbelievers both recognizing the essential mysteriousness of human existence.

Entheogens and Post-Secular Cosmopolitics

Having now explored the sociocultural particularities of Daime in Europe, it is important to recognize wider implications of the transnational movement of ayahuasca rituals for enduring disputes about the public place of religion in Western societies. Recall that religions are self-identified groups organizing themseves around moral principles and ritual practices oriented toward entities that cannot be detected by scientific measures. The question of criminalization or religious freedom for Santo Daime has real-life consequences for daimistas. One cannot interpret such issues without first addressing broader cosmopolitical disagreements about whether ayahuasca begets "hallucinogenic" delusions or "entheogenic" revelations. Speaking of intercultural debates in political ecology, Stengers (2005, 1002–1003) sets the "scene" this way:

> There is no knowledge that is both relevant and detached. It is not an objective definition of a virus or of a flood that we need, a detached definition everybody should accept, but the active participation of all those whose practice is engaged in multiple modes with the virus or with the river. As for the cosmopolitical perspective. . . . I suggest first distinguishing the figure of the expert and that of the diplomat. Experts are the ones whose practice is not threatened by the issue under discussion since what they know is accepted as relevant. Their role will require them to present themselves and to present what they know, in a mode that does not foresee the way in which that knowledge will be taken into account. By contrast, diplomats are there to provide a voice for those whose practice, whose mode of existence and whose identity are threatened by a decision. . . . Diplomats' role is therefore above all . . . to give a voice to those who define themselves as threatened, in a way likely to cause the experts to have second thoughts, and to force them to think about the possibility that their favorite course of action may be an act of war. (Stengers 2005, 1002–1003; see also Latour 2004; Stengers 2010; Stengers 2011)

With disputes about a mind-altering sacrament, this ethnography of Santo Daime acts as a cosmopolitical mediator between "expert" lawmakers and fardado "diplomats." Attempting to help attenuate fardados' sociolegal persecution in Europe, I appeal to post-secular cosmopolitics as an avenue for weathering intercultural disagreements about ayahuasca states of consciousness, for, as Mario Blaser (2016, 565) argues, "[I]t is not a matter of either/or but of both/and." Hereby, not only would non-daimistas have to suspend their disfavoring view of ayahuasca in order to recognize daimistas' religious freedom, in return the Daime churches would have to accept government oversight to curtail risks such as those catalogued above.

Dating back at least to the eighteenth-century writings of Voltaire and Hume, various European intellectuals have foretold the imminent obsolescence of religion in their homelands (see Gorski and Altınordu 2008). By the 1960s, the "secularization thesis" reigned across the social sciences (Cannell 2010, 86), with diminishing commitment to and attendance at traditional churches cited as conclusive evidence for the downfall of religion's public influence in the Western world. Commentators still point to Western Europe as the most secularized region on Earth (Soper and Fetzer 2002, 169). There is no denying a conspicuous decay in the number of parishioners attending traditional European (i.e., Christian) places of worship, and this fixture of the secularization thesis is not in doubt. Citing the comprehensive World Values surveys conducted in the last two decades of the twentieth century, Norris and Inglehart (2011, 86) confirm that "the existing evidence in Western Europe consistently and unequivocally shows two things: traditional religious beliefs and involvement in institutionalized religion (i) vary considerably from one country to another; and (ii) have steadily declined throughout Western Europe, particularly since the 1960s." Between 1981 and 2001, surveys showed decreases in the percentage of citizens who attend churches across Western Europe, especially in Ireland (from 82% to 65% [decline of −17%]), Spain (40% to 26% [−14%]), Belgium (31% to 19% [−12%]), and the Netherlands (26% to 14% [−12%]) (Norris and Inglehart 2011, 74). These declines in "traditional" church attendance are why many scholars and laypeople alike accept the notion that "in Western Europe, if nowhere else, the old secularization theory would seem to hold" (Berger 1999, 9). Others who look at the numbers showing chronological declines in European church attendance and membership see "a decisive, long-lasting, and ongoing trend toward secularization" (Bunzl 2005, 535). There is also a noticeable generational imbalance, where younger Europeans tend not to be as dedicated to the religions practiced by older generations (Voas and Doebler 2011, 45). But despite drastic drops in church attendance around the continent, today there remains a critical mass of spiritual believers in Europe.

In academic parlance, religion is habitually contrasted with the notion of the *secular*[16] (i.e., nonreligion, a prioritization of this-worldliness). The "secular" designates those aspects of social life that do not involve any recourse to supernatural beings. Instead, secular affairs are organized according to a reliance on nontheistic systems of logic. Yet in acknowledging the persistent importance of religion in today's world, many social theorists now refer to the current age as "post-secular" (see Green 2019). For Jürgen Habermas (2009, 59–77), the albeit clumsy adjective *post-secular* recognizes a reciprocal onus on both religious and nonreligious Europeans to learn to negotiate cooperatively. Habermas (2010a, 18) defines a "post-secular society" as that within which "secularization functions less as a filter separating out the contents of [religious] traditions than as a transformer which redirects the flow of tradition." Sociologist Grace Davie (2014, 29) reckons the "post-secular" as an ambiguous label that captures two concurrent trends impacting the status of faith in Western societies: "It is true that religion has re-entered the public square in new and unexpected ways . . . [and] it is equally true that the process of secularization is continuing." As Habermas (2005, 26–27) observes, in such a *post-secular* arena, "the expectation of a persisting disagreement between worldly knowledge and religious tradition deserves the predicate 'reasonable' only if religious convictions are granted, from the perspective of secular knowledge, an epistemic status that is not simply 'irrational.'"[17] Habermas (2010a, 16) argues that believers must repay this gesture when it comes to the practical concern of governing civil societies. Rather than project their religious values onto the state, religious minorities must accept that the secular value of separating church and state is necessary for arbitrating in diverse democratic societies. However, Taylor (2007, 427–429) identifies a secularist bias or "unthought which underpins much secularization theory," whereby "the exclusion/irrelevance of religion is often part of the unnoticed background of social science, history, philosophy, [and] psychology." Perhaps the greatest asset of anthropology is that its techniques of participant-observation and its holistic approach to human diversity help to spell out unfamiliar cultural territories. Accordingly, to hone the post-secular concept—which misleadingly implies an era after secularism—cosmopolitical framings of entheogens can promote what I would rename a *post-arrogant* paradigm, demoting both secularist and religious chauvinisms equally.

Over the past few decades, the entheogenic practice of Santo Daime has expanded across the world. After first establishing small congregations in Spain and Belgium, there are now Daime churches operating in twelve

European countries. Preceding chapters have shown that European fardados believe their Daime rituals help them find workable solutions to common physical and psychological problems. My informants consider ayahuasca a holy sacrament. These ideas conflict with current policies that prohibit the possession and consumption of entheogens. The initial response from Western governments has been to arrest and prosecute people who engage in Daime rituals. For instance, the latest legal decision handed down in the Belgian region of Flanders firmly rejected daimistas' appeal for religious freedom in that country (Belgium 2014; see also Labate and Taymans forthcoming).

Taking the legal limbo faced by Belgian fardados as an example, it is imperative that social facts about Santo Daime are revealed so as to counteract "anti-sect" stigmas found in mainstream society (Fautré 1999). As "the specifically Belgian context" is characterized by legal scholar Rik Torfs (2005, 659), "organized religious groups, including the traditional churches, do not always enjoy a favorable reputation in Belgium," and the secularist "climate in society is not against specific penal norms limiting activities of so-called harmful sectarian organisations." Created by an act of parliament in 1998, the Belgian government's Center for Information and Advice on Harmful Sectarian Organizations pursues a mandate "to publish, whether on its own initiative or at the request of any public authority, advice and recommendations about the phenomenon of harmful sectarian organizations and especially on the policy regarding the fight against these organizations" (Fautré 1999, 389). Through this anti-sect center, the Belgian state pays extra negative attention to new religions. State overreach is witnessed in the fact that new religions such as the Anthroposophical Society, the Universal Church of God, and Sahaja Yoga were successful in legal cases in which they accused the Belgian government of defamation (Fautré 2010, 321). A recent biennial report from this CIAOSN/IACSSO[18] (2010, 10), filed on behalf of the Belgian national and regional governments, outlined scholarly evidence pertaining to ayahuasca. Despite the overwhelmingly skeptical tone of this text, the authors take great pains to cite results of biomedical studies and the emic perspective of those who ingest ayahuasca for religious purposes. This report ends with a review of legal trials involving ayahuasca churches in Brazil, the United States, the Netherlands, and France, concluding that the French decision to prohibit ayahuasca was "slanted in favor of a strongly repressive option." When it comes to the all-important constitutional question of whether Santo Daime is a "religion" to be protected or a "sect" to be feared, these definitions are murky in Belgium. As itemized by legal scholar Norman Doe (2011, 99), "there are no formal legal requirements for a religious group to become a statutory *culte recconu* [recognized religion] in Belgium; according to unwritten administrative practice, the group must be: sufficiently large; well-structured; present in the territory for some decades; socially important; and it must be such as not to threaten social order." As the present book has demonstrated, except for fardados' small population size the Santo Daime meets all of the above conditions.

To the south, the French government's outright condemnation of Santo Daime seems to be a kind of secular inquisition, wherein citizens are punished for deviating from the state's officially monophasic ontology. In her detailed examination, Bourgogne (2011, 360) makes a blunt assessment of the French Daime case, concluding that "obsession with secularization combined with the fear surrounding sects threatens the freedom of spiritual minorities" such as Santo Daime. In contrast to the small number of fardados in France, the vehemence and inflexibility of governmental prohibitions against Daime activities expose a deep-seated antipathy toward polyphasic beliefs. After all, what else besides bigotry would compel a secular state to ignore science in continuing to forbid this entheogenic spirituality? From an anthropological perspective, this conflict is not so much about the substance of ayahuasca as it is about the ethno-philosophical nature of consciousness. The points of ontological dispute seem to be daimistas' beliefs that (1) ayahuasca is not a "hallucinogen," and (2) that Daime rituals can be therapeutic. European daimistas concur with the Brazilian fardado/intellectual Alex Polari de Alverga (2011, 203) that altered states of consciousness induced by their Daime sacrament assist one in healing oneself through "a difficult and hard journey to reach self-awareness"; more specifically, Polari frames Santo Daime as an opportunity to "confront all layers of resistance and illusion that separate us from the very fundamental truths about ourselves." Such polyphasic assertions are anathema to the monophasic bias of drug control regimes that now dictate the global governance of psychoactive substances (see Tupper and Labate 2014). Thus, in its banning of all mind-altering agents—other than profitable sales of alcohol, tobacco, and psychopharmaceuticals—the French state offers a textbook case of widespread prejudices against entheogens.[19] In general, court rulings against Santo Daime tend to cherry-pick publications that suggest negative effects, such as a toxicology study that was debunked for giving pregnant rats exorbitant doses out of proportion with the " 'real world,' human, ritual consumption of ayahuasca" (dos Santos 2010, 534).

Since popular assumptions in Europe tend to lump all new religions into a preformed category of dubiousness, it is imperative that social scientists disseminate accurate information to counteract lay inclinations. As one example, the Church of Scientology is also being prosecuted in Belgium because of charges that through aggressive recruiting practices church leaders committed "extortion, fraud, illegal practice of medicine and violation of privacy laws" (Jauregui 2012). Meanwhile, it is taboo in Santo Daime to actively recruit new members. Fardados believe that people find their own way to the Daime if it is part of their spiritual path, so they see no need to pressure anyone to join the works. Santo Daime and Scientology do share the ideal of helping people to overcome suffering in their lives, but such therapeutic ends are also found amid state-authorized religions such as Christianity and Buddhism. Potent objects are venerated in most religions, be they altars, icons, prayer beads, an entheogenic sacrament, or Scientology's Dianetics. But against the Euro-American habit of attributing words such as *cult* and *sect* to all new religions, important distinctions between Scientology and Santo Daime must be acknowledged. The mystical-shamanic worldview of fardados relies on gaining intimate knowledge of one's inner self through internal revelations instigated by the Daime tea. When one receives visions during Daime works, the interpretation of their meaning is left to the person who experiences them. Compare this to the "e-meter" technology of Scientology, a device registering electrical currents in a devotee's body, which are then interpreted by a designated church expert known as an "auditor" (Bromley 2009, 94). Santo Daime members' openness to scientific observation and research also differentiates this ayahuasca religion from the more secretive conduct of Scientology. Given the multiplicity of new spiritualities in Europe, it is necessary for legislators to demarcate how each group poses a unique cosmopolitical case, so as to differentiate between safe spiritual formats and harmful cults.

Before its recent legal backtracking on the issue (see Hartman 2018), the Netherlands had long stood out as the safest place for daimistas to practice their religion in Europe, as it would seem that the Dutch respect Article 9 of the European Convention on Human Rights (Doe 2011, 42[n15]). In Spain, the "Spanish Supreme Court . . . has legalized the shared consumption [of ayahuasca], as long as this happens among habitual consumers, without publicizing the event, when it is done by people who are sure and determined of what they are doing and there is no context of gain" (López-Pavillard and de las Casas 2011, 372). In other European countries, Daime practitioners worship within a legal grey area, such as with adjournments of legal prosecutions against fardados in Italy (Menozzi 2011). As Rohde and Sander (2011, 347) report, the case against Daime in Germany was "officially dismissed" in 2007 on a technicality "that although the Daimistas had offended the German drug law, they had acted without knowing that they committed a crime." With few exceptions, a strategy of harassing daimistas without bringing the case to trial is popular with governments that want to prevent decisive rulings akin to the original outcome in the Netherlands. We see this approach in the United Kingdom. At present, it appears that this piecemeal situation for the Santo Daime will continue until the European Court of Human Rights is consulted at the supranational level.

In approaching this cosmopolitical discord, one can refer to Habermas's (1989[1962]) contemplations on the *public sphere*. In post-Enlightenment societies, the public sphere is composed of mediated "social arenas in which . . . a conflict of opinions is fought out more or less discursively" (Habermas 1992, 430). Charles Taylor (2007, 192) maintains that the Euro-American public sphere is characterized by its "radical secularity." Existing in a "relational dynamic" with "religion," secularity circumscribes the operations of the state as segregated from theistic dogma (Hirschkind 2011, 641). Scholars engaged in the emerging subfield of the anthropology of secularism have begun to deconstruct how "liberal secularism's claims to tolerance" can veil an exclusionary political agenda that "permits and develops certain ways of being and living while disdaining, tacitly prohibiting, or stunting others" (Cannell 2010, 90–91). These scholars now scrutinize how "the Enlightenment doctrine of secularism that enabled the delimiting of a public sphere, in which tolerance and neutrality could be practiced, has been critical to a particular kind of authoritative definition of religion—that is, the demarcation of a line between what does and does not constitute the terms of *authentic religion*" (Abeysekara 2008, 176). As noted by Asad (2003, 183–85): "From the beginning the liberal public sphere excluded certain kinds of people: women, subjects without property, and members of religious minorities"; but, "the introduction of new discourses may result in the disruption of established assumptions structuring debates in the public sphere." The cosmopolitics of Santo Daime accentuate the secularist assumption that there are no supernatural phenomena outside the material realm as a metaphysical claim just as unprovable as any religious belief.

As stated at the outset, I am an agnostic, an ontological position I still hold even after my fieldwork. Counter to John Bialecki's (2014) survey of methodological atheism in the Anthropology of Christianity subfield or the conflation of methodological agnosticism with atheism in Dawson's (2013, 196) book on Santo Daime, we should beware the hegemonic "illusion of the rational 'obviousness'" of secular disenchantment (C. Taylor 2007,

539–593). I have herein advocated for a kind of "strong agnosticism" as necessary for social scientists who find themselves mediating betwixt religious-secularist cross-pressures within Western public spheres: whereas a "'weak agnosticism' . . . is nothing more than a confession that one does not know whether God exists. . . . Strong agnosticism . . . says that we *cannot* know whether or not God exists" (Le Poidevin 2010, 9; see also Dourley 2014, 5/92/162–63). On a specific cosmopolitical issue, I have tried to show that ethnographic interpretations of entheogenic therapies and religiosity are best served by acknowledging that

> theism and atheism start on pretty much the same footing. There should be no presumption of atheism, and indeed no presumption of theism either. The initial position should be [a strong] agnostic one, which means that theists and atheists share the burden of proof. Agnosticism is not redundant. (Le Poidevin 2010, 53)

As opposed to disenchanted approaches that operate according to a "presumption" or "default setting" that "the rational thing is to be atheist" (Le Poidevin 2010, 46), the strong agnostic tack of the present text assumes a receptivity that does not foreclose daimistas' mystical attitudes. Such a post-secular or post-arrogant approach discerns a common bias of false confidence underlying both methodological atheism and fundamentalist theology.

Like Narby's (1998, 6–9) reaction to ayahuasca shamanism in the Amazon, through ethnophenomenology at Daime works I have been repeatedly humbled at being forced to face the "bottomless arrogance of my presuppositions." Though I am not a daimista, I learned a great deal about the sources of my own existential struggles through participating in Daime rituals with an open mind. This is not unlike the self-confrontation and positive personal outcomes that an agnostic anthropologist might have in conducting ethnophenomenology with Buddhist monks or Catholic nuns. It has been my intention to demonstrate how an agnostic approach to anthropology can result in sympathetic insights that might otherwise be occluded by a stalwartly disenchanted approach committed to the ideological tenets of secularism. To be sure, my ethnophenomenological immersion within Santo Daime did reshape my previously disenchanted outlook into a more flexible, awestruck agnosticism. I now see no problem admitting that religiosity *may* be onto something, that God *might* very well exist. Hence, without taking a hard stance on either side of belief, an agnostic social scientist can operate with receptivity to the mystical healing of existential despair in Daime works. Given all I have personally experienced at ayahuasca rituals, it is fair to say that "Pascal's Wager" in favor of the existence of a divine Higher Power now seems like a wise bet to me (see Kearney 2011, 183; Letheby 2016, 33). From a standpoint of praxis, I now cast my existential lot with Pascal, erring on the side of considering myself a "person of faith" as regards those questions that opened the preface of this book. Unlike staunch theists or atheists who know it to be true that God does/doesn't exist, I make a self-conscious choice to trust Great Spiritual Teachers not because I possess self-assured belief, but rather as a pragmatic gamble with the life I live in the face of my mortality—I now feel most comfortable allying myself with philosopher Richard Kearney's (2001, 5) proposal for "*The God Who May Be*," a post-arrogant or "anatheist" theology of intellectual humility, which "reminds us that what seems impossible to us is only seemingly so" (see also Kearney 2011). As an anthropologist, I do not have to share my informants' worldview, I only have to consider it seriously. It is clear from my research that sacramental consumption of ayahuasca in the Santo Daime church is not dangerous; if anything it is perhaps quite advantageous for some people. Congruent with mounting scientific evidence, my encounters with fardados call into question the supposed necessity of harsh prohibitions against entheogenic practices like Santo Daime.

The above analyses show how fardados' perspectives on ayahuasca can highlight broader cosmopolitical struggles between secularist and spiritual stances in today's world. Instead of establishing one lone "fundamental ontology" (what Heidegger termed a "worlding"), Blaser (2014, 53) exhorts anthropologists to reconcile humanity's "multiple ontologies." Stimulating "conversation on political ontology," he targets the same cosmopolitics that assail fardados' ontological "stories" and all other societal "world-ings . . . enacting a reality" that is nonsecular and/or nonmodern: "In this context, carving out a space to listen is also carving out a space to tell another story to (and about) ourselves, to engage in other kinds of worlding that might be more conducive to a coexistence based on recognizing conflicts rather than brushing them off as irrelevant or nonexistent" (Blaser 2013, 551/559). When we listen to fardados, they advance a plausible hypothesis that ayahuasca's inconsistent legality is symptomatic of underlying tensions between hardline monophasic ("closed-spin") secularities and agnostic ("open-spin") secularities predisposed to tolerating polyphasic worldings (see Taylor 2007, 550–51). Irrespective of whether it is branded phenomenological (P) anthropology, existential (E) anthropology, or ontological (O) anthropology, the joint agendas of a PEO anthropology can be harnessed to mollify conflicts between secular Being-in-the-world (Heidegger 1962[1927], 32–38/78–79) and polyphasic ontologies of Being-in-otherworlds. Instead of prejudging alternative states of consciousness that most Europeans have never personally experienced, I agree with Jackson (1996, 19) that "what ethnography demands of phenomenology is resistance to [ontological and existential] generalizations made on the strength of one's own [etic] self-understanding." Like existential anthropology, the related strategies of ethnophenomenology and ethno-ontology operate as "less a repudiation of any one way of explaining human behavior—scientific, religious, humanist, animist—than a reminder that life is irreducible to the terms with which we seek to grasp it" (Jackson and Piette 2015b, 9). This PEO anthropology has been deployed herein to help etic outsiders sympathize with fardados' emic worldings, thus fostering more nuanced examinations of secular and non-secular cosmopolitics.

It is hoped that this presentation of my research with Santo Daime groups can inform renewed conciliations between monophasic and polyphasic ideologies. The way that Western countries handle the emergence of entheo-genic practices is a test case for Euro-American claims of liberalist tolerance. For fardados who believe that the global spread of Santo Daime is not a coincidence, the Christianity brought by Europeans to South America has returned to Europe in a new form. They esteem the Daime not only as a medicinal remedy to psychophysical illnesses; fardados believe that when one is committed to integrating lessons from these rituals into daily life, the ayahuasca sacrament is a divine source of "solutions" more broadly. Santo Daime is exemplary of how "new forms of religion are coming into Europe from outside . . . offering a significant challenge to the widely held assumptions about the place of religion in European societies" (Davie 2006, 33). How can post-secular/post-arrogant societies reconcile a commitment to protect citizens' freedom of religion with the arrival of exotic practices that violate existing legal norms? Applying anthropology to this cosmopolitical quandary is crucial for my informants, who are criminalized because their religion conflicts with controversial yet entrenched drug legislation. At the same time, as entheogens such as ayahuasca become integrated into Western societies, it is necessary to avoid appropriating or colonizing indigenous/non-Western voices and intellectual property all over again. It would thus be prudent for psychedelic science to welcome a more prominent role for applied anthropology—such ongoing consultation with the ethnographic record will help familiarize "expert" policymakers with cosmopolitcal claims of "diplomats" representing the newly arrived entheogenic groups.

Looking ahead, applied anthropology has a big role to play with shepherding the arrival of entheogenic medicines into Western contexts (see Apud 2017, 2020b; Re et al. 2016). My ethnographically informed position on psychedelic psychotherapy falls somewhere in the middle between those who argue for unbridled libertarianism and those who desire excessive clinical restrictions on the use of these treatments. Like the "Wild West" phase of all new and not yet regulated therapies, there are lots of charlatans who market themselves unjustifiably as "healers." But just thinking you are good at leading psychedelic rituals is not the same as being certified by established peers or an official regulatory body. While religious organizations such as Santo Daime must continue to be very cautious about who they endorse as legitimate ritual leaders,[20] in its secular contexts psychedelic therapy should probably be a "controlled act" like surgery or midwifery. The move to befittingly regulate psychedelic health care is being led by clinical psychologist Janis Phelps, who published a seminal paper entitled "Developing Guidelines and Competencies for the Training of Psychedelic Therapists" (2017). In her article, Phelps (2017, 473) argues that the rapid legitimization of psychedelics means that in the near future "there will be further need for therapeutic services from properly trained medical professionals, therapists, clergy, and chaplains to work in clinics and centers that have expanded access programs." She wisely proposes that anyone serving in the role of "sitter"/ guide for psychedelic therapy or supervising pre-/post-"integration" sessions should be certified according to "six therapist competencies," which she lists as "empathetic abiding presence; trust enhancement; spiritual intelligence; knowledge of the physical and psychological effects of psychedelics; therapist self-awareness and ethical integrity; and proficiency in complementary techniques" (Phelps 2017, 450). As attested herein, entheogens can elicit spontaneous erruptions of religious material, and people who ingest entheogens often need support from experienced guides like the *fiscal* "guardians" in Daime. How can a facilitator who lacks formal training in the discipline of spiritual care even hope to respond adequately when psychedelic patients have impactful visions of Jesus, Krishna, angels, or demons? Hence, future psychedelic therapists should be considered underqualified if they have not completed rigorous psychospiritual training with accredited programs, akin to multifaith models found with the Canadian Association for Spiritual Care[21] (CASC), the Association for Clinical Pastoral Education[22] (ACPE), or the European Council for Pastoral Care and Counselling[23] (ECPCC). One envisions that spiritual care training would be a vital component of specialized clinical education departments in emerging degree programs, such as the certificate in Psychedelic-Assisted Therapies & Research from the Center for Psychedelic Therapies and Research (CPTR) at California Institute of Integral Studies[24] (CIIS) or the Psychedelics & Spirituality Studies Initiative (PSSI) at University of Ottawa[25] (see Rochester et al., forthcoming)—other pedagogies include "interfaith" certification in entheogenic chaplaincy[26] (Keiman 2020), learning "empathic resonance" via "psychedelic apprenticeships" (Timmermann, Watts, and Dupuis forthcoming), or the MAPS Zendo (2015) Project's innovative approach to integration support in its *Psychedelic Harm Reduction Training Manual*[27] (see also Tai et al. 2021).

When it comes to the concurrent rise of entheogenic religions and psychedelic psychotherapy in "modern" societies, Stengers (2011, 299–304) is correct that mere "tolerance" of "nonmodern" worldviews can end up being a "curse" (*malédiction*) that reinforces dominions of physicalist secularism within the spheres of law and scholarship; she points out that it is rank disingenuousness whenever tolerance comes as a guise for patronizing forbearance, which "barely hides [the] immense pride" and ethnocentric "arrogance" maintained by "practitioners" of scientism. And yet, the cosmopolitical ideal of being taken seriously by secular policymakers is not the highest priority for my daimista informants—right now, they are confronted with more pressing fears about being harassed by police and even imprisoned for their sacramental use of ayahuasca. While they no doubt desire public approval of their entheogenic practices as a long-term goal, for the time being daimistas are content to receive begrudging legislative tolerance as a first step in cosmopolitical negotiations with governments, albeit with the hope of one day attaining mutually respectful legitimacy within their home countries. Only after fardados achieve the foothold of official tolerance can genuine cosmopolitical conversations about "sacred" entheogens begin in earnest; in other words, scientific and legal authorities must first embrace cosmopolitics as "a new and badly needed humility" to establish a forum for post-arrogant colloquies between "materialism, with its quantitative thinking…and 'controlled' experiments on one side, and… romantic supernaturalism on the other" (Stengers 2010, 78-79).

16

Closing Remarks

Toward Mutual Respect and Toleration

The persecution of new religious ideas and practices is an old story. With regard to entheogens in the Western world, European governments' misgivings about psychoactive sacraments are first documented in a "1620 inquisitorial edict prohibiting the use of peyote and other native herbs and mushrooms for the purposes of divination, healing, and witchcraft"; presuming work of the Devil, such decrees indicate how "the rapidly expanding use of these substances for magical and healing practices even among nonindigenous people in the early seventeenth century was for the inquisitors of New Spain evidence of a diabolic conspiracy between the indigenous shamanic users of these substances and a growing number of Spanish and other *castas* who consulted them and spread the use of peyote among non-Indians" (Chuchiak IV 2012, 308–309). So not only must ayahuasca forevermore be recognized as "intellectual property" that "belongs to the indigenous people of Western Amazonia" (Narby 1998, 152–55), it is also intriguing that Europeans with desires for healing are now drinking this mind-altering brew in Europe.

It may appear at first glance that daimistas are recolonizing ayahuasca by Christianizing a sacrament that originated in non-Christian indigenous contexts. Cultural appropriation is indeed a legitimate and extremely sensitive concern in emergent psychedelic communities. For instance, at a recent meeting of the Multidisciplinary Association for Psychedelic Studies (MAPS), an indigenous questioner called out the "white privilege" of conference attendees during a presentation by Gabor Maté, a Hungarian Canadian doctor now treating addictions with entheogenic intervention: "referring to the growing boom in American and European tourism to countries like Peru and Brazil for the purpose of taking part in healing ceremonies using psychedelic plants, which some people fear will threaten access for native populations to these ancient, sacred rites," this woman reminded Maté and his crowd that "cultural appropriation is a form of retraumatization to indigenous people" (Schwartz 2017). Maté has since rectified his initial oversight in the newer edition of *In the Realm of Hungry Ghosts*, his classic book on addiction. Modeling a chastened deference that should be emulated by all Western medical professionals and drug experts, Maté (2018, xxiii/xxvii–xxviii) recognizes that indigenous societies possess advanced knowledge of psychoactive plant medicines, such as ayahuasca:

> Preventing and healing trauma is a universal issue, not restricted to any one class or any particular ethnic or racial grouping. In fact, as I get to know more about Native ways I am often struck by the thought that we hurt ourselves when we dismiss cultures whose core teachings and values, if appreciated by modern society, could help heal our world. . . . We would have much to gain from respecting the resilience and age-old teachings of those who have suffered the most from trauma, dislocation, addiction: the Aboriginal people among us. . . . The more I assimilate the latest scientific research on human development, the brain, health and the interconnections between the individual and the social milieu, the greater respect I have for the traditional practices of those we have colonized and whose culture we did our best to destroy.

In line with Groisman's (2009) "reparations" and Dawson's (2013, 162/267) "neo-liberal, commodity capitalism"/"commoditization" critiques of Daime's expansion beyond its Amazonian roots, the threat of cultural appropriation always looms whenever Westerners selectively borrow ideas or ritual elements from non-Western traditions. This complex ethical dilemma has long been of interest to anthropologists (for example, see the work of Michael F. Brown 1994; 1997; 2009). And yet, overemphasis on neoliberal economics in the New Age movements[1] tends to obscure fardados' sincere desire to initiate heart-rending processes of truth and reconciliation with people of color in the former colonies. Unlike existentially immature New Agers, the present anthropological study has shown that Western fardados are serious practitioners of a genuine shamanic mysticism originally formulated by an Afro-Brazilian man in the Amazon rainforest. Rather than stealing the ayahuasca tradition, my informants want to bridge the destructive psychosocial chasm of European hegemony that has persisted for hundreds of years. Instead of profiting from neocolonial exploitation, fardados genuinely want to heal colonialist wounds by learning from native wisdoms of the Americas how to be less greedy and less egocentric people. To this end, I would suggest that Anglophone daimistas pay careful attention to Krippner's text on *Protecting Indigenous Knowledge from Ecopiratism* (1999), itself a translation of the "Charter of the Principles of Indigenous Knowledge" drafted in Portuguese by indigenous South American leaders (see also Indigenous Peoples of the Juruá Valley 2019). Moving forward, the most ethical option is for Western mental health "experts" to share power and demonstrate cosmopolitical humility in their explorations of psychedelic realms where they are the cultural neophytes—nonindigenous scholars can do this by supporting and learning from "indigenous epistemological research," as stipulated by authors of an important new article on the many ways social justice issues apply to all future psychedelic research by Western scientists (Bouso and Sánchez-Avilés 2020, 149).

I can confirm that whenever the topic arose, European fardados expressed gratitude to the indigenous peoples who invented ayahuasca. This thankfulness is illustrated in the words of Amos, a thirty-one-year-old Israeli-born fardado studying for his PhD in the Netherlands:

> *The Western people of Europe colonized a lot of places in the world and killed many indigenous people, destroyed the indians and the Africans. . . . In a way, this whole* [historical] *process . . .* [occurred] *in order for them to reach here and help us cure ourselves. So the spreading is a double movement: it's a movement of the West there and there's a movement from there back here; the Western movement there is a destructive movement, and now we get back the cure.*

A social justice perspective might understandably wince at European fardados' enjoyment of a ritual technology invented by the very indigenous groups who continue to be oppressed by Eurocentric forces of neocolonialism. Of course, if nonindigenous daimistas want to prove that they are *truly* grateful to the indigenous peoples for sharing their ayahuasca technology with Mestre Irineu, they would be wise to heed important warnings in publications by Roger K. Green (2019, 2020, 2021) about Westerners' ongoing inclination for blind neocolonialist mindsets. For sure, because of the nature of its history, theology, and sacramental drink, the Santo Daime is obligated to engage in truth and reconciliation endeavors throughout Africa and the Americas. It is a good question why there are no aboriginal names[2] atop European fardados' GST freelists, which are dominated by nonindigenous personalities. To rectify abuses of the colonialist past, in future daimistas must keep painstakingly improving relations with the indigenous traditions out of which ayahuasca first sprouted. Any Western daimista who doubts this culpability should read through Taussig's *Shamanism, Colonialism, and the Wild Man: A Study in Terror and Healing* (1987), which also exposes imperialist crimes against mestizos and South Americans of African descent. It is thus a paramount responsibility for daimistas of European ancestry to reckon with the ugly historical events that laid the groundwork for their beautiful religion to became a nucleus of Christian hybridization with indigenous shamanism and Afro-Brazilian spirituality. The same duty of postcolonial redress applies to all ayahuasca tourists of European heritage (see Fraser 2017). I am happy to report that we already see awareness growing among Brazilian daimistas, who are learning to work in partnership with local aboriginal peoples in ways that resemble Matthew Fox's (1988, 6/65/228–40) call for a "*deep ecumenism*" or the Anishinaabe people's "Eighth Fire" prophecy (Benton-Banai 2010[1988], 91)—for example, Céu do Mar, a Daime church in Rio de Janeiro, has an ongoing "alliance" with the Yawanawa nation, performing ayahuasca rituals together and raising money for charities (Platero 2018). One also witnesses signs of good faith efforts at long-term processes of truth and reconciliation in the *Inclusion and Diversity* initiative of the Chacruna Institute, which amplifies indigenous and other minority voices in psychedelic science (see George et al. 2020). No doubt, thorny questions about intersectional power imbalances remain for future research and activism.

To be sure, fardados do not want to pose as indigenous people; rather, they want to be edified by ayahuasca in a cultural language they can more readily understand. It is not only fardados' polyphasic beliefs that are running afoul of local authorities, but it is actually their possession and use of an indigenous psychoactive technology that is taboo in Europe. Whereas a Catholic inquisition forbade entheogens as demonic during the colonial era, now it is Western-centric bigotry assailing polyphasic ayahuasca spirituality—shamanism and Daime alike—because "hallucinogens" betray disenchanted norms of monophasic consciousness.

In justifying their spiritual practice, fardados understand Santo Daime to be an Amazonian renewal of Christ's teachings. Through the confluence of intercontinental forces, an Afro-Brazilian migrant in the rainforest ended up founding a Christian-inspired religion that eventually made its way around the world. In this way, Santo Daime can be seen as a composite reverberation of European conquests in Africa and the Americas, actions that are now returning to their derivation. Similar ideas about Daime as a shamanic prescription for Westerners infirmed by a corrupted Christianity are expressed in hymn #75 from Mestre Irineu:

Os caboclos já chegaram	*The* [Amazonian spirits] *already arrived*
De braços nus e pés no chão	*With bare arms and feet*
Eles trazem remédios bons	*They bring good remedies*
Para curar os cristãos	*To heal the Christians*

Most, but not all, of my informants are deeply suspicious of institutionalized Christianity in Europe. Many dislike what they see as a history of Jesus's model of peace and charity being perverted for the purposes of imperialist and commercial powers. Fardados look to the Daime to "bring good remedies" by reinstalling Jesus's original message. In other words, fardados believe that Daime coaches them how to be better Europeans—less Eurocentric, more xenophilic—by showing them they have much to learn from foreign ways of being and knowing.

Thus, for European fardados, Santo Daime is actually a way of curing psychospiritual sicknesses at the heart of the Western project. Unlike the violent European colonizers profiled by Taussig (1987), daimistas are engaged in a critical self-reflection housed within a moral system of compassion toward other people and responsibility for the whole Earth. For them, the Christ that returned from the Amazon jungle has been purified of colonialist pollutions, arriving back to Europe through the Daime liquid and Mestre Irineu's teachings. Fardados herald Daime as a newly reformed Christianity, whereby each individual devotee seeks to decolonize their own mind by stripping themselves of their Eurocentric/egocentric attachments. Daime is a means for folks raised within a Christian discourse to better comprehend the polyphasic worldview of indigenous peoples. Yes, there are real concerns about Western appropriations of indigenous entheogen traditions; but my fieldwork suggests that European fardados are themselves suffering condemnation from Western authorities because they have adopted a shamanic affinity for plant-based alterations of consciousness. If anything, the theology of Santo Daime represents the strategic appropriation of Christianity by Afro-Brazilian and indigenous ayahuasca traditions.

Whether it is Amazonian shamans or members of the Santo Daime religion, therapeutic and spiritual uses of ayahuasca fly in the face of "the axioms of Western knowledge," especially a "rational gaze" that "considers hallucinations to be at best illusions, at worst morbid phenomena" (Narby 1998, 42–43). A major purpose of Euro-American anthropology is to translate otherness into terms that can be understood by mainstream Western culture. But social scientists fail when instead of taking seriously the challenges that entheogens pose for monophasic presumptions about the nature of reality, they dismiss it as "veriest nonsense":

> Despite all the protestations of "entheogen" users, I can detect nothing of interest in what they claim to have learned. Their insights are trivial. They have brought nothing to the world that has been of any use. Interest in passing through doors in our minds seems to me to be self-indulgent, if not addictive in the worst sense of the word. Indeed, there is no evidence that there is any sort of "other realm" filled with wisdom, be it tucked away in our brains or "out there" in another dimension. (Lewis-Williams 2010, 172)

Fardados were shown the above statement from archaeologist David Lewis-Williams, to get their reaction. They all critiqued his lack of scientific rigor and his confident uttering of uninformed opinions. One informant said: "He's a scientist, but he says something about something he doesn't know, so that's not very scientific." Of course, Lewis-Williams merely reiterates mainstream presuppositions. On the contrary, ethnographic findings presented in this book show that entheogens like ayahuasca can be beneficial when ingested in a proper set and setting.

Citing internal divisions within nations around the world grappling with a "double pull" between "two continuously opposing tendencies," Geertz (2000, 256–57) underscores anthropology's relevance to "a practical politics of cultural conciliation." The double pull of religious and secular cross-pressures continues to be prominent in Western social life. This is present in Dawson's (2013, 184) puzzling criticism of the "preoccupations of academics sympathetic to the ritual use of psychoactive substances [who are] thereby keen to defend Santo Daime." The fieldwork results presented in my book demand such a "critically applied public anthropology," whereby ethnographers are duty-bound "to reduce the structurally imposed suffering of our research subjects" (Bourgois and Schonberg 2009, 297). I seek to live up to this objective by publicizing the facts about daimistas' earnest spiritual devotion, misunderstandings of which fuel continued discriminations against my informants. As stated by Hermann, a German Daime leader who was present when his government ordered police to raid a Daime ritual while toting automatic firearms: "We are victims . . . we just want tolerance!" Advocating on behalf of daimistas, a critically applied public anthropology overrides pretenses of detached objectivity in response to laws that make my informants criminals, ethnocentric legislation built on paranoia rather than on empirical research. I am aware that status quo stigmatizations against entheogens consider anything short of condemning these substances as promotional activism. But I also know that anthropologists must continue to be publicly engaged in upending all injustices, just as we are with the topics of economic disparity, homophobia/transphobia, sexism, and racism.

Today, Santo Daime abides in the face of legal codes prohibiting the entheogen my informants use in their ceremonies. Regarding my main research subjects, the Belgian government initiated a formal investigation of Daime activities in late 2011. Since the conclusion of my fieldwork, government inspectors have interrogated at least eight Belgian fardados, all of whom were consulted as informants in the present study. Authorities conducted a search of the home of the CdU commander and his wife, and detained a shipment of ayahuasca at customs, confiscating a total of forty-five liters of the Daime brew. To be fair, fardados report that the government interrogations were not overly aggressive. They say that investigators seemed to be concerned mainly with whether the ayahuasca was being used as a means of "drugging" unsuspecting participants and taking money against their will. Hopefully the present text can serve to dispel such unfounded presumptions about Santo Daime being a manipulative "sect." Still, out of fear of further police raids all Belgian Daime groups now organize their ritual works outside of Belgium. This means that unless the government recognizes their religious right to employ an entheogenic sacrament, daimistas in Belgium have effectively been forced into exile. As outlined in a statement released by scholarly experts in the field of ayahuasca studies:

> Persecution of the Brazilian ayahuasca religions has been mostly based on misinformed prejudice against the use of psychedelic substances in what are reasonably safe and socially controlled ritual contexts, and which constitute authentic cultural traditions and expressions that must be respected as such. (Anderson et al. 2012, 173)

It would thus be in accordance with Western liberalist values to reevaluate drug policies that currently deny daimistas their right to religious freedom.

With prohibition of ayahuasca, I am reminded of how philosopher Robert Pirsig spoke of the errors of arrogant "paternalism" he witnessed when psychiatrists forced him against his will to undergo electroshock "therapy" in the 1960s. His words echo cosmopolitical frustrations daimistas feel today with respect to state authorities who forbid sacramental uses of ayahuasca:

> Don't try to correct me, just understand me will you! . . . People say, "well we don't have time, and what you say really isn't very important. What we say is important, we know what's good." And this is the old act of the inquisition, saying "We know! Don't tell us! We know, you heretics!" . . .
>
> [I am aware] I could be completely wrong in what I'm saying, I hope I never forget that I might just be off on a tack of my own that's completely wrong, but so might they! I remember an old statement of Oliver Cromwell, a deep Christian, who used to say to others: "I beseech you in the bowels of Christ, bethink you that you may be wrong!" This is what I would say to the psychiatrists today: please, don't forget that you might be wrong! I don't ask you to believe that you're wrong, but believe that you *might* be [wrong] (Pirsig 2014, minute 42:40–44:55).

It is this value of cosmopolitical humility (aka "Cromwell's rule") that motivates daimistas' critique of biomedical and legalistic censures against "hallucinogens," an overconfidence that has resulted in the latter's overlooking therapeutic potentials of "entheogens" such as ayahuasca (see also Stengers 2005, 996/1003). Noting that the "history of medicine is tragically filled with discoveries of great significance that were initially ridiculed and dismissed," perhaps clinical and legal resistance to psychedelics is a display of what NYU School of Medicine Professor Jonathan Howard (2018, 468) defines as the *Semmelweis Reflex,* the academic or intellectual "tendency to reject new evidence or new knowledge because it contradicts established norms, beliefs, or scientific paradigms." As an awestruck, post-arrogant agnostic, I cannot say whether or not daimistas' worldview is indeed the correct one. But what my preceding analyses do demonstrate is that fardados represent a European subculture now reassessing mainstream ontological assumptions in light of mystical-shamanic ideas they imported from the Amazon rainforest. Considering the avalanche of new publications presenting results of empirical tests with entheogens, it would be prudent to apply Cromwell's rule when it comes to reevaluating Western culture's Semmelweis Reflex about controlled, nonrecreational uses of these substances.

In terms of religious uses of entheogens, Santo Daime's illegal status exemplifies how post-arrogant cosmopolitics might aid in settling cross-pressured disputes about ontological meaning and psychophysical well-being. A first step toward healthier dialogues would require policymakers to acknowledge scientific results, which suggest that entheogenic rituals might offer health breakthroughs. But such a step is hampered by ingrained monophasic presuppositions in mainstream Western society, according to which nothing worthwhile can be found outside the normal waking state of consciousness (see Blainey 2010; Walsh and Grob 2005, 224). By contrast, the post-secular scheme proposed by Habermas and others is a conciliatory program, urging governments to cherish positive contributions that religions make to society. What I call the post-arrogant is an appeal for inter- and intracultural dialogues rooted in cosmopolitical humility, mutual respect, and an applied ethics of anthropological relativism.

Through preceding chapters, I have sought to convey an ethnographic appreciation of Santo Daime. Equivalent to the stance of Calabrese's (2013, xi) book on peyote rituals in the Native American Church: "When we bracket our ethnocentrism and strive to understand this cultural tradition on its own terms and from a broad anthropological perspective . . . the bulk of the evidence reveals [Santo Daime] to be a cultural system of therapeutic, developmental, and spiritual intervention." Like Osto's (2016, xviii) book on psychedelics and Buddhism, the present volume has striven "in part to undermine the prejudicial outlook of the hegemonic cultural discourse on the nonmedical use of drugs." My research highlights an ostracized group of individuals who "might otherwise remain forgotten, with attention to the ways their own struggles and visions of themselves create holes in dominant theories and policies" (Biehl and Moran-Thomas 2009, 282). This book seeks to reframe the emergence of entheogenic religions in the West as necessitating post-arrogant compromises about alterations of consciousness.

More broadly, Santo Daime signifies the need to reassess presumptions about secularism and spirituality in the public spheres of twenty-first-century Europe. In some circles, spiritual faith is scorned by hardline critics, who point to the tortures, murders, and wars attributable to religion both throughout history and today (e.g., the best-selling books of "new atheists" such as Richard Dawkins [2006]). Inversely, there is now a rapidly growing critique of the old European secularization story being stoked by Habermas, who has softened his previously strong secularist convictions (Reder and Schmidt 2010, 5). Habermas is exemplary of a trend in prominent European intellectuals now questioning the fundamental assumptions of secularism. Yet even though several of this new group of post-secular scholars "have openly declared they are atheists, or at least agnostics . . . their intention is not to oppose religious faith, but to understand it and its inherent power—particularly its political potential" (Liedman 2010, 53). Jointly, they question the presumption that religious worldviews are obsolete and inferior compared to disenchanted science. In carefully distinguishing it from "esteem" for those whom one disagrees with, Habermas (2009, 69) builds his template for a post-secular society upon the value of tolerance: "Toleration means that believers, members of other religions, and non-believers must concede each other's right to observe convictions, practices, and ways of life which they themselves reject." The members of Santo Daime in Europe agree. They want to coexist with the ideals of both secularism and traditional religion, and they expect toleration of their mystical practices in turn. Exhibiting a cosmopolitical ethos, "post-secular" dialogues promote the replacement of secularist-religious cross-pressures with an ironclad cross-modesty, both sides admitting a lack of verifiable proof for their ontological postulates. Habermas (2010a, 15/19) conceives what I term cross-modesty as the "awareness of what's missing" in disenchanted secularism; in short, what is missing in Western public spheres are post-arrogant conversations based on a respectful[3] cooperation between nonbelievers and believers.

Atheist Alain de Botton (2012) displays this moderate compromise position for those modern agents who are tired of the intractable debate between extreme believers and nonbelievers. In a genuinely post-arrogant spirit, de Botton praises religions' facility for promoting community, kindness, aesthetic achievements, education, and intellectual rigor, while also providing existential comfort for those who are suffering. Instead of dismissing theistic beliefs (which he personally believes to be untrue), de Botton (2012, 11–12) advocates a "balanced" approach that acknowledges what atheists can learn from their religious counterparts: "It must be possible to remain a committed atheist and nevertheless find religions sporadically useful, interesting and consoling—and be curious as to the possibilities of importing certain of their ideas and practices into the secular realm." It is with this same posture that Habermas (2010b, 82) cautions secularist peers not to abandon the advantages of spiritual worldviews "too hastily." A post-secular view still condemns negative consequences of religion (e.g., violence, brainwashing, and sectarian oppression), while it also urges secularists to recognize many benefits that religions bestow on society (e.g., community, charity, education, and refuge). Therefore, these post-arrogant tactics embody a *solution* to religion-secularism conflicts by *integrating* positive contributions supplied by both interests.[4] Santo Daime offers a readymade test case for such post-arrogant compromises.

In principle, fardados' struggle for liberty around the world is akin to the struggles of any other religious minority. Because they were born and raised within a late-twentieth-century European culture, fardados' outlook acknowledges that science is really good at accounting for the material world. But they also believe that mystical contemplation allows individuals to acquire inner self-knowledge. As a group of polyphasic believers that gathers periodically, fardados evince a post-arrogant approach to the larger monophasic society in which they live. They desire a willingness on the part of secular society to work toward a reconsideration of Daime's criminal status in recognition of their religious freedom. Of course, secular European governments will not tolerate actions that bring harm to people. But as has been demonstrated throughout this text, empirical evidence verifies that entheogens like ayahuasca are not harmful when used in structured contexts. Correspondingly, a renewed cosmopolitical negotiation about the optimal way to regulate entheogens can commence in the European public sphere.

Before closing, for future researchers I want to highlight tantalizing parallels between entheogenic states of mind and the "overview effect" experienced by astronauts looking down on the Earth, a simultaneously secular/ mystical topic of "connectedness" broached by Carhart-Harris and colleagues (2018, 549; see also Carhart-Harris and Friston 2019, 332–333/336; Roberts 2006, xiii; Watts, Gandy, and Evans 2019). It is clear from reports such as National Geographic's television docuseries *One Strange Rock* that in space, astronauts can have moments of amplified existential enlightenment, and some seem to return to Earth with a more environmentally sane worldview and an acceptance that all of humanity is one with Nature (Aronofsky 2018). It costs millions of dollars to send each astronaut into outer space. I hope that if the reader has gained any insight from the present volume, it is that many psychonauts across the world are finding a much cheaper but nonetheless wondrous *innerview* effect from the entheogenic experience here on Earth (see Nelson 2018, xiv). Perhaps entheogenic rituals might be a "medicine" more like the indigenous idea of medicine: a biopsychosocial-spiritual therapy for soul and self and each other, which can heal our egoic wounds so we project less aggression at other people and become less covetous of the Earth's finite resources. Daimistas argue that we need to find inner ego balance before we can establish outer social balance. Perhaps the Climate Crisis might be partially addressed by allowing people to educate themselves with indigenous plant teachers about causal links between inner and outer disharmony? In a recent article entitled "From Egoism to Ecoism," a team of scientists from the Centre for Psychedelic Research at Imperial College London found that "nature relatedness . . . was positively correlated with concomitant increases in psychological well-being and was dependent on the extent of ego-dissolution and the perceived influence of natural surroundings during the acute psychedelic state"—these researchers argue that since people become more environmentally conscious up to two years after a psychedelic experience it "bears relevance for psychedelic treatment models in mental health and, in the face of the current ecological crisis, planetary health" (Kettner et al. 2019). Adapting Winkelman's (2001) secular relabeling of entheogens as psychointegrators, my fieldwork with daimistas teaches that a better term might be *anthro-integrators*. Just like any established *anthrointegration* modality—be it yoga, Buddhism, indigenous sweat lodges, etc.—Santo Daime involves time-honored mystical/shamanic techniques for harmonizing and repairing holistic connections within oneself (cognitive, existential, emotional, physical), connections between oneself and other selves, and connections between selfhood and all of Nature/Cosmos. I have proposed herein that existential anthropology is uniquely positioned to mediate new cosmopolitical dialogues between these traditions of anthrointegration therapy and Western biomedicine.

For my informants, the suiscope/innerview process of the self observing itself in Daime works has inspired their Cosmic Consciousness worldview. As Clara from Belgium proclaimed, the healing of conflicts within her self through ayahuasca rituals fuels her desire to transcend interpersonal conflicts and seek more social harmony:

> *At this time there's more and more separation and it's so hard to find unity, to find priorities that you want to serve. . . . I think also in the Daime if you feel that feeling of oneness, then I think it's the most happy feeling you can feel, because you recognize the other and you recognize yourself. It brings more love if you can work on a puzzle together than if you do it by yourself. If you see God or the power that can be God as a oneness, then we are all working on this together, we are all parts of the puzzle. It's so much more beautiful if you can help each other and bring all knowledge together. We try to see God in ourselves and in the other.*

These sentiments resonate with the spirit of the post-secular, contending that both believers and nonbelievers would profit from paying attention to each other's perspectives, partners rather than adversaries. In the spirit of cosmopolitics, entheogenic groups must recognize the need for secular states to operate apart from religious codes, and secular states must restrain monophasic disbelief to revisit the permissibility of entheogens in religious and psychotherapeutic contexts.

Surprisingly, despite my lack of allegiance to the religious tenets of Santo Daime, by employing ethnophenomenological methods of participant observation I obtained major personal benefits anyway. It is not uncommon for ethnographers to undergo personal transformations after experiencing scientifically inexplicable anomalies through indulging in spiritual practices of their informants (see Richards 2003; Young and Goulet 1994). I can say that simply by attending Daime works, I experienced lasting improvements in my own sense of well-being. Without going into too much detail, I can honestly report that my Daime experiences directly resulted in the disappearance of chronic acid reflux (I no longer take omeprazole pills I had ingested daily for over a decade). Along with increases of patience and inner peace, over the course of fieldwork I also saw marked decreases in my anxiety, bad temper, and desire to consume alcohol to excess, as well as a striking improvement in my "picky" eating habits. All of this prompted my wife to comment that since I began drinking ayahuasca I have become a better husband.

Evoking the *solutions* and technological themes woven throughout this study, Lars said about having an anthropologist attend the Daime works and conduct research with his church:

> *It's a good thing, because you translate this very weird religion or doctrine into scientific terms. You investigate it by the scientific method, so it's good for legal things. And it's good for us as far-dados to have a scientific approach to it, because we are curious also. . . . It's very interesting! It's in this one big melting pot of things happening around the Santo Daime. You're an instrument, like we are all instruments in the Santo Daime. But instruments of what? For what goal? That's the mystery that makes it interesting.*

This tendency to see scholars as just another "instrument" in the mystical (suiscope) apparatus of Santo Daime displays fardados' characteristic receptivity. It is this determined willingness on the part of fardados to merge and find common truths between seemingly distinct perspectives that arises repeatedly in conversations with them. As they face legal challenges around the world, Daime groups want to work with rather than against scientists and legal systems.

Veteran fardados warned me there is a danger when the material sacrament becomes an object of idolatry[5] or ego-inflation. Instead, they view Daime as a divinely molded vehicle, an astral "tool" that helps humans explore and repair themselves only when its suiscope mechanism is used judiciously. Paralleling Trungpa's (1973) warnings about humans' tendency to confuse spiritual values and egotistical attachment (i.e., Spiritual Materialism), Frederik put it this way:

> *It never occurred to me to put a word to this beverage. I don't see it as Christ or Light, I see it as Daime, just a drink. By drinking Daime there is another part of my consciousness that opens, and it gives me a doorway to that other realm. And then through that I can see some things that are useful to myself and to others. . . . I think the drink helps us get in contact with the* [Cosmic] *consciousness, the drink itself is not the* [Cosmic] *consciousness. It's a key, and there are many keys: meditation, the Daime, there are other plants that are used by indigenous people. There are all sorts of keys; you pick up the key that suits you best. . . .*
>
> *I'm afraid that* [Daime] *is like the other keys. It helps people who are aware that the key is just a key to the other thing. . . . I hear many people in the Daime say "The Daime will do it for me"; for me personally that's not correct. YOU have to do it! The Daime doesn't do it in your place, it just shows you* [aspects] *of your self and of your consciousness, and that's it! So you have to work very hard, because it shows you all the elements of your ego, and then you know what you have to work on. I also do meditation and it's the same thing: you get in a very beautiful layer where you see these wonderful visions, and then you have these layers where they show you all these elements in the ego that are still not cured, so you know what you have to do. But the meditation doesn't do it for you; it just makes you see it better, brighter.*

As ethnographic evidence was reviewed above, the reader was exposed to some meaningful facts about what Santo Daime is not: Santo Daime is not a drug-crazed cult[6] whose members are seeking to "trip out" or get "high."

Santo Daime is not a hedonistic indulgence into dangerous intoxication. On the contrary, throughout this volume the reader has witnessed how Santo Daime is many things at the same time. Santo Daime is Christian and it is shamanistic. Santo Daime is a sincere form of mysticism, a spiritual school of the self. Santo Daime is a periodic social group where people with a polyphasic worldview can assemble and tap into what they see as a personal connection with an inner God. Counter to prejudices that would characterize them as foolish drug fiends, the daimistas I met in my fieldwork are some of the most courageous people I have ever known. The battalions of Juramidam are indeed like a military brigade of love, joy, and peace, marching into battle not against fellow humans but against their own egoic demons. Month after month, year after year, decade after decade, they are warriors of compassion and universal altruism. In such an astral scenario, the anthropologist is like an embedded war journalist, living alongside self-styled soldiers of God's army, fighting the internal enemies of self-centred greed and pride, sometimes for one tour, sometimes as a lifelong commitment.

After more than ninety years and counting, Santo Daime has evolved and diversified its eclectic reach, incorporating a wide range of different religious traditions into its perpetually diversifying "melting pot." But as with the more highly publicized challenges to secularism raised by Islamic immigrant populations, the Santo Daime introduces a complex political problem for the European Union: trying to enforce laws against the use of substances like ayahuasca (commonly vilified as "hallucinogens"), while respecting freedom of religion. The continued prohibition of ayahuasca rituals relies upon a circular logic, inferring that because their religion is unlawful, fardados' religious rights are not subject to constitutional protections. So even while this book has focused on small Daime congregations in Europe, the question of whether accommodations are made for fardados speaks to larger cross-pressures about limitations on religious expression in Western societies.

Moreover, fardados assert that globalization of ayahuasca is the vegetal world's way of communicating a message to humankind; they affirm ayahuasca as an expression of the Earth's agency, such that threats of deforestation and pollution have prompted the planet's collective consciousness to warn us about our unsustainable habits (see also McKenna 2005). My informants maintain that Daime shows them how every thing (animals, plants, viruses, rocks, water, air, planets, stars) is a projection stemming from a single, foundational intelligence (see Narby 2005). Fardados intentionally imbibe their sacramental material in order to witness what they believe is the superphysical root of all being. Indeed, ayahuasca is a potent ritual object!

Whether we take a religious or secular approach in our personal life, an agnostic appreciation of Santo Daime allows for less arrogance in listening to what daimistas have to say. If there is one thing this ethnophenomenology proves, it is that a despairing Western world may have much to learn from indigenous technologies of entheogenic therapy. Fardados insisted to me that their lives are palpably more stable and pleasant because Daime acts as a "key" to solutions for their problems. These claims may appear incredible to some readers, but the empirical evidence shows there are very profound therapeutic results occurring for participants in these entheogenic rituals. Fardados believe that if ayahuasca religion is decriminalized, proper uses of this sacred beverage might help assuage many rampant plights: drug/alcohol abuse, anxiety/depression, existential malaise, ecological degradation, and so on. It remains to be seen whether the benefits of entheogens will be accepted in North Atlantic democracies. But with the continued growth of post-secular tolerance, the therapeutic potentials of ayahuasca rituals may one day be as admired in the West as Buddhist meditation or Hindu yoga. Time will tell.

I am not a member of any religion, but I have sought to adopt a post-arrogant demeanor in the pages of this book. Through my fieldwork I learned to marvel at how (despite intense piety) European fardados refrain from evangelizing with nonbelievers in their midst. In return, out of respect for my informants I now sign off with a nod to theological continuities between controversial Christianities in premodern Europe and the syncretic ayahuasca religion of Santo Daime. Since this text opened with quotations from two males, it closes with excerpts from the visionary writings of two female sages, one a beguine[7] mystic burned at the stake for heresy in medieval Paris and the other a world-renowned *Umban*-daimista[8] elder from Brazil:

> [I]t is a greater thing for this Soul that she becomes inebriated from what her Lover Himself drinks and has drunk and will drink from the divine beverage of His goodness. . . . In this barrel of divine beverage are, without fail, several taps. This is known to the humanity which is joined to the person of the Son of God, the humanity who drinks at the most noble tap after the Trinity. And the Virgin Mary drinks at the one after and this noble lady is intoxicated by the most High. And after her, the ardent Seraphim drink, on the wings of whom these Free Souls fly.

> —Marguerite Porete, *The Mirror of Simple Souls*

É com Deus que eu tomo Daime	*It is with God that I drink Daime*
E com Deus eu chego lá	*It is with God I'll go there*
Porque Deus é quem me ensina	*Because God is who teaches me*
Tudo que eu tenho que saber	*All that I have to know*

—hymn #106, "É Com Deus Que Eu Tomo Daime"
("It is with God that I drink Daime"), by Madrinha Baixinha

Figure 16.1. *Souls of Warriors of the Faith form a Cross*, engraving by Gustave Doré (1869), *Divine Comedy* by Dante Alighieri (1265–1321). Published with permission from the Bibliothèque nationale de France (BnF).

.

Appendix I

Glossary of Portuguese Santo Daime Terms

bailado	"dance"; the three types of movement (march, waltz, and *mazurka*) performed during special Daime rituals
comandante	"commander"; the church leader who directs the Daime work
comitivas	"entourages" of fardados that leave their home country to visit Santo Daime congregations in another country
daimistas	a generic term that refers to committed Santo Daime followers, both fardados and firmados
doutrina	"doctrine"; the corpus of hymns, ritual techniques, and moral teachings comprising the Santo Daime tradition
fardados / fardadas	male/female official members of Santo Daime, those who wear the farda uniform
fardas	"uniform" worn by fardados; in blue and white varieties
fardamento	initiation rite where the aspirant receives their "star" and wears the official farda (uniform) for the first time
feitio	"making"; the ritual of preparing and cooking the Daime beverage
firmados	those who regularly attend Daime works without a formal commitment

firmeza	"firmness"; a trait denoting a person's capacity to gracefully cope with ordeals encountered in both Daime works and life in general
fiscal (plural: *fiscais*)	"supervisor" or "guardian"; trained fardados designated with the task of overseeing the ritual work; it is their responsibility to come to the aid of individuals having difficulty during the ritual
fiscalização	"fiscalization" or "supervision"; the role of overseeing the safety and harmony of a work by a trained fiscal
hinos	"hymns"; considered as "received" by individual fardados from the astral plane; contain teachings and knowledge that is imparted to the devotee while they are sung during ritual works
hinário	"hymnal"; bound collections of multiple hymns received by past and present leaders of Santo Daime; sung in entirety at special works
igreja	"church"; official Santo Daime churches usually have names starting with Céu do/da "Sky/Heaven of"
Jagube	The name of the *Banisteriopsis caapi* vine in Santo Daime
Madrinha	"Godmother"; a term of respect for a female fardada elder
Mestre Ensinador	"Master Teacher"; the mystical presence that is contacted through the Santo Daime sacrament
músicos	"musicians" who play instruments to provide musical accompaniment for singing hymns during the works
Padrinho	"Godfather"; a term of respect for a male fardado elder
peia	karmic "obstacles" that offer lessons within the Daime works and in daily life
puxadoras	"pullers"; young females who lead the singing of the hymns
Rainha	The name of the *Psychotria viridis* shrub in Santo Daime

salão	"hall" or "salon"; the physical space in which Daime works take place
Santo Daime	"Holy Give-me"; the name for the religion and the ayahuasca sacrament
trabalhos	"works"; the name for rituals of the Santo Daime
união	"union"; a cosmological value of monism; for daimistas, experiencing states of mystical union is the epitome of the Daime practice, a feeling of oneness with all things

Short Form Abbreviations of Specific Hinários Quoted in the Text

MI = Mestre Irineu
PS = Padrinho Sebastião
PA = Padrinho Alfredo

Church Names / Locations

CCMI Casa da Cura Mestre Irineu / Brussels Capital Region, Belgium
CdAI Céu do Arco-Íris / Namur province, Belgium
CdSJ Céu do São João / Spain
CdSM Céu do Santa Maria / Amsterdam, the Netherlands
CdU Céu da União / East Flanders, Belgium
RaS Rendezvous avec Soi / the Netherlands and Brazil

Appendix II

Liturgical Calendar of Santo Daime

In CEFLURIS, the official annual calendar of works is established in the "Norms of Ritual" handbook (see CEFLURIS 1997: 21–22):

Day	Festivity	Hinário Sung at this work	Time	Farda
7th Jan	Pd. Alfredo's Birthday	Padrinho Sebastião	9:00	White
19th Jan	Saint Sebastian	Pd. Sebastião + Missa	18:30	White
18th March	Saint Joseph	Padrinho Alfredo	18:30	White
White Thursday	Holy Week	Hinário dos Mortos Companions of the Mestre	18:30	Blue
Good Friday	Holy Week	Missa	16:00	Blue
2nd Sunday of May	Mother's Day	Madrinhas Julia + Rita + Cristina	16:00	White
12th June	Saint Anthony	Maria Brilhante	18:30	White
23th June	São João	Mestre Irineu	18:30	White
25th June	Md. Rita's Birthday	Padrinho Sebastião	9:00	White
28th June	Saint Peter	Padrinho Alfredo	18:30	White
6th July	Day that Mestre Irineu died	Tetéo + Missa	18:30	White
2nd Sunday of August	Father's Day	Padrinho Sebastião	09:00	White

continued on next page

413

Day	Festivity	Hinário Sung at this work	Time	Farda
6th Oct	Pd. Sebastião's Birthday	Mestre Irineu	18:30	White
1st Nov	All Souls' Day	Hinário Dos Mortos + Missa	18:30	Blue
7th Dec	Immaculate Conception	Mestre Irineu	18:30	White
14th Dec	M. Irineu's Birthday	Padrinho Sebastião	18:30	White
24th Dec	Christmas	Mestre Irineu	18:30	White
31th Dec	New Years Eve	Padrinho Alfredo	18:30	White
5th Jan	Three Holy Kings	Mestre Irineu Entrega do trabalho	18:30	White

Since each participant must sign a record book, I was able to confirm the total attendance numbers for each of the June Festival works in Amsterdam, 2010. The division of the attendance by males and females gives an indication of the slight female majority in an otherwise gender-balanced congregation:

	Females	Males
Santo Antônio	80	66
São João	105	102 (The bookkeeper said that for CEFLURIS Churches, this [the feast day of St. John the Baptist] is the most important work of the year, because Pd. Sebastião is considered an avatar of St. John the Baptist)
Md. Rita's Birthday	54	53
São Pedro	72	71
Day M. Irineu died	61	50

Appendix III

Master List of Sacred Plants (Europe-wide Sample)

Anthropac tabulation of "Sacred Plants" freelist results (n = 42 European fardados)

FREELIST: SORTED BY "SMITH'S s"

Item	Frequency	Resp Pct	Avg Rank	Smith's s
1 AYAHUASCA	42	100	1.643	0.892
2 PEYOTE	33	79	3.394	0.530
3 CANNABIS	34	81	3.500	0.488
4 MUSHROOMS	31	74	3.613	0.461
5 SAN PEDRO	28	67	4.286	0.400
6 IBOGA	20	48	5.350	0.204
7 TOBACCO	11	26	5.182	0.128
8 DATURA	8	19	5.250	0.087
9 JUREMA	6	14	3.833	0.079
10 A. MUSCARIA	7	17	5.571	0.078
11 SALVIA	5	12	5.400	0.058
12 SAGE	4	10	7.250	0.046
13 COCA	5	12	6.600	0.034
14 ROSEROOT	2	5	4.500	0.033
15 PHARMALA	3	7	6.000	0.025
16 BASILIC	1	2	1.000	0.024
17 OPIUM PAPAVER	2	5	6.000	0.023
18 OREGANO	2	5	8.000	0.023
19 GOUDSBLOEM	1	2	3.000	0.021
20 MYRRH	1	2	2.000	0.020

continued on next page

Item	Frequency	Resp Pct	Avg Rank	Smith's s
21 LAVENDER	2	5	9.000	0.019
22 DIGITALIS	1	2	4.000	0.019
23 ANGELICA	1	2	3.000	0.019
24 BRANDNETEL	1	2	5.000	0.017
25 MORNINGGLORY	2	5	7.500	0.017
26 KHAT	1	2	6.000	0.016
27 SANDLEWOOD	1	2	3.000	0.016
28 COFFEE	1	2	7.000	0.014
29 PASSIONFRUIT	1	2	8.000	0.013
30 JUNIPER	1	2	9.000	0.012
31 HENBANE	2	5	8.500	0.012
32 DRAGON	1	2	6.000	0.012
33 ECHINACEA	1	2	9.000	0.011
34 APPLES	1	2	7.000	0.011
35 RUE	1	2	7.000	0.011
36 KAMBO	2	5	9.500	0.010
37 KAVAKAVA	2	5	10.500	0.010
38 FALARIS	1	2	7.000	0.010
39 TYME	1	2	11.000	0.009
40 TREES	1	2	8.000	0.009
41 ALCOHOL	1	2	9.000	0.008
42 MESCALINE	1	2	5.000	0.008
43 BRUGMANSIA	2	5	10.500	0.008
44 OAK	1	2	12.000	0.007
45 RAPÉ	2	5	9.500	0.007
46 LSD	1	2	6.000	0.007
47 BAY LEAF	1	2	9.000	0.006
48 GRASS	1	2	9.000	0.006
49 PARSLEY	1	2	12.000	0.006
50 NUNU	1	2	10.000	0.006
51 CEDAR	1	2	4.000	0.006
52 ATROPA BELLADONA	1	2	7.000	0.006
53 BODI	1	2	13.000	0.006
54 BETAL NUT	1	2	14.000	0.004
55 SEAWEED	1	2	10.000	0.004
56 MYRTL	1	2	10.000	0.004
57 PALO SANTO	1	2	6.000	0.004
58 FLOWERS	1	2	11.000	0.004
59 MANDRAKE	1	2	11.000	0.004

Item	Frequency	Resp Pct	Avg Rank	Smith's *s*
60 ACACIA	1	2	7.000	0.003
61 MDMA	1	2	7.000	0.003
62 NUTMEG	1	2	11.000	0.002
63 MICROORGANISMS	1	2	11.000	0.002
64 EVERYTHINGWITHDMT	1	2	12.000	0.002
65 FOOD	1	2	16.000	0.001
Total/Average:	298		7.095	

Appendix IV

Master List of Great Spiritual Teachers (Belgian Sample)

Anthropac tabulation of "Great Spiritual Teachers" freelist results (n = 32 Belgian fardados)
all time periods are Common Era (after 1 CE/AD) unless otherwise noted

FREELIST: SORTED BY "SMITH'S *s*"

Item	Frequency	Resp Pct	Avg Rank	Smith's *s*
1 JESUS CHRIST —Jewish spiritual teacher, founder of Christianity (1st century)	27	84	3.370	0.639
2 BUDDHA —Nepalese spiritual teacher, founder of Buddhism (6th–5th century BCE)	22	69	2.682	0.535
3 MESTRE IRINEU —Brazilian spiritual teacher, founder of Santo Daime (19th–20th century)	15	47	5.067	0.313
4 GANDHI —Indian political activist (19th–20th century)	10	31	4.700	0.212
5 PD. SEBASTIÃO —Brazilian spiritual teacher, Santo Daime elder (20th century)	8	25	3.500	0.171

continued on next page

Item	Frequency	Resp Pct	Avg Rank	Smith's s
6 MOHAMMED —religious/political/military leader, prophet, founder of Islam (6th–7th century)	6	19	5.000	0.141
7 KRISHNA —Hindu deity, avatar of Vishnu	5	16	2.600	0.134
8 VIRGIN MARY —mother of Jesus Christ (1st century BCE–1st century CE)	8	25	8.125	0.105
9 DALAI LAMA —Tibetan Buddhist leader, spiritual teacher (20th–21st century)	7	22	7.000	0.105
10 ECKHART TOLLE —German Canadian spiritual teacher, author (20th–21st century)	6	19	6.833	0.090
11 A FRIEND —they mentioned the name of a specific friend (a natural cut-off for triads)	4	13	5.750	0.074
12 SRI AUROBINDO —Indian public intellectual, spiritual leader (19th–20th century)	4	13	6.750	0.074
13 KRISHNAMURTI —Indian philosopher (20th century)	4	13	5.000	0.069
14 CONFUCIUS —Chinese philosopher (6th century BCE)	4	13	7.000	0.068
15 SOCRATES —Greek Philosopher (5th century BCE)	3	9	4.667	0.068
16 LAO TSE —Chinese philosopher (6th century BCE)	3	9	5.667	0.063
17 DEEPAK CHOPRA —Indian physician (20th century)	3	9	4.667	0.059

Item	Frequency	Resp Pct	Avg Rank	Smith's s
18 LUIZ MENDES —Brazilian Santo Daime elder (20th–21st century)	3	9	3.333	0.057
19 MY MOTHER —some fardados mentioned their own mother	3	9	5.000	0.052
20 NELSON MANDELA —South African politician (20th–21st century)	3	9	10.333	0.046
21 MD. RITA —Brazilian Santo Daime elder (20th–21st century)	2	6	4.500	0.046
22 RUDYARD KIPLING —English writer (19th–20th century)	2	6	6.500	0.045
23 MOTHER MEERA —Indian spiritual leader (20th–21st century)	2	6	6.500	0.043
24 SAI BABA —Indian guru (20th–21st century)	3	9	8.000	0.042
25 ST. FRANCIS OF ASSISI —Italian Catholic friar (12–13th century)	3	9	9.333	0.042
26 MARTIN LUTHER KING JR. —American spiritual and civil rights leader (20th century)	3	9	8.333	0.039
27 MAHAVATAR BABAJI —Indian saint (19th–20th century)	2	6	7.000	0.039
28 ST. TERESA OF AVILA —Spanish Catholic nun, mystic (16th century)	2	6	8.500	0.038
29 ST. JOHN THE BAPTIST —Jewish-Christian preacher, prophet (1st century)	3	9	9.000	0.038

continued on next page

Item	Frequency	Resp Pct	Avg Rank	Smith's s
30 AMMA —Indian spiritual leader, guru (20th–21st century)	4	13	10.000	0.034
31 MIRRA ALFASSA —French spiritual leader, known as "The Mother" (19th–20th century)	2	6	6.000	0.033
32 OSHO —Indian guru, mystic (20th century)	4	13	6.500	0.033
33 ANANDAMAYI MA —Indian spiritual leader (20th century)	2	6	8.500	0.032
34 KARMAPA —Rangjung Rigpe Dorje, Tibetan Buddhist spiritual leader (20th century)	1	3	1.000	0.031
35 PD. FERNANDO —Brazilian Santo Daime elder (20th–21st century)	1	3	1.000	0.031
36 ZARATHUSTRA —ancient Persian founder of Zoroastrianism	2	6	7.500	0.030
37 CAROLINE MYSS —American spiritual author (20th–21st century)	1	3	2.000	0.030
38 PD. ALFREDO —Brazilian Santo Daime elder (20th–21st century)	2	6	4.500	0.030
39 MY PSYCHOTHERAPIST	1	3	2.000	0.028
40 HANS STOLP —Dutch theologian and author (20th–21st century)	1	3	3.000	0.028
41 RAMANUJA —Indian theologian (11th–12th century)	1	3	3.000	0.028
42 DAIME PEOPLE	2	6	5.500	0.028

Item	Frequency	Resp Pct	Avg Rank	Smith's s
43 CARL JUNG —Swiss psychotherapist (19th–20th century)	2	6	9.500	0.028
44 WIFE	1	3	2.000	0.027
45 MOSES —Jewish religious leader, prophet (14th–13th century BCE)	1	3	3.000	0.026
46 ADI SHANKARA —Indian philosopher (8th–9th century)	1	3	4.000	0.026
47 MARIA ALICE —Brazilian Santo Daime elder (20th–21st century)	1	3	4.000	0.026
48 MOTHER TERESA —Albanian-Indian Catholic nun (20th century)	2	6	5.500	0.025
49 THE MAYA —the ancient civilization of Mesoamerica	2	6	10.000	0.025
50 LE PÂLE —"the pale" prophet, a legend that Jesus visited the Americas in Pre-Columbian times	1	3	4.000	0.025
51 SHAKESPEARE —English playright (16th–17th century)	1	3	5.000	0.025
52 RANANDA —American guru (20th–21st century)	1	3	2.000	0.025
53 MD. JULIA —Brazilian Santo Daime elder (20th–21st century)	1	3	3.000	0.025
54 PROPHETS	1	3	3.000	0.025

continued on next page

Item	Frequency	Resp Pct	Avg Rank	Smith's s
55 ST. JOHN OF THE CROSS —Spanish Catholic friar, mystic (16th century)	1	3	5.000	0.025
56 RAMAKRISHNA —Indian mystic (19th century)	1	3	5.000	0.024
57 MILAREPA —Tibetan Buddhest poet, yogi (11th–12th century)	1	3	3.000	0.024
58 YOGANANDA —Indian yogi, guru (20th century)	1	3	4.000	0.023
59 CHAMAN ARCO IRIS —a stone sculpture in St. Augustine, Columbia	1	3	5.000	0.023
60 ALAN WATTS —English American spiritual author (20th century)	1	3	2.000	0.023
61 WILLIAM BLAKE —English artist, poet, mystic (18th–19th century)	1	3	6.000	0.023
62 RAMANA MAHARSHI —Indian mystical ascetic (19th–20th century)	2	6	10.500	0.023
63 DAUGHTER	1	3	4.000	0.023
64 B. K. S IYENGAR —Indian yoga teacher, author (20th–21st century)	1	3	3.000	0.022
65 SONIA DINI —Brazilian Santo Daime elder (20th–21st century)	1	3	3.000	0.022
66 RUDOLF STEINER —Austrian philosopher (19th–20th century)	1	3	7.000	0.022
67 P. TEILHARD de CHARDIN —French Catholic priest, philosopher (19th–20th century)	1	3	7.000	0.022

Item	Frequency	Resp Pct	Avg Rank	Smith's *s*
68 ST. PETER —Israeli-Palestinian spiritual leader (1ˢᵗ century)	1	3	4.000	0.022
69 NISARGADATTA MAHARAJ —Indian philosopher, guru (20ᵗʰ century)	2	6	8.500	0.021
70 JAN VAN RUYSBROECK —Flemish priest, mystic (14ᵗʰ century)	1	3	4.000	0.021
71 ISIS —ancient Egyptian goddess	1	3	8.000	0.020
72 OMRAAM M. AÏVANHOV —Bulgarian philosopher, mystic (20ᵗʰ century)	2	6	9.500	0.020
73 TAISEN DESHIMARU —Japaense Zen Buddhist teacher (20ᵗʰ century)	1	3	7.000	0.020
74 PD. VALDETE —Brazilian Santo Daime elder (20ᵗʰ–21ˢᵗ century)	1	3	3.000	0.019
75 GRANDMOTHER	1	3	8.000	0.018
76 LUONG MINH DANG —Vietnamesse founder of Spiritual Human Yoga (20ᵗʰ–21ˢᵗ century)	1	3	6.000	0.018
77 SRI YUKTESWAR GIRI —Indian spiritual teacher (19ᵗʰ–20ᵗʰ century)	1	3	6.000	0.018
78 PATTABHI JOIS —Indian yoga teacher (20ᵗʰ–21ˢᵗ century)	1	3	4.000	0.018
79 ZÉ RICARDO —Brazilian Santo Daime elder (20ᵗʰ–21ˢᵗ century)	1	3	4.000	0.018

continued on next page

Item	Frequency	Resp Pct	Avg Rank	Smith's *s*
80 D. T. SUZUKI —Japanese spiritual teacher (19th–20th century)	1	3	8.000	0.018
81 MARCUS AURELIUS —Roman Emperor (2nd century)	1	3	9.000	0.017
82 GUANYIN —Buddhist *bodhisattva* (enlightened being)	1	3	10.000	0.017
83 ANTOINE de ST-EXUPÉRY —French writer (20th century)	1	3	10.000	0.017
84 CDAI COMMANDER —Belgian Santo Daime elder (20th–21st century)	1	3	6.000	0.017
85 HERMES TRISMEGISTUS —ancient Medditerranean spiritual author	1	3	7.000	0.017
86 OSIRIS —ancient Egyptian god	1	3	7.000	0.017
87 EDWARD BACH —English phystician, spiritual author (19th–20th century)	1	3	9.000	0.017
88 WRITERS and ARTISTS	1	3	6.000	0.016
89 ERICH FROMM —German social scientist (20th century)	1	3	11.000	0.016
90 WALT DISNEY —American animator, film director, businessman (20th century)	1	3	11.000	0.016
91 TERENCE MCKENNA —American ethnobotanist, philosopher, author (20th century)	1	3	3.000	0.016
92 BAIRD SPALDING —American author (19th–20th century)	1	3	10.000	0.015

Item	Frequency	Resp Pct	Avg Rank	Smith's *s*
93 MOZART —Austrian composer, musician (18th century)	1	3	12.000	0.014
94 G. I. GURDJIEFF —Armenian spiritual teacher, author (19th–20th century)	1	3	6.000	0.014
95 VOLTAIRE —French philosopher (18th century)	1	3	11.000	0.014
96 KRISHNAMACHARYA —Indian yoga teacher (19th–20th century)	1	3	5.000	0.013
97 GABRIEL COUSENS —American physician, nutritionist, spiritual author (20th–21st century)	1	3	11.000	0.013
98 EVA PIERRAKOS —Austrian spiritual teacher (20th century)	1	3	4.000	0.013
99 J. SEBASTIAN BACH —German composer, musician (17th–18th century)	1	3	13.000	0.013
100 ST. GERMAIN —aka "Master Rakoczi," fabled master of theosophy	1	3	9.000	0.012
101 FR. FRANÇOIS BRUNE —French Catholic priest, author (20th–21st century)	1	3	11.000	0.012
102 BRUNO BETTELHEIM —Austrian American psychologist, writer (20th century)	1	3	8.000	0.011
103 ST. JOSEPH —Israeli-Palestinian carpenter, father of Jesus Christ (1st century BCE–1st century CE)	1	3	14.000	0.011
104 ONESELF	2	6	7.000	0.011

continued on next page

Item	Frequency	Resp Pct	Avg Rank	Smith's s
105 ARTHUR RACKHAM —English book illustrator (19th–20th century)	1	3	14.000	0.011
106 GREGG BRADEN —American spiritual teacher, author (20th–21st century)	1	3	7.000	0.010
107 HINDUISM —the religion	1	3	12.000	0.010
108 ST. MICHAEL —archangel, leader of the Army of God	2	6	13.000	0.010
109 LEONARDO da VINCI —Italian artist, polymath (15th–16th century)	1	3	10.000	0.010
110 STEVE ROTHER —American spiritual teacher (20th–21st century)	1	3	8.000	0.009
111 MAHARISHI M. YOGI —Indian yogi, guru (20th–21st century)	1	3	8.000	0.009
112 ARABS —the ethnicity/culture centered in the Middle East	1	3	8.000	0.009
113 AVALOKITEŚVARA —Buddhist *bodhisattva* (enlightened being)	1	3	15.000	0.009
114 JAN DRIES —Dutch nutritionist, dietician (20th–21st century)	1	3	13.000	0.009
115 ALEX POLARI —Brazilian Santo Daime elder (20th–21st century)	1	3	6.000	0.009
116 FATHER	1	3	9.000	0.009
117 SANTO DAIME —the divine being in the ayahuasca drink	2	6	12.500	0.008

Item	Frequency	Resp Pct	Avg Rank	Smith's s
118 ALEJANDRO JODOROWSKY —Chilean French filmmaker, spiritual guru (20th–21st century)	1	3	13.000	0.008
119 SWAMI PREMANANDA —Sri Lankan/Indian spiritual teacher (20th–21st century)	1	3	10.000	0.008
120 ALAN PARSONS —English musician, record producer (20th–21st century)	1	3	10.000	0.008
121 HILDEGARD von BINGEN —German nun, mystic, author (12th century)	1	3	16.000	0.008
122 BLUE EAGLE —spiritual blogger (20th–21st century)	2	6	15.500	0.008
123 DIRK GHEKIERE —Belgian spiritual teacher, shaman (20th–21st century)	1	3	14.000	0.007
124 ST. MACHUTUS —Welsh Catholic evangelist (6th–7th century)	1	3	8.000	0.007
125 AL-GHAZALI —Persian theologian, mystic (11th–12th century)	1	3	15.000	0.007
126 MARY MAGDALENE —disciple of Jesus Christ (1st century)	1	3	16.000	0.007
127 ROBERVAL —Brazilian Santo Daime elder (20th–21st century)	1	3	5.000	0.006
128 BYRON KATIE —American author (20th–21st century)	1	3	5.000	0.006
129 INDIA —the country	1	3	9.000	0.006

continued on next page

Item	Frequency	Resp Pct	Avg Rank	Smith's s
130 MELLIE UYLDERT —Dutch writer, alternative healer, occultist, astrologer (20th–21st century)	1	3	17.000	0.006
131 KARLFRIED DÜRCKHEIM —German diplomat, psychotherapist and Zen Master (20th century)	1	3	6.000	0.005
132 IBN ARABI —Iberian Arab Sufi mystic, philosopher (12th–13th century)	1	3	16.000	0.005
133 PYTHAGORAS —Greek philosopher, mathmetician, spiritual leader (6th–5th century BCE)	1	3	12.000	0.005
134 RAPHAEL —the archangel	1	3	18.000	0.005
135 JEFF GREEN —American astrologer (20th–21st century)	1	3	18.000	0.005
136 LUCIANO DINI —Brazilian Santo Daime elder (20th–21st century)	1	3	7.000	0.004
137 ATTAR of NISHAPUR —Persian Sufi poet, hagiographer (12th–13th century)	1	3	17.000	0.003
138 FATHER DAMIEN —Belgian Catholic priest (19th century)	1	3	19.000	0.003
139 URIEL —the archangel	1	3	19.000	0.003
140 CHUCK BERRY —American musician (20th–21st century)	1	3	10.000	0.003
141 SON	1	3	11.000	0.003

Item	Frequency	Resp Pct	Avg Rank	Smith's s
142 PLATO —Greek philosopher (5th–4th century BCE)	1	3	13.000	0.002
143 UNKNOWN —???	1	3	17.000	0.002
144 RENÉ GUÉNON —French metaphysciaian, author (19th–20th century)	1	3	18.000	0.002
145 MEISTER ECKHART —German mystic, theologian (13th–14th century)	1	3	19.000	0.002
146 GABRIEL —the archangel	1	3	20.000	0.002
Total Items/Average Length of List:	308		9.625	

Appendix V

Master List of Great Spiritual Teachers
(Europe-wide Sample)

Anthropac tabulation of "Great Spiritual Teachers" freelist results (n = 42 European fardados)

FREELIST: SORTED BY "SMITH'S s"

Item	Frequency	Pct	Resp Rank	Avg Smith's s
1 JESUS CHRIST	34	81	2.941	0.650
2 MESTRE IRINEU	23	55	6.043	0.298
3 BUDDHA	16	38	4.500	0.259
4 OSHO	15	36	4.667	0.239
5 DALAI LAMA	13	31	5.462	0.179
6 PD SEBASTIÃO	13	31	7.923	0.154
7 PD ALFREDO	11	26	9.000	0.103
8 KRISHNAMURTI	7	17	6.143	0.100
9 ST JOHN the BAPTIST	6	14	6.667	0.099
10 VIRGIN MARY	9	21	7.333	0.095
11 GANDHI	6	14	4.167	0.095
12 YOGANANDA	5	12	4.200	0.079
13 FRANCIS ASSISI	6	14	6.833	0.077
14 MOSES	4	10	5.750	0.074
15 GURDJIEFF	4	10	4.750	0.072
16 MD RITA	5	12	5.000	0.068
17 BABAJI	3	7	4.000	0.061
18 CHICO CORRENTE	3	7	3.333	0.058
19 AMMA	4	10	9.000	0.057

continued on next page

Item	Frequency	Pct	Resp Rank	Avg Smith's s
20 FATHER	3	7	6.000	0.049
21 MOTHER	3	7	6.333	0.043
22 ZE RICARDO	3	7	7.667	0.043
23 MOHAMMED	4	10	7.250	0.042
24 SAI BABA	3	7	10.333	0.039
25 MARIA ALICE	2	5	4.000	0.038
26 SAINT ANTHONY	3	7	11.667	0.036
27 RAMAKRISHNA	2	5	6.000	0.035
28 APOSTLES	2	5	6.500	0.032
29 SHRIDHYANYOGI	3	7	11.333	0.029
30 EVERYONE	3	7	11.000	0.029
31 ST GERMAIN	2	5	8.500	0.029
32 CONFUCIUS	2	5	9.000	0.029
33 ST JOHN of the CROSS	2	5	5.500	0.028
34 MOTHER MEERA	2	5	5.000	0.028
35 FRIEND	3	7	8.667	0.028
36 SANTO DAIME	2	5	4.500	0.028
37 PD VALDETE	2	5	7.500	0.027
38 MEISTER ECKHART	2	5	8.500	0.027
39 MD CRISTINA	3	7	8.000	0.026
40 TIMOTHY LEARY	2	5	10.500	0.026
41 INNER VOICE	2	5	2.500	0.026
42 KING SOLOMON	2	5	9.500	0.025
43 ST MICHAEL	2	5	10.000	0.024
44 GRANDFATHER	1	2	1.000	0.024
45 PEDRO KUPFER	1	2	1.000	0.024
46 KEN KESEY	1	2	1.000	0.024
47 RAMAYANA	1	2	1.000	0.024
48 LUONG MINHDANG	1	2	1.000	0.024
49 ADEILDOCAX	1	2	1.000	0.024
50 STAN GROF	1	2	1.000	0.024
51 PLATO	1	2	1.000	0.024
52 CHOGYAL RINPOCHE	1	2	2.000	0.023
53 LINKAITING	1	2	2.000	0.022
54 SITTINGBULL	1	2	2.000	0.022
55 JOSEPH [New Testament]	2	5	9.500	0.022
56 MAHARISHI	1	2	2.000	0.022
57 DOG	1	2	2.000	0.022
58 SNGOENKA	1	2	3.000	0.022

Item	Frequency	Pct	Resp Rank	Avg Smith's *s*
59 JIGMELINGPA	1	2	2.000	0.021
60 ZARATHUSTRA	1	2	2.000	0.021
61 TERENCE MCKENNA	1	2	3.000	0.021
62 AMINA	1	2	3.000	0.021
63 BOB MARLEY	2	5	9.000	0.021
64 LAMEDEER	1	2	3.000	0.021
65 ABRAHAM	1	2	3.000	0.021
66 JODIE	2	5	6.000	0.021
67 RED PATH CHIEFS	2	5	16.000	0.021
68 PEKKAERVAST	1	2	4.000	0.020
69 MILAREPA	1	2	3.000	0.020
70 ALDOUS HUXLEY	1	2	4.000	0.020
71 SHAMANTEACHER	1	2	4.000	0.020
72 GERALDINE	1	2	4.000	0.019
73 NOAH	1	2	4.000	0.019
74 KRISHNA	2	5	9.500	0.019
75 ANNIE BESANT	1	2	5.000	0.019
76 SANTA CLARA	2	5	5.500	0.019
77 PADMASAMBHAVA	1	2	3.000	0.019
78 JACK KORNFIELD	1	2	2.000	0.019
79 BAIXINHA	2	5	11.000	0.019
80 STEVEN GASKIN	1	2	5.000	0.019
81 BABAR	1	2	6.000	0.018
82 MADAME BLAVATSKY	1	2	6.000	0.018
83 MD JULIA	1	2	5.000	0.018
84 LAO TSE	2	5	12.500	0.018
85 JOSEPH [Old Testament]	1	2	5.000	0.018
86 SAIMAA	1	2	4.000	0.018
87 DONVALOMERKABA	1	2	9.000	0.017
88 UNNAMEDTEACHER	1	2	4.000	0.017
89 ECKHART TOLLE	1	2	3.000	0.017
90 ALLAH	1	2	3.000	0.017
91 NARADAGURU	1	2	3.000	0.017
92 CASTANEDA	2	5	14.000	0.017
93 VICENTE FERRER	1	2	3.000	0.016
94 SHINSHIVASVAYAM-BHUMAHARAJ	1	2	8.000	0.016
95 RAIHNA da FLORESTA	1	2	3.000	0.016
96 ROLLING THUNDER	1	2	3.000	0.016

continued on next page

Item	Frequency	Pct	Resp Rank	Avg Smith's s
97 SWAMI PREMANANDA	1	2	7.000	0.015
98 KALEVALAPEOPLE	1	2	9.000	0.015
99 PRABHUPADA	2	5	4.500	0.015
100 AURELIODIAZ	1	2	9.000	0.015
101 ST TERESA of AVILA	2	5	7.500	0.015
102 CHILDREN	1	2	3.000	0.014
103 LADYPORTA	1	2	13.000	0.014
104 MENTOR	1	2	8.000	0.014
105 RAMANAMAHARASHI	2	5	14.000	0.014
106 CHAITANYA	1	2	4.000	0.014
107 SCHULGIN	1	2	4.000	0.014
108 RASTA ELDERS	1	2	10.000	0.014
109 NELSON MANDELA	1	2	8.000	0.013
110 SRIVIVEKANANDA	1	2	10.000	0.013
111 ANIMALS	1	2	6.000	0.013
112 CDAI LEADER	1	2	9.000	0.013
113 JOHN COLTRAINE	1	2	11.000	0.012
114 SHRIANANDIMA	2	5	13.000	0.012
115 KHENPOCHOGA	1	2	6.000	0.012
116 LUIS MENDEZ	1	2	7.000	0.012
117 4 EVANGELISTS	1	2	16.000	0.012
118 THICH NHAT HANH	2	5	7.000	0.012
119 PYTHAGORUS	1	2	3.000	0.012
120 RABBI ISAAC LURIA	1	2	10.000	0.012
121 MILES DAVIS	1	2	12.000	0.011
122 BEATRICE	1	2	10.000	0.011
123 KARMAPA	1	2	12.000	0.011
124 RABBI NACHMAN	1	2	11.000	0.011
125 BLACKELK	1	2	10.000	0.010
126 ST PETER	1	2	18.000	0.010
127 ST BRIDGETT	1	2	5.000	0.010
128 THELONIOUS MONK	1	2	13.000	0.010
129 LLAMA KOFINDA	1	2	5.000	0.010
130 HILDEGARD von BINGEN	1	2	8.000	0.010
131 BEBE STRATULAT	1	2	11.000	0.010
132 OSHO DISCIPLE	1	2	4.000	0.010
133 UMBANDA TRIBE	1	2	19.000	0.010
134 KHENZENPEIZE	1	2	7.000	0.010
135 BAALSHEMTOV	1	2	12.000	0.009

Item	Frequency	Pct	Resp Rank	Avg Smith's s
136 JOHN LENNON	1	2	11.000	0.009
137 LIEZI	1	2	11.000	0.009
138 HOPIS	1	2	6.000	0.009
139 SUN MOON STARS	1	2	20.000	0.009
140 ABRAHAM HICKS	1	2	8.000	0.009
141 YOGA TEACHER	1	2	12.000	0.008
142 CHE GUEVERA	1	2	5.000	0.008
143 EMERSON	1	2	13.000	0.008
144 RAMARINPOCHE	1	2	5.000	0.008
145 SPINOZA	1	2	5.000	0.008
146 GREAT SPIRIT	1	2	21.000	0.008
147 THE BEATLES	1	2	15.000	0.008
148 AHMEDELATTAR	1	2	12.000	0.007
149 DEELUZE	1	2	12.000	0.007
150 PADRE PIO	1	2	15.000	0.007
151 SWAMIDAYANANDA	1	2	6.000	0.007
152 JAWAHARLALNEHRU	1	2	6.000	0.007
153 TERESA CALCUTTA	1	2	6.000	0.007
154 CRISTINA TATI	1	2	16.000	0.007
155 KEITH JARRET	1	2	16.000	0.007
156 NOTHING	1	2	9.000	0.006
157 ZHUANGZI	1	2	13.000	0.006
158 NEIL DONALD WALSH	1	2	10.000	0.006
159 NATURE	1	2	4.000	0.006
160 INCAS	1	2	7.000	0.006
161 VALMIKI	1	2	13.000	0.006
162 KEN WILBER	1	2	17.000	0.006
163 SIBELIUS	1	2	17.000	0.006
164 JURAMIDAM	1	2	24.000	0.006
165 ST GEORGE	1	2	11.000	0.005
166 SOCRATES	1	2	9.000	0.005
167 BEIJA FLOR	1	2	25.000	0.005
168 TILOPA	1	2	9.000	0.005
169 JAMES HILLMAN	1	2	18.000	0.005
170 DERRIDA	1	2	14.000	0.004
171 TULSIDAS	1	2	14.000	0.004
172 ALAN KARDEC	1	2	10.000	0.004
173 IMAGINE-UNIMAGINE	1	2	10.000	0.004
174 SISTERS	1	2	15.000	0.004

continued on next page

Item	Frequency	Pct	Resp Rank	Avg Smith's *s*
175 RUMI	2	5	13.500	0.004
176 BAIRD T SPALDING	1	2	11.000	0.004
177 JIMI HENDRIX	1	2	6.000	0.004
178 PAPAPAUEH	1	2	26.000	0.004
179 WERNER ERHARD	1	2	7.000	0.003
180 DAFRIJOHN	1	2	7.000	0.003
181 RUDOLF STEINER	1	2	7.000	0.003
182 SHIVA	1	2	27.000	0.003
183 ANTONIO JORGE	1	2	15.000	0.003
184 WALTER BENJAMIN	1	2	15.000	0.003
185 HUSBAND	1	2	16.000	0.003
186 GANESH	1	2	28.000	0.002
187 NAROPA	1	2	10.000	0.002
188 NIETZSCHE	1	2	10.000	0.002
189 MYSELF	1	2	11.000	0.002
190 CHICO XAVIER	1	2	11.000	0.002
191 GOD	1	2	12.000	0.002
192 MANSUKHPATEL	1	2	12.000	0.002
193 BRAHMA	1	2	29.000	0.002
194 SHIVAPURIBABA	1	2	16.000	0.001
195 LOBSANGRAMPA	1	2	21.000	0.001
196 VISHNU	1	2	30.000	0.001
Total/Average:	414		9.857	

Appendix VI

Triad Test Results and Statistics

```
TRIADS
ffffffffffffffffffffffffffffffffffffffffffffffffffffffffffffffffffffffffffffffffffff
ff

New design each quest.?  NO
Input dataset:          C:\APAC\TRIAD-BE

Number of times each item was chosen in each triad:
```

MD (16)	KR (5)	BD (5)
VM (7)	ET (19)	BD (0)
MI (6)	VM (9)	GD (11)
DL (2)	JC (10)	ET (14)
VM (11)	DL (9)	MI (6)
ET (13)	GD (4)	PS (9)
KR (2)	MD (4)	ET (20)
JC (5)	DL (16)	KR (5)
JC (1)	KR (8)	PS (17)
BD (2)	JC (5)	GD (19)
MD (5)	VM (5)	DL (16)
DL (3)	MI (9)	ET (14)
BD (3)	KR (8)	DL (15)
BD (7)	PS (14)	VM (5)
ET (17)	GD (6)	BD (2)
MI (4)	KR (11)	ET (11)
ET (23)	JC (0)	VM (3)
GD (3)	MD (17)	DL (6)
KR (8)	MI (14)	GD (4)
MI (17)	JC (2)	BD (7)
MD (4)	JC (4)	GD (18)
PS (18)	DL (4)	GD (4)
BD (10)	DL (4)	PS (12)
ET (12)	PS (2)	MD (12)
BD (3)	MD (6)	MI (17)
KR (10)	VM (4)	PS (12)
JC (17)	MI (1)	PS (7)
MD (17)	JC (1)	VM (8)
PS (3)	MD (20)	MI (2)
GD (11)	KR (5)	VM (10)

Figure A.1. Triad Test results for top ten "Great Spiritual Teachers" (GST) from freelists (n = 26 Belgian fardados)

```
NON-METRIC MULTIDIMENSIONAL SCALING
fffffffffffffffffffffffffffffffffffffffffffffffffffffffffffffffffffffffffffffffff
ff

              1     2
           -----  -----
  1 JC    -0.88  -0.12
  2 BD    -0.18  -0.32
  3 MI     0.21   0.94
  4 GD     0.66  -0.70
  5 PS     0.01   1.12
  6 MD    -0.96  -0.70
  7 KR    -0.41  -0.74
  8 VM    -0.79   0.27
  9 DL     0.75  -0.06
 10 ET     1.58   0.32


Coordinates saved as dataset COORD
Stress 0.121 after 12 iterations.
```

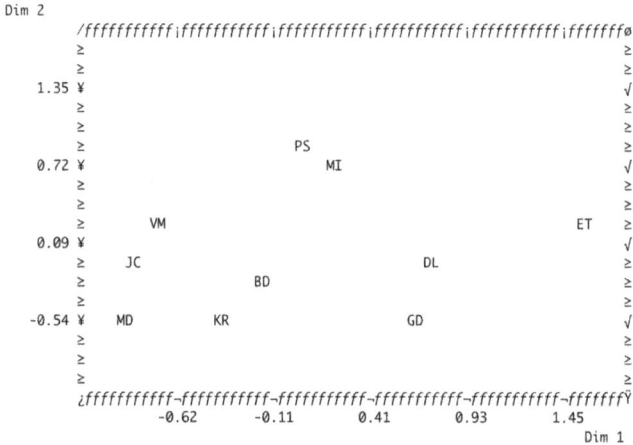

```
Dim 2
        /fffffffffffiffffffffffffiffffffffffffiffffffffffffiffffffffffffifffffff0
          ≥                                                                      ≥
          ≥                                                                      ≥
  1.35 ¥                                                                         √
          ≥                                                                      ≥
          ≥                                                                      ≥
          ≥                           PS                                         ≥
  0.72 ¥                                    MI                                   √
          ≥                                                                      ≥
          ≥                                                                      ≥
          ≥             VM                                              ET        ≥
  0.09 ¥                                                                         √
          ≥       JC                              DL                             ≥
          ≥                       BD                                             ≥
          ≥                                                                      ≥
 -0.54 ¥     MD          KR                          GD                          √
          ≥                                                                      ≥
          ≥                                                                      ≥
          ≥                                                                      ≥
        ¿fffffffffff¬fffffffffff¬fffffffffff¬fffffffffff¬fffffffffff¬ffffffΫ
            -0.62        -0.11        0.41         0.93         1.45
                                                                    Dim 1
Stress in 2 dimensions is 0.121
```

Figure A.2. GST Triad Multidimensional Scaling Map

```
JOHNSON'S HIERARCHICAL CLUSTERING
ffffffffffffffffffffffffffffffffffffffffffffffffff1
ff

Input dataset:          C:\APAC\AGPROX
Method:                 AVERAGE
Type of Data:           Similarities

HIERARCHICAL CLUSTERING

            M K B J V M P G D E
            D R D C M I S D L T

                           1
  Level     6 7 2 1 8 3 5 4 9 0
  ------     - - - - - - - - - -
  0.7692     . . . XXX . . . . .
  0.7500     . . . XXX XXX . . .
  0.6731     . . . XXX XXX XXX .
  0.6538     . . XXXXX XXX XXX .
  0.5288     . XXXXXXX XXX XXX .
  0.4115     XXXXXXXXX XXX XXX .
  0.3355     XXXXXXXXX XXXXXXX .
  0.3077     XXXXXXXXX XXXXXXXXX
  0.1671     XXXXXXXXXXXXXXXXXXX
```

Figure A.3. GST Triad Hierarchical Cluster Graph

```
 CONSENSUS ANALYSIS
ffffffffffffffffffffffffffffffffffffffffffffffffffffff1
ff

Type:                   MULTIPLE CHOICE
Proximity data?         NO
Input dataset:          C:\APAC\UNRANDOM.##D

Pseudo-Reliability = 0.908

EIGENVALUES
```

FACTOR	VALUE	PERCENT	CUM %	RATIO
1:	8.292	71.2	71.2	4.577
2:	1.812	15.5	86.7	1.169
3:	1.549	13.3	100.0	
	11.653	100.0		

Figure A.4. GST Triad Consensus Analysis

Notes

Preface

Regarding the first epigraph: the last sentence of Hegel's *Phenomenology* is an adaptation of a quote from Friedrich Schiller's *Die Freundschaft* (see Schulte-Sasse 2004, 88–89).

1. As pointed out by Tupper (2011, 16, n. 14), contrary to popular discourse ayahuasca is not a "tea," as it is "technically . . . a decoction (i.e., a brew) rather than an infusion of the plants."

2. Occasionally, daimista veterans will leave the church because they no longer feel inspired to remain members.

Chapter 1

1. Throughout this text, I refer to informants with pseudonyms (any resemblance to the names of real people is purely coincidental). With the exception of prominent Padrinhos and Madrinhas who are public figures, I am only publishing information that does not unduly intrude upon the privacy and anonymity of Santo Daime members. Since my informants are criminals in the eyes of most governments, I am determined that my research and subsequent publications are in accord with the American Anthropological Association's Ethics Code (AAA 2012); in particular, the "primary ethical obligation . . . to do no harm": "Among the most serious harms that anthropologists should seek to avoid are harm to dignity, and to bodily and material well-being, especially when research is conducted among vulnerable populations. Anthropologists should not only avoid causing direct and immediate harm but also should weigh carefully the potential consequences and inadvertent impacts of their work. When it conflicts with other responsibilities, this primary obligation can supersede the goal of seeking new knowledge."

2. The impetus to arrange my first Daime work in Europe was Benny Shanon's (2002, 42) short comments about daimista communities in the Netherlands; this

is what prompted me to find an email contact on the internet who then provided the necessary details for planning my first visit.

3. Specifically, the white room sequence in the final act called "Jupiter and Beyond the Infinite" (Kubrick 1968).

4. Unlike violent felons studied by Bourgois (1999) and Fleisher (1995), fardados are nonviolent. In contrast to prohibitions against street drugs such as heroin and crack cocaine, my informants are violating bans on ayahuasca, a substance that has proven to be safe and potentially beneficial within controlled circumstances.

5. In the decades after the 1971 UN Convention was passed, all Euro-American countries discussed herein signed and ratified the terms of the treaty (including Belgium [in 1995], the Netherlands [1993], France [1971], Germany [1971], the UK [1971], as well as Brazil [1971], Canada [1988], and the United States [1971]). The total list of signatories can be found here: http://treaties.un.org/doc/Publication/MTDSG/Volume%20I/Chapter%20VI/VI-16.en.pdf.

6. http://ayahuascadefense.com/index.php/national-legal-status/.

7. Although full legitimacy has yet to be granted (i.e., legal proceedings are ongoing), Daime groups have been acquitted of previous charges regarding the possession of ayahuasca in Italy (Menozzi 2011, 386–387).

8. See Haber (2011) and Rochester (2017).

9. Here, Jacoba broaches the existential dissatisfaction felt by many Western people today, a "malaise" of secular disenchantment that Charles Taylor (2007, 311/507) detects in the title of the Peggy Lee song "Is That All There Is?"

10. Original Portuguese: "Peia—Processo purgativo e mimético que às vezes ocorrecom o usa da bebida sacramental do Daime. É considerado uma limpeza ao nível físico e uma disciplina necessária para desbloquear resistências e cristalizações ao nível interior."

11. Although Castaneda presented his first book (*The Teachings of Don Juan*) as authentic ethnography, anthropologists are now aware that his work of literary fiction was largely the result of invented consultants and data (de Mille 1976).

12. Meaning "*a*-gnostic" (or "non-gnostic"), the "agnostic" label was invented by Thomas Henry Huxley in 1869 "to draw a contrast between his own uncertainty and the claims to secret and privileged knowledge that characterized the gnostics" (Le Poidevin 2010, 19–21).

13. It is important to note the strong affinities between Buber's I-You premise and Victor Turner's (1982, 250) anthropological concept of *communitas*: "It would be more correct to think of a ritual of affliction as a passionate attempt to heal the breaches caused by social structural conflict and competition and by egotistical or factional strivings for power, influence, wealth, etc., by reviving feelings of an underlying bedrock *communitas*, a generic human relationship undivided by status-roles or structural oppositions, which is also vouched for by myths and histories stressing the unity and continuity of the widest group to which all belong by birth and tradition."

14. Prominent examples include Michael Taussig (1987) with Marx or Walter Benjamin, Thomas Csordas (1997) with Merleau-Ponty, or Michael D. Jackson (2013) with Sartre.

15. According to the United Nations (2007, 7), in 2007 the total population for all of Europe was estimated to be approximately 731 million people, see: http://www.un.org/esa/population/publications/wpp2006/English.pdf.

16. European esoteric traditions incorporated into Santo Daime include influences from groups such as the *Esoteric Circle for the Communion of Thought*, the *Rosicrucian Order*, as well as various forms of *Kardecism* inspired by the nineteenth-century French medium Allan Kardec (Labate and Pacheco 2011, 75).

17. At some Daime works, I met seasoned visitors who distinguished themselves from less experienced non-fardados with the unofficial term *firmados*. This term is derived from the ubiquitous Daime ideal of *firmeza* or "firmness," a trait that denotes a person's capacity to gracefully cope with ordeals encountered in both Daime works and everyday life.

18. Some periods of the year involve special rituals that occur between the four standard monthly gatherings, such as the June Festival, which includes four extra works for a total of eight works within one month (see Appendix II).

19. Although the majority of interviews were conducted in English, I have taken the liberty to make slight grammatical corrections to some interview transcriptions quoted herein, so as to conform to Standard English.

20. http://ec.europa.eu/eurostat/statistics-explained/index.php/Unemployment_statistics.

21. One notable exception is the permanent community of daimistas living together on a compound in rural Spain (see chapter 7).

22. A militaristic term for the leader of a church. Dawson (2007, 73–74) describes this as a "military motif" prevalent in Daime discourse (with participants organized into *batalhões* ["battalions"] of age and gender, and fardado members wearing *fardas* ["uniforms"]).

23. Of thirty-one unmarried daimistas, seven had previously been married and four were currently involved in committed relationships with a significant other.

24. Fardado informants expressed to me their sympathetic concern for a transgendered participant who alternated between standing on the male and female sides of the gender-divided ritual space when attending works in Amsterdam. Apparently this individual eventually found they were most comfortable positioned in the aisle between the male and female sides of the salão. One wonders how Daime congregations will accommodate transgendered or nonbinary genderqueer folks in the future: Will they be able to choose which side of the gender-divided salão they wish to sit/stand on? Might they be permitted to wear a farda that conflates aspects of the men's and women's farda?

25. Of course, there are exceptions to this general rule. For instance, under police interrogation German daimistas admitted that "adolescents participated in the

ceremonies and in some cases also had drunk a symbolic dose of the tea" (Rohde and Sander 2011, 344–345/351[n. 15]). This is a complex and controversial topic that will eventually have to be worked out in the European court system.

26. Examples: *A Different Medicine*, by Joseph Calabrese (2013), Oxford University Press; *Altered States: Buddhism and Psychedelic Spirituality in America*, by Douglas Osto (2016), Columbia University Press; *Sacred Knowledge: Psychedelics and Religious Experiences*, by William A. Richards (2016), Columbia University Press; *Ayahuasca Shamanism in the Amazon and Beyond*, ed. Beatriz Labate and Clancy Cavnar (2014a) Oxford University Press; *Higher Wisdom: Eminent Elders Explore the Continuing Impact of Psychedelics*, ed. Roger Walsh and Charles Grob (2005), State University of New York Press; *Psychedelic Psychiatry: LSD from Clinic to Campus*, by Erika Dyck (2008), Johns Hopkins University Press; *American Trip*, by Ido Hartogsohn (2020), MIT Press.

Chapter 2

1. Any ethnographer who earnestly seeks to learn about religious behaviors is bound to absorb new ideas from their interaction with informants' worldview, what Tanya Luhrmann (1989, 307–15) calls "interpretive drift." With awareness of this tendency, the anthropologist can maintain objective distance while still obtaining new insights about religious cultures. The results of my own efforts to suspend disbelief in Daime works parallel Adam Klin-Oron's (2014, 645) participant-observation with practitioners of New Age "channeling": "Suspension of disbelief is not belief: It assumes temporality, an eventual resumption of disbelief."

2. Following Shanon (2002), a Swedish study (Kjellgren, Eriksson, and Norlander 2009, 310) employed phenomenological psychology to analyze questionnaires distributed to twenty-five northern Europeans who had experienced ayahuasca an average of seventeen times. One caveat is that on average, this study's respondents' last ayahuasca session was more than three hundred days prior to being interviewed, which makes it difficult to rely on such old memories.

3. In contrast to non-Brazilian scholars' tendency to refrain from "going native," many Brazilian anthropologists who study ayahuasca spiritualities end up becoming formal members of the groups they are researching (Labate, de Rose, and dos Santos 2008, 41); the latter issue is discussed in more detail by Labate (2004b).

4. Notable exceptions are hymns "received" in fardados' native language, which are sometimes performed in rituals.

5. For example, in the CEFLURIS Daime denomination the monthly fee (which includes a membership card) pays for one's admission to two "concentration" works, one *cura* ("healing") work, and one *santa missa* ("Holy Mass") work; during the month, a member is also able to participate for free in the works of any other CEFLURIS church.

6. Many people who use entheogens without identifying with a specific religious affiliation designate themselves as *psychonauts,* "sailors" of mind-space or explorers of inner-space. This lifestyle is widespread on the internet, where individual psychonauts exchange their experiences and advice based on quasi-scientific knowledge (Móró et al. 2011; Schifano et al. 2006). Although psychonauts seek visions and personal spiritual fulfillment through substances like ayahuasca, they tend to prefer to do so in autonomous and less structured contexts rather than in formal religious organizations such as Santo Daime. The ayahuasca tourists discussed in Part 2 are an example of independent psychonauts.

7. According to Taylor and Griffiths (2005, 94–95): "Talking to even a small number of drug users can produce a wealth of information for understanding behavior that often challenges commonly held beliefs about drug use. For this reason, researchers have often been content to dispense with the benefits offered by probability sampling theory and opt for any method that allows them access to sufficient numbers of drug users who exhibit the particular aspect of the behavior of interest. For many purposes the samples that are produced by conventional methods simply do not produce sufficient numbers for any meaningful analysis or may even exclude those who are often of most interest. Drug studies are sometimes criticized by those naive to the issues of this area for their lack of sampling rigor, when often in practice less insight would have been achieved by adopting a conventional approach to sample generation."

8. Bernard (2006, 186; emphasis added) confirms that: "Nonprobability samples are always appropriate for labor-intensive, in-depth studies of a few cases. Most studies of narratives are based on fewer than 50 cases, so every case must count. This means choosing cases on purpose, not randomly. In-depth research on sensitive topics requires nonprobability sampling. It can take months of participant-observation fieldwork before you can collect narratives about topics like sexual and reproductive history or bad experience with mental illness or *use of illegal drugs.*"

9. Employing a similar strategy, the MA thesis of Judith Sudhölter (2012, 8) demonstrates how a focus on "the interrelation between experience and narrative" is the most appropriate entry point for understanding the worldview of European Daime members.

10. In his ontological-existential phenomenology of the meaning of Being, Heidegger (1962[1927], 225–235/492[n.iv]) credits Kierkegaard as "the man who has gone farthest in analyzing the phenomenon of anxiety."

11. In a footnote, Walter Kaufmann justifies his translation of Buber's German: "*Eigenwesen,* literally own-being or self-being, is a highly unusual word. . . . 'Ego' works perfectly in all the many passages in which Buber speaks of *Eigenwesen.* . . . The only serious objection that comes to mind is that those who read Freud or subsequent psychoanalytic literature in English may have irrelevant and distracting associations with the word 'ego'. . . . Buber's *Ich* is closer to ordinary usage than Freud's; and 'ego' in [Buber] is closer to ordinary English usage than is the Freudian 'ego' " (see Buber 1996[1937], 111–12[n7]).

12. In his review of the empirical evidence, psychologist Robert S. Gable (2007) concludes that ayahuasca "used in religious ceremonies has a safety margin comparable to codeine, mescaline or methadone," and the risks of addiction or "sustained psychological disturbance are minimal."

13. "Faith is a state of openness or trust. To have faith is to trust yourself to the water. When you swim you don't grab hold of the water, because if you do you will sink and drown. Instead you relax, and float. And the attitude of faith is the very opposite of clinging to belief, of holding on. In other words, a person who is fanatic in matters of religion, and clings to certain ideas about the nature of God and the universe, becomes a person who has no faith at all. Instead they are holding tight. But the attitude of faith is to let go, and become open to truth, whatever it might turn out to be" (Watts 1977, 37).

Chapter 3

1. In contrast to the well-known entheogenic *phenethylamines* mescaline (found in peyote and San Pedro cacti) and MDMA (alias "Ecstasy"), DMT is part of the category of entheogens called *tryptamines* (see Callaway 2006; Jacob and Presti 2005; Shulgin 2003; Spinella 2001, 350–56; Strassman 2001, 32–37).

2. There remains a controversy regarding whether or not the β-carboline constituents of *Banisteriopsis caapi* are psychoactive by themselves, beyond their accepted emetic and purgative properties (Beyer 2009, 209–11). For instance, it has been demonstrated that harmaline is somewhat psychoactive, and arguably "hallucinogenic" (Naranjo 1967). There are reports that ayahuasca brews made exclusively from *B. caapi* (i.e., no other DMT plants added) have faint mind-altering effects (Beyer 2009, 217–18; Highpine 2012). However, because the most prevalent β-carboline in the vine (harmine) is apparently non-psychoactive, the issue of *B. caapi*'s entheogenic capacity remains uncertain (see Beyer 2009, 215–18). Since the present volume concerns Santo Daime, a religious context in which ayahuasca always contains both DMT and MAOI ingredients, it is this composite recipe that is emphasized herein.

3. https://en.oxforddictionaries.com/definition/us/jungle.

4. There are rising concerns about overharvesting and the future sustainability of the plants used to make ayahuasca, leading to growing calls for protective actions: https://chacruna.net/the-commodification-of-ayahuasca-how-can-we-do-better/.

5. Gates (1982, 10) states that "apparently in *B. caapi* the xylem paren-chyma form wide bands which traverse the secondary xylem and subdivide it into discrete lobes. . . . These lobes are often apparent on the outside of the stem as longitudinal ridges spiraling around the axis." In an exciting new development, a long overdue taxonomic and phytochemical reassessment of the diverse variety of

ayahuasca vine species found in the Amazon is currently underway, spearheaded by an interdisciplinary team of researchers in Brazil (Santos et al. 2020).

6. The Daime rituals I attended in Europe usually cost between US$40 and $80, a price that includes the considerable cost of importing ayahuasca from overseas.

7. Two recent documentary films (*Metamorphosis* [Aronowitz 2009] and *Vine of the Soul* [Meech 2010]) depict Western tourists traveling to the Amazon to take part in relatively safe ayahuasca ceremonies and their subsequent reactions to these maiden ayahuasca voyages.

8. A generic term for healers specializing in plant medicines, which can include ayahuasca.

9. A documentary aired on the "Nature of Things" program of the Canadian Broadcasting Corporation (CBC) proclaims that "the reported success rates for curing addicts at Dr. Mabit's detox centre are quadruple the average" (Ellam et al. 2011).

10. The official full name of UDV is *Centro Espírita Beneficente União do Vegetal* (CEBUDV).

11. Speaking of Irineu Serra's 1912 arrival in the rubber-tapping lands of the western Amazon, Edward MacRae (1992, 48) reports: "At first, he settled down in Xapuri, where he lived for two years, and then went on to Brasiléia, where he worked for three years, in the rubber plantations and then to Sena Madureira, for another three years. During this period he also worked as a civil servant for the Border Commission, created by the federal government to map the Acre frontier with Bolivia and Peru." The MA thesis of Sandra Goulart (1996) is the most detailed account of oral history relating to the birth of Santo Daime.

12. Although the Daime branch founded by Padrinho Sebastião was recently renamed *Igreja do Culto Eclético da Fluente Luz Universal Patrono Sebastião Mota de Melo* ("Church of the Eclectic Cultus of the Universal Flowing Light Patron Sebastião Mota de Melo," or ICEFLU), I refer to it herein as CEFLURIS because this is the standard acronym in the literature on ayahuasca religions and because in the common parlance of European fardados CEFLURIS is still the name used to designate the Daime branch affiliated with Céu do Mapiá (Labate, dos Santos et al. 2010, 210).

Chapter 4

1. Groisman's (2000) fieldwork experience with Santo Daime in Brazil dates back to 1988, whereas during his twelve months of intermittent fieldwork in the Netherlands between 1996–98, even his most experienced Dutch informants had only been involved in the church since 1992.

2. Many of the chapters in the volume I am citing here are reproductions of a special issue of the journal *Fieldwork in Religion*, organized by the same editors

in 2006, then reprinted as a complete volume called *The Light from the Forest: The Ritual Use of Ayahuasca in Brazil* (Labate and MacRae 2008).

3. There is an example of one Dutch church that has historically expressed a penchant for experimenting with mediumship training under the direction of Brazilian mentors (see Groisman 2009, 195–97).

4. Through my subsequent fieldwork with fardados in North America (2012–2015), I can confirm that there are Santo Daime communities holding works in three Canadian provinces and at least thirteen states in the U.S. (University of Toronto, Research Ethics Board (REB) approved Protocol Reference #: 30479).

5. The Umbanda religion is a twentieth-century outgrowth of Macumba, a loose religious affiliation that developed in southern Brazil in response to the need of people from diverse African backgrounds to harmonize their common experiences of subalterity. Eventually, Christian and Kardecist doctrine was incorporated into the already syncretic Macumba in its reconfiguration as Umbanda. Spiritualist beliefs and practices predominate in Umbanda alongside reverence for individual mediums whose primary purpose is to alleviate various health afflictions by conjuring help from a host of Afro-Brazilian, Christian, indigenous, and/or Kardecist characters (Bastide 1978, 322, 332; Bramly 1977, 6–7). In Umbanda, the healing of people's mental and physical sicknesses is carried out when "Umbanda spirits temporarily possess trained mediums": "Enacting the character traits and wielding the paraphernalia typical of the spirit whose possession has been induced, the medium serves as a conduit through which higher spirits offer counsel as to the most propitious means of remedying the supplicant's ills and staving off further spiritual assault. Prescribed remedies range from spiritual cleansing through ritual exorcism, the making of placatory offerings and counter alliances with other spirits, to visiting a doctor or adopting a more positive outlook on life. In acting as its conduit, the medium is considered to have faithfully served his adoptive spirit, furthering the likelihood of future success" (Dawson 2007, 26; see Brown 1994, 94-95).

Associations between Santo Daime and Umbanda continue to this day, as there is now a mutual exchange of practice and belief between the two otherwise distinct religions (see Dawson 2007, 84; Marques Junior 2009). There are now branches of CEFLURIS who actively combine Umbanda spiritualism within Daime ceremonies, a practice known as *Umbandaime*. This combination of the two faiths occurs according to the rationale that complex and often ambiguous visions induced with ayahuasca can be translated by Umbanda mediums into expressions that are personally meaningful for the supplicant (Groisman 2000, 148–150). The emergence of Umbandaime embodies a rebound effect where Santo Daime interpretations of Umbanda, which had originally been introduced into the Daime by Padrinho Sebastião, are being reflected back onto contemporary Umbanda in its southern Brazil homeland. Hence, whereas Padrinho Sebastião had initially sought out Santo Daime as a supplement to his mediumship training, some modern daimistas are now going back to Umbanda to complement their experiences with ayahuasca.

Unlike in Brazil, at least for now the Umbanda-mediumistic practices are muted if not largely absent in most European Daime communities.

Chapter 5

1. While colleagues and informants had advised me to ensure I get a direct boat to Mapiá, my canoe driver left late and so what is usually a one-day trip was broken up by many stops to make deliveries and included a night's stay in the jungle.

2. Original Portuñol: "Pode encontrar com Santo Daime um poder superior. O Santo Daime é uma bebida de poder, uma planta sagrada donde está feita para purificar os aparelhos porque o Daime tem poder de mostrar coises superiores fora de materia; como por exemplo perceber é deus dentro e fora de tudo. Quando nos tememos o Santo Daime é procurar amor, firmar o pensamento é na luz, nos consegemos perceber que existem coisas além da materia: espírito."

3. The leaves of *P. viridis* are seen as the feminine aspect of the brew. *Rainha* is a reference to the "Queen of the Forest," a Marian apparition who initiated Mestre Irineu as founder of Santo Daime (Polari de Alverga 1999, 253).

4. Although lack of access to raw materials means that *feitio* works (where the plants are prepared and cooked into Daime) are not carried out in Europe, many European fardados have participated in such works during their pilgrimages to Brazil.

5. Original Portuguese: "de muito união e também de muito diálogo entre o saber traditional dos povos da floresta (a importância da espiritualidade nesse das plantas sagradas), e também com a ciência, com o estado."

Chapter 6

1. Whereas the EU parliamentary capital is located in Strasbourg, France, and the EU judicial capital is situated in the Grand Duchy of Luxembourg, Brussels is the EU's executive capital because it is the permanent hub of both the European Commission and the Council of the European Union (Hein 2004). Brussels is often "misrepresented as the grey, scruffy and rather boring adopted capital of Europe" (Favell and Martiniello 2008, 137). However, along with the many other profound lessons that ethnographic fieldwork furnishes, one discovers that the beauty of a place is not always a quality that is immediately recognizable; rather, it is the observer that must find out how to appreciate what is being observed. Only after many weeks does one's eye adjust enough to notice the plethora of artistic gems dotted throughout this sprawling metropolis.

2. While anglophones are accustomed to "French Fries," Belgians insist that deep-fried cut potatoes are of Belgian origin. Indeed, the Frietmuseum in Brugge attests to this national heritage.

3. The significance of beer for Belgian culture cannot be overstated. The optimal examples of these delicious nectars are produced by monks at "Trappist" monasteries.

4. Indeed, Christianity gained its initial foothold in Belgium between the fourth and sixth centuries CE (Milis 1999, 7–8).

5. https://www.biodanza.org/en.

6. The two facets of the ECHR Article 9 stated in full (see Doe 2011, 42[n15]):

> "(1) Everyone has the right to freedom of thought, conscience and religion; this right includes freedom to change his religion or belief and freedom, either alone or in community with others and in public or private, to manifest his religion or belief, in worship, teaching, practice and observance.
>
> (2) Freedom to manifest one's religion or beliefs shall be subject only to such limitations as are prescribed by law and are necessary in a democratic society in the interests of public safety, for the protection of public order, health or morals, or for the protection of the rights and freedoms of others."

As Lemmens (1999, 94) point out, religious freedom is ensured in the Belgian Constitution; protections for religion in ECHR Article 9 are supported by Article 18 of the International Covenant on Civil and Political Rights, which "is drafted in practically identical terms."

7. For daimistas, the word *doctrine* (*doctrina* in Portuguese) is the most accurate label for the complex of teachings, rituals, and cosmological principles in Santo Daime. For fardados, the doctrine is not so much a codified system of beliefs as it is a straightforward method or manual for life that is compiled in the ever-growing corpus of *hinos* (hymns), believed to be "received" from the astral Otherworld. Especially in secular Europe, where a general distrust of hierarchical religious organizations is prevalent, I occasionally witnessed newcomers' discomfort with the term *doctrine* because of associations of this word with *indoctrinate.* The hinos do sometimes mention the term *indoctrinate,* but the emic intention of this word in Daime is to encourage the drinker to "indoctrinate" themselves, rather than the connotation of some outside human authority seeking to evangelize and convert others.

Chapter 7

1. *Caminho Rojo* (Spanish for "Red Path/Road/Way") is a "neo-shamanic" (Scuro 2016) or "neopagan . . . pan-Indian" (de la Torre 2015) movement that

combines various entheogens with *temazcal* sweat lodge rituals. Pd. Alfredo and the founders of Santo Daime are not indigenous peoples, but they acknowledge indebtedness to aboriginal South Americans and are wont to maintain close relations with native communities in Amazonia and abroad (see Part VII).

2. The MA thesis written in Spanish by Santiago López-Pavillard (2008) is a good general overview reporting on the author's ethnographic encounters with various forms of ayahuasca ritual in Spain (see also López-Pavillard 2018). Santo Daime members are subsumed into a corpus of interviews that also includes participants in the UDV and independent ayahuasca shamanism. López-Pavillard (2008, 138–141) acknowledges that ayahuasca rituals in Spain attract "seekers" (Spanish: *buscadores*) in search of deeper levels of self-knowledge. But he also admits that more in-depth ethnographic analysis is needed in order to understand how people integrate the lessons of ayahuasca into their spiritual worldview. The present book serves to satisfy this appeal, embarking on a detailed examination of how Europeans interpret their ayahuasca experiences relative to existing religious and secular norms of Europe.

3. This notion comes from the same kinds of esotericist "New Thought" or "Mind Cure" movements that influenced the early founders of Santo Daime (Jones et al. 2005, 3848–52; Meyer 2014; see also Bender 2010).

4. http://www.emcdda.europa.eu/data/treatment-overviews/Portugal.

5. http://www.emcdda.europa.eu/about/mission.

6. In an earlier article, Carsten Balzer (2005) recounted details about ceremonies in Germany held in 1993, which he incorrectly claimed to be the "first steps of the Brazilian Santo Daime religion in Europe." Balzer's article is to be commended, however, for acknowledging in his closing remarks that European Daime communities have progressively matured in the doctrine and the churches have developed a stable atmosphere for administering ayahuasca akin to that found in Brazil.

7. Some of my fardado informants were aware of Weinhold's (2007) article, which concentrates primarily on the "failures" of Europeans aspiring to practice Santo Daime. They criticized this research as giving undue attention to natural growing pains of importing the doctrine from Brazil, thereby neglecting more effectual functions of the rituals. Even so, Weinhold's article is interesting from an etic perspective, in that it surveys how ritual errors highlight some of the tacit social norms in Daime works.

8. Hermann confirmed that these flags do not necessarily indicate places where Daime rituals are being carried out; rather, it is that German fardados have made contact with fellow daimistas who hail from these countries. He said that it is not important for him whether or not countries actually host official Daime works; instead, for him it is crucial that at least one firmado citizen has "lit the fire" of Santo Daime in that country even if they have not yet become a full fardado.

9. The leader of the German Daime groups assured me that his Persian daimista friends were already in the process of creating an alternate Iranian flag for him to put up inside the German Daime works (based on the Lion and Sun logo from earlier in Iran's history).

10. While it is reasonable to presume that German fardados have a more comprehensive social network of daimistas than I do, my fieldwork can only confirm daimistas from the European countries **bolded** in this list.

11. There are no Palestinian daimistas yet, but an Israeli fardado living in Amsterdam advised Hermann that it is better to include the Palestinian flag beside the Israeli flag as a sign of good will and peace.

12. Apparently there is one daimista living in Germany who is from Armenia, which is significant to fardados because Armenia was the first nation to adopt Christianity as its official faith in the fourth century CE (Jones et al. 2005, 488).

13. It is safe to presume that ayahuasca rituals exist on a much larger geographical distribution than is here reported for Santo Daime in Europe. For example, there are already published studies focused on non-Daime uses of ayahuasca in the Baltic States (see Kaasik 2016; Kaasik and Kreegipuu 2020).

14. The recent work of graduate students in the Netherlands is also notable. Written in Dutch, the BA thesis of Jacqueline Braak (2009) considers the long-term significance of *inzichten* ("insights") that daimistas in the Netherlands gain through their ayahuasca rituals. Also written in Dutch, Jazmin Wuyts (2008) conducted a "multi-sited" study of urban Daime communities in Brazil and the Netherlands; like Groisman, she categorizes Santo Daime from an etic perspective as a *religie van de nieuwe tijd* ("religion of the New Age"). More accessibly written in English is Judith Sudhölter's MA thesis in religious studies. In between attending seven works with the Daime church of Amsterdam, Sudhölter (2012, 21) also interviewed eight Dutch daimistas. In her effort to compare and contrast the experiential narratives of Daime participants, she presents direct quotations from her interviewees, many of which evoke themes assessed in the present volume. For instance, Dutch daimistas told her that the ego is illusory, making statements like, "We are the universe that beholds itself," "All is one," and claiming that Daime helps to "dissolve" the ego (Sudhölter 2012, 45–46). However, though she hints at the "mystical" worldview of her informants, her analysis draws its main conclusions from the idiosyncratic distinctions between individual daimistas. Of course, she is right that European daimistas are "highly aware of the relativity of their own story-telling" (Sudhölter 2012, 59) as rooted in the subjectivity of their personal perspectives. As one can see in the quotations found throughout the present book, European fardados frequently attach disclaimers to truth statements (e.g., "for me") to indicate that they are not alleging universal or objective facts. But Sudhölter (2012, 47) makes the exaggerated declaration that Dutch daimistas' "cosmologies differ to . . . a large extent." Through the comprehensive research undertaken herein, it is clear there *are* common elements shared in fardados' worldview—in particular, Daime experiences reinforce the mystical conviction that the differences between individuals and cultures are superficial. Unanimously, fardados downplay these dissimilarities as a dualistic distraction, emphasizing how Daime teaches them to concentrate on elemental connections interlinking all things in the universe.

15. As an exception to pseudonyms, I give Md. Geraldine's true name here, both because of her status as a public figure in the global daimista community and for posterity, since she passed away in Spring 2016 at the age of seventy-one (more than twenty years after her initial brain tumor diagnosis). See: http://www.santodaime.org/site/site-antigo/archives/midia/geraldine.htm

16. Across daimista communities there is a widely held conviction that the Daime "can heal illnesses such as hepatitis, malaria, asthma, and even deadly illnesses like AIDS and cancer" (Schmidt 2007, 128). In more recent fieldwork in North America I met a Hungarian woman with breast cancer who has attended Daime works on and off as a non-fardada visitor for many years. She told me that even though her cancer symptoms are worsening, she is not taking chemotherapy because she does not believe in it. I met another fardada from the United States who has ceased taking her chemotherapy even though she was diagnosed with cancer because she says she finds the Daime is all she needs to maintain her health. Relatedly, I also have encountered some anti-vaccination sentiments among North American daimistas. On the other hand, I met a Canadian fardada who did undergo chemotherapy in combination with taking Daime during her breast cancer and she is now cancer free (for other examples of this variability in opinions, see Schmidt 2007, 174–87).

17. In the concluding paragraph of *The Sickness unto Death*, Kierkegaard (1989[1849], 165) puts it this way: "The formula for that state in which there is no despair at all: in relating itself to itself and in wanting to be itself, the self is grounded transparently in the power which established it. Which formula in turn, as has frequently been remarked, is the definition of faith."

18. See Appendix II

19. Religious freedom is protected in Article 9 of the European Convention on Human Rights (ECHR), a law that applies to all EU member states, which in 2012 included the pre-Brexit UK. Both the ECHR and UK national government laws include a pivotal disclaimer about the limits of religious freedom: "freedom of belief is absolute . . . [but] freedom to manifest belief, is qualified" (Doe 2011, 42[n19]; see also Walsh 2017).

20. Seamus presumes that most of his fellow Hare Krishna followers would not consider him to be a genuine Hare Krishna devotee because he uses a psychoactive substance such as the Daime beverage.

21. Although I can confirm that fardados living in Northern Ireland travel to Ireland to partake in Daime works, at the time of my fieldwork there were not any formal Daime groups holding regular works in Northern Ireland.

22. See http://www.unodc.org/pdf/convention_1971_en.pdf.

23. I leave out Romania, Poland, and Ukraine because my contact with daimistas from these places was too limited.

24. Original French: "Tout le monde a peur . . . et pour nous . . . c'est extrêmement lourd sur les épaules. On se cache . . . Moi les voisins, ils ne savent pas qui je suis; je suis obligé de me cacher. C'est triste. Parce que le . . . Santo

Daime nous donne accès à l'ouverture, et là on est . . . obligé de faire la fermeture. Donc c'est difficile à vivre pour nous. Mais, il faut la patience, le calme, et nous avons l'éternité pour [la justice]. Nous allons continuer de [pratiquer ailleurs] avec humilité et discrétion."

25. The way fardados relate this story of the Santo Daime's founding in Belgium implies Catholic connotations that she (like Saint Peter [*Petrus*, the "rock"]) was among the first to found a church in Europe.

26. While common Western parlance might instinctively refer to Santo Daime as a "sect" or "cult," these terms carry pejorative connotations in English. I use the term "church" (*igreja* in Portuguese) because this is how fardados prefer to label their individual organizations and the global Daime community as a whole.

27. Someone who "makes or repairs stringed instruments"; see https://www.ahdictionary.com/word/search.html?q=luthier

28. Some daimistas are tobacco smokers, but the tendency is to eventually quit. Among veteran Belgian fardados (i.e., those with more than ten years of experience in Daime), I counted only one who currently smokes tobacco. While the volume of alcohol consumed typically declines when people begin to follow Santo Daime, many daimistas do not quit entirely but merely moderate their alcohol consumption so as not to become overly intoxicated.

29. In Portuguese: *energia do mal.*

30. As summarized by Lemmens (1999, 89), those criteria indicating a "harmful sectarian organization" include: "fraudulent or misleading recruitment methods; recourse to mental manipulation; bad physical or mental treatment of the adepts or their family; denial to adepts or their family of adequate medical treatment; violence, including of a sexual nature, to the adepts, their family, third persons or even children; the obligation for the adepts to break with their family, their spouse, their children, their relatives and their friends, kidnapping of children, or their withdrawal from their parents; the deprivation of the freedom to leave the sect; disproportionate financial demands, fraud, and embezzlement of money and goods, at the expense of the adepts; abusive exploitation of the work of the adepts; a complete break with the democratic society, considered as evil; the will to destroy society in favor of the sect; recourse to illegal methods in order to acquire power."

Chapter 8

1. CdSM is also the place where I had my first ayahuasca experience in a Daime Mother's Day work in 2005.

2. This depends on whether or not it is a "dancing" work (for which chairs are not included).

3. One of the few ritual taboos in Daime (which is corrected when violated by a newcomer) is to never place a hymnbook directly on the floor. Instead, if one

needs to set down a hymnbook, it is best to have some other object (even a thin piece of material) between the book and the floor.

4. A French brand of juice glass; one of the veteran fardados who regularly served doses of Daime commented to me about the suitability of the company's Latin name for acting as a vessel of the Daime: *Dura-lex* (Latin: "Hard Law"). The hymns attest to the capacity of Daime to mete out karmic "justice," frankly and directly.

5. The openings of all glass jugs and Duralex *picardie* tumblers (whether they contain Daime or water) are covered with either white doilies or laminated paper marked with a six-pointed star; apparently, this is done to protect the liquid contents from foreign energies that are flowing throughout the salão during the work.

6. *Agua de Florida* cologne (made by Murray and Lanman) is not always included in Daime works, yet in some churches a bottle is used at the resting stations to freshen one's face and hands after vomit purges.

7. see English translation: https://www.erowid.org/chemicals/ayahuasca/ayahuasca_article4.shtml

8. Besides the numerous hinários (full hymnbooks) containing the many hymns received by individual leaders of Santo Daime, most CEFLURIS churches in Europe utilize what they call the "green book" (a publication of Amsterdam's Céu da Santa Maria), while non-CEFLURIS churches print their own hymnbooks (e.g., the CdAI book is modeled after the "green book" with a cover photograph of a rainbow arching over a beautiful mountain scene).

9. The *Our Father* prayer in Daime is slightly modified, with the passive phrase "Thy Kingdom Come" replaced by the more active "Let us go unto Thy Kingdom." Examples of other prayers recited in Daime works are the "Key of Harmony" and "Consecration of the Space" from the Sao Paulo–based Esoteric Circle of the Communion of Thought, as well as the "Prayer of *Caritas*" [Latin: Charity] originally from spiritual mediumship circles in France (see Dawson 2013, 16/63; Labate and Pacheco 2011, 77).

10. As pointed out by MacRae (2006, 397): "More recently, with the growth in number of followers, certain changes were made in the cooking process, in order to use the raw material in a more efficient manner, avoiding waste and cooking some batches a little more, so as to concentrate them for easier transport. Nevertheless, the ingredients used are still the same and differences in concentration are taken into account when the Daime is served during the rituals. But Daimistas have always been aware of the fact that the same dosage of the brew, taken from the same batch, will have different effects in different moments on the same person, so little attention is normally given to matters of a more pharmacological nature. Many Daimistas even dislike giving too much attention to such details, since this suggests a denial of the divine nature of the Daime by seeing it as 'just another drug.'"

11. So hallowed is the Daime liquid that the residue in the bottom of used storage containers is carefully saved to mix with water and then given to houseplants, which is believed to imbue those plants and their fruit with the Daime spirit.

12. Silva Sá (2010, 169–70) describes how different stages of the *feitio* preparation and cooking ritual result in different strengths of Daime tea: "This task is carried out by skilled specialists, who monitor the flavor, visual aspects, and the effects of the drink. Usually, the same liquid is boiled three times, together with fresh raw plant materials on each occasion. This produces a thick dark liquid that is then filtered through a cloth sieve. Depending on the stage of brewing, the Daime is classified as 'first,' 'second,' or 'third degree.' The strongest type is 'first degree,' having boiled three times. The quality of the brew is further regulated through the selective use of raw plant materials—in terms of quantity or of the specific parts of the plant (e.g., the branches of the vine are not as strong as the roots). Some samples can be stored successfully for several years, fully preserving their properties."

Depending on the strength of the Daime liquid being offered, my informants tell me that participants are served between 75 and 150 ml for the first dose. This means that approximately one liter of 2:1 or 3:1 Daime concentrate can provide the first dose for ten people. For the second and third servings, progressively smaller doses of usually stronger Daime are served (sometimes as little as 15ml of 9:1 strength distillate called *mel* ["honey"] for the final dose). Dawson (2013, 54) reports similar measures with his informants, that "weaker doses of Daime tend to be larger (about 80–100ml) than those containing a more potent concentration (approximately 40–60ml)."

13. The common daimista discourse of "energetic" or "subtle" bodies beyond the physical self (see Part VI) parallels the parlance of North American esoteric aficionados that Bender (2010, 95–100) calls "New Metaphysicals."

14. http://www.collinsdictionary.com/dictionary/english/astral-projection

15. Here he refers to ideas discussed by Hadot (2006).

16. Although it is a speculative "hypothesis" with "no proof," Narby's (1998, 124–31) ruminations on plays of light that typically occur with ayahuasca suggest intriguing avenues for future research; daimistas would no doubt commiserate with Narby's (albeit conjectural) notion that Amazonian "ayahuasqueros perceive DNA-emitted [biophotons] in their visions" (see also Barnard, forthcoming; Shanon 2002, ch. 17).

17. As with the entire "Consecration of the Space" prayer, concepts of "lower self" and "Higher Self" are derived from influences of the "Esoteric Circle of the Communion of Thought," of which Mestre Irineu was a member along with the Rosicrucian Order (Labate and Pacheco 2011, 75/78). Dawson (2007, 83–84) recounts how this Euro-Brazilian "esoteric-Spiritist repertoire served Irineu Serra as a template by which he orchestrated the progressive formalization of this community's discourse and practice."

18. I make reference to excerpts of specific hinários throughout this text by citing the person who "received" the hymn and its number within the hymnal. Name abbreviations can be referenced in the Appendix I glossary (e.g., Padrinho Sebastião # 143 = PS#143).

19. In the Amsterdam church CdSM, they follow the Parabens song with the Dutch version of Happy Birthday called "Lang zal hij/ze leven" (Long shall he/she live).

20. At one CdAI birthday work I attended, a fardado was presented with a large purple rock crystal. At CdU the tradition is to give a bouquet of flowers to people celebrating their birthday. I was honored that even though I was not officially a member, after a work at CdU near my birthday I was presented with flowers.

21. In my interview with Md. Geraldine, leader of the Dutch church Céu da Santa Maria and considered the "Madrinha of Europe," she concurred with this characterization of Santo Daime hymns as a "Third Testament."

22. To hear examples, many videos of Daime singing performances can be found on YouTube.

23. See McDonald (1984, 70): "[F]ertile meaning arises from the polyglot elements of *Finnegan's Wake*, Hart Crane, William Blake, or the Bible, Torah, Koran, or any other fractured, layered, polysemic text. The production of meaning, as Eliot saw, can only happen in a complex interaction among the performed word, the act of perceiving it, and the kaleidoscopic contexts produced in that magic moment of connection."

24. Receiving hymns is a prevalent but not uncontroversial phenomenon among daimistas; of course, one of the main sources of renown for figures of past and present Daime leadership is the quality and widely recognized authenticity of the hymnals they "received" from the astral. On the other hand, fardados are often suspicious of inauthentic hymns they believe to be a manifestation of the human ego, perceived as only a mimicry of the style and language of authentic hymns. There is also a tradition of the receiver dedicating or "offering" individual hymns to close friends/family as a gesture of camaraderie and gratitude (Labate and Pacheco 2011, 36).

25. It is common for artistically inclined ayahuasca participants to be inspired to compose music or visual art as a result of their experiences. For a vivid depiction of images encountered through ayahuasca from a viewpoint of indigenous Amazonian myths, see Luna and Amaringo (1993).

26. Original Portuguese: "A miração, que tem entre seus objetivos o auto-conhecimento, a assimilação da mensagem dos hinos, a integração social, a cura espiritual e a salvação da alma . . ."

27. To clarify, daimistas' carefulness about visionary states of mind mirrors the Buddhist approach described in Episode #90 of Jack Kornfield's (2019) *Heart Wisdom Podcast*, entitled "Healing Through Loving Awarness" (beginning at six minutes before the end): "So with deep listening, instead of possessing things, you shift your identity and you become instead the loving awareness itself. You rest in the consciousness. So when my teacher, Ajahn Chah, went to a great Master to tell him about all his meditation experiences (lights and visions and samadhi and so forth), the Master looked back and said, 'Chah, you missed the point: those

are just experiences, they're like movies (a war movie, and a romantic comedy and a documentary, and a super hero movie).' He said, 'They're just movies. The only question is: To Whom Do they Happen? Who is witnessing or seeing all this? Turn your attention back and become the one who knows, the knowing, become the awareness itself. And that is your gateway to Freedom.'"

28. A *wordcloud* shows a visual representation of how often words appear in a text; it does this by showing high frequency words as larger in the wordcloud (but their relative placement within the wordcloud is random). All wordclouds in this chapter were created using the open-source software www.wordle.net

Chapter 9

1. Pd. Alfredo's hymns #34 and #131 provide a representative list of these Afro-Brazilian *orixá* and *caboclo* spirits, and a general list with information can be found at http://www.nossairmandade.com/beings.php.

2. Citing Labate and Pacheco (2004), an official Daime website identifies *Tucum* as the "name of a caboclo, an entity with a lot of power and knowledge. In the native Brazilian Tupi language, tucum is also a name for the palm, *Bactris setosa*, from which strong fiber is made." The same website identifies *Currupipipiraguá* as "possibly a transformation of Curupira, a religious entity from the northeastern Brazilian state of Maranhão, where Mestre Irineu was born"; see http://www.nos-sairmandade.com/beings.php.

3. see www.neip.info/upd_blob/0000/272.pdf.

4. Taylor (2007, 278) frames the theology of *hypostasis* as assuming that "the person is the kind of being which can partake in communion"; in Christianity, hypostasis refers to "the one person of Christ in which the divine and human natures are united"; see http://www.collinsdictionary.com/dictionary/english/hypostasis.

5. The Greek word *kenosis* has been variously transated as "self-emptying, abandonment, self-divesting, renunciation, concealment, reduction, limitation, or humiliation" (Law 2013, 53).

6. Translation from Spanish: Daime theology "is rooted in the Christian tradition of *kenosis* that I understand from its literal sense 'empty,' 'emptying' (*emptiness*), and this can be interpreted as suspension of judgment, suppression of ego so the divine can" take control (Chávez 2008, 157).

7. See also Garrett 2008.

8. Hummingbirds (Portuguese: *beija-flor* [literally, "kisses flowers"]) are thought to symbolize the spirit of the Daime (Greganich 2010, 32). That is why there is a hummingbird on the cover of the book about Santo Daime by Dawson (2013).

9. Such esoteric doctrines and the associated "mind-cure" or New Thought movements were popular in Brazil in Mestre Irineu's time, and thus "these European-derived movements provided a theoretical framework for interpreting aya-

huasca," such as the ectoplasmic "force" that appears within rituals (Meyer 2014, 167–69/193/235–38; Mulford 1888). Further, daimistas' shared inclination to believe in multiple lives is virtually identical to neo-Rosicrucian ideas about karmic reincarnation: "The Rosicrucians hold as a very important part of the teaching the occult doctrine of Metempsychosis, Reincarnation, or Transmigration of Souls, the essence of which doctrine is the survival of the individual soul after it passes from the physical body in death, and its reembodiment in a physical body by rebirth after a sojourn in the resting place of the souls" (Atkinson 2012[1918], 141; see also Bender 2010).

10. Although it is not found often in Daime hymns, the word *solução* ("solution") shows up in hymn #129 of the *Luz na Escuridão* ("Light in the Darkness") hymnal (Paulo-Roberto n.d.).

11. Even though they are not officially part of Santo Daime doctrine, all but one of these people were identified as "Great Spiritual Teachers" by European fardados (see Part VI and Appendices IV and V); the one exception in Masaharu Taniguchi, founder of a Japanese new religious movement called *Seicho-no-Ie*.

12. See Chávez (2008).

13. According to Charlesworth (2010, 413): "As indicated by the caduceus . . . the serpent who brings death is bested by the serpent who brings life. As Moses lifted up a serpent, and Jesus, the Son of Man, was lifted up on a cross, the two serpents are lifted up out of the chalice." This iconography also recalls Chapter 20 in Jung's *Red Book*, entitled "The Way of the Cross", wherein a "transformative image of a black snake appears, winding up, becoming white and emerging through the mouth of the crucified Christ" (Dunne 2015, 13).

14. The Gnostic text *Hypostasis of the Archons*, also known as *The Reality of the Rulers*.

15. http://daimeluzsagrada.org/rape.html

16. Lab tests confirm that this frog's secretion has antimicrobial properties (Beeton, Gutman, and Chandy 2006, 410).

17. See Part VI for a thorough discussion of how fardados esteem a variety of religious traditions.

18. This concurs with the Buddhist teacher Chogyam Trungpa's (1973, 180) advice about *Cutting Through Spiritual Materialism*: "Many people make the mistake of thinking that, since ego is the root of suffering, the goal of spirituality must be to conquer and destroy the ego. . . . That struggle is merely another expression of ego."

19. *A Course in Miracles* talks about how "the ego's whole thought system . . . blocks your joy, so that you perceive yourself as unfulfilled," and how "the removal of blocks, then, is the only way to guarantee help and healing" (Schucman 2007[1976], 132/153).

20. A handy gloss for what daimistas believe ayahuasca teaches them about the unhealthy aspects of the human ego is the following inventory from the "Voice of Christ" narrator in Kempis's (2003[1418], 125) *The Imitation of Christ*: "Lament

and grieve because you are still so worldly, so carnal, so passionate and unmortified, so full of roving lust, so careless in guarding the external senses, so often occupied in many vain fancies, so inclined to exterior things and so heedless of what lies within, . . . so inclined to ease and the pleasures of the flesh and so cool to austerity and zeal, so curious to hear what is new and to see the beautiful and so slow to embrace humiliation and dejection, so covetous of abundance, so niggardly in giving and so tenacious in keeping, so inconsiderate in speech, . . . so quickly moved to anger, so apt to take offence at others, so prone to judge, so severe in condemning, so happy in prosperity and so weak in adversity, so often making good resolutions and carrying so few of them into action. When you have confessed and deplored these and other faults with sorrow and great displeasure because of your weakness, be firmly determined to amend your life day by day and to advance in goodness."

Chapter 10

1. Referring to when an ayahuasca state of consciousness is felt only faintly (rather than inner luminosity of the Holy Light), fardados will call this a "light work."

2. A tribute to Heidegger's (1962[1927], 27[n1]/94) existential concept of *being-in-the-world* as the ontological condition of *Dasein* (conscious awareness of "Being-there") in "everyday" situations. Unlike most metaphysical theorizing in Western philosophy, ethnographic tactics of participant observation in Daime works involve encounters with something wholly other than the "everyday." Hence, the etic neologism *being-in-the-astral* captures daimistas' emic idea about otherworldly states of consciousness induced by ayahuasca in a way that initiates fresh avenues for future ethnophenomenological inquiry.

3. And yet, a Daime leader in Canada alerted me to a rationale for why many fardados refuse to cut the taste with mints: since they consider the Daime sacrament a sacred gift of divine nectar, to scowl and cover up the tang shows a lack of gratitude to the medicine, the bitterness of which is itself a deep lesson about faithful surrender.

4. Along these lines, fardados view ayahuasca Christianity as retrofitting this psychoactive agent to catalyze human transfiguration, opening a portal to the Kingdom of God where communication with spiritual entities becomes possible, like Jesus speaking with Moses and Elijah on the mount of transfiguration (Matt. 17:1–13), daimistas believe they converse with various divine masters while under the influence of the sacramental brew. Much as the Jesus Prayer is employed in Eastern Orthodox mysticism (Ware 1974, 25), rituals with the Daime sacrament comprise a holy device that can lead aspirants to what they construe as *theosis* ("'deification' or 'divinization'").

5. This is most likely related to a Bible passage (Prov. 26:11): "As a dog returns to his own vomit, so a fool repeats his folly" (see also 2 Pet. 2:22).

Chapter 11

1. Historically, it is known that a beverage called the *kykeon* was imbibed in ancient Greek mystery rites at the temple of Eleusis. It has been hypothesized that the ecstatic transcendence achieved in these Eleusinian rituals occurred as a result of the kykeon's containing ergot, a parasitic fungus (*Claviceps purpurea*) containing entheogenic ergotamine that grows on common grain crops. But the inadvertent long-term ingestion of ergot can be poisonous, such as when contaminated grains are used to make bread, leading to public outbreaks of what is colloquially termed "St. Anthony's Fire" (Schultes et al. 2001, 102–105).

2. Borgatti (1999, 122) says "a conventional rule-of-thumb is to obtain lists from a minimum of 30" respondents. To determine whether or not one has collected enough freelists, Borgatti (1999, 122–23) states: "one heuristic . . . is to compute the frequency count after 20 or so lists from randomly chosen informants, then repeat the count after 30 lists. If the relative frequencies of the top items have not changed, this suggests that no more informants are needed" (see also Borgatti 1994, 264).

3. "Smith's *s*" is a statistical measure of the number of informants who mentioned an item relative to that item's average ranking within the freelists of informants who mentioned said item (Smith, 1993).

4. Like the "Great Spiritual Teachers" domain (see Part VI), "sacred plants" is an emic category common to European fardados (they used this term when speaking English). Though many fardados stated that "all plants are sacred," they proceeded to mention specific plants that are prototypical for their domain of "sacred plants."

5. Although a few informants distinguished between the labels Ayahuasca (*B. caapi* + *P. viridis*) and Santo Daime (the same plants called Jagube + Rainha), for the purposes of analyzing salience of plants contained in this beverage, my Anthropac input only counted first mentions of the common mixtures in Ayahuasca/Daime.

6. http://www.emcdda.europa.eu/online/annual-report/2011/cannabis/3.

7. http://www.erowid.org/plants/datura/.

8. Cécile's reference to the esoteric "egregore" concept evokes the metaphysical "theory that there exist immaterial energy complexes that are sustained by human beliefs and emotions, and consequently assume a quasi-independent, personal guise" (Godwin 2007, 63). See also Matthew 18:20 for her paraphrasing of Jesus's words in the Bible.

9. It is interesting to note that the notion of a "house" as a metaphor for the self was also present among Brazilian fardados (Polari de Alverga 2011, 205) and Dutch daimistas interviewed by Groisman (2000, 187).

10. For instance, hymn #35 of Germano Guilherme speaks from the point of view of the Daime spirit addressing a Daime initiate: "If you ask me, I will keep giving you."

11. Jung reread the alchemical *opus* ("work") as wrought on the inner self or soul. Although Jung himself ultimately dismissed entheogens as unnoteworthy for

psychotherapy, there is no denying the archetypal richness of ayahuasca experiences. Indeed, the ways daimistas describe what they get out of their Daime practice are stunningly similar to Jung's ideas about individuation as a mystical process of personal growth and healing (see Dourley 2014).

12. The genitive case reflexive pronoun (see Collins 1985, 243/248). In a more secular sense, fardados' framing of Daime rituals' suiscope function echoes psychotherapeutic connotations of Spinoza's phrase *causa sui* ("self-caused cause"); Ernest Becker's (1997[1973], 36/107) ideas about the egoic *causa sui* project as "a lie that must take its toll as one tries to avoid reality" amplifies fardados' view of Daime works as a method for discovering delusions of their own ego patterns, the subconscious myths of self that drive negative behavioral patterns.

13. http://www.collinsdictionary.com/dictionary/english/scope

14. In addition to their main objective of being charitable to suffering spirits in the astral, mediumship trends in Santo Daime can also be seen as an accessory to the mystical suiscope toolkit of Daime because spirit incorporation offers another vantage point from which to explore hidden aspects of self (see Barnard forthcoming; Dawson 2013; Schmidt 2007). When I attended a workshop with a prominent Daime elder from Oregon, he taught that daimista mediumship is tripartite, consisting of three interrelated parts/aspects: "inspiration, ego, and drama."

15. As seen in Appendices IV and V, a large number of yoga and meditation teachers from India are highly respected by European fardados, a testament to the continuity they see between Daime and the Eastern spiritual traditions.

16. Often employing Jungian language of the archetypal "shadow" (Grof 1998, 21), numerous fardados with whom I spoke claimed that Daime shows the destructive aspects of one's subconscious self, and that by illuminating this major source of life's problems, one can disengage from pathological fixations.

17. 2 Cor. 3:18—"But we all, with unveiled face, beholding as in a *mirror* the glory of the Lord, are being transformed into the same image from glory to glory, just as by the Spirit of the Lord."

18. This notion also appears in the *Course in Miracles* text, which claims that "in this world you can become a spotless mirror, in which the Holiness of your Creator shines forth from you to all around you" (Schucman 2007[1976], 292).

19. The main hymnbook used in Santo Daime works notes how the Prayer of Caritas was channeled on Christmas Day 1873 by the French medium Madam W. Krell.

Chapter 12

1. Scholars also refer to such states as "unitary consciousness," or a "Pure Conscious Event" (PCE) (Gellman 2014). Although he does not credit Underhill explicitly, Richards (2016, 34) construes the psychedelic journeys of clinical patients

as spontaneously occasioning mystical "glimpses of a return to unitive consciousness, coupled with becoming an increasingly compassionate presence in the everyday world."

Chapter 13

Regarding Figure 13.1, here is a description from a similar Blake Image at The Huntington Library, Art Museum, and Botanical Gardens: "In a vision of future times, the warrior angel Michael shows to Adam humanity's salvation through Christ's crucifixion. The nail through Christ's feet pierces the head of the serpent; Death and Sin . . . lie defeated below the cross. Eve sleeps at the bottom of the design; neither Milton nor Blake give her direct access to Michael's prophecy." http://emuseum.huntington.org/objects/60/illustration-11-to-miltons-paradise-lost-michael-foretel;jsessionid=F32E7E58828938D6BCD207F3DCB07873?ctx=634c0e39-7a1c-4c04-ba9d-c3e1dedbdc69&idx=11.

1. Groisman (2009, 186) hypothesizes that: "The presence of *daimista* religious groups in Europe, and especially in the Netherlands, has been sustained by (1) an empirical interest in sharing and appropriating the knowledge based in the experiences of 'indigenous' populations—in particular, focusing on the exploration of modified states of consciousness and shamanism; and (2) a sense of reparation for the revision and exploitative forms of European expansion to the 'New World' in the past five centuries."

2. One sees this with shifts in scholarly study of this cultural category away from the "New Age" label, rebranding these pursuits as "spiritualities of life" (Heelas 2008).

3. The eponymous first hymn of Pd. Alfredo's hymnal is *Nova Era* ("New Era/Age"); it is true that some ideas associated with the New Age have been incorporated as one of many elements in the eclectic and constantly expanding doctrinal inventory of Santo Daime.

4. In his comprehensive historical review, Taylor (2007, 510) observes that "much of the spirituality we call 'New Age' is informed by a humanism which is inspired by the Romantic critique of the modern disciplined, instrumental agent, which was central . . . to the 60s; the stress is on unity, integrity, holism, individuality" (see also Taylor 2007, 380–89/505–35).

5. In great detail, Taylor (1989, 526[n20]) echoes Berlin's identification of the counter-Enlightenment that is often obscured by the dominance of post-Enlightenment emphases on liberalist individualism: "We are also ethnocentric, or at least too narrow in our understanding and sympathy, if we take it as axiomatic that a self is what we ought to want to have to be. There are influential spiritual outlooks which want to have us escape or transcend the self. Buddhism is the best known. But there are also certain strands of modern Western culture, for whom the

demands in any case of the Western identity of the disengaged and independent agent have seemed unreal, or intolerably restricting, or oppressive."

6. "Great Spiritual Teacher/s" is an emic category that Lars made known in early interviews.

7. The vast majority of names on the GST lists were only mentioned by one or twofardados, and so these names were tangential to the core cognitive domain I am seeking to tease out here.

8. Follow-up interviews were conducted with those Belgian fardados who provided the longest lists because social science presumes that "individuals who know a lot about a subject list more terms than do people who know less" (Quinlan 2005, 2; see also de Munck and Sobo 1998, 79).

9. Unless otherwise indicated, birth-death dates of ancient GSTs are derived from the *Encyclopedia of Religion*, 2nd edition (Jones et al. 2005).

10. Tambor de Mina is somewhat distinct from Afro-Brazilian traditions found in the rest of Brazil. While Maranhão "cult houses" are related to some Bahian Afro-Brazilian churches of the "Jeje nation (*nação Jeje*) . . . in Maranhão the Jeje are known as Mina-Jeje and this denomination of Candomblé is mainly associated with the Casa das Minas, a cult house with strong Fon influences" (Parés 2001, 92). The Jeje nation of Brazil is headquartered in two primary locales, each boasting unique interpretations of their shared religious heritage: "The Candomblé in Bahia and the Tambor de Mina in Maranhão, although possessing basic conceptual and ritual similarities (i.e., drum-song-dance ritual format, spirit possession, initiation, sacrifice, healing, celebration aspects), present a wide range of differences in terms of ritual calendars, spiritual entities, song repertoires, drums, dances, costumes, and initiation rituals, making clear distinctions between both cults" (Parés 2001, 100). Most significant for our purposes here are the predilections of Jeje religions, which use drumming and dancing as techniques that encourage an ecstatic trance state. The initiates' altered consciousness is viewed as a way of accessing and communicating with spiritual realms where healing and self-knowledge can be attained, much like in Santo Daime.

11. In this way, it is known that "there exists between the capital city of Maranhão and the *sertão* [wilderness] a transitional zone where the African religions intermixed with the Indian *catimbó*. . . . In the rural areas, the white masters would not allow their slaves to perform their ritual dances, thus making priesthood impossible. All the blacks could do was to cherish and secretly hand down the names of a few especially powerful or revered gods and a nostalgia for their proscribed religion. Any of them who succeeded in escaping or revolting quickly merged with the Indians and found, in the *pajelança*, ceremonies that were in some ways similar to their ancestral ones, notably in the passionate pursuit of ecstasy" (Bastide 1978, 184).

12. The most famous early followers of Mestre Irineu were also from northeastern Brazil and are still revered for the hymnals they received; e.g., Maria Damião from Belém (Pará state), Germano Guilherme from Piauí state, João Pereira from Ceará state, and Antônio Gomes from Ceará state.

13. The mythic life history of Krishna's various incarnations is documented in an ancient Hindu text called the *Bhāgavata Purāṇa* (Jones et al. 2005).

14. Mestre Oswaldo was part of a World War II–era wave of "migrations into the Amazon from the coastal areas during an economic boom, the same process that had earlier brought Afro-Brazilian religions to this area . . . [which then brought] several Umbandista religious specialists and federation leaders who had undergone their religious training and orientation in Rio and São Paulo and who began to organize federations in Manaus" (Brown 1994, 211).

15. It is estimated that Mary was thirteen years old at the time of Jesus's conception/birth, but there are conflicting reports about exactly when she died/ascended, sometime in the first century CE (Tavard 1996, 24–28/210).

16. Merton (2004[1960], 192) wrote this in his journal: "It was like awakening for the first time from all the dreams of my life—as if the Blessed Virgin herself, as if Wisdom had awakened me. We do not hear the soft voice, the gentle voice, the feminine voice, the voice of the Mother: yet she speaks everywhere and in everything. . . . My heart is broken for all my sins and the sins of the whole world, for the rottenness of our spirit of gain that defiles wisdom in all beings—to rob and deflower wisdom as if there were only a little pleasure to be had, only a little joy, and it had to be stolen, violently taken and spoiled. When all the while the sweetness of the 'Woman,' her warmth, her exuberant silence, her acceptance, are infinite, infinite! Deep is the ocean, boundless sweetness, kindness, humility, silence of wisdom that is *not* abstract, disconnected, fleshless."

17. The Marian apparition that appeared in the face of the moon to Mestre Irineu and instructed this first fardado about how to organize the syncretic doctrine of Santo Daime.

18. I do not have statistics but, anecdotally, I met many daimistas who were raised Catholic; most notably, I observed that there are numerous daimistas of Catholic heritage who live in majority-Protestant countries such as the Netherlands, Germany, and England. It would be interesting for future studies to explore the religious background demographics of daimistas in different parts of the world.

19. http://alchemyguild.memberlodge.org/page-311919.

20. Owing to a Catholic legend identifying Mary as the supernatural entity who gave the rosary to St. Dominic in an ecstatic vision—from Latin *rosarium,* rosary means "rose garden"—Mary has many alchemical honorifics, such as "Mystical rose" and "Queen of the most holy Rosary" (note that fardadas wear a fabric "rose" on their white farda); see: http://www.vatican.va/special/rosary/documents/litanie-lauretane_en.html & https://www.rosarycenter.org/homepage-2/rosary/the-rosary-st-dominic/.

21. Triad tests are only useful for "very small domains (12 items or less)" (Borgatti 1999, 142). Anthropac will generate "a series of individually randomized questionnaires in a standard format" to avoid "order bias" (Borgatti 1994, 266–267). These randomized questionnaires are then printed and distributed to informants.

22. Weller and Romney (1988, 16) confirm that "there are no absolute rules for inclusion and exclusion of items. . . . The researcher should be sure that items included in the study domain are known by the vast majority of the informants." Although there is no rigid rule about where to make the "cut-off" of freelist items on the triads, I included the top ten names because these were mentioned with relatively high frequency and they are names familiar to all informants.

23. Including all possible groupings of three items from the top ten items would produce 120 separate triads, which is too burdensome for respondents (see D'Andrade 1995, 48–54). Following Borgatti (1999, 143), I used a "balanced incomplete block or BIB design. . . . In a BIB design, every pair of items occurs a fixed number of times. The number of times the pair occurs is known as lambda (λ). . . . Thus, it is much better to have at least a λ = 2 design, where each pair of items occurs against two different third items." Thus, using a λ = 2 BIB design allowed me to gather the same information about these ten GST items with only thirty triads by taking a controlled and "manageable sample of triples" (Borgatti 1999, 143).

24. It is important to check the "stress" measure for multidimensional scaling (MDS) maps: "Of course, it is not necessary that an MDS map have zero stress in order to be useful. A certain amount of distortion is tolerable. Different people have different standards regarding the amount of stress to tolerate. The rule of thumb we use is that anything under 0.1 is excellent and anything over 0.15 is unacceptable." (Borgatti 1996 [Methods], 31/33). The stress of the MDS produced from Belgian fardados' triad tests had an acceptable stress of 0.121 (see Appendix VI).

25. With triad data, it is necessary to determine that informants actually do share common cognitive models regarding the cultural domain being explored. Thus, one must run a "consensus analysis" on the triad data (Romney et al. 1986). In the consensus analysis for Belgian fardados' GST triads (see Appendix VI), the first eigenvalue was more than four times larger than the second eigenvalue (a ratio of 4:1). This means that the GST triad data are acceptable, since one only need have a 3:1 ratio between the first and second eigenvalues to show that there is sufficient consensus between informants (Borgatti and Halgin 2011, 176).

26. In order to get each informant to focus on one level of clustering at a time, I showed them each hierarchical cluster level sequentially from the most similar to the least similar as they appeared in the hierarchical clustering graph (see Figures 13.2 and 13.3 and Appendix VI). For instance, I showed them the map with only JC and VM circled, and recorded their interpretation. Then I showed them a second page with MI and PS also circled, then one with GD and DL also circled, and so on until they had interpreted each hierarchical cluster level.

27. Wilber (1998, 89–90) uses the following metaphor to depict what he means by the "pre/trans fallacy" that is pervasive in Cartesian ontologies of the modern West: "Freud was a reductionist, Jung an elevationist—the two sides of the pre/trans fallacy. And the point is that they are *both* half right and half wrong. A

good deal of neurosis is indeed a fixation/regression to prerational states, states that are not to be glorified. On the other hand, *mystical* states do indeed exist, beyond (not beneath) rationality, and those states are not to be reduced."

28. As the Austrian philosopher Ludwig Wittgenstein (2001[1921], 89) famously declared: "There are, indeed, things that cannot be put into words. They make themselves manifest. They are what is *mystical*. The correct method in philosophy would really be the following: to say nothing except what can be said, i.e., propositions of natural science . . . and then, whenever someone else wanted to say something metaphysical, to demonstrate to him that he had failed to give a meaning to certain signs in his propositions."

Chapter 14

1. https://newchurch.org/contact/locations/.

2. Swedenborg writes in *Divine Love & Wisdom*: "Every single thing that comes to light in the created universe has such an equivalence with every single thing in us that you could call us a kind of universe as well. There is a correspondence of our affective side and its consequent thought with everything in the animal kingdom, a correspondence of our volitional side with its consequent discernment with everything in the plant kingdom, and a correspondence of our outermost life with everything in the mineral kingdom" (Dole, Cooper, and Rose 2011, 98).

3. In the next sentence, Swedenborg then cites Matt. 8:11–12.

4. For further information, I refer readers to online resources of the *Swedenborg Foundation,* such as this rendering of "regeneration" that would sound very familiar to daimistas: "The will is the part of our mind that moves us, that urges us to action. In the context of regeneration, you could think of our old, unregenerated will as the egotistical part of ourselves that wants everything for itself, that wants all its desires to be satisfied, that doesn't care about anybody else. Part of the process of regeneration is reforming the old will, or, as Swedenborg says, subjugating it so that a new will might be born within us" (see https://swedenborg.com/emanuel-swedenborg/explore/regeneration/).

I would also suggest that the Swedenborg Foundation's *Swedenborg and Life* podcast is quite consistent with the ways daimistas talk about their spirituality, especially the episode called "The Spiritual Battles of Jesus Christ"; see: https://swedenborg.com/spiritual-battles-jesus-christ/.

5. While the prominence of Jesus on fardados GST freelists has necessitated a focus on Christ in this volume, future research might explore more deeply the relations between Santo Daime and other religious ideologies. For instance, I know that a daimista community in the eastern United States holds large works at a Buddhist establishment and a Daime group in western Canada includes a high proportion of Muslim fardados.

6. Fardados are deeply suspicious of hierarchical religious institutions that build up around the GST, which they see as a corruption of the original message. As their doctrine expands, some fardados express concern that Santo Daime may one day become corrupted by the same mistakes of conceit and lust for power.

7. Anthropologist Jane Granskog (2003) links *transmodernism* with emergent *integral cultures* discussed in the previous chapter: "Integral Culture is concerned with values focused on spiritual transformation, self actualization, ecological sustainability, and the worth of the feminine; one that places primary emphasis on personal accountability, taking individual responsibility for finding new creative ways to bring balance and harmony back into a world gone awry."

8. Ray and Anderson (2000, 171) itemize in detail what is meant by the label "consciousness movements": "they include the human potential movement; *psychedelic explorations*; the so-called new spirituality, which is extensively based on quite ancient Buddhism, Hinduism, Taoism, Native American traditions, Celtic practices, and mystical Judaism and Sufism and Christianity, as well as Wicca (which is very old or very new, or both); bodywork, yoga, and the various marital arts; healing practices, including acupuncture, therapeutic touch, and laying on of hands; and a wide spectrum of prayer and meditation."

9. For another example of interfaith perennialist thought in the twentieth century, see Schuon (2013).

10. Following Ray and Anderson (2000, 17), both CC and fardados "are disenchanted with 'owning more stuff,' materialism, greed, me-firstism, status display, glaring social inequalities of race and class, society's failure to care adequately for elders, women, and children, and the hedonism and cynicism that pass for realism in modern society"; at the same time, fardados are like CC in that they "reject the intolerance and narrowness of social conservatives."

11. This idea corresponds to the teachings of *A Course in Miracles*, with its special focus on how every individual can choose to be a spiritual teacher by exemplifying their understanding that all is one and that this finite world is an illusion. Or in the words of the supplementary Manual for Teachers: "Into this hopeless and closed learning situation, which teaches nothing but despair and death, God sends His teachers" (Schucman 2007[1976], Manual for Teachers, 2).

12. As this cosmic momentum is summarized by Dourley (2014, 176): "The pleromatic process is the ongoing cyclical re-immersion of the ego in its return to its source as that source becomes itself more conscious in the ego's return to a consciousness more attuned to its source and so to all that is as an expression of that source."

13. Like the author of the present text, Bucke hailed from southern Ontario.

14. The fardados I met all evinced an affinity for the kinds of ideas associated with Cosmic Consciousness, even though it seemed clear to me that they had never read the classic book of the same name by Bucke (1995[1901]).

15. This thinking matches the scheme of futurologist Willis Harman (1998, 30), who predicted that "transcendental monism" will eventually replace the "materialistic

monism" that has reigned since the Enlightenment: Transcendental Monism "finds the ultimate stuff of the universe to be consciousness. Mind (or consciousness, or spirit) is primary, and matter-energy arises in some sense out of mind. The physical world is to the greater mind as a dream image is to the individual mind. . . . Consciousness is not the end-product of material evolution; rather, consciousness was here first" (see also Granskog [2003]).

16. See the lyrics in the Daime hymn PA#126, entitled "Connected to Nature."

17. This much is stated in hymn #152 of Padrinho Alex Polari's hinario Nova Anunciação [*New Annunciation*], titled "O Daime E O Dharma" ("The Daime and the Dharma").

Chapter 15

For the artwork of Figure 15.1, here is the "public access description" from London's Victoria and Albert Museum: "The Dutch captured the British colony of Suriname during the Second Anglo-Dutch War (1667). Under the West India Company it was developed as a plantation slave society and became a primary destination for the Dutch slave trade. The brutal regime caused high mortality. . . . In 1774 the Scottish-Dutch soldier John Gabriel Stedman witnessed the brutal oppression of slaves during a campaign against the maroons, which he described in his *Narrative of a Five Years Expedition Against the Revolted Negroes of Surinam*. . . . This allegorical image is in the tradition of 'The Four Continents,' in which the continents are depicted as female figures. Blake, the abolitionist, has included gold arm bands on the arms of Africa and America to symbolise their enslavement to the central figure of Europe. However, the fact that Europe is being physically supported by her companions suggests the possibility of a more equitable relationship." See: http://m.vam. ac.uk/collections/item/O127397/europe-supported-by-africa-and-print-blake-william/.

1. https://www.imperial.ac.uk/psychedelic-research-centre/.

2. https://www.philosophyforlife.org/blog/robin-carhart-harris-on-psychedelics-and-the-unconscious

3. https://hopkinspsychedelic.org/.

4. Similar to Kierkegaard's (1989[1849], 87–88) comment that when people are confronted with existential despair "most soon run away," a passage from hymn #13 in Cristina Tati's Daime hymnal *Flores de São João* ("Flowers of St. John") gives this declaration from the perspective of the spirit in the Daime beverage: "All come to look for me, But I drive many to run [away]" (*Todos vêm me procurar; Mas botou muitos para correr*).

5. However, exceptions to this rule against badmouthing other daimistas must surely be made for more serious misdeeds. I did meet one estranged daimista who said they felt "betrayed" by prominent leaders of several European Daime churches, because they say they were ignored when they reported having been a victim of deception and "bullying" by fellow fardados, one of whom "stole" a valuable object

from them during a Daime work. Although I was unable to verify this story one way or the other, it nevertheless raises the spectre of cover-ups and the suppression of dissent; in the case of this one interviewee, their claim that they were cruelly ostracized by their daimista community via silent treatment demands attention from fardado authorities, as failure to properly address such accusations could expose the Daime to charges of criminal negligence in the future.

6. Unlike a journalist seeking sensational scoops, as an anthropologist I am not at liberty to reveal *everything* I saw and heard during fieldwork with daimistas. Other than their drinking of ayahuasca, a substance that is technically illegal, I will remain discreet about other esoteric aspects of Daime because it is not my place to publicize all that daimistas would prefer to keep classified. As summarized by one of my German informants, even though Santo Daime is very open about its beliefs and its use of the sacramental beverage, the doctrine also has "secrets" that must be protected because he believes these would be misconstrued by the outside world. Some of my scholarly colleagues have already revealed these more "secret" components of Daime in their publications (so they are already a matter of public record), but I am uncertain whether or not these authors received fardados' permission to do so. While I want to be as truthful as possible, I believe that sometimes the ethnographer must defer to his/her informants to determine what is safe/unsafe to disclose about their private activities. This omission does not apply to what European daimistas might perceive as uncomfortable or embarrassing revelations, such as the recent appearance of polygamous marriage among some of the Daime leaders in South America (see Cavnar 2011, 29). Instead, it is customary that "most anthropologists privilege their informants' major concerns" by erring on the side of caution when our consultants reveal sensitive information with the "understanding that the secrets will be kept" (Krech III and Sturtevant 1995, 90–91). Of course, as this book outlines, I make an exception to secrecy when it comes to actions that (after careful reflection) I have come to deem as high-risk and/or nefarious.

7. In response to the growing awareness of how charisma and power imbalances can lead to sexual exploitation within psychedelic subcultures, a very helpful *Ayahuasca Community Guide for Sexual Abuse Awareness* has recently been published in multiple languages by the Chacruna Institute for Psychedelic Plant Medicines (Sinclair and Labate 2019), see https://chacruna.net/community/ayahuasca-community-guide-for-the-awareness-of-sexual-abuse/.

8. See: https://erowid.org/chemicals/ayahuasca/ayahuasca_death.shtml

9. http://www.parismatch.com/Actu/International/Chili-un-nouveau-ne-sacrifie-par-une-secte-512012.

10. https://www.lapresse.ca/international/amerique-latine/201910/06/01-5244358-perou-un-quebecois-se-suicide-dans-un-centre-consacre-a-layahuasca.php. A Canadian Daime leader subsequently gave an interview to the *Montreal Gazette* to address public concerns by explaining that such tragedies are very rare and can be mitigated by the careful screening and ritual regulations of the ayahuasca religions: https://montrealgazette.com/opinion/columnists/ahahuasca-conference-aims-to-demystify-and-educate.

11. http://www.cbc.ca/news/world/canadian-ayahuasca-killing-1.3371062.

12. I asked Julia, a veteran fardado from England, about the rumor I heard concerning a man who burned down a building in Japan subsequent to attending a Daime work there. As UK fardados still keep in contact with Japanese daimistas, Julia confirmed that Daime activities are ongoing in Japan amid the heightened scrutiny that the doctrine has received since this tragedy occurred. Despite the alarming implications of this incident, she demurred that "it was just a crazy guy," who should never have been allowed to partake of Santo Daime in the first place.

13. http://afamiliajuramidam.org/english/liturgy/decree.html.

14. As an ethnographer, I can relate to this account because I had some adverse reactions in many of the early ayahuasca rituals I attended (vomiting, chills, intense fear, disorientation). Although I have not passed out during a work (yet), on rare occasions daimistas faint and fall to the ground, a risk that fiscal supervisors are trained to stay alert to so they can catch people before they fall. But not all daimistas go through this difficult initiation with Santo Daime; indeed, some individuals who already have a background in mystical disciplines such as yoga or meditation reported to me that their previous practice had prepared them for Santo Daime, so their first experiences with ayahuasca were blissful; it appears that for many, mystical ayahuasca encounters can be a jarring shock, but for others it is akin to deep introspective states with which they are already familiar.

15. She attends one of the Brazilian-run Daime churches that promotes total abstinence from all psychoactive substances except ayahuasca; this pessimistic attitude about alcohol and smoking does not apply to all daimistas.

16. As Taylor (2007, 264–65) explains, the term *secular* comes from " 'saeculum,' the Latin word for a big tract of time, an age . . . the adjective 'secular,' come[s] to be used in Latin Christendom as one term in a contrast; in fact, several related contrasts. As a description of time, it comes to mean ordinary time, the time which is measured in ages, over against higher time, God's time, or eternity. . . . Or, by an easy extension, 'secular' can refer to the affairs of this world, 'temporal' affairs, and it contrasts with the affairs of the City of God, which are 'spiritual.' "

17. See also Habermas's (2008) article *Notes on Post-Secular Society*.

18. Published in both French and Flemish, the report also discusses the African entheogen *Iboga*.

19. No doubt there will be continued resistance as Santo Daime spreads around the world. For example, I fret about what daimistas might face if they enter territories governed by repressive drug-control regimes in Russia, China, Southeast Asia, or the Middle East.

20. Because they feel under assault, I have heard North American Daime commanders refer to themselves as "protectors," enshrined with responsibility to safeguard the liquid light from being snuffed out by adversarial sociolegal and political adversaries.

21. https://spiritualcare.ca/cascacss_competencies/.

22. http://www.professionalchaplains.org/files/2017%20Common%20 Qualifications%20and%20Competencies%20for%20Professional%20Chaplains.pdf.

23. http://wp.ecpcc.info/about-ecpcc/.

24. https://www.ciis.edu/research-centers/center-for-psychedelic-therapies-and-research/about-the-certificate-in-psychedelic-assisted-therapies-and-research.

25. https://arts.uottawa.ca/cla-srs/en/psychedelics-and-spirituality-studies-initiative.

26. https://www.synthesisretreat.com/about-us (and) https://www.youtube.com/watch?v=49jAyeoWYYE.

27. https://maps.org/images/pdf/Psychedelic-Harm-Reduction-2015.pdf.

Chapter 16

1. Beyond the New Age, a similar and provocative critique is now being leveled at for-profit motives underlying some aspects of the global Mindfullness movement (see Purser 2019).

2. Exceptions being scant mentions of Sitting Bull [#54], Lame Deer [#64], Red Path Chiefs [#67], Black Elk [#125], the Hopi [#138], and the Inca [#160] on European fardados' list and the Maya [#49] on Belgians' list.

3. Here I am thinking of the "attitude of respect and acceptance" demanded of counselors working in the helping professions: "All humans are fallible and possess good and poor human skills or capabilities that may result in either happiness or suffering for themselves and others. Respect comes from the Latin word *respicere,* meaning to look at. Respect means the ability to look at others as they are and to prize their unique individuality. Respect also means allowing other people to grow and develop on their own terms without exploitation and control. Though an accepting attitude involves respecting others as separate and unique human beings, this does not mean that you need to agree with everything [other people] say. Ideally, however, you are secure enough in yourself to respect what they say as being their versions of reality" (Nelson-Jones 2016, 48).

4. A similar ideal of mutual tolerance is endorsed by Canadian public intellectuals. With reference to debates about religious pluralism in secular Québécois society, Maclure and Taylor (2011) recast secularism as the liberalist project to protect citizens' "freedom of conscience."

5. While European fardados do not worship the Daime liquid itself, some of my informants do evince a belief that the physical beverage contains powerful spiritual properties. Like fardados in the Brazilian Amazon, my informants agree that the physical presence of the Daime brew can act as a kind of "talisman product . . . a form of protection" (Cemin 2006, 282).

6. Although what I observed with Santo Daime does not fit with the list of traits usually associated with exploitative religious cults (see http://www.cifs.org.au/CAWCG.pdf), daimistas must remain vigilant to suppress the misuse of their doctrine by nefarious personalities.

7. See Dourley 2014, 65–72.

8. See Dawson 2013, 29–30.

Bibliography

AAA (American Anthropology Association). 2012. "Code of Ethics, Section 1: Do No Harm. American Anthropology Association," November 1, 2012. http://ethics.americananthro.org/category/statement/.

Abramovitz, Rodrigo Sebastian de Moraes. 2002. "Música e Silêncio na Concentração do Santo Daime." *Cadernos do Colóquio* 1, no. 5: 20–29.

Adams, William Yewdale. 1998. *The Philosophical Roots of Anthropology*. Stanford: CSLI.

Adelaars, Arno, Christian Rätsch, and Claudia Müller-Ebeling. 2006. *Ayahuasca: Rituale, Zaubertränke und visionäre Kunst aus Amazonien*. Baden and München: AT-Verlag.

Agar, Michael. 2006. *Dope Double Agent: The Naked Emperor on Drugs*. Morrisvilee, NC: Lulubooks.

Ahern, Patrick. 1998. *Maurice and Therese: The Story of a Love*. New York: Doubleday.

Alfredo. n.d. *Nova Era (New Era)*.

———. n.d. "O Cruzeirinho (The Little Cross)."

Ali, Abdullah Yusuf, trans. 2004. *The Qur'an*. Elmhurst, NY: Tahrike Tarsile Quran.

Almaas, A. H. (2017). *The Alchemy of Freedom: The Philosophers' Stone and the Secrets of Existence*. Boulder: Shambhala.

Alter, Torin. 2007. "The Knowledge Argument." In *The Blackwell Companion to Consciousness*, edited by Max Velmans and Susan Schneider, 396–405. Malden, MA: Blackwell.

Anderson, Brian T. 2012. "Ayahuasca as Antidepressant? Psychedelics and Styles of Reasoning in Psychiatry." *Anthropology of Consciousness* 23, no. 1:44–59.

———, Beatriz C. Labate, Matthew Meyer, Kenneth W. Tupper, Paulo C. R. Barbosa, Charles S. Grob, Andrew Dawson, and Dennis McKenna. 2012. "Statement on Ayahuasca." *International Journal of Drug Policy* 23, no. 3: 173–75.

Andritzky, Walter. 1989. "Sociopsychotherapeutic Functions of Ayahuasca Healing in Amazonia." *Journal of psychoactive drugs* 21, no. 1.

Apud, Ismael. 2017. "Science, Spirituality, and Ayahuasca: The Problem of Consciousness and Spiritual Ontologies in the Academy." *Zygon* 52, no. 1:100–23.

———. 2020a. "Personality Traits in Former Spanish Substance Users Recovered with Ayahuasca." *Journal of Psychoactive Drugs* 52, no. 3: 264–72.

———. 2020b. *Ayahuasca: Between Cognition and Culture—Perspectives from an Interdisciplinary and Reflexive Ethnography.* Vol. 32. PUBLICACIONS URV, Universitat Rovira i Virgili, Catalonia (Spain).Apud, Ismael, and Oriol Romaní. 2017. "Medicine, Religion and Ayahuasca in Catalonia. Considering Ayahuasca Networks from a Medical Anthropology Perspective." *DRUPOL International Journal of Drug Policy* 39: 28–36.

Araújo, Jussara Rezende. 2001. "O Cristianismo e os Fundamentos da Barbárie: Análise do Discurso do Santo Daime." *Paper Presented at the CELACOM—XIX Colóquio Internacional da Escola Latino-Americana de Comunicação.*

Araújo, Wladimyr Sena. 2006. "The Barquinha: Symbolic Space of a Cosmology in the Making." *Fieldwork in Religion* 2, no. 3: 350–62.

Arberry, Arthur John. 2009[1947]. *Discourses of Rumi.* Richmond, UK: Routledge Curzon.

Arendt, Hannah. 1998[1958]. *The Human Condition.* Chicago: University of Chicago Press.

Argento, Elena, Rielle Capler, Gerald Thomas, Philippe Lucas, and Kenneth W. Tupper. 2019. "Exploring Ayahuasca-Assisted Therapy for Addiction: A Qualitative Analysis of Preliminary Findings among an Indigenous Community in Canada." *Drug and alcohol review* 38, no. 7: 781–89.

Aronofsky, Darren. 2018. *One Strange Rock.* New York: National Geographic.

Aronowitz, Keith. 2009. *Metamorphosis.* Mono Blanco Films, USA.

Arweck, Elisabeth. 2006. *Researching New Religious Movements: Responses and Redefinitions.* London and New York: Routledge.

Asad, Talal. 1993. *Genealogies of Religion: Discipline and Reasons of Power in Christianity and Islam.* Baltimore: Johns Hopkins University Press.

———. 1996. "Comments on Conversion." In *Conversion to Modernities: The Globalization of Christianity,* edited by Peter van der Veer, 263–73. New York: Routledge.

———. 2003. *Formations of the Secular: Christianity, Islam, Modernity.* Stanford: Stanford University Press.

———. 2006. "Responses." In *Powers of the Secular Modern: Talal Asad and His Interlocutors,* edited by David Scott and Charles Hirschkind, 206–41. Stanford: Stanford University Press.

Atkinson, William Walker. 2012[1918]. *The Secret Doctrine of the Rosicrucians: A Lost Classic by Magus Incognito.* Newburyport: Red Wheel Weiser.

Bach, Edward, and F. J. Wheeler. 1997. *The Bach Flower Remedies.* New Canaan, CT: Keats.

Badone, Ellen. 1990. *Religious Orthodoxy and Popular Faith in European Society.* Princeton: Princeton University Press.

Baixinha. n.d. "Guia Mestre (Master Guide)."

Balée, William L. 2012. *Inside Cultures: A New Introduction to Cultural Anthropology.* Walnut Creek, CA: Left Coast Press.

Balzer, Carsten. 2005. "Ayahuasca Rituals in Germany: The First Steps of the Brazilian Santo Daime Religion in Europe." *Curare* 28, no. 1:53–66.

Barbosa de Almeida, Mauro. 2002. "The Politics of Amazonian Conservation: The Struggles of Rubber Tappers." *Journal of Latin American Anthropology* 7, no. 1:170–219.

Barbosa, P. C., I. M. Cazorla, J. S. Giglio, and R. Strassman. 2009. "A Six-Month Prospective Evaluation of Personality Traits, Psychiatric Symptoms, and Quality of Life in Ayahuasca-Naïve Subjects." *Journal of psychoactive drugs* 41, no. 3: 205–12.

Barbosa, Paulo Cesar Ribeiro, Luís F. Tófoli, Michael P. Bogenschutz, Robert Hoy, Lais F. Berro, Eduardo AV Marinho, Kelsy N. Areco, and Michael J. Winkelman. (2018). "Assessment of Alcohol and Tobacco Use Disorders among Religious Users of Ayahuasca. *Frontiers in psychiatry* 9: 136.

Barker, Eileen. 1999. "New Religious Movements: Their Incidence and Significance." In *New Religious Movements: Challenge and Response,* edited by Bryan R. Wilson and Jamie Cresswell, 15–32. London and New York: Routledge.

Barnard, G. William. 2014. "Entheogens in a Religious Context: The Case of the Santo Daime Religious Tradition." *Zygon* 49, no. 3:666–84.

———. Forthcoming. *Liquid Light: Ayahuasca Visions and Embodying Divinity in the Santo Daime Religious Tradition.* New York: Columbia University Press.

Baruš, Imants. 2003. *Alterations of Consciousness: An Empirical Analysis for Social Scientists.* Washington, DC: American Psychological Association.

Bastide, Roger. 1978. *The African Religions of Brazil: Toward a Sociology of the Interpenetration of Civilization.* Baltimore: Johns Hopkins University Press.

Bastos, Abguar. 1979. "Culto do Santo Daime [The Santo Daime Cult]." In *Os Cultos Mágico-religiosos no Brasil [The Magico-Religious Cults in Brazil],* edited by A. Bastos. São Paulo: Hucitec.

Becker, Ernest. 1997[1973]. *The Denial of Death.* New York: Free Press.

Beeton, Christine, George A. Gutman, and K. George Chandy. 2006. "Targets and Therapeutic Properties of Venom Peptides." In *Handbook of Biologically Active Peptides,* edited by Abba J. Kastin, 403–14. Amsterdam and Boston: Academic Press.

Belgium. 2014. "Court of First Instance of Bruges (Fourteenth Chamber)." Judgement no. *849.*

Bender, Courtney. 2010. *The New Metaphysicals: Spirituality and the American Religious Imagination.* Chicago: University of Chicago Press.

Benton-Banai, Edward. 2010[1988]. *The Mishomis Book: The Voice of the Ojibway.* Minneapolis: University of Minnesota Press.

Berger, Peter L. 1999. "The Desecularization of the World: A Global Overview." In *The Desecularization of the World: Resurgent Religion and World Politics*, edited by Peter L. Berger, 1–18. Grand Rapids: W. B. Eerdmans.

Berlin, Isaiah. 1979. *Against the Current: Essays in the History of Ideas.* London: Hogarth Press.

Bernard, H. Russell. 2000. *Social Research Methods: Qualitative and Quantitative Approaches.* Thousand Oaks, CA: SAGE.

———. 2006. *Research Methods in Anthropology: Qualitative and Quantitative Approaches.* Lanham, MD: AltaMira Press.

———. 2011. *Research Methods in Anthropology: Qualitative and Quantitative Approaches.* Lanham, MD: AltaMira.

———, and Gery Wayne Ryan. 2010. *Analyzing Qualitative Data: Systematic Approaches.* Los Angeles: SAGE.

Bessire, Lucas, and David Bond. 2014. "Ontological Anthropology and the Deferral of Critique." *American Ethnologist* 41, no. 3: 440–56.

Beyer, Peter. 1994. *Religion and Globalization.* London, Thousand Oaks, CA: SAGE.

Beyer, Stephan V. 2009. *Singing to the Plants: A Guide to Mestizo Shamanism in the Upper Amazon.* Albuquerque: University of New Mexico Press.

———. 2012. "Special Ayahuasca Issue Introduction: Toward a Multidisciplinary Approach to Ayahuasca Studies." *Anthropology of Consciousness* 23, no. 1:1–5.

Beyerstein, Barry L., and Mark Kalchik. 2003. "History of the Psychedelic Experience." In *Hallucinogens: A Forensic Drug Handbook*, edited by Richard R. Laing, 1–36. San Diego: Academic Press.

Bialecki, Jon. 2014. "Does God Exist in Methodological Atheism?: On Tanya Luhrmann's When God Talks Back and Bruno Latour." *Anthropology of consciousness* 25, no. 1: 32–52.

BIBLE. https://www.biblegateway.com.

Biehl, João, and Amy Moran-Thomas. 2009. "Symptom: Subjectivities, Social Ills, Technologies." *Annual Review of Anthropology* 38, no. 1: 267–88.

Bilhimer, M. H., Schult, R. F., Higgs, K. V., Wiegand, T. J., Gorodetsky, R. M., and Acquisto, N. M. 2018. "Acute Intoxication Following Dimethyltryptamine Ingestion." *Case Reports in Emergency Medicine* 2018: 1–3.

Blain, Jenny. 2002. *Nine Worlds of Seid-Magic: Ecstasy and Neo-Shamanism in Northern European Paganism.* London and New York: Routledge.

Blainey, Marc G. 2010. "The Future of a Discipline: Considering the Ontological/Methodological Future of the Anthropology of Consciousness, Part II: Towards an Ethnometaphysics of Consciousness: Suggested Adjustments in SAC's Quest to Reroute the Main (Stream)." *Anthropology of Consciousness* 21, no. 2: 113–38.

———. 2015. "Forbidden Therapies: Santo Daime, Ayahuasca, and the Prohibition of Entheogens in Western Society." *Journal of Religion and Health* 54, no. 1: 287–302.

———. 2016a. "Groundwork for the Anthropology of Belgium: An Overlooked Microcosm of Europe." *Ethnos* 81, no. 3: 478–507.

———. 2016b. "Techniques of Luminosity: Iron-Ore Mirrors and Entheogenic Shamanism among the Ancient Maya." In *Manufactured Light: Mirrors in the Mesoamerican Realm*, edited by Emiliano Gallaga and Marc G. Blainey, 179–206. Boulder: University Press of Colorado.

Blaser, Mario. 2013. "Ontological Conflicts and the Stories of Peoples in Spite of Europe: Toward a Conversation on Political Ontology." *Current Anthropology* 54, no. 5: 547–68.

———. 2014. "Ontology and Indigeneity: On the Political Ontology of Heterogeneous Assemblages." *Cultural Geographies* 21, no. 1: 49–58.

———. 2016. "Is Another Cosmopolitics Possible?" *Cultural Anthropology* 31, no. 4: 545–70.

Blavatsky, Helena P. 1891. *Glossary of Theosophical Terms Used in The Key to Theosophy*. London: Theosophical Publishing Society.

Blom, J. C. H., and E. Lamberts. 1999. "Epilogue: Unity and Diversity in the Low Countries." In *History of the Low Countries*, edited by J. C. H. Blom and Emiel Lamberts, 471–85. New York: Berghahn Books.

Bogers, H. (1999). *Words from the Earth & the Astral*. Netherlands: Self-Published booklet.

Boggan, S. 2008. "Santo Daime: The Drug-Fuelled Religion." *The Times*, April 7.

Borgatti, Stephen P. 1991. "ANTHROPAC." *Anthropology News* 32, no. 2: 2.

———. 1994. "Cultural Domain Analysis." *Journal of Quantitative Anthropology* 4: 261–78.

———. 1996. *ANTHROPAC 4.0 User's Guide*. Natick, MA: Analytic Technologies.

———. 1999. "Elicitation Techniques for Cultural Domain Analysis." In *Enhanced Ethnographic Methods: Audiovisual Techniques, Focused Group Interviews, and Elicitation Techniques (The Ethnographer's Toolkit, Volume 3)*, edited by Jean J. Schensul, Margaret D. Lecompte, Bonnie K. Nastasi, and Stephen P. Borgatti, 115–51. Walnut Creek, CA: Altamira Press.

———, and Daniel S. Halgin. 2011. "Consensus Analysis." In *A Companion to Cognitive Anthropology*, edited by David B. Kronenfeld, Giovanni Bennardo, Victor C. de Munck, and Michael D. Fischer, 171–90. Malden, MA: Wiley-Blackwell.

Bourgogne, Ghislaine. 2011. "One Hundred Days of Ayahuasca in France: The Story of a Legal Decision." In *The Internationalization of Ayahuasca*, edited by B. C. Labate and KH. Jungaberle, 353–63. Berlin: Lit Verlag.

Bourgois, P. 1999. "Theory, Method, and Power in Drug and HIV-Prevention Research: A Participant-Observer's Critique." *Substance Use & Misuse* 34, 14: 2155–72.

———. 2003. *In Search of Respect: Selling Crack in El Barrio*. Cambridge: Cambridge University Press.

———, and Jeff Schonberg. 2009. *Righteous Dopefiend*. Berkeley: University of California Press.

Bouso, José Carlos, and Jordi Riba. 2014. "Ayahuasca and the Treatment of Drug Addiction." In *The Therapeutic Use of Ayahuasca*, edited by Beatriz Caiuby Labate and Clancy Cavnar, 95–110. Berlin: Springer-Verlag.

Bouso, José Carlos, and Constanza Sánchez-Avilés. 2020. "Traditional Healing Practices Involving Psychoactive Plants and the Global Mental Health Agenda: Opportunities, Pitfalls, and Challenges in the 'Right to Science' Framework." *Health and Human Rights* 22, no. 1: 145–50.

Boyer, Pascal. 2008. "Being Human: Religion: Bound to Believe?" *Nature* 455 (7216): 1038–39.

Braak, Jacqueline. 2009. "Inzicht in Ayahuasca." BA Thesis: Religiestudies, Universiteit van Amsterdam.

Brabec de Mori, Bernd. 2011. "Tracing Hallucinations: Contributing to a Critical Ethnohistory of Ayahuasca Usage in the Peruvian Amazon." In *The Internationalization of Ayahuasca*, edited by B. C. Labate and KH. Jungaberle, 23–47. Berlin: Lit Verlag.

Bramly, Serge. 1977. *Macumba: The Teachings of Maria-Jose, Mother of the Gods*. New York: St. Martin's Press.

Brissac, Sérgio. 2006. "An Approach to the Religious Experience of Participants of the União Do Vegetal." *Fieldwork in Religion* 2, no. 3: 319–49.

Bromley, David G. 2009. "Making Sense of Scientology: Prophetic, Contractual Religion." In *Scientology*, edited by James R. Lewis, 83–102. New York: Oxford University Press.

Bronfman, Jeffrey. 2011. "The Legal Case of the União do Vegetal vs. The Government of The United States." In *The Internationalization of Ayahuasca*, edited by B. C. Labate and KH. Jungaberle, 287–300. Berlin: Lit Verlag.

Brown, Diana DeG. 1994. *Umbanda: Religion and Politics in Urban Brazil*. New York: Columbia University Press.

Brown, Jerry B., and Julie M. Brown. 2016. *The Psychedelic Gospels: The Secret History of Hallucinogens in Christianity*. Rochester, VT: Park Street Press.

———. 2019. "Entheogens in Christian Art: Wasson, Allegro, and the Psychedelic Gospels." *Journal of Psychedelic Studies*: 1–22.

Brown, Michael F. 1994. "Who Owns What Spirits Share—Reflections on Commodification and Intellectual Property in New Age America." *PoLAR: Political and Legal Anthropology Review* 17, no. 7: 7–18.

———. 1997. *The Channeling Zone: American Spirituality in an Anxious Age*. Cambridge: Harvard University Press.

———. 2009. *Who Owns Native culture?* Cambridge: Harvard University Press.

Bruce, Steve. 1992. *Religion and Modernization: Sociologists and Historians Debate the Secularization Thesis*. Oxford and New York: Clarendon Press, Oxford University Press.

Buber, Martin. 1996[1937]. *I and Thou*. New York: Touchstone.

Bucke, Richard Maurice. 1995[1901]. *Cosmic Consciousness: Classic Investigation of the Development of Man's Mystic Relation to the Infinite*. New York: Penguin.

Buckser, Andrew. 1999. "Modern Identities and the Creation of History: Stories of Rescue among the Jews of Denmark." *Anthropological Quarterly* 72, no. 1: 1–17.

Budriūnaitė, Agnė 2009. "The Knight of Faith—Between Existentialism and Mysticism." *Logos (Lithuania)* 61: 31–42.

Bunzl, Matti. 2005. "Methods and Politics." *American Ethnologist* 32, no. 4: 533–37.

Burger, Richard Lewis. 1992. *Chavin and the Origins of Andean Civilization*. London: Thames and Hudson.

Burroughs, William Seward, and Allen Ginsberg. 1968. *The Yage Letters*. San Francisco: City Lights Books.

Calabrese, Joseph D. 2008. "Clinical Paradigm Clashes: Ethnocentric and Political Barriers to Native American Efforts at Self-Healing." *Ethos* 36, no. 3: 334–53.

Calabrese, Joseph D. 2013. *A Different Medicine: Postcolonial Healing in the Native American Church*. New York: Oxford University Press.

Callaway, Jace C. 2006. "Phytochemistry and Neuropharmacology of Ayahuasca." In *Sacred Vine of Visions: Ayahuasca*, edited by R Meltzer, 94–116. Rochester, VT: Park Street Press.

———, and Charles S. Grob. 1998. "Ayahuasca Preparations and Serotonin Reuptake Inhibitors: A Potential Combination for Severe Adverse Interactions." *Journal of psychoactive drugs* 30, no. 4: 367–69.

Cannell, Fenella. 2006. "Introduction." In *The Anthropology of Christianity*, edited by Fenella Cannell, 1–50. Durham: Duke University Press.

———. 2010. "The Anthropology of Secularism." *Annual Review of Anthropology* 39: 85–100.

Carhart-Harris, R. L., and K. J. Friston. 2019. "REBUS and the Anarchic Brain: Toward a Unified Model of the Brain Action of Psychedelics. *Pharmacological reviews* 71, no. 3: 316–44.

Carhart-Harris, R. L., D. Erritzoe, E. Haijen, M. Kaelen, and R. Watts. 2018. "Psychedelics and Connectedness." *Psychopharmacology* 235, no. 2: 547–50.

Carlini, E. A., and Lucas O. Maia. 2017. "Plant and Fungal Hallucinogens as Toxic and Therapeutic Agents." In *Plant Toxins*, edited by Célia R. Carlini P. Gopalakrishnakone, Rodrigo Ligabue-Braun, 37–80. Netherlands: Springer.

Carmody, Denise Lardner, and John Carmody. 1996. *Mysticism: Holiness East and West*. New York: Oxford University Press.

Castaneda, Carlos. 2016[1968]. *The Teachings of Don Juan; A Yaqui Way of Knowledge*. Berkeley: University of California Press.

Cavnar, Clancy. 2011. *The Effects of Participation in Ayahuasca Rituals on Gays' and Lesbians' Self Perception*. PsyD Thesis, John F. Kennedy Graduate School of Professional Psychology, Pleasant Hill, CA.

Cécile. n.d. *Doçura da Luz* ("Sweetness of the Light").

CEFLURIS. 1997. *Norms of Ritual.* Vila Ceu do Mapia, Amazonas, Brazil.
———. n.d. *Guidelines for Guardians.* Unpublished Manuscript.
Cemin, Arneide. 1998. *Ordem, Xamanismo e D·Diva:O Poder do Santo Daime,* PhD Thesis, Social Anthropology, Universidade de São Paulo, São Paulo, Brazil.
———. 2006. "The Rituals of Santo Daime: 'Systems of Symbolic Constructions.'" *Fieldwork in Religion* 2, no. 3: 256–85.
———. 2010. "The Rituals of Santo Daime: Systems of Symbolic Constructions." In *Ayahuasca, Ritual, and Religion in Brazil,* edited by Beatriz Caiuby Labate and Edward Macrae, 39–64. London and Oakville, CT: Equinox.
Central Intelligence Agency, United States. 2008. *CIA World Factbook (2008).* Available from http://www.credoreference.com/book/cia.
Charlesworth, J. H. (2010). *The Good and Evil Serpent: How a Universal Symbol Became Christianized.* New Haven: Yale University Press.
Chávez, Maurici Genet Guzmán. 2008. Kenosis o la Idea de Dios en Mí en el Ritual del Santo Daime. *Ciências Sociais Unisinos* 44, no. 2: 157–61.
Chelini-Pont, Blandine. 2005. "INTERNATIONAL LAW AND RELIGION SYMPOSIUM—Religion in the Public Sphere: Challenges and Opportunities." *Brigham Young University Law Review* 3: 611–27.
Chryssides, George D., and Margaret Z. Wilkins. 2014. *Christians in the Twenty-first Century.* New York: Routledge.
Chuchiak IV, John F. 2012. *The Inquisition in New Spain, 1536–1820: A Documentary History.* Baltimore: Johns Hopkins University Press.
CIAOSN/IACSSO. 2010. *Rapport bisannuel / Tweejaarlijks verslag.* Brussels, Belgium: Centre d'Information et d'Avis sur les Organisations Sectaires Nuisibles / Informatie- en Adviescentrum inzake Schadelijke Sektarische Organisaties.
Clark, Carlton F. "Perk." 1998. "Transpersonal Group Psychotherapy: Theory, Method, and Community." *Journal for Specialists in Group Work,* 23, no. 4: 350–71.
Clark, Walter Houston. 1969. *Chemical Ecstasy; Psychedelic Drugs and Religion.* New York: Sheed and Ward.
Coleman, Simon. 2000. *The Globalisation of Charismatic Christianity Spreading the Gospel of Prosperity.* Cambridge and New York: Cambridge University Press.
Collier, Richard. 1968. *The River that God Forgot; The Story of the Amazon Rubber Boom.* New York: Dutton.
Collins, John F. 1985. *A Primer of Ecclesiastical Latin.* Washington, DC: Catholic University of America Press.
Corbett, M. K. 1983. "Ashmole and the Pursuit of Alchemy: The Illustrations to the Theatrum Chemicum Britannicum, 1652." *The Antiquaries Journal* 63, no. 2: 326–36.
Cormier, Zoe. 2015. "No Link Found between Psychedelics and Psychosis." *Nature News* https://www.nature.com/news/no-link-found-between-psychedelics-and-psychosis-1.16968.

Cougar, Michael. 2005. *An Investigation of Personal Transformations and Psychoactive Plant Use in Syncretic Ritual Ceremonies in a Brazilian Church*. PhD thesis, Institute of Transpersonal Psychology, Palo Alto, CA.

Course, Magnus. 2010. "Of Words and Fog: Linguistic Relativity and Amerindian Ontology." *Anthropological theory* 10, no. 3: 247–63.

Crick, Francis. 1966. "Letter to the Editor." *Varsity, the University of Cambridge newspaper (The Wellcome Library)*.

Cross, John of the. 2003[1619]. *Dark Night of the Soul*. Mineola, NY: Dover.

———. 2010[1618]. *Ascent of Mount Carmel*. Brewster, MA: Paraclete Press.

Csordas, Thomas J. 1997. *The Sacred Self A Cultural Phenomenology of Charismatic Healing*. Berkeley, Los Angeles, and London: University of California Press.

———. 2004. "Asymptote of the Ineffable: Embodiment, Alterity, and the Theory of Religion." *Current Anthropology* 45, no. 2: 163–85.

———. 2007. "Introduction: Modalities of Transnational Transcendence." *Anthropological Theory* 7, no. 3: 259–72.

Culp, John. 2009. "Panentheism." In *The Stanford Encyclopedia of Philosophy*, edited by Edward N. Zalta. https://plato.stanford.edu/entries/panentheism/.

Dalai Lama. 2005. *The Essential Dalai Lama: His Important Teachings*. New York: Penguin.

D'Andrade, Roy. 1995. *The Development of Cognitive Anthropology*. Cambridge: Cambridge University Press.

Davie, Grace. 2006. "Is Europe an Exceptional Case?" *Hedgehog Review* 8, no. 1/2: 23–34.

———. 2014. "Thinking Sociologically about Religion: A Step Change in the Debate?" In *Sociological Theory and the Question of Religion*, edited by Andrew McKinnon and Marta Trzebiatowska, 19–32. Surrey, UK: Ashgate.

Davies, Norman. 1996. *Europe: A History*. Oxford and New York: Oxford University Press.

Davis, Alan K., John M. Clifton, Eric G. Weaver, Ethan S. Hurwitz, Matthew W. Johnson, and Roland R. Griffiths. 2020. "Survey of Entity Encounter Experiences Occasioned by Inhaled N, N-dimethyltryptamine: Phenomenology, Interpretation, and Enduring Effects." *Journal of Psychopharmacology* 34, no. 9: 1008–20.

Davis, Wade. 1995. "Ethnobotany: An Old Practice, a New Discipline." In *Ethnobotany: Evolution of a Discipline*, edited by Richard Evans Schultes and Siri Von Reis, 40–51. Portland, OR: Dioscorides Press.

———. 1996. *One River: Explorations and Discoveries in the Amazon Rain Forest*. New York: Simon and Schuster.

Dawkins, Richard. 2006. *The God Delusion*. Boston: Houghton Mifflin.

Dawson, Andrew. 2007. *New Era, New Religions: Religious Transformation in Contemporary Brazil*. Aldershot, England and Burlington, VT: Ashgate.

———. 2010. "Positionality and Role-Identity in a New Religious Context: Participant Observation at Ceu do Mapia." *Religion* 40, no. 3: 173–81.

———. 2013. *Santo Daime: A New World Religion*. London: Bloomsbury.

Dawson, Lorne L. 2003. "Who Joins New Religious Movements and Why: Twenty Years of Research and What Have We Learned?" In *Cults and New Religious Movements: A Reader*, edited by Lorne L. Dawson, 116–30. Malden, MA: Blackwell.

de Assis, Glauber Loures. 2020. "Mestre Irineu: A Black Man Who Changed the History of Ayahuasca." *Chacruna—Inclusion & Diversity*, August 13, 2020. https://chacruna.net/mestre-irineu-ayahuasca/.

De Botton, Alain. 2012. *Religion for Atheists: A Non-Believer's Guide to the Uses of Religion*. New York: Pantheon Books.

de la Torre, Renée. 2015. "Red Path (Camino Rojo)." In *Encyclopedia of Latin American Religions*, edited by Henri Gooren, 1–5. https://link.springer.com/referenceworkentry/10.1007/978-3-319-08956-0_8-1.

De Mille, Richard. 1976. *Castaneda's Journey: The Power and the Allegory*. Santa Barbara: Capra Press.

de Munck, Victor C., and Elisa Janine Sobo. 1998. *Using Methods in the Field: A Practical Introduction and Casebook*. Walnut Creek, CA: AltaMira Press.

Dean, Warren. 1987. *Brazil and the Struggle for Rubber: A Study in Environmental History*. Cambridge and New York: Cambridge University Press.

Dente, Karen. 2011. "Disputed EU Herbal Medicine Rules Take Force." *Nature Medicine* 17, no. 6: 636.

Desjarlais, Robert, and C. Jason Throop. 2011. "Phenomenological Approaches in Anthropology." *Annual Review of Anthropology* 40: 87–102.

Desjarlais, Robert R. 1992. *Body and Emotion: The Aesthetics of Illness and Healing in the Nepal Himalayas*. Philadelphia: University of Pennsylvania Press.

Dias Junior, Walter. 1991. "O Culto ao Santo Daime: Um Paradoxo da Modernidade?" ("The Cult of Santo Daime: A Paradox of Modernity?"). *Electronic document: NEIP—Núcleo de Estudos Interdisciplinares sobre Psicoativos* www.neip.info/downloads/walter_1.pdf.

———. 1992. *O Império de Juramidam nas Batalhas do Astral: Uma Cartografia do Imaginário no Culto do Santo Daime*. Master's Thesis in Anthropology, São Paulo, Pontifica Universidade Católica.

Dobbelaere, Karel. 2008. "Two Different Types of Manifest Secularization: Belgium and France Compared." In *The Centrality of Religion in Social Life: Essays in Honour of James A. Beckford*, edited by Eileen Barker and James A. Beckford, 69–82. Burlington, VT: Ashgate.

Dobkin de Rios, Marlene. 1972. *Visionary Vine: Psychedelic Healing in the Peruvian Amazon*. San Francisco: Chandler.

———. 1984. *Hallucinogens, Cross-Cultural Perspectives*. Albuquerque: University of New Mexico Press.

————. 2009. *The Psychedelic Journey of Marlene Dobkin de Rios: 45 Years with Shamans, Ayahuasqueros, and Ethnobotanists*. Rochester, Vt.: Park Street Press.

Dobkin de Rios, Marlene, Charles S. Grob, Enrique Lopez, Dartiu Xavier da Silviera, Luisa K. Alonso, and Evelyn Doering-Silveira. 2005. "Ayahuasca in Adolescence: Qualitative Results." *Journal of Psychoactive Drugs* 37, no. 2: 135–39.

Dobkin de Rios, Marlene, and Roger Rumrrill. 2008. *A Hallucinogenic Tea, Laced with Controversy: Ayahuasca in the Amazon and the United States*. Westport: Praeger.

Doe, Norman. 2011. *Law and Religion in Europe: a Comparative Introduction*. Oxford and New York: Oxford University Press.

Doering-Silveira, Evelyn, Charles S. Grob, Marlene Dobkin de Rios, Enrique Lopez, Luisa K. Alonso, Cristiane Tacla, and Dartiu Xavier Da Silveira. 2005. "Report on Psychoactive Drug Use Among Adolescents Using Ayahuasca Within a Religious Context." *Journal of Psychoactive Drugs* 37, no. 2: 141–44.

Dolder, P. C., Y. Schmid, F. Muller, S. Borgwardt, and M. E. Liechti. 2016. "LSD Acutely Impairs Fear Recognition and Enhances Emotional Empathy and Sociality." *Neuropsychopharmacology* 41, no. 11: 2638–46.

Dole, George F., Lisa Hyatt Cooper, and Jonathan S. Rose (2011). *A Swedenborg Sampler: Selections from Heaven and Hell, Divine Love and Wisdom, Divine Providence, True Christianity, and Secrets of Heaven*. West Chester, PA: Swedenborg Foundation.

dos Santos, Rafael Guimarães. 2010. "Toxicity of Chronic Ayahuasca Administration to the Pregnant Rat: How Relevant Is It Regarding the Human, Ritual Use of Ayahuasca?" *Birth Defects Research Part B: Developmental and Reproductive Toxicology* 89, no. 6: 533–35.

————. 2013a. "Safety and Side Effects of Ayahuasca in Humans—An Overview Focusing on Developmental Toxicology." *Journal of Psychoactive Drugs* 45, no. 1: 68–78.

————. 2013b. "A Critical Evaluation of Reports Associating Ayahuasca with Life-Threatening Adverse Reactions." *Journal of Psychoactive Drugs* 45, no. 2: 179–88.

Dos Santos, Rafael G., Fermanda M. Balthazar, José C. Bouso, and Jaime E. C. Hallak. 2016. "The Current State of Research on Ayahuasca: A Systematic Review of Human Studies Assessing Psychiatric Symptoms, Neuropsychological Functioning, and Neuroimaging." *Journal of Psychopharmacology* 30, no. 12: 1230–47.

dos Santos, R., J. Landeira-Fernandez, R. J. Strassman, V. Motta, and A. P. Cruz. 2007. "Effects of Ayahuasca on Psychometric Measures of Anxiety, Panic-like, and Hopelessness in Santo Daime Members." *Journal of Ethnopharmacology* 112, no. 3: 507–13.

Dourley, John P. 2014. *Jung and his Mystics: In the End It All Comes to Nothing*. New York: Routledge.

Doyle, Richard. 2012. "Healing with Plant Intelligence: A Report from Ayahuasca." *Anthropology of Consciousness* 23, no. 1: 28–43.

Droogers, André, and Sidney M. Greenfield. 2001. "Recovering and Reconstructing Syncretism." In *Reinventing Religions: Syncretism and Transformation in Africa and the Americas*, edited by Sidney M. Greenfield and André Droogers, 21–42. Oxford: Rowman and Littlefield.

Dunne, C. 2015. *Carl Jung: Wounded Healer of the Soul*. New York: Watkins.

Durkheim, Émile. 1915. *The Elementary Forms of the Religious Life, a Study in Religious Sociology*. London and New York: G. Allen and Unwin, Macmillan.

Dyck, Erika. 2008. *Psychedelic Psychiatry: LSD from Clinic to Campus*. Baltimore: Johns Hopkins University Press.

Eade, John, and Michael J. Sallnow. 2013. *Contesting the Sacred: The Anthropology of Pilgrimage*. Eugene, OR: Wipf and Stock.

Easwaran, Eknath, trans. 2004. *Bhagavad Gita*. Boston: Shambhala.

Eberle, Thomas S. 2010. "The Phenomenological Life-World Analysis and the Methodology of the Social Sciences." *Human Studies* 33: 123–39.

———. 2014. "Phenomenology as a Research Method." In *The Sage Handbook of Qualitative Data Analysis*, edited by U. Flick, 184–202. Thousand Oaks, CA: SAGE.

Eisenstein, Charles. 2011. *Sacred Economics: Money, Gift, and Society in the Age of Transition*. Berkeley: Evolver Editions.

Eliade, Mircea. 1964. *Shamanism: Archaic Techniques of Ecstasy*. Princeton: Princeton University Press.

Ellam, Mark, Jeronimo M. M., and Robin McKenna. 2011. The Jungle Prescription. The Nature of Things (Canadian Broadcasting Corporation). Canada.

Ellenberger, Henri F. 1968. "The Concept of Creative Illness." *Psychoanalytic review* 55, no. 3: 442–56.

Ellens, J. Harold, and Thomas B. Roberts. 2015. *The Psychedelic Policy Quagmire: Health, Law, Freedom, and Society*. Santa Barbara: Praeger; Imprint of ABC-CLIO.

EMCDDA (European Monitoring Centre for Drugs and Drug Addiction). 2011. *Annual Report 2011: The State of the Drug Problem in Europe*. Luxembourg: Office for Official Publications of the European Communities.

Esslemont, J. E. 2006[1923]. *Bahá'u'lláh and the New Era: An Introduction to the Bahá'í Faith*. Wilmette, IL: Bahá'í Pub. Trust.

European Commission. 2005. *Social Values, Science, and Technology (Special Eurobarometer 225)*. Luxembourg: Office for Official Publications of the European Communities.

———. 2010. *Biotechnology (Special Eurobarometer 341)*. Bruxelles: TNS Opinion and Social.

Evans-Wentz, W. Y. 1980[1927]. *The Tibetan Book of the Dead or The After-Death Experiences on the Bardo Plane, According to Lama Kazi Dawa-Samdup's English Rendering*. Oxford: Oxford University Press.

Fautré, Willy. 1999. "Belgium's Anti-Sect War." *Social Justice Research* 12, no. 4: 377–92.

———. 2010. "Belgium." In *Religions of the World: A Comprehensive Encyclopedia of Beliefs and Practices*, edited by J. Gordon Melton and Martin Baumann, 317–19. Santa Barbara: ABC–CLIO.

Favell, Adrian, and Marco Martiniello. 2008. "Multi-national, Multi-cultural, and Multi-levelled Brussels: National and Ethnic Politics in the 'Capital of Europe.'" In *Cities in Movement: Migrants and Urban Change*, edited by L. Fonseca, 137–64. Lisbon: Centro de Estudoes Geograficos.

Favret-Saada, Jeanne. 1980. *Deadly Words: Witchcraft in the Bocage*. New York: Cambridge University Press.

Fernández, Xavier, and Josep Maria Fábregas. 2014. "Experience of Treatment with Ayahuasca for Drug Addiction in the Brazilian Amazon." In *The Therapeutic Use of Ayahuasca*, edited by Beatriz Caiuby Labate and Clancy Cavnar, 161–82. Berlin: Springer-Verlag.

Ferrari, Silvio. 2006. "New Religious Movements in Western Europe." *Religioscope* 9 (October 2006); http://religion.info/pdf/2006_10_ferrari_nrm.pdf.

Ferreira, M. Jamie. 1998. "Faith and the Kierkegaardian leap." In *The Cambridge Companion to Kierkegaard*, edited by Alastair Hannay and Gordon Daniel Marino, 207–34. Cambridge and New York: Cambridge University Press.

Ferrer, Jorge N. 2002. *Revisioning Transpersonal Theory: A Participatory Vision of Human Spirituality*. Albany: State University of New York Press.

———. 2017. *Participation and the Mystery: Transpersonal Essays in Psychology, Education, and Religion*. Albany: State University of New York Press.

Fischer, Edward F. 2014. *The Good Life: Aspiration, Dignity, and the Anthropology of Wellbeing*. Stanford: Stanford University Press.

Fischer, Louis. 1954. *Gandhi: His Life and Message for the World*. New York: New American Library.

Fleisher, Mark S. 1995. *Beggars and Thieves: Lives of Urban Street Criminals*. Madison: University of Wisconsin Press.

Flierman, Robert. 2016. "Religious Saxons: Paganism, Infidelity, and Biblical Punishment in the Capitulatio de partibus Saxoniae." In *Religious Franks: Religion and Power in the Frankish Kingdoms: Studies in Honour of Mayke de Jong*, edited by Rob Meens, Dorine Van Espelo, Bram van den Hoven van Genderen, Janneke Raaijmakers, Irene van Renswoude, Carine van Rhijn, and Mayke De Jong, 181–201. Manchester: Manchester University Press.

Ford, James A., and Julian H. Steward. 1954. "On the Concept of Types." *American Anthropologist* 56, no. 1: 42–57.

Fotiou, Evgenia. 2010. *From Medicine Men to Day Trippers: Shamanic Tourism in Iquitos, Peru*. PhD Dissertation, Cultural Anthropology, University of Wisconsin—Madison.

———. 2012. "Working with La Medicina: Elements of Healing in Contemporary Ayahuasca Rituals." *Anthropology of Consciousness* 23, no. 1: 6–27.

Foucault, Michel. 1988. "Technologies of the Self." In *Technologies of the Self: A Seminar with Michel Foucault*, edited by Luther H. Martin, Huck Gutman, and Patrick H. Hutton, 16–49. Amherst: University of Massachusetts Press.

Fox, Matthew. 1988. *The Coming of the Cosmic Christ*. San Francisco: Harper and Row.

Fox, Renée C. 1988. *Essays in Medical Sociology*. New Brunswick, NJ: Transaction.

———. 1994. *In the Belgian Château: The Spirit and Culture of a European Society in an Age of Change*. Chicago: Ivan R. Dee.

Frager, Robert. 1999. *Heart, Self, and Soul: A Sufi Approach to Growth, Balance, and Harmony*. Wheaton, IL: Quest Books.

Frankl, Viktor E. (2006[1959]). *Man's Search for Meaning: An Introduction to Logotherapy*. Boston: Beacon Press.

Fraser, Barbara. 2017. "The Perils and Privileges of an Amazonian Hallucinogen: Tourism Based on Consumption of the Plant Brew Known as Ayahuasca is Booming, for Better and for Worse." *SAPIENS, https://www.sapiens.org/culture/ayahuasca-tourism-amazon/*.

Frecska, Ede. 2011. "The Risks and Potential Benefits of Ayahuasca Use from a Psychopharmacological Perspective." In *The Internationalization of Ayahuasca*, edited by Beatriz Caiuby Labate and Henrik Jungaberle, 151–65. Berlin: Lit Verlag.

Frederik. n.d. "A Pilgrimage to the Angelic Realm."

Frenopoulo, Christian. 2006. "Healing in the Barquinha Religion." *Fieldwork in Religion* 2, no. 3: 363–92.

Frith, Chris, and Geraint Rees. 2007. "A Brief History of the Scientific Approach to the Study of Consciousness." In *The Blackwell Companion to Consciousness*, edited by Max Velmans and Susan Schneider, 9–22. Malden, MA: Blackwell.

Fróes, Vera. 1986. *Santo Daime, Cultura Amazônica: História do Povo Juramidam*. Manaus, Brazil: SUFRAMA.

Fuller, Robert C. 2000. *Stairways to Heaven: Drugs in American Religious History*. Boulder: Westview.

———. 2001. *Spiritual, but not Religious: Understanding Unchurched America*. Oxford: Oxford University Press.

Furst, Peter T. 1976. *Hallucinogens and Culture*. San Francisco: Chandler and Sharp.

Gable, Robert S. 2007. "Risk Assessment of Ritual Use of Oral Dimethyltryptamine (DMT) and Harmala Alkaloids." *Addiction* 102, no. 1: 24–34.

Gallup, George, and D. Michael Lindsay. 1999. *Surveying the Religious Landscape: Trends in U.S. Beliefs*. Harrisburg, PA: Morehouse.

Garrett, Susan R. 2008. *No Ordinary Angel: Celestial Spirits and Christian Claims about Jesus*. New Haven: Yale University Press.

Gasser, P., D. Holstein, Y. Michel, R. Doblin, B. Yazar-Klosinski, T. Passie, and R. Brenneisen. 2014. "Safety and Efficacy of Lysergic Acid Diethylamide–Assisted Psychotherapy for Anxiety Associated with Life-Threatening Diseases." *Journal of Nervous and Mental Disease* 202, no. 7: 513–20.

Gates, Bronwen. 1982. *Banisteriopsis, Diplopterys (Malpighiaceae)*. Bronx: The New York Botanical Garden.

Gayle, Damien. 2015. "Psychoactive Substances Ban Will 'End Brain Research' in Britain, Experts Warn." *The Guardian*, https://www.theguardian.com/politics/2015/may/29/psychoactive-substances-ban-end-brain-research-britain-david-nutt.

Gearin, Alex K. 2015. "Whatever You Want to Believe: Kaleidoscopic Individualism and Ayahuasca Healing in Australia." *TAJA The Australian Journal of Anthropology* 26, no. 3: 442–55.

———. 2017. "Dividual Vision of the Individual: Ayahuasca Neo-shamanism in Australia and the New Age Individualism Orthodoxy." *IJSNR International Journal for the Study of New Religions* 7, no. 2: 199–220.

Geertz, Clifford. 1973. *The Interpretation of Cultures: Selected Essays*. New York: Basic Books.

———. 2000. *Available Light: Anthropological Reflections on Philosophical Topics*. Princeton: Princeton University Press.

Gellman, Jerome. 2014. "Mysticism." In *The Stanford Encyclopedia of Philosophy*, edited by Edward N. Zalta. http://plato.stanford.edu/entries/mysticism/.

Gellner, David N. 2001. "Studying Secularism, Practising Secularism. Anthropological Imperatives." *Social Anthropology* 9, no. 3: 337–40.

Gimello, Robert. 1979. "Mysticism and Meditation." In *Mysticism and Philosophical Analysis*, edited by S. T. Katz, 170–99. New York: Oxford University Press.

George, Jamilah R., Timothy I. Michaels, Jae Sevelius, and Monnica T. Williams. 2020. "The Psychedelic Renaissance and the Limitations of a White-Dominant Medical Framework: A Call for Indigenous and Ethnic Minority Inclusion. *Journal of Psychedelic Studies* 4: 4–15.

Godwin, Joscelyn. 2007. *The Golden Thread: The Ageless Wisdom of the Western Mystery Traditions*. Wheaton, IL: Quest Books/Theosophical Pub. House.

Goldhill, Olivia. 2018. "A Millionaire Couple Is Threatening to Create a Magic Mushroom Monopoly." *Quartz*, November 8, 2018: https://qz.com/1454785/a-millionaire-couple-is-threatening-to-create-a-magic-mushroom-monopoly/.

Goldman, Jonathan. 1999. "Preface." In *Forest of Visions: Ayahuasca, Amazonian Spirituality, and the Santo Daime Tradition*, xx–xxxiii. Rochester, VT: Park Street Press.

González, Débora, María Carvalho, Jordi Cantillo, Marc Aixalá, and Magí Farré. In Press. "Potential Use of Ayahuasca in Grief Therapy." *OMEGA—Journal of Death and Dying*.

Gorski, Philip S., and Ateş Altınordu. 2008. "After Secularization?" *Annual Review of Sociology* 34, no. 1: 55–85.

Goulart, Sandra Lucia. 1996. *Raízes Culturais do Santo Daime*. MA Thesis, Social Anthropology, Universidade de São Paulo, São Paulo, Brazil.

———. 2004. *Contrastes e Continuidades em uma Tradição Amazonica: As Religiões da Ayahuasca*. PhD Dissertation, Social Anthropology, Universidade de Campinas, Brazil, Campinas, Brazil.

———. 2006. "Religious Matrices of the União do Vegetal." *Fieldwork in Religion* 2, no. 3: 286–318.

Gow, Peter. 1994. "River People: Shamanism and History in Western Amazonia." In *Shamanism, History, and the State*, edited by N. Thomas and C. Humphrey, 90–113. Ann Arbor: University of Michigan Press.

Granskog, Jane E. 2003. "Spirit Matters: An Exploration of Shamanic Techniques to Transform the Environment." *Southwestern Anthropological Association Newsletter* 44: 22–26.

Green, Roger K. 2019. *A Transatlantic Political Theology of Psychedelic Aesthetics: Enchanted Citizens*. Cham, Switzerland: Springer.

———. 2020. *Ayahuasca's Religious Diaspora in the Wake of the Doctrine of Discovery*. PhD Dissertation. University of Denver, Denver, CO.

———. 2021. "At Cross-Purposes: Conversion, Conscripted Compromise, and the Logic of Eurochristian Religious Poetics," In *The Colonial Compromise: The Threat of the Gospel to the Indigenous Worldview*, edited by Miguel A. De La Torre, 55–70. Lanham, MD: Lexington Books / Fortress Academic.

Greenhouse, Linda. 2006. "Sect Allowed to Import Its Hallucinogenic Tea." *New York Times* (February 22).

Greenwood, Susan. 2005. *The Nature of Magic: An Anthropology of Consciousness*. Oxford and New York: Berg.

Greganich, Jéssica. 2010. *"Entre a Rosa e o Beija-Flor": Um Estudo Antropológico de Trajetórias na União Vegetal (UDV) e no Santo Daime*. MA thesis, Social Anthropology, Federal University of Rio Grande do Sul, Brazil.

Griffiths, R., W. Richards, U. McCann, and R. Jesse. 2006. "Psilocybin Can Occasion Mystical-type Experiences Having Substantial and Sustained Personal Meaning and Spiritual Significance." *Psychopharmacology* 187, no. 3: 268–83.

Grof, Stanislav. 1976. *Realms of the Human Unconscious: Observations from LSD Research*. New York: Dutton.

———. 1998. *The Cosmic Game: Explorations of the Frontiers of Human Consciousness*. Albany: State University of New York Press.

Groisman, Alberto. 1991. *"Eu Venho Da Floresta": Ecletismo E Práxis Xamânica Daimista No "Céu Do Mapiá*. Masters thesis, Anthropology, UFSC, Florianópolis, Brazil.

———. 2000. *Santo Daime in the Netherlands: An Anthropological Study of a New World Religion in a European Setting*. PhD Thesis, Social Anthropology, University of London, London, UK.

———. 2009. "Trajectories, Frontiers, and Reparations in the Expansion of Santo Daime to Europe." In *Transnational Transcendence: Essays on Religion and Globalization*, edited by Thomas J. Csordas, 185–203. Berkeley: University of California Press.

Guilherme, Germano. n.d. "Vós Sois Baliza [Thou Art a Beacon]."

Guimarães, Oswaldo. 2019. *Jornal do Céu*, edition 11. Vila Céu do Mapiá, Floresta Nacional do Purus, Pauiní-AM, Brazil. https://www.santodaime.org/site/files/sdadmin/JORNAL-2019-EN-WEB.pdf.

Gupta, Akhil, and James Ferguson. 1997. "Discipline and Practice: 'The Field' as Site, Method, and Location in Anthropology." In *Anthropological Locations: Boundaries and Grounds of a Field Science*, edited by Akhil Gupta and James Ferguson, 1–46. Berkeley: University of California Press.

Guthrie, Stewart. 1993. *Faces in the Clouds: A New Theory of Religion*. New York: Oxford University Press.

Güzeldere, Güven. 1997. "The Many Faces of Consciousness: A Field Guide." In *In The Nature of Consciousness: Philosophical Debates*, edited by Ned Block, Owen Flanagan, and Güven Güzeldere, 1–67. Cambridge: MIT Press.

Haber, Roy. 2011. "The Santo Daime Road to Seeking Religious Freedom in the USA." In *The Internationalization of Ayahuasca*, edited by B. C. Labate and KH. Jungaberle, 301–17. Berlin: Lit Verlag.

Habermas, Jürgen. 1989[1962]. *The Structural Transformation of the Public sphere: An Inquiry into a Category of Bourgeois Society*. Cambridge: MIT Press.

———. 1992. "Further Reflections on the Public Sphere." In *Habermas and the Public Sphere*, edited by Craig J. Calhoun, 421–61. Cambridge: MIT Press.

———. 2005. "Equal Treatment of Cultures and the Limits of Postmodern Liberalism." *Journal of Political Philosophy* 13, no. 1: 1–28.

———. 2008. "Notes on Post-Secular Society." *New Perspectives Quarterly* 25, no. 4: 17–29.

———. 2009. *Europe: the Faltering Project*. Cambridge and Malden, MA: Polity.

———. 2010a. "An Awareness of What Is Missing." In *An Awareness of What Is Missing: Faith and Reason in a Post-Secular Age*, edited by Jürgen Habermas et al., 15–23. Malden, MA: Polity.

———. 2010b. "A Reply." In *An Awareness of What Is Missing: Faith and Reason in a Post-Secular Age*, edited by Jürgen Habermas et al., 72–83. Malden, MA: Polity.

Haden, Mark, Brian Emerson, and Kenneth W. Tupper. 2016. "A Public-Health-Based Vision for the Management and Regulation of Psychedelics." *Journal of Psychoactive Drugs* 48, no. 4: 243–52.

Hadot, Pierre. 2006. *The Veil of Isis: An Essay on the History of the Idea of Nature*. Cambridge: Belknap Press of Harvard University Press.

Hall, Anthony. 2007. "Extractive Reserves: Building Natural Assets in the Brazilian Amazon." In *Reclaiming Nature Environmental Justice and Ecological Restoration*, edited by James K. Boyce, Sunita Narain, and Elizabeth A. Stanton, 151–79. New York: Anthem Press.

Hall, Linda B. 2004. *Mary, Mother and Warrior: The Virgin in Spain and the Americas*. Austin: University of Texas Press.

Hall, Wayne, and Louisa Degenhardt. 2007. "Prevalence and Correlates of Cannabis Use in Developed and Developing Countries." *Current Opinion in Psychiatry* 20, no. 4: 393–97.

Halman, Loek, and Thorleif Pettersson. 2003. "Differential Patterns of Secularization in Europe: Exploring the Impact of Religion on Social Values." In *Religion in Secularizing Society: The Europeans' Religion at the End of the 20th Century*, edited by Loek Halman and Ole Riis, 48–75. Leiden and Boston: Brill.

Halpern, J. H., A. R. Sherwood, T. Passie, K. C. Blackwell, and A. J. Ruttenber. 2008. "Evidence of Health and Safety in American Members of a Religion Who Use a Hallucinogenic Sacrament." *Medical Science Monitor* 14, no. 8: 15–22.

Hamill, Jonathan, Jaime Hallak, Serdar M. Dursun, and Glen Baker. 2019. "Ayahuasca: Psychological and Physiologic Effects, Pharmacology, and Potential Uses in Addiction and Mental Illness." *Current neuropharmacology* 17, no. 2: 108–28.

Hanegraaff, Wouter. 1998. *New Age Religion and Western Culture Esotericism in the Mirror of Secular Thought*. Albany: State University of New York Press.

———. 2002. "New Age Religion." In *Religions in the Modern World: Traditions and Transformations*, edited by Linda Woodhead, Christopher Partridge, Hiroko Kawanami and David Smith, 287–304. London: Routledge.

———. 2011. "Ayahuasca Groups and Networks in the Netherlands: A Challenge to the Study of Contemporary Religion." In *The Internationalization of Ayahuasca*, edited by B. C. Labate and KH. Jungaberle, 85–103. Berlin: Lit Verlag.

———. 2014. "Entheogenic Esotericism." In *Contemporary Esotericism*, edited by Egil Asprem and Kennet Granholm. New York: Routledge.

Hannay, Alastair. 1989. "Translator's Introduction." In Søren Kierkegaard, *The Sickness Unto Death: A Christian Psychological Exposition for Edification and Awakening*, 1–32. New York: Penguin Books.

———. 1998. "Kierkegaard and the Variety of Despair." In *The Cambridge Companion to Kierkegaard*, edited by A. Hannay and G. D. Marino, 329–48. New York: Cambridge University Press.

Harman, Willis W. 1998. *Global Mind Change The Promise of the 21st Century*. Institute of Noetic Sciences: Berret-Koehler Publishers. http://search.ebscohost. com/login.aspx?direct=true&scope=site&db=nlebk&db=nlabk&AN=41456.

Harmless, William. 2008. *Mystics*. Oxford and New York: Oxford University Press.

Harner, Michael J. 1973. *Hallucinogens and Shamanism*. New York: Oxford University Press.

Harris, Marvin. 1979. *The Rise of Anthropological Theory: A Hhistory of Theories of Culture*. London: Routledge and Kegan Paul.

Hartelius, Glenn. 2017. "Zombie Perennialism: An Intelligent Design for Psychology? A Further Response to Taylor's Soft Perennialism." *International Journal of Transpersonal Studies* 36, no. 2: 93–110.

Hartman, Rini. 2018 "Dutch Freedom of Religion on Pause for Santo Daime." *Chacruna Institute for Psychedelic Plant Medicines*, March 15, 2018. https:// chacruna.net/dutch-freedom-religion-pause-santo-daime/.

Hartman, Shelby. 2019. "Why LGBTQI+ Members Are Creating Their Own Ayahuasca Circles." *Chacruna*. https://chacruna.net/why-lgbtqi-members-are-creating-their-own-ayahuasca-circles/.

Hartogsohn, Ido. 2018. "The Meaning-Enhancing Properties of Psychedelics and Their Mediator Role in Psychedelic Therapy, Spirituality, and Creativity." *Frontiers in neuroscience* 12: 129.

———. 2020. *American Trip: Set, Setting, and the Psychedelic Experience in the Twentieth Century*. Cambridge: MIT Press.

Harvey, Andrew. 1996. *Light upon Light: Inspirations from Rumi*. Berkeley: North Atlantic Books.

Harvey, Graham. 2004. "Performing and Constructing Research as Guesthood in the Study of Religions." In *Anthropologists in the Field Cases in Participant Observation*, edited by L. Hume and J. Mulcock, 168–82. New York: Columbia University Press.

———. 2006. *Animism: Respecting the Living World*. New York: Columbia University Press.

———. 2012. "Rituals in New Religions." In *The Cambridge Companion to New Religious Movements*, edited by O. Hammer and M. Rothstein, 97–112. New York: Cambridge University Press.

Heelas, Paul. 1991. "Cults for Capitalism: Self Religions, Magic, and the Empowerment of Business." In *Religion and Power: Decline and Growth. London: British Sociological Association*, edited by Peter Gee and John Fulton, 27–41. Twickenham: British Sociological Association, Sociology of Religion Study Group.

———. 1996. *The New Age Movement: The Celebration of the Self and the Sacralization of Modernity*. Oxford and Cambridge, MA: Blackwell.

———. 2008. *Spiritualities of Life: New Age Romanticism and Consumptive Capitalism*. Malden, MA: Blackwell.

Hefner, Robert W. 1998. "Multiple Modernities: Christianity, Islam, and Hinduism in a Globalizing Age." *Annual Review of Anthropology* 27: 83–104.

Hegel, Georg Wilhelm Friedrich. 1977[1807]. *Phenomenology of Spirit*. Oxford: Oxford University Press.

Heidegger, Martin. 1962[1927]. *Being and Time*. New York: Harper Collins.

Hein, Carola. 2004. *The Capital of Europe: Architecture and Urban Planning for the European Union*. Westport, CT: Praeger.

Henderson, Joseph Lewis, and Maud Oakes. 1990. *The Wisdom of the Serpent: The Myths of Death, Rebirth, and Resurrection*. Princeton: Princeton University Press.

Henman, Anthony Richard. 2009[1985]. "Ayahuasca Use in a Religious Context: The Case of the União Do Vegetal in Brazil." Adapted from a 1985 paper presented at the 45th Congresso Internacional de Americanistas Erowid.org. Feb 2009.: https://www.erowid.org/chemicals/ayahuasca/ayahuasca_article2.shtml.

Heywood, Paolo. 2012. "Anthropology and What There Is: Reflections on 'Ontology.'" *The Cambridge Journal of Anthropology* 30, no 1: 143–51.

Highpine (Sachahambi), Gayle. 2008. *What Indigenous Groups Traditionally Use Ayahuasca?* http://www.ayahuasca.com/?p=12.

———. 2012. "Unraveling the Mystery of the Origin of Ayahuasca." Paper published online: http://www.neip.info/html/objects/_downloadblob.php?cod_blob=1184.

Hildburgh, Walter L. 1940. "'Caravaca' Crosses and Their Uses as Amulets in Spain." *Folklore* 51, no. 4: 241–58.

Hirschkind, Charles. 2011. "Is There a Secular Body?" *Cultural Anthropology* 26, no. 4: 633–47.

Hobbs, Jonathan. 2018. "'Altered by the Hand of Man': Contextualizing Ayahuasca Law in Britain and Europe." In *The Expanding World Ayahuasca Diaspora: Appropriation, Integration, and Legislation*, edited by B. C. Labate and C. Cavnar, 40–60. New York: Routledge.

Holbraad, Martin, and Morten Axel Pedersen. 2014. "The Politics of Ontology." *Theorizing the Contemporary*, Cultural Anthropology website, January 13, 2014. http://www.culanth.org/fieldsights/461-the-politics-of-ontology.

Horák, Miroslav, Petr Novák, and Wanda Vozáryová. 2016. "Legal Aspects of the Ayahuasca Consumption in the European Union." In *Conference Proceedings: Region v rozvoji spolecnosti 2016*, edited by In. FAKULTA REGIONÁLNÍHO ROZVOJE A MEZINÁRODNÍCH STUDIÍ: Mendel University in Brno.

Horák, Miroslav, Nahanga Verter, and Kristina Somerlíková. 2014. "Efficacy of Drug Rehab Centres in Nicaragua, Peru, and the Czech Republic." *Adiktologie* 14, no. 4:428–39.

Horák, Miroslav, Lea Hasíková, and Nahanga Verter. 2018. "Therapeutic Potential Ascribed to Ayahuasca by Users in the Czech Republic." *Journal of psychoactive drugs* 50, no. 5: 430–36.

Horák, Miroslav, and Nahanga Verter. 2019. *Ayahuasca in the Czech Republic* (Extended Version). Brno: Mendel University.

Howard, Jonathan. 2018. *Cognitive Errors and Diagnostic Mistakes*. Berlin/Heidelberg: Springer.

Husserl, Edmund. 1960[1929]. *Cartesian Meditations: An Introduction to Phenomenology*. The Hague: M. Nijhoff.

Huxley, Aldous. 1990[1956]. *The Doors of Perception and Heaven and Hell*. New York: Harper and Row.

———. 2009[1945]. *The Perennial Philosophy*. New York and London: Harper and Brothers.

Indigenous Peoples of the Juruá Valley. 2019. *Declaration of the 3rd Brazilian Indigenous Conference on Ayahuasca, Marechal Thaumaturgo*, Acre State, Brazil. https://chacruna.net/declaration-of-the-3rd-brazilian-indigenous-conference-on-ayahuasca/.

Jackson, Joe. 2008. *The Thief at the End of the World: Rubber, Power, and the Seeds of Empire*. New York: Viking.

Jackson, Michael D. 1996. *Things as They Are: New Directions in Phenomenological Anthropology*. Bloomington: Indiana University Press.

———. 2005. *Existential Anthropology: Events, Exigencies, and Effects*. New York: Berghahn Books.

———. 2013. *Lifeworlds: Essays in Existential Anthropology*. Chicago and London: The University of Chicago Press.

Jackson, Michael D., and Albert Piette. 2015a. *What Is Existential Anthropology?* New York: Berghahn.

———. 2015b. "Introduction: Anthropology and the Existential Turn." In *What Is Existential Anthropology?*, edited by Michael D. Jackson and Albert Piette. New York: Berghahn.

Jacob, M. S., and D. E. Presti. 2005. "Endogenous Psychoactive Tryptamines Reconsidered: An Anxiolytic Role for Dimethyltryptamine." *Medical hypotheses* 64, no. 5: 930–37.

James, William. 1985[1902]. *The Varieties of Religious Experience.* Cambridge: Harvard University Press.

Jansen, Yolande. 2006. "Laïcité, or the Politics of Republican Secularism." In *Political Theologies: Public Religions in a Post-Secular World*, edited by Hent de Vries and Lawrence Eugene Sullivan, 475–93. New York: Fordham University Press.

Jauregui, Andres. 2012. "Belgium To Prosecute Scientology As Criminal Organization; Church Faces Charges Of Extortion, Fraud." *Huffington Post.* http://www.huffingtonpost.com/2012/12/28/belgium-prosecutes-scientology-extortion-fraud_n_2375823.html.

Jespersen, Julie Dalsgaard. 2016. *The Reality of Illusion and the Illusion of Reality An Anthropological Study of Entheogenic Ceremonies in a Dutch Spiritual Group.* Master's Thesis, Anthropology, Aarhus University, Denmark. http://encontro-comseueu.nl/wp-content/uploads/2017/09/The-Reality-of-Illusion-and-the-Illusion-of-Reality.pdf.

Johnson, Frank. 1985. "The Western Concept of Self." In *Culture and Self: Asian and Western Perspectives*, edited by Anthony J. Marsella, George A. De Vos and Francis L. K. Hsu, 91–138. New York: Tavistock.

Johnson, Todd M. 2010. "A Statistical Approach to the World's Religious Adherents, 2000–2050 CE." In *Religions of the World: A Comprehensive Encyclopedia of Beliefs and Practices* edited by J. Gordon Melton and Martin Baumann, lv–lxxii. Santa Barbara: ABC-CLIO.

Jones, Lindsay, Mircea Eliade, and Charles J. Adams. 2005. *Encyclopedia of Religion.* 2nd edition. Detroit: Macmillan Reference USA.

Kaasik, Helle. 2016. *Psychology of Ayahuasca Users in Estonia*, MA Thesis, Psychology, University of Tartu, Tartu, Estonia. http://kodu.ut.ee/~hellex/aya/Ayaeng.htm.

Kaasik, Helle, and Kairi Kreegipuu. 2020. "Ayahuasca Users in Estonia: Ceremonial Practices, Subjective Long-Term Effects, Mental Health, and Quality of Life." *Journal of Psychoactive Drugs* 52, no. 3: 255–63.

Kaasik, Helle, Rita C. Z. Souza, Flávia S. Zandonadi, Luís Fernando Tófoli, and Alessandra Sussulini. 2020. "Chemical Composition of Traditional and Analog Ayahuasca." *Journal of Psychoactive Drugs*: 1–11.

Kapferer, Bruce. 2001. "Anthropology. The Paradox of the Secular." *Social Anthropology* 9, no. 3: 341–44.

Kardec, Allan. 1874. *Experimental Spiritism: Book on Mediums; Or, Guide for Mediums and Invocators: Containing the Special Instruction of the Spirits on the Theory of All Kinds of Manifestations, the Development of Mediumship; the Difficulties and the Dangers that Are to be Encountered in the Practice of Spiritism.* Boston: Colby and Rich.

Kavenská, Veronika, and Hana Simonová. 2015. "Ayahuasca Tourism: Participants in Shamanic Rituals and their Personality Styles, Motivation, Benefits, and Risks." *Journal of Psychoactive Drugs Journal of Psychoactive Drugs* 47, no. 5: 351–59.

Kazantzakis, Nikos. 2000[1955]. *God's Pauper, St. Francis of Assisi.* London: Faber and Faber.

Kearney, Richard. 2001. *The God Who May Be: A Hermeneutics of Religion.* Bloomington, IN: Indiana University Press.

———. 2011. *Anatheism: Returning to God after God.* New York: Columbia University Press.

Keiman, Daan. 2020. Psychedelic Chaplaincy—Integrating Interfaith Spiritual Care into Psychedelic Therapies and Science. Presentation at the *Interdisciplinary Conference on Psychedelics Research.* Amsterdam, NL: OPEN Foundation.

Kempis, Thomas à. 2003[1418]. *The Imitation of Christ.* Mineola, NY: Dover.

Kettner, Hannes, Sam Gandy, Eline C. H. M. Haijen, and Robin L. Carhart-Harris. 2019. "From Egoism to Ecoism: Psychedelics Increase Nature Relatedness in a State-Mediated and Context-Dependent Manner." *International Journal of Environmental Research and Public Health* 16, no. 24: 5147.

Kierkegaard, Søren 1980[1844]. *The Concept of Anxiety: A Simple Psychologically Orienting Deliberation on the Dogmatic Issue of Hereditary Sin.* Princeton: Princeton University Press.

———. 1989[1849]. *The Sickness unto Death: A Christian Psychological Exposition for Edification and Awakening.* New York: Penguin Books.

———. 1990[1851/1876]. *For Self-Examination; Judge for Yourself!* Princeton: Princeton University Press.

———. 2003[1843]. *Fear and Trembling: Dialectical Lyric by Johannes de silentio.* London: Penguin.

King, Anthony. 2003. *The European Ritual: Football in The new Europe.* Aldershot, UK, and Burlington, VT: Ashgate.

Kjellgren, A., A. Eriksson, and T. Norlander. 2009. "Experiences of Encounters with Ayahuasca—'The Vine of the Soul.'" *Journal of psychoactive drugs* 41, no. 4: 309–15.

Klin-Oron, Adam. 2014. "How I Learned to Channel: Epistemology, Phenomenology, and Practice in a New Age Course." *American ethnologist* 41, no. 4: 635–47.

Knibbe, Kim Esther, and Peter Versteeg. 2008. "Assessing Phenomenology in Anthropology: Lessons from the Study of Religion and Experience." *Critique of anthropology* 28, no. 1: 47–62.

Knoblauch, Hubert, and Bernt Schnettler. 2001. "Die Kulturelle Sinnprovinz Der Zukunftsvision Und Die Ethnophänomenologie." *Psychotherapie und Sozial-wissenschaft: Zeitschrift für Qualitative Forschung* 3, no. 3: 182–203.

Kornfield, Jack. 2000. *After the Ecstasy, the Laundry: How the Heart Grows Wise on the Spiritual Path.* New York: Bantam Books.

———. 2019. "Healing through Loving Awareness." Episode 90, *Heart Wisdom Podcast.* Be Here Now Network. March 21, 2019. https://beherenownetwork. com/jack-kornfield-ep-90-healing-through-loving-awareness/.

Krech III, Shepard, and William C. Sturtevant. 1995. "The Uses of Ethnographic Records." In *Preserving the Anthropological Record,* edited by Sydel Silverman and Nancy J. Parezo, 85–94. New York: Wenner-Gren Foundation for Anthropological Research.

Kripal, Jeffrey J. 2014. *Comparing Religions.* Malden, MA: John Wiley and Sons.

Krippner, Stanley. 1999. "Protecting Indigenous Knowledge from Ecopiratism." *Shaman's Drum* 52: 8–11.

———. 2000. "The Epistemology and Technologies of Shamanic States of Con-sciousness." *Journal of Consciousness Studies* 7, no. 11: 93–118.

Krishnamurti, Jiddu. 1969. *Freedom from the Known.* New York: HarperCollins.

Kubrick, Stanley. 1968. *2001: A Space Odyssey.*

Kukla, André. 1988. "Cross-Cultural Psychology in a Post-Empiricist Era." In *The Cross-Cultural Challenge to Social Psychology,* edited by Michael Harris Bond, 141–52. Newbury Park, CA: SAGE.

La Rocque Couto, Fernando. 1989. *Santos e Xamãs,* MA thesis, Social Anthropology, Universidade Nacional de Brasilia, Brazil.

Labate, Beatriz Caiuby. 2004a. "A Literatura Brasileira Sobre as Religiões Ayahuasquei-ras." In *O Uso Ritual da Ayahuasca (The Ritual Use of Ayahuasca),* edited by Beatriz Caiuby Labate and Wladimyr Sena Araújo, 231–73. São Paulo: Mercado de Letras.

———. 2004b. *A Reinvenção do Uso da Ayahuasca nos Centros Urbanos.* Campinas, Brasil: FAPESP: Mercado de Letras.

———. 2006. "Brazilian Literature on Ayahuasca Religions." *Fieldwork in Religion* 2, no. 3: 200–34.

———. 2011a. "Consumption of Ayahuasca by Children and Pregnant Women: Medical Controversies and Religious Perspectives." *Journal of Psychoactive Drugs* 43, no. 1: 27–35.

———. 2011b. *Ayahuasca Mamancuna Merci Beaucoup: Internacionalização e Diversificação do Vegetalismo Ayahuasqueiro Peruano (Ayahuasca Mamancuna Merci Beaucoup: Internationalization and Diversification of Peruvian Ayahuasca Vegetalismo),* PhD Diss., Social Anthropology, Universidade Estadual de Campinas, Campinas, SP, Brazil.

———. 2012a. "Ayahuasca Religions in Acre: Cultural Heritage in the Brazilian Borderlands." *Anthropology of Consciousness* 23, no. 1: 87–102.

———. 2012b. "The Shaman Who Turned into a Frog: A Promise of Patented Medicine." Erowid.org (Originally published in Portuguese in Comunidade Virtual de Antropologia) no. http://www.erowid.org/animals/phyllomedusa/ phyllomedusa_article3.shtml.

Labate, Beatriz Caiuby, Brian Anderson, and Henrik Jungaberle. 2011. "Ritual Ayahuasca Use and Health: An Interview with Jacques Mabit." In *The Internationalization of Ayahuasca*, edited by B. C. Labate and KH. Jungaberle, 223–43. Berlin: Lit Verlag.

Labate, Beatriz Caiuby, and Wladimyr Sena Araújo. 2004. *O Uso Ritual da Ayahuasca (The Ritual Use of Ayahuasca)*. 2nd ed. São Paulo: Mercado de Letras.

Labate, Beatriz Caiuby, and Clancy Cavnar. 2014a. *Ayahuasca Shamanism in the Amazon and Beyond*. New York: Oxford University Press.

———. 2014b. *The Therapeutic Use of Ayahuasca*. Berlin: Springer-Verlag.

———. 2018a. *Plant Medicines, Healing and Psychedelic Science: Cultural Perspectives*. Cham, CH: Springer.

———. 2018b. *The Expanding World Ayahuasca Diaspora: Appropriation, Integration, and Legislation*. New York: Routledge.

Labate, Beatriz Caiuby, Clancy Cavnar, and Alex K Gearin. 2017. *The World Ayahuasca Diaspora: Reinventions and Controversies*. New York: Routledge.

Labate, Beatriz Caiuby, and Tiago Coutinho. 2014. " 'My Grandfather Served Ayahuasca to Mestre Irineu': Reflections on the Entrance of Indigenous Peoples into the Urban Circuit of Ayahuasca Consumption in Brazil." *Curare* 37, no. 3: 181–94.

Labate, Beatriz Caiuby, Isabel Santana de Rose, and Rafael Guimarães dos Santos. 2008. *Ayahuasca Religions: A Comprehensive Bibliography and Critical Essays*. Santa Cruz, CA: MAPS, Multidisciplinary Association for Psychedelic Studies.

Labate, Beatriz Caiuby, and Kevin Feeney. 2012. "Ayahuasca and the Process of Regulation in Brazil and Internationally." *International Journal of Drug Policy* 23, no. 2: 154–61.

Labate, Beatriz Caiuby, Antonio Marques Alves Jr., Isabel Santana de Rose, and José Augusto Lemos. 2010. "A Tribute to Glauco Vilas Boas: Beloved Brazilian Cartoonist and a Leader in the Santo Daime Religion, Slain in São Paulo." Erowid.org. May 6, 2010: Erowid.org/chemicals/ayahuasca/ayahuasca_info14. shtml.

Labate, Beatriz Caiuby, and Henrik Jungaberle. 2011. *The Internationalization of Ayahuasca*. Berlin: Lit Verlag.

Labate, Beatriz Caiuby, and Edward Macrae. 2008. *The Light from the Forest: The Ritual Use of Ayahuasca in Brazil*. London: Equinox Publishing.

———. 2010. *Ayahuasca, Ritual and Religion in Brazil*. London and Oakville, CT: Equinox.

Labate, Beatriz Caiuby, Edward MacRae, and Sandra Lucia Goulart. 2010. "Brazilian Ayahuasca Religions in Perspective." In *Ayahuasca, Ritual, and Religion in*

Brazil, edited by Beatriz Caiuby Labate and Edward Macrae, 1–20. London and Oakville, CT: Equinox.

Labate, Beatriz Caiuby, and Glauber Loures de Assis. 2017. "The Religion of the Forest: Reflections on the International Expansion of a Brazilian Ayahuasca Religion." In *The World Ayahuasca Diaspora: Reinventions and Controversies*, edited by Beatriz Caiuby Labate, Clancy Cavnar, and Alex K. Gearin, 57–78. New York: Routledge.

Labate, Beatriz Caiuby, Glauber Loures de Assis, and Clancy Cavnar. 2017. "A Religious Battle: Musical Dimensions of the Santo Daime Diaspora." In *The World Ayahuasca Diaspora: Reinventions and Controversies*, edited by Beatriz Caiuby Labate, Clancy Cavnar, and Alex K. Gearin, 99–122. New York: Routledge.

Labate, Beatriz Caiuby, and Gustavo Pacheco. 2004. "Matrizes Maranhenses do Santo Daime [Maranhão Matrices of the Santo Daime]." In *O Uso Ritual da Ayahuasca* (*The Ritual Use of Ayahuasca*), edited by Beatriz Caiuby Labate and Wladimyr Sena Araújo, 303–44. São Paulo: Mercado de Letras.

———. 2010. *Opening the Portals of Heaven: Brazilian Ayahuasca Music*. Münster: Lit Verlag.

———. 2011. "The Historical Origins of Santo Daime: Academics, Adepts, and Ideology." In *The Internationalization of Ayahuasca*, edited by B. C. Labate and KH. Jungaberle, 71–84. Berlin: Lit Verlag.

Labate, Beatriz Caiuby, Rafael Guimarães dos Santos, Brian Anderson, Marcelo Mercante, and Paulo César Ribeiro Barbosa. 2010. "The Treatment and Handling of Substance Dependence with Ayahuasca: Reflections on Current and Future Research." In *Ayahuasca, Ritual, and Religion in Brazil*, edited by Beatriz Caiuby Labate and Edward MacRae, 205–27. London: Equinox.

Labate, Beatriz Caiuby, and Olivier Taymans. Forthcoming. *Ayahuasca Defence Fund Legal Situation in Belgium*. http://ayahuascadefense.com/index.php/national-legal-status/.

Lafrance, Adele, Anja Loizaga-Velder, Jenna Fletcher, Marika Renelli, Natasha Files, and Kenneth W. Tupper. 2017. "Nourishing the Spirit: Exploratory Research on Ayahuasca Experiences along the Continuum of Recovery from Eating Disorders." *Journal of psychoactive drugs* 49, no. 5: 427–35.

Lambek, Michael. 2007. "The Cares of Alice Alder: Recuperating Kinship and History in Switzerland." In *Ghosts of Memory: Essays on Remembrance and Relatedness*, edited by Janet Carsten, 218–40. Malden, MA: Blackwell.

———. 2015. "Both/And." In *What Is Existential Anthropology?*, edited by M. Jackson and A. Piette, 58–83. New York: Berghahn.

Landes, Ruth. 1940. "A Cult Matriarchate and Male Homosexuality." *The Journal of Abnormal and Social Psychology* 35, no. 3: 386–97.

Laqueur, Walter. 1997. *Fin de Siècle and Other Essays on America and Europe*. New Brunswick, NJ: Transaction Publishers.

Latour, Bruno. 1993. *We Have Never Been Modern*. Cambridge: Harvard University Press.

———. 2004. Whose Cosmos, which Cosmopolitics? Comments on the Peace Terms of Ulrich Beck. *Common Knowledge* 10(3): 450–462.

Laughlin, Charles. 1997. "The Cycle of Meaning: Some Methodological Implications of Biogenetic Structural Theory." In *Anthropology of Religion: A Handbook*, edited by Stephen D. Glazier, 471–88. Westport, CT: Greenwood.

———. 1999. "Biogenetic Structural Theory and the Neurophenomenology of Consciousness." In *Toward a Science of Consciousness III: The Third Tucson Discussions and Debates*, edited by Stuart R. Hameroff, Alfred W. Kaszniak, and David J. Chalmers, 459–74. Cambridge: MIT Press.

Law, David R. 2013. *Kierkegaard's Kenotic Christology*. Oxford: Oxford University Press.

Le Poidevin, Robin. 2010. *Agnosticism: A Very Short Introduction*. New York: Oxford University Press.

Leadbeater, Charles W. 2005[1896]. *The Astral Plane: Its scenery, Inhabitants, and phenomena*. New York: Cosim Classics.

Lemmens, Paul. 1999. "New Religious Movements and the Law in Belgium." In *New Religious Movements and the Law in the European Union*, edited by European Consortium for Church-State Research, 87–104. Milan: A. Giuffrè.

Lemons, J. D. 2018. *Theologically Engaged Anthropology*. Oxford: Oxford University Press.

Letheby, Chris. 2016. "The Epistemic Innocence of Psychedelic States." *Consciousness and Cognition* 39: 28–37.

Lewis, James R. 2004. "New Religion Adherents: An Overview of Anglophone Census and Survey Data." *Marburg Journal of Religion* 9, no. 1: 1–17.

Lewis-Williams, J. David. 2010. *Conceiving God: The Cognitive Origin and Evolution of Religion*. London: Thames and Hudson.

Liedman, Sven-Eric. 2010. "Intellectual Challenges from Religion." In *Religion in the 21st Century Challenges and Transformations*, edited by Lisbet Christoffersen, Jans Raun Iverson, Hanne Petersen, and Margit Warburg, 51–66. Farnham, UK, and Burlington, VT: Ashgate.

Loizaga-Velder, Anja, and Rolf Verres. 2014. "Therapeutic Effects of Ritual Ayahuasca Use in the Treatment of Substance Dependence: Qualitative Results." *Journal of Psychoactive Drugs* 46, no. 1: 63–72.

López-Pavillard, Santiago. 2008. *Recepción de la ayahuasca en España*, Master's thesis, Social Anthropology, Universidad Complutense de Madrid, Madrid, Spain.

———. 2018. *Chamanes, ayahuasca y sanación*. Madrid, ES: Consejo Superior de Investigaciones Científica (CSIC).

———, and Diego de las Casas. 2011. "Santo Daime in Spain: A Religion with a Psychoactive Sacrament." In *The Internationalization of Ayahuasca*, edited by B. C. Labate and KH. Jungaberle, 365–74. Berlin: Lit Verlag.

Lowell, Jonathan Thomas. 2013. *Into and out of the Forest: Change and Community in Céu do Mapiá*, Masters Thesis, Geography and the Environment, University of Texas at Austin, Austin, TX.

———, and Paul C. Adams. 2016. "The Routes of a Plant: Ayahuasca and the Global Networks of Santo Daime." *Social & Cultural Geography* 18, no. 2: 137–57.

Lüdtke, Karen. 2009. *Dances with Spiders: Crisis, Celebrity, and Celebration in Southern Italy*. New York: Berghahn Books.

Luhrmann, Tanya M. 1989. *Persuasions of the Witch's Craft: Ritual Magic in Contemporary England*. Cambridge: Harvard University Press.

———. 2012. *When God Talks Back: Understanding the American Evangelical Relationship with God*. Toronto: Random House.

———. 2018. The Real Ontological Challenge. *HAU: Journal of Ethnographic Theory* 8, no. 1–2: 79–82.

Luke, David. 2014. "Psychedelic Possession: The Growing Incorporation of Incorporation into Ayahuasca Use." In *Talking with the Spirits: Ethnographies from between the Worlds*, edited by Jack Hunter and David Luke, 229–54. Brisbane: Daily Grail.

———. 2020. "Anomalous Psychedelic Experiences: At the Neurochemical Juncture of the Humanistic and Parapsychological." *Journal of Humanistic Psychology*: 1–41.

Luna, Luis Eduardo. 1986. *Vegetalismo: Shamanism among the Mestizo Population of the Peruvian Amazon*. Stockholm: Almqvist and Wiksell International.

Luna, Luis Eduardo, and Pablo Amaringo. 1993. *Ayahuasca Visions: The Religious Iconography of a Peruvian Shaman*. Berkeley: North Atlantic Books.

Luna, Luis Eduardo, and Steven F. White. 2000. *Ayahuasca Reader: Encounters with the Amazon's Sacred Vine*. Santa Fe, NM: Synergetic Press.

Lyotard, Jean-François. 1984. *The Postmodern Condition: A Report on Knowledge*. Minneapolis: University of Minnesota Press.

Mabit, J., R. Giove, and J. Vega. 1996. "Takiwasi: The Use of Amazonian Shamanism to Rehabilitate Drug Addicts." In *Yearbook of Cross-Cultural Medicine and Psychotherapy, Zeitschrift für Ethnomedizin (Journal of Ethnomedicine)*, 257–85. Berlin: Publishing House for Science and Education, VWB.

MacLean, Katherine, Matthew Johnson, and Roland Griffiths. 2011. "Mystical Experiences Occasioned by the Hallucinogen Psilocybin Lead to Increases in the Personality Domain of Openness." *Journal of Psychopharmacology* 25, no. 11: 1453–61.

Maclure, Jocelyn, and Charles Taylor. 2011. *Secularism and Freedom of Conscience*. Cambridge: Harvard University Press.

Macquarrie, John. 1996. *Mediators between Human and Divine: From Moses to Muhammad*. New York: Continuum.

MacRae, Edward 1992. *Guiado por la Luna: Shamanismo y Uso Ritual de la Ayahuasca en el Culto de Santo Daime (Guided by the Moon: Shamanism and the Ritual Use of Ayahuasca in the Santo Daime Religion in Brazil)*. Sao Paulo: Brasiliense.

———. 2004. "The Ritual Use of Ayahuasca by Three Brazilian Religions." In *Drug Use and Cultural Contexts "Beyond the West": Tradition, Change, and Post-Colonialism*, edited by R. Coomber and N. South, 27–45. UK: Free Association Books.

———. 2006. "The Religious Uses of Licit and Illicit Psychoactive Substances in a Branch of the Santo Daime Religion." *Fieldwork in Religion* 2, no. 3: 393–414.

———. 2010. "The Development of Brazilian Public Policies on the Religious Use of Ayahuasca." In *Ayahuasca, Ritual, and Religion in Brazil*, edited by Beatriz Caiuby Labate and Edward MacRae, 191–204. London: Equinox.

Madera, Lisa Maria. 2009. "Visions of Christ in the Amazon: The Gospel According to Ayahuasca and Santo Daime." *Journal for the Study of Religion, Nature & Culture* 3, no. 1: 66–98.

Magliocco, Sabina. 2012. "Neopaganism." In *The Cambridge Companion to New Religious Movements*, edited by Olav Hammer and Mikael Rothstein, 150–66. Cambridge and New York: Cambridge University Press.

Malinowski, Bronislaw. 1939. "The Group and the Individual in Functional Analysis." *American Journal of Sociology* 44, no. 6: 938–64.

Marguerite, Porette. 1993. *The Mirror of Simple Souls*. New York: Paulist Press.

Marino, Gordon Daniel. 1998. "Anxiety in the Concept of Anxiety." In *The Cambridge Companion to Kierkegaard*, edited by A. Hannay and G. D. Marino, 308–28. New York: Cambridge University Press.

Marques Junior, Antonio Alves. 2009. *Drums for the Queen of the Forest: The Insertion of Umbanda in Santo Daime*, Masters Thesis, Religious Sciences, PUC-SP; http://www.neip.info/upd_blob/0001/1281.pdf.

Maté, Gabor. 2018. *In the Realm of Hungry Ghosts*. Toronto: Penguin-Random House.

Mathews, Gordon, and Carolina Izquierdo. 2009. *Pursuits of Happiness: Well-Being in Anthropological Perspective*. New York: Berghahn Books.

Mathews, J., and M. Tomlinson. 2018. "Introduction: Conversations between theology, anthropology, and history." *St Mark's Review* 244: 1–8. https://stmarks.edu.au/wp-content/uploads/2018/07/SMR244-2018-extract.pdf.

Matory, James Lorand. 2005. *Black Atlantic Religion: Tradition, Transnationalism, and Matriarchy in the Afro-Brazilian Candomblé*. Princeton: Princeton University Press.

McDonald, John J. 1984. "Religion and Literature." *Religion & Literature* 16, no. 1: 61–71.

McGrane, Bernard. 1989. *Beyond Anthropology: Society and the Other*. New York: Columbia University Press.

McGraw, John J. 2004. *Brain and Belief: An Exploration of the Human Soul*. Del Mar, CA: Aegis Press.

McKanan, Dan. 2017. *Eco-Alchemy: Anthroposophy and the History and Future of Environmentalism*. Berkeley: University of California Press.

McKenna, Dennis J. 2005. "Ayahuasca and Human Destiny." *Journal of Psychoactive Drugs Journal of Psychoactive Drugs* 37, no. 2: 231–234.

————. 2006. "Ayahuasca: An Ethnopharmacologic History." In *Sacred Vine of Visions: Ayahuasca*, edited by R Meltzer, 40–62. Rochester, VT: Park Street Press.

————, J. C. Callaway, and C. S. Grob. 1998. "The Scientific Investigation of Ayahuasca: A Review of Past and Current Research." *Heffter Review of Psychedelic Research* 1: 65–77.

McLeod, Hugh, and Werner Ustorf. 2003. *The Decline of Christendom in Western Europe, 1750–2000*. Cambridge and New York: Cambridge University Press.

Meech, Richard. 2010. *Vine of the Soul: Encounters with Ayahuasca*. Canada: Meech Grant Productions.

Melton, J. Gordon, and Martin Baumann. 2010. "Religious Adherents of the World by Continent." In *Religions of the World: A Comprehensive Encyclopedia of Beliefs and Practices*, edited by J. Gordon Melton and Martin Baumann, lix–lxxii. Santa Barbara: ABC-CLIO.

Mendes do Nascimento, Luiz. 2005[1992]. *Report: [Interview with] Luiz Mendes doNascimento*. Translated by Rodrigo Conti Tavares, English revision by Lou Gold. https://www.mestreirineu.org/luiz-eng.htm.

Menozzi, Walter. 2011. "The Santo Daime Legal Case in Italy." In *The Internationalization of Ayahuasca*, edited by B. C. Labate and KH. Jungaberle, 379–88. Berlin: Lit Verlag.

Mercante, Marcelo S. 2006. *Images of Healing: Spontaneous Mental Imagery and Healing Process of the Barquinha, a Brazilian Ayahuasca Religious System*, PhD Dissertation, Human Sciences, Saybrook Graduate School and Research Center, San Francisco, CA.

Merton, Thomas. 2004[1960]. *A Year with Thomas Merton: Daily Meditations from His Journals*. New York: HarperCollins.

Metzner, Ralph. 1993. "The Split between Spirit and Nature in European Consciousness. *the Trumpeter Journal of Ecosophy* 10, no. 1: http://trumpeter.athabascau.ca/index.php/trumpet/article/view/407/658.

————. 2006. "Introduction: Amazonian Vine of Visions." In *Sacred Vine of Visions: Ayahuasca*, edited by Ralph Metzner, 1–39. Rochester, VT: Park Street Press.

Meyer, Matthew. 2014. *"In the Master's House": History, Discourse, and Ritual in Acre, Brazil*. Department of Anthropology, University of Virginia.

Mikosz, José Eliézer. 2009. *A Arte Visionária e a Ayahuasca: Representações Visuais de Espirais e Vórtices Inspiradas nos Estados não Ordinários de Consciência (ENOC)*, PhD Dissertation, Interdisciplinar em Ciências Humanas, Universidade Federal de Santa Catarina, Florianópolis, SC, Brazil.

Milis, L. J. R. 1999. "A Long Beginning: The Low Countries through the Tenth Century." In *History of the Low Countries*, edited by J. C. H. Blom and Emiel Lamberts, 1–21. New York: Berghahn Books.

Miller, Melanie. 2019. "Chemical Hints of Ayahuasca Use in Pre-Columbian Shamanic Rituals. *PNAS: Proceedings of the National Academy of Sciences of the United States of America* 116, no. 23: 11079–81.

Monroe, Rachel. 2017. "Sexual Assault in the Amazon: As the Ayahuasca Tourism Industry Grows, So Do Accounts of Abuse." *New York Magazine*. *https://www. thecut.com/2017/01/sexual-assault-ayahuasca-tourism.html*.

Monteiro da Silva, Clodomir. 2004. "O Uso Ritual da Ayahuasca e o Reencontro de Duas Tradições: A Miração e a Incorporação no Culto do Santo Daime." In *O Uso Ritual da Ayahuasca*, 2nd edition, edited by Beatriz Caiuby Labate and Wladimyr Sena Araújo, 413–43. São Paulo: Mercado de Letras.

Moreira, Paulo, and Edward MacRae. 2011. *Eu Venho de Longe: Mestre Irineu e seus Companheiros*. Salvador, Bahia: SciELO-EDUFBA-UFMA.

Móró, Levente, Katalin Simon, Imre Bárd, and József Rácz. 2011. "Voice of the Psychonauts: Coping, Life Purpose, and Spirituality in Psychedelic Drug Users." *Journal of Psychoactive Drugs* 43, no. 3: 188–98.

Mota de Melo, Sebastião n.d. "*O Justiceiro* [The Justice Maker]."

Moura da Silva, Eliane. 2006. "Similaridades e Diferenças entre Estilos de Espiritual-idade Metafísica: O Caso do Círculo Esotérico da Comunhão do Pensamento (1908–1943)." In *Orixás e Espíritos: O Debate Interdisciplinar na Pesquisa Contemporânea*, edited by Artur Cesar Isaia, 225–40. Uberlândia: Editora da Universidade Federal de Uberlândia.

Mulford, Prentice. 1888. *Your Forces, and How to Use Them*. New York: F. J. Needham.

Müller, Tim, and Anja Neundorf. 2012. "The Role of the State in the Repression and Revival of Religiosity in Central Eastern Europe." *Social Forces* 91, no. 2: 559–82.

Naranjo, Claudio. 1967. "Psychotropic Properties of the Harmala Alkaloids." In *Ethnopharmacological Search for Psychoactive Drugs*, edited by Daniel H. Efron, Bo Holmstedt, and Nathan S. Kline, 385–91. Washington, DC: U.S. Department of Health, Education and Welfare.

Naranjo, Plutarco 1986. "El ayahuasca in la arqueología ecuatoriana." *America Indigena* 46: 117–28.

Narby, Jeremy. 1998. *The Cosmic Serpent: DNA and the Origins of Knowledge*. New York: Jeremy P. Tarcher/Putnam.

———. 2005. *Intelligence in Nature: An Inquiry into Knowledge*. New York: Jeremy P. Tarcher/Penguin.

———, and Francis Huxley. 2001. *Shamans through Time*. New York: J. P. Tarcher/ Putnam.

Nelson, Christopher AP. 2006. "Kierkegaard, Mysticism, and Jest: The story of little Ludvig." *Continental Philosophy Review* 39, no. 4: 435–64.

Nelson, M. 2018. *Pushing Our Limits: Insights from Biosphere 2*. Tucson: University of Arizona Press.

Nelson-Jones, Richard. 2016. *Basic Counselling Skills: A Helper's Manual*. Washing-ton, DC: SAGE.

Nešpor, Zdeněk R. 2010. "Attitudes towards Religions(s) in a 'Non-Believing' Czech Republic." *Anthropological Journal of European Cultures* 19, no. 1: 68–84.

Neto, Fernando Dini. 2006. *Histórias para Acordar Gente Grande [Stories to Awaken Great People]*. Sorocaba, SP, Brazil: Para Todos; TCM Comunicação.

Noorani, Tehseen. 2019. "Making Psychedelics into Medicines: The Politics and Paradoxes of Medicalization." *Journal of Psychedelic Studies*: 1–6.

Norris, Pippa, and Ronald Inglehart. 2011. *Sacred and Secular: Religion and Politics Worldwide*. Cambridge and New York: Cambridge University Press.

Nutt, David, Leslie A King, William Saulsbury, and Colin Blakemore. 2007. "Development of a Rational Scale to Assess the Harm of Drugs of Potential Misuse." *The Lancet* 369 (9566): 1047–53.

Oakley, Peter. 1980. "Participation in Development in N. E. Brazil." *Community Development Journal* 15, no. 1: 10–22.

Obadia, Lionel. 1999. *Bouddhisme et Occident : la diffusion du bouddhisme tibétain en France [Buddhism and the West: The Diffusion of Tibetan Buddhism in France]*. Paris: l'Harmattan.

Oliveira, Isabela. 2009. "Santo Daime: Um Sacramento Cristão em Formação." *Revista Brasileira de História das Religiões* 1, no. 3: 397–418.

Ona, Genís, Maja Kohek, Tomàs Massaguer, Alfred Gomariz, Daniel F. Jiménez, Rafael G. Dos Santos, Jaime EC Hallak, Miguel Ángel Alcázar-Córcoles, and José Carlos Bouso. 2019. "Ayahuasca and Public Health: Health Status, Psychosocial Well-Being, Lifestyle, and Coping Strategies in a Large Sample of Ritual Ayahuasca Users." *Journal of psychoactive drugs* 51, no. 2: 135–45.

Orcutt, Jacqueline S. (2019). *A Phenomenological Study of Ayahuasca Experiences Reported by Selected Members of the Santo Daime Church* (Doctoral dissertation, Saybrook University).

Osho. 1995. *Life's Mysteries: An Introduction to the Teachings of Osho*. New York: Penguin.

Osorio, F. L., R. F. Sanches, L. R. Macedo, R. G. dos Santos, L. Wichert-Ana, J. A. Crippa, J. E. Hallak, F. L. de Osorio, J. Riba, J. P. Maia-De-Oliveira, and D. B. de Araujo. 2015. "Antidepressant Effects of a Single Dose of Ayahuasca in Patients with Recurrent Depression: A Preliminary Report." *Rev. Bras. Psiquiatr. Revista Brasileira de Psiquiatria* 37, no. 1: 13–20.

Osto, Douglas. 2016. *Altered States: Buddhism and Psychedelic Spirituality in America*. New York: Columbia University Press.

Ott, Jonathan. 2011. "Psychonautic Uses of 'Ayahuasca' and its Analogues: Panacea or Outré Entertainment?" In *The Internationalization of Ayahuasca*, edited by B. C. Labate and KH. Jungaberle, 105–22. Berlin: Lit Verlag.

Pagels, Elaine. 1989. *The Gnostic Gospels*. New York: Vintage.

———. 2011. *Adam, Eve, and the Serpent: Sex and Politics in Early Christianity*. New York: Vintage.

Pahnke, Walter Norman. 1963. *Drugs and Mysticism An Analysis of the Relationship between Psychedelic Drugs and the Mystical Consciousness*, PhD. Diss., History and Philosophy of Religion, Harvard University, Cambridge, MA.

————. 1969. "The Psychedelic Mystical Experience in the Human Encounter with Death." *The Harvard Theological Review* 62, no. 1: 1–21.

————, and William A. Richards. 1966. "Implications of LSD and Experimental Mysticism." *Journal of Religion and Health* 5, no. 3: 175–208.

Palhano-Fontes, Fernanda, Dayanna Barreto, Heloisa Onias, Katia C. Andrade, Morgana M. Novaes, Jessica A. Pessoa, Sergio A. Mota-Rolim, Flávia L. Osório, Rafael Sanches, Rafael G. dos Santos, Luís Fernando Tófoli, Gabriela de Oliveira Silveira, Mauricio Yonamine, Jordi Riba, Francisco R. Santos, Antonio A. Silva-Junior, João C. Alchieri, Nicole L. Galváo-Coelho, Bruno Lobão-Soares, Jaime E. C. Hallak, Emerson Arcoverde, João P. Maia-de-Oliveira, and Dráulio B. Araújo (2019). Rapid Antidepressant Effects of the Psychedelic Ayahuasca in Treatment-Resistant Depression: A randomized Placebo-Controlled Trial. *Psychological medicine* 49, no. 4: 655–63.

Pantoja, Mariana Ciavatta, and Osmildo Silva da Conceição. 2006. "The Use of Ayahuasca among Rubber Tappers of the Upper Juruá." *Fieldwork in Religion* 2, no. 3: 235–55.

Parés, Luis Nicolau. 2001. "The Jeje in the Tambor de Mina of Maranhão and in the Candomble of Bahia." In *Rethinking the African Diaspora: The Making of a Black Atlantic World in the Bight of Benin and Brazil*, edited by Kristin Mann and Edna G. Bay, 91–115. London and Portland, OR: F. Cass.

Parman, Susan. 1998. "The Meaning of 'Europe' in the American Anthropologist (Part I)." In *Europe in the Anthropological Imagination*, edited by Susan Parman, 169–96. Upper Saddle River, NJ: Prentice-Hall.

Parsons, William B. 2008. "Psychologia Perennis and the Academic Study of Mysticism." In *Mourning Religion*, edited by William B. Parsons, 97–123. Charlottesville: University of Virginia Press.

————. 2010. "On Mapping the Psychology and Religion Movement: Psychology as Religion and Modern Spirituality." *Pastoral Psychology* 59, no. 1: 15–25.

————. 2011a. "Teaching Mysticism: Frame and Content." In *Teaching Mysticism*, edited by W. B. Parsons, 3–10. New York: Oxford University Press.

————. 2011b. "Mysticism, Spirituality, and the Undergraduate: Reflections on the Use of Psychosocial Theory." In *Teaching Mysticism*, edited by W. B. Parsons, 209–23. New York: Oxford University Press.

————. 2013. *Freud and Augustine in Dialogue: Psychoanalysis, Mysticism, and the Culture of Modern Spirituality*. Charlottesville: University of Virginia Press.

Partridge, Christopher. 2004. *The Re-Enchantment of the West Vol. 1: Alternative Spiritualities, Sacralization, Popular Culture, and Occulture*. London: T and T Clark International.

————. 2018. *High Culture: Drugs, Mysticism, and the Pursuit of Transcendence in the Modern World*. Oxford, UK: Oxford University Press.

Paulo-Roberto. n.d. "Luz na Escuridão [Light in the Darkness]."

Pendergrast, Mark. 2003. *Mirror Mirror: A History of the Human Love Affair with Reflection.* New York: Basic Books.

Perraudin, Frances. 2015. "Lib Dems: Legalise Medicinal Cannabis and Possession of Drugs for Personal Use." *The Guardian.* https://www.theguardian.com/society/2015/jun/23/lib-dems-legalise-medicinal-cannabis-and-possession-of-drugs-for-personal-use.

Phelps, Janis. 2017. Developing Guidelines and Competencies for the Training of Psychedelic Therapists. *Journal of Humanistic Psychology* 57, no. 5: 450–87.

Piette, Albert. 1992. "Play, Reality, and Fiction: Toward a Theoretical and Methodological Approach to the Festival Framework." *Qualitative Sociology* 15, no. 1: 37–52.

Pirsig, Robert. 2014. "The Motorcycle Is Yourself: Revisiting "Zen and the Art of Motorcycle Maintainence.'" CBC Ideas podcast. http://www.cbc.ca/radio/ideas/the-motorcycle-is-yourself-revisiting-zen-and-the-art-of-motorcycle-maintenance-1.2914205.

Platero, Lígia Duque. 2018. *Fazer Parentes: Uma Descrição da "Aliança" entre os Yawanawa (Pano) e o Céu do Mar, uma Igreja Urbana do Santo Daime,* Tese de Doutorado em Antropologia, Universidade Federal do Rio de Janeiro. http://neip.info/tese/fazer-parentes-uma-descricao-da-alianca-entre-os-yawanawa-pano-e-o-ceu-do-mar-uma-igreja-urbana-do-santo-daime-em-meio-urbano-tese-de-doutorado-em-antropologia-universidade-fed/.

Polari de Alverga, Alex. 1996. "Seriam os Deuses Alcalóides? [Might the Gods be Alkaloids?]." *Paper Presented at the Congresso Internacional de Psicologia Transpessoal, Manaus, Brazil.* http://www.santodaime.org/archives/alex1.htm.

———. 1998. *O Evangelho Segundo Sebastião Mota.* Céu do Mapiá: CEFLURIS editorial.

———. 1999. *Forest of Visions: Ayahuasca, Amazonian Spirituality, and the Santo Daime Tradition.* Translated by Rosana Workman. Rochester, VT: Park Street Press.

———. 2011. "'Mr. Chico, Please Heal Yourself'—Spiritual Healing in the Santo Daime Doctrine and Its Interface with Medical-Scientific Knowledge." In *The Internationalization of Ayahuasca,* edited by B. C. Labate and KH. Jungaberle, 201–21. Berlin: Lit Verlag.

———. n.d. "Nova Anunciação [New Annunciation]."

Pollan, Michael. 2018. *How to Change Your Mind: What the New Science of Psychedelics Teaches us about Consciousness, Dying, Addiction, Depression, and Transcendence.* New York: Penguin Books.

Purser, Ronald. 2019. *McMindfulness: How Mindfulness Became the New Capitalist Spirituality.* London: Repeater Books.

Quinlan, Marsha. 2005. "Considerations for Collecting Freelists in the Field: Examples from Ethobotany." *Field Methods* 17, no. 3: 219–34.

Rabinow, Paul. 1996. *Essays on the Anthropology of Reason*. Princeton: Princeton University Press.

Ram, Kalpana, and Christopher Houston. 2015a. *Phenomenology in Anthropology: A Sense of Perspective*. Bloomington: Indiana University Press.

———. 2015b. "Introduction: Phenomenology's Methodological Invitation." In *Phenomenology in Anthropology: A Sense of Perspective*, edited by Kalpana Ram and Christopher Houston, 1–25. Bloomington: Indiana University Press.

Rambo, Lewis R. 2003. "Anthropology and the Study of Conversion." In *The Anthropology of Religious Conversion*, edited by Andrew Buckser and Stephen D. Glazier, 211–22. Lanham, MD: Rowman and Littlefield.

Rapport, Nigel. 2002. " 'The Truth Is Alive': Kierkegaard's Anthropology of Dualism, Subjectivity, and Somatic Knowledge." *Anthropological Theory* 2, no. 2: 165–83.

Rätsch, Christian. 2005. *The Encyclopedia of Psychoactive Plants: Ethnopharmacology and Its Applications*. Rochester, VT: Park Street Press.

Ray, Paul H. 1998. *The Integral Culture Survey: A Study of the Emergence of Transformational Values in America*. Sausalito: Institute of Noetic Sciences and Fetzer Institute.

Ray, Paul H., and Sherry Ruth Anderson. 2000. *The Cultural Creatives: How 50 Million People Are Changing the World*. New York: Harmony Books.

Re, Tania, J. Palma, J. E. Martins, and M. Simões. 2016. "Transcultual Perspective on Consciousness: Traditional Use of Ayahuasca in Psychiatry in the 21st Century in the Western World." *Cosmos and History: The Journal of Natural and Social Philosophy* 12, no. 2: 237–49.

Reder, Michael, and Josef Schmidt. 2010. "Habermas and Religion." In *An Awareness of What Is Missing: Faith and Reason in a Post-Secular Age*, edited by Jürgen Habermas et al., 1–14. Cambridge, UK, and Malden, MA: Polity.

Reichel-Dolmatoff, Gerardo. 1990[1972]. "The Cultural Context of an Aboriginal Hallucinogen: *Banisteriopsis Caapi*." In *Flesh of the Gods: The Ritual Use of Hallucinogens*, edited by Peter T. Furst, 84–113. Long Grove, IL: Waveland Press.

Riba, J., M. Valle, G. Urbano, M. Yritia, A. Morte, and M. J. Barbanoj. 2003. "Human Pharmacology of Ayahuasca: Subjective and Cardiovascular Effects, Monoamine Metabolite Excretion, and Pharmacokinetics." *The Journal of pharmacology and experimental therapeutics* 306, no. 1: 73–83.

Ricardo, Ze. n.d. "Harmonia Cósmica [Cosmic Harmony]."

Richards, Cara. 2003. "Problems Reporting Anomalous Observations in Anthropology." *Journal of Scientific Exploration* 17, no. 1: 5–18.

Richards, William A. 2005. "Entheogens in the Study of Religious Experiences: Current Status." *Journal of Religion and Health* 44, no. 4: 377–89.

———. 2016. *Sacred Knowledge: Psychedelics and Religious Experiences*. New York: Columbia University Press.

Richardson, James T., and Massimo Introvigne. 2001. " 'Brainwashing' Theories in European Parliamentary and Administrative Reports on 'Cults' and 'Sects.' " *Journal for the Scientific Study of Religion* 40, no. 2: 143–68.

Richman, Gary Dale. 1990/1991. "The Santo Diame Doctrine: An Interview with Alex Polari de Alverga." *Shaman's Drum* 22: 30–41.

Riding, Alan. 1994. "48 in Sect Are Killed in Grisly Ritual in Switzerland." *New York Times.* http://www.nytimes.com/1994/10/06/world/48-in-sect-are-killed-in-grisly-ritual-in-switzerland.html?pagewanted=all.

Robbins, Joel. 2006. "Anthropology and Theology: An Awkward Relationship?" *Anthropological Quarterly* 79, no. 2: 285–94.

———. 2014. "The Anthropology of Christianity: Unity, Diversity, New Directions." *Current Anthropology* 55: 157–71.

Roberts, Thomas B. 2006. *Psychedelic Horizons.* Exeter: Imprint Academic.

Robertson, Roland. 1992. *Globalization: Social Theory and Global Culture.* London: SAGE.

Rochester, Jessica Williams. 2012. *Ceu do Montreal: From Orthodoxy to Universalism,* Thesis, All Faiths Seminary International, New York, NY.

———. 2017. "How Our Santo Daime Church Received Religious Exemption to Use Ayahuasca in Canada." Chacruna.net http://chacruna.net/how-ayahuasca-church-received-religious-exemption-canada/.

Rochester, J., A. Vallely, P. Grof, M. Williams, H. Chang, and K. Caldwell (Forthcoming). Entheogens and Psychedelics in Canada, Proposals for a New Paradigm. Manuscript accepted for publication in *Journal of the Canadian Psychological Association.*

Rogers, Charlotte. 2012. *Jungle Fever: Exploring Madness and Medicine in Twentieth--Century Tropical Narratives.* Nashville: Vanderbilt University Press.

Rohde, Silvio A., and Hajo Sander. 2011. "The Development of the Legal Situation of Santo Daime in Germany." In *The Internationalization of Ayahuasca,* edited by B. C. Labate and KH. Jungaberle, 339–52. Berlin: Lit Verlag.

Rohr, Richard. 2012. *Falling Upward: A Spirituality for the Two Halves of Life.* London: SPCK.

Romney, A. Kimball, Susan C. Weller, and William H. Batchelder. 1986. "Culture as Consensus: A Theory of Culture and Informant Accuracy." *American Anthropologist* 88, no. 2: 313–38.

Ruck, Carl A. P., Jeremy Bigwood, Danny Staples, Jonathan Ott, and Gordon Wasson. 1979. "Entheogens." *Journal of Psychedelic Drugs* 11, no. 1–2.

Šajda, Peter. 2015. "Kierkegaard's Mystical and Spiritual Sources: Meister Eckhart to Tersteegen." In *A Companion to Kierkegaard,* edited by Jon Stewart, 167–79. Malden, MA: Wiley Blackwell.

Santos, B. W. L., R. C. D. Oliveira, J. Sonsin-Oliveira, C. W. Fagg, J. B. F. Barbosa, and E. D. Caldas. 2020. "Biodiversity of β-Carboline Profile of Banisteriopsis caapi and Ayahuasca, a Plant and a Brew with Neuropharmacological Potential." *Plants* 9, no. 7: 870.

Sarrouh, Maria. 2020. *Santo Daime in Toronto.* Major Research Project, Master of Journalism thesis. Ryerson University, Toronto. https://santodaimetoronto.squarespace.com/.

Scheper-Hughes, Nancy. 2001. *Saints, Scholars, and Schizophrenics: Mental Illness in Rural Ireland*. Berkeley: University of California Press.

Schifano, F., P. Deluca, A. Baldacchino, T. Peltoniemi, N. Scherbaum, M. Torrens, M. Farre, I. Flores, M. Rossi, D. Eastwood, C. Guionnet, S. Rawaf, L. Agosti, L. Di Furia, R. Brigada, A. Majava, H. Siemann, M. Leoni, A. Tomasin, F. Rovetto, and A. H. Ghodse. 2006. "Drugs on the Web; The Psychonaut 2002 EU Project." *Progress in Neuropsychopharmacology & Biological Psychiatry* 30, no. 4: 640–46.

Schillebeeckx, Edward. 1963. *Christ, the Sacrament of the Encounter with God*. New York: Sheed and Ward.

Schmid, Janine Tatjana. 2011. "Ayahuasca Healing: A Qualitative Study about Fifteen European People Handling their Diseases." In *The Internationalization of Ayahuasca*, edited by B. C. Labate and KH. Jungaberle, 245–59. Berlin: Lit Verlag.

Schmid, Janine Tatjana, Henrik Jungaberle, and Rolf Verres. 2010. "Subjective Theories about (Self-)Treatment with Ayahuasca." *Anthropology of Consciousness* 21, no. 2: 188–204.

Schmidt, Titti Kristina. 2006. "Conflicts and Violence in Structuring Metaphors of the Santo Daime, a Religious and Environmental Movement in the Brazilian Amazon." *Scripta Instituti Donneriani Aboensis* 19: 322–38.

———. 2007. *Morality as Practice: The Santo Daime, an Eco-Religious Movement in the Amazonian Rainforest*. Department of Cultural Anthropology and Ethnology, Uppsala Universitet, Uppsala, Sweden.

Schneider, Kirk J. 2007. "Enchanted Agnosticism." In *Tikkun Reader: 20th Anniversary*, edited by Michael Lerner, 33–38. Lanham, MD: Rowman and Littlefield.

Schucman, Helen. 2007[1976]. *A Course in Miracles: Combined Volume*. Mill Valley, CA: Foundation for Inner Peace.

Schultes, Richard Evans. 1963. *Botanical Sources of the New World Narcotics*. Cambridge, MA: Psychedelic Review.

Schultes, Richard Evans, Albert Hofmann, and Christian Rätsch. 2001. *Plants of the Gods: Their Sacred, Healing, and Hallucinogenic Powers*. Rochester, VT: Healing Arts Press.

Schultes, Richard Evans, and Robert F. Raffauf. 2004[1992]. *Vine of the Soul: Medicine Men, Their Plants and Rituals in the Colombian Amazonia*. Santa Fe, NM: Synergetic Press.

Schulte-Sasse, Jochen. 2004. Mediality in Hegel: From Work to Text in the Phenomenology of Spirit." In *Idealism without Absolutes: Philosophy and Romantic Culture*, edited by T. Rajan and A. Plotnitsky, 73–92. Albany: State University of New York Press.

Schuon, Frithjof. 2013. *Splendor of the True: A Frithjof Schuon Reader*. Albany: State University of New York Press.

Schwartz, Casey. 2017. "Molly at the Marriott: Inside America's Premier Psychedelics Conference." *New York Times*. https://www.nytimes.com/2017/05/06/style/psychedelic-drug-resurgence-daily-life.html.

Scott, David. 2006. "Appendix: The Trouble of Thinking: An Interview with Talal Asad." In *Powers of the Secular Modern: Talal Asad and His Interlocutors*, edited by David Scott and Charles Hirschkind, 243–303. Stanford: Stanford University Press.

Scott, Gregory, and Robin L. Carhart-Harris. Forthcoming. "Psychedelics as a Treatment for Disorders of Consciousness." *Neuroscience of consciousness* 2019, no. 1.

Scuro, Juan. 2016. *Neochamanismo en América Latina: Una Cartografía desde el Uruguay*, PhD Dissertation, Antropologia Social, Universidade Federal do Rio Grande do Sul, Porto Alegre, Brazil. http://neip.info/novo/wp-content/uploads/2016/09/Scuro_Neochamanismo_Tese_Doutorado_2016.pdf.

Seager, William. 2000. "Physicalism." In *A Companion to the Philosophy of Science*, edited by W. H. Newton-Smith, 340–42. Malden, MA: Blackwell.

Selby, Jennifer A. 2012. *Questioning French Secularism: Gender Politics and Islam in a Parisian Suburb*. New York: Palgrave Macmillan.

Sententia, Wrye. 2004. "Neuroethical Considerations: Cognitive Liberty and Converging Technologies for Improving Human Cognition." *Annals of the New York Academy of Sciences* 1013: 221–28.

Serra, Raimundo Irineu. n.d. "O Cruzeiro [The Cross]."

Sessa, Ben, and Matthew W. Johnson. 2015. "Can Psychedelic Compounds Play a Part in Drug Dependence Therapy?" *The British journal of psychiatry* 206, no. 1: 1–3.

Shanon, Benny. 2002. *The Antipodes of the Mind: Charting the Phenomenology of the Ayahuasca Experience*. Oxford; New York: Oxford University Press.

———. 2008. "Biblical Entheogens: A Speculative Hypothesis." *Time and Mind* 1, no. 1: 51–74.

———. 2011. "Music and Ayahuasca." In *Music and Consciousness: Philosophical, Psychological, and Cultural Perspectives*, edited by David Clarke and Eric F. Clarke, 281–94. Oxford and New York: Oxford University Press.

Shaw, Rosalind, and Charles Stewart. 1994. "Introduction: Problematizing Syncretism." In *Syncretism/Anti-Syncretism: The Politics of Religions Synthesis*, edited by Rosalind Shaw and Charles Stewart, 1–26. New York: Routledge.

Shulgin, Alexander T. 2003. "Basic Pharmacology and Effects." In *Hallucinogens: A Forensic Drug Handbook*, edited by Richard R. Laing, 67–137. San Diego: Academic Press.

Silva Sá, Domingos Bernardo Gialluisi da. 2010. "Ayahuasca: The Consciousness of Expansion." In *Ayahuasca, Ritual and Religion in Brazil*, edited by Beatriz Caiuby Labate and Edward MacRae, 161–89. London: Equinox.

Silveira, Dartiu Xavier da, Charles S. Grob, Marlene Dobkin de Rios, Enrique Lopez, Luisa K. Alonso, Cristiane Tacla, and Evelyn Doering-Silveira. 2005. "Ayahuasca in Adolescence: A Preliminary Psychiatric Assessment." *Journal of Psychoactive Drugs* 37, no. 2: 129–33.

Sinclair, Emily, and Beatriz Labate. 2019. "Ayahuasca Community Guide for the Awareness of Sexual Abuse." *MAPS Bulletin* 29, no. 1 (Spring): 34–36.

Smith, Allan L., and Charles T. Tart. 1998. "Cosmic Consciousness Experience and Psychedelic Experiences: A First Person Comparison." *Journal of Consciousness Studies* 5, no. 1: 97–107.

Smith, David Woodruff. 2013. "Phenomenology." *The Stanford Encyclopedia of Philosophy*, edited by Edward N. Zalta. http://plato.stanford.edu/entries/phenomenology/.

Smith, Huston. 2000. *Cleansing the Doors of Perception: The Religious Significance of Entheogenic Plants and Chemicals*. New York: Jeremy P. Tarcher/Putnam.

Smith, J. Jerome. 1993. "Using ANTHROPAC 3.5 and a Spreadsheet to Compute a Free-list Salience Index." *Cultural Anthropology Methods Journal* 5, no. 3: 1–3.

Soares, Edson Lodi Campos, and Cristina Patriota de Moura. 2011. "Development and Organizational Goals of the União do Vegetal as a Brazilian and International Religious Group." In *The Internationalization of Ayahuasca*, edited by B. C. Labate and KH. Jungaberle, 277–86. Berlin: Lit Verlag.

Soares, Luiz Eduardo. 2010. "Santo Daime in the Context of the New Religious Consciousness." In *Ayahuasca, Ritual, and Religion in Brazil*, edited by Beatriz Caiuby Labate and Edward MacRae, 65–72. London: Equinox.

Sobiecki, Jean-Francois. 2013. "An Account of Healing Depression Using Ayahuasca Plant Teacher Medicine in a Santo Daime Ritual." *Indo Pacific Journal of Phenomenology* 12, no. 1: 1–12.

Soibelman, Tania. 1995. *"My Father and My Mother, Show Me Your Beauty": Ritual Use of Ayahuasca in Rio De Janeiro*, Masters Thesis, Social and Cultural Anthropology, The California Institute of Integral Studies (CIIS). http://www.neip.info/upd_blob/0000/728.pdf.

Soper, J. Christopher, and Joel Fetzer. 2002. "Religion and Politics in a Secular Europe." In *Religion and Politics in Comparative Perspective: The One, the Few, and the Many*, edited by Ted Gerard Jelen and Clyde Wilcox, 169–94. New York: Cambridge University Press.

Spillane, Joseph, and William B. McAllister. 2003. "Keeping the Lid on: A Century of Drug Regulation and Control." *Drug and alcohol dependence* 70, no. 3: 5–12.

Spinella, Marcello. 2001. *The Psychopharmacology of Herbal Medicine: Plant Drugs that Alter Mind, Brain, and Behavior*. Cambridge: MIT Press.

Spruce, Richard. 1908. *Notes of a Botanist on the Amazon and Andes: Being Records of Travel on the Amazon and Its Tributaries, the Trombetas, Rio Negro, Uaupés, Casiquiari, Pacimoni, Huallaga, and Pastasa: As Also to the Cataracts of the Orinoco, along the Eastern Side of the Andes of Peru and Ecuador, and the Shores of the Pacific, During the years 1849–1864*. London: Macmillan.

Srinivas, Tulasi. 2012. "The Sathya Sai Baba Movement." In *The Cambridge Companion to New Religious Movements*, edited by Olav Hammer and Mikael Rothstein, 184–97. Cambridge and New York: Cambridge University Press.

St. John, Graham. 2015. *Mystery School in Hyperspace: A Cultural History of DMT*. Berkeley: Evolver Editions.

Star, Jonathan. 2008. *Laozi's Tao Te Ching: The New Translation*. New York: Jeremy P. Tarcher/Penguin.

Stark, Rodney. 1993. "Europe's Receptivity to New Religious Movements: Round Two." *Journal for the Scientific Study of Religion* 32, no. 4: 389–97.

Steinbock, Anthony J. 2009. *Phenomenology and Mysticism: The Verticality of Religious Experience*. Bloomington: Indiana University Press.

Steinhardt, Joanna, and Tehseen Noorani. 2020. "The Psychedelic Revival." *Cultural Anthropology*—Hot Spots/Fieldsights series, July 21. https://culanth.org/fieldsights/series/the-psychedelic-revival.

Stengers, Isabelle. 2005. "The Cosmopolitical Proposal." In *Making Things Public: Atmospheres of Democracy*, edited by Bruno Latour and Peter Weibel, 994–1003. Cambridge: MIT Press.

———. 2010. *Cosmopolitics I*. Minneapolis: University of Minnesota Press.

———. 2011. *Cosmopolitics II*. Minneapolis: University of Minnesota Press.

Stewart, Dianne M. 2005. *Three Eyes for the Journey: African Dimensions of the Jamaican Religious Experience*. Oxford and New York: Oxford University Press.

Stoeber, Michael. 2015. "The Comparative Study of Mysticism." *Oxford Research Encyclopedia of Religion*. http://religion.oxfordre.com/view/10.1093/acrefore/9780199340378.001.0001/acrefore-9780199340378-e-93.

Stokes, Charles E. 2000. *The Amazon Bubble: World Rubber Monopoly*. Fort McKavett, TX: C. E. Stokes Jr.

Stoljar, Daniel. 2009. Physicalism. *The Stanford Encyclopedia of Philosophy*, edited by Edward N. Zalta. https://plato.stanford.edu/entries/physicalism/.

Strassman, Rick. 2001. *DMT—The Spirit Molecule: A Doctor's Revolutionary Research into the Biology of Near-Death and Mystical Experiences*. Rochester, VT: Park Street Press.

Strikwerda, Carl. 1997. *A House Divided Catholics, Socialists, and Flemish Nationalists in Nineteenth-Century Belgium*. Lanham, MD: Rowman and Littlefield.

Sudhölter, Judith. 2012. *When Experience Turns into Narrative: Playing the Game of Narrative Making with the Religious Experiences of Dutch Santo Daime Members*. MA thesis, Religious Studies, University of Amsterdam.

Sutcliffe, Steven. 2003. *Children of the New Age: A History of Alternative Spirituality*. London: Routledge.

Swedenborg, Emanuel. 1980[1764]. *Angelic Wisdom about Divine Providence*. New York: Swedenborg Foundation.

Tai, Sara J., Elizabeth M. Nielson, Molly Lennard-Jones, Riikka-Liisa Johanna Ajantaival, Rachel Winzer, William A. Richards, Frederick Reinholdt, Brian D. Richards, Peter Gasser, and Ekaterina Malievskaia. 2021. "Development and Evaluation of a Therapist Training Program for Psilocybin Therapy for Treatment-Resistant Depression in Clinical Research." *Frontiers in Psychiatry*, 12: 1–27.

Tati, Cristina. n.d. *Flores de São João (Flowers of St. John)*.

Taussig, Michael T. 1987. *Shamanism, Colonialism, and the Wild Man: A Study in Terror and Healing*. Chicago: University of Chicago Press.

Tavard, George H. 1996. *The Thousand Faces of the Virgin Mary*. Collegeville, MN: Liturgical Press.

Taylor, Bron. 2007. "Exploring Religion, Nature, and Culture—Introducing the Journal for the Study of Religion, Nature and Culture." *Journal for the Study of Religion, Nature, and Culture* 1, no. 1: 5–24.

———. 2010. *Dark Green Religion: Nature Spirituality and the Planetary Future*. Berkeley: University of California Press.

Taylor, Charles. 1989. *Sources of the Self: The Making of the Modern Identity*. Cambridge: Harvard University Press.

———. 2007. *A Secular Age*. Cambridge: Belknap Press of Harvard University Press.

Taylor, Colin, and Paul Griffiths. 2005. "Sampling Issues in Drug Epidemiology." In *Epidemiology of Drug Abuse*, edited by Zili Sloboda, 79–98. New York: Springer.

Taylor, Steve. 2016. "From Philosophy to Phenomenology: The Argument for a 'Soft' Perennialism." *International Journal of Transpersonal Studies* 35, no. 2: 17–41.

———. 2017. "The Return of Perennial Perspectives? Why Transpersonal Psychology Should Remain open to Essentialism." *International Journal of Transpersonal Studies* 36, no. 2: 75–92.

Teresa of Avila. 2007[1577]. *Interior Castle*. Mineola, NY: Dover.

Thiessen, Michelle S., Zach Walsh, Brian M. Bird, and Adele Lafrance (2018). Psychedelic Use and Intimate Partner Violence: The Role of Emotion Regulation. *Journal of psychopharmacology* 32, no. 7: 749–55.

Thomas, G., P. Lucas, N. R. Capler, K. W. Tupper, and G. Martin. 2013. "Ayahuasca-Assisted Therapy for Addiction: Results from a Preliminary Observational study in Canada." *Current Drug Abuse Reviews* 6, no. 1: 30–42.

Tillich, Paul. 2014[1952]. *The Courage to Be*. New Haven: Yale University Press.

Timmermann, Christopher, Rosalind Watts, and David Dupuis. Forthcoming. "Towards Psychedelic Apprenticeship: Developing a Gentle Touch for the Mediation and Validation of Psychedelic-Induced Insights and Revelations. *Transcultural Psychiatry* (preprint).

Tolle, Eckhart. 1999. *The Power of Now: A Guide to Spiritual Enlightenment*. Novato, CA: New World Library.

———. 2005. *A New Earth: Awakening to Your Life's Purpose*. New York: Plume.

Tomlinson, Matt. 2014. "Bringing Kierkegaard into Anthropology: Repetition, Absurdity, and Curses in Fiji." *American ethnologist* 41, no. 1: 163–75.

Torchinov, Evgeny. 2003. "Mysticism and Its Cultural Expression: An Inquiry into the Description of Mystical Experience and Its Ontological and Epistemological Nature." *International Journal of Transpersonal Studies* 22: 40–46.

Torfs, Rik. 2005. "The Permissible Scope of Legal Limitations on the Freedom of Religion or Belief in Belgium." *Emory international law review* 19, no. 2: 637–83.

Torres, Constantino Manuel. 1995. "Archaeological Evidence for the Antiquity of Psychoactive Plant Use in the Central Andes." *Annali dei Musei Civici-Rovereto* 11: 291–326.

Torres, Constantino Manuel, and David B. Repke. 2006. *Anadenanthera: Visionary Plant of Ancient South America.* New York: Haworth Herbal Press.

Townsend, Joan B. 2001. "Modern Non-Traditional and Invented Shamanism." In *Shamanhood: Symbolism and Epic*, edited by Juha Pentikainen, 257–64. Budapest: Akademiai Kiado.

Trungpa, Chögyam. 1973. *Cutting through Spiritual Materialism.* Berkeley: Shambhala.

Tupper, Kenneth W. 2002. "Entheogens and Existential Intelligence: The Use of Plant Teachers as Cognitive Tools." *Canadian Journal of Education* 27, no. 4: 499–516.

———. 2008. "The Globalization of Ayahuasca: Harm Reduction or Benefit Maximization?" *International Journal of Drug Policy* 19, no. 4: 297–303.

———. 2009. "Ayahuasca Healing beyond the Amazon: The Globalization of a Traditional Indigenous Entheogenic Practice." *Global Networks* 9, no. 1: 117–36.

———. 2011. *Ayahuasca, Entheogenic Education, and Public Policy.* University of British Columbia, Vancouver, BC.

Tupper, Kenneth W., and Beatriz Caiuby Labate. 2012. "Plants, Psychoactive Substances, and the International Narcotics Control Board: The Control of Nature and the Nature of Control." *Human Rights and Drugs* 2, no. 1: 17–28.

———. 2014. "Ayahuasca, Psychedelic Studies, and Health Sciences: The Politics of Knowledge and Inquiry into an Amazonian Plant Brew." *Current Drug Abuse Reviews* 7, no. 2: 71–80.

Tupper, K. W., E. Wood, R. Yensen, and M. W. Johnson. 2015. "Psychedelic Medicine: A Re-emerging Therapeutic Paradigm." *Canadian Medical Association Journal* 187, no. 14: 1054–64.

Turner, Victor. 1982. "Images of Anti-Temporality: An Essay in the Anthropology of Experience." *The Harvard Theological Review* 75, no. 2: 243–65.

Turney-High, Harry Holbert. 1953. *Château-Gérard: The Life and Times of a Walloon Village.* Columbia: University of South Carolina Press.

Underhill, Evelyn. 2002[1911]. *Mysticism: A Study in the Nature and Development of Spiritual Consciousness.* Mineola, NY: Dover.

———. 1914. *Ruysbroeck.* London: G. Bell and Sons/Toronto, ON: University of Toronto reprint.

Valdete. n.d. *Livrinho do Apocalipse (Little Book of Revelation)*: CEFLURIS.

van Amsterdam, Jan, Antoon Opperhuizen, and Wim van den Brink. 2011. "Harm Potential of Magic Mushroom Use: A review." *Regulatory Toxicology and Pharmacology* 59, no. 3: 423–29.

van den Plas, Adèle. 2011. "Ayahuasca under International Law: The Santo Daime Churches in the Netherlands." In *The Internationalization of Ayahuasca*, edited by B. C. Labate and H. Jungaberle, 327–38. Berlin: Lit Verlag.

Velmans, Max. 2007. "Dualism, Reductionism, and Reflexive Monism." In *The Blackwell Companion to Consciousness*, edited by Max Velmans and Susan Schneider, 346–58. Malden, MA: Blackwell.

Villavicencio, Manuel. 1858. *Geografîa de la republica del Ecuador*. New York: Impr. de R. Craighead.

Vitz, Paul C. 1998. "The Future of the University: From Postmodern to Transmodern." In *Rethinking the Future of the University*, edited by David Lyle Jeffrey and Dominic Manganiello, 105–16. Ottawa: University of Ottawa Press.

Voas, David. 2009. "The Rise and Fall of Fuzzy Fidelity in Europe." *European Sociological Review* 25, no. 2: 155–68.

———, and Stefanie Doebler. 2011. "Secularization in Europe: Religious Change between and within Birth Cohorts." *Religion and Society in Central and Eastern Europe* 4(1): 39–62.

Von Reis, Siri, and Harvard University Botanical Museum. 1972. *The Genus Anadenanthera in Amerindian Cultures*. Cambridge: Botanical Museum, Harvard University.

Wallace, Anthony F. C. 1966. *Religion: An Anthropological View*. New York: Random House.

Walsh, Charlotte. 2017. "Ayahuasca in the English Courts: Legal Entanglements with the Jungle Vine." In *The World Ayahuasca Diaspora: Reinventions and Controversies*, edited by Beatriz Labate, Clancy Cavnar and Alex K. Gearin, 243–62. New York: Routledge.

Walsh, Roger. 1989. "Shamanism and Early Human Technology: The Technology of Transcendence." *ReVision* 21: 34–40.

Walsh, Roger N. 2007. *The World of Shamanism: New Views of an Ancient Tradition*. Woodbury, MN: Llewellyn Publications.

———, and Charles S. Grob. 2005. *Higher Wisdom: Eminent Elders Explore the Continuing Impact of Psychedelics*. Albany: State University of New York Press.

Ware, Kallistos. 1974. *The Power of the Name: The Jesus Prayer in Orthodox Spirituality*. Fiacres, Oxford: SLG Press, Convent of the Incarnation.

Watt, Gillian. 2014. "Santo Daime in Ireland: A 'Work' in Process." *DISKUS: The Journal of the British Association for the Study of Religions* 16, no. 3: 47–56.

———. 2017. "Santo Daime in the Diaspora." In *Handbook of Contemporary Religions in Brazil*, edited by Bettina E. Schmidt and Steven Engler, 333–45. Boston: Brill.

———. 2018. "Santo Daime in a 'Post-Catholic' Ireland: Reflecting and Moving on." In *The Expanding World Ayahuasca Diaspora: Appropriation, Integration, and Legislation*, edited by B. C. Labate and C. Cavnar, 61–75. New York: Routledge.

Watts, Alan. 1965. *The Joyous Cosmology: Adventures in the Chemistry of Consciousness*. New York: Vintage Books.

———. 1977. *The Essence of Alan Watts*. Millbrae, CA: Celestial Arts.

———. 1999[1957]. *The Way of Zen*. New York: Vintage Books.

Watts, Rosalind, Sam Gandy, and Alex Evans. 2019. "The Whole-Planet View: Psychedelics Offer a Sense of Expansive Connectedness, Just Like Astronauts Have Felt Looking Back to Earth from Space." *Aeon*, Sep 17, 2019. https://aeon.co/essays/psychedelics-can-have-the-same-overview-effect-as-a-space-journey.

Weber, Max. 1948[1922]. "Science as a Vocation [*Wissenschaft als Beruf*]." In *From Max Weber: Essays in Sociology*, edited by Hans H. Gerth and C. Wright Mills, 129–56. New York: Oxford University Press.

Weil, Simone. 2002[1947]. *Gravity and Grace*. London and New York: Routledge.

Weinhold, Jan. 2007. "Failure and Mistakes in the Rituals of the European Santo Daime Church: Experiences and Subjective Theories of Participants." In *When Rituals Go Wrong: Mistakes, Failure, and the Dynamics of Ritual*, edited by Ute Hüsken, 49–72. Leiden: Brill.

Weinstein, Barbara. 1983. *The Amazon Rubber Boom, 1850–1920*. Stanford: Stanford University Press.

Weller, Susan C., and A. Kimball Romney. 1988. *Systematic Data Collection*. Newbury Park, CA: SAGE.

Whorf, Benjamin. 1941. "The Relation of Habitual Thought and Behavior to Language." In *In Language, Culture, and Personality, Essays in Memory of Edward Sapir*, edited by Leslie Spier, 75–93. Menasha, WI: Sapir Memorial Publication Fund.

Wiegele, Katharine L. 2005. *Investing in Miracles : El Shaddai and the Transformation of Popular Catholicism in the Philippines*. Honolulu: University of Hawai'i Press.

Wilber, Ken. 1998. *The Essential Ken Wilber: An Introductory Reader*. Boston: Shambhala.

———. 2000. *Integral Psychology: Consciousness, Spirit, Psychology, Therapy*. Boston: Shambhala.

Wilbert, Johannes. 1987. *Tobacco and Shamanism in South America*. New Haven: Yale University Press.

Willerslev, Rane, and Christian Suhr. 2018. "Is There a Place for Faith in Anthropology? Religion, Reason, and the Ethnographer's Divine Revelation." *HAU Journal of Ethnographic Theory* 8, no. 1–2: 65–78.

Williams-Hogan, Jane. 2003. "Field Notes: The Swedenborgian Church in South Africa." *Nova Religio: The Journal of Alternative and Emergent Religions* 7, no. 1: 90–97.

Wilson, Peter Lamborn. 1994. *Angels: Messengers of the Gods*. London: Thames and Hudson.

Winkelman, Michael J. 2000. *Shamanism: The Neural Ecology of Consciousness and Healing*. Westport, CT: Bergin and Garvey.

———. 2001. "Psychointegrators: Multidisciplinary Perspectives on the Therapeutic Effects of Hallucinogens." *Complementary Health Practice Review* 6: 219–38.

———. 2005. "Drug Tourism or Spiritual Healing? Ayahuasca Seekers in Amazonia." *Journal of psychoactive drugs* 37, no. 2: 209–18.

———. 2015. "Psychedelics as Medicines for Substance Abuse Rehabilitation: Evaluating Treatments with LSD, Peyote, Ibogaine and Ayahuasca." *CDAR Current Drug Abuse Reviews* 7, no. 2: 101–16.

———, and Ben Sessa, eds. 2019. *Advances in Psychedelic Medicine: State-of-the-Art Therapeutic Applications.* Santa Barbara, CA: ABC–CLIO.

Wittgenstein, Ludwig. 2001[1921]. *Tractatus Logico-Philosophicus.* London: Routledge.

Wolff, Tom J., and Torsten Passie. 2018. "Motivational Structure of Ayahuasca Drinkers in Social Networks. *Journal of Psychedelic Studies* 2, no. 2: 89–96.

Wolff, Tom John, Simon Ruffell, Nigel Netzband, and Torsten Passie (2019). "A Phenomenology of Subjectively Relevant Experiences Induced by Ayahuasca in Upper Amazon Vegetalismo Tourism. *Journal of Psychedelic Studies*: 1–13.

Wuthnow, Robert. 1998. *After Heaven: Spirituality in America since the 1950s.* Berkeley: University of California Press.

Wuytz, Jazmin. 2008. *Een religie van de nieuwe tijd: een multi-sited casestudy.* MA Thesis: Culturele Antropologie en Ontwikkelingssociologie, Universiteit Leiden.

York, Michael. 2005. "Shamanism and Magic." In *Witchcraft and Magic: Contemporary North America*, edited by Helen A. Berger, 81–101. Philadelphia: University of Pennsylvania Press.

Young, David E., and Jean-Guy Goulet. 1994. *Being Changed: The Anthropology of Extraordinary Experience.* Peterborough, ON, and Orchard Park, NY: Broadview Press.

Zaehner, R. C. 1961. *Mysticism Sacred and Profane: An Inquiry into Some Varieties of Praeternatural Experience.* Oxford: Oxford University Press.

Zammito, John H. 2002. *Kant, Herder, and the Birth of Anthropology.* Chicago: University of Chicago Press.

Zeifman, Richard, Fernanda Palhano-Fontes, Jaime Hallak, Emerson Arcoverde Nunes, João Paulo Maia-de-Oliveira, and Draulio Barros de Araujo. 2019. "The Impact of Ayahuasca on Suicidality: Results from a Randomized Controlled Trial." *Frontiers in Pharmacology* 10: 1325.

Zendo. 2015. *Zendo Project Training Manual.* Santa Cruz, CA: Multidisciplinary Association for Psychedelic Studies (MAPS).

Ziebertz, Hans-Georg, and Ulrich Riegel. 2008. *Europe: Secular or Post-Secular?* Berlin: Lit Verlag.

Zinberg, Norman E. 1984. *Drug, Set, and Setting: The Basis for Controlled Intoxicant Use.* New Haven: Yale University Press.

Znamenski, Andrei A. 2007. *The Beauty of the Primitive: Shamanism and the Western Imagination.* Oxford and New York: Oxford University Press.

Zuluaga, Germán. 2004. "A Cultura do Yagé, Um Caminho de Indios." In *O Uso Ritual da Ayahuasca* (*The Ritual Use of Ayahuasca*), edited by Beatriz Caiuby Labate and Wladimyr Sena Araújo, 129–46. São Paulo: Mercado de Letras.

Index

Page numbers in *italics* indicate illustrations.